A Reference Grammar of Modern Standard Arabic

A Reference Grammar of Modern Standard Arabic is a comprehensive handbook on
the structure of Arabic. Keeping technical terminology to a minimum, it
provides a detailed yet accessible overview of Modern Standard Arabic in
which the essential aspects of its phonology, morphology, and syntax can be
readily looked up and understood. Accompanied by extensive carefully
chosen examples, it will prove invaluable as a practical guide for supporting
students' textbooks, classroom work, or self-study and will also be a useful
resource for scholars and professionals wishing to develop an understanding
of the key features of the language. Grammar notes are numbered for ease of
reference, and a section on how to use an Arabic dictionary is included, as
well as helpful glossaries of Arabic and English linguistic terms and a useful
bibliography. Clearly structured and systematically organized, this book is set
to become the standard guide to the grammar of contemporary Arabic.

KARIN C. RYDING is Sultan Qaboos bin Said Professor of Arabic, Department of
Arabic Language, Literature and Linguistics, Georgetown University. She has
written a variety of journal articles on Arabic language and linguistics, and
her most recent books include *Early Medieval Arabic* (1998) and *Formal Spoken
Arabic: Basic Course* (second edition, with David Mehall, 2005).

A Reference Grammar of Modern Standard Arabic

KARIN C. RYDING

Georgetown University

CAMBRIDGE
UNIVERSITY PRESS

University Printing House, Cambridge CB2 8BS, United Kingdom

Cambridge University Press is part of the University of Cambridge.

It furthers the University's mission by disseminating knowledge in the pursuit of education, learning and research at the highest international levels of excellence.

www.cambridge.org
Information on this title: www.cambridge.org/9780521777711

First published 2005
8th printing 2013

A catalogue record for this publication is available from the British Library

Library of Congress Cataloguing in Publication data

Ryding, Karin C.
   A reference grammar of modern standard Arabic / Karin C. Ryding.
       p.   cm.
   Includes bibliographical references and index.
   ISBN 0 521 77151 X – ISBN 0 521 77771 2 (pb.)
       1. Arabic language–Grammar.   I. Title.

   PJ6303.R93 2005   492.7´82421–dc22

ISBN 978-0-521-77151-1 Hardback
ISBN 978-0-521-77771-1 Paperback

I am especially indebted to His Majesty Sultan Qaboos bin Said, Sultan of Oman, who generously endowed the position I occupy at Georgetown University, and whose patronage of study and research about Arabic language, literature, and culture is well known and widely respected. It is for this reason that I dedicate this book, with profound gratitude, to His Majesty.

Contents

Preface   *xvii*
List of abbreviations   *xxii*
Acknowledgments   *xxv*

1 Introduction to Arabic   1
   1 Afro-Asiatic and the Semitic language family   1
   2 An overview of Arabic language history   2
   3 Classical Arabic   2
   4 The modern period   4
   5 Arabic today   5

2 Phonology and script   10
   1 The alphabet   10
   2 Names and shapes of the letters   11
   3 Consonants: pronunciation and description   12
   4 Vowels   25
   5 MSA pronunciation styles: full form and pause form   34
   6 MSA syllable structure   35
   7 Word stress rules   36
   8 Definiteness and indefiniteness markers   40

3 Arabic word structure: an overview   44
   1 Morphology in general   44
   2 Derivation: the Arabic root-pattern system   45
   3 Word structure: root and pattern combined   49
   4 Dictionary organization   49
   5 Other lexical types   50
   6 Inflection: an overview of grammatical categories in Arabic   51
   7 Distribution of inflectional categories: paradigms   55
   8 MSA inflectional classes   55
   9 Case and mood: special inflectional categories in Arabic   56

4 Basic Arabic sentence structures   57

  1 Essential principles of sentence structure   57

  2 The simple sentence   58

  3 Other sentence elements   72

  4 Compound or complex sentences   72

5 Arabic noun types   74

  1 Verbal noun (*al-maSdar* المصدر)   75

  2 Active and passive participle (*ism al-faaᶜil* اسم الفاعل, *ism al-mafᶜuul* اسم المفعول)   83

  3 Noun of place (*ism makaan* اسم مكان)   86

  4 Noun of instrument (*ism al-ʾaala* اسم الآلة)   87

  5 Nouns of intensity, repetition, profession   88

  6 Common noun (*al-ism* الاسم)   88

  7 Generic noun (*ism al-jins* اسم الجنس) and noun of instance (*ism al-marra* اسم المرة)   89

  8 Diminutive (*al-taSghiir* التصغير)   90

  9 Abstraction nouns ending with *-iyya*   90

  10 Nouns not derived from verb roots   92

  11 Common nouns from quadriliteral and quinquiliteral roots: (*ʾasmaaʾ rubaaᶜiyya wa xumaasiyya* أسماء رباعية وخماسية)   93

  12 Collective nouns, mass nouns, and unit nouns (*ism al-jins* اسم الجنس; *ism al-waHda* اسم الوحدة)   94

  13 Borrowed nouns   95

  14 Arabic proper nouns   96

  15 Complex nouns, compound nouns, and compound nominals (*naHt* نحت and *tarkiib* تركيب)   99

6 Participles: active and passive   102

  1 Active participle (AP): (*ism al-faaᶜ il* اسم الفاعل)   103

  2 Passive participle (PP): (*ism al-mafᶜuul* اسم المفعول)   113

7 Noun inflections: gender, humanness, number, definiteness, and case   119

  1 Gender   119

  2 Humanness   125

  3 Number   129

  4 Definiteness and indefiniteness   156

  5 Case inflection   165

8 **Construct phrases and nouns in apposition** 205
 1 The construct phrase or ʾiDaafa الإضافة 205
 2 Nouns in apposition (badal بدل) 224

9 **Noun specifiers and quantifiers** 228
 1 Expressions of totality 228
 2 Expressions of limited number, non-specific number, or partiality 230
 3 Expressions of "more," "most," and "majority" 234
 4 Scope of quantifier agreement 235
 5 Non-quantitative specifiers 236

10 **Adjectives: function and form** 239
    Part one: Function 239
 1 Attributive adjectives 239
 2 Predicate adjectives 240
 3 Adjectives as substantives 240
 4 Arabic adjective inflection 241
 5 The adjective ʾiDaafa, the "false" ʾiDaafa
    (ʾiDaafa ghayr Haqiiqiyya إضافة غير حقيقية) 253
    Part two: Adjective derivation: the structure of Arabic adjectives 254
 1 Derivation patterns from Form I triliteral roots 255
 2 Quadriliteral root adjective patterns 258
 3 Participles functioning as adjectives 258
 4 Derivation through suffixation: relative adjectives (al-nisba النسبة) 261
 5 Color adjectives 270
 6 Non-derived adjectives 273
 7 Compound adjectives 274

11 **Adverbs and adverbial expressions** 276
 1 Adverbs of degree 277
 2 Adverbs of manner 281
 3 Place adverbials 288
 4 Time adverbials 290
 5 Numerical adverbials 295
 6 Adverbial accusative of specification (al-tamyiiz التمييز) 295
 7 Adverbial accusative of cause or reason (al-mafʿuul li-ʾajl-i-hi المفعول لأجله,
    al-mafʿuul la-hu المفعول له) 296
 8 Adverbs as speech acts 297

12 Personal pronouns   298

   1 Independent personal pronouns (*Damaaʾir munfaSila* ضمائر منفصلة)   298
   2 Suffix personal pronouns (*Damaaʾir muttaSila* ضمائر متصلة)   301
   3 Reflexive expressions with *nafs* plus pronouns   312
   4 Independent possessive pronoun: *dhuu* + noun   312

13 Demonstrative pronouns   315

   1 Demonstrative of proximity: 'this; these' هذا *haadhaa*   315
   2 Demonstrative of distance: 'that; those' ذلك *dhaalika*   316
   3 Functions of demonstratives   316
   4 Other demonstratives   319

14 Relative pronouns and relative clauses   322

   1 Definite relative pronouns   322
   2 Definite relative clauses   323
   3 Indefinite relative clauses   324
   4 Resumptive pronouns in relative clauses   324
   5 Indefinite or non-specific relative pronouns: *maa* ما and *man* مَنْ   325

15 Numerals and numeral phrases   329

   1 Cardinal numerals (*al-ʾaʿdaad* الأعداد)   329
   2 Ordinal numerals   354
   3 Other number-based expressions   360
   4 Expressions of serial order: "last"   364

16 Prepositions and prepositional phrases   366

   1 Overview   366
   2 True prepositions (*Huruuf al-jarr* حروف الجرّ)   367
   3 Locative adverbs or semi-prepositions
      (*Zuruuf makaan wa-Zuruuf zamaan* ظروف مكان وظروف زمان)   386
   4 Prepositions with clause objects   400

17 Questions and question words   401

   1 *ʾayn-a* أيْنَ 'where'   401
   2 *ʾayy-un* أيّ 'which; what'   402
   3 *kam* كَمْ 'how much; how many'   402
   4 *kayf-a* كَيْفَ 'how'   403
   5 *li-maadhaa* لِماذا 'why; what for'   403

6 *maa* ما and *maadhaa* ماذا 'what' 403

7 *man* مَنْ 'who; whom' 405

8 *mataa* متى 'when' 405

9 *hal* هَلْ and *ʾa-* أ- interrogative markers 405

18 Connectives and conjunctions 407
1 *wa-* 'and' (*waaw al-ʿaTf* واو العطف) 409
2 *fa-* ف 'and so; and then; yet; and thus' 410
3 Contrastive conjunctions 411
4 Explanatory conjunctions 412
5 Resultative conjunctions 412
6 Adverbial conjunctions 413
7 Disjunctives 417
8 Sentence-starting connectives 419

19 Subordinating conjunctions: the particle *ʾinna* and her sisters 422
1 Introduction 422
2 The particles 425

20 Verb classes 429
1 Verb roots 429
2 Verb derivation patterns: *ʾawzaan al-fiʿl* أوزان الفعل 433

21 Verb inflection: a summary 438
1 Verb inflection 438
2 Complex predicates: compound verbs, *qad*, and verb strings 446

22 Form I: The base form triliteral verb 455
1 Basic characteristics 455
2 Regular (sound) triliteral root (*al-fiʿl al-SaHiiH al-saalim* الفعل الصحيح السالم) 456
3 Geminate verb root (*al-fiʿl al-muDaʿʿaf* الفعل المضعّف) 458
4 Hamzated verb root (*al-fiʿl al-mahmuuz* الفعل المهموز) 460
5 Assimilated verb root (*al-fiʿl al-mithaal* الفعل المثال) 460
6 Hollow root (*al-fiʿl al-ʾajwaf* الفعل الأجوف) 461
7 Defective verb root (*al-fiʿl al-naaqiS* الفعل الناقص) 463
8 Doubly weak or "mixed" verb root 464
9 Verbal nouns of Form I 465
10 Form I participles 470

23 Form II   491
   1 Basic characteristics   491
   2 Regular (sound) triliteral root   492
   3 Geminate (doubled) root Form II   492
   4 Hamzated roots in Form II   492
   5 Assimilated roots in Form II   493
   6 Hollow roots in Form II   493
   7 Defective roots in Form II   493
   8 Doubly weak roots in Form II   494
   9 Examples of Form II verbs in context   494
  10 Form II verbal nouns   494
  11 Form II participles   496

24 Form III triliteral verb   503
   1 Basic characteristics   503
   2 Regular (sound) triliteral root   503
   3 Geminate (doubled) root Form III   504
   4 Hamzated roots in Form III   504
   5 Assimilated roots in Form III   505
   6 Hollow roots in Form III   505
   7 Defective roots in Form III   505
   8 Doubly weak roots in Form III   506
   9 Examples of Form III verbs in context   506
  10 Form III verbal noun   506
  11 Form III Participles: 508

25 Form IV triliteral verb   515
   1 Basic characteristics   515
   2 Regular (sound) triliteral root   516
   3 Geminate (doubled) root Form IV   516
   4 Hamzated roots in Form IV   517
   5 Assimilated roots in Form IV   517
   6 Hollow roots in Form IV   517
   7 Defective roots in Form IV   518
   8 Doubly weak roots in Form IV   518
   9 Exclamatory Form IV   518
  10 Examples of Form IV verbs in context   519
  11 Verbal noun of Form IV   519
  12 Form IV participles   521

26 Form V triliteral verb   530
  1 Basic characteristics   530
  2 Regular (sound) triliteral root   531
  3 Geminate (doubled) root Form V   531
  4 Hamzated roots in Form V   531
  5 Assimilated roots in Form V   532
  6 Hollow roots in Form V   532
  7 Defective roots in Form V   532
  8 Doubly weak roots in Form V   533
  9 Examples of Form V verbs in context   533
10 Form V verbal nouns   533
11 Form V participles   534

27 Form VI triliteral verb   543
  1 Basic characteristics   543
  2 Regular (sound) triliteral root   543
  3 Geminate (doubled) root Form VI   544
  4 Hamzated roots in Form VI   544
  5 Assimilated roots in Form VI   545
  6 Hollow roots in Form VI   545
  7 Defective roots in Form VI   545
  8 Examples of Form VI verbs in context   545
  9 Form VI verbal noun   546
10 Form VI participles   547

28 Form VII triliteral verb   555
  1 Basic characteristics   555
  2 Regular (sound) triliteral root   556
  3 Geminate (doubled) root Form VII   556
  4 Hamzated roots in Form VII   556
  5 Assimilated roots in Form VII   557
  6 Hollow roots in Form VII   557
  7 Defective roots in Form VII   557
  8 Examples of Form VII verbs in context   557
  9 Form VII verbal noun   557
10 Form VII participles   558

29 Form VIII triliteral verb   565
  1 Basic characteristics   565
  2 Regular or sound roots   568

3 Geminate (doubled) root Form VIII   568

4 Hamzated roots in Form VIII   568

5 Assimilated roots in Form VIII   569

6 Hollow roots in Form VIII   569

7 Defective roots in Form VIII   569

8 Examples of Form VIII verbs in context   569

9 Verbal nouns of Form VIII   570

10 Form VIII participles   571

30 Form IX triliteral verb   579

1 Basic characteristics   579

2 Sound/regular roots in Form IX   579

3 Geminate (doubled) roots Form IX   580

4 Hamzated roots in Form IX   580

5 Assimilated roots in Form IX   580

6 Hollow roots in Form IX   580

7 Defective roots in Form IX: rare   580

8 Form IX verbs in context   580

9 Verbal nouns of Form IX   580

10 Form IX participles   581

31 Form X triliteral verb   584

1 Basic characteristics   584

2 Sound/regular root   585

3 Geminate (doubled) roots in Form X   585

4 Hamzated roots in Form X   585

5 Assimilated roots in Form X   585

6 Hollow roots in Form X   585

7 Defective roots in Form X   586

8 Examples of Form X verbs in context   586

9 Form X verbal nouns   586

10 Form X participles   587

32 Forms XI–XV triliteral verb   596

1 Form XI: *if*ᶜ*aall-a* افعالّ /*ya-f*ᶜ*aall-u* يَفعالّ   596

2 Form XII: *if*ᶜ*aw*ᶜ*al-a* افْعَوْعَلَ/*ya-f*ᶜ*aw*ᶜ*il-u* يفْعَوْعِل   596

3 Form XIII: *if*ᶜ*awwal-a* افْعَوَّلَ / *ya-f*ᶜ*awwil-u* يفْعَوِّل   597

4 Form XIV: *if*ᶜ*anlal-a* افْعَنْلَلَ / *ya-f*ᶜ*anlil-u* يفْعَنْلِل   597

5 Form XV: *if*ᶜ*anlaa* افْعَنْلى /*ya-f*ᶜ*anlii* يفْعَنْلى   597

33 Quadriliteral verbs 599
  1 Basic characteristics of quadriliteral verb roots
    (ʾafʿaal rubaaʿiyya أفعال رباعيّة) 599
  2 Form I 599
  3 Form II 601
  4 Form III 602
  5 Form IV 603
  6 Examples of quadriliteral verbs in context 603
  7 Quadriliteral verbal nouns 604
  8 Form I quadriliteral participles 604

34 Moods of the verb I: indicative and subjunctive 606
  1 The indicative mood: al-muDaariʿ al-marfuuʿ المضارع المرفوع 606
  2 The subjunctive mood: al-muDaariʿ al-manSuub المضارع المنصوب 608

35 Moods of the verb II: jussive and imperative 616
  1 The jussive: al-jazm الجزم 616
  2 The imperative: al-ʾamr الأمر 622
  3 The permissive or hortative imperative: laam al-ʾamr لام الأمر 632
  4 The negative imperative: laa لا + jussive 632

36 Verbs of being, becoming, remaining, seeming
(kaan-a wa-ʾ axawaat-u-haa) 634
  1 The verb kaan-a كان /ya-kuun-u يَكون 'to be' 634
  2 The verb lays-a لَيْس 'to not be' 637
  3 Verbs of becoming: baat-a بات ʾaSbaH-a أصبَح, Saar-a صار 637
  4 Verbs of remaining: baqiy-a بَقِي, Zall-a ظلّ, maa zaal-a ما زالَ,
    maa daam-a ما دامَ 638
  5 Verbs of seeming or appearing 640

37 Negation and exception 641
  1 The verb lays-a لَيْس 'to not be' 641
  2 Negative particles and their effects 644
  3 Exceptive expressions 650

38 Passive and passive-type expressions 657
  1 Introduction 657
  2 The internal or inflectional passive 659
  3 Passive with derived forms of the verb 668

39 Conditional and optative expressions   671
   1 Possible conditions: *idhaa* إذا and *ʾin* إِنْ   671
   2 Conditional expressed with *-maa* ما 'ever'   674
   3 Contrary-to-fact conditionals: *la-* لَ *law . . .* لَوْ   675
   4 Optative constructions   676

Appendix I: How to use an Arabic dictionary   677
Appendix II: Glossary of technical terms   682
References   691
Index   701

Preface

This basic reference grammar is intended as a handbook for the general learner – a step on the way toward greater understanding of the Arabic language. Many excellent and effective textbooks for teaching Classical Arabic and Modern Standard Arabic (MSA) exist, as well as published research on a range of topics in Arabic linguistics (e.g., phonology, morphology, syntax, variation theory), but information in English on MSA grammatical topics tends to be scattered, and if a complete answer to a question regarding contemporary usage is needed, sometimes a number of sources need to be consulted.

The idea behind this reference grammar is to gather together in one work the essentials of MSA in such a way that fundamental elements of structure can be readily looked up and illustrated. It is intended primarily for learners of MSA as a practical guide for supporting their textbook lessons, classroom work, or self-study. This book is not intended in any way to supplant the exhaustive and profound analyses of classical and literary Arabic such as those by Wright (1896, reprint 1967) and Cantarino (1974–76). Those monumental books stand on their own and are irreplaceable reference works. This book is a work of considerably more modest goals and proportions.

1 Goals
This book is not designed to cover the entire field of literary or classical Arabic grammar. A comprehensive accounting of Arabic grammar is an undertaking of great complexity and depth, of competing indigenous paradigms (Basran and Kufan), of several dimensions (diachronic, synchronic, comparative), and of theoretical investigation across the spectrum of contemporary linguistic fields (e.g., phonology, morphology, syntax, semantics, pragmatics, sociolinguistics, and discourse analysis).

The Arabic language is a vast treasure-house of linguistic and literary resources that extend back into the first millennium. Its grammatical tradition is over a thousand years old and contains resources of extraordinary depth and sophistication. Works in English such as Lane's dictionary (1863, reprint 1984), Wehr's dictionary (fourth edition, 1979), Wright's grammar (1896, reprint 1967), and

Howell's grammar (reprint 1986) are seminal contributions in English to under-standing the wealth of the Arabic linguistic tradition. Yet, for the neophyte, for the average learner, or for the non-specialized linguist, easily usable reference works are still needed. This is, therefore, not a comprehensive reference grammar covering the full range of grammatical structures in both Classical and Modern Standard Arabic; rather, it centers on the essentials of modern written Arabic likely to be encountered in contemporary Arabic expository prose.

2 Methodology

The choices of explanations, examples, and layouts of paradigms in this book are pragmatically motivated rather than theoretically motivated and are not intended to reflect a particular grammatical or theoretical approach. I have been eclectic in providing descriptions of Arabic language features and structures, always with the intent of providing the most efficient access to Arabic forms and structures for Eng-lish speakers. For example, I have assigned numbers to noun declensions for ease of reference. Also, I refer throughout the text to "past tense" and "present tense" verbs rather than "perfect" tense and "imperfect" tense verbs, although this has not been standard practice for Arabic textbooks or grammars.[1] I refer to the "locative adverbs" (*Zuruuf makaan wa-Zuruuf zamaan*) as "semi-prepositions" (following Kouloughli 1994) because it captures their similarities to prepositions.[2]

Many Arabic terms and classifications, however, such as the "sisters of *'inna*" and the "sisters of *kaan-a*" are highly useful and pragmatic ways of organizing and presenting morphological and syntactic information, even to nonnative speakers of Arabic, so they have been retained. I have endeavored to provide both English and Arabic technical terms for categorized phenomena.

There are those, both traditionalists and non-traditionalists, who will no doubt disagree with the mode of presentation and grammatical descriptions used in this book. However, since this text is aimed at learners and interested laypeople as well as linguists, I hope that the categories devised and the descriptions and examples provided will be useful, readable, and readily understandable. Translit-eration is provided for all examples so that readers who do not have a grasp of Arabic script may have access to phonological structure.

3 The database

This reference grammar is based on contemporary expository prose, chiefly but not exclusively from Arabic newspapers and magazines, as the main resource for

---

[1] See the rationale for this choice in Chapter 21 on verb inflection, section 1.2.2.
[2] *Grammaire de l'arabe d'aujourd'hui*, D. E. Kouloughli refers to *Zuruuf makaan wa-Zuruuf zamaan* as "quasi-prépositions." (152).

topics and examples of current everyday Arabic writing practice. The grammatical description that emerges therefore calibrates closely with contemporary written usage. Media Arabic was chosen as a main source of data for this text because of its contemporaneousness, its coverage of many different topics, and the extemporary nature of daily reporting and editing. As a primary source of information about and from the Arab world, newspaper and magazine language reflects Arab editorial and public opinion and topics of current interest.[3] Various subject matter and texts were covered, ranging from interviews, book reviews, feature stories, religion and culture, and sports reports, to straight news reports and editorials. In addition to newspapers, other sources used for data collection included contemporary novels and nonfiction. This is therefore strictly a descriptive grammar that seeks to describe MSA as it is within the parameters noted above, and not to evaluate it or compare it with earlier or more elegant and elaborate forms of the written language.

There are doubtless those who would assert that the ordinariness of media language causes it to lack the beauty and expressiveness of literary Arabic, and therefore that it is unrepresentative of the great cultural and literary achievements of the Arabs.[4] To those I would reply that the very ordinariness of this type of language is what makes it valuable to learners because it represents a widely used and understood standard of written expression. As Owens and Bani-Yasin (1987, 736) note, "the average Arab is probably more exposed to this style than to most others, such as academic or literary writing." In fact, it is a vital and emergent form of written language, being created and recreated on a daily basis, covering issues from the mundane to the extraordinary. With limited time to prepare its presentation style, media Arabic reflects more closely than other forms of the written language the strategies and structures of spontaneous expression.[5]

Media Arabic is straightforward enough in its content and style to form the basis for advanced levels of proficiency and comprehension, to expand vocabulary, to create confidence in understanding a wide range of topics, and particu-

---

[3] Media discourse is described by Bell and Garrett (1998, 3) as "a rich resource of readily accessible data for research and teaching" and its usage "influences and represents people's use of and attitudes towards language in a speech community." They also state that "the media reflect and influence the formation and expression of culture, politics and social life" (1998, 4).

[4] Cantarino, for example, in the introduction to his major work, *The Syntax of Modern Arabic Prose*, vol. I, states that in compiling his illustrative materials, he consulted a variety of literary sources, but "Newspapers have generally been disregarded, since Arabic journalism – like most news writing around the world – does not necessarily offer the best or most representative standard of literary language" (1974, 1:x).

[5] The discipline of "media discourse research" or "media discourse analysis" is a rapidly growing one in linguistics. See Cotter 2001 for an overview of developments in this field. See also the cogent discussion of Arabic newspapers and the teaching of MSA in Taha 1995, and Mehall 1999.

larly to provide clear reference points for issues of structural accuracy.[6] As Widdowson has stated, students whose future contexts of use are broad and not clearly predictable need fundamental exposure to "a language of wider communication, a language of maximal generality or projection value" (1988, 7). I see media language as a cornerstone of linguistic and cultural literacy in Arabic; a medium which can be a useful goal in itself, but also a partial and practical goal for those who ultimately aim to study the Arabic literary tradition in all its elegance, diversity, and richness.

4 Contents

The book is arranged so that grammar notes are numbered and indexed for ease of reference; examples provided are based on information in the database. I have omitted or avoided names of persons and sometimes I have changed the content words to be less specific. For the most part, I have not created ad hoc examples; illustrations of syntactic structure are based on authentic usage. A section on how to use an Arabic dictionary is provided, as well as lists of Arabic and English technical terms, a bibliography that includes specialized and general works in Arabic, English, French, and German, and indexes based on Arabic terms and English terms.

Although I have tried to cover a wide range of aspects of contemporary written Arabic usage, there are bound to be lacunae, for which I am responsible. In terms of accuracy of description, the entire book has been submitted to native Arabic-speaking scholars and professional linguists for checking the grammatical descriptions and examples, but I alone am responsible for any shortcomings in that respect.

Procedures:

- Proper names have been left unvoweled on the final consonant, except where the voweling illustrates the grammatical point under discussion.
- For individual words or word groups taken out of context, the nominative case is used as the base or citation form.
- In giving English equivalents for Arabic structures, I have included in square brackets [ ] words inserted into English that are not present in the Arabic text but are necessary for understanding in English.
- I have included in parentheses and single quotes (' ') a more or less exact wording in the Arabic text that does not appear in the English equivalent.

---

[6] In his article "Broadcast news as a language standard," Allan Bell discusses the central role of media in reinforcing and disseminating a prestige standard language, especially in multilingual, multi-dialectal, or diglossic societies. See Bell 1983.

- In running text, English equivalents of Arabic lexical items are referred to in single quotes ''.
- In giving English equivalents for Arabic lexical items, essentially synonymous English meanings are separated by commas, whereas a semicolon separates equivalents with substantially different meanings.
- For purposes of brevity, in providing English equivalents of lexical items with broad semantic ranges, I have selected only one or two common meanings. These are not meant to be full definitions, only very basic glosses.

Abbreviations

acc.	accusative
adj.	adjective
adv.	adverb
AP	active participle
C	any consonant
CA	Classical Arabic
comp.	comparative
def.	definite
demons.	demonstrative pronoun
ESA	Educated Spoken Arabic
f./ fem.	feminine
Fr.	French
FSA	Formal Spoken Arabic
fut.	future
g.	gender
gen.	genitive
imp.	imperative
indef.	indefinite
indic.	indicative
intr.	intransitive
lw	loanword
m./masc.	masculine
MSA	Modern Standard Arabic
n.	noun
neg.	negative
no.	number
nom.	nominative
NP	noun phrase
o.s.	one's self
obj.	object
p./pers.	person

pass.	passive
perf.	perfect
pers.	person
pl./plur.	plural
plup.	pluperfect
pos.	positive
PP	passive participle
pres.	present
pron.	pronoun
quad.	quadriliteral
QAP	quadriliteral active participle
QPP	quadriliteral passive participle
refl.	reflexive
rel. pron.	relative pronoun
s.o.	someone
s.th.	something
sg./sing.	singular
subj.	subjunctive
superl.	superlative
trans.	transitive
v.	verb
V	any short vowel
vd.	voiced
vl.	voiceless
VN	verbal noun (*maSdar*)
VP	verb phrase
VV	any long vowel

Other diacritics:

boldface words (in examples)	indicate key words in examples
boldface syllables	indicate primary word stress
–	morpheme boundary[1]

---

[1] For purposes of structural clarity I have indicated inflectional morpheme boundaries within words when possible. There are points where morpheme boundaries merge (as in the endings of defective verbs and nouns); in these cases I have omitted a specific boundary marker.

/	separates singular and plural forms of substantives and past/present citation forms of verbs, e.g.,
	dars/duruus 'lesson/s'
	daras-a/ya-drus-u 'to study'
//	encloses phonemic transcription
' '	encloses glosses or translations
*	indicates a hypothetical or reconstructed form
~	'alternates with; or'

Acknowledgments

I am indebted to my first editor at Cambridge University Press, Kate Brett, for encouraging and shepherding this project in its initial stages. I gratefully acknowledge the support and help of my subsequent Cambridge editor, Helen Barton, who saw this project through its final stages, to Alison Powell and her production team, and to Jacque French for her careful copy editing. Deepest thanks go to Roger Allen and Mahdi Alosh, to my Georgetown colleagues Mohssen Esseesy, Serafina Hager, Margaret Nydell, Irfan Shahid, and Barbara Stowasser; and especially to David Mehall, who worked closely with me in editing and providing the Arabic script of the text.

I would also like to express my deep appreciation to Dr. Omar Al-Zawawi, Special Advisor to His Majesty Sultan Qaboos bin Said, Sultan of Oman.

Much gratitude is owed to my colleague Amin Bonnah who advised me throughout my research on knotty grammatical questions, and whose insight into and knowledge of the Arabic grammatical system is encyclopedic and unmatched. Invariably, when I had doubts or questions about particular structures or usages, I consulted Dr. Bonnah. Invariably, he had the answer or was able to find it out. If this reference grammar is found useful and valid, it is largely due to his guidance and contributions.

Any gaps, omissions, errors, or other infelicities in this text are my responsibility alone.

Sincere thanks go to all the faculty and students in the Arabic Department at Georgetown University who tolerated my obsession with collecting data, drafting, and compiling the book over a number of years. And I want to thank my husband, Victor Litwinski, who through his caring support and virtuoso editing skills made it possible for me to complete this project.

1

Introduction to Arabic

Arabic is a Semitic language akin to Hebrew, Aramaic, and Amharic, and more distantly related to indigenous language families of North Africa. It possesses a rich literary heritage dating back to the pre-Islamic era, and during the rise and expansion of the Islamic empire (seventh to twelfth centuries, AD), it became the official administrative language of the empire as well as a leading language of international scholarly and scientific communication. It is today the native language of over 200 million people in twenty different countries as well as the liturgical language for over a billion Muslims throughout the world.

1 Afro-Asiatic and the Semitic language family

The Semitic language family is a member of a broader group of languages, termed Afro-Asiatic (also referred to as Hamito-Semitic). This group includes four subfamilies in addition to Semitic, all of which are indigenous languages of North Africa: (1) Tamazight (Berber) in the Northwest (Morocco, Mauretania, Algeria, Tunisia and Libya); (2) the Chad languages (including Hausa) in the Northwest Central area; (3) ancient Egyptian and Coptic; and (4) the Cushitic languages of Northeast Africa (Somalia, the Horn of Africa).[1] The Semitic part of the family was originally based farthest East, in the Levant, the Fertile Crescent, and the Arabian peninsula.

Arabic, Hebrew, Aramaic (including Syriac), and Amharic are living language members of the Semitic group, but extinct languages such as Akkadian (Assyrian and Babylonian), Canaanite, and Phoenician are also Semitic. The Semitic language family has a long and distinguished literary history and several of its daughter languages have left written records of compelling interest and importance for the history of civilization.[2]

---

[1] See Zaborski 1992 for a brief description of the Afro-Asiatic language family and its general characteristics.

[2] For a general description of Arabic and the Semitic group, see Bateson 1967 (2003), 50–58 and Versteegh 1997, 9-22. For a more detailed discussion of the Semitic family and an extensive bibliography, see Hetzron 1987 and especially 1992, where he provides a list of fifty-one Semitic languages. For book-length introductions to comparative Semitic linguistic structure, see Wright 1966, Gray 1934, and especially Moscati 1969.

2 An overview of Arabic language history

The earliest stages of the Arabic language (Proto-Arabic or Old Arabic) are docu-
mented from about the seventh century BC until approximately the third century
AD, but because of the paucity of written records, little is known about the nature
of the language of those times. The only written evidence is in the form of
epigraphic material (brief rock inscriptions and graffiti) found in northwest and
central Arabia.[3]

   The next period, the third through fifth centuries, is usually referred to as Early
Arabic, a transitional period during which the language evolved into a closer sem-
blance of Classical Arabic. There are again few literary artifacts from this age, but
it is known that there was extensive commercial and cultural interaction with
Christian and Jewish cultures during this time, an era of both Roman and Byzan-
tine rule in the Levant and the Fertile Crescent.[4]

3 Classical Arabic

The start of the literary or Classical Arabic era is usually calculated from the sixth
century, which saw a vigorous flourishing of the Arabic literary (or poetic) language, especially in public recitation and oral composition of poetry, a refined
and highly developed formal oral art practiced by all Arab tribal groups and
held in the highest esteem. During the sixth century, the Arabic ode, or *qaSîda*,
evolved to its highest and most eloquent form. It was characterized by sophisticated metrics and a "highly conventionalized scheme . . . upwards of sixty cou-
plets all following an identical rhyme."[5]

   The form of language used in these odes is often referred to as the standard
poetic language or the poetic koinè, and there are conflicting theories as to its
nature – whether it was an elevated, distinctive, supra-tribal language shared by
the leadership of the Arabic-speaking communities, or whether it was the actual
vernacular of a region or tribe which was adopted by poets as a shared vehicle
for artistic expression. In particular, debate has centered around the existence
and use of desinential (i.e., word-final) case and mood inflection, a central feature of classical poetry but one which fell increasingly out of use in spoken Arabic, and which no longer exists in the urban vernaculars of today. Since little is

---

[3] A condensed but authoritative overview of the history and development of Arabic is provided in
the article "Arabiyya" in the *Encyclopedia of Islam* (1960, I:561–603). See also Kaye 1987 and Fischer 1992.
On the pre-Islamic period in particular, see Beeston 1981 and Versteegh 1997, 23–52. A good general
reference in Arabic is Hijazi 1978.

[4] For a comprehensive, multi-volume study of the Arab world and its relations with Rome and
Byzantium in late classical antiquity see Shahîd 1981, 1984, 1989, and 1995.

[5] Arberry 1957, 15. For further discussion of pre-Islamic Arabic poetry, see Nicholson 1987. See also
Zwettler 1978 for a survey and analysis of the Arabic oral poetry tradition.

known about the nature of the everyday spoken Arabic of pre-Islamic times or the different levels of linguistic formality that might have been used on different occasions, certainty has not been reached on this point, although theories abound.[6]

In the seventh century AD the Prophet Muhammad was gifted over a period of years (622–632 AD) with the revelation of verses which constituted a holy book, the *Qurʾân*, in Arabic, which became the key text of the new monotheistic religion, Islam. The text was rendered into an official version during the reign of the Caliph ʿUthmân (644–656 AD). From that time on, Arabic was not only a language of great poetic power and sophistication, but also permanently sacralized; as the chosen language for the *Qurʾân*, it became the object of centuries of religious study and exegesis, theological analysis, grammatical analysis and speculation.[7] Throughout the European medieval period, from the seventh through the twelfth centuries, the Arabic-speaking world and the Islamic empire expanded and flourished, centered first in Mecca and Madina, then Damascus, and then Baghdad.[8] Arabic became an international language of civilization, culture, scientific writing and research, diplomacy, and administration. From the Iberian peninsula in the West to Central and South Asia in the East stretched the world of Islam, and the influence of Arabic. The vast empire eventually weakened under the growing influence and power of emerging independent Muslim dynasties, with inroads made by the Crusades, Mongol invasions from the East, and with the expulsion of Muslims from the Iberian peninsula in the West. Arabic remained the dominant language in North Africa, the Levant, the Fertile Crescent, and the Arabian Peninsula, but lost ground to indigenous languages such as Persian in the East, and Spanish in the West.[9]

The language era from the thirteenth century to the eighteenth is generally known as "Middle Arabic," although there is some ambiguity to this term.[10] During this time, the Classical Arabic of early Islam remained the literary language, but the spoken Arabic of everyday life shifted into regional variations, each geographical

---

[6] On the nature of the standard poetic language and the pre-Islamic koinè, see Zwettler 1978, especially Chapter 3; Rabin 1955; Fück 1955; Corriente 1976; and Versteegh 1984, especially Chapter 1.

[7] For a brief introduction to the origins of Islam and the Qurʾânic revelations, see Nicholson 1930, especially Chapter 4.

[8] The main dynasties of the Caliphate are: the Orthodox Caliphs (632–661 AD); the Umayyads, based in Damascus (661–750 AD); and the Abbasids, based in Baghdad (750–1258 AD).

[9] Arabic has remained the dominant language in countries where the substratum language was originally Semitic or Afro-Asiatic, but not where the substratum languages were Indo-European, such as Persia or the Iberian peninsula. Aside from nationalistic and political considerations, linguistic compatibility between Arabic and its sister languages may have enabled certain populations to adapt more easily and throughly to Arabic. See Bateson 1967 (2003), 72–73 on this topic.

[10] Versteegh (1997, 114–29) has a cogent discussion of the issues related to "Middle Arabic." See also Blau 1961.

area evolving a characteristic vernacular.[11] The spoken variants of Arabic were not generally written down and therefore not preserved or anchored in any way to formalize them, to give them literary status or grammatical legitimacy. They continued to evolve along their own lively and supple paths, calibrating to the changes of everyday life over the centuries, but never reaching the status of separate languages.[12]

4 The modern period

The modern period of Arabic dates approximately from the end of the eighteenth century, with the spread of literacy, the concept of universal education, the inception of journalism, and exposure to Western writing practices and styles such as editorials, short stories, plays, and novels. Many linguists make a distinction between Classical Arabic (CA), the name of the literary language of the previous eras, and the modern form of literary Arabic, commonly known (in English) as Modern Standard Arabic (MSA). Differences between CA and MSA are primarily in style and vocabulary, since they represent the written traditions of very different historical and cultural eras, from the early medieval period to the modern. In terms of linguistic structure, CA and MSA are largely but not completely similar. Within MSA, syntax and style range from complex and erudite forms of discourse in learned usage to more streamlined expression in the journalistic, broadcasting, and advertising worlds. The high degree of similarity between CA and MSA gives strong continuity to the literary and Islamic liturgical tradition.

In Arabic, both CA and MSA are referred to as *al-lugha al-fuSHâ* اللغة الفصحى, or simply, *al-fuSHâ* الفصحى, which means "the most eloquent (language)." Badawi (1985) draws a helpful distinction between *fuSHâ al-ʿaSr* فصحى العصر (of the modern era) (MSA) and *fuSHâ al-turâth* فصحى التراث (of heritage) (CA). This is by no means a clear or universally accepted delineation, and opinion in the Arab world is apparently divided as to the scope and definition of the term *fuSHâ* فصحى.[13]

---

[11] There is speculation that the written/spoken Arabic dichotomy began much earlier, during the ninth century. See Blau 1961, Versteegh 1984, Fück 1955. For an evaluation of the main theories of Arabic dialect evolution and an extensive bibliography on the topic, see Miller 1986 and Bateson 1967 (2003), 94–114.

[12] This contrasts distinctively with the situation in the Scandinavian countries, for example, where a similar situation prevailed in that a mother language, known as Common Scandinavian, prevailed from about AD 550–1050, and then evolved into six official, literary languages (Danish, Dano-Norwegian, New-Norwegian, Swedish, Faroese, and Icelandic), plus many dialects. Despite the fact that the offshoots are all considered independent languages, "within this core [mainland Scandinavia] speakers normally expect to be understood [by each other] when speaking their native languages" (Haugen 1976, 23–24).

[13] See Parkinson's informative 1991 article for an extensive discussion of *fuSHâ*. In his study of Egyptian native Arabic speakers' ability with *fuSHâ*, he came to the conclusion that "The important point here is that people do not agree on a term, and that further they do not agree on what specific part of the communicative continuum, i.e., what specific varieties, any particular term should refer to" (33).

5 Arabic today

The Arab world today is characterized by a high degree of linguistic and cultural continuity. Arabic is the official language of all the members of the Arab League, from North Africa to the Arabian Gulf.[14] Although geography (including great distances and land barriers such as deserts and mountains) accounts for much of the diversity of regional vernaculars, a shared history, cultural background and (to a great extent) religion act to unify Arab society and give it a profound sense of cohesion and identity.

MSA is the language of written Arabic media, e.g., newspapers, books, journals, street signs, advertisements – all forms of the printed word. It is also the language of public speaking and news broadcasts on radio and television. This means that in the Arab world one needs to be able to comprehend both the written and the spoken forms of MSA. However, in order to speak informally with people about ordinary everyday topics, since there is no universally agreed-upon standard speech norm, Arabs are fluent in at least one vernacular form of Arabic (their mother tongue), and they understand a wide range of others. This coexistence of two language varieties, the everyday spoken vernacular and a higher literary form is referred to in linguistic terms as "diglossia."

5.1 Diglossia

The divergence among the several vernacular forms of Arabic, and between the vernaculars as a whole and the standard written form, make the linguistic situation of the Arab world a complex one.[15] Instead of having one universally agreed-upon standard speech norm, each major region of the Arab world (such as the Levant, the Arabian Gulf, the western Arabian peninsula, western North Africa, Egypt, and the Sudan) has as its own speech norm, a spoken vernacular coexistent with the written standard – MSA. Vernacular speech is much more flexible and mutable than the written language; it easily coins words, adapts and adopts foreign expressions, incorporates the latest cultural concepts and trends, and propagates slang, thus producing and reflecting a rich, creative, and constantly changing range of innovation. Vernacular or colloquial languages have evolved their own forms of linguistic artistry and tradition in terms of popular songs, folk songs, punning and jokes, folktales and spontaneous performance art.

---

[14] Morocco, Algeria, Tunisia, Libya, Egypt, Sudan, Mauretania, Jordan, Lebanon, Palestine, Syria, Iraq, Kuwait, Bahrein, Qatar, UAE, Oman, Saudi Arabia, and Yemen.

[15] For more on diglossia, see Ferguson 1959a and 1996, and Walters, 1996. See also *Southwest Journal of Linguistics* 1991, which is a special issue devoted to diglossia. Haeri 2003 is a book-length study of the relationships among Classical Arabic, MSA, and colloquial Arabic in Egypt.

Their changeability, however, also means that Arabic vernaculars may vary substantially from one another in proportion to their geographical distance. That is, neighboring vernacular dialects such as Jordanian and Syrian are easily mutually intelligible to native Arabic speakers; however, distant regional dialects, such as Moroccan and Kuwaiti, have evolved cumulative differences which result in the need for conscious effort on the part of the speakers to accommodate each other and adjust their everyday language to a more mainstream level. Educated native Arabic speakers have enough mutual awareness of dialect characteristics that they can identify and adjust rapidly and naturally to the communicative needs of any situation.[16] This spontaneous yet complex adjustment made by Arabic speakers depends on their knowledge of the vast reservoir of the mutually understood written language, which enables them to intercommunicate. Therefore, Arabic speakers share a wealth of resources in their common grasp of the literary language, MSA, and they can use this as a basis even for everyday communication.

In the re-calibration of Arabic speech to be less regionally colloquial and more formal, however, some researchers have identified another variation on spoken Arabic, an intermediate level that is termed "cultivated," "literate," "formal," or "educated" spoken Arabic.[17] Thus, the Arabic language situation is characterized not simply as a sharp separation between written forms and spoken forms, but as a spectrum or continuum of gradations from "high" (very literary or formal) to "low" (very colloquial), with several levels of variation in between.[18] As Elgibali states (1993, 76), "we do not . . . have intuition or scholarly consensus concerning the number, discreteness and/or stability of the middle level(s)."

These levels are characterized by (at least) two different sociolinguistic dimensions: first, the social function; that is, the situations in which speakers find themselves – whether those situations are, for example, religious, formal, academic, casual or intimate. Secondly, these levels are conditioned by the educational and regional backgrounds of the speakers. In this intricate interplay of speech norms, situations, and backgrounds, educated native Arabic speakers easily find their way, making spontaneous, subtle linguistic adjustments to suit the dimensions of the occasion and the interlocutors.

---

[16] For a detailed discussion of variation in Arabic see Elgibali 1993.

[17] This is known as "cultivated" speech in Arabic: ʿâmmiyyat al-muthaqqafīn المثقّفين عامّية, or *lughat al-muthaqqafīn* المثقّفين لغة. A number of Arabic linguists have researched and discussed this phenomenon, but there is no consensus as to the nature, extent, definition, and use of this part of the Arabic language continuum. The focus of the dispute centers around the ill-defined and unstable nature of this particular form of spoken Arabic and whether or not it can be distinguished as an identifiable linguistic level of Arabic. For more discussion of this point, see Badawi 1985, Elgibali 1993, El-Hassan 1978, Hary 1996, Mitchell 1986, Parkinson 1993, and Ryding 1990 and 1991.

[18] See, for example, the five levels distinguished in Badawi 1985 and the "multiglossia" of Hary 1996.

5.2 Modern Standard Arabic: MSA

MSA is the written norm for all Arab countries as well as the major medium of communication for public speaking and broadcasting.[19] It serves not only as the vehicle for current forms of literature, but also as a resource language for communication between literate Arabs from geographically distant parts of the Arab world. A sound knowledge of MSA is a mark of prestige, education, and social standing; the learning of MSA by children helps eliminate dialect differences and initiates Arab children into their literary heritage and historical tradition. It aids in articulating the connections between Arab countries and creating a shared present as well as a shared past. Education in the Arab countries universally reinforces the teaching and maintenance of MSA as the single, coherent standard written language.

A number of excellent Western pedagogical texts have been developed over the past fifty years in which MSA is discussed, described, and explained to learners of Arabic as a foreign language.[20] However, up to this point, there has been no comprehensive reference grammar designed for use by western students of MSA.

5.3 Arabic academies

Grammatical and lexical conservatism are hallmarks of MSA. Arabic language academies exist in several Arab capitals (Cairo, Damascus, Baghdad, Amman) to determine and regulate the procedures for incorporation of new terminology, and to conserve the overall integrity of MSA.[21] Although foreign words are often borrowed into Arabic, especially for ever-expanding technical items and fields, the academies try to control the amount of borrowing and to introduce and encourage Arabic-derived equivalents, such as the Arabic word *hâtif* هاتف (pl. *hawâtif* هواتف) for 'telephone' (based on the Arabic lexical root *h-t-f*), to counteract the widespread use of the Arabized European term: *tiliifûn* تليفون.

According to Versteegh (1997, 178) "From the start, the goal of the Academy was twofold: to guard the integrity of the Arabic language and preserve it from dialectal and foreign influence, on the one hand, and to adapt the Arabic language to the needs of modern times, on the other." Another researcher states

> Arab academies have played a large role in the standardization of modern written and formal Arabic, to an extent that today throughout the Arab world there is more or less one modern standard variety. This is the variety used in newspapers, newsreel

---

[19] For a discussion and definition of this particular term, see McLaughlin 1972.

[20] See, for example, Abboud and McCarus 1983; Abboud, Attieh, McCarus, and Rammuny 1997; Brustad, Al-Batal, and Al-Tonsi 1995 and 1996; Cowan 1964; Middle East Centre for Arab Studies (MECAS) 1959 and 1965; Rammuny 1994; Ziadeh and Winder 1957.

[21] For more detail on Arabic language academies see Holes 1995, 251–55 and Stetkevytch 1970, 23–25 and 31–33.

broadcasting, educational books, official and legal notices, academic materials, and instructional texts of all kinds. The three academies that have had the greatest influence are those based in Cairo, Damascus and Baghdad. Among the common objectives of these academies is the development of a common MSA for all Arabic-speaking peoples.   (Abdulaziz 1986, 17).

5.4 Definitions of MSA

A fully agreed-upon definition of MSA does not yet exist, but there is a general consensus that modern Arabic writing in all its forms constitutes the basis of the identity of the language. Modern writing, however, covers an extensive range of discourse styles and genres ranging from complex and conservative to innovative and experimental. Finding a standard that is delimited and describable within this great range is a difficult task; however, there is an identifiable segment of the modern Arabic written language used for media purposes, and it has been the focus of linguists' attention for a number of years because of its stability, its pervasiveness, and its ability to serve as a model of contemporary written usage. Dissemination of a written (and broadcast) prestige standard by the news media is a widespread phenomenon, especially in multilingual, diglossic, and multi-dialectal societies.

One of the most complete descriptions of MSA is found in Vincent Monteil's *L'arabe moderne* in which he refers to "le néo-arabe" as "l'arabe classique, ou régulier, ou écrit, ou littéral, ou littéraire, sous sa forme moderne" (1960, 25). That is, he understands "modern Arabic" to be the modern version of the old classical language. He also states that "on pourrait aussi le traiter d'arabe 'de presse', étant donné le rôle déterminant qu'a joué, et que joue encore, dans sa diffusion ... *lughat al-jarâ'id*" (1960, 27). Defining MSA through its function as the language of the Arabic news media is a useful way to delimit it since it is not officially codified as a phenomenon separate from Classical Arabic and because Arabic speakers and Arabic linguists have differing opinions on what constitutes what is referred to as *al-lugha al-fuSHâ*. As Monteil also remarks, "s'il est exact de reconnaître ... que l'arabe moderne 'se trouve être une langue assez artificielle, une langue plus ou moins fabriquée' plutôt qu'un 'usage codifié,' il faut déclarer ... que 'c'est une langue vivante' et qui 'correspond à un besoin vital'" (1960, 28). It is these characteristics of newspaper language, its vitality and practicality, that make it a prime example of modern written Arabic usage.

Elsaid Badawi's phrase, *fuSHâ al-ʿaSr* العصر فصحى, is his Arabic term for MSA (1985, 17), which he locates on a continuum (at "level two") between Classical Arabic ("level one") and Educated Spoken Arabic ("level three"). As he points out, the levels "are not segregated entities," (1985, 17) but shade into each other gradually. He identifies level two (MSA) as "mostly written" rather than spoken, and levels two and three as essentially "in complementary distribution" with each other (1985, 19), that is, they function in separate spheres, with some overlap.

Leslie McLoughlin, in his 1972 article "Towards a definition of Modern Standard Arabic," attempts to identify distinctive features of MSA from one piece of "quality journalism" (57) and provides the following definition which he borrows from M. F. Saʿîd: "that variety of Arabic that is found in contemporary books, newspapers, and magazines, and that is used orally in formal speeches, public lectures, learned debates, religious ceremonials, and in news broadcasts over radio and television" (58). Whereas Saʿîd states that MSA grammar is explicitly defined in grammar books (which would bring it close to CA), McLoughlin finds several instances in which MSA differs from CA, some of which are lexical and some of which are syntactic (72–73).

In her *Arabic Language Handbook* (1967; 2003, 84), Mary Catherine Bateson identified three kinds of change that differentiate MSA from CA: (1) a "series of 'acceptable' simplifications" in syntactic structures, (2) a "vast shift in the lexicon due to the need for technical terminology," and (3) a "number of stylistic changes due to translations from European languages and extensive bilingualism."

In the research done for this book, a wide variety of primarily expository texts, including Arabic newspaper and magazine articles, as well as other forms of MSA, were consulted and put into a database over a period of ten years. The morphological and syntactic features of the language used in these writings were then analyzed and categorized. This resulted in the finding that few structural inconsistencies exist between MSA and CA; the major differences are stylistic and lexical rather than grammatical. Particular features of MSA journalistic style include more flexible word order, coinage of neologisms, and loan translations from western languages, especially the use of the *ʾiDaafa* إضافة or annexation structure to provide equivalents for compound words or complex concepts. It is just this ability to reflect and embody change while maintaining the major grammatical conventions and standards that make journalistic Arabic in particular, a lively and widely understood form of the written language and, within the style spectrum of Arabic as a whole, a functional written standard for all Arab countries.

2

Phonology and script

This chapter covers the essentials of script and orthography as well as MSA phonological structure, rules of sound distribution and patterning, pronunciation conventions, syllable structure, and word stress. Four features of Arabic script are distinctive: first, it is written from right to left; second, letters within words are connected in cursive style rather than printed individually; third, short vowels are normally invisible; and finally, there is no distinction between uppercase and lowercase letters. These features can combine to make Arabic script seem impenetrable to a foreigner at first. However, there are also some features of Arabic script that facilitate learning it. First of all, it is reasonably phonetic; that is, there is a good fit between the way words are spelled and the way they are pronounced. And secondly, word structure and spelling are very systematic.

1 The alphabet

There are twenty-eight Arabic consonant sounds, twenty-six of which are consistently consonants, but two of which – *waaw* and *yaa'* – are semivowels that serve two functions, sometimes as consonants and other times as vowels, depending on context.[1] For the most part, the Arabic alphabet corresponds to the distinctive sounds (phonemes) of Arabic, and each sound or letter has a name.[2] Arabic letter shapes vary because Arabic is written in cursive style, that is, the letters within a word are systematically joined together, as in English handwriting. There is no option in Arabic for "printing" or writing each letter of a word in independent form. There is no capitalization in Arabic script and therefore no distinction between capital and small letters. Letters are instead distinguished by their position in a word, i.e., whether they are word-initial, medial, or final. This is true

---

[1] "Certain consonants have some of the phonetic properties of vowels . . . they are usually referred to as approximants (or frictionless continuants), though [/w/ and /y/] are commonly called semivowels, as they have exactly the same articulation as vowel glides. Although phonetically vowel-like, these sounds are usually classified along with consonants on functional grounds" Crystal 1997, 159. See also section 4.2.2. this chapter.

[2] For further reading about the Arabic alphabet and its close conformity with the phonemes of the language, see Gordon, 1970, 193–97.

both in printed Arabic and in handwriting. Handwriting is not covered in this text, but there are several excellent books that provide instruction in it.[3]

Every letter has four possible shapes: word-initial, medial, final, and separate. The following table gives the names of the sounds of Arabic listed in dictionary or alphabetical order, along with their shapes:[4]

2 Names and shapes of the letters

Arabic letter shape

Name	Final	Letter	Initial	Independent
(hamza)				ء
ʾalif	ـا	ـا	ا	ا
baaʾ	ـب	ـبـ	بـ	ب
taaʾ	ـت	ـتـ	تـ	ت
thaaʾ	ـث	ـثـ	ثـ	ث
jiim	ـج	ـجـ	جـ	ج
Haaʾ	ـح	ـحـ	حـ	ح
xaaʾ	ـخ	ـخـ	خـ	خ
daal	ـد	ـد	د	د
dhaal	ـذ	ـذ	ذ	ذ
raaʾ	ـر	ـر	ر	ر
zaay	ـز	ـز	ز	ز
siin	ـس	ـسـ	سـ	س
shiin	ـش	ـشـ	شـ	ش
Saad	ـص	ـصـ	صـ	ص
Daad	ـض	ـضـ	ضـ	ض
Taaʾ	ـط	ـطـ	طـ	ط

---

[3] McCarus and Rammuny, 1974; Brustad, Al-Batal, and Al-Tonsi, 1995; Abboud and McCarus 1983, part 1:1–97.

[4] There is an older order which is not used for organizing dictionary entries, but which is used in presenting elements of a text in outline, much as English speakers would make points A., B., and C. That order is called the *ʾabjad*, and is usually recited in the form of words: *ʾabjad, hawwaz, HuTTii, kalaman, saʿfaS, qurishat, thaxadh-un DaZagh-un* (أَبْجَدَ هَوَّزْ حُطِّي كَلَمَنْ سَعْفَصْ قُرِشَتْ ثَخَذْ ضَظَغْ).

Arabic letter shape (cont.)

Name	Final	Letter	Initial	Independent
Zaaʾ	ظ	ظـ	ظـ	ظ
ʿayn	ع	ـعـ	عـ	ع
ghayn	غ	ـغـ	غـ	غ
faaʾ	ف	ـفـ	فـ	ف
qaaf	ق	ـقـ	قـ	ق
kaaf	ك	ـكـ	كـ	ك
laam	ل	ـلـ	لـ	ل
miim	م	ـمـ	مـ	م
nuun	ن	ـنـ	نـ	ن
haaʾ	ـه	ـهـ	هـ	ه
waaw	و	و	و	و
yaaʾ	ي	ـيـ	يـ	ي

The cursive nature of Arabic script, as shown above, requires several forms for each letter. Most letters are joined to others on both sides when they are medial, but there are a few that are called "non-connectors" which are attached to a preceding letter, but not to a following letter. The non-connectors are: *ʾalif, daal, dhaal, raaʾ, zaay,* and *waaw,* as shown in the following examples:

country	bilaad	بلاد
decision	qaraar	قرار
soldier	jundiyy	جندي
delicious	ladhiidh	لذيذ
ministry	wizaara	وزارة
star	kawkaba	كوْكَبة

3 Consonants: pronunciation and description

It is impossible to provide a fully accurate description of Arabic sounds solely through written description and classification. Some sounds are very similar to English, others slightly similar, and others quite different. This section provides a phonemic chart and some general principles of pronunciation as well as descriptions of Arabic sounds. The descriptions given here are for standard MSA pronunciation. Some sounds have allophones, or contextual variations, as noted.[5]

3.1 Phonemic chart of MSA consonants

	Labial	Labio-dental	Interdental	Alveolar	Palatal	Velar	Uvular	Pharyngeal	Glottal

Stops
  Voiceless
  Voiced
	b ب			ط T ت t
				ض D د d
						k ك	q ق		ء ʾ

Affricates
  Voiceless
  Voiced
					j ج				

Fricatives
  Voiceless
  Voiced
		f ف	th ث
			dh ذ Z ظ
				ص S س s
				z ز
					sh ش	x خ
						gh غ
								H ح
								ʿ ع
									h ه

Nasals	m م			n ن					
Laterals				l ل					
Flaps				r ر					
Semivowels (approximants)	w و				y ي				

3.2 Description of Arabic consonants

These descriptions are both technical and nontechnical, with examples relating to English sounds wherever possible.[6]

1 *hamza* (ʾ) (ء)   voiceless glottal stop: like the catch in the voice between the syllables of "oh-oh";[7]

2 *baaʾ* (b) (ب)   voiced bilabial stop; /b/ as in "big";

3 *taaʾ* (t) (ت)   voiceless alveolar stop; /t/ as in "tin";

---

[5] Colloquial regional variants, such as the pronunciation of /j/ as /y/ in the Arab Gulf region, or /k/ plus front vowel as /ch/ in Iraqi colloquial, are not provided here because they are nonstandard for formal pronunciation of MSA.

[6] For an in-depth, traditional account of Arabic phonetics, see Gairdner 1925. For technical analyses of Arabic phonology and its history, see Al-Ani 1970 and Semaan 1968.

[7] As Gairdner points out, another good example of this in English would be the hiatus prefixed to the stressed word "our" in the sentence "It wasn't our fault" (1925, 30).

4	*thaaʾ* (th) (ث)	voiceless interdental fricative; /θ/ or /th/ as in "thin";[8]
5	*jiim* (j) (ج)	There are three standard regional variants:
		(a) voiced alveopalatal affricate; / j/ as in "jump";
		(b) voiced alveopalatal fricative (zh): as the /z/ in "azure" or the medial sound in "pleasure";
		(c) voiced velar stop; /g / as in "goat";[9]
6	*Haaʾ* (H) (ح)	voiceless pharyngeal fricative; a sound produced deep in the throat using the muscles involved in swallowing. Constrict these muscles while at the same time pushing breath through – as though you were trying to stage-whisper "Hey!"[10]
7	*xaaʾ* (x) (خ)	voiceless velar fricative; like the /ch/ in Bach or Scottish loch; in some romanization systems it is represented by /kh/;
8	*daal* (d) (د)	voiced alveolar stop; /d/ as in "door";
9	*dhaal* (dh) (ذ)	voiced interdental fricative: /ð/ or /dh/ pronounced like the /th/ in "this";
10	*raaʾ* (r) (ر)	voiced alveolar flap or trill: as /r/ in Italian or Spanish; a good example in English is to pronounce the word "very" as "veddy";
11	*zaay* (z) (ز)	voiced alveolar fricative: /z /as in zip;
12	*siin* (s) (س)	voiceless alveolar fricative: /s/ as in sang;
13	*shiin* (sh) (ش)	voiceless palatal fricative: /sh/ as in ship;
14	*Saad* (S) (ص)	voiceless velarized alveolar fricative: /s/ but pronounced farther back in the mouth, with a raised and tensed tongue;
15	*Daad* (D) (ض)	voiced velarized alveolar stop: /d/ but pronounced farther back in the mouth, with a raised and tensed tongue;
16	*Taaʾ* (T) (ط)	voiceless velarized alveolar stop: /t/ pronounced farther back in the mouth, with a raised and tensed tongue;

---

[8] Arabic has two different symbols for the two phonemes or different kinds of "th" in English - the voiceless, as in "think" (often transcribed as /θ/) and the voiced interdental as in "them" (often transcribed as / ð /). *Thaaʾ* /ث/ is the voiceless one whereas *dhaal* /ذ/ is voiced. In this text, the voiceless version /θ/ is romanized as /th/, and the voiced / ð / as /dh/.

[9] The variations are essentially as follows: the first is more characteristic of the Arabian Peninsula and Iraq, the second more Levantine and North African, and the third specifically Egyptian and Sudanese pronunciation. Occasionally, a mixed pronunciation of *jiim* is found, with one variant alternating with another, especially /j/ and /zh/.

[10] The nature of the pharyngeal consonants *Haaʾ* and ʿ*ayn* is described in detail in McCarus and Rammuny 1974, 124–34 and in Gairdner 1925, 27–29.

17 *Zaa'* (Z) (ظ)	There are two standard variants of this phoneme: (a) voiced velarized interdental fricative: /dh/ as in "this" pronounced farther back in the mouth, with a raised and tensed tongue; (b) voiced velarized alveolar fricative: /z/ pronounced farther back in the mouth with a raised and tense tongue;[11]
18 *ᶜayn* (ᶜ) (ع)	voiced pharyngeal fricative: this is a "strangled" sound that comes from deep in the throat, using the muscles used in swallowing;[12]
19 *ghayn* (gh) (غ)	voiced velar fricative: a "gargled" sound, much like French /r/;
20 *faa'* (f) (ف)	voiceless labiodental fricative: as /f / in "fine";
21 *qaaf* (q) (ق)	voiceless uvular stop: this is made by "clicking" the back of the tongue against the very back of the mouth, where the uvula is;
22 *kaaf* (k) (ك)	voiceless velar stop: /k/ as in "king";
23 *laam* (l) (ل)	voiced lateral: this has two pronunciations: (a) /l/ as in "well" or "full" (back or "dark" /l/);[13] (b) /l/ as in "lift" or "leaf" (fronted or "light" /l/);[14]
24 *miim* (m) (م)	voiced bilabial continuant: /m/ as in "moon";
25 *nuun* (n) (ن)	voiced nasal continuant: /n/ as in "noon";
26 *haa'* (h) (ه)	voiceless glottal fricative: /h/ as in "hat";
27 *waaw* (w) or (uu) (و)	bilabial semivowel: /w/ as in "wind" or long vowel /uu/ pronounced like the "oo" in "food";
28 *yaa'* (y) or (ii) (ي)	palatal semivowel: /y/ as in "yes" or long vowel /ii/ pronounced like the long /i/ in "machine."[15]

The notation of Arabic consonants and their use in orthography is quite straightforward, except for the following considerations, which are described in detail: the orthography and pronunciation of the letter *hamza*, the spelling and pronunciation variants of the the *taa' marbuuTa*, and the doubling of consonant

---

[11] Pronunciation of *Dhaa / Zaa'* varies regionally; the interdental and alveolar fricatives are the most widely accepted.

[12] See note 10.

[13] Technically, this variant of /l/ is velarized. The tongue is raised in the back of the mouth. Although primarily an allophonic variant, for a theory of its status as a separate phoneme in Arabic, see Ferguson 1956.

[14] This variant of /l/ is more fronted and palatalized even than the light /l/ in English and is closer to French /l/ as in "belle." See Gairdner 1925, 17–19 for discussion of "dark" and "light" /l/.

[15] When *yaa'* is the final letter of a word, it is printed without dots in Egyptian publications; elsewhere in the Arab world, it receives its two dots at all times and in all positions.

strength (gemination). The nature of the approximants (semivowels) *waaw* and *yaa'* is also discussed at greater length under the section on vowels.

3.3 *hamza* rules: orthography and pronunciation

There are two kinds of *hamza*, strong and weak. Strong *hamza* is a regular consonant and is pronounced under all circumstances, whether in initial, medial, or final position in a word. Weak *hamza* or "elidable" *hamza* is a phonetic device that helps pronunciation of consonant clusters and only occurs at the beginning of a word. It is often deleted in context.

3.3.1 Strong *hamza* (*hamzat al-qaT^c* هَمْزَة القَطْع):

The Arabic letter *hamza* (') is often written with what is termed a "seat," or "chair" (*kursii* كُرْسي in Arabic), but sometimes the *hamza* sits aloof, by itself. There is a set of rules to determine which chair, if any, *hamza* will take, depending on its position within a word, as follows:

3.3.1.1 CHAIR RULES

(1)   The chairs used for *hamza* are identical with the letters for long vowels: *'alif, waaw,* and *yaa'*. When *yaa'* is used as a seat for *hamza*, it loses its two dots.

(2)   When used as chairs, the long vowels are not pronounced. They appear in the script only as seats for the *hamza*, not as independent sounds.

(3)   The choice of which chair to use (*'alif, waaw,* or *yaa'*) is determined by two things: position of the *hamza* in the word and/or the nature of the vowels immediately adjacent to *hamza*.

3.3.1.2 INITIAL *hamza* CHAIR RULES: When *hamza* is the initial consonant in a word, it has an *'alif* seat. When the vowel with *hamza* is a *fatHa* or *Damma*, the *hamza* is written on top of the *'alif*, and when the vowel with the *hamza* is *kasra*, the *hamza* is usually written under the *'alif*.[16] Note that the vowel after *hamza* can be a short or a long one. In written Arabic, *hamza* in initial position is usually invisible, along with its short vowel. Here it is provided.

mother	*'umm*	أُمّ
professor	*'ustaadh*	أُسْتاذ
where?	*'ayna*	أَيْنَ
bigger	*'akbar*	أَكْبَر
Islam	*'islaam*	إسْلام
Iran	*'iiraan*	إيران

---

[16]   In certain kinds of script, the *hamza* with *kasra* is split, with the *hamza* remaining on top of the *'alif* and the *kasra* being written below.

3.3.1.3 MEDIAL *hamza* When *hamza* occurs in the middle of a word, it normally has a seat determined by the nature of its adjacent vowels. The vowel sounds contiguous to *hamza*, on either side, whether short or long, have a firm order of priority in determining the seat for *hamza*. That order is: *i-u-a*. That is, the first priority in seat-determination is an /i/, /ii/, or /y/ sound, which will give *hamza* a *yaaʾ* seat (*yaaʾ* without dots). In the absence of an /i/ sound, an /u/ or /uu/ sound gives *hamza* a *waaw* seat, and this has second priority. If there is no /i/ or /u/ sound, an /a/ or /aa/ gives *hamza* an *ʾalif* seat, and this has the lowest priority. This system is easier to understand with examples:

(1) *yaaʾ* seat:

organization	*hayʾa*	هَيْئَة
deputy	*naaʾib*	نائِب
Israel	*ʾisraaʾiil*	إِسْرائيل
well	*biʾr*	بِئر
refuge	*mawʾil*	مَوْئِل
he was asked	*suʾila*	سُئِل

(2) *waaw* seat:

educator	*muʾaddib*	مُؤَدِّب
affairs	*shuʾuun*	شُؤُون
he composes	*yuʾallif*	يُؤَلِّف
question	*suʾaal*	سُؤال
feminine	*muʾannath*	مُؤَنَّث

(3) *ʾalif* seat:

visa	*taʾshiira*	تَأْشيرة
she asked	*saʾalat*	سَأَلَتْ
head	*raʾs*	رَأْس
late, delayed	*mutaʾaxxir*	مُتَأَخِّر

(4) **Medial aloof *hamza*:** When *hamza* occurs medially after *waaw* as long vowel /uu/, or after *ʾalif* followed by an /a/ sound, it sits aloof. In general, Arabic script avoids having two adjacent *ʾalifs*.

measures	ʾijraaʾaat	إجْراءات
attacks	iʿtidaaʾaat	اعتداءات
manliness, valor	muruuʾa	مروءة
he wondered	tasaaʾala	تَساءَل

3.3.1.4 FINAL *hamza*: When *hamza* is the final letter of a word, it can either sit aloof or have a seat.

(1) **Aloof:** *Hamza* sits aloof at the end of a word when it is preceded by a long vowel:

calmness	huduuʾ	هدوء
port	miinaaʾ	ميناء
free; innocent	bariiʾ	بريء

Or when it is preceded by a consonant (with *sukuun*):

part	juzʾ	جزْء
thing	shayʾ	شيْء
burden	ʿibʾ	عبْء

(2) **On a seat:** Final *hamza* sits on a seat when it is preceded by a short vowel. The nature of the short vowel determines which seat *hamza* will have. A *fatHa* gives it an *ʾalif* seat, a *kasra* gives it a *yaaʾ* (without dots) seat, and a *Damma* gives it a *waaw* seat.

prophecy	tanabbuʾ	تنبّؤ
shore	shaaTiʾ	شاطئ
warm	daafiʾ	دافئ
principle	mabdaʾ	مبْدأ

(3) **Shift of seat with suffixes:** It is important to note that word-final *hamza* may shift to medial *hamza* if the word gets a suffix and *hamza* is no longer the final consonant. Suffixes such as possessive pronouns (on nouns) and verb inflections cause this to happen. Short vowel suffixes (case and mood-markers) normally do not influence the writing of *hamza*. Here are some examples:

| friends (nom.) | ʾaSdiqaaʾ-u | أصْدقاء |
| our friends (nom.) | ʾaSdiqaaʾ-u-naa | أصْدقاؤُنا |

our friends (gen.)	ʾaSdiqaaʾ-i-naa	أَصْدِقائِنا
our friends (acc.)	ʾaSdiqaaʾ-a-naa	أَصْدِقاءَنا
he read	qaraʾ-a	قَرَأ
we read	qaraʾ-naa	قَرَأْنا
they (m.) read	qaraʾ-uu[17]	قَرَؤُوا
you (f.) are reading	ta-qraʾ-iina	تَقْرَئِينَ

3.3.2 *hamza* plus long /aa/ *madda*

A special symbol stands for *hamza* followed by a long /aa/ sound: /ʾaa/. The symbol is called *madda* ('extension') and looks like this: آ. It is always written above ʾalif and is sometimes referred to as ʾalif *madda*. It can occur at the beginning of a word, in the middle, or at the end. Even if it occurs at the beginning of a word, the *madda* notation is visible, unlike the regular initial *hamza*.

Asia	ʾaasiyaa	آسيا
final	ʾaaxir	آخِر
mirror	mirʾaah	مِرْآة
minarets	maʾaadhin	مَآذِن
the Qurʾân	al-qurʾaan	الْقُرآن
establishments	munshaʾaat	مُنْشَآت
they (2 m.) began	badaʾaa	بَدَآ

3.3.3 Weak *hamza* (*hamzat al-waSl* همزة الوصل)

Hamzat al-waSl, elidable *hamza*, is a phonetic device affixed to the beginning of a word for ease of pronunciation. It is used only in initial position, and is accompanied by a short vowel: /i/, /u/, or /a/.[18] For purposes of phonology and spelling it is necessary to know whether an initial *hamza* is a strong one or an elidable one, since elidable *hamza* drops out in pronunciation unless it is utterance-initial. When elidable *hamza* drops out, its ʾalif seat remains in spelling, but it gets a different symbol on top of it, called a *waSla*, which indicates deletion of the glottal stop and liaison between the previous vowel and the following consonant.[19] If a word starting with

---

[17] It is the style in certain Arab countries to write even the third person masculine plural with *hamza* sitting on ʾalif, e.g., *qaraʾuu* قَرَأوا. Either way is correct.

[18] It is a phonological rule that no word may start with a consonant cluster in Arabic, but certain morphological processes result in patterns or groupings of affixes that cause consonant clusters.

[19] The technical term for this process is aphaeresis or aphesis, deletion of an initial vowel of a word and substituting for it the final vowel of the previous word, as the deletion of the initial "a" in "are" in the contraction "we're" or the initial "i" of "is" in "she's."

elidable *hamza* is preceded by a consonant, a "helping vowel" is affixed to the consonant in order to facilitate pronunciation. Neither *hamzat al-waSl* nor *waSla* are visible in ordinary text.

In the transcription system used in this text, words that start with initial *hamzat al-waSl* do not have the transliterated *hamza* symbol ('). The main categories of words that begin with *hamzat al-waSl* are as follows:

3.3.3.1 DEFINITE ARTICLE, *al-* الـ: The short vowel that accompanies elidable *hamza* of the definite article is *fatHa*.

(1)   **Sentence-initial:** The sentence-initial *hamza* is pronounced.

الْوِزارَةُ هُناك.   الْمُنافَسَةُ قَوِيَّةٌ.

al-wizaarat-u hunaaka.   *al-munaafasat-u qawiyyat-un.*

The ministry is (over) there.   Competition is strong.

(2)   **Non-sentence-initial:** The *hamza* and its short vowel /a/ on the definite article are deleted, although the '*alif* seat remains in the spelling.

هُمْ في الْوِزارَةِ.   لكِنَّ الْمُنافَسَةَ قَوِيَّةٌ.

hum fii l-wizaarat-i.   *laakinna l-munaafasat-a qawiyyat-un.*

They are at the ministry.   But the competition is strong.

3.3.3.2 CERTAIN COMMON WORDS: The short vowel that accompanies elidable *hamza* of this set of words is *kasra*.

son	*ibn*	اِبن
name	*ism*	اِسْم
woman	*imra'a*	اِمْرَأة
two	*ithnaan*	اِثْنان

(1)   **Utterance-initial:** The *hamza* is pronounced.

اِبْني مُسافِرٌ.   اسْمُ اللّه

***ibn-ii** musaafir-un.*   ***ism-u** llaah-i*

My son is travelling.   **the name** of God

(2)   **Non-utterance-initial:** The *hamza* and its *kasra* are omitted in pronunciation. Sometimes the '*alif* seat of the *hamza* is also omitted in these words.

سافَرَ مَعَ ابْني.   باسْمْ اللّه

*saafar-a maʿa **bn-ii**.*   *bi-**sm**-i-llaaah-i*

He traveled with **my son**.   in **the name** of God

3.3.3.3 FORMS VII–X VERBAL NOUNS AND PAST TENSE VERBS:

The short vowel that accompanies elidable *hamza* of this set of words is *kasra*. The *ʾalif* seat remains in spelling.

انْتَخَبَ الشَّعْبُ رئيساً جديداً.

intaxab-a l-shaʿb-u raʾiis-an jadiid-an.

The people **elected** a new president.

وانْتَخَبَ الشَّعْبُ رئيساً جديداً.

wa-ntaxab-a l-shaʿb-u raʾiis-an jadiid-an.

And the people **elected** a new president.

3.3.3.4 IMPERATIVE VERBS OF FORMS I AND VII–X:

The short vowel that accompanies these imperative forms is either *kasra* or *Damma*. The *ʾalif* seat remains.

اسْتَمِعْ.	فَاسْتَمِعْ.
istamiʿ.	*fa-stamiʿ.*
Listen.	So listen.
اقْرأ هذه الكَلِمات.	واقْرأ هذه الكَلِمات.
iqraʾ haadhihi l-kalimaat-i.	*wa-qraʾ haadhihi l-kalimaat-i.*
Read these words.	And read these words.

3.3.3.5 SPELLING BORROWED WORDS THAT START WITH CONSONANT CLUSTERS:

Terms borrowed from other languages into Arabic and which start with consonant clusters, need a helping vowel to facilitate the onset of the pronunciation of the consonant cluster. The helping vowel is written with *hamza* and seated on an *ʾalif Tawiila*. For example:

studio	*istuudyuu*	اسْتوديو
strategic	*istraatiijiyy*	اسْتراتيجِيّ
stable; barn	*isTabl*	اسْطَبَل

3.4 *taaʾ marbuuTa* (تاء مَرْبوطَة)

3.4.1 Spelling

The *taaʾ marbuuTa* is a spelling variant of regular *taaʾ*. It occurs only in word-final position on nouns and adjectives. It is not an optional variant, but determined by word meaning and morphology. In shape, it looks like a *haaʾ* with two dots over it.

corner	*zaawiya*	زاوِيَة
necessity	*Daruura*	ضَرورة
basket	*salla*	سَلَّة

3.4.2 Meaning and use

In most cases, *taaʾ marbuuTa* is a marker of feminine gender. For example, an Arabic word that refers to a person's occupation may be either masculine or feminine, depending on whether one is referring to a man or woman (i.e., engineer, teacher, doctor, student). The masculine singular is a base or unmarked form, and the feminine singular is marked by the presence of a *taaʾ marbuuTa*.

ambassador (m./f.)	*safiir /safiira*	سفير/سفيرة
king/queen	*malik/malika*	مَلِك/مَلِكَة
prince/princess	*ʾamiir/ ʾamiira*	أمير/أميرة
student (m./f.)	*Taalib/Taaliba*	طالِب/طالِبَة

Some nouns, however, are inherently feminine in gender and always spelled with *taaʾ marbuuTa*. For example:

storm	*ʾaaSifa*	عاصِفَة
island	*jaziira*	جَزيرة
culture	*thaqaafa*	ثقافة
flower	*zahra*	زَهْرة

In addition to showing feminine gender on nouns, *taaʾ marbuuTa* also shows feminine gender on adjectives:

مُنَظَّمَة دُوَلِيَّة
munaZZama duwaliyya
an international organization

الطَّالِبَة المُسْلِمَة
al-Taaliba l-muslima
the Muslim student (f.)

فُرْصَة سَعيدة
furSa saʿiida
a happy occasion

مَمْلَكة مُسْتَقِلَّة
mamlaka mustaqilla
an independent kingdom

3.4.3 Pronunciation

In pronunciation, *taaʾ marbuuTa* sometimes has the *haaʾ* sound and other times, *taaʾ*, so that it is a combination of *taaʾ* and *haaʾ* in terms of its written shape and its pronunciation. One consistent feature of *taaʾ marbuuTa* is that it is always preceded by an /a/ sound, usually short /a/ (*fatHa*), but sometimes, long /aa/ (*ʾalif*).

ship	*safiina*	سَفينة
apple	*tuffaaHa*	تُفّاحة
giraffe	*zaraafa*	زَرافة
life	*Hayaat*	حَياة
canal; channel	*qanaat*	قَناة
prayer	*Salaat*	صَلاة

3.4.3.1 FULL FORM: In full form pronunciation, the *taa' marbuuTa* plus final inflectional vowel is pronounced as /t/:

شَبْكَةٌ مَعْلوماتِيَّةٌ   في حَياةٍ طَويلةٍ

shabkat-un ma'luumaatiyyat-un   *fii Hayaat-in Tawiilat-in*
information network   in a long lifetime

الْجامِعةُ الْوَطَنِيَّةُ   عاصِمةُ الْبَلَدِ

al-jaami'at-u l-waTaniyyat-u   *'aaSimat-u l-balad-i*
the national university   the capital of the country

3.4.3.2 PAUSE FORM PRONUNCIATION: In pause form, the final inflectional vowel is not pronounced, and, usually, **neither is the *taa' marbuuTa***. In most pause form situations, the pronunciation of *taa' marbuuTa* becomes *haa'*. Because a final /h/ sound is hard to hear, it sounds as though the word is pronounced only with a final /a/, the *fatHa* that precedes the *taa' marbuuTa*.[20]

a democratic republic	*jumhuuriyya dimuqraaTiyya*	جُمْهوريَّة دِمقْراطيَّة
a large island	*jaziira kabiira*	جَزيرة كَبيرة

(1)   **Exceptions:**

(1.1) If the *taa' marbuuTa* is preceded by a long /aa/, pronunciation of the /t/ in pause form is optional:

life	*Hayaat or Hayaa(h)*	حَياة
young woman	*fataat or fataa(h)*	فَتاة
equality	*musaawaat or musaawaa(h)*	مُساواة

---

[20] For pronunciation of *taa' marbuuTa* as the first term of an annexation phrase (*'iDaafa*), see Chapter 8, section 1.2.1.5.

(1.2)   If the word ending in *taa' marbuuTa* is the first term of an annexation structure (*'iDaafa*), the *taa'* is usually pronounced, even in pause form:

مَدينَة دِمَشق	قِصّة حُبّ
madiinat dimashq	*qiSSat Hubb*
(both words in pause form)	(both words in pause form)
the city of Damascus	a love story

3.5 Consonant doubling (gemination): *tashdiid* تَشْديد

Sometimes consonants are doubled in Arabic. This is both a spelling and pronunciation feature and means that the consonants are pronounced with double strength or emphasis.[21] The technical term for this kind of doubling is "gemination." In Arabic, the doubling process is called *tashdiid*, and instead of writing the letter twice, Arabic has a diacritical symbol that is written above the doubled consonant which shows that it is pronounced with twice the emphasis. The name of the symbol is *shadda* ('intensification'), and it looks like this: ّ. Like the short vowels, *shadda* does not normally appear in written text, but it is necessary to know that it is there. Here are some examples of words that include doubled or geminated consonants:

freedom	*Hurriyya*	حرِّية	surgeon	*jarraaH*	جرّاح
pomegranate	*rummaan*	رُمّان	very	*jidd-an*	جِدّاً
to appoint	*'ayyana*	عيَّن	pilgrimage	*Hajj*	حجّ
love	*Hubb*	حبّ	to sing	*ghannaa*	غنّى
doubt	*shakk*	شكّ	to destroy	*xarraba*	خرّب

3.5.1 Reasons for gemination

Gemination can result from a lexical root that contains a doubled root consonant (such as the root *H-b-b* for *Hubb*, 'love'), or it can result from a derivational process, that is, it can change word meaning and create words. For example, the verb stem *daras* means 'to study,' but a derived form of that verb, *darras*, with doubled *raa'*, means 'to teach.' The meanings are related, but not the same.

Gemination can also be the result of assimilation, the absorption of one sound into another. In these cases, the process is phonetic and not phonemic, i.e., it is a

---

[21] In English, the spelling of a word with a double consonant does not indicate that the pronunciation of that consonant is stronger (e.g., kitten, ladder, offer). However, when an identical consonant is pronounced across word boundaries, it is pronounced more strongly. For example, in the following phrases, the last letter of the first word and the first letter of the last word combine together and result in stronger pronunciation: "shelf-full," "good deed," "hot tea," or "still life." This kind of consonant strengthening resembles the process of gemination in Arabic.

rule of pronunciation and does not affect the meaning of a word. For example, the /l/ of the definite article /al-/ is assimilated to certain consonants when they begin words (e.g., *al-daftar*, 'the notebook,' is pronounced *ad-daftar*).[22]

4 Vowels

The Modern Standard Arabic sound system has six vowel phonemes: three "long" ones and three "short": / *ii*/ and /*i*/, /*uu*/ and /*u*/, /*aa*/ and /*a*/. The difference in length is not a difference in vowel quality, but in the length of time that the vowel is held. The distinction between short and long is similar to difference in length in musical notation, where there are quarter notes, half notes, and whole notes, each one held twice as long as the other. It is possible to think of short vowels as resembling quarter notes and long vowels as half notes, the long vowels being held approximately double the length of time of the short vowels. Long vowels are represented in the Arabic alphabet by the letters ʾ*alif* (*aa*), *waaw* (*uu*) and *yaaʾ* (*ii*). They are written into words as part of the words' spelling. Short vowels, on the other hand, are not independent letters and are written only as diacritical marks above and below the body of the word. In actual practice, short vowels are not indicated in written Arabic text; they are invisible.

The pronunciation of vowels, especially /*aa*/ and /*a*/, varies over a rather wide range, depending on word structure and the influence of adjacent consonants, but also on regional variations in pronunciation. Moreover, the letter ʾ*alif* has several different spelling variants and the letters *waaw* and *yaaʾ* function both as vowels and as consonants.

4.1 Phonemic chart of MSA vowels

	Front	Central	Back
High	i/ii ـي		u/uu ُو
Mid			
Low		a/aa َ١	

4.2 Long vowels

4.2.1 ʾalif

4.2.1.1 PRONUNCIATION: The letter ʾ*alif* represents a long /*aa*/ sound. The quality of this sound varies from being fronted (as in the English word "fad"), a low

---

[22] See section 8.1 on the definite article in this chapter.

central vowel (as in "far"), or a low back vowel (as in the English word "saw.") Here are some words with long /aa/:

	Fronted:			Backed:	
people	*naas*	ناس	fire	*naar*	نار
during	*xilaal*	خلال	system	*niZaam*	نظام
door	*baab*	باب	leader	*qaaʾid*	قائد
peace	*salaam*	سلام	lighthouse	*manaara*	منارة
ruler	*Haakim*	حاكم	neighbor	*jaar*	جار

Usually, in order to have the central or backed pronunciation, the word has a back consonant, either a velarized one (S, D, T, or Z) or a *qaaf*, as the ones above illustrate. The backed pronunciation is also used when ʾalif is followed immediately by *raaʾ* (as in the words *manaara, naar,* and *jaar*). However, in certain parts of the Arab world, especially the Eastern regions (such as Iraq), the backed pronunciation is more frequent.

4.2.1.2 SPELLING VARIANTS OF ʾ*alif.* There are three variations of the letter ʾ*alif:* ʾ*alif qaSiira* ('dagger' ʾ*alif*), ʾ*alif maqSuura* ('shortened' ʾ*alif*) and regular ʾ*alif* (ʾ*alif Tawiila* – 'tall' ʾ*alif*). These variants are not optional but are determined by derivational etymology and spelling conventions.

4.2.1.3 ʾ*alif Tawiila* ألِف طَويلَة. This is the standard form of ʾ*alif.* It is a non-connecting letter written into the word:
(1) ʾ*alif Tawiila* in initial position: In initial position, ʾ*alif* is not a vowel; it is always a seat for *hamza* (accompanied by a short vowel) or *madda* (*hamza* plus long /aa/).

(1.1) ʾ*alif* with *hamza* and short vowel:

four	ʾ*arbaʿa*	أَرْبَعَة
brothers	ʾ*ixwaan*	إخْوان
pipe	ʾ*unbuub*	أُنْبوب

(1.2) ʾ*alif* with *madda:*

August	ʾ*aab*	آب
instrument	ʾ*aala*	آلَة
other (m.)	ʾ*aaxar*	آخَر

(2) *ʾalif* **in medial position:** In medial position, *ʾalif Tawiila* is connected to the letter that precedes it, but it does not connect to the following letter:

north; left	*shamaal*	شَمال
she said	*qaalat*	قالَتْ
side	*jaanib*	جانِب

The letter *ʾalif* has a special relationship with a preceding *laam*: it sits inside the curve of the *laam* at an angle. This special combination of letters is called a "ligature," and is even occasionally cited as part of the alphabet ("*laam-ʾalif*").

peace	*salaam*	سَلام
Jordan	*al-ʾurdun*	الأُرْدُن
no	*laa*	لا

(3) *ʾalif Tawiila* **in final position:**

(3.1) *ʾalif* **as long vowel in word-final position:** At the end of a word *ʾalif Tawiila* may occur:

here	*hunaa*	هُنا
Malta	*maalTaa*	مالْطا
this (m.)	*haadhaa*	هذا

(3.2) *ʾalif Tawiila* **with nunation:** A word-final *ʾalif* may be written with two *fatHas* above it, signaling that the word is nunated, that is, marked for indefinite accusative case (and pronounced *-an*). In this case, the *ʾalif* is not pronounced; it is only a seat or "chair" for the two *fatHas* that mark the indefinite accusative. The accusative case often indicates that a noun is an object of a transitive verb, or it may mark an adverbial function. For further description and examples of the accusative, see Chapter 7 on noun inflections. Some examples of adverbial accusatives ending with *ʾalif* plus nunation include:

welcome	*ʾahl-an*	أهْلاً
tomorrow	*ghad-an*	غَداً
thanks	*shukr-an*	شُكْراً
greatly	*kathiir-an*	كثيراً
very	*jidd-an*	جِداً
finally	*ʾaxiir-an*	أخيراً

(3.3)   **silent inflectional ʾalif Tawiila**: The ʾalif Tawiila is written as part of the third person masculine plural past tense inflection, but it is only a spelling convention and **it is not pronounced**. If a pronoun suffix is added to this verb inflection, then the silent ʾalif is deleted:[23]

لاحَظوا.	كانوا كَذلكَ.	حملوها على ظهورهم.
laaHaZ-uu.	kaan-uu ka-dhaalika.	Hamal-uu-haa ʿalaa Zuhuur-i-him.
They noticed.	They were like that.	They carried it on their backs.

4.2.1.4 "DAGGER" ʾalif: ʾalif qasiira ألف قَصيرة: This form of ʾalif is a spelling convention used only with certain words. It is a reduced version of ʾalif Tawiila written **above** the consonant (hanging above it rather like a dagger), rather than beside it in the body of the word. As with the short vowels written above or below the word, this form of ʾalif is not normally visible in ordinary text. It is therefore necessary to know that a word is spelled with ʾalif qaSiira in order to pronounce it correctly. The words spelled with ʾalif qaSiira are not many in number, but some of them are used with great frequency. The most common ones include:

God	allaah '	الله	اللـه
god	ʾilaah	إله	إلـه
this (m.)	haadha	هذا	هـذا
this (f.)	haadhihi	هذه	هـذه
these	haaʾulaaʾi	هؤلاء	هـؤلاء
that (m.)	dhaalika	ذلك	ذلك
thus	haakadhaa	هكذا	هـكذا
but	laakinna	لكنَّ	لكنَّ

4.1.2.4 ʾalif maqSuura ألف مقصورة: The ʾalif maqSuura looks like a yaaʾ without dots. This form of ʾalif occurs only at the end of a word. It is a spelling convention occurring with certain words because of their derivational etymology. Sometimes a dagger ʾalif is added above the ʾalif maqSuura to distinguish it from a final yaaʾ. Some words spelled with ʾalif maqSuura are proper names, such as:

Leila	laylaa	لَيلى	Moses	muusaa	موسى
Mona	munaa	مُنى	Mustafa	muSTafaa	مصطفى

---

[23] This ʾalif is called ʾalif al-faaSila or "separating ʾalif." It is also sometimes referred to as "otiose ʾalif."

Other words ending in *ʾalif maqSuura* may be any form class: verb, preposition, noun, adjective:

he built	*banaa*	بَنى	piety	*taqwaa*	تَقْوى
upon	*ʿalaa*	عَلى	greatest (f.)	*kubraa*	كُبْرى
to, toward	*ʾilaa*	إلى			

Sometimes, in an indefinite noun or adjective, the *ʾalif maqSuura* is a seat for the indefinite accusative marker, *fatHataan*, and the word is pronounced with an /-an / ending instead of -*aa*. This depends on the word's etymology. For declension and more examples of these words, see Chapter 7 on noun inflections.

hospital	*mustashfan*	مُسْتَشْفى
echo	*Sadan*	صدى
coffeehouse	*maqhan*	مَقْهى

Most words spelled with final *ʾalif maqSuura* have to change it to *ʾalif Tawiila* if the word receives a suffix and the *ʾalif* is no longer final:

مُسْتَوى	مُسْتَواهُ	قُرى	قُرانا	رمى	رَماها
mustawan	*mustawaa-hu*	*quran*	*quraa-naa*	*ramaa*	*ramaa-haa*
level, status	his status	villages	our villages	he threw	he threw it (f.)

Certain function words spelled with *ʾalif maqSuura* shift from *ʾalif* to a diphthongized *yaaʾ* when they receive pronoun suffixes:[24]

لَدى	لَدَيْها	إلى	إلَيْهِم	عَلى	عَلَيْكُم
ladaa	*laday-haa*[25]	*ʾilaa*	*ʾilay-him*	*ʿalaa*	*ʿalay-kum*
with, at	with her	to, toward	to them (m.)	on, upon	upon you (pl.)

4.2.2 Semivowels/semi-consonants *waaw* and *yaaʾ*

The letters *waaw* and *yaaʾ* have two functions. They represent the consonant sounds /w/ and /y/, respectively, and they also represent the long vowels /uu/ and /ii/. English has something similar to this because the letter "y" can act as a consonant, as in the word "yellow" or it can act as a vowel, as in the word "sky."[26] The Arabic /ii/ sound symbolized by *yaaʾ* is like the /i/ in English "machine." The /uu/ sound symbolized by *waaw* is like the /u/ in "rule."

---

[24] For rules and full paradigms of these prepositions, see Chapter 16 on prepositions and prepositional phrases.

[25] This particle also has the sense of possession: 'she has.'

[26] See note 1.

4.2.2.1 THE SOUNDS OF *waaw*: The letter *waaw* represents either the sound of
| w| or the long vowel |uu|. For example, in the following words, it is |w|:

boy	*walad*	وَلَد	state	*wilaaya*	وِلاية
season	*mawsim*	مَوْسِم	first	*ʾawwal*	أوَّل

And in the following it is |uu|:

breakfast	*faTuur*	فَطور	entry	*duxuul*	دُخول
light	*nuur*	نور	forbidden	*mamnuuᶜ*	مَمْنوع

4.2.2.2 THE SOUNDS OF *yaaʾ*: The letter *yaaʾ* represents either the sound of |y| as
in "young" or the long vowel |ii| as the "i" in "petite." For example, in the
following words it is |y|:

Yemen	*yaman*	يَمَن
white	*ʾabyaD*	أبْيَض
day	*yawm*	يَوْم

In the following words it is pronounced as |ii|:

elephant	*fiil*	فيل
dune	*kathiib*	كَثيب
religion	*diin*	دين

4.3 Short vowels and *sukuun* (*al-Harakaat wa l-sukuun* الْحَرَكات وَالسّكون)

The set of three short vowels consists of the sounds |a|,| i|, and |u|. They are not
considered part of the Arabic alphabet and are not as a rule visible in written Arabic. The short vowels are referred to in Arabic not as letters (*Huruuf*) but as
"movements" (*Harakaat*). That is, they are seen as a way of moving the voice from
one consonant to another.

Short vowels can be written into a text, but ordinarily they are not. Two exceptions to this are the Qurʾân and children's schoolbooks. In the Qurʾân, the short
vowels are made explicit so that readers and reciters can be absolutely certain of
the correct pronunciation of the sacred text. In schoolbooks, they are inserted so
that children can study and master word structure and spelling as they learn how
to read MSA. As reading skill progresses, the use of short vowels in pedagogical
texts is phased out. This is done because the patterning of short vowels is largely
predictable and therefore marking them is considered redundant.

For learners of Arabic as a foreign language, the absence of short vowels
requires extra attention to word structure and morphological patterning, and

memorization of the exact sound of the word as well as its spelling. Just because the vowels are invisible doesn't mean they don't exist.

4.3.1 *fatHa*: فَتْحَة short /a/

The short vowel /a/, called *fatHa*, ranges in pronunciation from low central (as in "dark") to lowered mid front (as in "best"), depending on context. The short vowel /a/ is represented, when written, by a small diagonal mark sloping downward to the left (َ). It is placed *above* the consonant that it follows in pronunciation. Examples:

country	*balad*	بَلَد
she danced	*raqaSat*	رَقَصَتْ
mint	*na*ᶜ*na*ᶜ	نَعْنَع

4.3.2 *kasra* : كَسْرَة short /i/

The short vowel /i/, called *kasra*, ranges in pronunciation from a high front vowel (as in "petite") to a lower front vowel (as in "sit"). *Kasra* is represented by a mark similar to *fatHa*, but is written **underneath** the consonant it follows (ِ). Examples:

pepper	*filfil*	فِلْفِل
skin	*jild*	جِلْد
apricots	*mishmish*	مِشْمِش

4.3.3 *Damma*: ضَمَّة short /u/

The short /u/ sound in Arabic, called *Damma*, ranges from a high back vowel (as in "duke") to a lower rounded back vowel (as in "bull"). The *Damma* is represented by what looks like a small *waaw*, or an English apostrophe (ُ). It is written **above** the consonant which it follows. Examples:

cities	*mudun*	مُدُن
ear	ᵓ*udhun*	أُذُن
quarter	*rub*ᶜ	رُبْع

4.3.4 Absence of vowel: *sukuun* سُكون

A consonant is not always followed by a vowel. Sometimes one consonant comes immediately after another, or a consonant will end a word. In order to indicate clearly that a consonant is not followed by a vowel, Arabic uses a diacritical mark called a *sukuun* ('silence') which looks like a mini-zero (ْ)placed directly above the consonant.

As with the short vowel indicators, the *sukuun* is invisible in ordinary script. It is shown here in the following examples:

room	*ghurfa*	غُرْفَة	we drink	*nashrab*	نَشْرَب
temple	*ma°bad*	مَعْبَد	sand	*raml*	رَمْل

4.3.5 Extra short or helping vowels

An epenthetic or helping vowel may be inserted at the end of a word in context in order to prevent consonant clusters and facilitate smoothness of pronunciation within a sentence. In a sentence, these helping vowels are added to words that would otherwise end with *sukuun* when the following word begins with a consonant cluster. The determination of the helping vowel is as follows:

4.3.5.1 HELPING VOWEL *kasra*: The short vowel *kasra* is by far the most frequent helping vowel.

نَشَرَتِ الْجَرِيدَةُ الأَخْبَارَ.

nasharat-i l-jariidat-u l-ʾaxbaar-a.
The newspaper published the news.

هَلِ انْتَهَى الْمُؤْتَمَرُ؟

hal-i ntahaa l-muʾtamar-u?
Did the conference end?

4.3.5.2 HELPING VOWEL *Damma*: The helping vowel *Damma* is used with the second person plural personal pronouns and third person plural pronouns when they are spelled with *Damma*:

اسْتَقْبَلَتْهُمُ الْبِعْثَةُ الرَّسْمِيَّةُ.

istaqbal-at-hum-u l-biʿthat-u l-rasmiyyat-u.
The official delegation met them.

يَعْتَبِرُونَكُمُ الرُّوَّادَ.

ya-ʿtabir-uuna-kum-u l-ruwwaad-a.[27]
They consider you (m. pl.) the pioneers.

هَلِ اشْتَرَيْتُمُ الطَّعَامَ؟

hal-i shtaray-tum-u l-Taʿaam-a?[28]
Did you (m. pl.) buy the food?

---

[27] Phonetically, *ya-ʿtabir-**uuna-kum-u** r-ruwwaad-a.*
[28] Phonetically, *hal-i shtaray-**tum-u** T-Taʿaam-a?* There are two helping vowels here, a *kasra* on the question-word *hal* in order to prevent a consonant cluster with the past tense Form VIII verb, and *Damma* after the subject marker *-tum* affixed to the past tense verb.

4.3.5.3 LONG VOWEL *waaw* AS HELPING VOWEL: A special case of a **long helping vowel** /uu/ occurs when the object of the verb following the second person masculine plural past tense suffix /-tum/ happens to be a pronoun. A long /uu/ is inserted as a buffer between the subject marker on the verb and the object pronoun:

هَلْ نَشَرْتمُوهَا ؟

hal nashar-tum-uu-haa?

Did you (m. pl.) publish it?

4.3.5.4 HELPING VOWEL *fatHa*: The short vowel *fatHa* has restricted use as a helping vowel. With the word *min* 'from,' the helping vowel is *fatHa* before the definite article and otherwise, *kasra*.

مِنَ الْكُوَيْتِ	مِنَ الْغَرْبِ
min-a l-kuwayt-i	*min-a l-gharb-i*
from Kuwait	from the west

مِنِ انْتهَاءِ الْحَرْب	مِنِ اسْمِنَا
min-i ntihaaʾ-i l-Harb-i	*min-i sm-i-naa*
from the end of the war	from our name

4.4 Diphthongs and glides

Diphthongs or glides in Arabic are combinations of short vowels and semivowels. The sequences that occur are /aw/, /ay/, /iy/, and /uw/. The sequences */iw/ and */uy/ are usually prohibited.

4.4.1 Diphthongs

4.4.1.1 /aw/ (PRONOUNCED LIKE THE "ow" IN "power")[29]

above	*fawqa*	فَوْق	almonds	*lawz*	لَوْز
pine-nuts	*Sanawbar*	صَنَوْبَر	appointment	*mawʿid*	مَوْعِد

4.4.1.2 /ay/ (PRONOUNCED LIKE ENGLISH "eye," OR "aye")[30]

egg	*bayDa*	بَيْضَة	car	*sayyaara*	سَيَّارَة
to change	*ghayyar*	غَيَّر	night	*layl*	لَيْل

---

[29] In less formal spoken Arabic and in colloquial Arabic the diphthong /aw/ changes to a long vowel /oo/, pronounced like the /o/ in "note."

[30] Again, in less formal Arabic and colloquial Arabic, the diphthong /ay/ changes to the long vowel /ee/, pronounced like the long /a/ in "date."

4.4.2 Glides

Glides are vowel–consonant combinations where the vowel and consonant have very close points of articulation, such as /iy/ (high front vowel plus palatal sonant) and /uw/ (high back vowel plus rounded bilabial sonant). In most cases the glide consonant is doubled.

4.4.2.1 HIGH FRONT GLIDE /iy/:

Arab (f.)	ʿarabiyya	عربية	Egyptians	miSriyy-uun	مصريّون
denied	manfiyy	منفيّ	yearly	sanawiyy-an	سنويّاً

4.4.2.2 HIGH BACK GLIDE /uw/:

growth	numuww	نُمُوّ	enemy	ʿaduww	عدوّ
youth	futuwwa	فتوّة	height	ʿuluww	علوّ

5 MSA pronunciation styles: full form and pause form

When reading MSA formally, aloud, words are pronounced according to certain rules.

5.1 Full form

When complete voweling is observed, all vowels are pronounced, including all the short vowels that are contained in the words but not visible in the text. This also includes any word-final inflectional vowels and is called "full" form pronunciation.

حَضَرَ رئيسُ الْجُمْهوريّةِ إلى الْعاصمةِ لَيْلَةَ أمْسِ.

HaDar-a raʾiis-u l-jumhuuriyyat-i ʾilaa l-ʿaaSimat-i laylat-a ʾams-i.
The president of the republic came to the capital last night.

5.2 Pause form

There is also a standard Arabic pronunciation principle that a word-final short vowel may be left unpronounced. This is called "pause form" in English and *waqf* وقْف ('stopping') in Arabic. There are two variants of this principle:

5.2.1 Formal pause form

When reading MSA aloud, the standard practice is to use pause form on the final word of a sentence, or (if it is a long sentence) wherever there is a natural "pause" for breath.

حَضَرَ رَئِيسُ الْجُمْهُورِيَّةِ إِلَى الْعَاصِمَةِ لَيْلَةَ أَمْسِ.

HaDar-a raʾiis-u l-jumhuuriyyat-i ʾilaa l-ʿaaSimat-i laylat-a ʾams.[31]

The president of the republic came to the capital last night.

5.2.2 Informal pause form:

When reading MSA aloud or when speaking MSA less formally, pause form is sometimes used on most or all words ending with a short vowel.

حَضَرَ رئِيس الْجُمْهُوريَّة إِلَى الْعَاصِمَة لَيْلَةَ أَمْسِ.

HaDar raʾiis l-jumhuuriyya ʾilaa l-ʿaaSima laylat ʾams.[32]

The president of the Republic came to the capital last night.

5.2.2.1 PAUSE FORM FOR WORDS ENDING IN *taaʾ marbuuTa*: A word that terminates in *taaʾ marbuuTa* is usually pronounced as ending in -a or -ah in pause form unless it is the first term of an *ʾiDaafa*, in which case it is pronounced as a /-t-/ sound.

capital	ʿaaSima	عَاصِمَة
university	jaamiʿa	جَامِعَة
organization	munaZZama[33]	مُنَظَّمَة

جَامِعَة بَيْروت	عَاصِمَة عُمَان
jaamiʿat bayruut	ʿaaSimat ʿumaan
the university of Beirut	the capital of Oman

6 MSA syllable structure

There are a limited number of possible syllable sequences for MSA word structure.

First of all, no word or syllable may start with a vowel. If a word appears to start with a vowel, such as *ʾislaam* or *ʾumma* or *ʾabadan*, what is actually heard is a vowel preceded by a glottal stop (*hamza*). English speakers tend not to hear the glottal stop because it is not phonemic (meaningful) in English. It is, however, a real consonant in Arabic.

I	ʾanaa	أَنَا
week	ʾusbuuʿ	أُسْبُوع
if	ʾidhaa	إِذَا

[31] Final short vowel /-i/ is unpronounced.
[32] Note that in order to avoid consonant clusters and ease pronunciation, when speaking in pause form, sometimes helping vowels have to be inserted.
[33] For a more detailed description of *taaʾ marbuuTa* pronunciation, see McCarus and Rammuny 1974, 112–13. See also section 1.2 of Chapter 7, on feminine gender marking.

The second rule is that no word or syllable may begin with a consonant cluster, such as /sk/ or /br/. Consonant clusters within syllables are prohibited, except for one situation: In pause form, a word may end in a consonant cluster, such as: *fahimt* 'I understood' فهمْت or *istaᶜmalt* 'I used' استعملْت. Syllable structure in MSA is therefore limited to the following five combinations of consonants and vowels.

6.1 Full form pronunciation syllables

(1)   "Short" or "weak" syllable: CV (consonant–short vowel)
> e.g., *-ma, -bi, -hu*

(2)   "Long" or "strong" syllables: CVV (consonant–long vowel)
> or CVC (consonant–short vowel–consonant)
> e.g., *-faa, -dii, -ras, -tab*

6.2 Additional pause form pronunciation syllables

(1)   "Super-strong" syllables: CVVC (consonant–long vowel–consonant)
> or CVCC (consonant–short vowel–consonant–consonant)
> e.g., *-riim, -nuun, -sart, -rabt*

These super-strong sequences occur primarily in word-final position.[34]

7 Word stress rules

Stress rules refer to the placement of stress or emphasis (loudness) within a word. In English, stress is not fully predictable and is learned by ear or along with word spelling. Some words in English are differentiated only by stress, for example: invalid (noun and adjective), present (noun, adjective, and verb), suspect (noun and verb), conduct (noun and verb).

Stress in Modern Standard Arabic, on the other hand, is essentially predictable and adheres to some general rules based on syllable structure. Because MSA is not a spontaneously spoken language, the rules given here for stress patterns are for the way MSA is pronounced when read out loud or used in speaking from pre-pared texts in the Eastern Arab world. In Egypt and the Sudan, stress rules are different for MSA as well as the colloquial language. Nonetheless, the standard Eastern form is "a nearly universal norm," acceptable and understandable throughout the Arab world.[35]

---

[34] Active participles of geminate Form I verbs contain an internal CVVC sequence, for example, حاجّ
Ḥaajj 'pilgrim,' مادّة *maadda,* 'substance,' كافّة *kaaffa* 'entirety,' سامّ *saamm* 'poisonous,' جافّ *jaaff* 'dry,'
عامّ *ᶜaamm* 'public; general,' خاصّ *xaaSS* 'private; special,' or حارّ *Ḥaarr* 'hot.' Some borrowed words
also contain this sequence, such as *raad-yuu* راديو 'radio.' See Chapter 6 on participles, section 1.1.2.

[35] McCarthy and Prince 1990a, 252. They also note that "there is inconsistency in the stressing of
standard Arabic words between different areas of the Arab world, and no direct testimony on this
subject exists from the Classical period."

Different sets of rules are used for full form pronunciation and pause form pronunciation. They overlap to a great extent, but there are some differences. The major feature of all these stress rules is that **stress placement is calculated from the end of a word** – not the beginning. Note that some Arabic words are composed of several morphological elements, including case endings and pronoun suffixes of various sorts, so that the length of words may vary substantially.

7.1 Full form stress rules

7.1.1 Stress is never on the final syllable

Therefore, in words of two syllables, stress is on the first, no matter what that first syllable is like (strong or weak). Examples (stress is indicated by **boldface**):

to, towards	*'ilaa*	إلى	we	*naHnu*	نَحْنُ
what	*maadhaa*	ماذا	they visited	*zaaruu*	زاروا
she	*hiya*	هِي	here	*hunaa*	هُنا

7.1.2 Stress on penult

Stress is on the second syllable from the end of the word (the penult) if that syllable is strong (CVC or CVV). Examples:

efforts (nom.)	*juhuudun*	جُهودٌ
students (acc.)	*Tullaaban*	طلّاباً
they taught her	*darrasuuhaa*	درّسوها
they (f.) write	*yaktubna*	يكتبْنَ
you (m. pl.) worked	*ʿamiltum*	عملتُم

7.1.3 Stress on the antepenult

If the second syllable from the end of the word is weak (CV), then the stress falls back to the third syllable from the end (the antepenult):

a capital	*ʿaaSimatun*	عاصِمةٌ
all of us	*kullunaa*	كلُّنا
a library (nom.)	*maktabatun*	مكتبةٌ
he tries	*yuHaawilu*	يُحاوِلُ
Palestinian (f.)	*filasTiiniyyatun*	فلِسطينيّةٌ

7.1.4 Summary: word length

Therefore, in full-form pronunciation, MSA stress falls either on the second or third syllable from the end of the word. Note that if a suffix is attached to a word, it increases the number of syllables and may change the stress pattern, e.g.,

university	*jaamiʿatun*	جامعة
our university	*jaamiʿatunaa*	جامعتنا
office	**maktabun**	مكتب
his office	*maktabuhu*	مكتبه
we studied	*darasnaa*	درسنا
we studied it (f.)	*darasnaahaa*	درسناها

7.2 Pause form stress rule

The same basic set of rules applies to pause form, but there is an important additional rule for pause form pronunciation: Stress falls on the final syllable of a word if that syllable is a super-strong one (CVCC or CVVC).

| minister | *waziir* | وزير | discussions | *mubaaHathaat* | مباحثات |
| boundaries | *Huduud* | حدود | I tried | *Haawalt* | حاولت |

7.2.1 Summary

To summarize, MSA stress falls on either the second or the third syllable from the end of the word or, in pause form, on the final syllable if it is super-strong.[36]

7.2.2 Other pause form conventions

7.2.2.1 PAUSE FORM *nisba*:
Words in pause form that end with the *nisba* (relative adjective) suffix *-iyy* should technically have stress placed on that final syllable (CVCC), e.g.,

| Yemeni | *yamaniyy* | يمني | official | *raʾiisiyy* | رئيسي |
| Arab | *ʿarabiyy* | عربي | Bedouin | *badawiyy* | بدوي |

And this is done in very formal spoken MSA. However, it is often the case in spoken MSA (as in colloquial Arabic) that this ending is treated not as *-iyy* but simply

---

[36] As McCarthy and Prince concisely note: "The stress system is obviously weight-sensitive: final syllables are stressed if superheavy CvvC or CvCC; penults are stressed if heavy Cvv or CvC; otherwise the antepenult is stressed" (1990a, 252).

as long *ii*, in which case the stress is placed as though the last syllable contained an open long vowel:

Yemeni	*yamanii*	يَمَنِي	official	*ra'iisii*	رَئِيسِي
Arab	*'arabii*	عَرَبِي	Bedouin	*badawii*	بَدَوِي

7.2.2.2 PAUSE FORM CHANGE IN STRESS FOR CERTAIN WORDS SPELLED WITH *taa'* *marbuuTa*: In pause form, *taa' marbuuTa*, along with its case ending, is not pronounced, and this eliminates a syllable from the word. Therefore, stress has to be recalculated, and certain words spelled with *taa' marbuuTa* shift the stress when pronounced in pause form.

	Full form (includes case ending)	Pause form	
university	*jaami'at-un*	*jaami'a*	جَامِعَة
school	*madrasat-un*	*madrasa*	مَدْرَسَة
lecture	*muHaaDarat-un*	*muHaaDara*	مُحَاضَرَة

The shift in stress in the above examples occurs because when the *taa' marbuuTa* plus case ending is deleted, the third syllable from the end becomes the second syllable from the end, and because it is weak (CV), it cannot receive the stress, so the stress shifts back to the previous syllable. There are also cases where the deletion of *taa' marbuuTa* plus case ending does not alter the stress pattern. This happens if the syllable that originally had the stress is a strong syllable. In this case the strong syllable retains the stress, in keeping with the general rules.[37]

	Full form	Pause form	
city	*madiinat-un*	*madiina*	مَدِينَة
dove	*Hamaamat-un*	*Hamaama*	حَمَامَة
heroism	*buTuulat-un*	*buTuula*	بُطُولَة

---

[37] For additional reading on Arabic word stress and generative phonology, see Brame 1970 and Abdo 1969.

8 Definiteness and indefiniteness markers

8.1 Definite article *al-* الـ

8.1.1 Spelling

The definite article in Arabic is spelled with *ʾalif-laam* and is attached as a prefix. This spelling convention makes a word with the prefixed definite article look like just one word. The definite article thus never occurs independently (*al-* الـ). It is a proclitic particle, i.e., always attached to a word – either a noun or an adjective.

the sheikh	*al-shaykh*	الشّيخ	the night	*al-layla*	اللّيْلَة
the genie	*al-jinnii*	الْجنّي	the women	*al-nisaa'*	النِّساء

8.1.2 Pronunciation

In general, the definite article is pronounced "al" but many speakers shorten the /a/ sound so that it sounds more like "el" (as in English "elbow"). It is spelled with elidable *hamza* (*hamzat al-waSl*) (see above), so if the definite article is not utterance-initial, the *hamza* drops out in pronunciation and the vowel pronounced with the *laam* of the definite article is actually the final vowel of the preceding word (see also above under *hamzat al-waSl*).

8.1.2.1 SUN AND MOON LETTERS

(1)   Sun Letters (*Huruuf shamsiyya* شمْسيّة حُروف): Certain sounds assimilate or absorb the sound of the *laam* in the definite article. These sounds or letters are called "sun letters" (*Huruuf shamsiyya*). When a word begins with one of these sounds, the *ʾalif-laam* of the definite article is written, but the *laam* is not pronounced; instead, it is absorbed or assimilated into the first letter or sound in the word and that letter is doubled in strength. A *shadda* is written over the sun letter itself to show that the /l/ is assimilated into it and strengthens it, but the shadda does not show in normal printed Arabic.

The sun letters or sounds that absorb the /l/ of the definite article are as follows:

ت ث د ذ ر ز س ش ص ض ط ظ ل ن

taaʾ, thaaʾ, daal, dhaal, raaʾ, zaay, siin, shiin, Saad, Daad, Taaʾ, Zaaʾ, laam, nuun

English	Pronounced	Arabic
the commerce	*at-tijaara*	التّجارة
the culture	*ath-thaqaafa*	الثّقافة

English	Pronounced	Arabic
the religion	ad-diin	الدِّين
the gold	adh-dhahab	الذَّهَب
the lord	ar-rabb	الرَّبّ
the flowers	az-zuhuur	الزُّهور
the secret	as-sirr	السِّر
the sun	ash-shams	الشَّمس
the wool	aS-Suuf	الصَّوف
the noise	aD-Dajja	الضَّجَّة
the doctor	aT-Tabiib	الطَّبيب
the shadow	aZ-Zill	الظِّلّ
the clothing	al-libaas	اللِّبـاس
the light	an-nuur	النّور

(2) Moon letters (*Huruuf qamariyya* حُروف قَمَريَّة): "Moon letters" do not absorb the /l/ of the definite article. The moon letters are:

أ ب ج ح خ ع غ ف ق ك م ه و ي

hamza, baa', jiim, Haa', xaa', 'ayn, ghayn, faa', qaaf, kaaf, miim, haa', waaw, yaa'

English	Pronounced	Arabic
Islam	al-'islaam	الإسْلام
the bedouin	al-badw	البَدْو
the pocket	al-jayb	الجَيْب

English	Pronounced	Arabic
the luck	al-HaZZ	الْحَظّ
the mustard	al-xardal	الْخَرْدَل
the Arabs	al-ʿarab	الْعَرَب
the west	al-gharb	الْغَرْب
the pepper	al-filfil	الْفِلْفِل
the moon	al-qamar	الْقَمَر
the treasure	al-kanz	الْكَنْز
the center	al-markaz	الْمَرْكَز
the engineering	al-handasa	الْهَنْدَسَة
the ministry	al-wizaara	الْوِزارَة
the hand	al-yad	الْيَد

8.1.2.2 SUMMARY: SUN AND MOON LETTERS: The Arabic alphabet, or inventory of consonant sounds, is therefore divided into two groups: sounds that assimilate the /l/ of the definite article and sounds that do not. The sounds are best learned through memorization, listening, and speaking practice. Note that in many transliteration systems (Library of Congress, for example), when written Arabic is romanized into Latin letters, the definite article is spelled "*al*" even though in pronunciation the /l/ may be assimilated. That is the case in the romanization in this text.

8.2 Indefinite marker: nunation (*tanwiin* تَنْوِين)

Indefiniteness, which corresponds to the use of "a" or "an" in English, is not marked with a separate word in Arabic. Instead, it is marked with a suffix, an /n/ sound that comes at the **end** of a word. This /n/ sound is not written with a regular letter /nuun/. It is indicated by writing the final inflectional vowel on a word twice. In the case of *Damma*, nunation is often indicated by giving the *Damma* a "tail" or flourish at the end, rather than doubling it.[38]

---

[38] The writing conventions for this indefinite marking are described in detail in Chapter 7, section 4.2.1.

Nunation as a marker of indefiniteness may appear on nouns, adjectives, and adverbs. Certain classes of words (e.g., diptotes) are restricted from having nunation.

a house (nominative)	*bayt-u-n*	بيتٌ
a house (genitive)	*bayt-i-n*	بيتٍ
a house (accusative)	*bayt-a-n*	بيتاً

Note that the accusative form of nunation often needs a "seat" or "chair" which is usually *'alif Tawiila*.[39] For example:

place	*makaan-an*	مَكاناً
bridge	*jisr-an*	جِسْراً
many	*kathiir-an*	كَثيراً

In words spelled with *taa' marbuuTa*, the nunation sits atop the final letter and the accusative nunation does not require an *'alif* chair. This is also the case in words that end with *hamza* preceded by a long vowel.

an embassy (nominative)	*sifaarat-u-n*	سفارةٌ
an embassy (genitive)	*sifaarat-i-n*	سفارةٍ
an embassy (accusative)	*sifaarat-a-n*	سفارةً
an evening (nominative)	*masaa'-u-n*	مَساءٌ
an evening (genitive)	*masaa'-i-n*	مَساءٍ
an evening (accusative)	*masaa'-a-n*	مَساءً

---

[39] Certain "defective" nouns use *'alif maqSuura* as a seat for the *fatHataan* in both the nominative and the accusative cases, e.g., معنى *ma'nan* 'meaning' or مقهى *maqhan* 'coffeehouse.' See section 5.4.4 of Chapter 7 for further details of this declension.

3

Arabic word structure: an overview

"The Semitic root is one of the great miracles of man's language."[1]

1 Morphology in general

Morphology, or word structure, pertains to the organization, rules, and processes concerning meaningful units of language, whether they be words themselves or parts of words, such as affixes of various sorts. Meaningful components and subcomponents at the word level are referred to as morphemes.[2] Arabic morphology is different from English in some very basic respects but it is highly systematic. In fact, Arabic and the Semitic languages have had substantial influence on the development of certain key concepts in theoretical morphology.[3]

Theories of word structure, or morphology, usually focus on two essential issues: how words are formed (**derivational or lexical morphology**) and how they interact with syntax (**inflectional morphology**, e.g., marking for categories such as gender, number, case, tense). Arab grammarians, starting in the late eighth and early ninth centuries AD, developed sophisticated analyses of Arabic morphology that differ from modern Western theories, but interrelate with them in interesting ways.[4] Because this reference grammar is intended primarily for the use of Western readers, it is organized along the lines of traditional Western categories, with inclusion of the Arabic terminology.

Derivational or lexical morphology has to do with principles governing word formation (such as analysis of the English words "truthful" or "untruthfulness"

---

[1] Lohmann 1972, 318.

[2] Aronoff (1976, 7) gives this general definition of morphemes: "the units into which words are analyzed and out of which they are composed." This definition is adequate as a start, although Aronoff notes that it is problematic in certain ways for morphological theory. For a general introduction to traditional morphology a good place to begin is Matthews 1974. He writes: "the morpheme is established as the single minimal or primitive unit of grammar, the ultimate basis for our entire description of the primary articulation of language. Words, phrases, etc., are all seen as larger, complex or non-primitive units which are built up from morphemes in successive stages" (1974, 78). For further developments in morphological theory see Aronoff 1976 and 1994, Anderson 1992, and Spencer 1991.

[3] "It may thus well be that all Western linguistic morphology is directly rooted in the Semitic grammatical tradition" (Aronoff 1994, 3).

[4] For discussion of how Arabic morphological categories interrelate with Western theories, see Ryding 1993. See also discussions in Aronoff 1994, esp. 123–64 and Anderson 1992, 57–58; Monteil (1960, 105–223) has an excellent overview of MSA morphological issues.

derived from the base word "true").[5] **Inflectional morphology** describes how words vary or inflect in order to express grammatical contrasts or categories, such as singular/plural or past/present tense. Derivation, since it is the process of creating words or lexical units, is considered procedurally prior to inflection, which subsequently acts upon the word stem and modifies it, if necessary, for use in context (by affixing /-s/ in English for plural, for example, or /-ed/ for past tense). These are two fundamental categories, therefore, in approaching language structure. However, the boundaries between derivation and inflection are not as clear-cut in Arabic as they are in English because Arabic morphology works on different principles, and because Arabic morphological theory views elements of word structure and sentence structure from a different perspective.[6]

Readers who are consulting this reference grammar for answers to specific questions may want to skip over the morphological theory and consult the paradigms (inflectional charts), and the book is designed to allow them to do so. However, those who are studying Arabic with goals of understanding the processes and categories of Arabic language structure will find that descriptions of the morphological structure are helpful not only in understanding the theoretical framework of Arabic, but also in organizing their knowledge in order to serve as a foundation for higher levels of achievement and proficiency. Moreover, without a sound grasp of Arabic morphological principles, learners will be unable to make use of Arabic dictionaries.

2 Derivation: the Arabic root-pattern system

Arabic morphology exhibits rigorous and elegant logic. It differs from that of English or other Indo-European languages because it is to a large extent based on **discontinuous** morphemes. It consists primarily of a system of consonant **roots** which interlock with **patterns** of vowels (and sometimes certain other consonants) to form words, or word stems. This type of operation is not unknown in English. If one looks at the consonant sequence s-ng, one knows that its meaning

---

[5] In the word "untruthfulness," for example, there are five morphemes: un-, true, -th, -ful, and -ness. Four of these morphemes are bound, i.e., they cannot occur on their own, and one ("true") is "free."

[6] The two major categories of grammatical analysis in Arabic are *Sarf* صرف and *naHw* نحو, which are often translated as morphology and syntax, respectively. However, the boundary between them is not the same boundary as in Western grammatical theory. The category of *Sarf* covers many areas of derivational morphology (e.g., the ten forms of the verb) and some inflectional morphology (e.g., the past tense paradigm); but it does not include the study of case and mood. A further category of Arabic grammatical analysis, *ishtiqaaq*, is often translated as 'etymology' but actually deals more with Arabic derivational morphology. It is etymology (the study of word origins and development) in the sense that it deals extensively with the creation of words from the lexical root system, but not in the Western diachronic sense that examines the evolution of lexical items and their meanings over time and through different, though related stages of language evolution.

has to do with vocal music. By inserting different vowels into the vowel slot between the /s-/ and the /-ng/ several different English words can be formed:

sing   (v.)
sang   (v.)
sung   (v.)
song   (n.)

All of these items are words, or stems that can have suffixes such as "sing-ing," "song-s," "sing-s," "song-'s," "sing-er," or prefixes, such as "un-sung." As a comparison, the consonant sequence *s-ng* corresponds roughly to the concept of an Arabic consonantal **root**, whereas the vowels and affixes would correspond approximately to the Arabic concept of **pattern**. The procedure of differentiating meaning by means of word-internal vowel change is known technically as "ablaut" or "introflection," defined as a word-internal change that signals a grammatical change. Other examples in English include: man/men, foot/feet, mouse/mice, know/knew, sink/sank/sunk. In English, the change usually involves just one vowel; however, in Arabic, it can involve several, for example:

he wrote	*katab-a* (v.)	كَتَبَ
he corresponded	*kaatab-a* (v.)	كاتَبَ
it was written	*kutib-a* (v.)	كُتِبَ
book	*kitaab* (n.)	كِتاب
books	*kutub* (n.)	كُتُب
writer; (adj.) writing	*kaatib* (n.)	كاتِب
writers	*kuttaab* (n.)	كُتّاب
write! (2 m.s.)	*uktub!* (v.)	أُكْتُبْ!

These words, or stems, can have inflectional suffixes such as *katab-at* 'she wrote,' or *kutub-an* 'books' (accusative case). The root or three-consonant ordered sequence *k-t-b* has to do with "writing," and most words in the Arabic language that have to do with writing are derived from that root, through modifying patterns of vowels (and sometimes also adding certain consonants). This is a typically Semitic morphological system. In Arabic, this **root-pattern** process has evolved extensively and very productively in order to cover a vast array of meanings associated with each semantic field (such as "writing"). A few more examples:

| office; desk | *maktab* (n.) | مَكْتَب |
| offices; desks | *makaatib* (n.) | مَكاتِب |

library	*maktaba* (n.)	مَكْتَبَة
she writes	*ta-ktub-u* (v.)	تَكْتُب
we write	*na-ktub-u* (v.)	نَكْتُب
writing	*kitaaba* (n.)	كِتَابة
written	*maktuub* (PP)	مَكْتُوب

As seen in the above examples, the shifting of **patterns** around the consonantal **root** accomplishes a great deal in terms of word creation (derivation) and to some extent, word inflection (e.g., pluralization). The consonant root can be viewed as a nucleus or core around which are constellated a wide array of potential meanings, depending on which pattern is keyed into the root. Roots and patterns are interacting components of word meaning and are both bound morphemes. They each convey specific and essential types of meaning, but neither one can exist independently because they are abstract mental representations.[7]

2.1 A definition of root

A **root** is a relatively invariable discontinuous bound morpheme, represented by two to five phonemes, typically three consonants in a certain order, which interlocks with a pattern to form a stem and which has lexical meaning.[8]

The **root** morpheme (for example, /k-t-b/) is "discontinuous" because vowels can be interspersed between those consonants; however, those consonants must always be present and be in the same sequence: first /k/, then /t/, then /b/. The usual number of consonants in an Arabic root is three and these constitute "by far the largest part of the language" (Haywood and Nahmad, 1962: 261). However, there are also two-consonant (biliteral), four-consonant (quadriliteral) (such as z-l-z-l, b-r-h-n, t-r-j-m), and five-consonant roots (quinquiliteral) (such as b-r-n-m-j).[9]

The root is said to contain lexical meaning because it communicates the idea of a real-world reference or general field denotation (such as "writing"). It is useful to think of a lexical root as denoting a semantic field because it is within that

---

[7] The fact that they are abstract does not diminish the fact that they are strong psychological realities for Arabic speakers. According to Frisch and Zawaydeh (2001, 92) "there is clear psycholinguistic evidence that Arabic consonantal roots are a distinct component of the Arabic mental lexicon."

[8] I am indebted to Professor Wallace Erwin for this definition.

[9] Aside from the reduplicated four-consonant root, such as w-s-w-s or h-m-h-m, which is inherently Arabic, four- and five-consonant roots can be borrowings from other languages. Some have been part of the Arabic lexicon for hundreds of years; others are recent borrowings (such as t-l-f-n 'to telephone'). The Arab grammarian al-Khalil ibn Ahmad (d.791) made an extensive study of Arabic lexical roots and determined which were Arabic and which were not according to rules of Arabic phonology and phonotactics. See Sara 1991 on al-Khalil's phonology.

field that actual words come into existence, each one crystalizing into a specific lexical item. The number of lexical roots in Arabic has been estimated between 5,000 and 6,500.[10]

2.2 A definition of pattern

A **pattern** is a bound and in many cases, discontinuous morpheme consisting of one or more vowels and slots for root phonemes (radicals), which either alone or in combination with one to three derivational affixes, interlocks with a root to form a stem, and which generally has grammatical meaning.[11]

The pattern is defined as discontinuous because it intersperses itself among the root consonants (as in the word *kaatib*).[12] It is useful to think of it as a kind of template onto which different roots can be mapped.[13] The "derivational affixes" mentioned in the definition include the use of consonants that mark grammatical functions, such as the derivational prefix *mu-* for many participles, the prefix *ma-* for a noun of place, or the relative adjective suffix /-*iyy*/. Consonants that are included in Arabic pattern formation are: /ʾ/ (*hamza*), /t/ (*taaʾ*), /m/ (*miim*), /n/ (*nuun*), /s/ (*siin*), /y/ (*yaaʾ*), and /w/ (*waaw*). These consonants may be used as prefixes, suffixes or even infixes.[14] One further component of patterning is gemination or doubling of a consonant. Therefore, the components of MSA pattern-formation include: six vowels (three long: /aa/, /ii/, /uu/; three short: /a/, /i/, and /u/); seven consonants (ʾ, t, m, n, s, y, w); and the process of gemination.[15]

Patterns are said to possess grammatical (rather than lexical) meaning because they signify grammatical or language-internal information; that is, they distinguish word types or word classes, such as nouns, verbs, and adjectives. They can even signal very specific information about subclasses of these categories. For example, noun patterns can readily be identified as active participle, noun of place, noun of instrument, or verbal noun, to name a few. Because patterns are

[10] Kouloughli (1994, 60) cites about 6,500 lexical roots found in a dictionary of 50,000 lexical items. Greenberg (1950) bases his study of lexical root phonotactics on 3,775 verb roots found in Lane (1863) and Dozy (1881).

[11] This definition is also from Professor Wallace Erwin.

[12] There are a few patterns that consist of just one vowel (such as _a_ _), for example, *Harb* 'war' or *nawm* 'sleep,' and these patterns are not considered discontinuous. Most patterns, however, involve more than one vowel.

[13] Patterns are sometimes referred to as "prosodic templates" or "stem templates" in discussions of morphological theory (see, e.g., Aronoff 1994, 134, Spencer 1994). For the concept of "templatic morphology" see McCarthy and Prince 1990.

[14] Such as the *taaʾ* infixed between the root consonants *jiim* and *miim* in the Form VIII verb *ijtamaʿ-a* 'to meet,' for example, from the root *j-m-ʿ* 'gathering together.' Another example is the infixing of *waaw* in the word *shawaariʿ*, the plural of *shaariʿ* 'street.' Again, the infix is inserted between the first and second consonants of the root.

[15] A traditional mnemonic device for remembering Arabic morphological components is the invented word *saʾaltumuuniihaa* سألتمونيها 'you (pl.) asked me it.'

limited to giving grammatical or intralinguistic information, there are fewer Arabic patterns than roots.

3 Word structure: root and pattern combined

Most Arabic words, therefore, are analyzed as consisting of two morphemes – a root and a pattern – interlocking to form one word. Neither an Arabic root nor a pattern can be used in isolation; they need to connect with each other in order to form actual words. A word such as *kaatib* 'writer,' for example, consists of two bound morphemes: the lexical root *k-t-b* and the active participle pattern _*aa*_*i*_ (where the slots stand for root consonants).[16] When a root is mapped onto a pattern, they together form a word, "writer," ("doer of the action of writing"). This word can then act as a stem for grammatical affixes such as case-markers. For example, the accusative indefinite suffix -*an*:

قابلنا كاتباً.

qaabal-naa kaatib-an.

We met a writer.

Understanding the system of root–pattern combinations enables the learner to deduce or at least wisely guess at a wide range of word meanings through compositional semantics by putting together root and pattern meanings to yield a word meaning. This ultimately lightens the load of vocabulary learning.[17]

4 Dictionary organization

Arabic dictionaries are based on lexical roots and not word spelling.[18] Instead of relying on the exact orthography of a word, Arabic dictionaries are organized by the root or consonant core of a word, providing under that entry every word derived from that particular root. The root is therefore often called a "lexical root" because it is the actual foundation for the lexicon, or dictionary. The lexical root

---

[16] In their work on Arabic templatic morphology, McCarthy and Prince propose separating Arabic root and pattern components into distinct "tiers" in accordance with the "Prosodic Morphology Hypothesis" (1990, 3–6).

[17] It is important to note that not all Arabic word-meanings are semantically transparent, despite the rigor of the system. Many words have come to have particular connotations due to cultural, historical, and regional factors and need to be learned through use of the dictionary. (See Bateson 2003, 1–3.) For a helpful analysis of Arabic morphology as it relates to the lexicon, see Stowasser 1981.

[18] The roots in an Arabic dictionary are listed alphabetically according to the order of letters in the Arabic alphabet. For example, the root *k-t-f* comes after *k-t-b* because /f/ comes after /b/ in the alphabet. Therefore, in order to find the root, one has to know the order of the alphabet. This is dealt with further in Appendix 1. This system applies to genuinely Arabic words or words that have been thoroughly Arabized. However, loanwords – words borrowed from other languages – are listed in an Arabic dictionary by their spelling. Note that pre-modern Arabic dictionaries may have alternative arrangements of the root consonants. See Haywood 1965 on the history of Arabic lexicography.

provides a semantic field within which actual vocabulary items can be located. In this respect, an Arabic dictionary might be seen as closer to a thesaurus than a dictionary, locating all possible variations of meaning in one referential domain or semantic field under one entry. See Appendix 1 for a summary of how to use an Arabic dictionary.

5 Other lexical types

5.1 Compounding into one word (*naHt* نحت)

Another word-formation process exists in Arabic: compounding, composing a word by conjoining other words. There are several subprocesses or variations on this procedure, and although it is not common in traditional Arabic morphology, it is used in MSA for recently coined items and for loan-translations, especially technical terms. The classic MSA example is the word *ra'smaal* 'capital' formed from conjoining the words *ra's* 'head' and *maal* 'money.' Another example is *laa-markaziyya* 'decentralization,' from the words *laa* 'no' and *markaziyya* 'centralization.' Sometimes only part of a word is used in the compound, as in the word for 'supersonic,' *faw-SawTiyy*, abbreviating the word for 'above, super' *fawq* to *faw-* , joining it with the noun *SawT* 'sound,' and suffixing the adjectival /-iyy/ ending.[19]

5.2 Compounding into two words (*tarkiib* تركيب)

Sometimes the lexical item created is not one single word in Arabic, but a noun phrase, such as *ᶜadam wujuud* 'non-existence' or *kiis hawaa'* 'airbag,' or a combined participle-noun phrase such as *mutaᶜaddid-u l-'aTraaf*, 'multilateral.' With the necessity for rapid translation of technical and computational terms from Western languages into Arabic, these kinds of lexical compounds have become more prevalent over the past two or three decades. See Chapter 5, section 15.2 for further detail on this type of lexical innovation.

5.3 Solid stems

Solid stems are words which cannot be reduced or analyzed into the root–pattern paradigm. They consist of primarily three sets in Arabic: pronouns, function words, and loanwords. Solid-stem words are listed in Arabic dictionaries according to their spelling.

5.3.1 Pronouns

Arabic pronoun categories include personal pronouns, demonstrative pronouns, and relative pronouns. These categories do not fit precisely into the standard root and pattern system, although they show definite phonological relationships to

---

[19] See Stetkevych 1970, 48–55. See also Chapter 5, section 15.1.

each other within their categories, such as the relation between *haadhaa* 'this (m.)' and *haadhihi* 'this (f.)'.

5.3.2 Function words

Another common subset of solid stems consists of Arabic function words – such as prepositions and conjunctions. These are high-frequency items, and in terms of their structure, they are usually short or even monosyllabic. For example: *fii*, 'in; at,' *ʾilaa*, 'to, towards,' or *wa-* 'and.'

5.3.3 Loanwords

There are also a number of words (primarily nouns) in MSA that are borrowed directly from other languages, and these are considered, for the most part, to have solid stems, e.g., they cannot be broken down into roots and patterns, such as the words *raadyuu* 'radio' and *kumbyuutir* 'computer.'[20]

Many proper nouns fall into this category, as well, including Middle Eastern place names such as *baghdaad*, 'Baghdad' and *bayruut* 'Beirut.'[21] Such words are discussed at greater length in Chapter 5.

6 Inflection: an overview of grammatical categories in Arabic

The term "inflection" generally refers to phonological changes a word undergoes as it is being used in context. In English, some common inflectional categories are: number (singular and plural), tense (e.g., past, present), and voice (active and passive).

Generally speaking, Arabic words are marked for more grammatical categories than are English words. Some of these categories are familiar to English speakers (such as tense and number) while others, such as inflection for case or gender, are not. There are eight major grammatical categories in Arabic: tense/aspect, person, voice, mood, gender, number, case, definiteness. Six of these apply to verbs (tense/aspect, person, voice, mood, gender, number), four apply to nouns and adjectives (gender, number, case, definiteness), and four apply to pronouns (person, gender, number and – to a limited extent – case).

Here is a brief summary of these categories and their roles in Arabic. Details on all these topics are found as noted under specific reference points.

6.1 Tense/Aspect

Tense and aspect can be seen as two different ways of viewing time. Tense usually deals with linear points extending from the past into the future. Aspect sees the

---

[20] A few words borrowed from Western languages, such as "film" and "bank" fit so well into the root–pattern system that Arabic plurals have evolved for them – *ʾaflaam* and *bunuuk*, respectively.
[21] These names are not originally Arabic but derive from other languages of the region such as Aramaic or Persian.

completeness of an action or state as central: is the action over with and completed, ongoing, or yet to occur? The points of view of the two terms are different:
one focuses on when the action occurs and the other focuses on the action itself –
whether it is complete or not. These two grammatical categories do overlap to
some extent and have in practice blended into one in MSA.[22]

There are two basic morphological tenses in Arabic: past and present, also
called perfective and imperfective, respectively. In dealing with the modern written language, many linguists and teachers find it more pragmatic to describe
Arabic verbs in terms of tense, and the terms *past/present* (referring to time or
tense) and *perfect/imperfect* (referring to aspect) are often used interchangeably.
There is also a future tense, indicated by prefixing either *sa-* or *sawfa* to a present
tense form. Other tenses exist, such as the past perfect, the future perfect, and the
past continuous, but they are **compound tenses** involving the use of auxiliary
verbs and particles.[23]

6.2 Person

Arabic verbs and personal pronouns inflect for three persons: first person (I, we),
second person (you), and third person (she, he, they). There are differences with
English, however, in the gender and number of these persons. For the Arabic first
person (*'anaa, naHnu*) there is no gender distinction. For the second person, there
are five forms of "you": masculine singular (*'anta*), feminine singular (*'anti*), dual
(*'antumaa*), masculine plural (*'antum*) and feminine plural (*'antunna*). For the third
person, there are six verbal distinctions and five pronoun distinctions: he (*huwa*),
she (*hiya*), they-two masculine (*humaa*), they-two feminine (*humaa*), they masculine
(*hum*) and they feminine (*hunna*). (See charts in Chapter 12.) Thus, the total number of person categories in Arabic is thirteen, as opposed to the seven of English
(I, you, he, she, it, we, they).

6.3 Voice

The category of voice refers to whether an Arabic verb or participle is active or passive. Generally speaking, the passive is used in Arabic only if the agent or doer of
the action is unknown or not to be mentioned for some reason. There are sets of

---

[22] In his description of "the states (tenses) of the verb" in Classical Arabic, Wright (1967, I:51) says:
"The temporal forms of the Arabic verb are but *two* in number, the one expressing a *finished* act,
one that is done and completed in relation to other acts (the *Perfect*); the other an *unfinished* act,
one that is just commencing or in progress (the *Imperfect*)" (emphasis in original). On the same
page he gives an indication of the complexity of Arabic tense/aspect relations when he states that
"The Arabian Grammarians . . . have given an undue importance to the idea of time, in connection
with the verbal forms, by their division of it into the past (*al-maaDii* الماضي) the present (*al-Haal*
الحال or *al-HaaDir* الحاضر) and the future (*al-mustaqbal* المستقبل) the first of which they assign
to the Perfect and the other two to the Imperfect."

[23] See Chapter 21 on verb inflection.

morphological inflections and syntactic constructions particular to the passive and these are dealt with in Chapter 38.

6.4 Mood

Mood or "mode" refers to verb categories such as *indicative, subjunctive, imperative,* or (in Arabic) *jussive*. These categories reflect contextual modalities that condition the action of the verb. For example, whereas the indicative mood tends to be characteristic of straightforward statements or questions, the subjunctive indicates an attitude toward the action such as doubt, desire, wishing, or necessity, and the imperative mood indicates an attitude of command or need for action on the part of the speaker.

The issue of mood marking is a central one in Arabic grammar (along with case marking). Moods fall under the topic of morphology because they are reflected in word structure; they are usually indicated by suffixes or modifications of suffixes attached to the present tense verb stem, and the phonological nature of the verb stem determines what form the suffix will take. The mood markers are often short vowel suffixes, for example, /-u/ for indicative and /-a/ for subjunctive.

In Arabic, mood marking is done only on the imperfective or present tense stem; there are no mode variants for the past tense. The Arabic moods are therefore non-finite; that is, they do not refer to specific points in time and are not differentiated by tense. Tense is inferred from context and other parts of the clause.

Mood marking is determined either by particular particles which govern or require certain moods (e.g., the negative particle *lam* requires the jussive mood on the following verb) or by the narrative context in general, including attitude of the speaker and intended meaning. See Chapters 34 and 35 on verb moods.

6.5 Gender

Arabic exhibits two genders: masculine and feminine.[24] For the most part, gender is overtly marked, but there are words whose gender is covert and shows up only in agreement sequences. The gender category into which a noun falls is semantically arbitrary, except where nouns refer to human beings or other living creatures. Gender is marked on adjectives, pronouns, and verbs, as well, but is not inherent, as it is in nouns. Gender is discussed at greater length in Chapter 7.

6.6 Number

Arabic has three number categories: singular, dual, and plural. Whereas singular and plural are familiar categories to most Western learners, the dual is less

---

[24] A very few nouns are both masculine and feminine, for example: 'salt' *milH* and 'spirit' *ruuH* (see Chapter 7 for further discussion).

familiar.[25] The dual in Arabic is used whenever the category of "two" applies, whether it be in nouns, adjectives, pronouns, or verbs.

The concept of plural therefore applies to three or more entities. This category interacts in specific ways with the category of gender and also with a morphological category which is peculiar to Arabic: humanness. Both gender and humanness affect the way in which a noun, participle, or adjective is pluralized.

Numerals themselves, their structural features and the grammatical rules for counting and sequential ordering, constitute one of the most complex topics in Arabic. They are discussed in Chapter 15.

6.7 Case

Arabic nouns and adjectives normally inflect for three cases: nominative, genitive, and accusative. Cases fall under the topic of morphology because they are part of word structure; they are usually suffixes attached to the word stem, and the nature of the word stem determines what form the suffix will take.[26] In general, the case markers are short vowel suffixes: *-u* for nominative, *-i* for genitive and *-a* for accusative, but there are substantial exceptions to this.[27] A case-marking paradigm is usually referred to as a *declension*; there are eight different nominal declensions in Arabic and these are discussed in Chapter 7.

Cases also fall under the topic of syntax because they are determined by the syntactic role of a noun or adjective within a sentence or clause.[28] To indicate roughly how the system works, the nominative case typically marks the subject role (most often the agent or doer of an action); the accusative marks the direct object of a transitive verb or it may mark an adverbial function; and the genitive is used mainly in two roles: marking the object of a preposition and marking the possessor in a possessive structure. For case roles and rules, see Chapter 7, section 5.

6.8 Definiteness: determiners

Arabic has both definite and indefinite markers. The definite marker is a word (*al-*) which is not independent but is prefixed to nouns and adjectives; the indefiniteness marker is an affix (*-n*), normally suffixed to the case-marking vowel on nouns and adjectives; thus, *al-bayt-u* ('the house' – nominative, definite), but *bayt-u-n* ('a house' – nominative, indefinite). The suffixed /-n/ sound is not written with the

---

[25] In English, there are some words that refer specifically to two items such as "both" and "pair."

[26] For example, a diptote word such as *wuzaraaʾ* 'ministers' will show the genitive marker as *fatHa*, not *kasra*, because of the nature of its morphological pattern: *CuCaCaaʾ*.

[27] The exceptions fall into two categories: exceptions determined by morphological rules (such as the word pattern) and exceptions determined by phonological rules (such as the rule that two vowels cannot combine).

[28] Traditional Arabic grammar deals with case inflections as a category of syntax (*naHw*) rather than morphology (*Sarf*).

letter /n/ (*nuun*) but is indicated by modifying the short vowel case-marker (see Chapter 7, section 4). Whereas the definite article is visible in Arabic script, the indefinite marker normally is not.[29]

7 Distribution of inflectional categories: paradigms

In terms of the distribution of the above eight categories of inflection, Arabic verbs inflect for the first six: tense/aspect, person, voice, mood, gender, and number. Nouns and adjectives inflect for the last four: gender, number, case, and definiteness. Pronouns inflect for gender, number, and – to some extent – case. Any verb, for example, can be analyzed as being marked for six categories; any noun can be analyzed for four categories and any pronoun for three. This means that word structure in MSA is complex, and that verbs have the most complex structure of all.

Grammatical paradigms are charts or frameworks for words which show all their possible inflections.[30] In traditional Western grammars, there are two major divisions of paradigms: verbs and nominals (nouns, adjectives and pronouns). A verb paradigm is called a conjugation; a nominal paradigm is called a declension. Verbs are said to "conjugate" or inflect for verbal categories of tense, person, number, gender, mood, and voice. Nominals are said to "decline," to inflect for case, number, gender, and definiteness.

The forms or phonological realizations that these categories take in any particular word are determined by that word's membership in an **inflectional class**.[31]

8 MSA inflectional classes

An inflectional class contains words whose inflections (either declension or conjugation) are identical, or at least highly similar.

Criteria for inflectional classes: Verbs fall into several classes by virtue of their phonological structure, which affects how they inflect (e.g., hollow verbs, defective verbs, assimilated verbs). So do nouns and adjectives (e.g., triptotes and diptotes). In addition, nouns and/or adjectives may fall into certain classes because of their origins and etymology. In order to help learners with these many categories and the forms that they take, this reference grammar provides **paradigms** or

---

[28] The exception to this is the accusative indefinite suffix -*an*, which is often written into the script with an *ʾalif* and two *fatHas*.

[30] Carstairs-McCarthy points out that there is an abstract notion of paradigm ("the set of combinations of morphosyntactic properties or features . . . realized by inflected forms of words (or lexemes) in a given word-class (or major category or lexeme class) in a given language") as well as a concrete one: "the set of inflectional realizations expressing [an abstract paradigm] for a given word (or lexeme) in a given language" (1994, 739).

[31] I am following Aronoff's (1994, 65) definition of inflectional class: "a set of lexemes whose members each select the same set of inflectional realizations." Carstairs-McCarthy gives a similar definition: "a set of words (lexemes) displaying the same paradigm in a given language" (1994, 739).

inflectional charts for each inflectional class as well as descriptions of the main morphophonemic processes underlying the resulting forms.

9 Case and mood: special inflectional categories in Arabic

As can be seen in the above descriptions, there are two Arabic inflectional categories that interface with syntax: case and mood. Both of them mark this interfacing by short vowel suffixes, called in English "moods" or "modes" when they apply to verbs, and "cases" when they apply to nouns or adjectives. One of the interesting features of Arabic structure is that the nominative case (on nouns and adjectives) and the indicative marker (on verbs) are to a large extent identical: suffixed /-u/; and the accusative and subjunctive markers are largely identical as well: suffixed /-a/.[32] It is important for learners of Arabic to know that in Arabic grammar these two categories are referred to as one; that is, nominative and indicative are considered one category: *raf*ᶜ or *marfuu*ᶜ, and accusative and subjunctive are considered another: *naSb* or *manSuub*.

Because of these formal similarities, case and mood are treated as categories of syntax (*naHw*) in traditional Arabic grammar, and for very sound and compelling reasons. Moreover, there is no theoretical distinction in Arabic between case and mood. Readers who are interested in morphological theory or in studying Arabic grammar more extensively should keep in mind that Arabic sets these categories apart, and that they are of great – even central – importance in Arabic syntactic theory. One can certainly say that these two categories are closer to the syntactic level of analysis than to the semantic or lexical level.[33]

---

[32] This is, of course, a generalization. Other formal realizations of these categories exist, but this is the major one.

[33] See Ryding 1993 for more on this topic. See also the entries *Sarf* and *naHw* in the *Encyclopedia of Islam*; and Bohas, Guillaume and Kouloughli 1990, especially Chapters 3 and 4.

4

Basic Arabic sentence structures

This chapter deals with very basic sentence structure and relations among sentence elements.

1. Essential principles of sentence structure

There are two major syntactic principles that affect the structure of Arabic phrases and clauses: agreement/concord and government.

1.1 Agreement or concord (*muTaabaqa* مطابقة)

Agreement or concord is where words in a phrase or clause show feature compatibility, that is, they match or conform to each other, one reflecting the other's features. For example, a verb is masculine singular if it has a masculine singular subject. A feminine singular noun takes a feminine singular adjective, and so forth. In order to undertake this matching or agreement of features, one needs to be aware of the rules for agreement, and of the categories that constitute feature compatibility.

Generally, in discussion of case systems, the term **concord** is used to refer to matching between nouns and their dependants (typically adjectives, other nouns, or pronouns), whereas **agreement** refers to matching between the verb and its subject.[1] Often, however, these terms are used synonymously. Categories of concord and agreement in Arabic include: gender, number, definiteness, and case for nouns and adjectives, and inflection for gender, number, and person for verbs and pronouns.[2]

1.2 Government (*ʿamal* عمل)

Government is a syntactic principle wherein certain words *cause* others to inflect in particular ways — not in agreement with the "governing" word (the ʿaamil عامل), but **as a result of the effect of the governing word**.[3]

---

[1] See Blake 1994, 186, footnote 6.
[2] For a detailed historical overview of Arabic and Semitic agreement structures, see Russell 1984.
[3] The term "government" as an equivalent for the Arabic term ʿamal is used extensively, but other terms such as "operation" and "regimen" are also used in English translations. All these terms refer to the power of one word, one structure, or one concept to affect the inflection of another word.

In his four-volume grammar of modern Arabic, *al-naHw al-waafii*, Abbaas Hasan defines *ʿaamil* as "what supervenes on a word and thereby affects its ending by making it nominative/indicative, accusative/subjunctive, genitive, or jussive" (*maa ya-dxul-u ʿalaa l-kalimat-i fa-yu-ʾaththir-u fii ʾaaxir-i-haa bi-l-raf ʿ-i, ʾaw-i l-naSb-i, ʾaw-i l-jarr-i ʾaw-i l-jazm-i*).[4]

Typical "governors" (*ʿawaamil* عوامل) in Arabic are verbs, prepositions, and particles. For example, a transitive verb takes or "governs" a direct object in the accusative case. Or a certain particle, such as the negative future marker *lan*, requires the subjunctive mood on the following verb; a preposition requires that its noun object be in the genitive case, and so on.

Case (on substantives) and mood (on verbs) are the two categories affected by **government** in Arabic.[5]

1.3 Dependency relations

Because of these essential principles that characterize the structure of words in phrases and clauses, Arabic can be seen as a language that has a network of **dependency relations** in every phrase or clause. These relations are **key components** of the grammatical structure of the language.

2. The simple sentence

Traditional Arabic grammatical theory divides sentences into two categories depending on **the nature of the first word in the sentence.** Sentences whose first word is a noun or noun phrase are termed *jumal ismiyya* جملة اسمية, or 'nominal sentences,' and sentences whose initial word is a verb are termed *jumal fiʿliyya* جملة فعلية, or 'verbal sentences.' This first-word criterion is not based on whether the sentence contains a verb, but on whether the verb is initial or not.[6]

In the teaching of Arabic as a foreign language, however, a different distinction is often used for classifying Arabic sentences. This distinction is based on **whether or not the sentence contains a verb.** The English term "equational sentence" is used to refer to verbless predications. The term "verbal sentence" refers to predications that contain a verb. As Abboud and McCarus state, "Arabic sentences are of two types, those with verbs, called *verbal sentences*, and those not containing verbs, called *equational sentences*" (emphasis in original; 1983, Part 1:102).

Confusion sometimes arises with the term "verbal sentence" because if one uses it to refer to the traditional Arabic term, one means "sentence starting with

---

[4] Hasan 1987, I:441. The definition is given in an extensive footnote that describes the types of *ʿaamil*.

[5] Sometimes the governor is an abstraction (*ʿaamil maʿnawiyy* عامل معنوي), such as the concept "subject of an equational sentence" (*ibtidaaʾ* ابتداء). For a general outline of the Arabic theory of government in English see Bohas, Guillaume, and Kouloughli 1991, 57-62. See also Hasan 1987 for further description in Arabic of *ʿaamil lafZiyy* 'overt governor' and *ʿaamil maʿnawiyy* 'abstract governor.'

[6] This theoretical distinction, however, is disputed. See Ayoub and Bohas 1983 for a counter argument to the word-order criterion. For more on this, see Cantarino 1974, I:2.

a verb." But if "verbal sentence" is used to refer to the distinction between verbless and verb-containing sentences, it means "sentence containing a verb." Similarly, sometimes the terms *jumla ismiyya* and "equational sentence" are taken to be equivalents, but they are not. A *jumla ismiyya* is a sentence that starts with a noun, including those that contain verbs. An equational sentence refers to a predication that is specifically verbless. These terms are not equivalent because they are based on different criteria.

In this text, in keeping with the terms used by Abboud and McCarus, I use the term "equational" to refer to verbless sentences, and "verbal sentence" to refer to those containing a verb.

2.1 Equational sentences in general

Equational sentences are verbless. The reason these sentences are verbless is because the Arabic verb 'to be' (*kaan-a*) is not normally used in the present tense indicative; it is simply understood. These sentences consist of a subject or topic (*mubtadaʾ*: 'what is begun with') and predicate (*xabar*: 'piece of information; news'). That is, they typically begin with a noun phrase or pronoun and are completed by a comment on that noun phrase or pronoun. The comment or predicate may take the form of different classes of words and phrases: nouns, predicate adjectives, pronouns, or prepositional phrases. These sentences are "equational" because the subject and predicate "equate" with each other and balance each other out in a complete proposition, or equation.

2.1.1 The structure of equational sentences

The subject or topic of an equational sentence is in the nominative case, and so is the predicate, if it is a noun or adjective. When the predicate is a noun, pronoun, or adjective, it agrees with the subject in gender and number, but not in definiteness.[7] Generally, the subject is the first element in the sentence, but sometimes the order is reversed, and the predicate comes first.

2.1.1.1 COMMON TYPES OF EQUATIONAL SENTENCES:

(1) **Noun/adjective:** Here the subject is a noun with the definite article, and the predicate is an adjective (or adjective phrase) marked for indefiniteness.

العالم قرية صغيرة.	الطريق طويل.
al-ʿaalam-u qaryat-un Saghiirat-un.	al-Tariiq-u Tawiil-un.
The world [is] a small village.	The road [is] long.

---

[7] Blake (1994, 191, note 2) gives a clear description of the subject-predicate relationship for equational sentences when he states that "the concord between a predicative noun or adjective and a subject would normally be described as concord of the predicative word with the subject, since it typically involves inherent features of the subject being marked on the predicate."

المنافسة قوية.

al-munaafasat-u qawwiyyat-un.

Competition [is] strong.

الكرز أحمر.

al-karaz-u ʾaHmar-u.

Cherries [are] red.

الرياح جنوبية شرقية معتدلة.

al-riyaaH-u januubiyyat-un sharqiyyat-un muᶜ tadilat-un.

The winds [are] moderate southeasterly.

(2) **Noun phrase/adjective:** Here the subject is a noun phrase and the predicate an indefinite adjective or adjective phrase.

قصر الملك ضخم.

qaSr-u l-malik-i Daxm-un.

The king's palace [is] huge.

كلها أفلام سياسية.

kull-u-haa ʾaflaam-un siyaasiyyat-un.

All of them [are] political films.

(3) **Pronoun/adjective or adjective phrase:**

هو ذكي.

huwa dhakiyy-un.

He [is] intelligent.

هي أمريكية من أصل عربي.

hiya ʾamriikiyyat-un min ʾaSl-in ᶜarabiyy-in

She [is] an American of Arab origin.

(4) **Pronoun/noun:**

أنت صديقتي.

ʾanti Sadiiqat-ii.

You (f.) [are] my friend.

هو خبير.

huwa xabiir-un.

He [is] an expert.

نحن عرب.

naHn-u ᶜarab-un.

We [are] Arabs.

(5) **Demonstrative pronoun/noun:**

هذا دفتري.

haadhaa daftar-ii.

This [is] my notebook.

هذه تجربة مهمة.

haadhihi tajribat-un muhimmat-un.

This [is] an important experiment.

(6) **Demonstrative pronoun/adjective or adjective phrase:**

هذا غير صحيح.

haadhaa ghayr-u SaHiiH-in.

This [is] untrue.

هذا جديد.

haadhaa jadiid-un.

This [is] new.

(7) **Noun/noun or noun/noun phrase:**

زوجتي طبيبة.

zawjat-ii Tabiibat-un.

My wife [is] a doctor.

الزراعة لغة عالمية.

al-ziraaᶜat-u lughat-un ᶜaalamiyyat-un.

Agriculture [is] a world language.

(8)   Noun/prepositional phrase:

الحمد لله.
al-Hamd-u li-llaah-i.
Praise [be] to God.

السلام عليكم.
al-salaam-u ʿalay-kum.
Peace [be] upon you.

(9)   **Reversal of subject and predicate:** Sometimes the predicate of an equational sentence will come before the subject. This most often happens when the subject lacks the definite article.

هنا حمّامنا.
hunaa Hammaam-u-naa.
Here [is] our bathroom.

بينهما سيدتان.
bayn-a-humaa sayyidat-aani.
Between ('the two of') them [are] two women.

(10)   **Expression of possession:** Possession is usually predicated by means of a preposition or semi-preposition, and it often is the first element of the equational sentence. Because the predication is in the form of a prepositional phrase, the item that is possessed is in the nominative case, being the subject of an equational sentence.

عندي مشكلة.
ʿind-ii mushkilat-un.
I have ('at-me is') a problem.

لديهم القدرة.
laday-him-i l-qudrat-u.
They have ('at-them is') the capability.

لها أربع أرجل.
la-haa ʾarbaʿ-u ʾarjul-in.
They have ('to-them are') four legs.

(11)   **Existential predications:** "there is/there are"

(11.1)   With *hunaaka* "there is; there are":

هناك موضوعان مهمان.
hunaaka mawDuuʿ-aani muhimm-aani.
There [are] two important topics.

هناك عوامل كثيرة.
hunaaka ʿawaamil-u kathiirat-un.
There [are] many factors.

(11.2)   With *thammat-a* "there is; there are":

فثمة قيم مختلفة.
fa-thammat-a qiyam-un muxtalifat-un.
For **there** [are] different values.

(12)   **Equational sentences with definite predicates: the copula pronoun:** These require the copula or "pronoun of separation" to distinguish the

subject from the predicate.[8] The pronoun agrees with the subject (or *mub-tada*ʾ) in gender and number:

المهم هو العودة.

al-muhimm-u huwa l-ʿawdat-u.

The important [thing] [is] to return ('returning').

المهم هو العمل.

al-muhimm-u huwa l-ʿamal-u.

The important [thing] [is] work.

الأمّ هي نموذج كل النساء.

al-ʾumm-u hiya namuudhaj-u kull-i l-nisaaʾ-i.

The mother [is] the model for all women.

(13) **Equational sentence with clause as predicate:** In the following equational sentence, the subject is a compound one, and the predicate actually consists of another equational sentence "their source is one."

المسيحية والإسلام أصلهما واحد.

al-masiiHiyyat-u wa-l-ʾ islaam-u ʾaSl-u-humaa waaHid-un.

Christianity and Islam [are from] one source ('**their source is one**').

(14) **Negation of verbless sentences:** Verbless sentences are usually made negative with the use of the verb *lays-a* 'to not be' (see Chapter 37 for further description of *lays-a*). When *lays-a* is used, it changes the predicate of the sentence from the nominative case to the accusative case.[9]

(14.1) **Positive statement:**   **Negation:**

أنت صديقتنا.   لست صديقتنا.

ʾanti Sadiiqat-u-naa.   *las-ti Sadiiqat-a-naa.*

You [are] our friend.   You **are not** our friend.

(14.2) **Positive statement:**   **Negation:**

هو خبير.   ليس خبيرا.

huwa xabiir-un.   *lays-a xabiir-an.*

He [is] an expert.   He **is not** an expert.

---

[8] Eid (1991, 33) suggests that "the copula pronoun be analyzed as a predicate expressing the relation of identity."

[9] It is therefore one of what are called the *nawaasix* or 'converters-to-accusative' described in Chapter 7, section 5.3.3.8.

(14.3) Positive statement: Negation:

الطريق طويل.   ليس الطريق طويلا.
al-Tariiq-u Tawiil-un.   ***lays-a** l-Tariiq-u Tawiil-**an**.*
The road [is] long.   The road **is not** long.

(14.4) Positive statement: Negation:

زوجتي طبيبة.   ليست زوجتي طبيبة.
zawjat-ii Tabiibat-un.   ***lays-at** zawjat-ii Tabiibat-**an**.*
My wife [is] a doctor.   My wife **is not** a doctor.

(15) **Non-present tense indicative equational sentences:** Sentences that are
      equational in the present tense indicative need a form of the verb *kaan-a* in
      other tenses or moods. The verb *kaan-a*, like *lays-a*, requires that the predi-
      cate of the equational sentence be in the accusative case (see Chapter 36):

(15.1) Present: Past:

قصر الملك ضخم.   كان قصر الملك ضخما.
qaSr-u l-malik-i Daxm-un.   ***kaan-a** qaSr-u l-malik-i Daxm-**an**.*
The king's palace [is] huge.   The king's palace **was** huge.

(15.2) Present: Past:

الطريق طويل.   كان الطريق طويلا.
al-Tariiq-u Tawiil-un.   ***kaan-a** l-Tariiq-u Tawiil-**an**.*
The road [is] long.   The road **was** long.

(15.3) Present: Future:

زوجتي طبيبة.   ستكون زوجتي طبيبة.
zawjat-ii Tabiibat-un.   ***sa-ta-kuun-u** zawjat-ii Tabiibat-**an**.*
My wife [is] a doctor.   My wife **will be** a doctor.

2.2 The simple verbal sentence (*jumla fiᶜliyya* جملة فعلية)

2.2.1 Subject as verb inflection only

The simplest verbal sentence consists of a verb and its pronoun subject. The
subject pronoun is incorporated into the verb as part of its inflection. It is not
necessarily mentioned separately, as it is in English.[10] Past tense verbs inflect with
a subject suffix; present tense verbs have subject prefix and also a suffix.

---

[10] In current linguistic terms, Arabic is a "pro-drop" language. That is, its verbs incorporate their
subject pronouns as part of their inflection, and separate subject pronouns are not necessary for
indicating person.

عاد.	نتشرّف.	نجحت.	يحاولون.
ʿaad-a.	*na-tasharraf-u.*	*najaH-at.*	*yu-Haawil-uuna.*
He returned.	We are honored.	She succeeded.	They try.

2.2.2 Specification of noun subject

When a **subject noun or noun phrase is specified**, it usually follows the verb and is in the nominative case. The verb **agrees** with the specified subject in gender. The subject and verb together form a structural unit, or *jumla* جملة.

عاد السفير.	عاد سفير تونس.
ʿaad-a l-safiir-u.	*ʿaad-a safiir-u tuunis-a.*
The ambassador returned.	The ambassador of Tunisia returned.

نجحت الحكومة.	نجحت الحكومة الجديدة.
najaH-at-i l-Hukuumat-u.	*najaH-at-i l-Hukuumat-u l-jadiidat-u.*
The government succeeded.	The new government succeeded.

2.2.3 Intransitive verbs (al-ʾafʿaal ghayr al-mutaʿaddiya; al-ʾafʿaal al-laazima الأفعال غير المتعدية الأفعال اللازمة)

If the verb is intransitive, it does not take a direct object, but it may be complemented by an adverbial or prepositional phrase:

عاشوا في البلاد العربية.	يَهْطِل الثلج على الجبال.
ʿaash-uu fii l-bilaad-i l-ʿarabiyyat-i.	*ya-hTil-u l-thalj-u ʿalaa l-jibaal-i.*
They lived in Arab countries.	Snow falls on the mountains.

2.2.4 Transitive verbs (al-ʾafʿaal al-mutaʿaddiya الأفعال المتعدية)

If the verb is transitive, it takes a **direct object**, which is in the **accusative case**. It may be a noun, a noun phrase, or a pronoun.

لا أعرف شيئًا.	لقي مقاومة.	أجروا محادثات.
laa ʾa-ʿrif-u shayʾ-an.	*laqiy-a muqaawamat-an.*	*ʾajraw muHaadathaat-in.*
I do not know anything.	He encountered resistance.	They conducted talks.

حزمت حقيبتها.	رفع يده.	شكّلا لجنة مشتركة.
Hazam-at Haqiibat-a-haa.	*rafaʿ-a yad-a-hu.*	*shakkal-aa lajnat-an mushtarakat-an.*
She packed her suitcase.	He raised his hand.	They (two) formed a joint committee.

2.2.5 Mention of both subject and object

If both the subject and the object of the verb are specified, the word order is usually Verb–Subject–Object (VSO). **This is the standard word order of verbal sentences in Arabic.**

فتح كريم فمه.

fataH-a kariim-un fam-a-hu.

Karim opened his mouth.

وقّعت مصر اتفاقية.

waqqaᶜ-at miSr-u ttifaaqiyyat-an.

Egypt signed an agreement.

يحمل السفير رسالة.

ya-Hmil-u l-safiir-u risaalat-an.

The ambassador is carrying a letter.

2.3 Summary of basic sentence relations

The basic dependency relations in a simple Arabic verbal sentence are therefore as follows:

(1) The subject is incorporated in the verb as part of its inflection.
(2) The subject may **also** be mentioned explicitly, in which case it usually follows the verb and is in the nominative case. The verb agrees in gender with its subject.
(3) A transitive verb, in addition to having a subject, also takes a direct object in the accusative case. This object follows the verb and any mentioned subject.
(4) The basic word order is thus VSO: Verb–Subject–Object.
(5) The word order may vary to SVO (Subject–Verb–Object) or even VOS (Verb–Object–Subject) under certain conditions.[11]

2.4 Further dependency relations

There are a few issues that add to the complexity of the basic structure of syntactic relations. These have to do with verb–subject agreement and word order.

2.4.1 Verb–subject agreement

In a verb-initial sentence or clause, the verb agrees with its subject in gender, but not always in number. **If the verb precedes the subject and the subject is dual or plural, the verb remains singular.**[12] Thus a dual or plural noun subject when it follows the verb, does not influence verb inflection for number.[13]

2.4.1.1 PLURAL OR DUAL SUBJECT FOLLOWING VERB: If the subject is plural or dual, and it follows the verb, the verb inflects only for gender agreement, and not number agreement. The verb remains singular.

---

[11] See Parkinson 1981 for a study of word-order shift in MSA.
[12] This restriction on the number inflection of the Arabic verb is sometimes referred to as "agreement asymmetry." See Bolotin 1995 for further analysis of this topic.
[13] See Mohammed 1990 for extensive analysis of issues in subject–verb agreement in MSA.

ضحك الطلاب.
DaHik-a l-Tullab-u.
The students laughed. ('**He-laughed**, the students.')

يظهر الروس نبلاء وكراماً.
ya-Zhar-u l-ruus-u nubalaaʾ-a wa-kiraam-an.
The Russians appear [as] noble and generous. ('**He-appears**, the Russians . . .')

وصل الرئيسان إلى دمشق أمس.
waSal-a l-raʾiis-aani ʾilaa dimashq-a ʾams-i.
The two presidents arrived in Damascus yesterday. ('**He-arrived**, the two presidents . . .')

تشتري النساء خبزا.
ta-shtarii l-nisaaʾ-u xubz-an.
The women buy bread. ('**She-buys**, the women . . .')

شاهدت المدن إضرابا واسعا.
shaahad-at-i l-mudun-u ʾiDraab-an waasiᶜ-an.[14]
The cities **witnessed** an extensive strike. ('**She witnessed**, the cities . . .)

2.4.1.2 VARIATION IN WORD ORDER: Occasionally, the subject of a verbal sentence or clause precedes the verb. **In that case the verb agrees with it in gender and in number:**

(1) **Subject–Verb–Object (SVO):** Within the body of a text the writer may choose to start a sentence with a noun or noun phrase for stylistic reasons or for emphasis. This inverted word order also happens in embedded clauses. Moreover, certain fixed expressions are in the SVO order. When the subject precedes the verb, the verb agrees with it in gender **and in number.**[15] Technically, this word order converts a *jumla fiᶜliyya* (verbal sentence) into a *jumla ismiyya* (nominal sentence).

المدينة تملك تراثا إسلاميا.
al-madiinat-u ta-mlik-u turaath-an ʾislaamiyy-an.
The city possesses an Islamic heritage.

السعادة تغمرني.
al-saᶜaadat-u ta-ghmur-u-nii.
Happiness overwhelms me.

---

[14] Note that the subject here is nonhuman, and therefore takes feminine singular agreement.
[15] When a noun or noun phrase is sentence-initial, the sentence is considered a *jumla ismiyya* even if it contains a verb, in accordance with traditional Arabic grammatical theory which bases sentence categories on the nature of the sentence-initial word. See also note 6.

كثيرون منهم يسافرون في رحلة منظمة.

*kathiir-uuna min-hum **yu-saafir-uuna** fii riHlat-in munaZZamat-in.*

Many of them **are traveling** on an organized tour.

الله يسلمك.

allaah-u yu-sallim-u-ka.

[May] **God keep you safe.**

القوات تشن حملة واسعة بحثا عن أسلحة.

*al-quwwaat-u **ta-shunn-u** Hamlat-an waasiʿat-an baHth-an ʿan ʾasliHat-in.*

The forces are launching an extensive campaign to search for weapons.

وهناك أيضا فتيات يمارسن كرة القدم.

*wa-hunaaka ʾayD-an **fatayaat-un yu-maaris-na** kurat-a l-qadam-i.*

(And) there are also **young women** who **play** ('practice') soccer.

(2) **Headlines and topic sentences:** In Arabic newspapers it is often the case that the headline will be SVO whereas the first or lead sentence in the article, recapping the same thing, will be VSO. This shift in word order illustrates the attention-getting function of the SVO word order.[16]

Headline: SVO:

فرنسا تحذّر الناشطين الإسلاميين.

*faransaa **tu-Hadhdhir-u** l-naashiT-iina l-ʾislaamiyy-iina.*

France warns Islamic activists.

Lead sentence: VSO:

حذّرت فرنسا أمس إسلاميين متشددين.

Hadhdhar-at faransaa ʾams-i ʾislaamiyy-iina mutashaddid-iina.

France yesterday **warned** Islamic extremists.

(3) **Preposed direct object (topic and comment):** For stylistic reasons, an **object of a verb or preposition** may be preposed at the beginning of a sentence. In this case, a transitive verb (or prepositional phrase) requires a pronoun object to replace and refer to the preposed noun object. The pronoun object on the verb agrees with the noun it refers to in gender and number.

هذه الفرصة لا نجدها إلا في القاهرة.

haadhihi l-furSat-u laa na-jid-u-haa ʾillaa fii l-qaahirat-i.

This opportunity can only be found in Cairo.

('**This opportunity**, we do not find it except in Cairo.')

---

[16] See Watson's (1999) article on the syntax of Arabic headlines for more on this topic.

العرب كانت لهم علاقة بحياة إسبانيا.

al-ʿarab-u kaan-at la-hum ʿalaaqat-un bi-Hayaat-i ʾisbaanyaa.

The Arabs had a relationship with the life of Spain.

(**The Arabs**, [there] was **to-them** a relationship . . .')

Sometimes, when this is done, the connectives *ʾamma . . . fa-* ('as for . . .') are used to identify the topic and comment on parts of the sentence:

أما هذه الفرصة فلا نجدها إلا في القاهرة.

ʾammaa haadhihi l-furSat-u fa-laa na-jid-u-haa ʾillaa fii l-qaahirat-i.

As for this opportunity, it can only be found in Cairo.

(4) **Verb–Object–Subject (VOS):** In some cases, the verb will come first, and the object will come before the subject of the verb. This is especially true **if the object is substantially shorter** than the subject. In the following sentences, the object is set in boldface type.

حضر اللقاء عدد من أصحاب الاختصاص.

HaDar-a l-liqaaʾ-a ʿadad-un min ʾaSHaab-i l-ixtiSaaS-i.

A number of specialists attended **the meeting.**

('Attended **the meeting** a number of specialists.')

غطّى أحداثها عشرون ألف صحفي.

ghaTTaa ʾaHdaath-a-haa ʿishruuna ʾalf-a SuHufiyy-in.

Twenty thousand reporters covered **its events.**

('Covered **its events** twenty thousand reporters.')

سيشارك في الندوة عدد من الأساتذة.

sa-yu-shaarik-u fii l-nadwat-i ʿadad-un min-a l-ʾasaatidhat-i.

A number of professors will participate in the seminar.

('Will participate **in the seminar** a number of professors.')

(4.1) **Object plus adverb:** Sometimes an adverb will also be placed before the subject, especially if it is short.

يغادر القاهرة اليوم متوجها إلى باريس وفد مصري.

yu-ghaadir-u l-qaahirat-a l-yawm-a mutawajjih-an ʾilaa baariis wafd-un miSriyy-un.

An Egyptian delegation left **Cairo today** heading for Paris.

('Left **Cairo today** heading for Paris an Egyptian delegation.')[17]

وغادر عمان أمس مساعد وزير الخارجية.

wa-ghaadar-a ʿammaan-a ʾams-i musaaʿid-u waziir-i l-xaarijiyyat-i.

---

[17] In this sentence, the object (*al-qaahirat-a*), a short adverb (*l-yawm-a*), and an adverbial phrase (*mutawajjih-an ʾilaa baariis*) 'heading for Paris' have all been inserted before the subject.

The assistant minister of foreign affairs left **Amman yesterday.**
('Left **Amman yesterday** the assistant minister of foreign affairs.')

2.5 Doubly transitive verbs

There are a number of verbs in Arabic that take two objects. Both objects may be expressed as nouns or noun phrases, or one or both may be expressed as a pronoun.

2.5.1 Both objects expressed as nouns or noun phrases

This occurs especially with verbs of asking, considering, requesting, and appointing.

سألوا الطلاب أسئلة كثيرة.

sa'al-uu l-Tullab-a 'as'ilat-an kathiirat-an.

They asked **the students many questions.**

اعتبر العمانيون هذه الخطوة إنجازا تاريخيا كبيرا.

i'tabar-a l-'umaaniyy-uuna haadhihi l-xuTwat-a 'injaaz-an taariixiyy-an kabiir-an.

The Omanis considered **this step a great historical accomplishment.**

اعتبروا الهجوم نوعا من الدفاع عن النفس.

i'tabar-uu l-hujuum-a naw'-an min-a l-difaa'-i 'an-i l-nafs-i.

They considered **the attack a type** of self-defense.

2.5.2 One object expressed as noun or noun phrase, the other as pronoun

أعطتهم تمرينات.

'a'T-at-hum tamriinaat-in.

She gave **them exercises.**

يعتبرونهم نجومهم المفضلين.

ya-'tabir-uuna-hum nujuum-a-hum-u l-mufaDDal-iina.

They consider **them their favorite stars.**

يعتبره آخرون ضمانة.

ya-'tabir-u-hu 'aaxar-uuna Damaanat-an.

Others consider **it an assurance.**

ناشدوه القيام بدور.

naashad-uu-hu l-qiyaam-a bi-dawr-in

They implored **him to take** a role.

2.5.3 Both objects expressed as pronouns

In this case, one object pronoun is suffixed onto the verb and the other attached to the pronoun-carrier *'iyyaah-.* This occurs mainly with verbs of giving and sending.

أهداني إياه أهل فاطمة.

'ahdaa-nii 'iyyaa-hu 'ahl-u faaTimat-a.

Fatima's family sent it to me ('sent me it').

أعطانا إياها.

*'a*ʿ*Taa-naa 'iyyaa-haa.*

He gave it to us ('gave us it').

2.5.4 One object a noun or noun phrase, the other a predicate adjective

In this kind of double accusative, a definite noun serves as object of the verb and an indefinite adjective describes the state or condition of that noun.

شاهد الدنيا جميلة.

shaahad-a l-dunyaa jamiilat-an.

He saw the world [as] beautiful.

ترك الباب مفتوحا.

tarak-a l-baab-a maftuuH-an.

He left the door open.

2.5.5 Passive constructions with doubly transitive verbs

When a doubly transitive verb is in a passive construction, one object becomes the subject of the passive verb (an in the nominative case if mentioned specifically) and the other object remains in the accusative case:

تُوِّج بطلا.

tuwwij-a baTal-an.

He was crowned champion.

تُوِّج اللاعب بطلا.

*tuwwij-a l-laa*ʿ*ib-u baTal-an.*

The athlete was crowned champion.

سئل الطلاب أسئلة كثيرة.

su'il-a l-Tullaab-u 'as'ilat-an kathiirat-an.

The students were asked many questions.

عُيِّن طبيبا خاصًا للخليفة.

ʿ*uyyin-a Tabiib-an xaaSS-an li-l-xaliifat-i.*

He was appointed [as] special physician to the Caliph.

2.5.6 Dative movement with doubly transitive verbs

Where one of the objects of the verb is an indirect object, or beneficiary of the action, an optional structure using the dative-marking prepositions *li-* or *'ilaa* is possible. It is only permissible, however, if the beneficiary noun follows the direct object, e.g.:

أعطيت الكتاب للبنت.

*'a*ʿ*Tay-tu l-kitaab-a li-l-bint-i.*

I gave the book to the girl.

Otherwise, the beneficiary noun precedes the object noun and is in the accusative case.[18]

---

[18] These examples are taken from Ryding 1981, 19–23.

أعطيت البنت الكتاب.

*ʾaᶜTay-tu **l-bint-a** l-kitaab-a.*

I gave **the girl** the book.

2.5.7 Semantic structure of doubly transitive verbs

These verbs fall into four semantic classes:

2.5.7.1 Where the second object is what would be termed an **indirect object** or beneficiary of the action ("I gave **Noura** the book," i.e., "I gave the book to Noura");

أعطتــهم تمرينات.

*ʾaᶜT-at-**hum** tamriinaat-in.*

She gave **them** exercises.

2.5.7.2 Where the second object is **equivalent to the first** ("We consider him a great author.") This includes evaluative verbs of deeming, judging, and considering, such as *iᶜtabara*.[19]

يعتبرونــهم نجومهم المفضلين.

*ya-ᶜtabir-uuna-**hum** nujuum-a-hum-u l-mufaDDal-iina.*

They consider **them their favorite stars.**

2.5.7.3 Where the first accusative is **caused to be the second** ("They appointed her **ambassador**") but both refer to the same entity. These verbs include actions such as making, creating, naming, and appointing.

عيّنوها سفيرة.

*ᶜayyan-uu-**haa** safiirat-an.*

They appointed **her ambassador.**

2.5.7.4 Where **each object is different** ("He taught **the students English**" = "He caused the students to learn English."). These are usually Form II or Form IV verbs, causatives of transitive base verbs, such as (Form II) *darras-a* 'to teach' ('to cause **someone** to study **something**') or (Form IV) *ʾaraa* 'to show' ('to cause **someone** to see **something**').[20]

---

[19] This group has a special designation in Arabic called *ʾafᶜaal al-qalb, ʾafᶜaal qalbiyya* or *ʾafᶜaal quluub* 'verbs of the heart' because they denote intellectual or emotional evaluations. See Chapter 7, section 5.3.3 on accusative case.

[20] For detailed analysis of double accusatives in MSA see Abboud and McCarus 1983, Part 2:93–96 and for Classical Arabic, see Wright 1967, II:47–53.

درّسـنـي الـتـاريخ.

darras-a-nii l-taariix-a.

He taught **me history.**

3. Other sentence elements

Sentence elements other than verb, subject, and object (in verbal sentences) and subject and predicate (in equational sentences) include various types of adverbials.[21]

3.1 Placement of adverbials in basic sentences

Arabic adverbial expressions are considered "extras" in the sentence (*faDla* فضلة) because they give information external to the core VS or VSO structure. They are usually quite flexible in their placement and can occur at almost any point in a clause, especially if they consist of short words. More than one may occur in a sentence.

يقضي ليالـيه في الصلاة.

ya-qDii layaalii-hi fii l-Salaat-i.

He spends his nights **in prayer.**

غـادر القـاهرة أمس السفير الأمريكي الجديد.

ghaadar-a l-qaahirat-a ʾams-i l-safiir-u l-ʾamriikiyy-u l-jadiid-u.

The new American ambassador left Cairo **yesterday.**

تنمو بـبطء.

ta-nm-uu bi-buTʾ-in.

They grow **slowly.**

تأكيدا لـمـا قاله أمس

taʾkiid-an li-maa qaal-a-hu ʾams-i

affirming what he said **yesterday**

4. Compound or complex sentences

Compound or complex sentences consist of more than one predication. They contain clauses related by means of coordinating conjunctions such as *wa-* 'and,' *fa-* 'and; and so,' or *bal* 'but rather.' These conjunctions have little or no effect on the syntax or morphology of the following clause but build up the sentence contents in an additive way.

Complex sentences, on the other hand, consist of a main clause and one or more subordinate or embedded clauses. Subordinate clauses are of three main

---

[21] For further discussion of this, see Chapter 11.

types – complement clauses, adverbial clauses, and relative clauses. In each case, there is usually a linking or connective element (such as *'anna* 'that' or *li-kay* 'in order that' or *alladhii* 'who; which') bringing the two clauses into relation with each other. Many Arabic subordinating conjunctions have a grammatical effect on the structure of the following clause. For example, *'anna* and related particles are followed by a clause whose subject is either a suffixed pronoun or a noun in the accusative; *li-kay* is followed by a verb in the subjunctive mood.

Specific compound and complex sentence types are dealt with in the following chapters:

Chapter 14: Relative pronouns and relative clauses
Chapter 18: Connectives and conjunctions
Chapter 19: Subordinating conjunctions: the particle *'inna* and her sisters
Chapter 34: Moods of the verb I: indicative and subjunctive
Chapter 35: Moods of the verb II: jussive and imperative
Chapter 36: Verbs of being, becoming, remaining, seeming (*kaan-a wa-'axawaat-u-haa*)
Chapter 37: Negation and exception
Chapter 39: Conditional and optative expressions

5

Arabic noun types

Arabic nouns fall into a number of different categories depending on their morphology and their relationship to Arabic lexical roots.[1] The extensive range of noun types yields a wealth of lexical possibilities that contribute to what Charles Ferguson has called the sense of "vastness and richness of the Arabic lexicon."[2] Two morphological criteria traditionally define Arabic nouns: they can take the definite article and/or they can take nunation.

Most Arabic nouns are derived from triliteral or quadriliteral lexical roots, and all nouns derived from a particular root are found in an Arabic or Arabic–English dictionary clustered under that root entry. Some nouns, however, have restricted roots; certain ones have only two root consonants, others have up to five root consonants. Yet other nouns have solid stems, unanalyzable into roots and patterns. This chapter is intended to give an overview of these noun types, with examples. It is by no means exhaustive and does not go into derivational detail within categories.[3] For inflectional characteristics of nouns, see the chapter on noun inflection.

Arabic nouns are usually derived from lexical roots through application of particular morphological patterns. The use of patterns interlocking with root phonemes allows the formation of actual words or stems. Noun patterns themselves carry certain kinds of meaning, such as "place where action is done," "doer of action," "name of action," or "instrument used to carry out action." The most frequent MSA noun patterns are as follows.[4]

---

[1] In traditional Arabic grammar, the term *ism* 'noun' covers a wide range of form classes. As Abboud et al. (1997, 67) state: "Nouns are divided into five subclasses: nouns, pronouns, demonstratives, adjectives and noun-prepositions." In this chapter, the topic is restricted to nouns per se. Note that the traditional Arabic definition of a noun is: *kalimat-un dall-at ʿalaa maʿnan fii nafs-i-hi, wa-lays-a l-zaman-u juzʾ-an min-haa*; 'a word indicating a meaning in itself and not containing any reference to time' (ʿAbd al-Latif et al. 1997, 9).

[2] Ferguson 1970, 377. On the same page he points to the "very complex but highly regular and symmetrical structure of the derivational system."

[3] For further analysis of Classical Arabic noun types, consult Wright 1967, I:106 ff. and Fleisch 1961, I:349–469.

[4] Fleisch 1961, I:267 has a useful chart of noun types: "Tableau du développement morphologique en arabe."

1 Verbal noun (*al-maSdar* المصدر)

Verbal nouns are systematically related to specific verb forms and can come from triliteral or quadriliteral roots. The verbal noun or *maSdar* names the action denoted by its corresponding verb, for example, *wuSuul* وصول 'arrival' from the Form I verb *waSal-a* وَصَلَ 'to arrive,' or *ʾidaara* إدارة 'administration; management' from the Form IV verb *ʾadaar-a* أدار / يُدير *yu-diir-u* 'to manage, direct.'[5] Each *maSdar* is systematically related to a specific verb form and can be derived from triliteral or quadriliteral roots. Verbal nouns are often abstract in meaning, but some of them have specific, concrete reference e.g., *binaaʾ* بناء 'building' (either the act of building, or the structure itself). In terms of their syntactic usage, verbal nouns may also express in Arabic what an infinitive expresses in English.[6]

This section provides an outline of the typical verbal noun derivation patterns from verb forms I–X and for quadriliterals I–IV. There is further elaboration on these forms in each section devoted to the particular form and its derivations. In this section also there are examples of the typical functions of verbal nouns in context.

1.1 Triliteral root verbal nouns

These nouns name the action denoted by the forms of the verb. The Form I verbal noun patterns are abundant and hard to predict; the derived form verbal nouns are much more predictable in their patterns. These patterns and noun classes are described in detail in the chapters on the various verb forms. Examples here serve to illustrate the extent of this noun class and the types of meaning conveyed by verbal nouns.

1.1.1 Form I

The morphological patterns for creation of verbal nouns from Form I are many and not predictable.[7] Wright lists forty-four possible verbal noun patterns for Form I or as he terms it, "the ground form" of the ordinary triliteral verb (1967, I:110–12); Ziadeh and Winder (1957, 71–72) list eighteen of the most commonly

---

[5] The Arabic term *maSdar/maSaadir* also means 'source,' an indication that the term for this type of noun refers to its essential nature as the name of an activity or state. The different schools of medieval Arabic grammatical analysis, the Basrans and Kufans, debated whether the noun or the verb is the most basic element of language, the Basrans arguing that the verbal noun is prior, and the Kufans that the verb is prior.

[6] Note that the citation form of the verb in Arabic is not an infinitive but a finite, inflected verb form (third person masculine singular past tense). The *maSdar* is much closer in meaning to an infinitive, but it is not used as a citation form in Arabic.

[7] ʿAbd al-Latif, ʿUmar, and Zahran state that "The verbal nouns of the base form are many and varied and cannot be known except by resorting to language [reference] books" *maSaadir-u l-thulaathiyy-i kathiirat-un wa-mutanawwiʿat-un laa tu-ʿraf-u ʾillaa bi-l-rujuu-ʿ-i ʾilaa kutub-i l-lughat-i* (1997, 83).

used ones in MSA. ʿAbd al-Latif, ʿUmar, and Zahran give an extensive list (in Arabic) with examples and some explanations (1997, 83–86). Following are examples of some of the most common Form I verbal noun patterns found in MSA:

swimming	*sibaaHa*	(*fiʿaala*)	سِبـاحَة
invitation	*daʿwa*	(*faʿla*)	دَعْوَة
forgiveness	*ghufraan*	(*fuʿlaan*)	غُفْران
clarity	*wuDuuH*	(*fuʿuul*)	وُضوح
bravery	*buTuula*	(*fuʿuula*)	بُطولَة
honor	*sharaf*	(*faʿal*)	شَرَف
glory	*majd*	(*faʿl*)	مَجْد
part	*juzʾ*	(*fuʿl*)	جُزْء
blessing	*baraka*	(*faʿala*)	بَرَكة
knowledge	*maʿrifa*	(*mafʿila*)	مَعْرِفة

1.1.2 Form II

Patterns: *tafʿiil* تَفْعيل and (for defective roots, especially) *tafʿila* تَفْعِلة; occasionally *tafʿiila* تَفْعيلة.[8] Less common variants include *tafʿaal* تَفْعال or *tifʿaal* تِفْعال.

strengthening	*taʿziiz*	تَعْزيز
equalization	*taswiya*	تَسْوِية
implementation	*tanfiidh*	تَنْفيذ
reminder; souvenir	*tadhkaar*	تِذْكار
ticket	*tadhkira*	تَذْكِرَة
experiment	*tajriba*	تَجْرِبة

1.1.3 Form III

Patterns: *mufaaʿala* مُفاعَلة and *fiʿaal* فِعال

attempt	*muHaawala*	مُحاوَلة
debate	*munaaqasha*	مُناقَشة
struggle	*jihaad*	جِهاد
defense	*difaaʿ*	دِفاع

---

[8] For an extensive list of Form II verbal noun variants in Classical Arabic see Wright 1967, I:115–16.

1.1.4 Form IV

Pattern: *ʾifʿaal* إفْعـال; for hollow verb roots *ʾifaala* إفالة; for defectives, *ʾifʿaaʾ* إفْعاء

exportation	*ʾiSdaar*	إصْدار
preparation	*ʾiʿdaad*	إعْداد
administration	*ʾidaara*	إدارة
abolition	*ʾilghaaʾ*	إلْغاء

1.1.5 Form V

Pattern: *tafaʿʿul* تَفَعُّل; for defectives *tafaʿʿ-in* تفَعّ

tension	*tawattur*	توتّر
delay	*taʾaxxur*	تأَخُّر
behavior	*taSarruf*	تصرُّف
challenge	*taHadd-in*	تحدّ
wish, desire	*tamann-in*	تمنٍّ

1.1.6 Form VI

Pattern: *tafaaʿul* تَفاعَل; for defectives *tafaaʿ-in* تَفاع

disparity	*tafaawut*	تَفاوُت
mutual exchange	*tabaadul*	تبـادُل
rivalry	*tanaafus*	تنـافُس
meeting, encounter	*talaaq-in*	تَلاقٍ
avoidance	*tafaad-in*	تَفادٍ

1.1.7 Form VII

Pattern: *infiʿaal* انْفعـال; hollow verb roots, *infiyaal* انْفيـال; for defectives, *infiʿaaʾ* انْفعـاء

reflection	*inʿikaas*	انعِكـاس
preoccupation	*inshighaal*	انْشغـال
compliance	*inqiyaad*	انْقيـاد
elapsing	*inqiDaaʾ*	انْقضـاء

1.1.8 Form VIII

Pattern: *iftiʿaal* افْتِعَال; hollow verb root, *iftiyaal* افْتِيَال; defective, *iftiʿaaʾ* افْتِعَاء

acquisition	*iktisaab*	اكْتِسَاب
election	*intixaab*	انْتِخَاب
choosing	*ixtiyaar*	اخْتِيَار
end	*intihaa*	انْتِهَاء

1.1.9 Form IX

Pattern: *ifʿilaal* افْعِلَال

greenness	*ixDiraar*	اخْضِرَار
reddening	*iHmiraar*	احْمِرَار
crookedness	*iʿwijaaj*	اعْوِجَاج

1.1.10 Form X

Pattern: *istifʿaal* اسْتِفْعَال; hollow root, *istifaala* اسْتِفَالَة; defective, *istifʿaaʾ* اسْتِفْعَاء

readiness	*istiʿdaad*	اسْتِعْدَاد
investment	*istithmaar*	اسْتِثْمَار
benefit	*istifaada*	اسْتِفَادَة
exception	*istithnaaʾ*	اسْتِثْنَاء

1.1.11 Forms XI–XV

These Forms of the verb are rare in MSA. For information about their structure see Chapter 33.

1.2 Quadriliteral root verbal nouns

Verbal nouns from quadriliteral verbs are primarily from Forms I, II, and IV of those verbs, as follows:

1.2.1 Form I: *faʿlal-a* فَعْلَلَة

The most common Form I quadriliteral verbal noun patterns are: *faʿlala* فَعْلَلَة and *fiʿlaal~fuʿlaal~faʿlaal* فَعْلَال~فُعْلَال~فِعْلَال:

explosion	*farqaʿa*	فَرْقَعَة
somersault	*shaqlaba*	شَقْلَبَة

earthquake	zilzaal	زِلْزَال
evidence	burhaan	بُرْهَان

1.2.2 Form II: *tafaʿlal-a* تَفَعْلَلَ

The Form II quadriliteral verbal noun pattern is *tafaʿlul* تَفَعْلُل:

oscillation	tadhabdhub	تَذَبْذُب
decline	tadahwur	تَدَهْوُر
serial	tasalsul	تَسَلْسُل

1.2.3 Form III: *ifʿanlala* افْعَنْلَلَ

The quadriliteral Form III verbal noun pattern is: *ifʿinlaal* افْعِنْلال. It is extremely rare.

1.2.4 Form IV: *ifʿalalla* افْعَلَلَّ

The form IV verbal noun pattern is *ifʿilaal* افْعِلال:

serenity	iTmiʾnaan	اطْمِئْنان
shuddering	ishmiʾzaaz	اشْمِئْزاز

1.3 Special characteristics of verbal nouns in context

The function and distribution of verbal nouns parallel that of other nouns except that in addition to those functions, the verbal noun may retain some of its verbal force. There are three ways in which verbal nouns are distinctive in their use:

(1) they may serve as the equivalent of an infinitive;
(2) when the verbal noun is from a transitive verb and serves as the first term in an ʾiDaafa إضافة structure, it may take an object in the accusative case;
(3) they may be used as verb intensifiers in the cognate accusative (*mafʿuul muTlaq* مَفْعول مُطْلَق) construction.

1.3.1 Verbal noun as equivalent to gerund or infinitive

The verbal noun may be used as the object of a verbal expression where the English equivalent would be either a gerund or an infinitive.[9]

سَأُحَاوِل إلْقاء ضوء.

sa-ʾu-Haawil-u ʾilqaaʾ-a Daw ʾ-in.

I shall try **to shed/shedding** light.

---

[9] In such constructions, the verbal noun is normally interchangeable with the particle ʾan plus a subjunctive verb.

حاولت كسر التقليد.

*Haawal-at **kasr-a** l-taqliid-i.*

She tried **to break/breaking** tradition.

حاول إنقاذ حياة رجل.

*Haawal-a **ʾinqaadh-a** Hayaat-i rajul-in.*

He tried **to save/saving** a man's life.

لا يمكن التهرب منه.

*laa yu-mkin-u **l-taharrub-u** min-hu.*

It is inescapable ('it is not possible **to escape/escaping** from it').

بهدف جعل الخريجات يعملن فيه

*bi-hadaf-i **jaʿl-i** l-xariijaat-i ya-ʿmal-na fii-hi*

with the aim of **having ('making')** the graduates (f.) work in it

تتيح للجانب الأمريكي التأكيد.

*tu-tiiH-u li-l-jaanib-i l-ʾamriikiyy-i **l-taʾkiid-a.***

It grants the American side **assurance.**

1.3.2 Verbal nouns in *ʾiDaafas* or with pronoun suffix

The verbal noun may be used in any part of an *ʾiDaafa*, as the first or second term:

1.3.2.1 VERBAL NOUN AS FIRST TERM OF CONSTRUCT:

انشغال المسؤولين	استثمار بلايين الدولارات
***inshighaal-u** l-masʾuul-iina*	***istithmaar-u** balaayiin-i l-duulaaraat-i*
the **preoccupation** of the officials	the **investment** of billions of dollars

زيارة القصر	تعيين القضاة
***ziyaarat-u** l-qaSr-i*	***taʿyiin-u** l-quDaat-i*
visiting the castle	the **appointing** of judges

1.3.2.2 AS SECOND TERM:

حزام أمان	فرصة الزيارة
Hizaam-u ʾamaan-in	*furSat-u **l-ziyaarat-i***
safety belt	the chance **to visit**

1.3.2.3 OR EVEN AS BOTH TERMS:

حق اللجوء	دفع التعويض
*Haqq-u **l-lujuuʾ-i***	***dafʿ-u** l-taʿwiiD-i*
the **right of asylum**	the **payment of compensation**

تعزيز التفاهم
ta'ziiz-u l-tafaahum-i
strengthening of understanding

دعا إلى تعزيز التعاون.
da'aa 'ilaa ta'ziiz-i l-ta'aawun-i.
He called for **strengthening cooperation.**

1.3.2.4 VERBAL NOUNS FROM TRANSITIVE VERBS: SPECIAL CONSIDERATIONS. When a verbal noun derived from a transitive verb is the first term of an *'iDaafa*, a number of possibilities exist for expressing both the doer of the action (the subject of the verb underlying the verbal noun) and the recipient of the action (the object of the underlying verb).

(1)   The first term of the *'iDaafa* is a verbal noun and the second term is **the subject of the underlying verb:**

استقبال الرئيس
istiqbaal-i l-ra'iis-i
the president's reception
(the president is receiving)

مغادرة السفير
mughaadarat-u l-safiir-i
the departure of the ambassador
(the ambassador departs)

(2)   The second term of the *'iDaafa* may be the **object of the underlying verb.** Here the first term of the *'iDaafa* is a verbal noun derived from a transitive verb and the second term is the object of the verb.

the raising of the flag	raf'-u l-'alam-i	رفع العلم
entering the church	duxuul-u l-kaniisat-i	دخول الكنيسة
playing a role	la'b-u dawr-in	لعب دور
by using its tail	bi-stixdaam-i dhayl-i-hi	باستخدام ذيله

دعا إلى تشكيل جيش.
da'aa 'ilaa tashkiil-i jaysh-in.
He called for **the formation of an army.**

أدى إلى منع الكتاب.
'addaa 'ilaa man'-i l-kitaab-i.
It led to **banning the book.**

(3)   **Verbal noun + subject and object:** When the subject of the underlying verb is the second term of the *'iDaafa*, or when it takes the form of a pronoun suffix on the verbal noun, the object of the underlying verb may still be mentioned. It follows the *'iDaafa* or the verbal noun plus pronoun and is in the accusative case. Thus the verbal noun retains some of its verbal force in making the object noun accusative.

In most cases in the data covered for this work, the subject of the underlying verb takes the form of a pronoun suffix on the verbal noun.

قبل مغادرته العاصمة
qabl-a mughaadarat-i-hi l-'aaSimat-a
before **his leaving the capital**

خلال استقباله أمس وفدا من أهالي المفقودين

xilaal-a **stiqbaal-i-hi** *ʾams-i* **wafd-an** *min ʾaahaalii l-mafquud-iina*

during **his meeting** yesterday **a delegation** of families of the missing

ولدى رفضهم ذلك

wa-ladaa **rafD-i-him** *dhaalika*

upon **their refusal of that/their refusing that**

منذ نيلها جائزتها الأولى

mundh-u **nayl-i-haa** *jaaʾizat-a-haa l-ʾuulaa*

since **her winning** her first prize

عقب إعلانه الانسحاب من الحياة العامة

ʿaqib-a ʾ **iʿlaan-i-hi** *l-insiHaab-a min-a l-Hayaat-i l-ʿaammat-i*

just after **his announcing** [his] withdrawal from public life

سماعهم الأصوات

samaaʿ-u-hum-u l-ʾaSwaat-a

their hearing the sounds

1.3.2.6 DOUBLY TRANSITIVE VERBAL NOUN: The verb underlying the verbal noun in an *ʾiDaafa* may be doubly transitive, taking two objects, one of which becomes the second term of the *ʾiDaafa*, and the other of which remains in the accusative case, coming after the *ʾiDaafa*:

تعيين اللواء مديرا للدائرة

taʿyiin-u l-liwaaʾ-i mudiir-an li-l-daaʾ irat-i

appointment of the general [as] director of the department

تعيين مراد قائدا لقوات الأمن

taʿyiin-u muraad-in qaaʾid-an li-quwwaat-i l-ʾamn-i

appointing Murad [as] leader of the security forces

1.3.3 Verbal noun and preposition

If a verbal noun derives from a verb-preposition idiom, the preposition is still part of the verbal noun expression:

للفوز بالرئاسة

li-l-fawz-i bi-l-riʾaasat-i

in order **to win** the presidency

(*faaz-a bi-* = 'to win s.th.')

تحويل الحلم إلى حقيقة

taHwiil-u l-Hulm-i ʾilaa Haqiiqat-in

transforming the dream into reality
(*Hawwal-a ʾilaa* = 'to transform s.th. into s.th.')

أكد نائب الرئيس رغبة بلاده في تحقيق السلام.
*ʾakkad-a naaʾ ib-u l-raʾ iis-i **raghbat-a** bilaad-i-hi **fii** taHqiiq-i l-salaam-i.*
The vice-president affirmed the **desire** of his country **for** achieving peace.
(*raghib-a fii* = 'to desire s.th.')

استمروا في البحث عن تفسيرات.
*istamarr-uu fii l-**baHth-i** ʿan tafsiiraat-in.*
They continued **to search for** explanations.
(*baHath-a ʿan* = 'to search for s.th.')

1.3.4 The cognate accusative: *al-mafʿuul al-muTlaq* المفعول المطلق

The cognate accusative emphasizes or intensifies a statement by using a verbal
noun derived from the main verb or predicate (which may also be in the form of
a participle or verbal noun). The verbal noun and any modifying adjectives are
usually in the indefinite accusative. For more on this topic, see Chapter 7, section
5.3.3.4.

غضب غضبا شديدا.	وخافوا خوفا شديدا.
*ghaDib-a **ghaDb-an** shadiid-an.*	*wa-xaaf-uu **xawf-an** shadiid-an.*
He became **extremely angry**.	They became **extremely afraid**.

مصالحنا مرتبطة ارتباطا وثيقا بمصالح الدول العربية.
*maSaaliH-u-naa **murtabiTat-un** ʾirtibaaT-an wathiiq-an bi-maSaaliH-i l-duwal-i
l-ʿarabiyyat-i.*
Our interests are **firmly entwined** with the interests of the Arab states.

2 Active and passive participle (*ism al-faaʿil* اسم الفاعل, *ism al-mafʿuul* اسم المفعول)

Arabic participles are descriptive terms derived from verbs. The active participle
describes or refers to the doer of the action and the passive participle describes or
refers to the object of the action. An entire chapter (Chapter 6) is devoted to these
multifunctional words but they are also included briefly here in order to provide
examples of yet another noun type in Arabic.

In terms of their structure, participles are predictably derived according to the
ten forms of the verb and have characteristic shapes. They may occur as masculine
or feminine. When participles refer to human beings, they reflect the gender of
the individual referred to. Some participles have acquired specific noun meanings and may be either masculine in form (e.g., *shaariʿ* شارع 'street') or feminine
(*qaaʾima* قائمة 'list').

Arabic verbs have both active and passive participles.[10] This section lists examples of both, but more extensive descriptions of base and variant forms are found in Chapter 6 and in the chapters on each form (I–X) of the verb.

2.1 Form I active participle (AP): *faaᶜil* فاعِل

The Form I AP has the typical pattern of *faaᶜil* or *faaᶜila*. For AP nouns, the form of the plural depends on whether the AP refers to a human being or not. APs referring to humans take either a sound plural or the broken plural *fuᶜᶜaal*; those referring to nonhuman entities often take the *fawaaᶜil* plural but may take other plurals as well.

rider/s	*raakib/rukkaab*	راكِب / رُكّاب
spokesman/men	*naaTiq/naaTiquuna*	ناطِق / ناطِقون
street/s	*shaariᶜ/shawaariᶜ*	شارِع / شَوارِع
circle/s	*daaʾira/dawaaʾir*	دائِرَة / دَوائِر
base; rule/s	*qaaᶜida/qawaaᶜid*	قاعِدَة / قَواعِد
suburb/s	*DaaHiya/DawaaHin*	ضاحِيَة /ضَواحٍ

2.2 The extended Form II–X AP nouns

Form II–X APs are typified by having a prefix /mu-/ and a stem vowel *kasra* (/-i/). Hollow and defective forms have special patterns described in Chapters 22–31. As a general rule, the plurals for nonhuman referents are formed with the sound feminine plural and for human referents with either the sound masculine or the sound feminine plural.

II: *mufaᶜᶜil* مُفَعِّل

coordinator	*munassiq*	مُنَسِّق	drug, narcotic	*muxaddir*	مُخَدِّر
inspector	*mufattish*	مُفَتِّش	singer	*mughannin*	مُغَنٍّ

III: *mufaaᶜil* مُفاعِل

assistant	*musaaᶜid*	مُساعِد	lecturer	*muHaaDir*	مُحاضِر

IV: *mufᶜil* مُفْعِل

supervisor	*mushrif*	مُشْرِف	Muslim	*muslim*	مُسْلِم

V: *mutafaᶜᶜil* مُتَفَعِّل

volunteer	*mutaTawwiᶜ*	مُتَطَوِّع	specialist	*mutaxaSSiS*	مُتَخَصِّص

---

[10] For the most part, only transitive verbs have passive participles.

VI: *mutafaaʿil* مُتَفاعِل

synonym   *mutaraadif*   مُتَرادِف

VII: *munfaʿil* مُنْفَعِل is rarely used as a noun.

VIII: *muftaʿil* مُفْتَعِل

listener   *mustamiʿ*   مُسْتَمِع   elector   *muntaxib*   مُنْتَخِب

X: *mustafʿil* مُسْتَفْعِل

orientalist   *mustashriq*   مُسْتَشْرِق   importer   *mustawrid*   مُسْتَوْرِد

2.3 Quadriliteral AP nouns: *mufaʿlil* مُفَعْلِل

Quadriliteral active participles of Form I are also characterized by a prefix /mu-/ and a stem vowel *kasra* (/-i-/). QAPs with human referents take either the sound masculine or sound feminine plural; with those referring to nonhuman entities, the sound feminine plural is usually used. Further discussion of quadriliteral participles is found in Chapter 33.

engineer/s	*muhandis/muhandisuuna*	مُهَنْدِس/مُهَنْدِسون
translator/s (m.)	*mutarjim/mutarjimuuna*	مُتَرْجِم/مُتَرْجِمون
translator/s (f.)	*mutarjima/mutarjimaat*	مُتَرْجِمة/مُتَرْجِمات
explosive/s	*mufarqiʿ/mufarqiʿaat*	مُفَرْقِع/مُفَرْقِعات

2.4 Passive participles (PP)

Passive participles that have evolved into use as nouns have a wide range of meanings, and it is not always possible to see immediately how their form relates to their meaning. In the derived forms (II–X), the passive participle often functions as the noun of place for that particular form of the verb (e.g., Form X PP: *mustashfan* 'hospital, place of healing' or Form VIII PP: *muxtabar* 'laboratory, place of experiment').

2.4.1 Form I: *mafʿuul* مَفْعول

The PP of Form I has the typical pattern of *mafʿuul* or *mafʿuula*. The plural for non-human PP nouns in this form is often *mafaaʿiil* or the sound feminine plural; for human referents, the sound plural is usually used.

concept/s	*mafhuum/mafaahiim*	مَفْهوم / مَفاهيم
plan; project/s	*mashruuʿ/mashaariiʿ*	مَشْروع/مَشاريع ~ مَشْروعات
	~*mashruuʿaat*	

group/s	*majmuuʿa /majmuuʿaat*	مَجْموعة / مَجْموعات
delegate/s	*manduub/ manduubuuna*	مَنْدوب / مَنْدوبون
official/s (n.)	*masʾuul/masʾuuluuna*	مَسْؤول / مَسْؤولون

2.4.2 Forms II–X

The PPs of the extended forms used as nouns have a /mu-/ prefix and *fatHa* (/-a-/) as their stem vowel:

Form II: *mufaʿʿal* مُفَعَّل

| organization | *munaZZama* | مُنَظَّمة | volume (book) | *mujallad* | مُجَلَّد |

Form III: *mufaaʿal* مُفاعَل is rare

Form IV: *mufʿal* مُفْعَل

| attaché | *mulHaq* | مُلْحَق | lexicon | *muʿjam* | مُعْجَم |

Form V: *mutafaʿʿal* مُتَفَعَّل

| requirements | *mutaTallabaat*[11] | مُتَطَلَّبات |

Form VI: *mutafaaʿal* مُتَفاعَل

| availability; reach | *mutanaawal* | مُتَناوَل |

Form VII: *munfaʿal* مُنْفَعَل

| slope | *munHadar* | مُنْحَدَر | lowland | *munxafaD* | مُنْخَفَض |

Form VIII: *muftaʿal* مُفْتَعَل

| society | *mujtamaʿ* | مُجْتَمَع | laboratory | *muxtabar* | مُخْتَبَر |

Form X: *mustafʿal* مُسْتَفْعَل

| future | *mustaqbal* | مُسْتَقْبَل | hospital | *mustashfan* | مُسْتَشْفى |

2.4.3 Quadriliteral PP nouns: *mufaʿlal* مُفَعْلَل

These PPs have the same characteristics as the derived form triliteral PPs: a pre-fixed /mu-/ and stem vowel *fatHa* (/-a-/).

| camp | *muʿaskar* | مُعَسْكَر | series | *musalsal* | مُسَلْسَل |

3 Noun of place (*ism makaan* اسم مكان)

Certain noun patterns refer to the place where the activity specified by the verb occurs. These nouns are systematically related to triliteral verbs.

---

[11] Usually occurs in the plural.

3.1 Form I nouns of place: *mafʿal* مَفْعَل

For Form I, most nouns of place are of the pattern *mafʿal* مَفْعَل or *mafʿala* مَفْعَلَة, or, in some cases *mafʿil* مَفْعِل. The plural of this type of noun is most often of the *mafaaʿil* مَفاعِل pattern or *mafaaʿiil* مَفاعيل pattern.

English	Arabic		English	Arabic	
center	*markaz*	مَرْكَز	library	*maktaba*	مَكْتَبَة
entrance	*madxal*	مَدْخَل	school	*madrasa*	مَدْرَسَة
exit	*maxraj*	مَخْرَج	mosque	*masjid*	مَسْجِد
playground	*malʿab*	مَلْعَب	(Arab) west	*maghrib*	مَغْرِب
restaurant	*maTʿam*	مَطْعَم	(Arab) east	*mashriq*	مَشْرِق
swimming pool	*masbaH*	مَسْبَح	bank	*maSrif*	مَصْرِف

Some nouns of place have both *mafʿal* and *mafʿil* forms:

foothold   *mawTiʾ* and *mawTaʾ*   مَوْطِئ / مَوْطَأ

3.2 Forms II–X nouns of place

For nouns of place from derived forms (II–X), the passive participle is used. The most common derived nouns of place are from forms VII, VIII and X. The sound feminine plural is used for the plural of these nouns.

lowland	*munxafaD*	VII	مُنْخَفَض
level	*mustawan*	VIII	مُسْتَوى
colony	*mustaʿmara*	X	مُسْتَعْمَرة
settlement	*mustawTana*	X	مُسْتَوْطَنة
future	*mustaqbal*	X	مُسْتَقْبَل
hospital	*mustashfan*	X	مُسْتَشْفى

4 Noun of instrument (*ism al-ʾaala* اسم الآلة)

A specific derivational pattern is used to denote nouns of instrument, i.e., nouns that denote items used in accomplishing a certain action. The patterns are *mifʿaal* مِفْعال, *mifʿal* مِفْعَل, and *mifʿala* مِفْعَلَة. See also section 5.2 below.

Some examples include:

key	*miftaaH*	مِفْتاح	elevator	*miSʿad*	مِصْعَد
broom	*miknasa*	مِكْنَسة	scissors	*miqaSS*	مِقَصّ
scale	*miqyaas*	مِقْياس	refinery	*miSfaat*	مِصْفاة

5 Nouns of intensity, repetition, profession

A special noun pattern exists to denote intensity of action or repeated action: *faʿʿaal* فَعّال.[12] For human beings the nouns usually denote profession, for example:

artist (m./f.)	*fannaan/fannaana*	فَنّان / فَنّانة
baker (m./f.)	*xabbaaz/xabbaaza*	خَبّاز / خَبّازة
tailor (m./f.)	*xayyaaT/xayyaaTa*	خَيّاط / خَيّاطة
weightlifter (m./f.)	*rabbaaʿ/rabbaaʿa*	رَبّاع / رَبّاعة

5.1 Nouns of profession

The abstract noun denoting the **name of a profession** is often of the verbal noun pattern *fiʿaala* فِعالة, as follows:

beekeeping	*niHaala*	نِحالة	surgery	*jiraaHa*	جِراحة
carpentry	*nijaara*	نِجارة			

5.2 Nouns of intensity as nouns of instrument

Occasionally, the pattern for nouns of intensity (*faʿʿaal* فَعّال or *faʿʿaala* فَعّالة) is used to denote an **instrument**. For machines or instruments that perform specified tasks, the feminine form of the noun of intensity is often used:

opener	*fattaaHa*	فَتّاحة	freezer	*thallaaja*	ثَلّاجة
dryer	*nashshaafa*	نَشّافة	car	*sayyaara*	سَيّارة
washer	*ghassaala*	غَسّالة			

6 Common noun (*al-ism* الاسم)

This is a vast category. Common nouns derived from **triliteral** lexical roots include an extensive range of items which can be of either gender. These nouns may or may not be related to lexical roots that generate verbs.

---

[12] Nouns of intensity usually have a *shadda* on the middle radical, just as the Form II verb doubles the middle radical in order to denote frequency or intensity. A certain iconicity appears to exist in Arabic between doubling the strength of a consonant and reference to intensity or frequency of action. For more on iconicity and sound symbolism in Arabic see E. K. Wright 2000.

basket	salla	سَلّة	coffee	qahwa	قَهْوة
man	rajul	رجُل	fog	Dabaab	ضَباب
homeland	waTan	وطَن	horse; mare	faras	فَرَس
bridge	jisr	جِسْر	tree	shajara	شَجَرة
saddle	sarj	سَرْج	book	kitaab	كِتاب

7 Generic noun (*ism al-jins* اسم الجنس) and noun of instance (*ism al-marra* اسم المرة)

Generic nouns refer to something in general, such as "laughter" or "agriculture." Sometimes they refer to something that can be counted and sometimes it is not possible to pluralize the noun because it is an abstraction and a generality. It can be said that the concept of "generic" contrasts with "specific."[13] Examples of generic nouns in Arabic would be:

| dancing | raqS | رَقْص | support | da‘m | دَعْم |
| safety | ’amaan | أمان | victory | fawz | فَوْز |

Nouns that refer to actions in general, such as "laughing" or "dancing," can be contrasted with a singular occurrence or instance of that action, such as "a short laugh" or "a traditional dance." The generic term is often masculine singular, whereas the individual instance is often feminine singular, marked by *taa’ marbuuTa*. This is a general rule, but sometimes the generic term comes to be used to refer to individual, concretized instances (e.g., *binaa’* – see below).

dancing	raqS	رَقْص	waves	mawj	مَوْج
a dance	raqSa	رَقْصَة	a wave	mawja	مَوْجة
shipping	shaHn	شَحْن	building	binaa’	بِناء
a shipment	shaHna	شَحْنة	a building	binaa’ ~binaaya	بِناء ~بِناية

The plural used for counting or referring to a number of these instances of action is often the sound feminine plural, but may also be a broken plural, especially if the feminine singular is not used as the instance noun (e.g., *binaa’* 'a building').

many laughs	DaHkaat-un kathiirat-un	ضَحْكات كَثيرة
traditional dances	raqSaat-un taqliidiyyat-un	رَقْصات تَقْليديَّة
heat waves	mawjaat-un Haarrat-un	مَوْجات حارَّة

[13] See Hurford 1994, 81–82, for good examples of generic nouns and noun phrases in English.

| sound waves | ʾamwaaj-un Sawtiyyat-un | أَمْواج صَوْتِيَّة |
| new buildings | ʾabniyat-un jadiidat-un | أَبْنِية جَديدة |

There is thus a formal distinction in Arabic between a noun that denotes a generic activity or state and a semelfactive noun, that is, a noun that denotes a single occurrence or instance of that activity and which is usually feminine. The units or instances can be pluralized or counted using a plural form of the "noun of instance."

8 Diminutive (*al-taSghiir* التصغير)

There are specific noun patterns used to denote smallness or endearment. These nouns can refer to small things such as a pocket dictionary, a short period of time, or to people and people's names.[14] The main pattern is *CuCayC* or *CuCayyaC*.

		root	
very small state	duwayla	d-w-l	دُوَيْلَة
little garden	junayna	j-n-n	جُنَيْنة
little tree, sapling	shujayra	sh-j-r	شُجَيْرة
lake ('little sea')	buHayra	b-H-r	بُحَيْرة
a little before	qubayl-a	q-b-l	قُبَيْل
electron	kuhayrib	k-h-r-b	كُهَيْرِب
a little while (adv.)	hunayhat-an	h-n-h	هُنَيْهة
little daughter	bunayya	b-n	بُنَيّة
Hussein	Husayn	H-s-n	حُسَيْن

9 Abstraction nouns ending with -*iyya*

Although many nouns with abstract meaning exist in Arabic, there is a morphological process for creating even more through suffixing the feminine *nisba* ending -*iyya* (يّة) to an already existing word stem. In this way, new concepts can be readily created, and this category is an important one in MSA.[15] In fact, its prevalence has led the Arabic Language Academy in Cairo to declare that this type of noun may be derived from any word at all.[16] Nouns created with this process take

---

[14] The diminutive can also express contempt, but no examples of this occurred in the data.

[15] For a survey of these types of nouns in modern Arabic, see Monteil 1960, 124–26.

[16] ʿAbd al-Latif, ʿUmar, and Zahran 1997, 91: "*li-kathrat-i haadhaa l-nawʿ-i min-a l-maSaadir-i wa-ʾahammiyyat-i-hi ʾaSdara majmaʿ-u l-lughat-i l-ʿarabiyyat-i bi-l-qaahirat-i qaraar-an bi-qiyaasiyyat-i-hi min ʾayy-i kalimat-in.*"

the sound feminine plural if they are count nouns. Some examples include the following.

9.1 Derivation from a singular noun

This noun can be of any sort, derived or non-derived:

theory	naZariyya	نَظَرِيَّة	Christianity	al-masiiHiyya	المَسيحِيَّة
diversification	taʿaddudiyya	تَعَدُّدِيَّة	operation	ʿamaliyya	عَمَلِيَّة
legitimacy	sharʿiyya	شَرْعِيَّة	terrorism	ʾirhaabiyya	ارهَابِيَّة
diary	yawmiyya	يَوْمِيَّة			

Sometimes from a noun stem which is otherwise not regularly in use:

| divinity | ʾuluuhiyya | أُلوهِيَّة | oneness, unity | waHdaaniyya | وَحْدانية |

9.2 Derivation from a plural noun

| stardom | nujuumiyya | نُجومِيَّة | horsemanship | furuusiyya | فُروسِيَّة |

9.3 Derivation from an adjective

The adjective can be in the comparative form as well as in the base form.

importance	ʾahammiyya	أَهَمِّيَّة	priority	ʾafDaliyya	أَفْضَلِيَّة
majority	ʾakthariyya	أَكْثَرِيَّة	effectiveness	faʿʿaaliyya	فَعّالِيَّة
minority	ʾaqalliyya	أَقَلِّيَّة	priority	ʾawwaliyya~ ʾawlawiyya	أَوَّلِيَّة~أَوْلَوِيَّة

فَهُناكَ أولويات أهمّ.

fa-hunaaka **ʾawlawiyyaat-un** *ʾahamm-u.*

There are more important **priorities.**

هناك أفضلية لمن يجيد اللغة الإنكليزية.

hunaaka **ʾafDaliyyat-un** *li-man yu-jiid-u l-lughat-a l-ʾ inkliiziyyat-a.*

There is **a preference** for those who have mastered English.

9.4 Derivation from a particle or pronoun

| identity | huwiyya | هُوِيَّة | quantity | kammiyya | كَمِّيَّة |
| quality | kayfiyya | كَيْفِيَّة | | | |

9.5 Derivation from a participle

| responsibility | masʾuuliyya | مَسْؤولِيَّة | majority | ghaalibiyya | غالِبِيَّة |

9.6 Derivation from a borrowed word

chauvinism   *shuufiiniyya*   شوفينيّة   diplomacy   *diibluumaasiyya*   ديبلوماسيّة

transcendentalism   *tiraansindantaliyya*   ترانْسِنْدَنْتَليّة

10 Nouns not derived from verb roots

10.1 Primitive nouns

Certain nouns in Arabic are not derived from verb roots. Some of these are what Wright (1967) and others refer to as "primitive,"[17] i.e., well-attested substantives that form part of the core lexicon of the language but are not verbal derivatives.[18] In certain dictionaries, verbs may be listed with these nouns, but the verbs are usually denominative – derived from the noun.

10.1.1 Triliteral

man	*rajul*	رَجُل	trap	*faxx*	فَخّ
eye	*ʿayn*	عَيْن	day	*yawm*	يوم
head	*raʾs*	رَأْس	panther; cheetah	*fahd*	فَهْد

10.1.2 Biliteral primitives

A few archaic nouns in Arabic have just two consonants (sometimes just one) in the root. These often refer to basic family relationships, body parts, or essential physical or social concepts. Some of the most frequently used ones include:

mother	*ʾumm*	أُمّ	hand	*yad*	يَد
father	*ʾab*	أَب	mouth	*fam/fuu*	فَم / فو
brother	*ʾax*	أَخ	name	*ism*	اسم
son	*ibn/bin*	ابن / بِن	water	*maaʾ*	ماء
father-in-law	*Ham*	حَم	possessor	*dhuu*	ذو
blood	*dam*	دَم			

10.1.3 The five nouns (*al-ʾasmaaʾ al-xamsa* الأسماء الخمسة)

A subset of five of these nouns (*ʾab, ʾax, fuu, Ham, dhuu*)[19] inflect for case by using a long vowel instead of a short vowel when they are the first term of an annexation structure or when they have a personal pronoun suffix.[20]

---

[17] See Wright 1967, I:106; Lecomte 1968, 64, and Holes 1995, 127.

[18] As Lecomte states (1968, 64) "Certains noms sont irréductibles à une racine verbale, et paraissent bien constituer le glossaire fondamental de la langue concrète."

[19] In some cases, a sixth noun is included. It did not occur in the corpus consulted for this text.

[20] For more information on these nouns and their inflectional paradigms, see Chapter 7, section 5ff.

أبو ظبي	من أخيها	أبونا
ʾab-uu Zabiyy	*min ʾax-ii-haa*	*ʾab-uu-naa*
Abu Dhabi	from her brother	our father

كان ذا مغزى	ديوان أبي نواس	
kaan-a dhaa maghz-an	*diiwaan-u ʾab-ii nuwaas-in*	
it was significant	the collected poetry of Abu Nuwas	
('possessing significance')		

11 Common nouns from quadriliteral and quinquiliteral roots: (ʾasmaaʾ rubaaʿiyya wa xumaasiyya أسماء رباعية وخماسية)

11.1 Quadriliteral

A number of Arabic common nouns are **quadriliteral**. Some of these words are of Arabic origin, and some of them derive from other languages. These quadriliteral nouns rarely have corresponding verb forms. For example:

eternity	*sarmad*	سَرْمَد	hedgehog	*qunfudh*	قُنْفُذ
scorpion	*ʿaqrab*	عَقْرَب	crocodile	*timsaaH*	تِمْساح
bomb	*qunbula*	قُنْبُلَة	dagger	*xanjar*	خَنْجَر
box	*Sanduuq*	صَنْدوق	wasp	*zunbuur*	زُنْبور
noise; uproar	*DawDaaʾ*	ضَوْضاء	amulet; talisman	*Tilsam*	طِلْسَم

11.2 Reduplicated quadriliterals

Certain quadriliteral noun roots consist of reduplicated pairs of consonants. These often refer to naturally occurring phenomena. Some of these nouns are associated with quadriliteral verbs that denote a particular repetitive sound or motion.

skull	*jumjuma*	جُمْجُمَة	pepper	*filfil*	فِلْفِل
sesame	*simsim*	سِمْسِم	pearl	*luʾluʾ*	لُؤْلُؤ
mint	*naʿnaʿ*	نَعْنَع	bat (animal)	*waTwaaT*	وَطْواط

11.2.1 Nouns from quadriliteral reduplicated verbs

زِلْزال

رَفْرَفَة

zilzaal earthquake (to shake: *zalzal-a* زَلْزَلَ)   *rafrafa* fluttering (to flutter: *rafraf-a* رَفْرَفَ)

وَسْوَسَة

waswasa rustling, whispering (to whisper: *waswas-a* وَسْوَسَ)

11.3 Nouns from quinquiliteral roots

Some common nouns are based on quinquiliteral (five-consonant) roots.[21]

chess	*shaTranj*	شَطْرَنْج
program	*barnaamaj*	بَرْنامَج
parsley	*baqduunis*	بَقْدونِس
spider	*ʿankabuut*	عَنْكَبوت
violet	*banafsaj*	بَنَفْسَج
quince	*safarjil*	سَفَرْجِل
salamander	*samandal~ samandar*	سَمَنْدَل ~ سَمَنْدَر
cauliflower	*qarnabiiT*	قَرْنَبيط
ginger	*zanjabiil*	زَنْجَبيل

12 Collective nouns, mass nouns, and unit nouns (*ism al-jins* اِسم الجنس; *ism al-waHda* اِسم الوحدة)

Certain Arabic nouns are terms that refer to groups of individual things in general (grapes, bananas, trees) or to something which occurs as a "mass," such as wood or stone. Normally, these nouns refer to naturally occurring substances and forms of life. In these cases, reference can also be made to an individual component of the collection or the mass, and so Arabic provides a morphological way of noting this distinction through use of a "unit" noun (*ism al-waHda* اِسم الوحدة). Most mass nouns or collective nouns are masculine singular, whereas most unit nouns (or "count" nouns, as they are sometimes called) are feminine singular. Here are some examples:

12.1 Collective/mass term

chicken(s)	*dajaaj*	دَجاج	eggs	*bayD*	بَيْض
owls	*buum*	بوم	fish	*samak*	سَمَك
bees	*naHl*	نَحْل	stone	*Hajar*	حَجَر
almonds	*lawz*	لَوْز	feathers	*riish*	ريش

---

[21] Many of these nouns have a peculiarity in that in the plural, in order to fit into the Arabic broken plural system, they actually lose a consonant, for example, *ʿankabuut/ʿanaakib* 'spider/s'. See Chapter 7, section 3.2.3 for more detail.

12.2 Unit term

a chicken	dajaaja	دَجاجَة	an egg	bayDa	بَيْضَة
an owl	buuma	بومَة	a fish	samaka	سَمَكَة
a bee	naHla	نَحلَة	a stone	Hajara	حَجَرة
an almond	lawza	لَوْزَة	a feather	riisha	ريشَة

12.3 Plural of unit nouns

If there is a need to count individual nouns or units, or imply variety, the counted noun takes a specific kind of plural that refers not to the generic grouping, but to a number of individual units. That countable plural is often the sound feminine plural, but it may also be a broken plural.

five chickens	xams-u dajaajaat-in	خَمْسُ دَجاجاتٍ
six owls	sitt-u ʾabwaam-in	سِتُّ أَبْوامٍ
three eggs	thalaath-u bayDaat-in	ثَلاثُ بَيْضاتٍ
types of fish	ʾanwaaʿ-u l-ʾasmaak-i	أَنْواعُ الأَسْماكِ

13 Borrowed nouns

In addition to incorporating terms from other Middle Eastern languages, over the centuries Arabic has incorporated words from European languages, such as Latin and Greek. In recent times, much of the borrowing has been from English and French. Most of these borrowed nouns are considered solid-stem words, not analyzable into root and pattern.

music	muusiiqaa	موسيقى	camera	kaamiiraa	كاميرا
comedy	kuumiidiyaa	كوميديا	doctor	duktuur	دكتور
petroleum	batruul	بترول	ton	Tann	طن
computer	kumbiyuutir	كمبيوتر	film	film	فلم
television	talfizyuun	تلفزيون	bank	bank	بنك
telephone	talifuun	تلفون			

Certain common everyday terms, such as "telephone," "camera," and "doctor," also have Arabic-based equivalents (loan translations) (e.g., *haatif, ʾaalat taSwiir, Tabiib*, respectively), most of which have been coined by consensus of authorities on Arabic language in the Arabic language academies in Cairo, Baghdad, and

Damascus. These academies are scholarly research institutes whose primary goal is to maintain the accuracy, richness, and liveliness of the Arabic language through defining standards, prescribing correct usage, and setting procedures for the coining of new terms.

The actual choice of using the borrowed term or the Arabic term varies from country to country, author to author, and from publication to publication. The largest category of current loanwords is in rapidly developing technology fields such as biology, medicine, and computer science. Efforts have been made to keep coining Arabic-based equivalents to these technical terms, but it is a challenge to keep pace with the amount of technical data used in the media every day. Here are just a few terms found in current Arabic newspapers:

video	*fiidyuu*	فيديو	hormones	*hurmuunaat*	هرمونات
cassette	*kaasitt*	كاست	cocaine	*kuukaayiin*	كوكايين
radar	*raadaar*	رادار	viruses	*fiiruusaat*	فيروسات

13.1 Borrowed acronyms

Arabic newspaper writing in particular also borrows acronyms for international bodies and uses them as individual words, spelled in Arabic:

UNESCO	*al-yuuniiskuu*	اليونيسكو	أعلنه اليونيسكو.
			ʾaʿlan-a-hu l-yuuniiskuu.
			UNESCO announced it.
OPEC	*ʾuubik*	أوبك	داخل أوبك وخارجه
			daaxil-a ʾuubiik wa-xaarij-a-hu
			inside **OPEC** and outside of it
UNICEF	*al-yuuniisiif*	اليونيسيف	

14 Arabic proper nouns

Proper nouns include names of people and places. These come from a variety of sources, many of them Arabic, but some non-Arabic.

14.1 Geographical names

Names of cities, countries, geographical features. Sometimes these include the definite article, sometimes they do not. If the name does not have the definite article, then it is diptote.

Tunisia	*tuunis*	تونس	The Nile	*al-niil*	النيل
Morocco	*al-maghrib*	المغرب	Jidda	*jidda*	جدة
The Euphrates	*al-furaat*	الفرات	Cairo	*al-qaahira*	القاهرة

14.2 Personal names

Arabic personal names are a rich source of cultural information.[22] Most given names consist of one word, but some names are actually phrases that include family information (e.g., "son of," "mother of," "father of," "daughter of") or else reference to religious concepts (e.g., "servant of the merciful," "light of the religion"). The structure of Arabic family names is highly complex and may include reference to family information, place of origin (e.g., *bayruutiyy* بيروتي, 'from Beirut'), profession (e.g., *Haddaad*, حدّاد 'blacksmith'), religion (e.g., *nuur-u l-diin* نور الدين 'light of religion'), or even physical characteristics (e.g., *'aHdab* أحدب 'humpbacked'). Moreover, naming practices vary throughout the Arab world.[23]

Because of the absence of capitalization in Arabic script, learners of Arabic sometimes find it challenging to distinguish proper names from ordinary adjectives and nouns within a text.

14.2.1 Women's given names

Women's names may be Arabic or borrowed from another language; if Arabic, they are usually nouns or adjectives denoting attractive qualities. Sometimes a mother will be known by a matronymic, referring to her as the mother of her eldest child.

Karima	'generous'	*kariima*	كريمة
Farida	'incomparable'	*fariida*	فريدة
Afaf	'chastity'	*'afaaf*	عفاف
Yasmine	'jasmine'	*yaasamiin*	ياسمين
Susan	'lily of the valley'	*sawsan*	سوسن

14.2.1.1 MATRONYMICS: Arabic uses teknonymics – names derived from a child's given name. It is not uncommon for an Arab mother to acquire a female teknonym or matronymic once she has had a child.

| Umm Hasan | Mother of Hasan | *'umm-u Hasan-in* | أم حسن |
| Umm Ahmad | Mother of Ahmad | *'umm-u 'aHmad-a* | أم أحمَد |

14.2.2 Men's given names

Men's names include descriptive adjectives and nouns, but also include a wide selection of phrasal names. Here are just a few examples:

---

[22] See Nydell 2002, 57–61, for a succinct description of Arab naming systems and traditions.
[23] See Badawi et al. 1991, for a comprehensive Arabic reference work on Arab names.

(1) **Adjectives:**

Sharif	'noble'	*shariif*	شريف
Karim	'generous'	*kariim*	كريم
Said	'happy'	*saᶜiid*	سعيد

(2) **Nouns:**

Raad	'thunder'	*raᶜd*	رعد
Leith	'lion'	*layth*	ليث
Fahd	'panther'	*fahd*	فهد

(3) **Participles:**

Mahmoud	'praised'	*maHmuud*	محمود
Adil	'just'	*ᶜaadil*	عادل
Mukhtar	'chosen'	*muxtaar*	مختار

(4) *Nisba* **adjectives:**

Shukri	'thankful'	*shukriyy*	شكريّ
Lutfi	'kind'	*luTfiyy*	لطفيّ

(5) **Traditional Semitic names:** These are names shared within the Semitic languages and traditions.

Ibrahim (Abraham)	*ʾibraahiim*	إبراهيم
Yousef (Joseph)	*yuusuf*	يوسف
Younis (Jonas)	*yuunus*	يونس
Suleiman (Solomon)	*sulaymaan*	سليمان
Musa (Moses)	*muusaa*	موسى

(6) **Inflected verbs:** These names are actually inflected verb forms:

Yazid	'he increases'	*ya-ziid*	يزيد
Ahmad	'I praise'	*ʾa-Hmad*	أحمد

(7) **Phrase names:** Arabic has phrasal names, usually in the form of construct
phrases:

Aladdin	'nobility of the religion'	*ᶜalaaʾ -u l-diin*	علاء الدين
Abdallah	'servant of God'	*ᶜabd-u llaah*	عبد الله
Abdurahman	'servant of the merciful'	*ᶜabd-u l-raHmaan*	عبد الرحمن

(8) Teknonymics: The Arabic term for this kind of name is *kunya* كنية. It is common in many parts of the Arab world for a man to acquire a teknonym once he has had a child, especially a male child, and he is often known by the name of his first male child.

Abu Hassan	'Father of Hassan'	*ʾabuu Hasan-in*	أبو حسن
Abu Bakr	'Father of Bakr'	*ʾabuu bakr-in*	أبو بكر

(9) Patronymics: A patronymic is a name derived from the father's given name:

Ibn Fadlan	'Son of Fadlan'	*ibn-u faDlaan*	ابن فضلان
Ibn Khaldoun	'Son of Khaldoun'	*ibn-u xalduun*	ابن خلدون
Ibn Saud	'Son of Saud'	*ibn-u saʿuud*	ابن سعود

15 Complex nouns, compound nouns, and compound nominals (*naHt* نحت and *tarkiib* تركيب)

Sometimes there is a need to express semantically complex concepts in noun form. This area of noun formation in Arabic is not as clear-cut as the other areas. "The debate on compounding in Arabic has long been bedeviled by failure to define terms precisely and apply consistent criteria. There are two fundamental definitional problems: the term for compounding itself, and the status of the components of a compound" (Emery 1988, 34).

Here three categories are distinguished: complex nouns, compound nouns, and compound nominals (phrases). Complex nouns are created from parts of words fused into one word. Compound nouns are created by combining two full words into one, and compound nominals are phrases of two words that are used to refer to one concept. In general in Arabic, the term *naHt* refers to complex and compound nouns, whereas the term *tarkiib* refers to compound nominals.

15.1 Complex nouns

Complex nouns are created through fusing two (or more) word stems into one. This is called *naHt* (literally 'chiseling') in traditional Arabic grammar. There are several sub-processes or variations on this procedure, and although it is not common in traditional Arabic morphology, it tends to be used in MSA for recently coined items and for loan translations, especially technical terms.

15.1.1 Blending word segments into one word

In this process, parts of words are segmented and re-blended into a word that combines parts of two word stems:

boulder	*julmuud~jalmad*	جلمود ~ جلمد

(from *jalida* جلد 'to freeze' and *jamuda* جمد 'to harden')

supranationalism	*al-fawqawmiyya*	الفوقومية

(from *fawq-a* فوق 'above' and *qawmiyya* قومية 'nationalism')

amphibian	*barmaa'iyy*	برمائي

(from *barr* بر 'land' and *maa'* ماء 'water' with *nisba* suffix *-iyy*)

15.1.2 Formula nouns

This word-formation process consists of using the initial letters or syllables of a string of words in a traditional, formulaic saying to create a quadriliteral noun, usually ending with a *taa' marbuuTa.*

basmalah	بسملة

the act of saying: *bi-ism-i llaah-i* باسم الله ('in the name of God')

Hawqalah	حوقلة

the act of saying: *laa Hawl-a wa-laa quwwat-a' illaa bi-llaah-i* لا حول ولا قوة إلا بالله ('There is no power and no strength save in God')

15.2 Compound nouns

Compounding refers to combining two complete word stems into one syntactic unit. The classic MSA example is the word *ra's-maal* رأسمال 'capital' formed from conjoining the words *ra's* 'head' and *maal* 'money.'[24] Another example is *laa-markaziyya* لا مركزية for 'decentralization,' from the words *laa* 'no' and *markaziyya* 'centralization.' Other examples include:

invertebrate	*laa-faqaariyy* ('no spinal column')	لا فقاري
invertebrates	*al-laa-faqaariyyaat*	اللا فقاريات
petition, application	*ʿarD-u-Haal* ('presentation of situation')	عرضحال
petitions	*ʿard-u-Haalaat*	عرضحالات
course of events	*maa jaraa* ('what flows')	ما جرى
courses of events	*maa jarayaat*	ما جريات
lottery	*yaa-naSiib* ('O chance! O fate! O luck!')	يا نصيب

---

[24] The plural of *ra's-maal* is found both as *rasaamiil* رساميل and as *ru'uus 'amwaal* رؤوس أموال.

the lottery	*al-yaa-naSiib*	اليا نصيب
lottery ticket	*waraqat-u yaa-nasiib*	ورقة يا نصيب

Note that compound nouns function as word stems and may receive plurals or definite articles.

15.3 Compound nominals: (*tarkiib* تركيب): Coherent composite phrases

Sometimes the noun concept is not expressed as a single word in Arabic, but as a noun phrase, usually an *ʾiDaafa*, such as *ʿadam-u wujuud-in* عدم وجود 'nonexistence' or *kiis-u hawaaʾ-in* كيس هواء 'airbag.' In such cases, the dual or plural is usually made by adding the dual suffix to or pluralizing the head noun, the first noun in the phrase.

bedroom	*ghurfat-u nawm-in*	غرفة نوم
two bedrooms	*ghurfat-aa nawm-in*	غرفتا نوم
bedrooms	*ghuraf-u nawm-in*	غرف نوم
reaction	*radd-u fiʿl-in*	ردّ فعل
two reactions	*radd-aa fiʿl-in*	ردّا فعل
reactions:	*ruduud-u fiʿl-in*	ردود فعل
passport	*jawaaz-u safar-in*	جواز سفر
two passports	*jawaaz-aa safar-in*	جوازا سفر
passports:	*jawaazaat-u safar-in*	جوازات سفر

Examples:

كرد فعل للاعتداءات
ka-radd-i fiʿl-in li-l-iʿ tidaaʾ aat-i
as a reaction to the attacks

خمس غرف نوم
xams-u ghuraf-i nawm-in
five **bedrooms**

6

Participles: active and passive

Arabic participles are descriptive words derived from particular stem classes, or Forms, of a verbal root. The **active participle** (*ism al-faaᶜil* اسم الفاعل) describes the doer of an action and the **passive participle** (*ism al-mafᶜuul* اسم المفعول) describes the entity that receives the action, or has the action done to it.[1] Arabic participles therefore describe or refer to entities involved in an activity, process, or state.

Arabic participles are based on a distinction in **voice**: they are either active or passive. This contrasts with English, where participles are based on **tense** (present or past) and are used as components of compound verb forms. Arabic participles are **not** used in the formation of compound verb tenses.[2]

In form, participles are substantives, that is they inflect as nouns or adjectives (for case, definiteness, gender, number).[3] In terms of their **function**, however, they may serve as nouns, adjectives, adverbs or even verb substitutes.[4] As Beeston notes (1970, 34), "it may be impossible when quoting a word out of context to assert that it is either [substantive or adjective], this being determinable only by the syntactic context." This is particularly true for Arabic participles. They are distinguishable by their form, but their syntactic functions are multiple.[5]

---

[1] According to Holes (1995, 122) "The basic difference between the two types of participle is that the active describes the state in which the subject of the verb from which it is derived finds itself as a result of the action or event which the verb describes, while the passive refers to the state in which the object or complement of the verb from which it is derived finds itself after the completion of the action/event."

[2] "The participles have no fixed time reference – this has to be interpreted from the context" (Holes, 1995, 122). Also, as Kouloughli states in this context, "Il est plus éclairant de penser que le participe actif renvoie au sujet du verbe actif alors que le participe passif renvoie, lui, au sujet du verbe passif" (1994, 217) rather than associating either participle with any sort of temporal notion.

[3] Lecomte (1968, 95) refers to Arabic participles as "the hinge between the verb and the noun" ("la charnière entre le verbe et le nom") because of their noun form combined with verbal qualities.

[4] "The active participle can function syntactically as a noun, verb or attributive adjective . . . while the passive participle is often used predicatively as quasi-verbal adjective to indicate the result or present relevance of a completed action" (Holes, 1995, 122–23).

[5] The description of Arabic participles varies substantially because of their wide-ranging functional nature. For example, they are referred to by Depuydt (1997, 494) as "adjectival verb forms," whereas Beeston (1970, 35) states that "the participle is a noun (substantive or adjective) which like the verbal abstract [i.e., verbal noun], matches the verb." Arabic grammar classifies both nouns and adjectives under the term *ism* 'noun; name' and thus refers to the participles as *ism al-faaᶜil* and *ism al-mafᶜuul*.

The meanings of active and passive participles are directly related to their descriptive nature and the verb from which they derive. However, within that semantic range participles have a wide range of meanings. "Many words which have the pattern of a participle contain highly specialized senses within their semantic spectrum, in addition to the fundamental value" (Beeston 1970, 35).

The derivational rules for participles are described in greater detail in the chapters on the individual forms (I–X, XI–XV, and quadriliteral).

1 Active participle (AP): (*ism al-faaᶜil* اسم الفاعل)

When an active participle is used as a substantive to refer to the doer of an action, often the English equivalent would be a noun ending in /-er/ or /-or/, such as 'inspector' or 'teacher.' In Arabic, the term for 'teacher' (*mudarris* مدرّس), for example, is an active participle, as is the term for 'visitor' (*zaaʾir* زائر). As a noun, when the AP refers to or describes a human being, it takes the natural gender of the person; when referring to something abstract, it may be either masculine or feminine. Also as a noun, it will take a particular form of the plural, which is not always predictable.

Used as an adjective, the active participle acts as a descriptive term, as, for example, the AP *jaaff* 'dry' in the phrase *jaww-un jaaff-un* 'dry air.' It may also correspond to an English adjective ending in /-ing/, such as the Form VIII AP *mubtasim* 'smiling' in the phrase *bint-un mubtasimat-un*, 'a smiling girl.' As a predicate adjective, it may serve as a verb substitute. For example, using the Form III AP *musaafir* 'traveling': *huwa musaafir-un* 'He is traveling.'[6]

The active participle (AP) can be derived from any form (stem class) of Arabic verbs, from I–X. AP's can be derived from quadriliteral verbs as well as triliteral. They describe the doer of the action.[7] They have predictable and distinctive forms.

1.1 Form I AP

The pattern of the active participle in Form I of the triliteral verb is **CaaCiC** (*faaᶜil* فاعل). This pattern shows slight modification when used with irregular root types, as described in Chapter 22, section 10.

1.1.1 Form I AP nouns

APs that refer to human beings take either a sound plural or a plural of the *fuᶜᶜaal* pattern. The nonhuman AP noun may be masculine or feminine and it may take the sound feminine plural or a broken plural, usually *fawaaᶜil*.

---

[6] Note, however, the temporal and aspectual ambiguity of the AP in context. It may refer to a state of current activity, or of having accomplished a certain activity. As Depuydt notes, "the inability to distinguish unambiguously between simultaneity and anteriority may occasionally be an impediment to using a participle" (1997, 494).

[7] In terms of meaning, note that an active participle (e.g., *raaD-in* 'satisfied' from *raDiya* 'to be satisfied') may have an English equivalent that ends in /-ed/, but it is still an active participle.

Strong/regular root: *faaᶜil* فاعل

guard/s	Haaris/Hurraas	حارِس/حُرّاس
researcher/s	baaHith/-uuna	باحِث/باحثون
rider/s; passenger/s	raakib/rukkaab	راكِب/رُكّاب
coast/s; shore/s	saaHil/sawaaHil	ساحِل/سواحِل
floor/s; storey/ies[8]	Taabiq/Tawaabiq	طابِق/طَوابِق
side/s	jaanib/jawaanib	جانِب/جوانِب
rule/s; base/s	qaaᶜida/qawaaᶜid	قاعِدة/قَواعِد
fruit/s	faakiha/fawaakih	فاكِهة/فَواكِه
university/ies	jaamiᶜa/-aat	جامِعة/جامِعات

Geminate root:

material/s	maadda/mawaadd[9]	مادّة/موادّ
pilgrim/s	Haajj/Hujjaaj~Hajiij	حاجّ/حُجّاج ~ حجيج

Hamzated root:

reader/s	qaari'/qurraa'	قارِئ/قُرّاء
accident/s; emergency/ies	Taari'a/Tawaari'	طارِئة/طَوارِئ

Assimilated root:

mother/s	waalida/-aat	والِدة/والِدات
father/s	waalid/-uuna	والِد/والِدون
import/s	waarid/-aat	وارِد/وارِدات
duty/ies; homework	waajib/-aat	واجِب/واجِبات

Hollow root:

visitor/s	zaa'ir/zuwwaar	زائِر/زُوّار
leader/s	qaa'id/quwwaad	قائِد/قُوّاد
fluid/s; liquid/s	saa'il/ sawaa'il	سائِل/سوائِل
being/s	kaa'in/-aat	كائِن/كائِنات

---

[8] Of a building. Also pronounced *Taabaq*.
[9] The plural *mawaadd* is the form that the plural pattern *fawaaᶜil* takes in geminate nouns because of the phonological restriction on sequences that include a vowel between identical consonants. **mawaadid → mawaadd*.

menu/s; list/s	qaaʾima/-aat~qawaʾim	قائم/قائمات ~ قوائم
circle/s; department/s	daaʾira/dawaaʾir	دائرة/دوائر

Defective root:

judge/s	qaaD-in/quDaah	قاضٍ/قُضاة
club/s	naad-in/nawaadin	نادٍ/نوادٍ
corner/s	zaawiya/zawaayaa	زاوِية/زوايا

Examples of Form I APs as nouns in context:

الوالدة والمولود في خير.
al-waalidat-u wa-l-mawluud-u fii xayr-in
Mother and child are well ('in goodness').

النادي العربي
al-naadii l-ʿarabiyy-u
the Arabic **club**

ناطق باسم الملكة
naaTiq-un bi-ism-i l-malikat-i
a **spokesman** in the name of the queen

1.1.2 Form I APs as adjectives

APs functioning as adjectives reflect the gender of the noun that they modify. In context they may function either as noun modifiers or predicate adjectives.

Strong/regular root:

able, capable	qaabil	قابِل	former	saabiq	سابِق
frowning; stern	ʿaabis	عابِس	unable	ʿaajiz	عاجِز
ruling	Haakim	حاكِم	next, coming	qaadim	قادِم

Assimilated root:

wide, broad	waasiʿ	واسِع	clear	waaDiH	واضِح

Geminate root:
This form of AP creates a unique monosyllabic stem consisting of a long vowel followed by a doubled consonant: CVVCC.[10]

dry	jaaff	جافّ	harmful	Daarr	ضارّ
important	haamm	هامّ	special; private	xaaSS	خاصّ
hot	Haarr	حارّ	poisonous	saamm	سامّ

---

[10] See also Chapter 2, note 34.

Hamzated root:

sorry, regretful	*ʾaasif*	آسِف	calm, peaceful	*haadiʾ*	هادِئ
final; last	*ʾaaxir*[11]	آخِر			

Hollow root:

visiting	*zaaʾir*	زائِر	frightful; amazing	*haaʾil*	هائِل

Defective root:

growing	*naam-in*	نامٍ	satisfied; pleased	*raaD-in*	راضٍ
high	*ʿaal-in*	عالٍ	last; past	*maaD-in*	ماضٍ
remaining	*baaq-in*	باقٍ			

Examples of APs in context as adjectives:

الثلاثاء الماضي
al-thulaathaaʾ-a **l-maaDiy-a**
last Tuesday

الوثب العالي
al-wathab-u **l-ʿaalii**
the high jump

المرّة القادمة
al-marrat-a **l-qaadimat-a**
the next time

وزير الاقتصاد الأردنيّ السابق
waziir-u l-iqtiSaad-i l-ʾurduniyy-u
    l-saabiq-u
the former Jordanian minister of
    economy

المشاريع الباقية
al-mashaariiʿ-u **l-baaqiyat-u**
the remaining projects

قال المدرب إنه راض.
qaal-a l-mudarrib-u ʾinna-hu **raaD-in**.
The coach said that he was satisfied.

الاستخدام الضارّ بالبيئة
al-istixdaam-u **l-Daarr-u** *bi-l-biiʾat-i*
use injurious to the environment

يفتح مجالات واسعة.
ya-ftaH-u majaalaat-in **waasiʿat-an**.
It opens wide fields.

آخر التطورات
ʾaaxir-u l-taTawwuraat-i
the latest developments

الخلفاء الراشدون
al-xulafaaʾ-u **l-raashid-uuna**
the orthodox caliphs

المعلومات اللازمة
al-maʿluumaat-u **l-laazimat-u**
the necessary information

في قائمة الدول الداعمة للارهاب
fii qaaʾimat-i l-duwal-i **l-daaʿimat-i**
    li-l-ʾirhaab-i
on the list of countries supporting
    terrorism

---

[11] From the hamzated roots *ʾ-s-f* and *ʾ-x-r*; the initial *hamza* followed by the long /aa/ of the *faaʿil* pattern create /ʾaa/, spelled with *ʾalif madda*.

1.1.3 Identical noun and adjective AP

It may happen that the AP for a particular verb is used both as a noun and as an adjective. In that case, they look identical in the singular, but the plurals usually differ.

1.1.3.1 AP NOUN PLURAL: The Form I AP **masculine human noun takes a broken plural of the form (***fuˁˁaal* فعّال**).** The feminine human noun takes the sound feminine plural.

visitor/s (m.)	*zaaʾir/zuwwaar*	زائر/زوّار
visitor/s (f.)	*zaaʾira/-aat*	زائرة/زائرات
worker/s (m.)	*ˁaamil/ˁummaal*	عامل/عمّال
worker/s (f.)	*ˁaamila/-aat*	عاملة/عاملات
writer/s (m.)	*kaatib/kuttaab*	كاتب/كتّاب
writer/s (f.)	*kaatiba/-aat*	كاتبة/كاتبات
ruler/s (m.)	*Haakim/Hukkaam*	حاكم/حكّام
ruler/s (f.)	*Haakima/-aat*	حاكمة/حاكمات

1.1.3.2 AP ADJECTIVE PLURAL: The Form I AP **adjective takes the sound masculine or the sound feminine plural** if it modifies or refers to a human plural noun.

visiting	*zaaʾir/-uuna~zaaʾira/-aat*	زائر/زائرون ~ زائرة/زائرات
working	*ˁaamil/-uuna~ˁaamila/-aat*	عامل/عاملون ~ عاملة/عاملات
writing	*kaatib/-uuna~kaatiba/-aat*	كاتب/كاتبون ~ كاتبة/كاتبات
ruling	*Haakim/-uuna/~Haakima/-aat*	حاكم/حاكمون ~ حاكمة/حاكمات

1.2 Derived form active participles (II–X)

As with Form I, the derived form AP may refer to humans or nonhuman entities and may function either as a noun or adjective, many of them doing double-duty. When referring to or denoting human beings, the plural is either masculine sound plural or feminine sound plural, depending on the natural gender of the head noun.

If, however, the participle noun refers to a nonhuman entity, such as *muxaddir* مخدّر 'drug,' its plural is sound feminine plural, *muxaddir-aat* مخدّرات 'drugs.'

1.2.1 Form II AP: *mufaˁˁil* مفعّل

coordinator	*munassiq/-uuna*	منسّق/منسّقون
inspector	*mufattish/-uuna*	مفتّش/مفتّشون

teacher	*mudarris/-uuna*	مُدَرِّس/مُدَرِّسون
hors d'oeuvres	*muqabbilaat*[12]	مُقَبِّلات
drug, narcotic	*muxaddir/-aat*	مُخَدِّر/مُخَدِّرات
note; reminder	*mudhakkira/-aat*	مُذَكِّرة/مُذَكِّرات
historian	*muʾarrix /-uuna*	مُؤَرِّخ/مُؤَرِّخون
distinctive feature; characteristic	*mumayyiza/-aat*	مُمَيِّزة/مُمَيِّزات
singer	*mughann-in/mughannuuna*	مُغَنٍّ/مُغَنّون
person praying	*muSall-in/muSalluuna*	مُصَلٍّ/مُصَلّون

Form II AP's in context:

عدد من الـمؤرخين العرب
ʿadad-un min-a l-muʾarrix-iina l-ʿarab-i
a number of Arab **historians**

عدسة مكبرة
ʿadasat-un mukabbirat-un
magnifying glass ('lens')

منسق نشاطات الأمم المتحدة
munassiq-u nashaaT-aat-i l-ʾumam-i l-muttaHidat-i
coordinator of the activities of the United Nations

1.2.2 Form III AP: *mufaaʿil* مُفاعِل

assistant	*musaaʿid*	مُساعِد	citizen	*muwaaTin*	مُواطِن
lecturer	*muHaaDir*	مُحاضِر	on duty	*munaawib*	مُناوِب
lawyer	*muHaam-in*	مُحامٍ	traveler/traveling	*musaafir*	مُسافِر
observer	*muraaqib*	مُراقِب	neutral	*muHaayid*	مُحايِد

Form III APs in context:

ابني مسافر.
ibn-ii musaafir-un.
My son is **traveling**.

دولة محايدة
dawlat-un muHaayidat-un
a **neutral** country

1.2.3 Form IV AP: *mufʿil* مُفْعِل

Muslim	*muslim*	مُسْلِم	rainy	*mumTir*	مُمْطِر
ocean	*muHiiT*	مُحيط	snowy	*muthlij*	مُثْلِج

---

[12] This expression usually occurs in the plural.

manager	*mudiir*	مُدير	boring	*mumill*	مُمِلّ
sunny	*mushmis*	مُشْمِس	possible	*mumkin*	مُمْكِن

Form IV APs in context:

الأيّام الـمشمسة	شيء مؤسف جدّاً
al-ʾayyaam-u l-mushmisat-u	*shayʾ-un muʾsif-un jidd-an*
the **sunny** days	a very **distressing** thing

أقرب وقت ممكن	المحيط الأطلسي
ʾaqrab-a waqt-in mumkin-in	*al-muHiiT-u l-ʾaTlasiyy-u*
the soonest **possible** time	the Atlantic **Ocean**

اللجنة المشرفة	النسائم المنعشة
al-lajnat-u l-mushrifat-u	*al-nasaaʾim-u l-munʿishat-u*
the **supervisory** committee	the **refreshing** breezes

1.2.4 Form V AP: *mutafaʿʿil* مُتَفَعِّل

volunteer	*mutaTawwiʿ*	مُتَطَوِّع	sorry	*mutaʾassif*	مُتَأَسِّف
specialist	*mutaxaSSiS*	مُتخصِّص	abundant	*mutawaffir*	مُتوفِّر
extremist	*mutaTarrif*	مُتطرِّف	diverse, various	*mutanawwiʿ*	مُتنوِّع

Note that some Form V APs can have passive meanings:

married	*mutazawwij*	مُتزوِّج
late; delayed	*mutaʾaxxir*	مُتَأَخِّر
frozen	*mutajammid*	مُتجمِّد

Form V APs in context:

تثير حماس المتفرّجين.
tu-thiir-u Hamaas-a l-mutafarrij-iina.
It arouses the excitement of **the spectators.**

المتحدّث باسم الحكومة
al-mutaHaddith-u bi-sm-i l-Hukuumat-i
the spokesperson in the name of the government

المحيط المتجمّد الشمالي
al-muHiiT-u l-mutajammid-u l-shimaaliyy-u
the Arctic Ocean ('the **frozen** northern ocean')

1.2.5 Form VI AP: *mutafaaⁿil* مُتَفَاعَل

successive	*mutataal-in*	مُتَتَال	equal, commensurate	*mutakaafiⁿ*	مُتَكَافِئ
increasing	*mutazaayid*	مُتَزَايِد	optimistic	*mutafaaⁿil*	مُتَفَائِل
scattered	*mutanaathir*	مُتَنَاثِر	pessimistic	*mutashaaⁿim*	مُتَشَائِم

Form VI APs in context:

سنوات متتالية
*sanawaat-un **mutataaliyat-un***
successive years

علب متناثرة
*ⁿilab-un **mutanaathirat-un***
scattered containers

الاهتمام المتزايد بالإسلام
*al-ihtimaam-u l-**mutazaayid-u** bi-l-ⁿislaam-i*
the **increasing** interest in Islam

مباراة متكافئة
*mubaaraat-un **mutakaafiⁿat-un***
an **equal** contest

1.2.6 Form VII AP: *munfaⁿil* مُنْفَعَل

No noun forms were encountered in the data, only adjectival APs of Form VII:

sliding	*munzaliq*	مُنْزَلِق	isolated	*munⁿazil*	مُنْعَزِل
originating	*munbathiq*	مُنْبَثِق	notched, indented	*munbaⁿij*	مُنْبَعِج

باب منزلق
*baab-un **munzaliq-un***
a **sliding** door

1.2.7 Form VIII AP: *muftaⁿil* مُفْتَعَل

listener	*mustamiⁿ*	مُسْتَمَع	respectful	*muHtarim*	مُحْتَرِم
waiting	*muntaZir*	مُنْتَظِر	smiling	*mubtasim*	مُبْتَسِم
agreeing	*muttafiq*	مُتَّفِق	moderate	*muⁿtadil*	مُعْتَدِل

1.2.7.1 FORM VIII AP WITH PP MEANING: A Form VIII AP may occasionally have the meaning of a passive participle:

full of; filled with	*mumtaliⁿ (bi-)*	مُمْتَلِئ (ب)
united	*muttaHid*	مُتَّحِد
hidden	*muxtabiⁿ*	مُخْتَبِئ

Form VIII APs in context:

الأمم المتحدة
al-ʾumam-u **l-muttaHidat-u**
the **United** Nations

لإرضاء مختلف الأذواق
li-ʾirDaaʾ-i **muxtalif-i** *l-ʾadhwaaq-i*
in order to please **various** tastes

الفتاة المبتسمة
al-fataat-u **l-mubtasimat-u**
the **smiling** girl

خصمك مختبئ
xaSm-u-ka **muxtabiʾ-un**
Your adversary **is hidden.**

1.2.8 Form IX AP: *mufʿall* مُفْعَلّ

The Form IX APs are rare.

1.2.9 Form X AP: *mustafʿil* مُسْتَفْعِل

orientalist	*mustashriq*	مُسْتَشْرِق	consumer; user	*mustaxdim*	مُسْتَخْدِم
continuous	*mustamirr*	مُسْتَمِرّ	impossible	*mustaHiil*	مُسْتَحِيل
circular	*mustadiir*	مُسْتَدِير			

Form X APs in context:

بصفة مستمرّة
bi-Sifat-in **mustamirrat-in**
in a **continous** way; continuously

ساحة مستديرة
saaHat-un **mustadiirat-un**
a **circular** courtyard

ثلاثة مستحيلات
thalaathat-u **mustaHiilaat-in**
three **impossible** [things]

لكل مستخدم
li-kull-i **mustaxdim-in**
for every **consumer**

1.3 Quadriliteral APs

Quadriliteral APs may function as nouns or adjectives. As with the derived-form triliteral-based APs, quadriliteral AP nouns, when referring to human beings, take the sound masculine or feminine plural, according to natural gender; when referring to nonhuman entities, the sound feminine plural is used.

Form I: *mufaʿlil* مُفَعْلِل

engineer/s	*muhandis-uuna*	مُهَنْدِس/مُهَنْدِسون
translator/s	*mutarjim-uuna*	مُتَرْجِم/مُتَرْجِمون
explosive/s	*mufarqiʿ/mufarqiʿaat*	مُفَرْقِع/مُفَرْقِعات

Form II: *mutafaʿlil* مُتَفَعْلِل

| deteriorating | *mutadahwir* | مُتَدَهْوِر |
| profound; far-reaching | *mutaghalghil* | مُتَغَلْغِل |

Form IV: *mufʿalill* مُفْعَلِلّ

serene, calm	*muTmaʾinn*	مُطْمَئِنّ
vanishing	*muDmaHill*	مُضْمَحِلّ
dusky, gloomy	*mukfahirr*	مُكْفَهِرّ

Quadriliteral APs in context:

هم في حال صحة متدهورة.
*hum fii Haal-i SiHHat-in **mutadahwirat-in**.*
They are in a **deteriorating** state of health.

خبراء المفرقعات
xubaraaʾ-u l-mufarqiʿaat-i
explosives experts

1.4 Special functions of APs

The active participle has a wide range of syntactic functions in Arabic. As noted, it may serve as a noun or adjective. As a predicate of an equational sentence, it may function to indicate a verb-like action:

هو مسافر.
*huwa **musaafir-un**.*
He **is traveling/has gone traveling**.

الطلاب زائرون.
*al-Tullaab-u **zaaʾir-uuna**.*
The students **are visiting**.

أنا فاهم.
*ʾanaa **faahim-un**.*
I understand ('I **am understanding**').

1.4.2 The *Haal* حال construction

A particular adverbial function of active participles is their use in the *Haal* or circumstantial accusative construction. The active participle is used to describe additional circumstances of a verbal action, coordinating a state or circumstances with the action denoted by the verb. The AP used in the *Haal* structure agrees with the doer or sometimes with the object of the action in number and gender, but is always in the accusative case.

دخل الصف متأخرا.
*daxal-a l-Saff-a **mutaʾaxxir-an**.*
He entered the classroom **late**.

دخلا البلد بالباخرة **قادمين** من الجزائر.

*daxal-aa l-balad-a bi-l-baaxirat-i **qaadim-ayni** min-a l-jazaaʾir-i.*

They (two) entered the country by ship, **coming** from Algeria.

انطلقوا **عائدين** إلى بيوتهم.

*inTalaq-uu **ʿaaʾ id-iina** ʾilaa buyuut-i-him.*

They departed, **returning** to their houses.

1.4.2.1 AP + NOUN OBJECT: If the *Haal* AP is from a transitive verb, it **may take an object in the accusative case:**

عاد إلى القاهرة **حاملا** رسالة من الزعيم الليبي.

*ʿaad-a ʾilaa l-qaahirat-i **Haamil-an risaalat-an** min-a l-zaʿiim-i l-liibiyy-i.*

He returned to Cairo **carrying a letter** from the Libyan leader.

وألقى الوزير كلمة **ناقلا** تحيات الرئيس.

*wa-ʾalqaa l-waziir-u kalimat-an **naaqil-an taHiyyaat-i** l-raʾiis-i.*

The minister gave a speech **transmitting the greetings** of the president.

For further discussion of the *Haal* construction, see Chapter 11, section 2.3.1.

2 Passive participle (PP): *ism al-mafʿuul* اسم المفعول

Like the active participle, the passive participle (PP) can be derived from any Form (stem class) of Arabic verbs, from I–X, and PPs can be formed from quadriliteral verbs as well as triliteral. In general, in order to have a passive participle a verb should be transitive, i.e., able to take an object complement or direct object, inasmuch as PPs describe the state of the object of the action.

Passive participles acting as nouns often correspond to English nouns ending in /-ee/ 'employee' (*muwaZZaf* موظّف), or they may correspond to an English past/ passive participle (e.g., *maktuub* مكتوب 'written').[13] However, a second important function of the **PPs of derived verb forms (II–X)** and **quadriliterals** is to function as **nouns of time and place**, so the requirement for transitivity is not always met. These include, for example, the nouns *mustashfan* مُسْتَشْفًى 'hospital' (X PP), *muxtabar* مُخْتَبَر 'laboratory' (VIII PP), and *muʿaskar* مُعَسْكَر 'camp' (Quad. I PP).

2.1 Form I passive participle: *mafʿuul* مفعول

This form of the PP describes the result of an action, whether it functions as a noun or an adjective. It may take a broken plural or the sound feminine plural if

---

[13] A good description of both present and past participles in English is found in Hurford 1994, 157–60 and 195–98. Note especially his description of the contrast between the English past participle and the Arabic passive participle, p. 159.

it refers to a nonhuman entity, and the sound masculine plural if it refers to human males.

Form I PP noun:

concept/s	*mafhuum/mafaahiim*	مفْهوم/مفاهيم
group/s	*majmuuʿa/–aat*	مجْموعة/مجْموعات
plan/s	*mashruuʿ/-aat~ mashaariiʿ*	مشْروع/مشْروعات ~ مشاريع
manuscript/s	*maxTuuT/-aat*[14]	مخْطوط/مخْطوطات
implication/s	*madluul/-aat*	مدْلول /مدْلولات
topic/s	*mawDuuʿ/mawDuuʿaat~ mawaaDiiʿ*	موْضوع /موْضوعات ~ مواضيع
creature/s	*maxluuq/-aat*	مخْلوق/مخْلوقات
sound/s	*masmuuʿ/-aat*	مسْموع/مسْموعات
prisoner/s	*masjuun/-uuna*	مسْجون/مسْجونون

PP adjective:

known	*maʿruuf*	معْروف	busy	*mashghuul*	مشْغول
blessed	*mabruuk*	مبْروك	forbidden	*mamnuuʿ*	ممْنوع

2.1.2 Form I PPs in context

في منشوراتها هذه
fii manshuuraat-i-haa haadhihi
in these of **its publications**

الوالدة والمولود في خير.
al-waalidat-u wa-**l-mawluud-u** fii xayr-in.
Mother and [new]**born** are well.

الجهود المبذولة لإعادة السلام
al-juhuud-u **l-mabdhuulat-u** li-ʾ iʿaadat-i l-salaam-i
the efforts **exerted** to re-establish peace

2.2 Derived form passive participles II–X

As nouns, these participles usually take sound plurals when referring to human beings. When referring to nonhuman entities, the sound feminine plural is usually used. Passive participles are less likely to occur in the reflexive/reciprocal and intransitive Forms V, VI, VII, and IX. Note that PPs as nouns of time and place are especially frequent in Forms VII–X.

---

[14] The singular occurs both as *maxTuuT* مخْطوط and as *maxTuuTa* مخْطوطة.

2.2.1 Form II PP: *mufaᶜᶜal* مُفَعَّل

Nouns:

organization	*munaZZama*	مُنَظَّمة	square	*murabbaᶜ*	مُرَبَّع
volume (book)	*mujallad*	مُجَلَّد	employee	*muwaZZaf*	مُوَظَّف
triangle	*muthallath*	مُثَلَّث	authorized agent	*mufawwaD*	مُفَوَّض

Adjectives:

illustrated	*muSawwar*	مُصَوَّر	complicated	*muᶜaqqad*	مُعَقَّد
preferred; favorite	*mufaDDal*	مُفَضَّل	cultured	*muthaqqaf*	مُثَقَّف
			armed	*musallaH*	مُسَلَّح

2.2.1.1 FORM II PPs IN CONTEXT:

مفوض الشركة	إلى العنف المسلّح
mufawwaD-u l-sharikat-i	*ʾilaa l-ᶜunf-i l-musallaH-i*
the company **agent**	to **armed** force
لـمجرد إثبات	في الميعاد المحدد
li-mujarrad-i ʾithbaat-in	*fii l-miiᶜaad-i l-muHaddad-i*
for **mere** proof	at the **designated** time

2.2.2 Form III PP: *mufaaᶜal* مُفاعَل

addressed, spoken to	*muxaaTab*	مُخاطَب

2.2.3 Form IV PP: *mufᶜal* مُفْعَل

attaché	*mulHaq/-uuna*	مُلْحَق/مُلْحَقون
lexicon	*muᶜjam/maᶜaajim*	مُعْجَم/مَعاجِم
compact/ed	*mudmaj*	مُدْمَج
cast; seamless	*mufragh*	مُفْرَغ
disused; disregarded	*muhmal*	مُهْمَل

2.2.3.1 FORM IV PPs IN CONTEXT:

الملحق العسكري	قرص مدمج
al-mulHaq-u l-ᶜaskariyy-u	*qurS-un mudmaj-un*
the military **attaché**	a **compact** disk

حلقة مفرغة	أشياء قديمة مهملة
Halqat-un **mufraghat-un**	*ʾashyaaʾ-u qadiimat-un* **muhmalat-un**
a **vicious** circle	old, **disused** things

2.2.4 Form V PP: *mutafaᶜᶜal* مُتَفَعَّل

change   *mutaghayyar*   مُتَغَيِّر   expected;   *mutawaqqaᶜ*   مُتَوقَّع
anticipated

مضوا وقتا أكثر من المتوقع.
maDaw waqt-an ʾakthar-a min-a **l-mutawaqqaᶜ-i.**
They spent more time than **expected.**

2.2.5 Form VI PP: *mutafaaᶜal* مُتَفَاعَل
The form VI PPs are rare.

2.2.6 Form VII PP: *munfaᶜal* مُنْفَعَل
These usually occur as nouns of place or time:

slope/s	*munHadar/-aat*	مُنْحَضَر/مُنْحَضَرات
lowland/s	*munxafaD/-aat*	مُنْخَفَض/مُنْخَفَضات
end of the month	*munsalax*[15]	مُنْسَلَخ

2.2.7 Form VIII PP: *muftaᶜal* مُفْتَعَل
When they occur as nouns, the Form VIII PPs sometimes denote nouns of place.

level/s	*mustawan/-ayaat*	مُسْتَوى/مُسْتَوَيات
content/s	*muHtawan/-ayaat*	مُحْتَوى/مُحْتَوَيات
society/s	*mujtamaᶜ/-aat*	مُجْتَمَع/مُجْتَمَعات
mid-point; half way	*muntaSaf/-aat*	مُنْتَصَف/مُنْتَصَفات
technical term/s	*muSTalaH/-aat*	مُصْطَلَح/مُصْطَلَحات
elected	*muntaxab*	مُنْتَخَب/مُنْتَخَبون
chosen	*muxtaar*	مُخْتار/مُخْتارون
occupied	*muHtall*	مُحْتَلّ

---

[15] Literally 'sloughed off, detached.'

2.2.7.1 FORM VIII PPs IN CONTEXT:

الأراضي المحتلة   في منتصف الليل

al-ʾaraaDii **l-muHtallat-u**   fii **muntaSaf-i** l-layl-i

the **occupied** lands   at **midnight**

Sometimes an **AP of Form VIII** will have a passive connotation, e.g.,

الولايات المتّحدة

al-wilaayaat-u **l-muttaHidat-u**

the **United** States

2.2.8 Form IX PP: *mufʿall* مُفْعَلّ

| greened | muxDarr | مُخْضَرّ |

2.2.9 Form X PP: *mustafʿal* مُسْتَفْعَل

future/s	mustaqbal/-aat	مُسْتَقْبَل/مُسْتَقْبَلات
hospital/s	mustashfan/-ayaat	مُسْتَشْفى/مُسْتَشْفَيات
warehouse/s	mustawdaʿ/-aat	مُسْتَوْدَع/مُسْتَوْدَعات
counselor/s	mustashaar/-uuna	مُسْتَشار/مُسْتَشارون
imported	mustawrad	مُسْتَوْرَد
borrowed	mustaʿaar	مُسْتَعار

2.2.9.1 FORM X PPs IN CONTEXT:

أسماء مستعارة   عطور مستوردة

ʾasmaaʾ-un **mustaʿaarat-un**   ʿuTuur-un **mustawradat-un**

pseudonyms ('**borrowed** names')   **imported** essences

أحد مستشاري الرئيس

ʾaHad-u **mustashaar-ii** l-raʾiis-i

one of the president's **counselors**

2.3 Quadriliteral PPs
Passive participles of quadriliteral verbs tend to occur chiefly in Forms I and II.

2.3.1 Form I QPP: *mufaʿlal* مُفَعْلَل

camp	muʿaskar	مُعَسْكَر	flattened	mufarTaH	مُفَرْطَح
series	musalsal	مُسَلْسَل	embellished	muzarkash	مُزَرْكَش
old-timer	muxaDram	مُخَضْرَم	crystallized	mubalwar	مُبَلْوَر

2.3.2 Form II QPP: *mutafaᶜlal* مُتَفَعْلَل

This form is rare.

2.3.3 Quadriliteral PPs in context

مسلسل جديد
musalsal-un jadiid-un
a new **series**

أمّا المخضرمة فقد جاءت رابعة.
ʾammaa l-muxaDramat-u, fa-qad jaaʾ-at raabiᶜat-an.
As for **the old-timer**, she came in fourth.

لسكّان الريف المبعثرين
li-sukkaan-i l-riif- **l-mubaᶜthar-iina**
to the **scattered** country dwellers

المقالاتُ الْمتَرْجمَةُ
al-maqaalaat-u **l-mutarjamat-u**
the **translated** articles

2.4 PP nouns in the plural

Certain **PP nouns** are used idiomatically in the plural. They refer to collective inanimate entities (often prepared foods), take the sound feminine plural, and include items such as the following:

edibles; foods	PP I *maʾkuulaat*	مَأْكولات
refreshments	PP I *mashruubaat*	مشْروبات
grilled [meats]	PP I *mashwiyyaat*	مشْويّات
information	PP I *maᶜluumaat*	معْلومات
canned [goods]	PP II *muᶜallabaat*	معلّبات
nuts	PP II *mukassaraat*	مكسّرات
variety; mixture	PP II *munawwaᶜaat*	منوّعات
products	PP IV *muntajaat*	منْتجات
selections	PP VIII *muxtaaraat*	مُخْتارات

7

Noun inflections: gender, humanness, number, definiteness, and case

Five inflectional features characterize Arabic nouns: **gender, humanness, number, definiteness,** and **case. Gender** and **humanness** are inherent in the noun; **number** and **definiteness** are determined semantically by the nature of the specific noun referent in context, and **case** is determined by the syntactic role of the noun (e.g., subject of the verb, object of a preposition) in a clause. Every Arabic noun in context manifests these five features, and all of these features are key components in determining agreement with phrase and clause constituents.

For example, gender, humanness, and number are essential factors in feature compatibility, or agreement, between the verb and its subject; whereas gender, humanness, number, definiteness, and case are all factors in feature compatibility between nouns and their modifiers.

Arabic nouns have a **base form**, or stem, which is used in a word list or looked up in a dictionary. This is also called the "**citation form.**" It is the bare-bones singular noun. Sometimes it is listed without any case ending, but often, in word lists, the nouns will be in the nominative case if read out loud. For example:

ambassador	*safiir-un*	سفير	poetry	*shiʿr-un*	شعر
map	*xariiTat-un*	خريطة	glory	*majd-un*	مجد
entrance	*madkhal-un*	مدخل	silver	*fiDDat-un*	فضة

1 Gender

Arabic nouns are classified as either feminine or masculine.[1] The gender category into which a noun falls is semantically arbitrary, except where a noun refers to a human being or other creature, when it normally conforms with natural gender. From the point of view of word structure, or morphology, the masculine form is the simplest and most basic shape, whereas feminine nouns usually have a suffix that marks their gender. For the most part, gender is overtly marked, but there are a few words whose gender is covert (see cryptomasculine and cryptofeminine nouns) and shows up only in agreement sequences.

---

[1] A very few nouns can be either masculine or feminine. See section 1.4 "dual gender nouns."

1.1 Masculine nouns

This is the base category, consisting of a vast range of nouns including male human beings and other living creatures, abstract and concrete nouns, and proper names. As a very general rule, if an Arabic noun does not have a feminine suffix, it is masculine.

river	*nahr*	نهر	minister	*waziir*	وزير
council	*majlis*	مجلس	progress	*taqaddum*	تقدم
proof	*burhaan*	برهان	peace	*salaam*	سلام

1.1.1 Masculine proper names

1.1.1.1 PERSONAL NAMES: Arabic male given names are considered masculine, even though some of them end with *taaʾ marbuuTa* or *ʾalif*:

Makram	*makram*	مكرم	Osama	*ʾusaama*	أسامة
Amin	*ʾamiin*	أمين	Moses	*muusaa*	موسى
Fouad	*fuʾaad*	فؤاد	Mustafa	*muSTafaa*	مصطفى

1.1.1.2 COUNTRIES: Country names are usually feminine, but there are a few masculine ones, including:

Morocco	*al-maghrib*	المغرب	Jordan	*al-ʾurdunn*[2]	الأردن
Iraq	*al-ʿiraaq*	العراق	Sudan	*al-suudaan*	السودان
Lebanon	*lubnaan*	لبنان			

1.1.2 Cryptomasculine nouns

A few words look overtly feminine because they are spelled with *taaʾ marbuuTa*, but they are actually masculine. Some of these are plural or collective forms. Some examples include:

Singular:

great scholar	*ʿallaama*[3]	علاّمة	Caliph	*khaliifa*	خليفة

---

[2] Wehr (1979) identifies the country of Jordan (*al-ʾurdunn*) as either masculine or feminine. As the name of the River Jordan, it is strictly masculine.

[3] This pattern, *faʿʿaala* فعّالة, is one that implies greatness or intensity. Another example is 'globe-trotter' *raHHaala* رحّالة.

Plural:

Pharaohs (pl.)	*faraaᶜina*	فراعنة	brothers	*ʾixwa*	إخوة
doctors (m. pl.)	*dakaatira*	دكاترة	students	*Talaba*	طلبة
Shiites (coll.)	*shiiᶜa*	شيعة	great men	*rijaalaat*[4]	رجالات

1.2 Feminine nouns

Most feminine nouns are marked by the *taaʾ marbuuTa* suffix (prounounced -*ah* or -*a* in pause form). Some of the most common categories for feminine nouns are: female human beings, female creatures, abstract concepts, individual units of naturally occurring classes (e.g., banana, tree), names of cities, names of most countries, and parts of the body that come in pairs (e.g., legs, hands, eyes).

1.2.1 Common nouns

picture	*Suura*	صورة	tribe	*qabiila*	قبيلة
storm	*ᶜaaSifa*	عاصفة	meal	*wajba*	وجبة

1.2.2 Concepts

Arabism	*ᶜuruuba*	عروبة	trust	*thiqa*	ثقة
culture	*thaqaafa*	ثقافة	civilization	*HaDaara*	حضارة

1.2.3 Abstract ideas

diversification	*taᶜaddudiyya*	تعددية	importance	*ʾahammiyya*	أهمّية
stardom	*nujuumiyya*	نجومية	freedom	*Hurriyya*	حرية

1.2.4 Instances (a single instance of an action)

a convulsion	*zaᶜzaᶜa*	زعزعة	a shipment	*shaHna*	شحنة
a coincidence	*Sudfa*	صدفة	a burst of laughter	*qahqaha*	قهقهة

1.2.5 Unit nouns (individual units of larger collective entities)

a tree	*shajara*	شجرة	a fish	*samaka*	سمكة
a grape	*ᶜinaba*	عنبة	a thorn	*shawka*	شوكة

---

[4] This is a "plural of a plural." (See section 3.2.5 for details on this structure.)

1.2.6 Cities

Names of cities are considered feminine because the Arabic word for 'city' is *madiina*, a feminine word. This is true for all cities, not just Arab cities.

Tunis	*tuunis*	تونس	Beirut	*bayruut*	بيروت
Cairo	*al-qaahira*	القاهرة	Paris	*baariis*	باريس
Jerusalem	*al-quds*	القدس	London	*landan*	لندن

Certain cities have titles or epithets which reflect the feminine gender of the city name. For example:

Medina "the Enlightened"	*al-madiinat-u l-munawwarat-u*	المدينة المنورة
Mecca "the Venerable"	*makkat-u l-mukarramat-u*	مكّة المكرّمة
Tunis "the Verdant"	*tuunis-u l-xaDraaʾ-u*	تونس الخضراء

1.2.7 Countries

Most countries are considered feminine, especially if their names end in *-aa*. Exceptions are noted above in section 1.1.1.2. Some examples of feminine gender countries are:

Egypt	*miSr*	مصر	America	*ʾamriikaa*	أمريكا
Syria	*suuriyaa*	سوريا	China	*al-Siin*	الصين
France	*faransaa*	فرنسا	Spain	*ʾisbaanyaa*	إسبانيا

Examples of phrases:

Muslim Spain	*ʾisbaanyaa l-muslimat-u*	إسبانيا المسلمة
North America	*ʾamriikaa l-shimaaliyyat-u*	أمريكا الشمالية
ancient Egypt	*miSr-u l-qadiimat-u*	مصر القديمة

1.2.8 Female proper names

Names of women and girls are considered feminine since they refer to female human beings. They may or may not end with *taaʾ marbuuTa*. Female names are diptote.

Zahra	*zahra*	زهرة	Zeinab	*zaynab*	زينب
Alia	*ʿaaliya*	عالية	Selma	*salmaa*	سلمى
Karima	*kariima*	كريمة	Hanan	*Hanaan*	حنان

1.2.9 Nouns spelled with final *taaʾ*

Two common words that are feminine by nature but spelled with a final *taaʾ* (rather than *taaʾ marbuuTa*):

daughter; girl	*bint*	بنت	sister	*ʾuxt*	أخت

1.2.10 Parts of the body

Certain parts of the body are considered feminine although not marked with *taaʾ marbuuTa*, especially those parts that come in pairs. For example:

foot	*qadam*	قدم	hand	*yad*	يد
eye	*ʿayn*	عين	ear	*ʾudhun*	أذن

1.2.11 Borrowed nouns

Nouns ending with an *-ah* or *-aa* sound, and which are borrowed from other languages, are usually treated as feminine:

doctorate (Fr. 'doctorat')	*duktuuraah*	دكتوراه
cinema (Fr. 'cinéma')	*siinamaa*	سينما
music	*muusiiqaa*	موسيقى
opera	*ʾuubiraa*	أوبرا
delta (Greek 'delta')	*daltaa*[5]	دلتا

1.2.12 Other feminine suffixes

Some nouns are marked feminine by suffixes other than *taaʾ marbuuTa*. These endings include: *ʾalif* plus *hamza* (-*aaʾ* اء) or *ʾalif Tawiila* (-*aa* ا) or *ʾalif maqSuura* (-*aa* ى). These endings are suffixed **after** the root consonants.[6] For example:

desert (root: *S-H-r*)	*SaHraaʾ*	صحراء
remembrance (root: *dh-k-r*)	*dhikraa*	ذكرى
universe; world (root: *d-n-y*)	*dunyaa*	دنيا

---

[5] As in *daltaa l-niil-i* 'the Nile Delta.'

[6] Note that there are also a number of masculine nouns that end with *ʾalif* plus *hamza*, *ʾalif Tawiila*, or *ʾalif maqSuura*. The *ʾalif* ending in those instances represents the final defective consonant of the lexical root and **is not an affix**. Some of these masculine nouns include:

song (root: *gh-n-y*)	*ghinaaʾ*	غناء
meaning (root: *ʿ-n-y*)	*maʿnan*	معنىً
stream (root: *j-r-y*)	*majran*	مجرىً
formal legal opinion (root: *f-t-y*)	*fatwaa*	فتوى

beautiful woman; belle (root: *H-s-n*)	*Hasnaaʾ*	حسناء
candy (root: *H-l-w*)	*Halwaa*	حلوى
fever (root *H-m-m*)	*Hummaa*	حمّى
chaos (root *f-w-D*)	*fawDaa*	فوضى

1.2.13 Cryptofeminine nouns

A few nouns are not overtly marked for feminine gender and yet are feminine. This is a small, defined set and includes:

bride	*ʿaruus*	عروس	self; soul	*nafs*	نفس
mother	*ʾumm*	أم	wine	*xamr*	خمر
fire	*naar*	نار	well	*biʾr*	بئر
house	*daar*	دار	cup	*kaʾs*	كأس
earth; ground; land	*ʾarD*	أرض	sun	*shams*	شمس
war	*Harb*	حرب	tooth; age	*sinn*	سن

Examples of cryptofeminine nouns and modifiers:

the afterlife	*al-daar-u l-ʾaaxirat-u*	الدار الآخرة
the Holy Land	*al-ʾarD-u l-muqaddasat-u*	الأرض المقدسة
common ground	*ʾarD-un mushtarakat-un*	أرض مشتركة
the First World War	*al-Harb-u l-ʿaalamiyyat-u l-ʾuulaa*	الحرب العالمية الأولى
in a deep well	*fii biʾr-in ʿamiiqat-in*	في بئر عميقة

1.3 Natural gender nouns

Many nouns that refer to human beings or other living creatures have both a masculine and a feminine form. They vary in gender depending on the nature of the referent, just as English has pairs of words such as "host" and "hostess." The general rule is that the masculine is the base form and the feminine is denoted by the addition of *taaʾ marbuuTa*. Examples of some of these include:

king/queen	*malik/malika*	ملك/ملكة
artist (m/f)	*fannaan/fannaana*	فنّان/فنّانة
ambassador/ambassadress	*safiir/safiira*	سفير/سفيرة

manager (m/f)	mudiir/mudiira	مدير/مديرة
grandfather/grandmother	jadd/jadda	جدّ/جدّة
cat (m/f)	qiTT/qiTTa	قطّ/قطّة
leopard (m/f)	namir/namira	نمر/نمرة

1.4 Dual gender nouns

A very small number of Arabic nouns are either masculine or feminine.[7] They can be treated syntactically as either one, although feminine agreement predominates in the data gathered for this study. There are not many nouns in this group, but some of them are fairly frequent:

market	suuq	سوق	spirit	ruuH	روح
road; path	Tariiq	طريق	sky	samaa'	سماء
bag	kiis	كيس	tongue	lisaan	لسان
salt	milH	ملح	condition	Haal	حال

Examples:

the black market	al-suuq-u l-sawdaa'-u	السوق السوداء
the Arab spirit	al-ruuH-u l-ʿarabiyyat-u	الروح العربية
in good condition	fii Haal-in jayyidat-in	في حال جيدة

2 Humanness

A unique and important morpho-semantic feature of Arabic nouns is humanness, that is, whether or not they refer to human beings. This is a crucial grammatical point for predicting certain kinds of plural formation and for purposes of agreement with other components of a phrase or clause. The grammatical criterion of humanness applies **only to nouns in the plural**.

2.1 Agreement

Agreement with nouns in the plural depends on whether the noun refers to human beings.

2.1.1 Nonhuman referent

If a plural noun refers to nonhuman entities, be they creatures or inanimate things, it takes **feminine singular** agreement. This is sometimes referred to as "deflected" agreement.[8] This applies to agreement with verbs, adjectives, and also pronouns.

---

[7] See Wright 1967, II:181–83 for a comprehensive list of dual gender nouns.
[8] See Belnap and Shabaneh 1992 on this topic.

الذئاب الرمادية
al-dhiʾaab-u l-ramaadiyyat-u
the gray wolves

حميره الهزيلة
Hamiir-u-hu l-haziilat-u
his scrawny donkeys

مخلوقات مفيدة جدا
maxluuqaat-un mufiidat-un jidd-an
very beneficial creatures

الفنون المعاصرة
al-funuun-u l-muʿaaSirat-u
contemporary arts

أشهر قليلة
ʾashhur-un qaliilat-un
a few months

في الأعوام الأخيرة
fii l-ʾaʿwaam-i l-ʾaxiirat-i
in the last years

2.1.2 Human referent

When the referent of the plural noun is human, then the agreement is straight-forward, using masculine or feminine plural forms as appropriate:

السفراء العرب
al-sufaraaʾ-u l-ʿarab-u
the **Arab** ambassadors

الخلفاء الراشدون
al-xulafaaʾ-u l-raashid-uuna
the **orthodox** caliphs

قادة عسكريون
qaadat-un ʿaskariyy-uuna
military leaders

النساء المتقدّمات في السن
al-nisaaʾ-u l-mutaqaddimaat-u fii l-sinn-i
women of **advanced** age

الإخوان المسلمون
al-ʾixwaan-u l-muslim-uuna
the **Muslim** Brotherhood ('Brothers')

أحد السكان الأصليّين
ʾaHad-u l-sukkaan-i l-ʾaSliyy-iina
one of the **indigenous** residents

2.1.3 Special cases

2.1.3.1 GROUPS OF HUMANS AS ABSTRACTIONS: Sometimes, although the noun referents are human, they are being referred to as abstractions, and thus the plural is treated as a nonhuman plural:

السلطات الرومانية
al-suluTaat-u l-ruumaaniyyat-u
the **Roman authorities**

جميع أسرهم الكريمة
jamiiʿ-u ʾusar-i-him-i l-kariimat-i
all their **distinguished families**

من أهم الشخصيات النسائية في التاريخ
min ʾahamm-i l-shaxSiyyaat-i l-nisaaʾiyyat-i fii l-taariix-i
among the most important **female personalities** in history

هناك فئات كثيرة من الشعب تعيش تحت الأرض
hunaaka fiʾaat-un kathiirat-un min-a l-shaʿb-i taʿiish-u taHt-a l-ʾarD-i
There are **many groups of people** [who] **live** underground.

فإن الغالبية انخرطت في جدل عنيف

fa-ʾinna l-ghaaⅼibiyyat-a nxaraT-at fii jadal-in ʿaniif-in

but **the majority plunged** into violent debate

قتلت خمسة أشخاص على الأقل.

qutil-at xamsat-u ʾashxaaS-in ʿalaa l-ʾaqall-i.[9]

At least **five persons were killed.**

2.1.3.2 'PEOPLE' WORDS: shaʿb شعب AND naas ناس

(1) *shaʿb* شعب: The word *shaʿb* 'people' although semantically plural, is usually treated as masculine singular, as a collective noun. Its plural, *shuʿuub*,
'peoples' is treated as a nonhuman plural with feminine singular
agreement:

مثل أي شعب آخر

mithl-a ʾayy-i shaʿb-in ʾaaxar-a

like any **other people**

الشعوب العربية والإسلامية

*al-shuʿuub-u l-ʿarabiyyat-u wa-l-
ʾislaamiyyat-u*

the Arab and Islamic **peoples**

مجرد شعوب وثنية

mujarrad-u shuʿuub-in wathaniyyat-in

mere **pagan peoples**

باركها الشعب كله.

baarak-a-haa l-shaʿb-u kull-u-hu.

All **the people** blessed it.

(2) *naas* ناس: The word *naas* 'people' has inconsistent agreement patterns.
From the triliteral root *ʾ-n-s*, and related to the words إنسان *ʾinsaan* 'human
being,' and آنسة *ʾaanisa* 'young lady,' it refers to people or folk in general.
Sometimes its agreement patterns follow the rules for words referring to
human beings, i.e., the agreement is masculine plural; other times (even
in the same text) it may be treated as an abstraction and the agreement is
feminine singular:

(2.1) **Plural agreement:**

الطليان ناس شرفاء.

al-Talyaan-u naas-un shurafaaʾ-u.

The Italians **are noble (pl.) people.**

فالناس يتناولون أنواعاً مختلفة من الأغذية.

fa-l-naas-u ya-tanaawal-uuna ʾanwaaʿ-an muxtalifat-an min-a l-ʾaghdhiyat-i.

People eat (pl.) different sorts of food.

---

[9] The agreement here is not with the feminine form of the number, since it is actually masculine
(agreeing via reverse gender with the singular of ʾashxaaS, shaxS).

(2.2)   Feminine singular agreement:

وكثير من **الناس** لا **تأكل** أغذية إلا من مصـادر نباتية.

*wa-**kathiir-un** min-a l-naas-i laa **ta-ʾkul-u** ʾaghdhiyat-an ʾillaa min maSaadir-a nabaatiyyat-in.*

Many **people** only **eat** (f. sg.) food from plant sources ('do not eat food except from plant sources').

2.2 Form of the noun plural

Certain plural patterns are used only with **nouns that denote human beings.**

2.2.1 The sound masculine plural

engineer/s	*muhandis/muhandis-uuna*	مهندس/مهندسون
cook/s	*Tabbaax/Tabbaax-uuna*	طبّاخ/طبّاخون
Omani/s	*ʿumaaniyy/ʿumaaniyy-uuna*	عماني/عمانيون
Lebanese	*lubnaaniyy/lubnaaniyy-uuna*	لبناني/لبنانيون

2.2.2 Broken plurals of certain patterns

a. *fuʿalaaʾ*

president/s	*raʾiis/ruʾasaaʾ*	رئيس/رؤساء
ambassador/s	*safiir/sufaraaʾ*	سفير/سفراء
prince/s	*ʾamiir/ʾumaraaʾ*	أمير/أمراء

b. *ʾafʿilaaʾ*

friend/s	*Sadiiq/ʾaSdiqaaʾ*	صديق/أصدقاء
doctor/s	*Tabiib/ʾaTibbaaʾ*	طبيب/أطباء

c. *fuʿʿaal*

writer/s	*kaatib/kuttaab*	كاتب/كتّاب
student/s	*Taalib/Tullaab*	طالب/طلاّب
guard/s	*Haaris/Hurraas*	حارس/حرّاس

2.2.3 Human/nonhuman homonyms

Sometimes two nouns may look identical (i.e., they are homonyms) but have different meanings, one human and one nonhuman, and so the plural is different, according to the noun referent:

worker/s	*ᶜaamil/ᶜummaal*	عامل/عمّال
factor/s	*ᶜaamil/ ᶜawaamil*	عامل/عوامل

3 Number

Arabic nouns are marked for three different kinds of number: **singular, dual, and plural**. Because Arabic has a special morphological category for the dual, plural in Arabic refers to three or more. The singular is considered the base form of the noun, and the dual and plural are extensions of that form in various ways.

3.1 The dual (*al-muthannaa* المثنى)

Arabic has a separate number category for two of anything. Instead of using the number "two" (*ithnaani* إثنان or *ithnataani* إثنتان) plus the plural noun, as does English ("two hands"), Arabic uses a dual suffix on the singular stem to mark the noun as being dual (e.g., *yad-aani* 'two hands'). The suffix has two case forms, the case being signaled by the change of the long vowel in the suffix from /-aa-/ to /-ay-/:

-aani (nominative)

-ayni (genitive/accusative)

Nominative:

وصل سفيران.
*waSal-a **safiir-aani**.*
Two ambassadors arrived.

Genitive:

بين سفيرين
*bayn-a **safiir-ayni***
between **two ambassadors**

Accusative:

زاروا السفيرين.
zaar-uu l-safiir-ayni.
They visited **the two ambassadors**.

3.1.1 Dual with *taaʾ marbuuTa*

When the dual suffix is added to a noun ending in *taaʾ marbuuTa*, the *taaʾ marbuuTa* is no longer the final letter in the word and it turns into regular *taaʾ*.

a year	*sanat-un*	سنة
two years	*sanat-aani*	سنتان
in (after) two years	* baʿd-a sanat-ayni*	بعد سنتين
a city	*madiinat-un*	مدينة
two cities	*madiinat-aani*	مدينتان
in two cities	*fii madiinat-ayni*	في مدينتين

3.1.2 Dual plus *waaw* or *yaaʾ*

When the dual suffix is added to certain words that are biliteral in origin, or to words in the defective declension, a *waaw* or *yaaʾ* is inserted before the dual suffix:[10]

أبوان	أخوان	محاميان
ʾab-a-w-aani	*ʾax-a-w-aani*	*muHaamiy-aani*
parents	two brothers	two lawyers

قاضيان	مقهيان	مستشفيان
qaaDiy-aani	*maqhay-aani*	*mustashfay-aani*
two judges	two cafés	two hospitals

3.1.3 Definiteness in the dual

One of the features of the dual suffix is that it shows no distinction between definite and indefinite. It cannot be marked for nunation.[11]

two smugglers	*muharrib-aani*	مهرّبان
the two smugglers	*al-muharrib-aani*	المهرّبان
with two smugglers	*maʿ-a muharrib-ayni*	مع مهرّبين
with the two smugglers	*maʿ-a l-muharrib-ayni*	مع المهرّبين

3.1.4 *Nuun*-deletion in *ʾiDaafa*

If a dual noun is the first term of an *ʾiDaafa* or annexation structure, the *nuun* plus *kasra* (/-ni/ نِ) of the dual suffix is deleted. Thus, -*aani* becomes -*aa* and -*ayni* becomes -*ay*.[12]

---

[10] Whether the additional consonant is *waaw* or *yaaʾ* depends on the root consonants and on derivational morphology. See Abboud and McCarus 1983, Part 2: 14–17.

[11] The dual suffixes -*aani* and -*ayni* as well as the sound masculine plural suffixes -*uuna* and -*iina* both terminate with the consonant *nuun*, followed by a short vowel, and this feature behaves to a certain extent as a form of nunation (being deleted if the noun has a possessive pronoun suffix, for instance). Additional nunation is not used for these suffixes.

[12] In Arabic annexation structures, there is a general prohibition on the first term (the *muDaaf*), against noun suffixes ending with an -*n* sound. This applies to nunation (indefiniteness marking), to the dual suffix, and to the sound masculine plural.

وزيرا العدل والإعلام

waziir-aa l-ʿadl-i wa l-ʾiʿlaam-i

the two ministers of Justice and Information

لـوزيري الخـارجية

li-waziir-ay-i l-xaarijiyyat-i

for the two foreign ministers

في سياستي الدفاع والتجارة

fii siyaasat-ay-i l-difaaʿ-i wa l-tijaarat-i[13]

in the two policies of defense and trade

في يومي السبت والأحد

fii yawm-ay-i l-sabt-i wa-l-ʾaHad-i

on the two days of Saturday
and Sunday

شقة مكونة من غرفتي نوم

shaqqat-un mukawwanat-un min ghurfat-ay nawm-in

a two-bedroom apartment ('an apartment consisting of two bedrooms')

3.1.5 *Nuun*-deletion with pronoun suffix

The same process occurs when a noun in the dual gets a possessive pronoun
suffix. The *-ni* of the dual suffix is deleted and the possessive pronoun suffix is
attached directly to the *-aa* or *-ay* of the dual suffix. For example:

بين يديه

bayn-a yad-ay-hi

in front of him ('between his two hands')

من جـانبيه

min jaanib-ay-hi

from its two sides

تفتح ذراعيها.

ta-ftaH-u dhiraaʿ-ay-haa.

She opens her arms.

وصل مندوباه.

waSal-a manduub-aa-hu.

His two delegates arrived.

3.1.6 Dual agreement

When a noun in the dual is modified by an adjective, is referred to by a pronoun,
or is the subject of a following verb, then these form classes conform to the dual
inflection as well. Thus, the concept of dual is present not only in nouns, but in
adjectives, pronouns and verbs. These are discussed separately under each of the
form-class headings, but here are some examples:

هناك موضوعان مهمان.

hunaaka mawDuuʿ-aani muhimm-aani.

There are two important subjects.

خلال السنتين الماضيتين

xilaal-a l-sanat-ayni l-maaDiyat-ayni

during the past two years

خـادم الحرمين الشريفين

xaadim-u l-Haram-ayni l-shariif-ayni[14]

the Servant of the two Holy Places

بين هاذين الحدثين

bayn-a haadh-ayni l-Hadath-ayni

between these two events

---

[13] In this and the following phrases the *-ay* dual ending is given a "helping vowel" *kasra* because of
the consonantal nature of the *-y* ending on the dual suffix *-ay*, in order to help pronunciation and
liaison with the following word. (See Wright 1967, I:21 on this point.)

[14] A traditional title of the ruler of Saudi Arabia.

3.2 The Plural (*al-jam*ᶜ الجمع)

Arabic nouns form their plurals in three ways. Two of these are "external" plurals
consisting of suffixes added to the singular stem (the sound feminine and sound
masculine plurals). The third way of pluralizing occurs inside the noun stem itself
(the "broken" or internal plural), shifting the arrangement of vowels, and sometimes inserting an extra consonant or two. To add to this diversity, a noun may
have two or three (or more) alternative plurals.

3.2.1 The sound feminine plural (*jam*ᶜ *mu*ʾ*annath saalim* جمع مؤنث سالم)

This form of plural is very common and applies to an extensive range of Arabic
noun classes, both human and nonhuman. It consists of a suffix *-aat* (ات-) attached
to the singular stem of the noun. Note that when this suffix is attached to a noun
that has *taa*ʾ *marbuuTa* in the singular, it **replaces** the *taa*ʾ *marbuuTa*:

power/s	*quwwa/* *quww-aat*	قوة/قوات	station/s	*maHaTTa/* *maHaTT-aat*	محطة/محطات
oasis/-es	*waaHa/* *waaH-aat*	واحة/واحات	society/ies	*mujtama*ᶜ/ *mujtama*ᶜ*-aat*	مجتمع/مجتمعات
company/ies	*sharika/* *sharik-aat*	شركة/شركات	airport/s	*maTaar/* *maTaar-aat*	مطار/مطارات

3.2.1.1 INFLECTION OF THE SOUND FEMININE PLURAL: The sound feminine plural
suffix has a special declension of its own. It inflects for definiteness (definite and
indefinite) and for case, but only shows two case variations instead of the normal
three: / -u/ or /-un/ for nominative and /-i/ or /-in/ for genitive/accusative. **The sound
feminine plural ending never takes *fatHa* / -a/.** For inflectional paradigms see
section 5.4.2.1, subsection (3), in this chapter.

Nominative:

companies	*sharik-aat-un*	شركاتٌ
the companies	*al-sharik-aat-u*	الشركاتُ

Genitive:

in companies	*fii sharik-aat-in*	في شركاتٍ
in the companies	*fii l-sharik-aat-i*	في الشركاتِ

Accusative:

He founded companies.	ʾ*assas-a sharik-aat-in.*	أسس شركاتٍ.
He founded the companies.	ʾ*assas-a l-sharik-aat-i.*	أسس الشركاتِ.

Examples:

يجري اتصالات.	لسنا مصريات.
*yu-jrii **ttiSaal-aat-in**.*	*las-na **miSriyy-aat-in**.*
He is implementing **contacts**.	We (f.) are not **Egyptian**.

3.2.1.2 VARIANTS: BUFFER SOUNDS INSERTED BEFORE SOUND FEMININE PLURAL SUFFIX:

Some nouns insert a *waaw* or *yaa'* or a *haa'* on the noun stem before affixing the */-aat/* ending. Most of these nouns end in the singular with a vowel or *'alif-hamza*, but some end with *taa'* or *taa' marbuuTa*:

(1) *waaw* insertion:

(1.1) Two common bi-consonantal nouns insert *waaw* before the *-aat* ending:

sister/s   *'uxt/ 'axa-w-aat*   أخت/أخوات   year/s   *sana/sana-w-aat*   سنة/سنوات

(1.2) Certain borrowed words ending in *'alif Tawiila* take the sound feminine plural with *waaw* as buffer between the two *'alifs*. Note that even though the referents of these nouns are human males, the plural is sound feminine.

pasha/s	*baashaa/baashaa-w-aat*	باشا/باشاوات
pope/s	*baabaa/baabaa-w-aat~baaba-w-aat*	بابا/باباوات ~ بابوات

(1.3) Nouns ending in the suffix *-aa'* often drop the final *hamza* and add a *waaw* between the stem and suffix:[15]

green (f.)/greens (vegetables)	*xaDraa' /xaDraa-w-aat*	خضراء/خضراوات
desert/s[16]	*SaHraa' /SaHraa-w-aat*	صحراء/صحراوات
parrot/s	*babbaghaa' /babbaghaa-w-aat*	ببّغاء/ببغاوات

(1.4) Nouns ending in *'alif* plus *taa' marbuuTa* usually shorten *'alif* to *fatHa*, and add a *waaw*:

channel/s; canal/s	*qanaat/qana-w-aat*	قناة/قنوات
prayer/s	*Salaat/ Sala-w-aat*	صلاة/صلوات

(2) *yaa'* insertion: Nouns that end with with *'alif maqSuura* shorten the *'alif* to *fatHa* and insert *yaa'* before the sound feminine plural suffix:

memory/ies	*dhikraa/dhikra-y-aat*	ذكرى/ذكريات
sweet/s	*Halwaa/Halwa-y-aat*	حلوى/حلويات

---

[15] Note that if the *hamza* in the *-aa'* ending is part of the root, then the *hamza* is not deletable, as in: *'ijraa'aat* إجراءات.

[16] Alternative plurals for *SaHraa'* are *SaHaaraa* صحارى and *SaHaar-in* صحار.

fever/s	*Hummaa/Humma-y-aat*	حمّى/حمّيات
level/s	*mustawan/mustawa-y-aat*	مستوى/مستويات
hospital/s	*mustashfan/mustashfa-y-aat*	مستشفى/مستشفيات

(3) ***haa'* insertion:** The word *'umm,* 'mother' inserts a *haa'* preceded by *fatHa* before suffixing the sound feminine plural:[17]

| mother/s | *'umm/ 'umm-ah-aat* | أمّ/أمّهات |

Borrowed words ending with a long vowel (especially *-uu*) often insert *haa'* as a buffer before the /-aat/ suffix in order to avoid two long vowels coming together:

casino/s	*kaaziinuu/kaaziinuu-h-aat*	كازينو/كازينوهات
radio/s	*raadyuu/raadyuu-h-aat*	راديو/راديوهات
studio/s	*(i)stuudyuu/(i)stuudyuu-h-aat*	ستوديو(١)/ستوديوهات(١)

3.2.1.3 WHERE THE SOUND FEMININE PLURAL IS USED: The following categories describe the types of nouns which make their plural using the sound feminine plural suffix *-aat.* Some categories are general, like number 1, and some are specific, like 3 and 4. In some cases there is more than one form of the plural. This is by no means an exhaustive list, but covers major categories.

(1) **Many (but not all) nouns ending in *taa' marbuuTa*:**

embassy/ies	*sifaara/sifaar-aat*	سفارة/سفارات
government/s	*Hukuuma/Hukuum-aat*	حكومة/حكومات
language/s	*lugha/lugh-aat*	لغة/لغات
ticket/s	*biTaaqa/biTaaq-aat~baTaa' iq*	بطاقة/بطاقات ~ بطائق
pharmacy/ies	*Saydaliyya/Saydaliyy-aat*	صيدلية/صيدليات
continent/s	*qaarra/qaarr-aat*	قارة/قارات
barracks	*thukna/thukn-aat~thukan*	ثكنة/ثكنات ~ ثكن

(1.1) **Vowel variation:** Feminine nouns ending with *taa' marbuuTa* or *taa'* that have *sukuun* on the second radical, often use the sound feminine plural with a slight internal vowel change, usually a shift to an additional vowel inserted after the second radical. When the original short vowel is *fatHa* or

---

[17] The word *'umm,* in addition to meaning literally 'mother,' also has abstract meanings such as 'source, origin, original version, essence.' See Wehr 1979 for examples and details.

kasra, the change tends to be to *fatHas*; if the short vowel is *Damma*, then the *Damma* may be copied or there may be a change to *fatHas*.

service/s	*xidma/xidam-aat~xidam*	خدمة/خدمات ~ خدم
experience/s	*xibra/xibar-aat*	خبرة/خبرات
girl/s; daughter/s	*bint/ban-aat*	بنت/بنات
session/s	*jalsa/jalas-aat*	جلسة/جلسات
sister/s	*ʾuxt/ ʾaxaw-aat*	أخت/أخوات
circle/s; ring/s	*Halqa/Halaq-aat*	حلقة/حلقات
authority/ies	*sulTa/suluT-aat*	سلطة/سلطات

(2) **Nouns referring strictly to female human beings.** Many of these nouns are actually participles used as substantives (nouns). Some denote professions, but others are simply common nouns. When the sound feminine plural is used to refer to groups of human beings, it only denotes **exclusively female groups.**[18]

lady/ies	*sayyida/sayyid-aat*	سيدة/سيدات
queen/s	*malika/malik-aat*	ملكة/ملكات
actress/es	*mumaththila/mumaththil-aat*	ممثلة/ممثلات
professor/s (f.)	*ʾustaadha/ ʾustaadh-aat*	أستاذة/أستاذات
customer/s (f.)	*zabuuna/zabuun-aat*	زبونة/زبونات
Muslim/s (f.)	*muslima/muslim-aat*	مسلمة/مسلمات
expert/s (f.)	*xabiira/xabiir-aat*	خبيرة/خبيرات

(3) **Verbal nouns from derived forms II–X of triliteral roots and also from Forms I–IV of quadriliteral roots.** These verbal nouns all take the sound feminine plural, even though most of them are masculine in the singular. In the Form II verbal noun, the *-aat* plural often alternates with a broken plural.[19]

Verbal nouns from triliteral roots:

| arrangement/s | II. *tartiib/tartiib-aat* | ترتيب/ترتيبات |
| negotiation/s | III. *mufaawaDa/mufaawaD-aat* | مفاوضة/مفوضات |

---

[18] If even one human male is present within the group, the masculine plural form is used.

[19] The optional Form II plural is usually of the **CaCaaCiiC** pattern. See section 3.2.3.2, subsection (4.1.4), in this chapter.

announcement/s	IV. *ʾiʿlaan/ ʾiʿlaan-aat*	إعلان/إعلانات
tension/s	V. *tawattur/tawattur-aat*	توتّر/توترات
exchange/s	VI. *tabaadul/tabaadul-aat*	تبادل/تبادلات
reflection/s	VII. *inʿikaas/ inʿikaas-aat*	انعكاس/انعكاسات
discovery/ies	VIII. *iktishaaf/iktishaaf-aat*	اكتشاف/اكتشافات
investment/s	X. *istithmaar/istithmaar-aat*	استثمار/استثمارات

Verbal nouns from quadriliteral roots:

mumbling/s	I. *hamhama/hamham-aat*	همهمة/همهمات
decline/s	II. *tadahwur/tadahwur-aat*	تدهور/تدهورات
serenity/ies	IV. *iTmiʾnaan/iTmiʾnaan-aat*	اطمئنان/اطمئنانات

The *nisba* of derived form verbal nouns, when functioning as a noun referring to nonhuman entities, also takes the sound feminine plural, e.g.,
'reserve/s' *iHtiyaaTiyy* احتياطيّ/*iHtiyaaTiyy-aat* احتياطيّات.

(4) **Active (AP) and passive (PP) participles of Form I that do not denote
human beings,** even though they may be masculine in the singular. Note
that some Form I participles have an alternate broken plural form.
Examples:

plan/s	I PP: *mashruuʿ/* *mashruuʿ-aat~mashaariiʿ*	مشروع/~ات~مشاريع
manuscript/s	I PP: *maxTuuT/maxTuuT-aat*[20]	مخطوط/مخطوطات
implication/s	I PP: *madluul/madluul-aat*	مدلول/مدلولات
topic/s	I PP: *mawDuuʿ/* *mawDuuʿ-aat~mawaaDiiʿ*	موضوع/~ات~مواضيع
creature/s	I PP: *maxluuq/maxluuq-aat*	مخلوق/مخلوقات
revenue/s	I AP: *ʿaaʾid/ʿaaʾid-aat*	عائد/عائدات
import/s	I AP: *waarid/waarid-aat*	وارد/واردات
duty/ies	I AP: *waajib/waajib-aat*	واجب/واجبات
being/s	I AP: *kaaʾin/kaaʾin-aat*	كائن/كائنات
menu/s; list/s	I AP: *qaaʾima/qaaʾim-aat ~ qawaaʾim*	قائمة/قائمات~قوائم

---

[20] The singular occurs both as *maxTuuT* مخطوط and *maxTuuTa* مخطوطة.

(5) **Active (AP) and passive (PP) participles of the derived verb forms (II–X) and quadriliterals if they do not refer to human beings.** These nouns may be either masculine or feminine in the singular.

volume/s	II PP: *mujallad/mujallad-aat*	مجلّد/مجلّدات
foundation/s	II PP: *muʾassasa/muʾassas-aat*	مؤسّسة/مؤسّسات
drug/s	II AP: *muxaddir/muxaddir-aat*	مخدّر/مخدّرات
note/s	II AP: *mudhakkira/mudhakkir-aat*	مذكّرة/مذكّرات
establishment/s	IV PP: *munshaʾa/munshaʾ-aat*	منشأة/منشآت
ocean/s	IV AP: *muHiiT/muHiiT-aat*	محيط/محيطات
change/s	V PP: *mutaghayyar/mutaghayyar-aat*	متغيّر/متغيّرات
synonym/s	VI AP: *mutaraadif/mutaraadif-aat*	مترادف/مترادفات
slope/s	VII PP *munHaDar/munHaDar-aat*	منحضر/منحضرات
conference/s	VIII PP: *muʾtamar/muʾtamar-aat*	مؤتمر/مؤتمرات
level/s	VIII PP: *mustawan/mustaway-aat*	مستوىً/مستويات
settlement/s	X PP: *mustawTana/mustawTan-aat*	مستوطنة/مستوطنات
hospital/s	X PP: *mustashfan/mustashfay-aat*	مستشفىً/مستشفيات
swamp/s	X PP: *mustanqaᶜ/mustanqaᶜ-aat*	مستنقع/مستنقعات
camp/s	Quad PP: *muᶜaskar/muᶜaskar-aat*	معسكر/معسكرات
explosive/s	Quad AP: *mufarqiᶜ /mufarqiᶜ-aat*	مفرقع/مفرقعات

Note that of course, participles of any verb form that refer (strictly) to female human beings will also take the sound feminine plural, in accordance with the rule in 3.2.1.3(2) above:

teacher/s (f.)	II AP: *mudarrisa/mudarris-aat*	مدرّسة/مدرّسات
citizen/s (f.)	III AP: *muwaaTina/muwaaTin-aat*	مواطنة/مواطنات
supervisor/s (f.)	IV AP: *mushrifa/mushrif-aat*	مشرفة/مشرفات
specialist/s (f.)	V AP: *mutaxaSSisa/mutaxaSSis-aat*	متخصصة/متخصصات
consumer/s (f.)	X AP: *mustahlika/mustahlik-aat*	مستهلكة/مستهلكات

(6)   With most (but not all) **loanwords borrowed directly from a foreign language into Arabic.**[21]

computer/s	*kumbiyuutir/kumbiyutir-aat*	كمبيوتر/كمبيوترات
telephone/s	*talifuun/talifuun-aat*	تلفون/تلفونات
taxi/s	*taaksii/taaksiiy-aat*	تاكسي/تاكسيات
dollar/s	*duulaar/duulaar-aat*	دولار/دولارات
hormone/s	*hurmuun/hurmuun-aat*	هرمون/هرمونات
virus/es	*fiiruus/fiiruus-aat*	فيروس/فيروسات
liter/s	*liitir/liitir-aat*	ليتر/ليترات
lord/s	*luurd/luurd-aat*[22]	لورد/لوردات

(7)   **The tens numbers (twenty through ninety), when referring to decades,** such as the "twenties" and "sixties." Note that the/ -aat/ plural suffix is **attached to the genitive/accusative form of the word stem (/-iin/, not /-uun/).**

sixty/sixties	*sittiina/sittiin-aat*	ستّين/ستّينات
seventy/seventies	*sabᶜiina/sabᶜiin-aat*	سبعين/سبعينات
ninety/nineties	*tisᶜiina/tisᶜiin-aat*	تسعين/تسعينات

(8)   **Feminine proper names** even if they do not end in *taaʔ marbuuTa:*

Zeinab/s	*zaynab/zaynab-aat*	زينب/زينبات
Amira/s	*ʔamiira/ ʔamiir-aat*	أميرة/أميرات

(9)   **Names of the letters of the alphabet:**

ʔalif/s	*ʔalif /ʔalif-aat*	ألف/ألفات
raaʔ/s	*raaʔ/raaʔ-aat*	راء/راءات
waaw/s	*waaw/waaw-aat*	واو/واوات

---

[21] Some examples of borrowed nouns with Arabic broken plurals are:

bank/s	*bank/bunuuk*	بنك/بنوك
ton/s	*Tann/ ʔaTnaan*	طنّ/أطنان
million/s	*milyuun/malaayiin*	مليون/ملايين
mile/s	*miil/ ʔamyaal*	ميل/أميال
meter/s	*mitr/ ʔaamtaar*	متر/أمتار

[22] As in *majlis-u l-luurdaat-i* 'The House of Lords.'

(10) **Names of the months**: There are three sets of names of the months used in Arabic: two sets for the solar calendar (one based on Semitic names and one on borrowed European names) and one for the lunar Muslim calendar.[23] All months make their plural with -*aat*.

April/s	*niisaan/niisaan-aat*	نيسان/نيسانات
July/s	*tammuuz/tammuuz-aat*	تموز/تموزات
Ramadan/s	*ramaDaan/ramaDaan-aat*	رمضان/رمضانات
Shawwal/s	*shawwaal/shawwaal-aat*	شوّال/شوّالات
December/s	*disambir/disambir-aat*	دسمبر/دسمبرات

(11) **Feminine adjectives that stand on their own as substantives**: for example, the feminine relative or *nisba* adjectives (adjectives ending in -*iyya*). Adjectives take the sound feminine plural when referring strictly to female human beings.

Yemeni/s (f.)	*yamaniyya/yamaniyy-aat*	يمنية/يمنيات
Tunisian/s (f.)	*tuunisiyya/tuunisiyy-aat*	تونسية/تونسيات
Arab/s (f.)	*ʿarabiyya/ ʿarabiyy-aat*	عربية/عربيات

(12) **Other**: The sound feminine plural is used on a number of other nouns that do not clearly fall into the above categories. One especially frequent use is with nouns whose final syllable contains a long /-*aa*-/ in the singular.

airport/s	*maTaar/maTaar-aat*	مطار/مطارات
orbit/s	*madaar/madaar-aat*	مدار/مدارات
field/s	*majaal/majaal-aat*	مجال/مجالات
animal/s	*Hayawaan/Hayawaan-aat*	حيوان/حيوانات
activity/ies	*nashaaT/nashaaT-aat*[24]	نشاط/نشاطات
decision/s	*qaraar/qaraar-aat*	قرار/قرارات
spice/s	*bahaar/bahaar-aat*	بهار/بهارات
security, guarantee/s	*Damaan/Damaan-aat*	ضمان/ضمانات
bath/s	*Hammaam/Hammaam-aat*	حمّام/حمّامات
current/s	*tayyaar/tayyaar-aat*	تيار/تيارات

---

[23] For complete sets of the Arabic names of months in the lunar and solar calendars see Ryding 1990, 409.

[24] Also *ʾanshiTa* أنشطة.

waterfall/s	*shallaal/shallaal-aat*	شلّال / شلّالات
call/s	*nidaaʾ /nidaaʾ-aat*	نداء / نداءات
folder/s	*milaff/milaff-aat*	ملفّ / ملفّات
location/s	*maHall/maHall-aat*	محلّ / محلّات

3.2.2 The sound masculine plural (*jam⁽ mudhakkar saalim* جمع مذكر سالم)

The sound masculine plural is much more restricted in occurrence than the sound feminine plural because, almost without exception, **it only occurs on nouns and adjectives referring to male human beings or mixed groups of male and female human beings.**[25]

3.2.2.1 INFLECTION OF THE SOUND MASCULINE PLURAL: This type of plural takes the form of a suffix that attaches to the singular noun (or adjective): *-uuna* (nominative) or *-iina* (genitive/accusative).

(1) **Case:** The sound masculine plural shows overtly only two case inflections instead of three. Note that the long vowel in the suffix (*-uu-* or *-ii-*) is the case marker, and is what changes when the case changes.[26] The short vowel ending (*fatHa*) (*-a*) remains the same in both the nominative and the genitive/accusative. This *fatHa* is not a case ending, but rather part of the spelling of the suffix. In pause form it is not pronounced. Examples:

observers (nom.)	*muraaqib-uuna*	مراقبون
observers (gen./acc.)	*muraaqib-iina*	مراقبين
surgeons (nom.)	*jarraaH-uuna*	جرّاحون
surgeons (gen./acc.)	*jarraaH-iina*	جرّاحين

(2) **Definiteness:** One of the features of the sound masculine plural suffix is that, like the dual suffix, there is no distinction between definite and indefinite:

assistants	*musaaⁱid-uuna*	مساعدون
the assistants	*al-musaaⁱid-uuna*	المساعدون
with assistants	*maⁱa musaaⁱid-iina*	مع مساعدين
with the assistants	*maⁱa l-musaaⁱid-iina*	مع المساعدين

[25] Exceptions are very few and include, for example, *ʾarD/* أرض-*ʾaraDuun* أرضون - 'land/s.' The noun *ʾarD* has a more common plural, however: *ʾaraaD-in* أراض.

[26] Arab grammarians consider the long vowel of the sound masculine plural as the inflectional vowel, the one that indicates case.

3.2.2.2 *Nuun*-DELETION:

(1) **As first term of *ʾiDaafa*:** A distinctive feature of the sound masculine plural suffix, like the dual suffix, is that because its final consonant is a *nuun*, the *nuun* and its vowel, *fatHa*, are deleted if the noun is the first term of an *ʾiDaafa* (annexation structure).[27] The long vowel of the suffix (-*uu*- or -*ii*-) is then left as the final element of the word.

فلسطينيّو الخارج	من متخرجي الجامعة
filisTiiniyy-uu l-xaarij-i	min ***mutaxarrij-ii*** *l-jaamiʿat-i*
Palestinians abroad	from the university **graduates**
مواطنو أوربا الغربية	بمسلمي شمال إفريقيا
muwaaTin-uu ʾuurubbaa l-gharbiyyat-i	bi-***muslim-ii*** *shimaal-i ʾ ifraaqiyaa*
the **citizens** of Western Europe	with the **Muslims** of North Africa
لمديري المنظمات	محبو العلم
*li-**mudiir-ii** l-munaZZamaat-i*	***muHibb-uu*** *l-ʿilm-i*
for the **administrators** of the organizations	**lovers** of knowledge
متابعو اللعبة	بنو قريش
mutaabiʿ-uu l-laʿbat-i	***ban-uu*** *quraysh-in*
followers of the game	Quraysh tribe (literally: 'the **sons** of Quraysh')

(2) **With a pronoun suffix:** Likewise, when a noun with the sound masculine plural is suffixed with a possessive pronoun, the *nuun* and short vowel /-a/ of the suffix are deleted:

from its supporters	*min muʾayyid-**ii-hi***	من مؤيديه
for their nominees	*li-murashshaH-**ii-him***	لمرشحيهم
our delegates	*manduub-**uu-naa***	مندوبونا
its publishers	*naashir-**uu-haa***	ناشروها
our sons	*ban-**uu-naa***	بنونا

3.2.2.3 WHERE THE SOUND MASCULINE PLURAL IS USED:
The following categories show the types of nouns which form their plural using the sound masculine suffix. Some categories are general, like number 1, and some are specific, like 3 and 4. This is not an exhaustive list, but covers major categories.

---

[27] See note 12 in this chapter.

(1)   **Participles as nouns**: Participles acting as substantives (nouns) often take the sound masculine plural when referring to human males or mixed groups of male and female.

(1.1)   **Form I**: Some Form I participle nouns take the sound masculine plural, but most take a broken plural (see section 3.2.3.1, subsection (1.2)) when referring to male human beings or mixed male/female groups. Some examples of the sound masculine plural are:

official/s	I PP: *mas'uul/mas'uul-uuna*	مسؤول/مسؤولون
researcher/s	I AP: *baaHith/baaHith-uuna*	باحث/باحثون
speaker/s	I AP: *naaTiq/naaTiq-uuna*	ناطق/ناطقون

(1.2)   **Forms II–X**: Derived form (II–X) triliteral and quadriliteral active and passive participles that refer to human males take the sound masculine plural:

Form II:

nominee/s	II PP: *murashshaH/murashshaH-uuna*	مرشّح/مرشحون
actor/s	II AP: *mumaththil/mumaththil-uuna*	ممثّل/ممثلون

Form III:

reporter/s	III AP: *muraasil/muraasil-uuna*	مراسل/مراسلون
citizen/s	III AP: *muwaaTin/muwaaTin-uuna*	مواطن/مواطنون
observer/s	III AP: *muraaqib/muraaqib-uuna*	مراقب/مراقبون

Form IV:

Muslim/s	IV AP: *muslim/muslim-uuna*	مسلم/مسلمون
attaché/s	IV PP: *mulHaq/mulHaq-uuna*	ملحق/ملحقون
manager/s	IV AP: *mudiir/mudiir-uuna*	مدير/مديرون
guide/s	IV AP: *murshid/murshid-uuna*	مرشد/مرشدون

Form V:

narrator/s	V AP: *mutakallim/mutakallim-uuna*	متكلّم/متكلمون
extremist/s	V AP: *mutaTarrif/mutaTarrif-uuna*	متطرّف/متطرفون
volunteer/s	V AP: *mutaTawwiʕ/mutaTawwiʕ-uuna*	متطوّع/متطوعون
rebel/s	V AP: *mutamarrid/mutamarrid-uuna*	متمرّد/متمردون

Form VI:

optimist/s	VI AP: *mutafaa'il/mutafaa'il-uuna*	متفائل/متفائلون
pessimist/s	VI AP: *mutashaa'im/mutashaa'im-uuna*	متشائم/متشائمون

Form VII: rare

Form VIII:

voter/s; elector/s	VIII AP: *muntaxib/muntaxib-uuna*	منتخب/منتخبون
listener/s	VIII AP: *mustamiᶜ /mustamiᶜ-uuna*	مستمع/مستمعون

Form IX: rare

Form X:

consumer/s	X AP: *mustahlik/mustahlik-uuna*	مستهلك/مستهلكون
renter/s	X AP: *mustaʾjir/mustaʾjir-uuna*	مستأجر/مستأجرون

(1.3) **Quadriliterals:**

engineer/s	QIAP: *muhandis/muhandis-uuna*	مهندس/مهندسون
translator/s	QIAP: *mutarjim/mutarjim-uuna*	مترجم/مترجمون

(2) **Names of professions:** Certain nouns in Arabic refer to those who engage in professions or other pursuits. The pattern is **CaCCaaC** (*faᶜᶜaal* فعّال). The masculine form of these nouns takes the sound masculine plural:

baker/s	*xabbaaz/xabbaaz-uuna*	خبّاز/خبّازون
hunter/s	*Sayyaad/Sayyaad-uuna*	صيّاد/صيّادون
money-changer/s	*Sarraaf/Sarraaf-uuna*	صرّاف/صرّافون
coppersmith/s	*naHHaas/naHHaas-uuna*	نحّاس/نحّاسون

(3) **Alternation with broken plural:** Sometimes the sound masculine plural alternates with a broken plural:

son/s	*ibn/ ʾabnaaʾ ~ban-uuna*	ابن/أبناء ~ بنون
director/s	*mudiir/ mudaraaʾ ~ mudiir-uuna*	مدير/مدراء ~ مديرون

(4) **Noun *nisbas*:** Nisba or relative adjectives may also function as nouns, in which case, if they refer to human males or mixed groups, they are often pluralized with the sound masculine plural:[28]

Lebanese	*lubnaaniyy/lubnaaniyy-uuna*	لبنانيّ/لبنانيّون
European/s	*ʾuurubbiyy/ʾuurubbiyy-uunaa*	أوربيّ/أوربيّون

---

[28] Some exceptions to this include the words for 'Arab,' 'bedouin,' and 'foreigner' which take broken plurals: *ᶜarabiyy/ ᶜarab* عربيّ/عرب, *badawiyy/badw* بدويّ/بدو, and *ʾajnabiyy/ ʾajaanib* أجنبيّ/ أجانب.

electrician/s	*kahrabaa'iyy/ kahrabaa'iyy-uuna*	كهربائيّ/كهربائيّون
statistician/s	*'iHSaa'iyy/'iHSaa'iyy-uuna*	إحصائيّ/إحصائيّون
politician/s	*siyaasiyy/siyaasiyy-uuna*	سياسيّ/سياسيّون
country dweller/s	*riifiyy/riifiyy-uuna*	ريفيّ/ريفيّون

(5) **Numbers in tens:** The tens numbers include the sound masculine plural suffix as part of their word structure. It inflects just as the regular sound masculine plural, *-uuna* for nominative and *-iina* for genitive/accusative.

twenty	*'ishruuna*	عشرون	sixty	*sittuuna*	ستّون
thirty	*thalaathuuna*	ثلاثون	seventy	*sab'uuna*	سبعون
forty	*'arba'uuna*	أربعون	eighty	*thamaanuuna*	ثمانون
fifty	*xamsuuna*	خمسون	ninety	*tis'uuna*	تسعون

علي بابا والأربعون لصّاً

'aliyy baabaa wa-l-'arba'-uuna liSS-an

Ali Baba and the **forty** thieves

في عشرين مجلداً

fii 'ishr-iina mujallad-an

in **twenty** volumes

بمشاركة ثلاثين باحثا

bi-mushaarakat-i thalaath-iina baaHith-an

with the participation of **thirty** researchers

If a plural is needed for these terms ("forties," "fifties," the sound feminine plural is suffixed to the genitive/accusative form of the number (see above 3.2.1.3(7)). For more on numerals, see Chapter 15.

3.2.3 The broken plural (*jam' al-taksiir* جمع التكسير)

The broken or internal plural is highly characteristic of Arabic nouns and adjectives. It involves a shift of vowel patterns within the word stem itself, as in English "man/men," "foot/feet" or "mouse/mice." It may also involve the affixation of an extra consonant (usually *hamza* or *waaw*). The relationship between singular nouns and their broken plural forms relates to syllable and stress patterns, so that there is often a characteristic rhythm to the singular/plural doublet when said aloud.

The structure and regularities of the Arabic broken plural system have been the subject of research in morphological theory over the past fifteen years, and considerable progress has been made in developing theories to identify and account for the underlying regularities in the broken plural system, the most prominent of those theories being templatic morphology and prosodic morphology.[29]

For nonnative speakers of Arabic, learning which nouns take which plurals can take some time, but if singulars and plurals are learned as doublets and grouped together, sound patterns of vowel–consonant distribution become evident and, at least to some extent, ascertainable. The most common broken plural patterns are listed here under triptote (fully inflected) and diptote (partially inflected) categories. (For the nature of diptote inflection see section 5.4.2.2 in this chapter.) Wherever possible, specific vowel patterns are identified.

Where patterns are more general, consonant–vowel structures are also given, using the convention that the symbol V stands for any vowel and VV for any long vowel. The letter C stands for any consonant.[30]

3.2.3.1 TRIPTOTE PATTERN PLURALS (*jam‘ mu‘rab* جمع معرب): These broken plural patterns are fully inflectable. They show all three case markers and can take nunation when indefinite.

(1) **Broken plural patterns with internal vowel change only:**

(1.1) **Plural: CuCuuC (*fu‘uul* فعول) from singular: CaCC (*fa‘l* فعل) or CaCiC (*fa‘il* فعل)**

The CuCuuC plural pattern is a frequent one, especially for plurals of geminate root Form I verbal nouns:

right/s	*Haqq/Huquuq*	حقّ/حقوق
doubt/s	*shakk/shukuuk*	شكّ/شكوك
art/s	*fann/funuun*	فنّ/فنون
army/ies	*jaysh/juyuush*	جيش/جيوش
century/ies	*qarn/quruun*	قرن/قرون
king/s	*malik/muluuk*	ملك/ملوك

---

[29] See, for example, McCarthy and Prince 1990a and 1990b, Paoli 1999, and Ratcliffe 1990. In particular, see Ratcliffe 1998 for an extensive analysis of Arabic broken plurals within comparative Semitic. As he describes it, it is "a historical and comparative study of a portion of the nominal morphology of Arabic and other Semitic languages on the basis of a fresh theoretical approach to non-concatenative or 'root and pattern' morphology" (1998, 1). As to the abundance of broken plural forms, Lecomte notes (1968, 72–73): "Le problème des pluriels internes est fort complexe, et rebelle à toute explication décisive. On notera toutefois que la fixation a été opérée par les lexicographes anciens aux IIe et IIIe siècles de l'Hegire à la suite de minutieuses enquêtes dans les tribus. Les différences dialectales constituent donc une des clés du problème. Elles expliquent en tout cas pourquoi les dictionnaires peuvent signaler plusieurs pluriels pour un même mot."

[30] For an extensive list and discussion of broken plural patterns, see Wright 1967, I:199–234. For further lists and analysis of broken plurals, see also Abboud and McCarus 1983, Part 2: 267–76; Blachère and Gaudefroy Demombynes 1975, 166–99; Cowan 1964, 23–28 and 200–202; Fleisch 1961, 470–505; MECAS 1965, 245–46; and Ziadeh and Winder 1957, 102.

A borrowed word that has taken this plural pattern:

bank/s	*bank/bunuuk*	بنك/بنوك

(1.2)   **Plural CuCCaaC (*fuᶜᶜaal* فعّال) from singular: CaaCiC (*faaᶜil* فاعل):** This plural, used with the Form I active participle (m.), is used only for human beings.[31]

deputy/ies	*naaᵓ ib/ nuwwaab*	نائب/نوّاب
worker/s	*ᶜaamil/ ᶜummaal*	عامل/عمّال
reader/s	*qaariᵓ / qurraaᵓ*	قارئ/قرّاء
guard/s	*Haaris/Hurraas~Harasa*	حارس/حرّاس~حرسة
rider/s	*raakib/rukkaab*	راكب/ركّاب
student/s	*Taalib/Tullaab~Talaba*	طالب/طلّاب~طلبة

(1.3)   **Plural CiCaaC (*fiᶜaal* فعال) from singular CVCVC or CVCC (*faᶜal* فعل, *faᶜul* فعل, *faᶜl* فعل)**

man/men	*rajul/rijaal*	رجل/رجال
mountain/s	*jabal/jibaal*	جبل/جبال
sand/s	*raml/rimaal*	رمل/رمال
earthenware jar/s	*jarra/jiraar*	جرّة/جرار
basket/s	*salla/silaal*	سلّة/سلال

(1.4)   **Plural CuCaC (*fuᶜal* فُعَل) from singular CVCCa (*faᶜla, fuᶜla, fiᶜla* فعلة)**

state/s	*dawla/ duwal*	دولة/دول
room/s	*ghurfa/ ghuraf*	غرفة/غرف
sentence/s	*jumla/ jumal*	جملة/جمل
opportunity/ies	*furSa/ furaS*	فرصة/فرص
time period/s	*mudda/mudad*	مدّة/مدد
picture/s	*Suura/Suwar*	صورة/صور
nation/s	*ᵓumma/ᵓumam*	أمّة/أمم

---

[31] For example, the noun *ᶜaamil* in the singular can mean either 'worker' or 'factor.' When it means 'worker' the plural is *ᶜummaal*; when it means 'factor,' the plural is *ᶜawaamil*.

(1.5) Plural CuCuC (*fuʿul* فعل) from singular: CVCVVC(a) (*faʿiil(a)* (ـة)فعيلـ,
       fiʿaal فعال)

city/ies	*madiina/mudun*	مدينة/مدن
ship/s	*safiina/ sufun*	سفينة/سفن
newspaper/s	*SaHiifa/SuHuf*	صحيفة/صحف
path/s	*Tariiq/Turuq*	طريق/طرق
book/s	*kitaab/kutub*	كتاب/كتب
foundation/s	*ʾasaas/ ʾusus*	أساس/أسس

(1.6) Plural CiCaC(*fiʿal* فعل) from singular CiCCa (*fiʿla* فعلة) or CaCiiC
       (*faʿiil* فعيل)

value/s	*qiima/qiyam*	قيمة/قيم
story/ies	*qiSSa/qiSaS*	قصّة/قصص
idea/s	*fikra/fikar*	فكرة/فكر
charm/s; enchantment/s	*fitna/fitan*	فتنة/فتن
team/s	*fariiq/firaq*	فريق/فرق

(1.7) Plural CaCCaa (*faʿlaa* فعلى) from singular CaCiiC (*faʿiil* فعيل) or CaCCiC
       (*faʿʿil* فعل): These plural forms go with certain adjectives that are also
       used as substantives referring to human beings:

dead	*mayyit/mawtaa*	ميّت/موتى
killed	*qatiil/qatlaa*	قتيل/قتلى
wounded	*jariiH/jarHaa*	جريح/جرحى
sick	*mariiD/marDaa*	مريض/مرضى

(2)   **Plurals with vowel change and affixation of consonant:**

(2.1) Plural: ʾaCCaaC (ʾafʿaal أفعال) from singular: CVCC (*faʿl* فعل) or CVCVC
       (*faʿal* فعل) or hollow: CVVC (*faal* فال, *fuul* فول, *fiil* فيل): This plural involves
       the prefixing of *hamza* plus *fatHa* to the word stem and the shift of vowel
       pattern to a long /aa/ between the second and third radicals:

dream/s	*Hulm/ ʾaHlaam*	حلم/أحلام
tower/s	*burj/ ʾabraaj*	برج/أبراج
profit/s	*ribH/ ʾarbaaH*	ربح/أرباح
section/s	*qism/ ʾaqsaam*	قسم/أقسام

thing/s	shay' / 'ashyaa'[32]	شيء/أشياء
color/s	lawn/ 'alwaan	لون/ألوان
error/s	ghalaT/ 'aghlaaT	غلط/أغلاط
foot/feet	qadam/ 'aqdaam	قدم/أقدام
door/s	baab/ 'abwaab	باب/أبواب
market/s	suuq/ 'aswaaq	سوق/أسواق
bag/s	kiis/ 'akyaas	كيس/أكياس
holiday/s	ʿiid/ 'aʿyaad	عيد/أعياد

Borrowed words that fit the pattern:

film/s	film/ 'aflaam	فلم/أفلام
ton/s	Tann/ 'aTnaan	طن/أطنان
mile/s	miil/ 'amyaal	ميل/أميال

Variants:

| day/s | yawm/ 'ayyaam[33] | يوم/أيّام |
| thousand/s | 'alf / 'aalaaf | ألف/آلاف |

(2.2)   **Plurals of 'paucity': 'aCCuC ('af ʿul أفعل) *and* CiCCa (f iʿla فعلة)**
(jamʿ al-qilla جمع القلّة): Certain nouns have an additional plural form
which denotes a 'plural of paucity,' usually considered to be in the range
of three to ten items:

river/s	nahr/ 'anhur	نهر/أنهر
month/s	shahr/ 'ashhur	شهر/أشهر
youth/s	fatan/fitya	فتىً/فتية

(2.2.1)   The plural of paucity can be contrasted with *jamʿ al-kathra* جمع الكثرة, the
plural that indicates many:

'anhur (a few rivers)	'anhaar~nuhuur (many rivers)	أنهر/أنهار ~ نهور
'ashhur (a few months)	shuhuur (many months)	أشهر/شهور
fitya (a few youths)	fityaan (many youths)	فتية/فتيان

---

[32] The plural *'ashyaa'* 'things' is diptote despite the fact that the final *hamza* is part of the root. See
section 5.4.2.2 in this chapter for further discussion of diptotes and diptote patterns.

[33] By virtue of phonological rules that prevent the sequence /-yw-/ in **'aywaam*, the plural form
becomes *'ayyaam*, with assimilation of the *waaw* to the *yaa'*. Likewise, **'a' laaf* is realized as *'aalaaf*
in order to avoid the sequence /'a'/. Other plurals of this pattern include 'literature' *'adab/
'aadaab* أدب/آداب and 'vestige' *'athar/ 'aathaar* أثر/آثار.

(2.3) Addition of *nuun*: Plural: CVCCaan (*faʿlaan* فعلان/*fiʿlaan* فعلان/*fuʿlaan* فعلان):

country/ies	*bilaad/buldaan*	بلاد/بلدان
neighbor/s	*jaar/jiiraan*[34]	جار/جيران
fire/s	*naar/niiraaan*	نار/نيران
worm/s	*duuda/diidaan*	دودة/ديدان
bull/s	*thawr/thiiraan*	ثور/ثيران

(2.4) **Addition of *taaʾ marbuuTa*:** Sometimes a *taaʾ marbuuTa* is suffixed as part of a plural pattern. When used with the plural, it does not signify feminine gender.

(2.4.1) **Plural CaCaaCiCa (*faʿaalila* فعاللة).** This is often used to pluralize names of groups or professions borrowed from other languages:

professor/s	*ʾustaadh / ʾasaatidha*	أستاذ/أساتذة
doctor/s	*duktuur/dakaatira*	دكتور/دكاترة
philosopher/s	*faylusuuf/falaasifa*	فيلسوف/فلاسفة
Bolshevik/s	*bulshifiyy/balaashifa*	بلشفي/بلاشفة
African/s	*ʾifriiqiyy/ʾafaariqa~ ʾifriiqiyy-uuna*	إفريقي/أفارقة~إفريقيون
pharaoh/s	*firʿawn/faraaʿina*	فرعون/فراعنة
bishop/s	*ʾusquf/ʾasaafiqa~ʾasaaqif*	أسقف/أساقفة ~ أساقف

(2.4.2) **Plural CaaCa (*faala* فالة):** Used with nouns derived from hollow verbs:

sir/s	*sayyid/saada*	سيّد/سادة
leader/s	*qaaʾ id/qaada*	قائد/قادة

(2.4.3) **Plural CuCaat (*fuʿaat* فعاة):** Used with active participles of Form I defective verbs:

infantryman/infantry	*maashin/mushaat*	ماشٍ/مشاة
judge/s	*qaaDin/quDaat*	قاضٍ/قضاة
reciter/s	*raawin/ruwaat*	راوٍ/رواة

---

[34] Phonological rules prevent the sequence /-iw-/ in the hypothetical form **jiwraan*, and it is realized as *jiiraan*, the /i/ sound assimilating the *waaw*. The same principle applies to *naar/niiraan* and others.

| marksman/-men | *raamin/rumaat* | رامٍ/رُماة |
| dilettante/s; fan/s | *haawin/huwaat* | هاوٍ/هواة |

(2.4.4)   **Plural CaCaCa** (*faʿala* فعلة) **from singular CaaCiC:** This plural often alternates with CuCCaaC.

student/s	*Taalib/Talaba~Tullaab*	طالب/طلبة ~ طلاب
servant/s	*xaadim/xadama~xuddaam*	خادم/خدمة ~ خدام
guard/s	*Haaris/Harasa~Hurraas*	حارس/حرسة ~ حراس

(2.4.5)   **Plural ʾaCCiCa** (*ʾafʿila* أفعلة) **from singular CVCaaC** (*faʿaal* فعال, *fiʿaal* فعال): In this broken plural pattern there is addition of both *hamza* at the start of the word and *taaʾ marbuuTa* at the end of the word:

carpet/s	*bisaaT /ʾabsiTa ~ busuT*	بساط/أبسطة ~ بسط
answer/s	*jawaab/ʾajwiba*	جواب/أجوبة
clothes	*libaas /ʾalbisa*	لباس/ألبسة
mixture/s	*mizaaj/ʾamzija*	مزاج/أمزجة
brain/s	*dimaagh/ʾadmigha*	دماغ/أدمغة

(2.4.6)   **Plural CaCaayaa** (*faʿaayaa* فعايا): This plural is used for certain feminine nouns, especially if they are defective or hamzated. It is invariable, always ending with *ʾalif*.

gift	*hadiyya/hadaayaa*	هدية/هدايا
sin	*xaTiiʾa/xaTaayaa*	خطيئة/خطايا
corner	*zaawiya/zawaayaa*	زاوية/زوايا

3.2.3.2 Diptote pattern broken plural (*mamnuuʿ min al-Sarf* ممنوع من الصرف): A number of common plural patterns are diptote and belong to conjugation five (see section 5.4.2.2). Among them are the following:

(1)   **Plural: CuCaCaaʾ** (*fuʿalaaʾ* فعلاء) **from singular: CaCiiC** (*faʿiil* فعيل): This plural is used only for human beings:

prince/s	*ʾamiir/ ʾumaraaʾ*	أمير/أمراء
president/s	*raʾiis/ ruʾasaaʾ*	رئيس/رؤساء
minister/s	*waziir/ wuzaraaʾ*	وزير/وزراء
leader/s	*zaʿiim/ zuʿamaaʾ*	زعيم/زعماء

| expert/s | *xabiir/xubaraaʾ* | خبير/خبراء |
| poor person/s | *faqiir/fuqaraaʾ* | فقير/فقراء |

(2) **Plural ʾaCCiCaaʾ** (*ʾafʿilaaʾ* أفعلاء) **from singular CaCiiC** (*faʿiil* فعيل). This broken plural pattern prefixes and suffixes *hamza*. It is used with humans only:

physician/s	*Tabiib/ ʾaTibbaaʾ*[35]	طبيب/أطباء
friend/s	*Sadiiq/ ʾaSdiqaaʾ*	صديق/أصدقاء
relative/s	*qariib/ʾaqribaaʾ*	قريب/أقرباء
loved one/s	*Habiib/ ʾaHibbaaʾ*	حبيب/أحباء

(3) **Plural CaCaaCiC** (*faʿaalil* فعالل). This is a frequent plural pattern. It is used primarily with words that have four consonants in the singular, but can also be used for plurals of words with three consonants in the singular. It has a number of variations, as follows:

(3.1) **Nouns derived from triliteral roots where the singular has a prefixed *miim*. For example:**

(3.1.1) **Nouns of place:**

center/s	*markaz/ maraakiz*	مركز/مراكز
kingdom/s	*mamlaka/ mamaalik*	مملكة/ممالك
restaurant/s	*maTʿam/maTaaʿim*	مطعم/مطاعم
mine/s	*manjam/manaajim*	منجم/مناجم

(3.1.2) **Nouns of instrument:**

towel/s	*minshafa/manaashif*	منشفة/مناشف
broom/s	*miknaas/makaanis*	مكناس/مكانس
elevator/s	*miSʿad/maSaaʿid*	مصعد/مصاعد

(3.1.3) **Participles: (Form IV AP nonhuman):**

| problem/s | *mushkila/ mashaakil* | مشكلة/مشاكل |

(3.2) **Other patterns of triliteral roots with added consonants:**

| ladder/s | *sullam /salaalim* | سلم/سلالم |
| foreigner/s | *ʾajnabiyy / ʾajaanib* | أجنبي/أجانب |

---

[35] Phonological rules prevent the sequence *ʾaTbibaaʾ, so the medial /i/ shifts and the form becomes *ʾaTibbaaʾ*.

middle part/s	ʾawsaT/ʾawaasiT	أوسط/أواسط
ticket/s	tadhkira/tadhaakir	تذكرة/تذاكر
fingertip/s	ʾunmula/ ʾanaamil	أنملة/أنامل

(3.3)   **Nouns derived from quadriliteral roots:**

frog/s	Dafdaʿ /Dafaadiʿ	ضفدع/ضفادع
element/s	ʿunSur/ ʿanaaSir	عنصر/عناصر
hotel/s	funduq/fanaadiq	فندق/فنادق
dagger/s	xanjar/xanaajir	خنجر/خناجر
bomb/s	qunbula/ qanaabil	قنبلة/قنابل
translation/s	tarjama/taraajim	ترجمة/تراجم

(3.4)   **Nouns that are borrowed from other languages, but fit the pattern:**

consul/s	qunSul/qanaaSil	قنصل/قناصل

(3.5)   **Certain quinquiliteral (five-consonant) nouns** reduce themselves by one consonant in order to fit this quadriliteral plural pattern:

spider/s	ʿankabuut/ ʿanaakib (omission of /t/)	عنكبوت/عناكب
program/s	barnaamaj/baraamij (omission of /n/)	برنامج/برامج
index/es	fihrist/fahaaris (omission of /t/)	فهرست/فهارس

(3.6)   **Variants on *faʿaalil* فعالل:**
A frequent variant on this plural pattern is the insertion of an extra sound in order to create the pattern: *waaw* or *hamza*, typically from singular CVCVVC or CVCVVCa:

(3.6.1)   **Plural CaCaaʾiC (*faʿaaʾil* فعائل): medial *hamza* insertion:**

newspaper/s	jariida/ jaraaʾid	جريدة/جرائد
minute/s	daqiiqa/ daqaaʾiq	دقيقة/دقائق
result/s	natiija/ nataaʾij	نتيجة/نتائج
church/es	kaniisa/ kanaaʾis	كنيسة/كنائس
garden/s	Hadiiqa/Hadaaʾiq	حديقة/حدائق
ode/s	qaSiida/qaSaaʾid	قصيدة/قصائد

(3.6.2)   **Plural ʾaCaaCiC (*ʾafaaʿil* أفاعل): initial *hamza* insertion:**

place/s	makaan/ ʾamaakin	مكان/أماكن
relative/s	qariib/ʾaqaarib	قريب/أقارب

(3.6.3) **Plural CawaaCiC (*fawaaⁱil* فواعل): *waaw* insertion:**

(3.6.3.1) **Active participles**

Used primarily with Form I active participles (**CaaCiC** or **CaaCiCa**) that do not refer to human beings:

salary/ies	*raatib/rawaatib*	راتب/رواتب
objection/s	*maaniᶜ / mawaaniᶜ*	مانع/موانع
capital/s	*ᶜaaSima/ ᶜawaaSim*	عاصمة/عواصم
fruit/s	*faakiha/fawaakih*	فاكهة/فواكه
mosque/s	*jaamiᶜ / jawaamiᶜ*	جامع/جوامع
street/s	*shaariᶜ / shawaariᶜ*	شارع/شوارع
ring/s	*xaatim/xawaatim*	خاتم/خواتم
incident/s	*Haadith/Hawaadith*	حادث/حوادث
last part/s	*ʾaaxir/ ʾawaaxir*	آخر/أواخر

(3.6.3.2) Used with a few words that have the Form I active participle pattern and that refer to human beings:

monarch/s	*ᶜaahil/ ᶜawaahil*	عاهل/عواهل
pregnant (one/s)	*Haamil/Hawaamil*	حامل/حوامل

(3.6.4) **Plural CaCaaCin (*faᶜaalin* فعال): defective noun variants:** When the *faᶜaalil* plural pattern is used with nouns from defective roots, or nouns with defective plural patterns, it ends with two *kasras* when it is indefinite. These *kasras* are not regular nunation but substitute for the missing *waaw* or *yaaʾ* from the root. These plural forms are still diptote and therefore do not take regular nunation.[36]

coffeehouse/s	*maqhan/maqaahin*	مقهى/مقاهٍ
range/s	*marman/maraamin*	مرمى/مرامٍ
night/s	*layl/layaalin*[37]	ليل/ليالٍ
effort/s	*masᶜan/masaaᶜin*	مسعى/مساعٍ

(4) **Diptote plural: CaCaaCiiC (*faᶜaaliil* فعاليل).** This is a four-consonant pattern with one short and two long vowels that applies mainly to the following types of singular nouns:

---

[36] See section 5.4.3 in this chapter for declensions of these words.
[37] A few words, such as *layl*, are not from defective roots, yet they have a plural form that uses the defective pattern. The words *ʾarD/ ʾaraaDin* أرض/أراضٍ ('earth, land') and *yad/ʾayaadin* يد/أياد ('hand') have these plurals as well.

(4.1) **Singular CVCCVVC:** Used with words where the singular has an added consonant and there is a long vowel between the second and third root consonants:

(4.1.1) **Prefixed *hamza*:**

pipe/s	ʾunbuub/ ʾanaabiib	أنبوب/أنابيب
week/s	ʾusbuuᶜ / ʾasaabiiᶜ	أسبوع/أسابيع
legend/s	ʾusTuura/ ʾasaaTiir	أسطورة/أساطير
fleet/s	ʾusTuul/ ʾasaaTiil	أسطول/أساطيل

(4.1.2) **Doubled middle root consonant:**

| window/s | shubbaak/shabaabiik | شبّاك/شبابيك |
| prayer rug/s | sajjaada/sajaajiid | سجّادة/سجاجيد |

(4.1.3) **Prefixed *miim*:**

(4.1.3.1) **Passive participles:** Form I passive participles serving as substantives:

decree/s	marsuum/maraasiim	مرسوم/مراسيم
topic/s	mawDuuᶜ / mawaaDiiᶜ	موضوع/مواضيع
concept/s	mafhuum/mafaahiim	مفهوم/مفاهيم
content/s	maDmuun/maDaamiin	مضمون/مضامين

(4.1.3.2) **Some nouns of instrument:**

| key/s | miftaaH/mafaatiiH | مفتاح/مفاتيح |
| saw/s | minshaar/manaashiir | منشار/مناشير |

(4.1.4) **Prefixed *taaʾ*:** Certain Form II verbal nouns as a plural variant:

report/s	taqriir/taqaariir	تقرير/تقارير
arrangement/s	tadbiir/-aat~tadaabiir	تدبير/-ات ~ تدابير
detail/s	tafSiil/-aat~tafaaSiil	تفصيل/-ات ~ تفاصيل
statue/s	timthaal/tamaathiil	تمثال/تماثيل
drill/s	tamriin/-aat~tamaariin	تمرين/-ات ~ تمارين

(4.2) **Quadriliteral root nouns** (singular pattern: CVCCVVC):

crocodile/s	timsaaH/tamaasiiH	تمساح/تماسيح
box/es	Sanduuq/Sanaadiiq	صندوق/صناديق
title/s; address/es	ᶜunwaan/ ᶜanaawiin	عنوان/عناوين

orchard/s	*bustaan/basaatiin*	بستان/بساتين
hornet/s	*zunbuur/zanaabiir*	زنبور/زنابير
volcano/es	*burkaan/baraakiin*	بركان/براكين

(4.3)   **Borrowed words that fit the singular CVCCVVC pattern:**

| million/s | *milyuun/malaayiin* | مليون/ملايين |
| billion/s | *bilyuun/balaayiin* | بليون/بلايين |

(5)   **Plural CawaaCiiC (*fawaaʿiil* فواعيل) from singular CaaCuuC (*faaʿuul* فاعول): variant from triliteral root with addition of *waaw*: This fits a triliteral root with two long vowels into a quadriliteral plural:**

spy/ies	*jaasuus/jawaasiis*	جاسوس/جواسيس
law/s	*qaanuun/qawaaniin*	قانون/قوانين
nightmare/s	*kaabuus/kawaabiis*	كابوس/كوابيس
dictionary/ies	*qaamuus/qawaamiis*	قاموس/قواميس
rocket/s	*Saaruux/Sawaariix*	صاروخ/صواريخ

3.2.4 Plurals from different or modified roots

A few nouns have plurals with different or slightly variant lexical roots.

woman/women	*imraʾa/nisaaʾ ~ niswa ~ niswaan*	امرأة/نساء ~ نسوة ~ نسوان
horse/es	*Hisaan/xayl*	حصان/خيل
water/s	*maaʾ /miyaah*	ماء/مياه
mouth	*fam / ʾafwaah*	فم/أفواه

3.2.5 Plural of the plural: (*jamʿ al-jamʿ* جمع الجمع)

Occasionally a noun will have **a plural form that can itself be made plural.** It is not clear whether there is a semantic difference between simple plural and plural of plural or if the use is purely stylistic choice. Some instances of plural of plural include:

hand/s	*yad / ʾaydِ-in/ʾayaad-in*	يد/أيدٍ/أياد
wound/s	*jurH / juruuH/ juruuHaat*	جرح/جروح/جروحات
path/s	*Tariiq/ Turuq/ Turuqaat*	طريق/طرق/طروقات
house/s	*bayt/ buyuut/ buyuutaat*	بيت/بيوت/بيوتات
pyramid/s	*haram/ ʾahraam/ʾahraamaat*	هرم/أهرام/أهرامات

In the following case, the plural of the plural has a semantic implication: the first plural is straightforward, but the plural of the plural implies distinction as well as plurality: 'distinctive men, men of importance.'

man/men/men of distinction   *rajul/rijaal/rijaalaat*   رجل/رجال/رجالات

4 Definiteness and indefiniteness

Arabic substantives may be marked for definiteness or indefiniteness. There is a definite article in Arabic, but it is not an independent word, it is a prefix *al-*. The indefinite marker ("a" or "an" in English) is not a separate word in Arabic. It is a suffix, *-n*, referred to technically as "nunation" (from the name of the letter/sound *nuun*). Thus, in Arabic, the definiteness marker is attached to the beginning of a word and the indefiniteness marker is attached to the end of a word. They are, of course, mutually exclusive.

4.1 Definiteness

Specifying definiteness, or determination, is a way of specifying or restricting the meaning of a noun. Arabic nouns are determined or made definite in three ways:

(1)   By prefixing the definite article /*al-*/;
(2)   By using the noun as first term of an *'iDaafa* (annexation structure);
(3)   By suffixing a possessive pronoun to the noun.

4.1.1 The definite article /*al-*/:
This function word has several important features:[38]

4.1.1.1 IT IS A PREFIX: It is not an independent word, it is a prefix, or proclitic particle. It is affixed to the beginning of a word and written as part of it.

the bread   *al-xubz*   الخبز

the pyramids   *al-'ahraam*   الأهرام

the joy   *al-faraH*   الفرح

4.1.1.2 IT IS SPELLED WITH *hamzat al-waSl:* Although spelled with *'alif-laam*, and most often transliterated as "al-," the *'alif* in this word is not a vowel and is therefore not pronounced; rather, it is a seat for a *hamza* and a short vowel *-a* (*fatHa*) which is pronounced when the word is utterance-initial.

When the definite article is not the first word in an utterance, then the *hamza* drops out, the /*a*/ vowel is replaced by the vowel that ends the previous word, and

---

[38] For more on the definite and indefinite articles, see Chapter 2, section 8.

there is no break between the words. There is, instead, a liaison, or smooth transition from one word to the next.[39]

to the city	*ʾilaa l-madiinat-i*	إلى المدينة
in Arabic	*bi-l-ʿarabiyyat-i*	بالعربية
the country's flag	*ʿalam-u l-balad-i*	علم البلد
The United Nations	*al-ʾumam-u l-muttaHidat-u*	الأمم المتّحدة

4.1.1.3 ASSIMILATION OF *laam*: The nature of the first letter of a noun or adjective determines the pronunciation of /al-/. The letters of the Arabic alphabet are divided into two sections, one section whose members assimilate the /l/ sound and another section whose members allow the full pronunciation of /l/ of the definite article. See also Chapter 2, section 8.1.2.

(1) **Sun letters** (*Huruuf shamsiyya* حروف شمسية): Certain sounds, or letters, when they begin a word, cause the *laam* of the definite article to assimilate or be absorbed into them in pronunciation (but not in writing). When this assimilation happens, it has the effect of doubling the first letter of the word. That letter is then written with a *shadda*, or doubling marker, and is pronounced more strongly. The list is:

تاء, ثاء, دال, ذال, راء, زاي, سين, شين, صاد, ضاد, طاء, ظاء, لام, نون

taaʾ, thaaʾ, daal, dhaal, raaʾ, zaay, siin, shiin, Saad, Daad, Taaʾ, Zaaʾ, laam, nuun

	Spelling	Arabic	Pronunciation
the leader	al-zaʿiim	الزعيم	az-zaʿiim
the fish	al-samak	السمك	as-samak
the honor	al-sharaf	الشرف	ash-sharaf
the fox	al-thaʿlab	الثعلب	ath-thaʿlab
the wolf	al-dhiʾb	الذئب	adh-dhiʾb

(2) **Moon letters** (*Huruuf qamariyya* حروف قمرية): Moon letters do not absorb or assimilate the /l/ of the definite article. They are:

همزة, باء, جيم, حاء, خاء, عين, غين, فاء, قاف, كاف, ميم, هاء, واو, ياء

hamza, baaʾ, jiim, Haaʾ, xaaʾ, ʿayn, ghayn, faaʾ, qaaf, kaaf, miim, haaʾ, waaw, yaaʾ

---

[39] For further discussion of the definite article and *hamzat al-waSl*, see Chapter 2, section 8.

the village	al-qarya	القرية
the institute	al-maʿhad	المعهد
the schedule	al-jadwal	الجدول
the government	al-Hukuuma	الحكومة

4.1.2 Uses of the definite article

The definite article is used in the following ways:

4.1.2.1 PREVIOUS SPECIFICATION: To specify a noun or noun phrase previously referred to or understood by the reader or hearer. For example:

المركز الجديد الذي أقيم
al-markaz-u l-jadiid-u lladhii ʾuqiim-a
the new center which has been established

وجد في الملعب.
wujid-a fii **l-malʿab-i.**
It was found in **the playground.**

أدرك أنه نسي الكلمة.
ʾadrak-a ʾanna-hu nasiy-a **l-kalimat-a.**
He realized that he had forgotten **the word.**

4.1.2.2 GENERIC USE: Here the definite article is used to specify a noun in general terms. In English, the generic use of the noun often omits the definite article, for example, "life is beautiful," "squirrels like nuts," "elephants never forget," "seeing is believing." Sometimes, also, in English, an indefinite article is used to refer to something in general: "a noun is a part of speech." In Arabic, the definite article is used when referring to something in general.

لا أحب المفاجآت.
I don't like **surprises.**
laa ʾu-Hibb-u **l-mufaaja\ʾaat-i.**

المهم هو العمل.
The important (thing) is **work.**
al-muhimm-u huwa **l-ʿamal-u.**

المنافسة قوية.
Competition is strong.
al-munaafasat-u qawiyyat-un.

أحب التنظيم في العمل.
I like **organization** at **work.**
ʾu-Hibb-u **l-tanZiim-a** fii l-ʿamal-i.

4.1.2.3 PLACE NAMES: Certain place names in Arabic contain the definite article. This includes names of places in the Arab world and elsewhere.

Khartoum	al-xarTuum	الخرطوم	Jordan	al-ʾurdunn	الأردن
Riyadh	al-riyaaD	الرياض	Iraq	al-ʿiraaq	العراق
Cairo	al-qaahira	القاهرة	Kuwait	al-kuwayt	الكويت

| Morocco | *al-maghrib* | المغرب | Austria | *al-nimsaa* | النمسا |
| Algeria | *al-jazaaʾir* | الجزائر | China | *al-Siin* | الصين |

4.1.2.4 NAMES OF THE DAYS OF THE WEEK: Names of the days of the week are considered definite and include the definite article. If they are modified by an adjective, it also carries the definite article:

الثلاثاء الماضي
al-thulaathaaʾ-a l-maaDiy-a
last Tuesday

أيام الجمعة والسبت
ʾayyaam-a l-jumʿat-i wa-l-sabt-i
on Fridays and Saturdays

بعد ظهر الثلاثاء الجاري
baʿd-a Zuhr-i l-thulaathaaʾ-i l-jaarii
next Tuesday afternoon

ليلَ الخميس والجمعة
layl-a l-xamiis-i wa-l-jumʿat-i
on Thursday and Friday night

4.1.2.5 TIMES OF THE DAY: Referring to times of the day, the hours are specified with the definite article:

بين السادسة والثامنة من مساء غد
bayn-a l-saadisat-i wa-l-thaaminat-i min masaaʾ-i ghad-in
between **six and eight** o'clock ('**the sixth and the eighth**') tomorrow evening

في السابعة والربع
fii l-saabiʿat-i wa-l-rubʿ-i
at **seven fifteen** ('**the seventh and the quarter**')

4.1.2.6 WITH ADJECTIVES: The definite article is used with adjectives when they modify definite nouns. This is described in greater detail in Chapter 10.

الأمين العام
al-ʾamiin-u l-ʿaamm-u
the secretary **general**

الهلال الخصيب
al-hilaal-u l-xaSiib-u
the **Fertile** Crescent

الحكاية القديمة
al-Hikaayat-u l-qadiimat-u
the **old** story

البحر المتوسط
al-baHr-u l-mutawassiT-u
the **Mediterranean** Sea

السفراء العرب
al-sufaraaʾ-u l-ʿarab-u
the **Arab** ambassadors

The article is also used on stand-alone adjectives when they serve as substitutes for nouns.

many of us	*al-kathiir-u min-naa*	الكثير منا
the greatest	*al-ʾakbar-u*	الأكبر
at least	*ʿalaa l-ʾaqall-i*	على الأقل

4.1.2.7 WITH CARDINAL NUMBERS IN DEFINITE PHRASES:

في السنوات الخمس المقبلة

fii l-sanawaat-i l-xams-i l-muqbilat-i

in the next five years

في الغرف التسع عشرة

fii l-ghuraf-i l-tisᶜ-a ᶜasharat-a

in the nineteen rooms

4.1.3 Definiteness through annexation (*ʾiDaafa* إضافة)

A noun can become definite through being added or annexed to another (Arabic: *ʾiDaafa* 'addition; annexation' also called the "genitive construct"). The first term of an annexation structure cannot have the definite article because it is made definite by means of its annexation to another noun. When the annexing noun is definite, or a proper noun, the whole phrase is considered definite.

زعماء القبائل

zuᶜamaaʾ-u l-qabaaʾil-i

the leaders of the tribes

حزب الله

Hizb-u llaah-i

the party of God

حلّ المشاكل

Hall-u l-mashaakil-i

the solution of the problems

مدينة دمشق

madiinat-u dimashq-a

the city of Damascus

If the annexing noun (the second noun in the phrase) is indefinite, the entire phrase is considered indefinite:[40]

Haqiibat-u yad-in	a handbag	حقيبة يد
Tabiib-u ʾasnaan-in	a dentist	طبيب أسنان
marmaa Hajr-in	a stone's throw	مرمى حجر

The *ʾiDaafa* is a very common syntactic structure in Arabic with a wide range of meanings, reflecting relationships of belonging, identification, and possession. For more detail and examples, see Chapter 8.

4.1.4 Definiteness through pronoun suffix

A third way for a noun to be made definite is to suffix a possessive pronoun. The pronoun is attached to a noun after the case marker. Note that a noun cannot have both the definite article and a pronoun suffix: they are mutually exclusive (just as one would not have "the my house" in English). Because a noun with a

---

[40] The first noun in the annexation structure *looks* definite because it does not have nunation, but it is not definite. For example, if it is modified, the adjective is indefinite:

| a beautiful handbag | *Haqiibat-u yad-in jamiilat-un* | حقيبة يد جميلة |
| an Egyptian dentist | *Tabiib-u ʾasnaan-in miSriyy-un* | طبيب أسنان مصري |

pronoun suffix is definite, any adjective modifying that noun has the definite article, in agreement with the definiteness of the noun.

طاقتها التكريرية	طاقتها

Taaqat-u-haa **l-takriiriyyat-u** | *Taaqat-u-haa*

its **refining** capacity | its capacity

بدأ مؤتمره الصحافي | بدأ مؤتمره

bada'a mu' tamar-a-hu **l-Sihaafiyy-a** | *bada'a mu'tamar-a-hu*

he began his **press** conference | he began his conference

في زيارته الرسمية الأخيرة | في زيارته

fii ziyaarat-i-hi **l-rasmiyyat-i** **l-'axiirat-i** | *fii ziyaarat-i-hi*

on his **last official** visit | on his visit

4.2 Indefiniteness

4.2.1 Writing and pronunciation: nunation (*tanwiin* تنوين)

Indefiniteness as a noun feature is usually marked by a suffixed /-n/ sound, which is written in a special way as a variation of the case-marking short vowel at the end of a word.[41] The technical term for this is "nunation" in English, and *tanwiin* تنوين in Arabic. The suffixed /-n/ sound is *not* written by using the Arabic letter *nuun*. Instead, it is signaled by writing the short case-marking vowel twice. Therefore, the names of the nunation markers are:

Dammataani	two Dammas	ٌ /
kasrataani	two kasras	ٍ
fatHataani	two fatHas	اً / ً

Whereas the definite article is visible in Arabic script, the indefinite marker normally is not, since it attaches itself to the inflectional short vowel suffixes.[42]

In general, the nominative (*Dammataani*) and genitive (*kasrataani*) forms of nunation are not pronounced in pause form. The accusative (*fatHataani*), however, is often pronounced, even in pause form, especially in common spoken Arabic adverbial phrases:

always	*daa'im-an*	دائماً	especially	*xuSuuS-an*	خصوصاً
never	*'abad-an*	أبداً	exactly	*tamaam-an*	تماماً

---

[41] See also Chapter 2, section 8.2.

[42] The exception to this is the accusative indefinite suffix, *-an*, which is written into the script with an *'alif* and two *fatHas*. See section 4.2.1.5(2) for further description.

4.2.1.1 MASCULINE SINGULAR INDEFINITE WORD:

bayt 'a house'		
Nominative	*bayt-un*	بيتٌ
Genitive	*bayt-in*	بيتٍ
Accusative	*bayt-an*	بيتاً

4.2.1.2 FEMININE SINGULAR INDEFINITE WORD:

ʿaaSifa 'a storm'		
Nominative	*ʿaaSifat-un*	عاصفةٌ
Genitive	*ʿaaSifat-in*	عاصفةٍ
Accusative	*ʿaaSifat-an*	عاصفةً

4.2.1.3 BROKEN PLURAL INDEFINITE WORD:

nujuum 'stars'		
Nominative	*nujuum-un*	نجومٌ
Genitive	*nujuum-in*	نجومٍ
Accusative	*nujuum-an*	نجوماً

4.2.1.4 SOUND FEMININE PLURAL INDEFINITE WORD: The sound feminine plural does not take *fatHa* or *fatHataani*; the genitive and accusative forms are identical:

kalimaat 'words'		
Nominative	*kalimaat-un*	كلماتٌ
Genitive	*kalimaat-in*	كلماتٍ
Accusative	*kalimaat-in*	كلماتٍ

4.2.1.5 NOTES ABOUT NUNATION: There are several things to note about the writing and pronunciation of nunation:

(1) First, the **nominative**, *Dammataan*, is more often written as a *Damma* with a "tail" or flourish, ⬚ rather than two separate *Dammas* ⬚.

a schedule	*jadwal-un*	جدولٌ	a colt	*muhr-un*	مُهرٌ
a steamship	*baaxirat-un*	باخرةٌ	a bell	*jaras-un*	جرسٌ

(2) **Second, the accusative,** *fatHataan*, is often accompanied by an *ʾalif*. This *ʾalif* is a spelling convention and is not pronounced. It is considered to be a chair or seat for the two *fatHas* to perch on. It is visible in Arabic script.

a rocket	*Saaruux-an*	صاروخًا	a knife	*sikkiin-an*	سكينًا
a rabbit	*ʾarnab-an*	أرنبًا	a saddle	*sarj-an*	سرجًا

(2.1) If a word in the accusative ends with a *taaʾ marbuuTa*, or a *hamza*, or preceded by *ʾalif*, then the *ʾalif* "chair" is not used and the *fatHataan* perch right on top of the *hamza* or *taaʾ marbuuTa*:

an evening	*masaaʾ-an*	مساءً	a melon	*baTTixat-an*	بطيخةً
a meeting	*liqaaʾ-an*	لقاءً	a permit	*ʾijaazat-an*	إجازةً
a breeze	*hawaaʾ-an*	هواءً	a language	*lughat-an*	لغةً

Examples:

واكتشف أيضاً أخطاءً.   حضروا لقاءً هامّاً.

wa-ktashaf-a ʾayD-an ʾaxTaaʾ-an.   *HaDar-uu liqaaʾ-an haamm-an.*

He also discovered **mistakes.**   They attended **an important meeting.**

(3) **Helping vowel with nunation:** Because nunation causes the pronunciation of a word to end with a consonant (/-n-/), there may be a need for a helping vowel after the nunation if, for instance, the nunated word is followed directly by a noun or adjective with the definite article thus creating a consonant cluster. That helping vowel is pronounced as *kasra* (/-i-/), but it is not written. Wright, in discussing this form of helping vowel, gives the example:

محمدٌ النبيِّ

muHammad-un-i l-nabiyy-u[43]

Muhammad the Prophet

---

[43] Wright 1967, I:22.

(4)   **Words that do not take nunation:** There are some words that do not take nunation when they are indefinite. This includes words that fall into the diptote declension (see section 5.4.2.2. in this chapter), words that end with the sound masculine plural (*-uuna* or *-iina*) (see section 5.4.2.1., subsection (2) in this chapter), words that end with the dual suffix (*-aani* and *-ayni*) and invariable words (see section 5.4.5. in this chapter).

Diptotes:

ambassadors	*sufaraaʾ-u*	سفراءُ	better	*ʾaHsan-u*	أحسنُ

Sound masculine plural:

engineers	*muhandis-uuna*	مهندسونَ	Egyptians	*miSriyy-uuna*	مصريونَ

Dual:

two states	*dawlat-aani*	دولتانِ	two poets	*shaaʿir-aani*	شاعرانِ

Invariable nouns:

chaos	*fawDaa*	فوضى	issues	*qaDaayaa*	قضايا

4.2.2 Uses of the indefinite

4.2.2.1 TO EXPRESS NON-DEFINITE STATUS: Nunation is used on Arabic nouns and adjectives to mark indefinite status. An adjective modifying an indefinite noun is also indefinite.

في عمرٍ مبكّرٍ
fii ʿumr-in mubakkir-in
at **an early age**

إلى دولةٍ جديدةٍ
ʾilaa dawlat-in jadiidat-in
to **a new state**

حققنا تقدماً كافياً.
Haqqaq-naa taqaddum-an kaafiy-an.
We have achieved **adequate progress.**

هذا الكتاب عملٌ رائدٌ.
haadhaa l-kitaab-u ʿamal-un raaʾ id-un.
This book is a **pioneering work.**

4.2.2.2 MASCULINE PROPER NAMES: A perhaps unusual (to English speakers) function of the indefinite marker is its use on many Arabic masculine given names. They are **semantically definite, but morphologically indefinite.** This is so because many of these Arabic names are derived from adjectives which describe particular attributes. Nonetheless, given names are considered definite and agreeing words are definite.

Muhammad 'praised'	*muHammad-un*	محمّدٌ	Salim 'flawless'	*saliim-un*	سليمٌ
Munir 'radiant'	*muniir-un*	منيرٌ	Ali 'exalted'	*ʿaliyy-un*	عليٌّ

Examples of agreement:

محمّدٌ الخَامِسُ

muHammad-un-i l-xaamis-u

Muhammad **the fifth**

Nunation is not marked on all masculine names, only those derived from Arabic adjectives or participles. For example, the names *ʾaHmad, ʾibraahiim, sulay-maan,* and *yuusuf* are diptote and do not take nunation.[44] Most female names are also diptote and do not take nunation.[45]

4.2.2.3 ADVERBIAL ACCUSATIVE EXPRESSIONS: Adverbial expressions in Arabic tend to be in the accusative case, and quite often in the indefinite accusative. It is therefore common to see the indefinite accusative marker when reading Arabic texts. Another characteristic of the indefinite accusative marker, especially with adverbs, is that it is pronounced as well as written, whereas the nominative and genitive forms of nunation are not normally pronounced in spoken Arabic.[46]

The adverbial use of the accusative is described in greater detail in the section on the accusative case, but here are some examples in the indefinite accusative (see also 4.2.1 above):

| immediately | *fawr-an* | فوراً | a little (bit) | *qaliil-an* | قليلاً |
| daily | *yawmiyy-an* | يومياً | very | *jidd-an* | جداً |

5 Case inflection

Arabic nouns, participles, adjectives and, to some extent, adverbs have word-final (or desinential) inflection. That is, they are marked for **case**, which indicates the syntactic function of the word and its relationship with other words in the sentence.[47] In Arabic, the term for case marking is (*ʾiʿraab* إعراب).[48] In respect to case

---

[44] For the reasons behind this see section 5.4.2.2 on the diptote declension.

[45] There are a few exceptions. The feminine name *hind-un,* for example, may take nunation. But this is exceptional.

[46] Pronunciation of nunation at the end of a word is apparently still heard in some rural vernacular forms of Arabic. For the most part, the only form of nunated ending that is regularly pronounced in spoken MSA or in the urban vernaculars is the accusative (/-an/).

[47] Blake (1994, 1) defines case as follows: "Case is a system of marking dependent nouns for the type of relationship they bear to their heads. Traditionally the term refers to inflectional marking, and, typically, case marks the relationship of a noun to a verb at the clause level or of a noun to a preposition, postposition or another noun at the phrase level."

[48] The Arabic term *ʾiʿraab* إعراب refers to desinential inflection in general: not only case markers on nouns, adjectives, and adverbs, but also mood markers (indicative, subjunctive, jussive) on verbs. Arab grammarians classify case marking and mood marking together in one category, and give them similar labels. For more on this see Bohas, Guillaume, and Kouloughli 1990, 53-55, and Ryding 1993.

inflection, Arabic resembles some European languages such as German, Russian, and Latin.

Arabic has three cases: nominative (*raf* رفع), genitive (*jarr* جر), and accusative (*naSb* نصب). As a general rule, these cases are indicated by short vowel suffixes: *-u* (*Damma*) for nominative, *-i* (*kasra*) for genitive, and *-a* (*fatHa*) for accusative. However, these short vowels are not the only ways to mark case. Words inflected for case fall into several declensions or inflection classes and therefore inflect for these three cases in different ways.

Case marking is placed at the end of a noun or adjective. If a noun or adjective is definite, then the case-marking short vowel is suffixed at the very end of the word. If a noun or adjective is indefinite, the case marker is followed by an indefinite marker (a final /-n/ sound, "nunation" in English and *tanwiin* in Arabic), indicated in writing by the convention of doubling the short vowel case ending, e.g., -*un* / ; /-*in*/ ; /-*an* / (see above).

Case is one of the most challenging inflectional categories in MSA for several reasons. First of all, it depends on rules of syntax for its implementation, and second, in many ways it is redundant. Moreover, colloquial forms of Arabic do not have case marking, so case is used only in written Arabic.[49] Even for native speakers of Arabic, therefore, the case system is learned through formal instruction.

5.1 Pronunciation and writing conventions

The Arabic case-ending system consists primarily of short, word-final vowels, *which are invisible* in conventional written Arabic texts.[50] This can hinder clear-cut understanding of case inflections and sentential relations. Furthermore, because the nature of these case marking vowels is dependent on a word's function in a sentence, they vary from one context to another, and only if one knows the rules of grammatical usage can one ascertain what the noun-final case markers are for any particular sentence.

The Arabic case-marking system, then, remains mostly hidden from view in written texts and is apparent only when the text is read out loud with complete

---

[49] This is true for the colloquial variants of spoken Arabic and even for educated spoken Arabic or formal spoken Arabic. Case does not play a significant role in these forms of the language.

[50] Exceptions to this general rule include case marking that occurs as long vowels in, for example, the dual suffixes (*-aani/ -ayni*), the sound masculine plural suffixes (*-uuna/-iina*) and the "five nouns" that inflect, under certain conditions, with long vowels (see section 5.4.1.c.). Another partial exception is the word-final *ʾalif* that appears in written Arabic script on many words as a seat for *fatHataan*, the indefinite accusative marker (e.g., *ʾaxiir-an* ('finally'), أخيراً, *ʾaHyaan-an* ('sometimes') أحياناً). This particular form of case ending (the indefinite accusative ending in *-an*) is often pronounced, even in pause form.

pronunciation of all vowels (i.e., in "full" form).[51] The ability to use and pronounce accurate case marking in written or literary Arabic is not an automatic skill but a rigorous task, even for educated native speakers. It is also therefore the mark of a well-educated or learned individual. The case-marking rules are used and understood primarily by scholars and specialists in Arabic grammar, linguistics, scripture, and literature.[52] Learners of Arabic as a foreign language need to know the basic rules of word order, inflection, agreement, and governance in order to make sense of Arabic texts. The degree to which they need knowledge of explicit case marking rules depends on the structure and goals of particular academic programs, and on the goals of individual learners.[53]

In this book the case-marking system is described in some detail, but not exhaustively. For those who wish to delve more deeply into Arabic morphosyntax, Wright (1967) is recommended as are Hasan (1987) especially volumes II and IV; Fleisch (1961, 268–82), Beeston (1970, 51–55), and Cowan (1958). For a recent theoretical study of case in general, a good reference is Blake 1994.

5.2 Case marking and declensions

Arabic case marking takes place either as a short vowel suffix or as a modification of a long vowel suffix. Cases are marked on nouns, adjectives, and certain adverbs. The categories described below show the most common instances of particular case functions in MSA. It has not been traditional to designate Arabic nouns as belonging to particular declensions or inflectional classes, except to refer to them as "triptote" (showing *three* different inflectional markers, one for each case) or "diptote" (showing only *two* different inflectional markers when indefinite, nominative, and genitive/accusative). However, for reference purposes here, each inflectional type is classified into a separate, numbered declension.[54]

---

[51] In reading written Arabic aloud, some narrators read most of the words in pause form, omitting desinential inflections. News broadcasters, for example, vary in their formality and in the degree to which they use case-marking in narrating news items. Some seldom use it; others use it partially, and some use it more consistently. Officials giving formal speeches also vary in the degree to which they pronounce case marking. Only in formal academic and religious contexts is pronunciation of full desinential inflection considered necessary or appropriate.

[52] Holes (1995, 142) states: "As a means of syntactic disambiguation in modern written Arabic, case plays almost no role (inevitably so, since in most cases it is carried by short vowel distinctions which are unmarked), and, despite the importance which the indigenous tradition of grammatical description and language pedagogy attaches to it, it is clear, when one examines ancient textual material, that the functional load of the case endings was no higher in the Classical period than it is now."

[53] See, for example, the article by Khaldieh (2001) titled: "The relationship between knowledge of i⁽raab, lexical knowledge, and reading comprehension of nonnative readers of Arabic."

[54] It should be understood that these declensional identifications are not standardized; they are named as such in this book to facilitate description and reference.

5.2.1 Shift of declension

In Indo-European languages a noun usually belongs to a particular inflectional class or declension in both the singular and the plural. However, in Arabic, the number suffixes (duals and sound plurals) and even the internal broken plural pattern, **can shift a noun into a different inflectional class**. The criteria for identifying declensions depend on the nature of the noun stem and also whether or not it includes a dual or plural number inflection.

5.3 Case categories and their functions

The type of case marking on a noun or adjective depends on its form and function. That is, it is determined by the inflectional class (declension) of the word involved and the role of the word within a specific sentence or clause (which case is appropriate under the circumstances). For example, in a sentence such as:

عقدَ المديرُ اجتماعاً مع الموظفينَ.

ʿaqad-a l-mudiir-u jtimaaʿ-an maʿ-a l-muwaZZaf-iina.

The director held a meeting with the employees.

There are three nouns in this sentence: *al-mudiir-u* 'director, manager,' *ijtimaaʿ-an* 'meeting,' and *al-muwaZZaf-iina* 'the employees.' Each noun is marked for its case role in the sentence.

The first noun, *mudiir*, belongs to the triptote declension or declension one and is marked for definiteness by means of the definite article. These facts provide information about the nature of the word itself. Its function in this particular sentence is as the subject of the verb *ʿaqad-a* 'held,' so this provides information about its syntactic role. Putting these pieces of information together, it is then possible to know that the case marker in this particular situation is *Damma*, which is the nominative marker for definite triptotes.

The second noun, *ijtimaaʿ*, also belongs to the triptote declension or declension one, and is marked for indefiniteness by nunation affixed at the end of the word. The noun functions in this sentence as direct object of the verb *ʿaqad-a* 'held,' so this provides information about its syntactic role. Putting these pieces of information together, it is then possible to know that the case marker in this particular situation is *fatHataani*, accusative.

The third noun is *al-muwaZZaf-iina*. It is plural and definite, and it follows the semi-preposition *maʿ-a*. It is therefore in the genitive case. It has a sound masculine plural suffix, which places it in a declension that shows the case inflection by means of the long vowel before the *nuun* of the plural suffix (the *-ii* of *-iina*).

Therefore, case as a system is both morphological (word-related) and syntactic (sentence-related) and is a hybrid "morphosyntactic" category. Each of the three Arabic cases is presented here with its typical functions. These lists are by no means exhaustive, but they cover the majority of occurrences of these cases in MSA.

5.3.1 Nominative case (*al-rafᶜ* الرفع, *al-marfuuᶜ* المرفوع)

The nominative inflection (typically *-u* or *-un*, *-uuna* in the sound masculine plural suffix, or *-aani* in the dual suffix) has five key functions.[55] It marks the subject of a verbal sentence, the subject and predicate of equational sentences, certain locative adverbs, the vocative, and citation forms.

5.3.1.1 THE SUBJECT (*al-faaᶜil* الفاعل) OF A VERBAL SENTENCE (*jumla fiᶜliyya* جملة فعلية): The subject of the verb is nominative because it forms, along with the verb, a structural unit, termed *jumla* جملة. This unit can stand independently of any other units and conveys a predication.

اتّفقَ الوزراءُ على تعزيز التعاونِ.

*ittafaq-a **l-wuzaraaʾ-u** ᶜalaa taᶜziiz-i l-taᶜaawun-i.*

The ministers agreed to strengthen cooperation.

عقدَ الجانبانِ مباحثاتٍ رسميةً.

*ᶜaqad-a **l-jaanib-aani** mubaaHathaat-in rasmiyyat-an.*

The two sides held official discussions.

تركَهُ المسلمونَ وراءَهم.

*tarak-a-hu **l-muslim-uuna** waraaʾ-a-hum.*

The Muslims left it behind them.

وُلدَ النبيُّ محمدٌ في مكةَ.

*wulid-a l-nabiyy-u **muHammad-un** fii makkat-a.*[56]

The Prophet Muhammad was born in Mecca.

5.3.1.2 THE SUBJECT (*al-mubtadaʾ* المبتدأ) AND PREDICATE (*al-xabar* الخبر) OF AN EQUATIONAL SENTENCE (*jumla ʾismiyya* جملة اسمية):[57]

المعلوماتُ خاطئةٌ.	قصرُ الملكِ ضخمٌ.
al-maᶜluumaat-u xaaTiʾat-un.	*qaSr-u l-malik-i Daxm-un.*
The information is wrong.	**The palace** of the king [is] **huge.**

---

55 In addition, the nominative case marking for defective nouns and adjectives fuses with the genitive (/-in/ for indefinite, /-ii/ for definite); for indeclinable nouns and adjectives it is realized as /-an/ or /-aa/, and for invariable nouns and adjectives, the nominative appears the same as all other cases; /-aa/. See the paradigms for declensions six, seven, and eight, 5.4.3–5.4.5.

56 The subject of an Arabic sentence with a passive verb, such as this one, is referred to as the *naaʾib al-faaᶜil* 'the deputy subject.' See Chapter 38 for the use of the passive.

57 The term for "subject" of an Arabic sentence differs depending on whether or not the sentence contains a verb. The subject of a verbal sentence (*al-faaᶜil*) is seen as the agent or doer of the action; the subject of an equational sentence (*al-mubtadaʾ*) is the topic of a verbless predication. For more on equational sentence structure, see Chapter 4, section 2.1ff.

الدفـع مسبّقٌ.   المهمُّ هوَ العودةُ.

al-daf ͨ-u musabbaq-un.   *al-muhimm-u huwa l-ͨawdat-u*

Payment [is] in advance.   **The important thing [is] to return.**

5.3.1.3 CERTAIN ADVERBS: A few adverbs retain a *Damma* (non-nunated) in many syntactic functions, even when they are preceded by a preposition. It has been hypothesized that this adverbial marker is a fossilized remnant of a locative case in previous stages of language development.[58] Certain function words, like *mundh-u* and *Hayth-u* have *Damma* consistently. Other words, such as *qabl-u* and *ba ͨd-u* have the *Damma* ending when they are used as independent adverbs, but not when used as prepositions followed by a noun or a pronoun (where they normally have *fatHa*).

since; ago	*mundh-u*	منذُ	only	*Hasb-u; fa-Hasb-u*	حسبُ
where; whereas	*Hayth-u*	حيثُ	yet	*ba ͨd-u*	بعدُ
at all	*qaTT-u*	قطُّ	before	*qabl-u; min qabl-u*	قبلُ ؛ من قبلُ

وسّعَ الأمريكيون الفارقَ منذُ البدايةِ.

*wassa ͨ-a l-ʾamriikiyy-uuna l-faariq-a **mundh-u** l-bidaayat-i.*

The Americans widened the margin [of points] from the beginning.

في مستشفىً حيثُ تقعُ قصصُ حبٍّ

*fii mustashfan **Hayth-u** ta-qa ͨ-u qiSaS-u Hubb-in*

in a hospital **where** love stories happen

لمْ تكشفْ هويتُهم بعدُ.

*lam tu-kshaf huwiyyaat-u-hum **ba ͨd-u.***

Their identities have not yet been revealed.

5.3.1.4 THE VOCATIVE (*al-nidaaʾ* النداء), where someone or some entity is addressed directly by the speaker. The nominative (without nunation) is used on the vocative noun unless that noun is the first term of an *ʾiDaafa* construction, in which case it shifts to accusative.[59]

يا رشيد   أيّها السيداتُ والسادةُ

*yaa **rashiid-u!**[60]   *ʾayyuhaa l-sayyidaat-u wa-l-saadat-u!*

O Rashid!   **Ladies and gentlemen!**

---

[58] See Fleisch 1961, I:280 and 1979, II:465–66 about the Semitic "adverbial case" with /-u/ suffix. For more on this see Chapter 11, section 4.1.3.

[59] See section 5.3.3.12 subsection (3) of this chapter for examples of the first terms of *ʾiDaafa* in the accusative after the vocative particle.

[60] If the vocative particle *yaa* ('O') is used, the following word has *Damma*, but not nunation or the definite article. If the vocative particle is *ʾayyu-haa* (m.) or *ʾayyatu-haa* (f.), the following word or words have the definite article.

Certain exclamations fall into this category:[61]

| O goodness! ('O peace!') | yaa *salaam-u*! | يا سلام! |
| What a loss! What a pity! | yaa *xasaarat-u*! | يا خسارة! |

5.3.1.5 THE CITATION FORM of nouns and adjectives in lists or lexicons, although they may also be cited without desinence, in "bare" form. This function of the nominative – as the default case marker for substantives in isolation, is in line with usage in other languages.[62] For example, a list of vocabulary words out of context:

monarch	*ʿaahil-un*	عاهل
forbidden	*mamnuuʿ-un*	ممنوع
treaty	*muʿaahadat-un*	معاهدة
The Sudan	*al-suudaan-u*	السودان
The Fertile Crescent	*al-hilaal-u l-xaSiib-u*	الهلال الخصيب

5.3.2 Genitive case (*al-jarr* الجر, *al-majruur* المجرور; *al-xafD* الخفض):

The genitive inflection (-*i* or -*in*, -*a* [in diptote declensions], -*iina* [for the sound masculine plural] or -*ayni* [in the dual]) has three chief functions. It marks:

5.3.2.1 THE OBJECT OF A PREPOSITION: Prepositions are followed by nouns or noun phrases in the genitive case.

في الظلام
fii l-Zalaam-i
in the shade

إلى اليمين
ʾilaa l-yamiin-i
to the right

من بيروت
min bayruut-a
from Beirut

كجسر حضاريّ
ka-jisr-in HaDaariyy-in
as a cultural bridge

من المماليك المصريين
min-a l-mamaaliik-i l-miSriyy-iina
from the Egyptian Mamelukes

في هذين الكتابين
fii haadh-ayni l-kitaab-ayni
in these two books

---

[61] Note that exclamations with *yaa* may also use the preposition *li-* 'for' + a definite noun in the genitive case:

| O the poor man! | yaa li-l-maskiin-i! | يا للمسكين! |
| How unfortunate! | yaa li-l-ʾasaf-i! | يا للأسف! |

[62] Blake notes (1994, 31) that in Greek (and other languages as well) the nominative "is the case used outside constructions, the case used in isolation, the case used in naming." He further states the proposition that (1994, 32) "the nominative simply delineates an entity not a relation between an entity and a predicate." See, for example, the Arabic vocabulary lists in Abboud and McCarus 1983.

5.3.2.2 THE OBJECT OF A LOCATIVE ADVERB (*Zarf makaan wa-Zarf zamaan* ظرف مكان وظرف زمان): Arabic locative adverbs function very much like prepositions. They are different from true prepositions in that they are derived from triliteral lexical roots and can also themselves be objects of prepositions. See section 5.3.3.2 following, and Chapter 16, section 3 on "semi-prepositions."

قبلَ أيّام
qabl-a ’ayyaam-in
[a few] **days** ago

تحتَ نورِ الشمسِ
taHt-a **nuur-i** l-shams-i
under **the sunlight**

5.3.2.3 THE SECOND TERM OF AN ’ *iDaafa* CONSTRUCTION: The second term of the annexation structure or ’*iDaafa* construction is normally a noun in the genitive case.

كيسُ فستقٍ
kiis-u *fustuq-in*
a bag **of nuts**

غرفةُ التجارةِ
ghurfat-u **l-tijaarat-i**
the chamber **of commerce**

لغةُ المثقّفين
lughat-u **l-muthaqqaf-iina**
the language **of cultivated [people]**

مديرُ المؤسسةِ
mudiir-u **l-mu’assasat-i**
the director **of the establishment**

مدينةُ بغدادَ
madiinat-u *baghdaad-a*
the city **of Baghdad**

5.3.3 Accusative case (*al-naSb* النصب; *al-manSuub* المنصوب)

The accusative inflection (-*a*, -*an*, -*in*, -*i*, -*iina* [in the sound masculine plural] or -*ayni* [in the dual]) has the most functions in Arabic because it not only marks nouns, adjectives, and noun phrases in a wide range of constructions, but it also marks adverbial expressions.[63] In MSA, it frequently occurs in the following constructions:

5.3.3.1 THE OBJECT OF A TRANSITIVE VERB (*al-maf‘uul bi-hi* المفعول به): A transitive verb is one which, in addition to having a subject or agent which accomplishes the action, also has an object or entity that is affected by the action. The object of the verb in Arabic is in the accusative case.[64]

حضروا اللّقاءَ.
HaDar-uu **l-liqaa’-a**.
They attended **the meeting**.

لا تشعلْ ناراً.
laa tu-sh‘il **naar-an**.
Don't ignite **a fire**.

---

[63] See Wright 1967, 2:45–129 for further discussion of the accusative in Classical Arabic.

[64] Blake, in his discussion of case roles in general, states (1994, 134): "The accusative is the case that encodes the direct object of a verb."

تعلّمَ كلمات معدودةً فقط.

ta'allam-a **kalimaat-in** ma'duudat-an faqaT.

He learned a limited number of **words** only.

5.3.3.2 LOCATIVE ADVERBS OF BOTH TIME AND PLACE (Zuruuf makaan wa-Zuruuf zamaan ظروف مكان وظروف زمان): These adverbs are usually in the accusative but may be made genitive if they follow a preposition.[65] They function in ways similar to prepositions, describing location or direction, and are followed by a noun in the genitive case. For that reason they are referred to in this work as semi-prepositions.[66] For a more extensive description and examples of prepositions and semi-prepositions see Chapter 16 section 3.

قبلَ سنة

qabl-a sanat-in

a year **ago**

عبرَ قارتَيْنِ

'abr-a qaarrat-ayni

across two continents

داخلَ الدولة الإسلاميّة

daaxil-a l-dawlat-i l-ʾ islaamiyyat-i

inside the Islamic state

عندَ إلقاء القبض

'ind-a ʾilqaaʾ-i l-qabD-i

at the time of arrest

5.3.3.3 ADVERBIAL EXPRESSIONS OF TIME, PLACE, AND MANNER (al-mafʿuul fii-hi المفعول فيه): The accusative case functions extensively in MSA to indicate the circumstances under which an action takes place.[67] In this function, the accusative can be used on nouns or adjectives. If the noun or adjective is by itself, it is normally in the indefinite accusative; if it is the first term of an ʾiDaafa, it does not have nunation.

تستمرُ يوماً واحداً.

ta-stamirr-u **yawm-an waaHid-an**.

It lasts **one day**.

جاءوا فجرَ يوم الاقتراع.

jaaʾ-uu **fajr-a** yawm-i l-iqtiraaʿ-i.

They came **at dawn** on the day of balloting.

حصلتُ حديثاً على الجنسية.

HaSal-tu **Hadiith-an** ʿalaa l-jinsiyyat-i.

I recently obtained citizenship.

اللجنةُ ستعقدُ اجتماعَيْنِ سنويّاً.

al-lajnat-u sa-ta-ʿqud-u jtimaaʿ-ayni **sanawiyy-an**.

The committee will hold two meetings **annually**.

---

[65] They seem to fall into the category of "relator nouns" described by Blake: "Relator nouns are a specialised subclass of nouns that behave like adpositions (prepositions)" (1994, 205).

[66] Wright states: "Many words, which are obviously substantives in the accusative of place . . . may be conveniently regarded in a certain sense as prepositions" (1967, II:178).

[67] Blake (1994, 182) notes that in a number of languages, "it is common for nouns in oblique cases to be reinterpreted as adverbs, particularly adverbs of place, time and manner."

سيعودُ قريباً إلى بغدادَ.

sa-ya‘uud-u qariib-an ’ilaa baghdaad-a.

He will return to Baghdad **soon**.

مدّةَ ثماني ساعاتٍ ليلَ الخميس

muddat-a thamaanii saa‘aat-in layl-a l-xamiis-i

[for] **a period of** eight hours on Thursday **night**

5.3.3.4 THE INTERNAL OBJECT OR COGNATE ACCUSATIVE STRUCTURE (*al-maf‘uul al-muTlaq* المفعول المطلق). In this structure, the action denoted is intensified through use of a verbal noun cognate with the verb (i.e., derived from the same root; usually from the same derivational form (I–X)). Often the verbal noun is modified by an adjective, also in the accusative:

حلّت الموضوعَ حلاً جذرياً.

Hall-at-i l-mawDuu‘-a Hall-an jidhriyy-an.

It solved the issue **fundamentally**.

تدركُه عمّانُ إدراكا كليّاً.

tu-drik-u-hu ‘ammaan-u ’idraak-an kulliyy-an.

Amman realizes it **fully**.

ساهما مساهمةً فعّالةً.

saaham-aa musaahamat-an fa‘‘aalat-an.

They (two) participated **effectively**.

5.3.3.5 THE CIRCUMSTANTIAL ACCUSATIVE (*al-Haal* الحال). Expressing a condition or circumstance that occurs concurrent with or ongoing at the time of the action of the main verb, a participle is often used to describe that condition (*al-Haal*). The participle agrees with the noun it modifies in number and gender, but is in the accusative case and usually indefinite. The active participle is widely used in this function, but occasionally the passive participle or a verbal noun is used. For more on this topic see Chapter 11, section 2.3.1.

(1) Using active participles:

دخلَ الصفَّ متأخّراً.

daxal-a l-Saff-a muta’axxir-an.

He entered the classroom **late**.

رفعَ يدَه معترضاً.

rafa‘-a yad-a-hu mu‘tariD-an.

He raised his hand **objecting**.

يغادرونَ القاهرةَ اليومَ متوجّهينَ إلى باريس.

yu-ghaadir-uuna l-qaahirat-a l-yawm-a mutawajjih-iina ’ilaa baariis.

They are leaving Cairo today **heading** for Paris.

ألقى الوزيرُ كلمةً **ناقلاً** تحيّاتِ الرئيسِ.

*ʾalqaa l-waziir-u kalimat-an **naaqil-an** taHiyyaat-i l-raʾiis-i.*

The minister gave a speech **transmitting** the greetings of the president.

(2) **Using passive participles:**

قفزتْ **مذعورةً**.

*qafaz-at **madhᶜuurat-an**.*

She jumped, **frightened**.

(3) **Using a verbal noun:**

وقالَ **رداً** على سؤالٍ...

*wa-qaal-a **radd-an** ᶜalaa suʾaal-in...*

(And) he said, **replying** to a question...

5.3.3.6 THE ACCUSATIVE OF PURPOSE (*al-mafᶜuul li-ʾajl-i-hi* المفعول لأجله) OR (*al-mafᶜuul la-hu* المفعول له) in order to show the motive, purpose, or reason for an action. It is usually used with an indefinite verbal noun.

القواتُ تشنُّ حملةً **بحثاً** عن أسلحةٍ.

*al-quwwaat-u ta-shunn-u Hamlat-an **baHth-an** ᶜan ʾasliHat-in.*

The forces are launching a campaign **searching** for weapons.

خلالَ حفلةِ استقبالٍ أقاموها **تكريماً** له.

*xilaal-a Haflat-i stiqbaal-in ʾaqaam-uu-haa **takriim-an** la-hu*

during a reception they gave **in his honor**

شهدتْ مختلفُ المدنِ إضراباً واسعاً **تضامناً** مع العمالِ.

*shahad-at muxtalif-u l-mudun-i ʾiDraab-an waasiᶜ-an **taDaamun-an** maᶜ-a l-ᶜummaal-i.*

Various cities witnessed a widespread strike **in solidarity** with the workers.

5.3.3.7 THE ACCUSATIVE OF SPECIFICATION (*al-tamyiiz* التمييز). This accusative is used on nouns in order to delimit and specify the application of a statement. It usually answers the question, "In what way?" It includes comparative and superlative expressions as well as counted nouns between 11 and 99, which are accusative and singular.

نعلنُ ذاكَ **قولاً** و**فعلاً**.

*nu-ᶜlin-u dhaaka **qawl-an** wa-**fiᶜl-an**.*

We announce that **in speech and in action**.

كانتْ أكبرَ عاصمة جاهاً وفخامةً.

kaan-at ʾakbar-a ʿaaSimat-in jaah-an wa-faxaamat-an.

It was the greatest capital **in fame and splendor.**

فقدْ بدا أكثرَ حذراً ودبلوماسيّةً.

fa-qad badaa ʾakthar-a Hidhr-an wa-dibluumaasiyyat-an.

It seemed more cautious and diplomatic ('greater in **caution and diplomacy**').

في عشرين مجلّداً	على مدى خمسةَ عشرَ عاماً
fii ʿishriina mujallad-an	*ʿalaa madaa xamsat-a ʿashr-a ʿaam-an*
in twenty **volumes**[68]	for fifteen **years**

بمشاركة ثلاثين باحثاً.

bi-mushaarakat-i thalaathiina baaHith-an

with the participation of thirty **researchers**

5.3.3.8 THE *nawaasix* النواسخ: CONVERTERS TO ACCUSATIVE.[69] Arabic grammar has a special category for words (verbs and particles) that shift one or more elements of a clause into the **accusative case**. There are three groups of these, each of which is composed of a typical word and what are termed its "sisters": **kaan-a and its sisters, ʾinna and its sisters,** and **Zann-a and its sisters.**[70]

(1) ***kaan-a* and its "sisters"** (*kaan-a wa-ʾaxawaat-u-haa* كان وأخواتها)[71] This set of verbs has the effect of shifting the predicate (*xabar*) of an equational sentence from the nominative case to the accusative case. According to Hasan (1987, I:545) there are thirteen of these verbs, the most common in MSA are:

lays-a	to not be[72]	ليس
Saar-a	to become	صار
baat-a	to become	بات
ʾaSbaH-a	to become	أصبح
Zall-a	to remain	ظل

---

[68] See Chapter 15 for further discussion of numerals and counting.

[69] "The *al-nawaasikh* group of words in Arabic is defined by the Arab grammarians according to formal criteria; specifically, the role played by these words in inflection. Thus, words classified as belonging to the *al-nawaasikh* category have the effect of inducing one or two elements of the nuclear sentence to 'fall' from the nominative to the accusative case" (Anghelescu 1999, 131).

[70] Hasan 1987, 1:543ff. and 630ff. has thorough descriptions of the *nawaasix* category in Arabic.

[71] See also Chapter 36 in this book.

[72] In addition to the verb *lays-a* there are certain negative particles that have similar meanings and effects, including *maa* and *laa*. See Hasan 1987 1:593ff. for more on these particles.

baqiy-a	to remain, to stay	بَقِيَ
daama and maa daama	to continue to be	دَامَ + مَا دَامَ
maa zaal-a	to continue to be; to still be; to not cease to be	مَا زَالَ
ʾamsaa	to become	أَمْسَى

These verbs all denote existential states of being (or not being), becoming, and remaining. They take accusative complements. That is, the predicate of the underlying equational predication is accusative.

مُؤلِّفُ الكتابِ ليسَ مؤرِّخاً.

muʾallif-u l-kitaab-i lays-a **muʾarrix-an.**

The author of the book is not **a historian.**

ليسَ جذاباً جداً.

lays-a **jadhdhaab-an** jidd-an.

It is not very **attractive.**

كانَ جزءاً من هذا الحلمِ.

kaan-a **juzʾ-an** min haadhaa l-Hulm-i.

It was a **part** of this dream.

أصبحَ همَّهم اليوميَّ.

ʾaSbaH-a **hamm-a-hum-u
l-yawmiyy-a.**

It became **their daily concern.**

كانتْ أكبرَ عاصمةٍ أوربيّةٍ.

kaan-at **ʾakbar-a** ʿaaSimat-in ʾuurubbiyyat-in.

It was **the largest** European capital.

الصناعةُ الشعبيّةُ ما زالتْ حيّةً.

al-Sinaaʿat-u l-shaʿbiyyat-u maa zaal-at **Hayyat-an.**

Folk handicraft is still **alive.**

(2) ʾinna **and her sisters** (ʾinna wa-ʾaxawaat-u-haa إن وأخواتها):

ʾinna	'verily; indeed; that'	إنَّ
ʾanna	'that'	أنَّ
laakinna	'but'	لكنَّ
li-ʾanna	'because'	لأنَّ
laʿalla	'perhaps'	لعلَّ

These particles are subordinating conjunctions which require that the **sub-ject** of the subordinate clause (also called the complement clause) be in the accusative case.[73]

---

[73] For more on ʾinna and her sisters, see Chapter 19 on subordinating conjunctions.

قالتَ إنّ أحداً لا يستطيعُ أنْ يوقفهم.

qaal-a ʾinna ʾaHad-an laa ya-staTiiʿ-u ʾan yu-waqqif-a-hum.

It said **that no one** could stop them.

أنّ الزراعةَ لغةٌ عالميّةٌ

ʾanna l-ziraaʿat-a lughat-un ʿaalamiyyat-un

that agriculture **is** a world language

لكنّ قليلين من الباحثينَ

laakinna qaliil-iina min-a l-baaHith-iina

but few of the researchers

لأنّ السنتينِ ا لأخيرتينْ كانتا من أفضل السنوات

li-ʾanna l-sanat-ayni l-ʾaxiirat-ayni kaan-ataa min ʾafDal-i l-sanawaat-i

because the last two years were among the best years

(3)   **Zann-a and her sisters** (*Zanna wa-ʾaxawaat-u-haa* ظنّ وأخواتها): The verb *Zann-a* 'to suppose, believe' is another one of the *nawaasix*. It has the effect of making both the subject and the predicate of an equational clause accusative.[74] This category includes verbs of "certainty and doubt" (Anghelescu 1999, 132). Hasan breaks this category down into two parts: *ʾafʿaal al-quluub*[75] أفعال القلوب or *ʾafʿaal qalbiyya* أفعال قلبيّة (verbs of perception or cognition) and *ʾafʿaal al-taHwiil* أفعال التحويل (verbs of transformation).[76] Hasan gives complete lists; here are some examples.[77]

(3.1)   **Verbs of perception:**

to suppose, believe   *Zann-a*   ظنّ

أظنُّ زيداً ذاهباً.

ʾa-Zunn-u Zayd-an dhaahib-an.

I believe Zayd [is] going.[78]

to consider, deem	*ʿadd-a*	عدّ	to perceive, deem, see	*raʾaa*	رأى
to find, deem	*wajad-a*	وجد	to consider	*iʿtabar-a*[79]	اعتبر

[74] One of these accusatives may take the form of an object pronoun suffix on the verb.

[75] Which Hasan explains as having to do with psychological perceptions: in particular, emotions and intellect (1987, II:4, note 4).

[76] As explained by Hasan, verbs that have to do with transformation of something from one state to another (Ibid., note 5).

[77] See especially Hasan's chart of *Zann-a* and her sisters (1987, II:10). Note also the discussion in Bohas, Guillaume, and Kouloughli 1990, 34–36.

[78] Example from Bohas, Guillaume, and Kouloughli 1990, 34.

[79] The verb *iʿtabar-a* 'to consider' is not included in older lists of *ʾafʿaal al-quluub*, but that is likely due to the fact that its usage is more modern and recent rather than traditional. Its meaning and its effect on the sentence components show that it is certainly a member of this category. I thank my colleague Amin Bonnah for this insight.

اعتبروا هذه الخطوةَ إنجازاً تاريخيّاً كبيراً.

i‘tabar-uu haadhihi l-xuTwat-a ’injaaz-an taariixiyy-an kabiir-an.

They considered this step a great historical accomplishment.

ونعتبر مكتبةَ المركزِ مهمةً.

wa-na-‘tabir-u maktabat-a l-markaz-i muhimmat-an.

We consider the library of the center important.

ما يراه البعضُ إيجابياتٍ يراه البعضُ الآخرُ سلبياتٍ.

maa ya-raa-hu l-ba‘D-u ’iijaabiyyaat-in ya-raa-hu l-ba‘D-u l-’aaxar-u
salbiyyaat-in.

What some see [as] positives others see [as] negatives.

(3.2)   Verbs of transformation: These verbs signify changing a thing into something else, changing its state or appearance, or designating one thing as something else.

| to convert | Sayyar-a | صير | to take, adopt (as) | ittaxadh-a | اتخذ |
| to make | ja‘al-a | جعل | to leave | tarak-a | ترك |

واتخذوا النهرَ حدوداً للمنطقة.

wa-ttaxadh-uu l-nahr-a Huduud-an li-l-mantiqat-i.

They took the river [as] borders of the region.

تركَ البابَ مفتوحاً.

tarak-a l-baab-a maftuuH-an.

He left the door open.

5.3.3.9 THE NOUN FOLLOWING THE *laa* OF ABSOLUTE OR CATEGORICAL NEGATION

(*laa l-naafiyat-u lil-jins-i* لا النافية للجنس).[80] In this construction the noun is devoid of the definite article or nunation. It carries only the accusative marker *fatHa*.

لا شكرَ على واجبٍ.

laa shukr-a ‘alaa waajib-in.

Don't mention it.

('There is no thanking for a duty.')

لا شكَّ في ذلكَ.

laa shakk-a fii dhaalika.

There's no doubt about that.

لا مبررَ لإلغائها.

laa mubarrir-a li-’ilghaa’-i-haa.

There is no excuse for its elimination.

لا مانعَ من دفعِ بعضِ الزيادة.

laa maani‘-a min daf ‘-i ba‘D-i l-ziyaadat-i.

There's no objection to paying
a bit more.

---

[80] See also Chapter 37, section 2.1.6.

من دونِهم لا استقرارَ ولا سلامَ في المنطقة.

min duun-i-him laa stiqraar-a wa laa salaam-a fii l-minTaqat-i.

Without them there is no **stability** and no **peace** in the region.

5.3.3.10 THE TEENS NUMBERS, both cardinal and ordinal, including eleven.[81] No matter what their function in a sentence, these compound numbers always have both parts marked with *fatHa*:

ثمنُهُ خمسةَ عشرَ درهماً.

thaman-u-hu xamsat-a ʿashar-a dirham-an.

Its cost is **fifteen** dirhams.

في الغرفِ التسعَ عشرةَ

fii l-ghuraf-i l-tisʿ-a ʿasharat-a

in the **nineteen** rooms

يبلغُ طولُهُ ثلاثةَ عشرَ متراً.

ya-blugh-u Tuul-u-hu thalaathat-a ʿashar-a mitr-an.

Its length reaches **thirteen** meters.

5.3.3.11 AS THE COMPLEMENT OF VERBS OF "SEEMING": Verbs that denote appearing or seeming also take accusative complements.

كانَ يبدو شخصيّةً بارزةً في مجتمعِه.

kaan-a ya-bduu shaxsiyyat-an baarizat-an fii mujtamaʿ-i-hi.

He had seemed [like] **a prominent personality** in his society.

تبدو أصغرَ بكثيرٍ من عمرِها.

ta-bduu ʾaSghar-a bi-kathiir-in min ʿumr-i-haa.

She appears much **younger** than her age.

يبدو عتيقاً جداً.

ya-bduu ʿatiiq-an jidd-an.

It looks very **ancient**.

5.3.3.12 LESS FREQUENT ACCUSATIVES: Further instances of the use of the accusative case in MSA are noted in most teaching texts and traditional grammars, but few or none appeared in the corpus of text studied for this book. Some of the most important include:

(1) *kam* **+ accusative singular noun:** A singular accusative, indefinite noun is used after the question word *kam* 'how much, how many?'

كم فصلاً قرأت؟

kam faSl-an qaraʾ-ti?

How many **chapters** did you (f.) read?

كم غرفةً في الفندقِ؟

kam ghurfat-an fii l-funduq-i?

How many **rooms** [are there] in the hotel?

---

[81] The only exception to this is the cardinal numeral "twelve" which occurs in both the nominative and the genitive/accusative cases. See Chapter 15 on numerals and numerical expressions.

(2) Exclamation of astonishment: *maa ʾafʿal-a!* ما أفعل! (*maa l-taʿajjub*
ما التعجّب): The accusative is used in the 'adjectival verb' construction
on the noun following the exclamation of wonder, astonishment or surprise
maa ʾafʿal-a! In this expression, the word *maa* is followed by "an elative in
the accusative of exclamation," (Cantarino, 1974, II:210), and then a noun
in the accusative case. Note that this form of the elative is identical with
a Form IV verb, and that it is described this way in some texts and called
fiʿl al-taʿajjub.[82]

ما أجملَ المنظرَ!
maa ʾajmal-a l-manZar-a!
How **lovely the view** is!

The noun may be replaced by a pronoun suffix:

ما أجملَهُ !
maa ʾajmal-a-hu!
How **lovely it** is![83]

(3) **Vocative first term of construct**: The accusative case is used with the vocative particles *yaa* or *ʾayy-u-haa* if the addressee is the first term of an *ʾiDaafa*
or noun construct, or if the noun has a pronoun suffix:

يا عبدَ اللّه !
yaa ʿabd-a llaah-i!
O Abdallah! (lit: 'servant of God')

يا أرضَ بلادي !
yaa ʾarD-a bilaad-ii!
O, **earth of my country!**

يا طلابَ الجامعة وأساتذَتها !
yaa Tullaab-a l-jaamiʿat-i wa-ʾasaatidhat-a-haa!
O **students and professors** of the university!

Even without the vocative particle, a noun in construct or with a pronoun
suffix, understood as the addressee, is put into the accusative:

أبانا الذي في السموات . . .
ʾab-aa-naa lladhii fii l-samawaat-i . . .
Our Father who [art] in heaven . . .

(4) **Nouns following exceptive expressions** (*al-istithnaaʾ* الاستثناء) in non-nega-
tive clauses: In clauses using an exceptive expression such as *maa ʿadaa*, or

[82] See Abboud and McCarus 1976, Part 2:272. See also Cowan 1964, 177. In this book, see Chapter 25
on the Form IV verb, section 9.
[83] For more examples see Cantarino 1974, II, 210–13.

ʾillaa, the noun following the exceptive is in the accusative case if the clause does not contain a negative.

حَضَرَ الجميعُ إلاّ رشيداً.

*HaDar-a l-jamiiᶜ-uʾ **illaa rashiid-an**.*

Everyone came **except Rashid**.

تكلّمتُ مع كلٌ الطالباتِ إلاّ ياسمينَ.

*takallam-tu maᶜa kull-i l-Taalibaat-i ʾ**illaa yaasamiin-a**.*

I spoke with all the [female] students **except Yasmine**.

This is the case in particular with time-telling, where the word *ʾillaa* is used to express how many minutes are lacking until a particular hour, e.g.:

الساعةُ الخامسةُ إلاّ ربعاً.

*al-saaᶜat-u l-xaamisat-u ʾ**illaa rubᶜ-an**.*

It is 4:45 ('five [o'clock] **less a quarter** [of an hour]').

الساعة السابعةُ إلاّ ثلثاً.

*al-saaᶜat-u l-saabiᶜat-u ʾ**illaa thulth-an**.*

It is 6:40 ('seven [o'clock'] **less a third** [of an hour]').

5.3.3.13 OTHER ACCUSATIVES: The accusative case is used in other constructions besides the ones mentioned, but these are infrequent in MSA. For more extensive discussion and listings, especially for literary and classical syntax, see Cantarino 1975, II:161–248; Wright 1967, II:44–129 and in Arabic, Hasan 1987, II:3–430.

5.4 Arabic declensions

Following the practice of Wright (1967, I:234 ff.) and Cowan (1964, 29ff.), this book refers to the various inflectional classes of substantives as "declensions." A declension is a class of substantives (nouns or adjectives) that exhibits similar inflectional markings for case and definiteness. Arabic nouns and adjectives fall into eight declensions:[84]

1   three-way inflection (called "triptote" in many Arabic grammars)
2   dual

---

[84] Note that Wright refers to declensions of "undefined" or "defined" nouns, referring to triptote nouns as the first declension (236) and diptote nouns as the second declension (239). He does not list other inflectional classes as declensions. Cowan (29) states that "there are three declensions in Arabic" allotting the first declension to triptotes, the second declension to diptotes and the third to the uninflectable and undeclinable substantives (32).

For ease of reference in this book, I have allotted declensional status not only to singular and broken plural noun stems, but also to words that incorporate suffixes denoting dual and plural number, since they inflect for case and definiteness in different ways.

3 sound feminine plural
4 sound masculine plural
5 diptote
6 defective
7 uninflectable (for case, but they show inflection for definiteness), and
8 invariable.

5.4.1 Three-way inflection: Triptote (*mu'rab* معرب)

The triptote is the base category or declension one for Arabic nouns and adjectives.[85] The term "triptote" refers to words (nouns and adjectives) that take all three short vowel case endings, each one differentiating a particular case (*Damma, kasra* and *fatHa*). The triptote declension also allows nouns and adjectives to be marked for indefiniteness with nunation.[86] This is considered the base or complete declension because it shows the full range of inflectional markers for all three cases.[87]

5.4.1.1 THE CASE MARKERS:

(1) **Nominative**: The nominative suffix in the triptote declension is *Damma* by itself ʾ (-*u*) for definite words or two *Dammas/Damma* with a tail ʾʾ or ʾ (-*u-n*) for indefinite words. Examples:

(1.1) **Noun in the nominative case:**

the honor/an honor	*al-sharaf-u/sharaf-un*	الشرفُ / شرفٌ
the secret/a secret	*al-sirr-u/sirr-un*	السرُ / سرٌ
the ship/a ship	*al-safiinat-u/safiinat-un*	السفينةُ / سفينةٌ

(1.2) **Adjective in the nominative case:**

short (def.)/short (indef.)	*al-qaSiir-u/qaSiir-un*	القصيرُ / قصيرٌ
new (def.)/new (indef.)	*al-jadiid-u/jadiid-un*	الجديدُ / جديدٌ

(2) **Genitive**: The genitive marker in the triptote declension is *kasra* by itself (-*i*) ِ for definite words or two *kasras* (-*i-n*) ِ for indefinite words. Note that when *kasra* is written together with *shadda*, it may be written either below the consonant or below the *shadda*.

---

85 The term *mu'rab* means 'fully inflectable.'
86 For more on nunation, see section 4.2 in this chapter.
87 Certain linguists have designated these cases differently in English. Beeston (1970, 51), for example, refers to the cases as "independent status (nominative)," "dependent status (genitive)," and "subordinate status (accusative)." See his Chapter 7 ("Syntactic markers of nouns") for a brief but comprehensive description of Arabic case marking.

(2.1)   **Noun in the genitive case:**

the honor/an honor	al-sharaf-i/sharaf-in	الشرفِ/شرفٍ
the secret/a secret	al-sirr-i/sirr-in	السرِّ / سرٍّ
the ship/a ship	al-safiinat-i/safiinat-in	السفينةِ / سفينةٍ

(2.2)   **Adjective in the genitive case:**

| short (def.)/short (indef.) | al-qaSiir-i/qaSiir-in | القصيرِ / قصيرٍ |
| new (def.)/new (indef.) | al-jadiid-i/jadiid-in | الجديدِ / جديدٍ |

(3)   **Accusative:** The accusative marker in the triptote declension is *fatHa* by itself (*-a*) for definite words or two *fatHas* to signal nunation (*-a-n*) for indefinite words. With the accusative form of nunation, a supporting *ʾalif* is used, except with words ending in *taaʾ marbuuTa* or in a *hamza* preceded by *ʾalif*. This support *ʾalif* is visible in writing, but it is not pronounced; it is only a seat for the two *fatHas*.

(3.1)   **Noun in the accusative case:**

the honor/an honor	al-sharaf-a/sharaf-an	الشرفَ / شرفاً
the secret/a secret	al-sirr-a/sirr-an	السرَّ / سرّاً
the ship/a ship	al-safiinat-a/safiinat-an	السفينةَ / سفينةً
the winter/a winter	al-shitaaʾ-a/shitaaʾ-an	الشتاءَ / شتاءً

(3.2)   **Adjective in the accusative case:**

| short (def.)/short (indef.) | al-qaSiir-a/qaSiir-an | القصيرَ / قصيراً |
| new (def.)/new (indef.) | al-jadiid-a/jadiid-an | الجديدَ / جديداً |

5.4.1.2 DECLENSION ONE PARADIGMS:

(1)   **Singular masculine noun:**

'house' *bayt* بيت				
	Definite:		**Indefinite:**	
Nominative	al-bayt-u	البيتُ	bayt-u-n	بيتٌ
Genitive	al-bayt-i	البيتِ	bayt-i-n	بيتٍ
Accusative	al-bayt-a	البيتَ	bayt-a-n	بيتاً

(2) **Plural noun:**

'houses' *buyuut* بيوت				
	Definite:		Indefinite:	
Nominative	al-buyuut-u	البيوتُ	buyuut-u-n	بيوتٌ
Genitive	al-buyuut-i	البيوتِ	buyuut-i-n	بيوتٍ
Accusative	al-buyuut-a	البيوتَ	buyuut-a-n	بيوتاً

(3) **Feminine singular noun:**

'ship' *safiina* سفينة				
	Definite:		Indefinite:	
Nominative	al-safiinat-u	السفينةُ	safiinat-u-n	سفينةٌ
Genitive	al-safiinat-i	السفينةِ	safiinat-i-n	سفينةٍ
Accusative	al-safiinat-a	السفينةَ	safiinat-a-n	سفينةً

(4) **Plural noun:**

'ships' *sufun* سفن				
	Definite:		Indefinite:	
Nominative	al-sufun-u	السفنُ	sufun-u-n	سفنٌ
Genitive	al-sufun-i	السفنِ	sufun-i-n	سفنٍ
Accusative	al-sufun-a	السفنَ	sufun-a-n	سفناً

(5) **Masculine singular adjective:**

'short' *qaSiir* قصير				
	Definite:		Indefinite:	
Nominative	al-qaSiir-u	القصيرُ	qaSiir-un	قصيرٌ
Genitive	al-qaSiir-i	القصيرِ	qaSiir-in	قصيرٍ
Accusative	al-qaSiir-a	القصيرَ	qaSiir-an	قصيراً

(6)   Broken plural adjective:

'short' *qiSaar* قصار				
	Definite:		Indefinite:	
Nominative	al-qiSaar-u	القصارُ	qiSaar-un	قصارٌ
Genitive	al-qiSaar-i	القصارِ	qiSaar-in	قصارٍ
Accusative	al-qiSaar-a	القصارَ	qiSaar-an	قصاراً

5.4.1.3 THE FIVE NOUNS (*al-ʾasmaaʾ al-xamsa* الأسماء الخمسة): Within the triptote declension there is a subset of Arabic nouns from biliteral or even monoliteral roots which show triptote case inflection in two ways: as a short vowel and as a long vowel. The long vowel is used when the word is used as the first term of a genitive construct (*ʾiDaafa*) or when it has a pronoun suffix.

The five nouns are:

father	*ʾab*	أب	mouth	*fam*	فم
brother	*ʾax*	أخ	possessor	*dhuu*	ذو
father-in-law	*Ham*	حم			

(1)   The five-noun paradigms: 'father' *ʾab* أب
(1.1)   As an independent word:

	Definite:		Indefinite:	
Nominative	al-ʾab-u	الأبُ	ʾab-u-n	أبٌ
Genitive	al-ʾab-i	الأبِ	ʾab-i-n	أبٍ
Accusative	al-ʾab-a	الأبَ	ʾab-an	أباً

(1.2)   With pronoun suffix: *–haa* 'her father':

Nominative	*ʾab-uu-haa*	أبوها
Genitive	*ʾab-ii-haa*	أبيها
Accusative	*ʾab-aa-haa*	أباها

(1.3) As first part of *ʾiDaafa*: 'the father of Hasan':

Nominative	*ʾab-uu Hasan-in*	أبو حسنٍ
Genitive	*ʾab-ii Hasan-in*	أبي حسنٍ
Accusative	*ʾab-aa Hasan-in*	أبا حسنٍ

Examples:

الأبُ يوسفُ

al-ʾab-u yuusuf-u

Father Joseph

أصبحَ أباً.

ʾaSbaH-a ʾab-an.

He became a **father**.

سألتُ أخاه.

saʾal-tu ʾax-aa-hu.

I asked **his brother**.

ذهبت إلى بيت أبيها.

dhahab-at ʾilaa bayt-i ʾab-ii-haa.

She went to **her father's** house.

5.4.2 Two-way inflection: declensions two, three, four, and five

Certain Arabic noun declensions **exhibit only two different case markers**, or two-way inflection. These declensions have a specific nominative inflectional marker but they merge the genitive and accusative into just one other inflectional marker.[88] Technically, these nouns are considered to exhibit all three cases; it is just that the genitive and accusative have exactly the same form.[89]

The declensions that have two-way inflection fall into two major categories, the suffix declensions and the diptote declension. The suffix declensions are determined by number suffixes and include the dual, the sound masculine plural, and the sound feminine plural, whereas the diptote declension includes words that fall into particular semantic and morphological categories, as described below.

5.4.2.1 SUFFIX DECLENSIONS: THE DUAL (DECLENSION TWO), THE SOUND MASCULINE PLURAL (DECLENSION THREE) AND THE SOUND FEMININE PLURAL (DECLENSION FOUR). Three sets of two-way inflections are based on dual and plural suffixes rather than word stems. That is, once the suffix is attached to a word, it is the suffix itself that determines how the word will be marked for case. These number-marking suffixes in Arabic are all restricted to two case markings rather

---

[88] Sometimes, in this latter category, the combined genitive/accusative inflection is referred to as the "oblique" or essentially, non-nominative case marker.

[89] Traditional Arabic grammatical theory evolved the concept that all nouns are marked for every case, but that in some of them the case marker is "virtual" or "implied" (*muqaddar*) rather than overt (*Zaahir*).

than three. These suffixes carry two kinds of information: number (dual or plural) and case (nominative or genitive/accusative).

(1) **Declension two: The dual** (*al-muthannaa* المثنى) As described in section 3.1 Arabic uses a suffix on the singular stem to mark the noun as being two in number, or in the dual. The dual suffix has two case forms, and is not inflected for definiteness.

-aani (nominative)   ان - ِ

-ayni (genitive/accusative)   يْنِ -

(1.1) **Masculine dual noun:**

'two houses' *bayt-aani* بيتان				
	Definite:		Indefinite:	
Nominative	al-bayt-aani	البيتانِ	bayt-aani	بيتانِ
Genitive	al-bayt-ayni	البيتينِ	bayt-ayni	بيتينِ
Accusative	al-bayt-ayni	البيتينِ	bayt-ayni	بيتينِ

(1.2) **Feminine dual noun:**

'two cities' *madiinat-aani* مدينتان				
	Definite:		Indefinite:	
Nominative	al-madiinat-aani	المدينتانِ	madiinat-aani	مدينتانِ
Genitive	al-madiinat-ayni	المدينتينِ	madiinat-ayni	مدينتينِ
Accusative	al-madiinat-ayni	المدينتينِ	madiinat-ayni	مدينتينِ

(1.3) **Masculine dual adjective:**

'big' *kabiir-aani* كبيران				
	Definite:		Indefinite:	
Nominative	al-kabiir-aani	الكبيرانِ	kabiir-aani	كبيرانِ
Genitive	al-kabiir-ayni	الكبيرينِ	kabiir-ayni	كبيرينِ
Accusative	al-kabiir-ayni	الكبيرينِ	kabiir-ayni	كبيرينِ

(1.4) Feminine dual adjective:

'big' kabiirat-aani كبيرتان				
	Definite:		Indefinite:	
Nominative	al-kabiirat-aani	الكبيرتان	kabiirat-aani	كبيرتان
Genitive	al-kabiirat-ayni	الكبيرتين	kabiirat-ayni	كبيرتين
Accusative	al-kabiirat-ayni	الكبيرتين	kabiirat-ayni	كبيرتين

Examples:

جرسانِ
jaras-aani
two bells

من مركزيْنِ
min markaz-ayni
from two centers

عاصفتانِ كبيرتانِ
ʿaaSifat-aani kabiirat-aani
two big storms

في مدينتيْنِ كبيرتيْنِ
fii madiinat-ayni kabiirat-ayni
in two big cities

(1.5) *Nuun-deletion with possessive pronouns and as first term of construct:*
When a dual noun is the first term of a construct, or if it has a pronoun
suffix, the *nuun* of the dual suffix (and its short vowel *kasra*) is deleted.[90]

بيديْهِ
bi-yad-ay-hi
in his two hands

مع مرشّحَي الحزبِ
maʿ-a murashshaH-ay-i l-Hizb-i
with the two nominees of the party

وحضرَ اللقاءَ عميدا كليتي الطبّ والهندسة.
wa-HaDar-a l-liqaaʾ-a ʿamiid-aa kulliyyat-ay-i l-Tibb-i wa-l-handasat-i.
The two deans of the schools of medicine and engineering attended the
meeting.

(2) Declension three: The sound masculine plural (*jamʿ mudhakkar saalim*
جمع مذكر سالم): The sound masculine plural has two forms, much like the

---

[90] The *nuun* of the dual can be considered a form of nunation, and since nunation cannot occur on a
noun that is the first term of a genitive construct or on a noun with a suffixed possessive pronoun, the *nuun* of the dual suffix (and the sound masculine plural) is likewise deleted. The dual
category is discussed at greater length in Chapter 15. Characteristics of the genitive construct, or
ʾiDaafa are discussed in Chapter 8.

dual. Note that the long vowel in the suffix (*-uu-* or *-ii-*) is what changes
when the case changes. The final short vowel (*fatHa* |*-a*/) remains the same
in both the nominative and the genitive/accusative. This *fatHa* is not a case
ending, but rather part of the spelling of the suffix. In pause form it is not
pronounced.

Note: This form of plural is used only to refer to human beings.

correspondents (nominative)	*muraasil-uuna*	مراسلون
correspondents (genitive/accusative)	*muraasil-iina*	مراسلين
Muslims (nominative)	*muslim-uuna*	مسلمون
Muslims (genitive/accusative)	*muslim-iina*	مسلمين

(2.1)   Sound masculine plural noun:

'citizens' *muwaaTin-uuna* مواطنون			
	Definite:		Indefinite:	
Nominative	*al-muwaaTin-uuna*	المواطنون	*muwaaTin-uuna*	مواطنون
Genitive	*al-muwaaTin-iina*	المواطنين	*muwaaTin-iina*	مواطنين
Accusative	*al-muwaaTin-iina*	المواطنين	*muwaaTin-iina*	مواطنين

(2.2)   Sound masculine plural adjective:

'many' *kathiir-uuna* كثيرون			
	Definite:		Indefinite:	
Nominative	*al-kathiir-uuna*	الكثيرون	*kathiir-uuna*	كثيرون
Genitive	*al-kathiir-iina*	الكثيرين	*kathiir-iina*	كثيرين
Accusative	*al-kathiir-iina*	الكثيرين	*kathiir-iina*	كثيرين

Examples:

مراقبون رسميّون

muraaqib-uuna rasmiyy-uuna

official observers

من المثقّفين المعتدلين

min-a l-muthaqqaf-iina l- muʕtadil-iina

from the moderate intelligensia

عددٌ من الباحثينَ والمفكرينَ المصريّينَ واللبنانيّينَ

ʿadad-un min-a l-baaHith-iina wa-l-mufakkir-iina l-miSriyy-iina wa-l-lubnaaniyy-iina

a number of Egyptian and Lebanese researchers and intellectuals

(2.3) *Nuun*-deletion with possessive pronouns and as first term of construct:
When a noun pluralized with the sound masculine plural suffix functions as the first term of a construct, or if it has a pronoun suffix, the *nuun*
(and its short vowel *fatha*) of the suffix is deleted (similar to what occurs
with the dual suffix above 5.4.2.1(1.5).[91] The long case-marking vowels /-uu-/
or /-ii-/ are then left as the remaining part of the suffix.

مراقبو الوفد

muraaqib-uu l-wafd-i

observers of the delegation

من مُتَخَرّجي الجامعة

*min **mutaxarrij-ii** l-jaamiʿat-i*

from **the graduates** of the university

ستطلبُ من ناخبيه التصويت.

*sa-ta-Tlub-u min **naaxib-ii-hi** l-taSwiit-a.*

It will ask its electors to vote.

(3) **Declension four: The sound feminine plural** (*jamʿ muʾannath saalim*
جمع مؤنث سالم). The sound feminine plural is also restricted to two
case markers. Unlike the dual and sound masculine plural, where the
case marking shows up on the long vowel of the suffix, the case marking
for the sound feminine plural occurs at the end of the suffix, just as normal triptote short vowel case marking would occur. However, the sound
feminine plural is restricted to only two of the short vowels: *Damma* and
kasra. It cannot take *fatHa*. The genitive/accusative form takes *kasra* or
kasrataan.

(3.1) **Sound feminine plural noun:**

‘elections’ *intixaabaat* انتخابات				
	Definite:		**Indefinite:**	
Nominative	*al-intixaabaat-u*	الانتخاباتُ	*intixaabaat-u-n*	انتخاباتٌ
Genitive	*al-intixaabaat-i*	الانتخاباتِ	*intixaabaat-i-n*	انتخاباتٍ
Accusative	*al-intixaabaat-i*	الانتخاباتِ	*intixaabaat-i-n*	انتخاباتٍ

---

[91] See also Chapter 8, 1.2.1.4.

(3.2) **Sound feminine plural adjective**: This form of the adjective is used only to refer to groups of female human beings:

'Egyptian' *miSriyyaat* مصريات				
	Definite:		Indefinite:	
Nominative	*al-miSriyyaat-u*	المصريات	*miSriyyaat-u-n*	مصريات
Genitive	*al-miSriyyaat-i*	المصريات	*miSriyyaat-i-n*	مصريات
Accusative	*al-miSriyyaat-i*	المصريات	*miSriyyaat-i-n*	مصريات

Examples of feminine plural accusative/genitive:

أجرى محادثات.	لسنا يمنيّات.	يفتحُ مجالات واسعة.
'ajraa **muHaadathaat-in**	*las-naa* **yamaniyyaat-in.**	*ya-ftaH-u* **majaalaat-in**
He held **talks**.	We are not **Yemeni** (f.pl.).	**waasi'at-an.**[92]
		It opens wide **fields**.

يجري اتصالاتٍ مع جميع الأطراف.

yu-jrii **ttiSaalaat-in** *ma'-a jamii'-i l-'aTraaf-i*

He is in contact with ('implementing **contacts**') with all sides.

دخلنَ الصفَّ منأخرات.	رابطةُ النساءِ العربيّاتِ
daxal-na l-Saff-a **muta'axxiraat-in.**	*raabiTat-u l-nisaa'-i* **l-'arabiyyaat-i**
They (f.) entered the classroom **late**.	the **Arab** women's club

5.4.2.2 DECLENSION FIVE: DIPTOTE (*al-mamnuu' min-a l-Sarf* الممنوع من الصرف): The term "diptote" refers to an inflectional category or declension of Arabic nouns and adjectives that are formally restricted *when they are indefinite*:

- They do not take nunation.
- They do not take *kasra* (the genitive marker).

Diptotes therefore, when indefinite, only exhibit two case-markers: final *-u* (*Damma*) for nominative case and final *-a* (*fatHa*) for both genitive and accusative. They look identical in the indefinite genitive and accusative cases.

---

[92] Note that the adjective agreeing with *majaalaat-in* shows the accusative as *fatHataan* because it is triptote and belongs to declension one. Both *majaalaat* and *waasi'a* are in the accusative, but they are marked differently because they fall into two different declensions.

(1)   Paradigms

(1.1)   Singular diptote noun:

'desert' *SaHraa'* صحراء				
	Definite:		Indefinite:	
Nominative	al-SaHraa'-u	الصحراء	SaHraa'-u	صحراء
Genitive	al-SaHraa'-i	الصحراء	SaHraa'-a	صحراء
Accusative	al-SaHraa'-a	الصحراء	SaHraa'-a	صحراء

(1.2)   Plural diptote noun:

'presidents' *ru'asaa'* رؤساء				
	Definite:		Indefinite:	
Nominative	al-ru'asaa'-u	الرؤساء	ru'assa'-u	رؤساء
Genitive	al-ru'asaa'-i	الرؤساء	ru'asaa'-a	رؤساء
Accusative	al-ru'saa'-a	الرؤساء	ru'asaa'-a	روؤ ساء

(1.3)   Singular masculine adjective

'red' *'aHmar* أحمر				
	Definite:		Indefinite:	
Nominative	al-'aHmar-u	الأحمر	'aHmar-u	أحمر
Genitive	al-'aHmar-i	الأحمر	'aHmar-a	أحمر
Accusative	al-'aHmar-a	الأحمر	'aHmar-a	أحمر

(1.4)   Singular feminine adjective:

'red' *Hamraa'* حمراء				
	Definite:		Indefinite:	
Nominative	al-Hamraa'-u	الحمراء	Hamraa'-u	حمراء
Genitive	al-Hamraa'-i	الحمراء	Hamraa'-a	حمراء
Accusative	al-Hamraa'-a	الحمراء	Hamraa'-a	حمراء

(1.5) Plural diptote adjective:

<table>
<tr><td colspan="5" align="center">'foreign' ʾajaanib أجانب</td></tr>
<tr><td></td><td colspan="2" align="center">Definite:</td><td colspan="2" align="center">Indefinite:</td></tr>
<tr><td>Nominative</td><td>al-ʾajaanib-u</td><td>الأجانبُ</td><td>ʾajaanib-u</td><td>أجانبُ</td></tr>
<tr><td>Genitive</td><td>al-ʾajaanib-i</td><td>الأجانبِ</td><td>ʾajaanib-a</td><td>أجانبَ</td></tr>
<tr><td>Accusative</td><td>al-ʾajaanib-a</td><td>الأجانبَ</td><td>ʾajaanib-a</td><td>أجانبَ</td></tr>
</table>

Examples of diptotes in context:

أربعةُ خناجرَ
ʾarbaʿat-u xanaajir-a
four **daggers**

سلطةٌ خضراءُ
salaTat-un xaDraaʾ-u
a **green** salad

بيتٌ أبيضُ
bayt-un ʾabyaD-u
a **white** house

إلى مدينة بغدادَ
ʾilaa madiinat-i baghdaad-a
to the city of **Baghdad**

سيؤدّي إلى علاقة أوثقَ بينَهما.
sa-yu-ʾaddii ʾilaa ʿalaaqat-in ʾawthaq-a bayn-a-humaa.
It will lead to a **firmer** relationship between the two of them.

(2) Categories of diptotes: Diptotes fall into categories based on their word structure. The main ones are: diptote by virtue of pattern (singular patterns and plural patterns) and diptote by nature or origin:[93]

(2.1) Diptote by pattern:

(2.1.1) Diptote plural patterns: Certain noun and adjective plural patterns are inherently diptote, including:

(a) <i>fuʿalaaʾ</i> فُعَلاء

Nouns:			Adjectives:		
ministers	<i>wuzaraaʾ</i>	وزراء	poor	<i>fuqaraaʾ</i>	فقراء
presidents	<i>ruʾasaaʾ</i>	رؤساء	strange	<i>ghurabaaʾ</i>	غرباء
princes	<i>ʾumaraaʾ</i>	أمراء	honorable	<i>shurafaaʾ</i>	شرفاء
leaders	<i>zuʿamaaʾ</i>	زعماء	generous	<i>kuramaaʾ</i>	كرماء

---

[93] See also section 3.2.3.2. in this chapter.

(b) *faʿaalil* فَعالِل

Nouns:			Adjectives:		
spices; herbs	*tawaabil*	توابل	foreign	*ʾajaanib*	أجانب
restaurants	*maTaaʿim*	مطاعم	relative(s)	*ʾaqaarib*	أقارب
offices	*makaatib*	مكاتب	greatest	*ʾakaabir*	أكابر
peppers	*falaafil*	فلافل			

(c) *faʿaaliil* فَعاليل

Nouns:		
crowds, throngs	*jamaahiir*	جماهير
topics	*mawaaDiiʿ*	مواضيع
legends	*ʾasaaTiir*	أساطير

(d) *ʾafʿilaaʾ* أفْعِلاء with variant *ʾafiʿlaaʾ* أفْعِلاء for geminate roots.

Nouns:			Adjectives:		
friends	*ʾaSdiqaaʾ*	أصدقاء	dear; strong	*ʾaʿizzaaʾ*	أعزّاء
few	*ʾaqillaaʾ*	أقلّاء	beloved	*ʾaHibbaaʾ*	أحبّاء
doctors	*ʾaTibbaaʾ*	أطبّاء			

(2.1.2) **Singular diptote patterns:**

(a) **Elative (comparative) adjectives and colors:** The diptote pattern is used to indicate the comparative state of the adjective and also for the basic color names.[94] Both the masculine and feminine forms of the elative are diptote:

(a.1) **Masculine singular comparative adjective *ʾafʿal* أفْعل:**

better, preferable	*ʾafDal*	أفضل	green (m.)	*ʾaxDar*	أخضر
happier	*ʾasʿad*	أسعد	blue (m.)	*ʾazraq*	أزرق
fewer; less	*ʾaqall*	أقلّ	yellow (m.)	*ʾaSfar*	أصفر

(a.2) **The feminine singular adjective used for colors and physical traits (*faʿlaaʾ* فعلاء):**

red	*Hamraaʾ*	حمراء	blonde	*shaqraaʾ*	شقراء
blue	*zarqaaʾ*	زرقاء	deaf	*Tarshaaʾ*	طرشاء

---

[94] For more description of comparative and superlative adjectives, see Chapter 10, section 4.2; for more about color adjectives, see Chapter 10, section 5.1.

(2.1.2.b)   **Nouns or adjectives that have a suffix -*aaᵓ* after the root consonants.**
Nouns of the *faʕlaaᵓ* فَعْلاء pattern. These words are usually feminine in
gender, e.g.,

desert	*SaHraaᵓ*	صحراء	beauty; belle	*Hasnaaᵓ*	حسناء

(2.2)   **Diptote by nature or origin:** Certain categories of words fall into the
diptote camp by virtue of their etymology or meaning.

(2.2.1)   **Most feminine proper names,** e.g.,

Fatima	*faaTima*	فاطمة	Zayna	*zayna*	زينة
Aida	*ʕaaᵓida*	عائدة	Afaf	*ʕafaaf*	عفاف

(2.2.2)   **Proper names of non-Arabic origin:** This includes a large number of
place names or names of geographical features in the Middle East
whose origins are from other Semitic languages or other (non-Semitic)
Middle Eastern languages. A salient characteristic of most of these
names is that they do not have the definite article.

Damascus	*dimashq*	دمشق	Tunis	*tuunis*	تونس
Baghdad	*baghdaad*	بغداد	Beirut	*bayruut*	بيروت
Egypt	*miSr*	مصر	Lebanon	*lubnaan*	لبنان
Mecca	*makka*	مكة	Tigris	*dijla*	دجلة

Examples:

from Damascus	*min dimashq-a*	من دمشقَ
in Tunis	*fii tuunis-a*	في تونسَ
to Egypt	*ᵓilaa miSr-a*	إلى مصرَ

Also, other non-Arab place names:[95]

Madrid	*madriid*	مدريد
Paris	*baariis*	باريس
Istanbul	*istaanbuul*	إسطانبول

---

[95] In MSA, names of places in other parts of the world, such as *nyuu yuurk* نيو يورك (New York), *waashinTun* واشنطن (Washington), or *istukhulm* استكهلم (Stockholm) are usually left uninflected, since
they are not readily accommodated into the Arabic inflectional class system.

A helpful rule of thumb with Middle Eastern place names in Arabic is that if they carry the definite article, then they inflect as triptotes, e.g.:

Rabat	*al-ribaaT*	الرباط	Khartoum	*al-xarTuum*	الخرطوم
Cairo	*al-qaahira*	القاهرة	Kuwait	*al-kuwayt*	الكويت

Examples:

from Cairo	*min-a l-qaahirat-i*	من القاهرة
in Khartoum	*fii l-xarTuum-i*	في الخرطوم
to Kuwait	*ʾilaa l-kuwayt-i*	إلى الكويت

(2.2.3)   **Certain masculine names:** Certain Arabic masculine proper names are diptote. These occur in the following categories:

(2.2.3.a)   **Derived from other Semitic languages:** These include many names mentioned in the Bible and in the Qurʾān.

Suleiman, Solomon	*sulaymaan*	سليمان	Jonah; Jonas	*yuunus*	يونس
Jacob; James	*yaʿquub*	يعقوب	Abraham	*ʾibraahiim*	إبراهيم

(2.2.3.b)   **Derived from verbs rather than adjectives:**

Ahmad 'I praise'	*ʾa-Hmad-u*	أحمد
Yazid 'He increases'	*ya-ziid-u*	يزيد

5.4.3 DECLENSION SIX: DEFECTIVE NOUNS AND ADJECTIVES (*ʾasmaaʾ naaqiSa* أسماء ناقصة; *al-ism al-manquuS* الاسم المنقوص).

This inflectional class includes primarily words derived from "defective" roots, that is, lexical roots whose final element is a semivowel rather than a consonant.

It includes masculine singular active participles from all forms (I–X) of defective verbs, verbal nouns from forms V and VI, and a set of noun plurals based primarily on the diptote plural pattern **CaCaaCiC**. The characteristic feature of this declension is that the final root consonant appears in the form of two *kasras* in the nominative and genitive indefinite. In an ordinary written text, these short vowels are not visible.[96]

Thus in this declension, the nominative and genitive inflections are identical; the accusative shows inflection for *fatHa* or *fatHataan*.

---

[96] The two *kasras* may be added into a printed text (in a newspaper article, for example) should there be ambiguity about the meaning of the word.

5.4.3.1 SINGULAR DEFECTIVE NOUN:

'lawyer' *muHaam-in*[97] محام				
	Definite:		**Indefinite:**	
Nominative	*al-muHaamii*	المحامي	*muHaam-in*	محام
Genitive	*al-muHaamii*	المحامي	*muHaam-in*	محام
Accusative	*al-muHaamiya*	المحامي	*muHaamiy-an*	محامياً

5.4.3.2 DIPTOTE DEFECTIVE PLURAL:[98]

'cafés' *maqaah-in* مقاه				
	Definite:		**Indefinite:**	
Nominative	*al-maqaahii*	المقاهي	*maqaah-in*	مقاه
Genitive	*al-maqaahii*	المقاهي	*maqaahin*	مقاه
Accusative	*al-maqaahiy-a*	المقاهي	*maqaah-iy-a*	مقاهي

Further examples:

Singular defectives:

club	*naad-in*	ناد	challenge	*taHadd-in*	تحدّ
judge	*qaaD-in*	قاض	singer	*mughann-in*	مغنّ

Plural defectives:

songs	*ʾaghaan-in*	أغان	nights	*layaal-in*	ليال
lands	*ʾaraaD-in*[99]	أراض	chairs	*karaas-in*	كراس
hands	*ʾayd-in ~ ʾayaad-in*	أيدٍ ~ أيادٍ	suburbs	*DawaaH-in*	ضواح

---

[97] Active participle from Form III defective verb *Haamaa/yu-Haamii*, 'to defend, protect.'
[98] Pattern **CaCaaCiC**.
[99] In this (ʾ-r-D) and the following three words, the defective ending has been added to a non-defective root (y-d, l-y-l, k-r-s).

من أيدينا	في ضواحي بيروتَ
min ʾaydii-naa	*fii DawaaHii bayruut-a*
from **our hands**	in the **suburbs** of Beirut
هوَ محامٍ.	كانَ محامياً.
huwa muHaam-in.	*kaan-a muHaamiy-an.*
He is **a lawyer.**	He **was a lawyer.**

5.4.4 Declension seven: indeclinable nouns (*al-ism al-maqSuur* الاسم المقصور)

Indeclinable nouns show **no variation in case, only definiteness**. They are chiefly derived from defective lexical roots and include, in particular, passive participles (m.) from all forms (I–X) and nouns of place from defective verbs.[100] They normally end with *ʾalif maqSuura*.

5.4.4.1 SINGULAR INDECLINABLE NOUN:

'hospital' *mustashfan* مستشفىً			
	Definite:		Indefinite:
Nominative	*al-mustashfaa*	المستشفى	*mustashfan*	مستشفىً
Genitive	*al-mustashfaa*	المستشفى	*mustashfan*	مستشفىً
Accusative	*al-mustashfaa*	المستشفى	*mustashfan*	مستشفىً

5.4.4.2 PLURAL INDECLINABLE NOUN:

'villages'[101] *quran* قرىً			
Nominative	*al-quraa*	القرى	*quran*	قرىً
Genitive	*al-quraa*	القرى	*quran*	قرىً
Accusative	*al-quraa*	القرى	*quran*	قرىً

---

[100] For a detailed explanation of the phonological rules applying to indeclinable nouns and adjectives, see Abboud and McCarus 1983, II:14–19.
[101] Singular *qarya* قرية.

5.4.4.3 FURTHER EXAMPLES:

(1)   **Nouns of place:**

coffeehouse	*maqhan*	مقهى	stream, course	*majran*	مجرى
goal, range	*marman*	مرمى	building	*mabnan*	مبنى

(2)   **Common nouns:**

stick, cane	*ʿaSan*	عصا	villages	*quran*	قرى

(3)   **Verbal nouns**

effort	*masʿan*	مسعى	meaning	*maʿnan*	معنى

(4)   **Passive participles of derived verb forms (II–X):**[102]

a level	*mustawan*	مستوى	a crossroad	*multaqan*	ملتقى
a hospital	*mustashfan*	مستشفى	required; requirement	*muqtaDan*	مقتضى

(5)   **Examples in context:**

نُقِلَ إلى مستشفى الجامعة الأميركيّة.

*nuqil-a ʾilaa **mustashfaa** l-jaamiʿat-i l-ʾamiirkiyyat-i.*

He was taken to **the hospital** of the American University.

تربطُ ثلاثَ قرىً كبيرة.	بمقتضى الاتّفاقيّة
*ta-rbiT-u thalaath-a **quran** kabiirat-in.*	*bi-**muqtaDaa** l-ittifaaqiyyat-i*
It links three big **villages**.	**in accordance with** the agreement

5.4.5 Declension eight: Invariable nouns

This noun class consists of a set of nouns which vary **neither in case nor in definiteness**. They are spelled with final ʾalif maqSuura unless the previous letter is yaaʾ, in which case, ʾalif Tawiila is used.[103]

---

[102] Some passive participles of the derived forms serve also as nouns of place.

[103] Abboud and McCarus 1983, II:19–20 provide an informative discussion of this declension. ʿAbd al-Latif et al. 1997, 54–55, describe these nouns as having a suffixed feminine marker, ʾalif maqSuura, and that they are therefore diptote, and do not take nunation.

5.4.5.1 INVARIABLE NOUN ENDING WITH ʾ*alif maqSuura*:

'complaint' *shakwaa* شكوى			
Nominative	*al-shakwaa*	الشكوى	*shakwaa*	شكوى
Genitive	*al-shakwaa*	الشكوى	*shakwaa*	شكوى
Accusative	*al-shakwaa*	الشكوى	*shakwaa*	شكوى

5.4.5.2 INVARIABLE NOUN ENDING WITH ʾ*alif Tawiila*:

'gifts' *hadaayaa* هدايا			
Nominative	*al-hadaayaa*	الهدايا	*hadaayaa*	هدايا
Genitive	*al-hadaayaa*	الهدايا	*hadaayaa*	هدايا
Accusative	*al-hadaayaa*	الهدايا	*hadaayaa*	هدايا

5.4.5.3 SINGULAR INVARIABLE ADJECTIVE:

'higher, highest' ʾ*aᶜlaa* أعلى			
Nominative	*al-ʾaᶜlaa*	الأعلى	ʾ*aᶜlaa*	أعلى
Genitive	*al-ʾaᶜlaa*	الأعلى	ʾ*aᶜlaa*	أعلى
Accusative	*al-ʾaᶜlaa*	الأعلى	ʾ*aᶜlaa*	أعلى

5.4.5.4 PLURAL INVARIABLE ADJECTIVE:

'sick' *marDaa* مرضى			
Nominative	*al-marDaa*	المرضى	*marDaa*	مرضى
Genitive	*al-marDaa*	المرضى	*marDaa*	مرضى
Accusative	*al-marDaa*	المرضى	*marDaa*	مرضى

5.4.5.5 TYPES OF DECLENSION EIGHT NOUNS AND ADJECTIVES. This declension or inflectional class includes a number of noun and adjective types:

(1)   **Singular nouns:** These nouns are feminine in gender, having an *'alif maq-Suura* suffixed after the root consonants, chiefly with patterns *fuʿlaa*, *fiʿlaa* and *faʿlaa*:

gift; benefit	*jadwaa*	جدوى	fever	*Hummaa*	حمى
candy, sweet	*Halwaa*	حلوى	dream	*ruʾyaa*	رؤيا
chaos	*fawDaa*	فوضى	world; universe	*dunyaa*	دنيا
memorial; anniversary	*dhikraa*	ذكرى	one; one of	*'iHdaa*	إحدى

وهذا بالإضافة إلى بقايا المشاكل.	إحداهما
*wa-haadhaa bi-l-'iDaafat-i 'ilaa **baqaayaa** l-mashaakil-i.*	***'iHdaa-humaa***
And this [is] in addition to **the rest** of the problems.	**one of [the two of] them**

شاهدَ الدنيا جميلةً.	هي إحدى أهمِّ المؤسّسات.
*shaahad-a **l-dunyaa** jamiilat-an.*	*hiya **'iHdaa** 'ahamm-i l-mu'assasaat-i.*
He saw **the world** [as] beautiful.	It is **one of the most** important establishments.

(2)   **Singular adjectives**

(2.1)   *fuʿlaa* فُعلى: The feminine singular superlative adjective has the form *fuʿlaa*, which puts it into this inflectional class. If the final *'alif* is preceded by a *yaa'*, it becomes *'alif Tawilla.*

finest, best	*Husnaa* (f. of *'aHsan*)	حسنى	middle, most central	*wusTaa* (f. of *'awsaT*)	وسطى
great, greatest	*kubraa* (f. of *'akbar*)	كبرى	highest	*ʿulyaa* (f. of *'aʿlaa*)	عُليا

أسماءُ اللّه الحسنى التسعةُ والتسعونَ
*'asmaa'-u llaah-i **l-Husnaa** l-tisʿat-u wa-l-tisʿuuna*
the ninety-nine **attributes** ('the finest names') of God

يمثّلُ خطوةً كبرى إلى الأمام.	خلالَ العصور الوسطى
*yu-maththil-u xuTwat-an **kubraa** 'ilaa l-'amaam-i.*	*xilaal-a l-ʿuSuur-i **l-wusTaa***
It represents a **great** step forward.	during the **Middle Ages**

(2.2)   *ʾafʿaa* أفعى: The comparative/superlative adjective from defective roots has
the form *ʾafʿaa*, which puts it also into this category.

من دون حد أدنى

min duun-i Hadd-in ʾadnaa

without a **lower** limit (minimum)

الشرق الأدنى

al-sharq-u l-ʾadnaa

the Near East

(2.3)   The feminine form of 'first' *ʾuulaa* أولى: This is a feminine adjective; it
usually follows a feminine noun.

للمرّة الأولى

li-l-marrat-i l-ʾuulaa

for the **first** time

الجملةُ الأولى

al-jumlat-u l-ʾuulaa

the **first** sentence

(2.4)   The feminine form of 'other' *ʾuxraa* أخرى

في دولٍ أخرى

fii duwal-in ʾuxraa

in **other** countries

مرّةً أخرى

marrat-an ʾuxraa

another time; one more time

(3)   **Invariable plurals:** Included in this set of words are a number of noun
and adjective plurals, such as the following:

Nouns:

Halaawaa	pl. of *Halwaa* 'sweet, candy'	حلاوى
zawaayaa	pl. of *zaawiya* 'corner'	زوايا
qaDaayaa	pl. of *qaDiyya* 'issue, problem'	قضايا
baqaayaa	pl. of *baqiyya* 'rest, remainder'	بقايا

Adjectives:

kaslaa	pl. of *kaslaan* 'lazy'	كسلى
ghaDaabaa	pl. of *ghadbaan* 'angry'	غضابى
naSaaraa	pl. of *naSraaniyy* 'Christian'	نصارى
qatlaa	pl. of *qatiil* 'killed (person), casualty'	قتلى
marDaa	pl. of *mariiD* 'sick (person)'	مرضى
jarHaa	pl. of *jariiH* 'wounded (person)'	جرحى

عددُ ضحايا الزلزالِ

ʿadad-u DaHaayaa l-zilzaal-i

the number of **victims** of the earthquake

(4) **Foreign nouns:** These nouns are not traditionally considered part of this class because they are not of Arabic origin. However, foreign proper names and borrowed words ending in /-aa/ are also invariable in their inflection.

Canada	*kanadaa*	كندا	cinema	*siinamaa*	سينما
France	*faransaa*	فرنسا	potato	*baTaaTaa*	بطاطا
Korea	*kuuriyaa*	كوريا	music	*muusiiqaa*	موسيقى
camera	*kaamiiraa*	كاميرا			

في زيارةٍ لفرنسا
fii ziyaarat-in li-faransaa
on a visit **to France**

في جنوبِ اسبانيا
fii januub-i isbaaniyaa
in southern **Spain**

السينما الحديثةُ
al-siinamaa l-Hadiithat-u
the modern **cinema**

في أنهار إفريقيا
fii ʾanhaar-i ʾifriiqiyaa
in the rivers of **Africa**

8

Construct phrases and nouns in apposition

1 The construct phrase or ʾiDaafa الإضافة

In Arabic, two nouns may be linked together in a relationship where the second noun determines the first by identifying, limiting, or defining it, and thus the two nouns function as one phrase or syntactic unit. Traditionally, in English descriptions of Arabic grammar, this unit is called the "genitive construct," the "construct phrase," or "annexation structure." In Arabic it is referred to as the ʾiDaafa ('annexation; addition'). As Beeston explains, "The link between a noun and an entity which amplifies it is termed by the Arab grammarians ʾiDaafa 'annexation', and the noun amplified is said to be muDaaf 'annexed'" (1970, 45).

Similar constructions in English, where two nouns occur together with one defining the other, might be, for example, "coffee cup," "university library," or (as one word) "eggshell." In fact, English often juxtaposes nouns to create new hybrid terms: "airbag," "seat belt," or "keyboard." Another English equivalent to the Arabic construct phrase is a possessive phrase using "of" ("the Queen of Sweden," "a bottle of wine") or the possessive suffix / -'s /on the possessing noun ("Cairo's cafés", "the newspaper's editorial").

The noun-noun genitive construct is one of the most basic structures in the Arabic language and occurs with high frequency. The first noun, the muDaaf ('the added'), has neither the definite article nor nunation because it is in an "annexed" state, determined by the second noun.[1] But, as the head noun of the phrase, the first noun can be in any case: nominative, genitive, or accusative, depending on the function of the ʾiDaafa unit in a sentence structure. The second, or annexing noun, is called the muDaaf ʾilay-hi.[2] It is marked either for definiteness or indefiniteness, and is always in the genitive case.

---

[1] "In Arabic it is the amplifying term whose definitional status yields the definitional status of the whole phrase: consequently, an annexed substantive will not itself have the article" (Beeston 1970, 46).

[2] Literally, the noun 'added to.' For an extensive discussion (in English) of ʾiDaafa constructions in literary Arabic, see Cantarino 1970, II: 92-119. See also Wright 1967, II:198-234 for a summary of the rules for Classical Arabic "Status constructus and the genitive." Hasan 1987, III:1-180 has a thorough analysis of the genitive construct (in Arabic).

In terms of semantic relationships between the nouns in an Arabic construct phrase, they are very wide-ranging.[3] Here they are classified in relatively discrete groups, but clear boundaries cannot always be established between the groups and sometimes membership blurs or overlaps. Eleven general categories are listed here.[4]

1.1 Types of *ʾiDaafa*s

1.1.1 Identity relationship

In this broad category, the second term specifies, defines, limits, or explains the particular identity of the first:[5]

Definite:

the city of Jerusalem	*madiinat-u l-quds-i*	مدينةُ القدسِ
the minister of justice	*waziir-u l-ʿadl-i*	وزيرُ العدلِ
starfish	*najmat-u l-baHr-i*	نجمةُ البحرِ

Indefinite:

a police officer	*DaabiT-u shurTat-in*	ضابطُ شرطة
a handbag	*Haqiibat-u yad-in*	حقيبةُ يدٍ
love letters	*rasaaʾil-u Hubb-in*	رسائلُ حبٍّ

1.1.2 Possessive relationship

In this kind of annexation structure, the first term can be interpreted as belonging (in the very broadest sense) to the second term. In certain respects, it is very close to the next category, the partitive relationship, and it is sometimes difficult to draw a line between the two.

Beirut airport	*maTaar-u bayruut-a*	مطارُ بيروت
the father of Hasan	*ʾab-uu Hasan-in*[6]	أبو حسنٍ
the leaders of the tribes	*zuʿamaaʾ-u l-qabaaʾil-i*	زعماءُ القبائلِ

1.1.3 Partitive relationship

Here the annexed term (the first term) serves as a determiner to describe a part or quantity of the annexing term. This includes the use of nouns that are quantifiers ("some," "all," "most"), certain numbers and fractions, and superlative constructions.

---

[3] Beeston refers to the "semantic polyvalency of the annexation structure" (1970, 46).

[4] Holes 1995, 166-67 (after Beeston 1970, 45-47) identifies six categories of constructs, including the adjective *ʾiDaafa* or "unreal" *ʾiDaafa* (*ʾiDaafa ghayr Haqiiqiyya*).

[5] Also called the epexegetical genitive, or genitive of explanation.

[6] Although the second noun, *Hasan*, has nunation, it is considered definite because it is a proper name.

Definite:

some of the films	*baʿD-u l-ʾaflaam-i*	بعضُ الأفلام
most of the seats	*muʿZam-u l-maqaaʿid-i*	معظمُ المقاعد
the first part of the month	*maTlaʿ-u l-shahr-i*	مطلعُ الشهر
the best conditions	*ʾafDal-u shuruuT-in*	أفضلُ شروط
the end of the line	*ʾaaxir-u l-Taabuur -i*	آخرُ الطابور
two-thirds of the members	*thulthaa l-ʾaʿDaaʾ-i*	ثلثا الأعضاء

Indefinite:

every day	*kull-a yawm-in*	كلَّ يَوْم
a quarter of a riyal	*rubʿ-u riyaal-in*	ربعُ ريال
any attempt	*ʾayy-u muHaawalat-in*	أيُّ محاولة
four daggers	*ʾarbaʿat-u xanaajir-a*	أربعةُ خناجر
a thousand pages	*ʾalf-u safHat-in*	ألفُ صفحة

For further discussion and examples of these categories, see sections on quantifiers, numerals, and superlative adjectives.

1.1.4 Agent relationship

In this type of construct, the **second term is the agent or doer of the action** and the first term is a verbal noun (*maSdar*), the name of an action:

the crowing of the rooster	*SiyaaH-u l-diik-i*	صياحُ الديك
the squeaking of the door	*Sariir-u l-baab-i*	صريرُ الباب
the departure of the minister	*mughaadarat-u l-waziir-i*	مغادرةُ الوزير
the arrival of the queen	*wuSuul-u l-malikat-i*	وصولُ الملكة

1.1.4.1 ACTION, AGENT, OBJECT: In this variant of the agent-relationship ʾiDaafa, where the object of the verbal action is mentioned in addition to the doer of the action, **then the object follows the ʾiDaafa construction, and is in the accusative case** (as object of the underlying transitive verb):

مغادرةُ الوزير العاصمةَ
mughaadarat-u l-waziir-i l-ʿaaSimat-a
the minister's leaving **the capital**

متابعةُ المركزِ الأحداثَ السياسيةَ

mutaabaᶜat-u l-markaz-i l-ʾaHdaath-a l-siyaasiyyat-a

the center's following [of] **political events**

تسلُمُ المرشحِ الرئاسةَ

tasallum-u l-murashshaH-i l-riʾaasat-a

the nominee's assuming [of] **the presidency**

1.1.5 Object relationship

In this type of construct, the **second term is the object of an action**, and the first term is either the name of the action (*maSdar*), or an active participle (*ism-u l-faaᶜil*) referring to the doer of the action.

1.1.5.1 FIRST TERM VERBAL NOUN: In this type, the first term is a verbal noun referring to the action itself:

Definite:

the raising of the flag	*rafᶜ-u l-ᶜalam-i*	رفعُ العلمِ
the protection of infants	*Himaayat-u l-ʾaTfaal-i*	حمايةُ الأطفالِ
the solution of the problems	*Hall-u l-mashaakil-i*	حلُ المشاكلِ
the regaining of the initiative	*istiᶜaadat-u l-mubaadarat-i*	استعادةُ المبادرة
entering the church	*duxuul-u l-kaniisat-i*	دخولُ الكنيسةِ
criticizing Orientalism	*naqd-u l-istishraaq-i*	نقدُ الاستشراقِ
riding horses	*rukuub-u l-xayl-i*	ركوبُ الخيلِ

Indefinite:

playing a role	*luᶜb-u dawr-in*	لعبُ دورٍ
establishing a state	*qiyaam-u dawlat-in*	قيامُ دولةٍ
opening fire	*ʾiTlaaq-u naar-in*	إطلاقُ نارٍ

1.1.5.2 FIRST TERM ACTIVE PARTICIPLE: In the second type of object-relationship *ʾiDaafa*, the first term is an active participle denoting the doer of an action:

Definite:

the decision-makers	*Saaniᶜ-uu l-qaraar-i*	صانعو القرارِ
companions of the delegation	*muraafiq-uu l-wafd-i*	مرافقو الوفدِ
the two leaders of the campaign	*qaaʾid-aa l-Hamlat-i*	قائدا الحملةِ

Indefinite:

an assistant minister; undersecretary	*musaaᶜid-u waziir-in*	مساعدُ وزيرٍ
a shoemaker	*Saaniᶜ-u ʾaHdhiyat-in*	صانعُ أحذيةٍ
an anteater	*ʾaakil-u naml-in*	آكلُ نملٍ

1.1.6 Compositional relationship

In this structure, the second noun of the construct expresses the nature or composition of the first:

Definite:

the railway ('road of iron')	*sikkat-u l-Hadiid-i*	سكةُ الحديد
bouquets of flowers	*baaqaat-u l-zuhuur-i*	باقاتُ الزهور

Indefinite:

a chain of mountains	*silsilat-u jibaal-in*	سلسلةُ جبالٍ
lentil soup	*shuurbat-u ᶜadas-in*	شوربةُ عدسٍ
a bunch of grapes	*ᶜunquud-u ᶜinab-in*	عنقودُ عنبٍ
a kindergarten ('garden of children')	*rawDat-u ʾaTfaal-in*	روضةُ أطفالٍ

1.1.7 Measurement relationship

Where the first noun expresses the nature of the measurement and the second (and third) the extent or the measurement itself. These occur mainly in indefinite *ʾiDaafas.*

a stone's throw	*marmaa Hajr-in*	مرمى حجرٍ
[for] a period of two days	*muddat-a yawm-ayni*	مدةَ يومينِ
to a distance of ten meters	*ʾilaa masaafat-i ᶜashrat-i ʾamtaar-in*	إلى مسافةِ عشرةِ أمتار
a kilo of bananas	*kiiluu mawz-in*	كيلو موزٍ

1.1.8 Contents relationship

Where the first term denotes a container and the second or annexing term the contents of the container:

Definite:

boxes of gold	*Sanaadiiq-u l-dhahab-i*	صناديقُ الذهب

Indefinite:

a cup of coffee	*finjaan-u qahwat-in*	فنجانُ قهوةٍ
a pack of gum	*ʿulbat-u ʿilkat-in*	علبةُ علكةٍ
a bag of nuts	*kiis-u fustuq-in*	كيسُ فستقٍ

1.1.9 Purpose relationship

Here the second term explains or defines the particular purpose or use of the first term:

a marble quarry	*maqlaʿ-u ruxaam-in*	مقلعُ رخامٍ
a rescue plane	*Taaʾ irat-u ʾinqaadh-in*	طائرةُ إنقاذٍ
greeting cards	*baTaaqaat-u tahniʾat-in*	بطاقاتُ تهنئةٍ

1.1.10 Quotation or title relationship

Here the second term is a title or a quotation. When this is the case, the words of the title or quotation in quotation marks are considered to be set off from the case-marking requirements of the second term of the *ʾiDaafa*, and are inflected independently, not necessarily in the genitive.

لفظ «الجهاد»   كتاب «ألف ليلة وليلة»

lafZ-u "al-jihaad-u"   *kitaab-u "ʾalf-u laylat-in wa-laylat-un"*

the expression "jihad"   the book "The Thousand and One Nights"

محاضرة بعنوان «الشرق الأوسط وتحدياته»

muHaaDarat-un bi-ʿunwaan-i "al-sharq-u l-ʾawsaT-u wa-taHaddiyaat-u-hu"

a lecture entitled "The Middle East and Its Challenges"

فلمُ «لحن السعادة»

film-u "laHn-u l-saʿaadat-i"

the film "The Sound of Music" ('the tune of happiness')

1.1.11 Clause relationship

A clause in its entirety may occasionally form the second term of an *ʾiDaafa*. For purposes of clarity, the boundary between first term and second term is indicated by a plus sign (+) in the Arabic transliteration:

في حال استمر الوضع على ما هو عليه

fii Haal-i + stamarr-a l-waDʿ-u ʿalaa maa huwa ʿalay-hi

in case the situation remains as it is

في وقت كان كل شيء معدا لتحقيق تقدم

fii waqt-i + kaan-a kull-u shayʾ-in muʿadd-an li-taHqiiq-i taqaddum-in

at a time [when] everything was prepared for achieving [some] progress

في وقت تدرك الحقيقة إدراكا كليا

fii waqt-i + tu-drik-u l-Haqiiqat-a ʾidraak-an kulliyy-an

at a time [when] it fully realizes the truth

1.2 Rules of the noun construct (ʾiDaafa إضافة):

1.2.1 The first term of the construct

The first term of a construct phrase **has neither the definite article nor nunation** because it is defined through the second term, which determines the definiteness or indefiniteness of the entire phrase. The first term of a construct phrase cannot have a possessive pronoun suffix.

The first term carries a case marker which is determined by the syntactic role of the phrase in the sentence or clause. Examples:

1.2.1.1 FIRST TERM OF CONSTRUCT IS NOMINATIVE:

مشكلةُ الشرق الأوسط معقّدةٌ.

mushkilat-u l-sharq-i l-ʾawsaT-i muʿaqqadat-un.

The problem of the Middle East is complex.

1.2.1.2 FIRST TERM OF CONSTRUCT IS ACCUSATIVE:

حضرَ حفلةَ وضع الحجر الأساس.

HaDar-a Haflat-a waDʿ-il-Hajr-i l-ʾasaas-i.

He attended **the party** for the laying of the cornerstone.

1.2.1.3 FIRST TERM OF CONSTRUCT IS GENITIVE:

هي على استعداد لـلعب دور نشيط.

hiya ʿalaa stiʿdaad-in li-laʿb-i dawr-in nashiiT-in.

She is ready to play an active role ('for **playing** an active role').

1.2.1.4 THE RESTRICTION ON NUNATION on the first term of the construct applies not only to the nunation which marks indefiniteness, but also to the **final *nuuns* of the dual and the sound masculine plural**. These *nuuns* are deleted on the first term of a construct phrase.

مهربو المخدّرات	وزيرا العدل والإعلام
muharrib-uu l-mukhaddiraat-i	*waziir-aa l-ʿadl-i wa l-ʾiʿlaam-i*
drug **smugglers** ('smugglers of drugs')	**the two ministers** of justice and information

لـوزيري الخارجية
li-**waziir-ay**-i l-xaarijiyyat-i
to the **two foreign ministers**

لـمديري المنظمات
li-**mudiir-ii** l-munaZZamaat-i
to **the directors** of the organizations

رياضيو كوبا
riyaaDiyy-**uu** kuubaa
the **athletes** of Cuba

مزارعو الزيتون
muzaari**ʿ-uu** l-zaytuun-i
olive **growers** ('growers of olives')

1.2.1.5 PAUSE FORM PRONUNCIATION OF *taaʾ marbuuTa* AS FIRST TERM OF CONSTRUCT When a word ending in *taaʾ marbuuTa* is the first word of a construct phrase, the *taaʾ* is pronounced, *even in pause form*. For more on this see Chapter 2, section 3.4.3.2.

مدينـة بيروت	سلسلـة جبـال	ثلاثـة أيام
madiinat bayruut	*silsilat jibaal*	*thalaathat ʾayyaam*
the city of Beirut	a chain of mountains	three days

1.2.2 The second or final term of the construct

The second or final term **is in the genitive case** (whether or not it is overtly marked); it may be either definite or indefinite; may be a noun or a demonstrative pronoun. It may have a possessive pronoun suffix.

1.2.2.1 SECOND TERM = NOUN:

Definite:

| the engineers' quarter | *Hayy-u l-muhandis-iina* | حيُّ المهندسين |
| the kings of India | *muluuk-u l-hind-i* | ملوك الهندِ |

Indefinite:

a lunch banquet	*maʾdabat-u ghadaaʾ- in*	مأدبةُ غداءٍ
a beauty queen	*malikat-u jamaal-in*	ملكةُ جمالٍ
six schools	*sitt-u madaaris-a*	ستُ مدارسَ

1.2.2.2 SECOND TERM = DEMONSTRATIVE PRONOUN: A demonstrative pronoun may serve as the second term of a construct phrase, but as an invariable word, it does not inflect for case.

the meaning of this	*maʿnaa haadhaa*	معنى هذا
all (of) this	*kull-u haadhaa*	كلُ هذا
the result of that	*natiijat-u dhaalika*	نتيجةُ ذلك

1.2.2.3 SECOND TERM HAS PRONOUN SUFFIX:

his birthplace	*masqaT-u ra's-i-hi*	مسقطُ رأسِه
marketing their (f.) production	*taswiiq-u 'intaaj-i-hinna*	تسويقُ إنتاجِهِنَّ
bearing their responsibilities	*taHammul-u mas'uuliyyaat-i-haa*	تحمل مسؤولياتِها
raising his level	*raf ʿ-u mustawaa-hu*	رفعُ مستواهُ
the withdrawal of its units	*saHb-u waHdaat-i-hi*	سحبُ وحداتِهِ

1.2.2.4 MORE THAN ONE NOUN MAY BE CONJOINED AS THE SECOND TERM OF THE CONSTRUCT:

في سياستي الدفاع والتجارة

fii siyaasatay-i l-difaaʿ-i wa-l-tijaarat-i

in the two policies of **defense and trade**

جرّاحُ الأنف والأذن والحنجرة

jarraaH-u l-'anf-i wa-l-'udhn-i wa-l-Hanjarat-i

nose, ear, and throat surgeon ('surgeon of nose, ('and') ear and throat')

1.3 Modifiers of the construct

1.3.1 Modifying the first term

A construct phrase cannot be interrupted by modifiers for the first term. Any adjectives or other modifiers applying to the first term of the *'iDaafa* must follow the entire *'iDaafa*. Modifiers for the first term agree with it in gender, number, case, and definiteness.

أشعة الشمس الدافئة

'ashiʿʿat-u l-shams-i l-daafi'at-u

the **warm rays** of the sun

منظمة التحرير الفلسطينية

munaZZamat-u l-taHriir-i l-filisTiiniyyat-u

the **Palestinian** Liberation Organization

إلى مطار أبو ظبي الدولي

'ilaa maTaar-i 'abuu Zabiyy-i l-duwaliyy-i[7]

to the Abu Dhabi **international airport**

طبيب أسنان جيد

Tabiib-u 'asnaan-in jayyid-un

a **good dentist** ('doctor of teeth')

أركان الإسلام الخمسة

'arkaan-u l-'islaam-i l-xamsat-u

the **five pillars** of Islam

جواز السفر المسروق

jawaaz-u l-safar-i l-masruuq-u

the **stolen** passport

---

[7] Technically this should be *'ilaa maTaar-i 'abii Zabiyy-i l-duwaliyy-i*, with inflection of *'ab* in the genitive, but in newspaper Arabic the name of the emirate is often treated as a lexical unit and not inflected.

1.3.2 Modifying the second term

The second term of the construct may be modified by adjectives directly following it and agreeing with it in definiteness, gender, number, and case.

في منطقة الشرق الأوسط

fii mintaqaT-i l-sharq-i l-ʾawsaT-i

in the region of **the Middle East**

ملحق الشؤون الثقافية

mulHaq-u l-shuʾuun-i l-thaqaafiyyat-i

cultural affairs officer ('attaché')

إسعاف الدفاع المدني

ʾisʿaaf-u l-difaaʿ-i l-madaniyy-i

civil defense ambulance

لبناء أسس جديدة وسليمة

li-binaaʾ-i ʾusus-in jadiidat-in
  wa-saliimat-in

to build **secure new foundations**

في افتتاح المعرض الدولي

fii ftitaaH-i l-maʿriD-i l-duwaliyy-i

at the opening of **the international exhibit**

1.3.3 Modification of both terms of the construct

When a construct or *ʾiDaafa* needs modifiers for both terms, the general order is to put the modifiers for the last term closest to the *ʾiDaafa*, and then modifiers for the first term(s), in ascending order. Each modifier agrees with its noun in case, gender, number, and definiteness.

مجمع اللغة العربية الأردني

majmaʿ-u l-lughat-i l-ʿarabiyyat-i l-ʾurduniyy-u

the Jordanian Arabic Language Academy

(literally: 'academy (of) the-language the-Arabic the-Jordanian')

رئيس مجمع اللغة العربية الأردني السابق

raʾ iis-u majmaʿ-i l-lughat-i l-ʿarabiyyat-i l-ʾurduniyy-i l-saabiq-u

the former president of the Jordanian Arabic Language Academy

(literally: 'president (of the) academy (of) the-language the-Arabic the-Jordanian the-former')

1.4 Demonstrative pronouns in construct phrases

1.4.1 Demonstrative with first term of construct

Normally, when a noun is modified by a demonstrative pronoun, that pronoun precedes the noun and the noun also has the definite article (for example, *haa-dhaa l-qarn-u* هذا القرن 'this century').[8] However, when a noun as **first term** of a construct is modified by a demonstrative pronoun, that **pronoun follows the entire**

---

[8] For further discussion of demonstrative pronouns, see Chapter 13.

'iDaafa structure because of the restriction that prevents the presence of the definite article on the first term of a construct. The pronoun agrees with the first term in gender and number.

لدعم وجهة النظر هذه
li-daᶜm-i wujhat-i l-naZar-i haadhihi
to support **this point** of view

في حملة التفتيش هذه
fii Hamlat-i l-taftiish-i haadhihi
in **this inspection** campaign

خلال مدة الانتظار تلك
xilaal-a muddat-i l-intiZaar-i tilka
during **that period** of waiting

مرحلة الجمود هذه
marHalat-u l-jumuud-i haadhihi
this level of solidity

1.4.2 Demonstrative with second term of construct

The second term of a construct or *'iDaafa* **may be preceded directly by a demonstrative pronoun** plus definite article because the second term can be marked for definiteness:

شمس ذلك العهد
shams-u dhaalika l-ᶜahd-i
the sun of **that time**

قيمة هذه المخدرات
qiimat-u haadhihi l-muxaddiraat-i
the value of **these drugs**

تدمير تلك الفيروسات
tadmiir-u tilka l-fiiruusaat-i
the destruction of **those viruses**

1.5 Complex or multi-noun construct

A construct phrase may consist of more than two nouns related to each other through the use of the genitive case. When this happens, the second and all subsequent nouns are in the genitive case and only the last noun in the entire construct phrase is marked for either definiteness or indefiniteness. Thus, the medial nouns, the ones which are neither first nor last, are all in the genitive, and none of them have nunation or the definite article. That is, the medial nouns combine certain features of being the first term of an *'iDaafa* (no definite article or nunation) with one feature of being the second term of an *'iDaafa* (marked for genitive case).

1.5.1 Construct with three nouns

تعيينُ وزيرِ الداخليّة
taᶜyiin-u waziir-i l-daaxiliyyat-i
the appointment of the minister of interior

جميعُ أفراد الأسرة
jamiiᶜ-u 'afraad-i l-'usrat-i
all the members of the family

مدُّ يدِ العونِ

madd-u yad-i l-ʿawn-i

extending a helping hand ('the hand of help')

رفعُ مستوى المعيشةِ

rafʿ-u mustawaa l-maʿiishat-i

raising the standard of living

رئيسُ تحريرِ المجلةِ

raʾiis-u taHriir-i l-majallat-i

the editor-in-chief of the magazine ('chief of the editing of the magazine')

1.5.2 Construct with four nouns

احتفالُ زرعِ شجرةِ أرزٍ

iHtifaal-u zarʿ-i shajarat-i ʾarz-in

celebration of the planting of a cedar tree

بمناسبةِ ذكرى استقلالِ بلادِه

bi-munaasabat-i dhikraa stiqlaal-i bilaad-i-hi

on the occasion of the commemoration of his country's independence

لمعالجةِ مشكلةِ إدمانِ المخدّراتِ

li-muʿaalajat-i mushkilat-i ʾidmaan-i l-mukhaddiraat-i

for handling the problem of drug addiction

تحتَ سماءِ جنوبِ فرنسا

taHat-a samaaʾ-i januub-i faransaa

under the skies of southern ('the south of') France

في دولِ جنوبِ شرقِ آسيا

fii duwal-i januub-i sharq-i ʾaasiyaa

in the countries of Southeast Asia

1.5.3 Construct with five nouns

تطبيقُ جميعِ قراراتِ مجلسِ الأمنِ

taTbiiq-u jamiiʿ-i qaraaraat-i majlis-i l-ʾamn-i

the application of all of the resolutions of the Security Council

سرقةُ جوازِ سفرِ أحدِ اللاعبينَ

sarqat-u jawaaz-i safar-i ʾaHad-i l-laaʿib-iina

the theft of the passport of one of the athletes

وزراءُ نفطِ دولِ مجلسِ التعاونِ

wuzaraaʾ-u nifT-i duwal-i majlis-i l-taʿaawun-i

the oil ministers of the states of the [Gulf] Cooperation Council

1.6 Joint annexation

Traditional Arabic style requires that the first term of the ʾiDaafa or annexation structure be restricted to one item. It cannot be two or more items joined with wa- 'and.' If more than one noun is to be included in the expression then they follow the ʾiDaafa and refer back to it by means of **a resumptive pronoun suffix.**

ويُرى في الصف الثاني مرافقو الوفد ومعاونوه.

*wa-yuraa fii l-Saff-i l-thaanii muraafiq-uu l-wafd-i **wa-muʿaawin-uu-hu**.*

Seen in the second row are the companions and assistants of the delegation ('the companions of the delegation **and its assistants**'). ·

بالنسبة إلى أساتذة التاريخ وطلابه

*bi-l-nisbat-i ʾilaa ʾasaatidhat-i l-taariix-i **wa-Tullaab-i-hi***

in relation to the professors and students of history ('the professors of history **and its students**')

وسط حماسة أعضاء المؤتمر وهتافاتهم

*wasT-a Hamaasat-i ʾaʿDaaʾ-i l-muʾtamar-i **wa-hutaafaat-i-him***

amidst the enthusiasm and cheers of the members of the conference ('the enthusiasm of the conference members **and their cheers**')

يضم أبرز الفنانين وأعظمهم.

*ya-Dumm-u ʾabraz-a l-fannaan-iina **wa-ʾaʿZam-a-hum.***

It brings together the most prominent and greatest artists ('most prominent artists **and the greatest of them**').

This rule is widely observed. However, it is also regularly broken, and "joint annexation is rapidly gaining ground" (Beeston 1970, 48), as the following examples show:

مساجد وقصور المدينة

***masaajid-u wa-quSuur-u** l-madiinat-i*

the mosques and castles of the city

في بحيرات وأنهار إفريقيا

*fii **buHayraat-i wa-ʾanhaar-i** ʾifriiqiyaa*

in **the lakes and rivers** of Africa

نمو وتطور اللغة العربية

***numuww-u wa-taTawwur-u** l-lughat-i l-ʿarabiyyat-i*

the growth and development of the Arabic language

احترام قيم وعادات الحضارات الأخرى

*iHtiraam-u **qiyam-i wa-ʿaadaat-i** l-HaDaaraat-i l-ʾ uxraa*

respecting the **values and customs** of other cultures

أكبر وأحسن النباتات

ʾakbar-u wa-ʾaHsan-u l-nabaataat-i

the **biggest and best** plants

باسم شعب وحكومة المملكة

bi-sm-i shaʿb-i wa-Hukuumat-i l-mamlakat-i

in the name of **the people and the government** of the kingdom

These examples and others show that joint annexation is an area of modern Arabic syntax where the traditional rules are still in use but routinely violated. This particular area of Arabic grammatical structure is in a state of flux, with the newer structure being widely used in everyday language.

1.7 Special cases of constructs

1.7.1 The use of ʿadam and ʾiʿaada

Two verbal nouns, *ʿadam* 'lack of' and *ʾiʿaada* 'repetition, resumption' are frequently used in **lexicalizing** functions, as the first term of *ʾiDaafas* to create compound lexical items.[9]

1.7.1.1 ʿadam + NOUN: The noun *ʿadam* is a privative term that expresses negative concepts or "lack of": it is used with verbal nouns to create compound Arabic expressions conveying concepts expressed in English by prefixes such as "non-," "in-," or "dis-," or to express what would be a negative infinitive.

impermissibility	*ʿadam-u jawaaz-in*	عدم جواز
nonexistence	*ʿadam-u wujuud-in*	عدم وجود
instability	*ʿadam-u stiqraar-in*	عدم استقرار
insincerity	*ʿadam-u jiddiyyat-in*	عدم جدية
discomfort	*ʿadam-u rtiyaaH-in*	عدم ارتياح
displeasure	*ʿadam-u riDaaʾ-in*	عدم رضاء

Examples:

من المهمّ عدم تقديم الكثير من التنازلات.

min-a l-muhimm-i ʿadam-u taqdiim-i l-kathiir-i min-a l-tanaazulaat-i.

It is important **not to offer** too many concessions.

---

[9] See also Chapter 37, section 2.2.5 in this book and Holes 1995, 266–67.

عدم ارتياح الجانبين
ᶜadam-u rtiyaaH-i l-jaanib-ayni
the **uneasiness** of both sides

1.7.1.2 *ʾiᶜaada* + NOUN 'RE-': The noun *ʾiᶜaada* used as the first term of a construct with a verbal noun, expresses concepts of repetition or renewal.[10]

إعادة تعمير
ʾiᶜaadat-u taᶜmiir-in
rebuilding

إعادة عدّ الأصوات
ʾiᶜaadat-u ᶜadd-i l-ʾaSwaat-i
recounting the vote

إعادة فرز الأصوات
ʾiᶜaadat-u farz-i l-ʾaSwaat-i
re-sorting the votes

إعادة فرض العقوبات
ʾiᶜaadat-u farD-i l-ᶜuquubaat-i
the **re-imposition** of sanctions

إعادة تعيين الوزير
ʾiᶜaadat-u taᶜyiin-i l-waziir-i
re-appointment of the minister

إعادة فتح سفارتها
ʾiᶜaadat-u fatH-i sifaarat-i-haa
the **reopening** of its embassy

1.7.2 Official titles as constructs

Many official titles of dignitaries and royalty consist of genitive constructs, for example:

His Highness the Prince	*sumuww-u l-ʾamiir-i*	سموُّ الأمير
His Highness the Crown Prince	*sumuww-u waliy-i l-ᶜahd-i*	سموُّ ولي العهد
His Majesty the King	*jalaalat-u l-malik-i*	جلالةُ الملك
His Majesty the Sultan	*jalaalat-u l-SulTaan-i*	جلالةُ السلطان
His Royal Highness	*SaaHib-u l-sumuww-i l-malikiyy-i*	صاحبُ السموِّ الملكيِّ
His Eminence	*SaaHib-u l-samaaHat-i*	صاحبُ السماحة
His Excellency the Minister	*maᶜaalii l-waziir-i*	معالي الوزير

1.7.3 Use of *nafs* 'same' as first term

A frequent genitive construct is the use of the noun *nafs* 'self' or 'same' as the first term in order to express the concept of "the same _____."[11]

ذكرت نفس الشيء.
dhakar-at nafs-a l-shayʾ-i.
It mentioned **the same thing**.

في نفس الوقت
fii nafs-i l-waqt-i
at **the same time**

---

[10] The noun *ʾiᶜaada* is a verbal noun from the Form IV verb *ʾaᶜaad-a /yu-ᶜiid-u* 'to renew, repeat, restore, re-do.'

[11] See also section 2.3.

تعمل جميعها على نفس المنوال.

ta-ʿmal-u jamiiʿ-u-haa ʿalaa nafs-i l-minwaal-i.

They all work **the same way**.

1.7.4 Coalescence of the construct

Certain frequently used constructs have come to function as solid units and are even occasionally written together as one word. This fusing of terms is rare in Arabic, but does happen occasionally:

1.7.4.1 FIXED EXPRESSIONS:

capital (financial resources)	*ra's-u maal-in*	رَأْسُ مالٍ
	ra'smaal	رأسمال
administrative officer (of a town or village)	*qaa'im-u maqaam-in*	قائمُ مقامٍ
	qaa'imaqaam	قائمقام

1.7.4.2 THREE TO NINE HUNDRED: Although optionally written as one word, the first term still inflects for case. For example:

five hundred	*xams-u mi'at-in*	خمسُ مئةٍ
	xams-u-mi'at-in	خمسمئة
nine hundred	*tisʿ-u mi'at-in*	تسعُ مئةٍ
	tisʿ-u-mi'at-in	تسعمئة

1.8 Avoiding the construct phrase or *ʾiDaafa*

Sometimes an *ʾiDaafa* is avoided by means of linking two nouns with a preposition, usually *min* or *li-*. This happens especially if the first noun is modified by an adjective or a phrase that would otherwise have to be placed after the *ʾiDaafa* construction. It is a stylistic option.

القسم الأخير من الكتاب

*al-qism-u l-ʾaxiir-u **min-a** l-kitaab-i*

the last part **of** the book

في النصف الثاني من القرن العشرين

*fii l-niSf-i l-thaanii **min-a** l-qarn-i l-ʿishriina*

in the second half **of** the twentieth century

خسوف جزئي للقمر

*xusuuf-un juz'iyy-un **li-l**-qamar-i*

a partial eclipse **of** the moon

المفوض العام لمكتب المقاطعة

*al-mufawwaD-u l-ʿaamm-u **li-**maktab-i l-muqaaTaʿat-i*

the general commissioner **of** the boycott office

ظهر العدد الجديد من المجلة.

Zahar-a l-ʿadad-u l-jadiid-u min-a l-majallat-i.

The new issue **of the magazine** appeared.

حضروا سباقا للخيل.

HaDar-uu sibaaq-an li-l-xayl-i.

They attended a horse race ('a race of horses').

1.9 Adjectives in construct phrases

Adjectives or participles functioning as adjectives may occur in construct phrases either as the first or second term, in the following types of constructions.

1.9.1 Modifier as first term of construct

Sometimes an adjective or a participle with adjectival meaning will appear as the first term of a construct phrase instead of following the noun as a modifier. In these phrases the adjective remains in the masculine gender, but it may be singular or plural. These expressions are often set phrases and tend to be used with particular adjectives, as follows.

في قديم الزمان

fii qadiim-i l-zamaan-i

in olden times

للشرقي المتوسط

li-sharqiyy-i l-muTawassit-i

to the eastern Mediterranean

مع كبار المسؤولين

maʿ-a kibaar-i l-masʾuul-iina

with the senior officials

لمجرد إثبات

li-mujarrad-i ʾithbaat-in

for mere confirmation

في مختلف المدن

fii muxtalif-i l-mudun-i

in various cities

لإرضاء مختلف الأذواق

li-ʾirDaaʾ-i muxtalif-i l-ʾadhwaaq-i

in order to please various tastes

في شتى مجلات الاقتصاد

fii shattaa majaalaat-i l-iqtiSaad-i

in diverse fields of economics

في شتى الأنشطة

fii shattaa l-ʾanshiTat-i

in various activities

1.9.2 The adjective or "false" ʾiDaafa (ʾiDaafa ghayr Haqiiqiyya إضافة غير حقيقية)

The "false" or "unreal" ʾiDaafa, also called the "adjective" ʾiDaafa, is a special case of the construct phrase where an adjective serves as the first term and acts as a modifier of a noun. Not only can an adjective serve as the first item in this structure, but, contrary to the general rules for the ʾiDaafa structure, this adjective may take the definite article if the phrase modifies a definite noun. Since this type of construct violates the rule against the first term of a construct phrase taking a definite article, it is termed "unreal" or "false."

This construction is a way of expressing a quality of a particular component of an item, often equivalent to hyphenated expressions in English such as: *long-term, hard-nosed*, or *cold-blooded*. It is generally used to express qualities of "inalienable possession," that is, qualities that are "naturally attributable" to their owners.[12]

The adjective *ʾiDaafa* is quite frequent in MSA because it is a construction that can be used to express recently coined, complex modifying terms such as "multi-lateral," or "long-range."

In this construction, the adjective agrees with the noun it modifies in case, number, and gender. The second term of the adjective *ʾiDaafa* is a definite noun in the genitive case and refers to a particular property of the modified noun.

1.9.2.1 ADJECTIVE *ʾiDaafa* AS NOUN MODIFIER:

(1) **Modifying a definite noun:** When modifying a definite noun, the first term of the adjective *ʾiDaafa* agrees with the noun in gender, number, and case, and it also has the definite article:

الرجل المثقف الطويل القامة

al-rajul-u l-muthaqqaf-u l-Tawiil-u l-qaamat-i

the cultured, tall ('**tall of height**') man

وقد أرسلت الآلة الأمريكية الصنع من العاصمة.

wa-qad ʾursil-at-i l-ʾaalat-u l-ʾamriikiyyat-u l-Sanʿ-i min-a l-ʿaaSimat-i.

The **American-made** instrument was sent from the capital.

في هذه القضية المتعددة الجوانب

fii haadhihi l-qaDiyyat-i l-mutaʿaddidat-i l-jawaanib-i

in this **multi-sided** issue

(2) **Modifying an indefinite noun:** When modifying an indefinite noun, the first term of the adjective *ʾiDaafa* does not have the definite article. However, neither does it have nunation, because this is prevented by its being the first term of an *ʾiDaafa*. It agrees with the noun it modifies in gender, number, and case:

هو أول مسؤول أمريكيّ رفيع المستوى يزور البحرين.

huwa ʾawwal-u masʾuul-in ʾamriikiyy-in rafiiʿ-i l-mustawaa ya-zuur-u l-baHrayn-a.

He is the first **high-level** American official to visit Bahrain.[13]

تسمى أشجاراً دائمةَ الخضرة.

tu-sammaa ʾashjaar-an daaʾimat-a l-xaDrat-i.

They are called **evergreen** trees.

---

[12] Killean 1970, 11. Killean's article "The false construct in Modern Literary Arabic" is one of the few that deal with the syntactic and semantic analysis of this structure from the point of view of generative syntax.

[13] Although the English equivalent of this sentence uses the definite article to refer to the "American official," the Arabic structure using the term *ʾawwal* 'first' is followed by an indefinite noun.

إمرأة مكتوفة الذراعين

*imraʾat-un **maktuufat-u l-dhiraaʿ-ayni***

a woman with **crossed arms**

ذلك عقب تدخل **عالي المستوى**

*dhaalika ʿaqib-a **tadaxxul-in ʿaalii l-mustawaa***

that [was] right after **a high-level intervention**

1.9.2.2 ADJECTIVE *ʾiDaafa* AS PREDICATE OF EQUATIONAL SENTENCE: When serving
as the predicate of an equational sentence, the first term of the adjective
ʾiDaafa does **not** have the definite article, in keeping with the rules for predicate
adjectives. It agrees with the noun it refers to in gender, number, and case.

اللهجة المصرية واسعة الانتشار.	إن الشطرنج هندي الأصل.
*al-lahjat-u l-miSriyyat-u **waasiʿat-u l-intishaar-i.***	*ʾinna l-shaTranj-a **hindiyy-u l-ʾaSl-i.***
The Egyptian dialect is **widespread**.	(Indeed) chess is **Indian in origin**.
الأرض مستديرة الشكل.	هذا صعب الاحتمال.
*al-ʾarD-u **mustadiirat-u l-shakl-i.***	*haadhaa **Saʿb-u l-iHtimaal-i.***
The earth is **circular in shape**.	This is **hard to bear**.

1.9.3 The descriptive construct with *ghayr* plus adjective

In this unique construction, an adjective serves as the second term of a construct
phrase. The noun *ghayr* ' non-; un-, in-, other than' is used as the first term of the
construct in order to express negative or privative concepts denoting absence of a
quality or attribute. As the first term of a construct, *ghayr* carries the same case
as the noun it modifies. As a noun which is the first term of an *ʾiDaafa*, it cannot have the definite article. The second term of the *ʾiDaafa* construction is an
adjective or participle in the genitive case which agrees with the noun being modified in gender, number, and definiteness. Here are some examples:

unsuitable	*ghayr-u munaasib-in*	غيرُ مناسبٍ
indirect	*ghayr-u mubaashir-in*	غيرُ مباشرٍ
untrue	*ghayr-u SaHiiH-in*	غيرُ صحيحٍ
insufficient	*ghayr-u kaaf-in*	غيرُ كافٍ
non-Arab	*ghayr-u ʿarabiyy-in*	غيرُ عربيٍّ
undesirable	*ghayr-u marghuub-in fii-hi*	غيرُ مرغوبٍ فيه

صعوبات غير متوقعة	بأساليب غير شريفة
*Suʿuubaat-un **ghayr-u mutawaqqaʿat-in***	*bi-ʾasaaliib-a **ghayr-i shariifat-in***
unexpected difficulties	in **unscrupulous** ('non-noble') ways

حسب أرقام غير رسمية

Hasab-a 'arqaam-in ghayr-i rasmiyyat-in

according to **unofficial figures**

2 Nouns in apposition (*badal* بدل)

Nouns or noun phrases are said to be in *apposition* with one another when they are juxtaposed and both refer to the same entity, but in different ways.[14] Phrases such as "my cat, Blondie," "Queen Victoria," "President Bush," or "King Hussein" consist of nouns in apposition. As a general rule, the nouns agree in case, number, gender, and definiteness, but one subset of appositional specifiers requires the accusative case.

2.1 Straight apposition

In straight apposition, the noun in apposition takes the same case as the noun with which it is in apposition.

2.1.1 Names and titles

The title (normally with the definite article) is followed directly by the name of the person:

King Fahd	*al-malik-u fahd-un*	الملكُ فهدٌ
The Emperor Constantine	*al-imbiraaTuur qusTanTiin*	الإمبراطور قسطنطين
The Prophet Muhammad	*al-nabiyy-u muHammad-un*	النبيُ محمدٌ
Queen Nur	*al-malikat-u nuur-u*	الملكةُ نورُ
Father Joseph	*al-'ab-u yuusuf-u*	الأبُ يوسفُ
Professor Faris	*al-'ustaadh-u faaris-un*	الأستاذُ فارسٌ
Colonel Qadhdhaafi	*al-ʿaqiid-u l-qadhdhaafiyy-u*	العقيدُ القذافيُ

2.1.2 Reduced relative clauses

In this form of apposition, the specifying noun is equivalent to a relative noun phrase:

---

[14] The term *badal* (literally, 'substitution; exchange') is used in traditional Arabic grammar to describe more than the noun-noun appositional relationship. It also covers the use of the demonstrative pronoun in demonstrative phrases, and modifying adjectives. In this section of the reference grammar, however, the discussion of *badal* is restricted to appositional structures that include nouns and personal pronouns. For a detailed discussion of apposition see Wright 1967, II: 272ff. Cachia (1973) gives the terms *tabʿ* or *tabʿiyya* for 'apposition,' and Hasan (1987) refers to nouns in apposition as *tawaabiʿ* (literally: 'followers').

بين نواب أعضاء في الحزب الوطني

bayn-a **nuwwaab-in** *ʾaʿDaaʾ-in fii l-Hizb-i l-waTaniyy-i*

among **deputies** [who are] **members** of the national party

ستطالب الدول الأعضاء بقطع هذه العلاقات.

sa-tu-Taalib-u **l-duwal-a l-ʾaʿDaaʾ-a** *bi-qaTʿ-i haadhihi l-ʿalaqaat-i.*

It will demand the **member states** sever these relations.

2.1.3 Apposition for specification

In more general terms, the noun or nouns in apposition further specify the head noun:

from **the mother company**	*min-a l-sharikat-i l-ʾumm-i*	من الشركة الأمِّ
in **the sister** [country] Jordan	*fii l-ʾurdunn-i l-shaqiiq-i*	في الأردنِّ الشقيق
my **friend**, Amira	*Sadiiqat-ii ʾamiirat-u*	صديقتي أميرةُ
the **creator** god	*al-rabb-u l-xaaliq-u*	الربُّ الخالقُ
She carried **her brother** Samir.	*Hamal-at ʾax-aa-haa samiir-an.*	حملت أخاها سميراً.
today, **Sunday**	*al-yawm-a l-ʾaHad-a*	اليومَ الأحد
the **guest** minister	*al-waziir-u l-Dayf-u*	الوزير الضيف

في العاصمة الأردنية عمان

fii **l-ʿaaSimat-i l-ʾurdunniyaat-i ʿammaan-a**

in the Jordanian capital, Amman

معرض الفنانين الشباب

maʿraD-u **l-fannaan-iina l-shabaab-i**

the exhibit of **young artists** ('artists youths')

2.2 Accusative Apposition

A noun in apposition to a pronoun is put into the accusative case because it specifies that noun in a particular way and is considered a form of *tamyiiz* or accusative of specification.

When an independent pronoun (often the first person plural) is further specified, the specifying noun is in the accusative case as the object of an understood verb such as *ʾaʿnii* 'I mean,' or *ʾaxuSS-u* 'I specify.'

we, **the Arabs**	*naHnu l-ʿarab-a*	نحنُ العربَ
we, **the people of the Gulf**	*naHnu l-xaliijiyy-iina*	نحنُ الخليجيين
we, **the Americans**	*naHnu l-ʾamriikiyy-iina*	نحنُ الأمريكيين

2.3 Appositive specification of quantity or identity

Arabic nouns may be further specified by other nouns in terms of quantity or
identity. In most of these cases, the specifying noun agrees in case with the head
noun and carries a personal pronoun suffix referring back to the head noun. The
pronoun agrees with the head noun in number and gender. Quantity nouns such
as *kull, jamii*ᶜ*, ba*ᶜ*D*, and fractions, as well as identity nouns such as *nafs* 'same; self'
are used in these expressions.[15]

ضحك الطلاب جميعهم
*DaHik-a l-Tullaab-u jamii*ᶜ*-u-hum*
all the students laughed
('the students, all of them')

الشعب كله
*al-sha*ᶜ*b-u kull-u-hu*
all the people
('the people, all of them')

على دول المنطقة كلها
ᶜ*alaa duwal-i l-minTaqat-i kull-i-haa*
on **all the states of the region**
('the states of the region, all of them')

في الوقت نفسه
fii l-waqt-i nafs-i-hi
at **the same time**

بالأسلوب نفسه
*bi-l-*ʾ*usluub-i nafs-i-hi*
in **the same way**

بالسرعة نفسها
*bi-l-sur*ᶜ*at-i nafs-i-haa*
at **the same speed**

بين العرب أنفسهم كقيسيين ويمنيين
*bayn-a l-*ᶜ*arab-i* ʾ*anfus-i-him ka-qaysiyy-iina wa-yamaniyy-iina*
among **the Arabs themselves** like the Qays and the Yamanis

2.3.1 Quantifier noun ᶜ*idda* (عدّة)

The noun ᶜ*idda* 'several' is often used in apposition with a head noun. It does not
carry a pronoun suffix. It agrees with the noun in case.

in **several cities**	*fii mudun-in* ᶜ*iddat-in*	في مدنٍ عدة
in **several regions**	*fii manaaTiq-a* ᶜ*iddat-in*	في مناطقَ عدة
in **several languages**	*bi-lughaat-in* ᶜ*iddat-in*	بلغاتٍ عدة
several years ago	*mundhu sanawaat-in* ᶜ*iddat-in*	منذ سنواتٍ عدة

وهناك سيّدات عدة برزن في هذا المجال.
wa-hunaaka **sayyidaat-un** ᶜ*iddat-un* *baraz-na fii haadhaa l-majaal-i.*
There are **several women** who have become eminent in this field.

---

[15] This is an alternative structure to using the quantifying nouns as the first term of an ʾ*iDaafa*, e.g.,
*kull-u l-wuzaraa*ʾ*-i* 'all the ministers' versus *al-wuzaraa*ʾ*-u kull-u-hum*, or *nafs-u l-fikrat-i* 'the same idea'
versus *al-fikrat-u nafs-u-haa*.

2.4 Relative pronoun *maa* in apposition

The indefinite relative pronoun *maa* can be used in apposition with a noun to indicate 'a certain,' or 'some.'

in a **certain place**	*fii makaan-in maa*	في مكانٍ ما
some day	*yawm-an maa*	يوماً ما
somewhat; to a **certain extent**	*naw ͨ-an maa*	نوعاً ما

لماذا تحب كاتباً ما؟	بعد فتح بلد ما
li-maadhaa tu-Hibb-u **kaatib-an maa**?	*ba ͨd-a fatH-i* **balad-in maa**
Why do you like **a certain writer**?	after conquering **a certain country**

9

Noun specifiers and quantifiers

Certain Arabic nouns act primarily as specifiers or determiners for other nouns. They may be used as first terms of construct phrases, in apposition with nouns, with pronouns, or independently. Many of these nouns express **quantities**; some express other kinds of specification.

Here are five major classes of specifiers and quantifiers in MSA.

1 Expressions of totality

1.1 *kull* كلّ 'all; every; the whole'

1.1.1 "Each, every"

When used as the first term of a construct phrase with a **singular, indefinite noun**, *kull* has the meaning of 'each' or 'every.'[1]

everything   *kull-u shay³-in* كل شيء   every one   *kull-u waaHid-in* كل واحد

every day   *kull-a yawm-in* كل يوم

لكلّ مستخدم | كل ريال من دخلنا | لـكلّ فنـان عربي
li-kull-i mustaxdim-in | *kull-u riyaal-in* min daxl-i-naa | *li-kull-i fannaan-in ⁽arabiyy-in*
for **every user** | **every riyal** of our income | for **every Arab artist**

1.1.2 "all, the whole"

When used with a **definite singular noun or a pronoun**, *kull* has the meaning of 'all of,' 'the whole,' or 'all.'

كل المساعدة الممكنة | كل هذا
kull-u l-musaa⁽adat-i l-mumkinat-i | *kull-u haadhaa*
all possible aid | all of this/that

---

[1] LeTourneau (1995, 30) refers to constructs with quantifiers as the first term as a "quantified construct state."

1.1.3 "all"

When used with a **definite plural noun**, *kull* means 'all.'

في كل الظروف	مع كل قضايا الشرق الأوسط
fii kull-i l-Zuruuf-i	*maʿa kull-i qaDaayaa l-sharq-i l-ʾawsaT-i*
in all circumstances	with **all the problems** of the Middle East

بهدف حل كل المشاكل

bi-hadaf-i Hall-i kull-i l-mashaakil-i

with the aim of solving **all the problems**

1.1.4 *kull-un min* كلٌّ من 'each; both; every one of'

The noun *kull* may be used as an indefinite noun with nunation, **followed by the preposition *min* 'of'** to convey the meaning of totality. When there are only two items, the phrase *kull min* functions as the equivalent of 'both.'

في كل من واشنطن وعمان بالتناوب

fii kull-in min waashinTun wa-ʿammaan-a bi-l-tanaawub-i

in **both** Washington and Amman, alternately

في كل من الحلقات قصة جديدة.	في كل من فرنسا والجزائر
fii kull-in min-a l-Halaqaat-i qiSSat-un jadiidat-un.	*fii kull-in min faransaa wa-l-jazaaʾir-i*
In **each installment** is a new story.	in **both** France and Algeria

1.1.5 *kull-un* كلٌّ; *al-kull* الكلّ 'everyone'

The noun *kull* may be **used alone** to express the idea of 'everyone.' It may occur with or without the definite article. Agreement is masculine singular.

كل يريد أن يلتقط صورا هناك.

kull-un yu-riid-u ʾan ya-ltaqiT-a Suwar-an hunaaka.

Everyone wants to take pictures there.

1.2 *jamiiʿ* جميع 'all'

The word *jamiiʿ* is used with **a following genitive noun (usually plural)** to mean 'all,' or 'the totality of.'

تطبيق جميع قرارات مجلس الأمن

taTbiiq-u jamiiʿ-i qaraaraat-i majlis-i l-ʾamn-i

the application of **all the decisions** of the security council

طاولت جميع أوجه المعرفة	إلى جميع إخوانهم
Taawal-at jamiiʿ-a ʾawjuh-i l-maʿrifat-i	*ʾilaa jamiiʿ-i ʾixwaan-i-him*
it rivaled **all aspects** of knowledge	to **all their brothers**

1.3 *kilaa~kilay/ kiltaa~kiltay* - كلتا - كلتي ~ كلا-كلي 'both; both of (m. & f.)'
The specialized dual quantifiers *kilaa/kilay* (m.) and *kiltaa/kiltay* (f.) are used to
express the idea of 'both.' They are followed by a **definite dual noun in the genitive or by a dual pronoun suffix**. These two words inflect as does the dual suffix
when it is the first term of a construct, but **they do not inflect for case when followed by a noun; only when followed by a pronoun**.

1.3.1 Masculine

both of the delegations	*kilaa l-wafd-ayni*	كلا الوفدين
in both worlds	*fii kilaa l-ʿaalam-ayni*	في كلا العالمين
with both of them (m.)	*maʿ-a kilay-himaa*	مع كليهما

1.3.2 Feminine

during both of the periods	*fii kiltaa l-fatrat-ayni*	في كلتا الفترتين
in both cases	*fii kiltaa l-Haalat-ayni*	في كلتا الحالتين
with both his hands	*bi-kiltaa yad-ay-hi*	بكلتا يديه
Both of them (f.) are affixes.	*kiltaa-humaa zaaʾidat-aani.*	كلتاهما زائدتان.
by both of them (f.)	*bi-kiltay-himaa*	بكلتيهما

1.4 *kaaffa* كافة 'totality; all'
The noun *kaaffa* is used as the first term of a construct phrase to express totality:

كافة اتجاهاتها   كافة شؤون الوزارة
kaaffat-u ttijaahaat-i-haa   *kaaffat-u shuʾuun-i l-wizaarat-i*
all of its inclinations   all the affairs of the ministry

وجّه التهنئة إلى كافة أفراد البعثة.
wajjah-a l-tahniʾat-a ʾilaa kaaffat-i ʾafraad-i l-biʿthat-i.
He directed congratulations to **all the members** of the delegation.

تتوفر كافّة الخدمات الأساسية.
ta-tawaffar-u kaaffat-u l-xidamaat-i l-ʾasaasiyyat-i.
All the basic **services** are provided.

2 Expressions of limited number, non-specific number, or partiality
There are several ways to express partial inclusion in Arabic.

2.1 *ba'D* بعض 'some,' 'some of'

The masculine singular noun *ba'D* is followed by a singular or plural noun in the genitive or by a pronoun suffix. It may also be used independently.

2.1.1 As first term of a construct

The quantifier *ba'D* is usually followed by a definite noun in the genitive case. Note that adjectives that follow the construct normally agree in gender and number with the second term, the noun being quantified.

بعض الجمعيات الخيرية
ba'D-u l-jam'iyyaat-i l-xayriyyat-i
some of the charitable associations

إعادة إخراج بعض الأفلام
'i'aadat-u 'ixraaj-i ba'D-i l-'aflaam-i
the re-release of some films

نجحوا بعض الشيء.
najaH-uu ba'D-a l-shay'-i.
They succeeded somewhat.

2.1.2 With pronoun suffix

The noun *ba'D* may also take a pronoun suffix.

يرى بعضهم في ذلك خطأ.
ya-raa ba'D-u-hum fii dhaalika xaTa'-an.
Some of them see in that a mistake.

2.1.3 Reciprocal بعض: Double use of *ba'D*

The concept of "each other" or "together" may be expressed with the use of *ba'D* as a reciprocal pronoun. The first *ba'D* has a pronoun suffix; the second has either the definite article or nunation.

هم يسألون بعضهم البعض.
hum ya-s'al-uuna ba'D-u-hum-u l-ba'D-a.
They are asking each other.

تعيش مع بعضها البعض.
ta-'iish-u ma'-a ba'D-i-haa l-ba'D-u.
They live all together.

وقوف اللاعبين بعضهم فوق البعض
wuquuf-u l-laa'ib-iina ba'D-u-hum fawq-a l-ba'D-i
the acrobats standing on top of each other

وعلى المواطنين أن يعرفوا بعضهم بعضا معرفة جيدة.
wa-'alaa l-muwaaTin-iina 'an ya-'rif-uu ba'D-u-hum ba'D-an ma'rifat-an jayyidat-an.
It is necessary for citizens to know each other well.

أعتقد أنهما منفصلان كثيرا عن بعضهما بعضا.
'a'taqid-u 'anna-humaa munfaSil-aani kathiir-an 'an ba'D-i-himaa ba'D-an.
I think that they (two) are very separate from each other.

2.2 *biD⁽* بضع and *biD⁽a* بضعة 'a few,' 'several'

This term is used in the **masculine with feminine nouns** and in the **feminine with masculine nouns**, reflecting **gender polarity** similar to that of the numeral system. The following noun is in the genitive plural. The nouns specified by *biD⁽* and *biD⁽a* are often numerals or terms of measurement:

2.2.1 With masculine noun

يتطلب بضعة أسابيع.
ya-taTallab-u biD⁽at-a ᵓasaabii⁽-a.
It requires **several weeks.**

بعد بضعة أيام
ba⁽d-a biD⁽at-i ᵓayyaam-in
after **a few days**

2.2.2 With feminine noun

أكثر من بضع مئات الأمثلة
ᵓakthar-u min biD⁽-i miᵓaat-i l-ᵓamthilat-i
more than **several hundred** examples

بعد بضع دقائق
ba⁽d-a biD⁽-i daqaaᵓ iq-a
in **a few minutes**

يعلق على بضع مئات الأصوات.
yu-⁽alliq-u ⁽alaa biD⁽-i miᵓaat-i l-aSwaat-i.
It hangs on **several hundred** votes.

أكثر من بضع ثوان
ᵓakthar-u min biD⁽-i thawaan-in
more than **a few seconds**

2.3 *⁽idda* عدّة 'several'

This noun is used in two ways: either as the first part of a construct phrase or as a noun in apposition with the noun it specifies.

2.3.1 As first term of construct

امتهن أهل المدينة عدة مهن.
imtahan-a ᵓahl-u l-madiinat-i ⁽iddat-a mihan-in.
The people of the city practiced **several trades.**

جاء هؤلاء المربّون من عدة دول عربية.
jaaᵓ-a haaᵓulaaᵓ i l-murabb-uuna min ⁽iddat-i duwal-in ⁽arabiyyat-in.
These educators came **from several Arab countries.**

2.3.2 In apposition with a noun

When *⁽idda* is in apposition with a noun, it carries the same case as the noun.

في مدن عدة
fii mudun-in ⁽iddat-in
in **various cities**

في مناطق عدة
fii manaaTiq-a ⁽iddat-in
in **several regions**

فهناك روايات عدة عما حدث.

fa-hunaaka riwaayaat-un ʿiddat-un ʿammaa Hadath-a.

There are **several stories** about what happened.

2.4 *shattaa* شتّى 'various, diverse; all kinds of'

This word, the plural of *shatiit* 'scattered; dispersed,' is used as the first term of an *ʾiDaafa*.

في شتّى أنحاء الأرض

fii shattaa ʾanHaaʾ-i l-ʾarD-i

in **various** parts of the earth

2.5 *muxtalif* مختلف 'various; several'

This active participle of Form VIII (literally 'differing') is often used as the first term of an *ʾiDaafa* to mean 'various' or 'different.'

من مختلف أنحاء الولاية

min **muxtalif-i** *ʾanHaaʾ-i l-wilaayat-i*

from **various** parts of the state

في مختلف المدن

fii **muxtalif-i** *l-mudun-i*

in **various** cities

2.6 *ʿadad-un min* عدد من 'a number of'

This is a widely used expression to denote a non-specific but significant number. Unlike other quantifiers, it is an indefinite noun followed by a preposition, so the noun that follows is the object of the preposition *min* 'of.'

دعوة عدد من الأساتذة والمربيين العرب

daʿwat-u **ʿadad-in min**-a *l-ʾasaatidhat-i wa-l-murabbiina l-ʿarab-i*

the invitation of **a number of Arab professors and educators**

حضر الاجتماع عدد من الباحثين والمفكرين.

HaDar-a l-ijtimaaʿ-a **ʿadad-un min**-a *l-baaHithiina wa-l-mufakkiriina.*

A number of researchers and intellectuals attended the conference.

2.7 *kathiir-un min* كثير من and *al-kathiir-u min* الكثير من 'many'

To indicate a large but indefinite number, these phrases are used.

يتذكر كثير من الناس.

ya-tadhakkar-u **kathiir-un min**-a *l-naas-i.*

Many ('of the') people remember.

أمامنا الكثير من الفرص والكثير من التحديات.

ʾamaam-a-naa **l-kathiir-u min**-a *l-furaS-i wa-l-kathiir-u min-a l-taHaddiyaat-i.*

Before us are **many opportunities** and **many challenges**.

3 Expressions of "more," "most," and "majority"

Arabic uses several expressions to convey concepts of "more," "most of," or "the majority of."

3.1 "More"

When discussing the concept of "more," there are two sides to it: a **quality** can be greater in intensity, which is expressed by the comparative (or "elative") form of the **adjective** (e.g., more important, more famous); this is discussed in Chapter 10, sections 4.2.1–4.2.3.

However, there is also another use of "more" to mean "more of something," "a greater quantity/amount of something" where the "more" expression is followed by a **noun or noun phrase**. In contemporary Arabic the phrase *al-maziid min* المزيد من (literally 'the increase of') is often used to express this concept of "more of."

للمزيد من الأراضي الزراعية
li-l-maziid-i min-a l-ᵓaraadii l-ziraaᵓiyyat-i
for **more** agricultural **lands**

لتحقيق المزيد من الإنجازات في جميع القطاعات
li-taHqiiq-i l-maziid-i min-a l-ᵓ injaazaat-i fii jamiiᶜ-i l-qiTaaᶜaat-i
to realize **more production** in all sectors

تعهدت بتقديم المزيد من الأموال للبنوك.
taᶜahhad-at bi-taqdiim-i l-maziid-i min-a l-ᵓamwaal-i li-l-bunuuk-i.
It pledged support for **more money** for banks.

3.2 'Most of': *muᶜZam* معظم and *ᵓakthar* أكثر

3.2.1 *muᶜZam*

The expression 'most of' is often accomplished with the word *muᶜZam* as the first term of an *ᵓiDaafa*:

معظم السفارات العربية
muᶜZam-u l-sifaaraat -i ᶜarabiyyat-i
most of the Arab embassies

حصل على معظم المقاعد.
HaSal-a ᶜalaa muᶜZam-i l-maqaaᶜid-i.
It obtained **most of the seats.**

في معظم القسم الثاني من الكتاب
fii muᶜZam-i l-qism-i l-thaanii min-a l-kitaab-i
in **most of the second part** of the book

3.2.2 *ᵓakthar* أكثر 'more; most'

The elative adjective *ᵓakthar* 'more; most' may also be used to express 'most' as first term of an *ᵓiDaafa*. The following noun is definite, may be singular or plural, and is in the genitive case.

أكثر الوقت	أكثر المواطنين	أكثر الناس
ʾakthar-u l-waqt-i	*ʾakthar-u l-muwaaTin-iina*	*ʾakthar-u l-naas-i*
most of the time	most of the citizens	most people

3.3 Expression of "majority"

The Arabic superlative adjective *ʾaghlab*, the derived noun *ʾaghlabiyya*, or the active participle *ghaalib* are all used to express the concept of "majority."

أغلبهم ليس مؤرخا.
ʾaghlab-u-hum lays-a muʾarrix-an.
The majority of them are not historians.

4 Scope of quantifier agreement

The scope of agreement or concord refers to agreement patterns that apply to "quantified construct states."[2] Agreement or concord is normally shown through adjectives and/or verbs.

Patterns of agreement with quantified construct states can vary in MSA and the phenomenon has been studied by both Parkinson and LeTourneau. As LeTourneau remarks (1995, 30), "a verb may agree in number and gender with either the quantifier (invariantly masculine singular) or with its complement."

Parkinson's findings (as paraphrased by LeTourneau 1995, 31) reveal that "certain grammatical features on the second term in the QCS [quantified construct state] license only one agreement option. Thus, if the second term to *kull* is either an indefinite feminine singular or a definite plural, the verb must agree with the second term (logical agreement, in traditional terms); if *baʿD* has a pronominal suffix and the verb follows, agreement with the quantifier (grammatical agreement) is mandatory (Parkinson 1975, 66)."

4.1 Agreement with quantifier

In conformity with the above-stated rule, the agreement is with the quantifier when it has a pronoun suffix (such as *baʿD* or *ʾaghlab*).

أغلبهم ليس مؤرخا.
ʾaghlab-u-hum lays-a muʾarrix-an.
The majority of them **are not historians** ('is not a historian').

4.2 Agreement with specified noun

The agreement may be with the noun that is the second term of the *ʾiDaafa*. This occurs especially with adjectives that immediately follow the noun.

---

2 LeTourneau, 1995, 30. In this article, "Internal and external agreement in quantified construct states," LeTourneau provides detailed analysis on this topic. See also Parkinson 1975 on the agreement of *baʿD* and *kull*.

تهم كل عربي مقيم في البلد

*ta-humm-u **kull-a** ᶜarabiyy-in **muqiim-in** fii l-balad-i*

it concerns **every Arab residing** in the country

بعض المثقفين العرب	يحملون كل الوثائق المطلوبة.
baᶜD-u l-muthaqqaf-iina l-ᶜarab-i	*ya-Hmil-uuna **kull-a** l-wathaaʾiq-i **l-maTluubat-i**.*
some of the Arab cultured elite	They are carrying **all the requested documents.**

كل الاحتمالات ممكنة.	كل المحاولات الّتي بذلت
*kull-u l-iHtimaalaat-i **mumkinat-un**.*	*kull-u l-muHaawalaat-i llatii budhil-at*
All probabilities **are possible.**	**all** the attempts that were made

4.3 Ambiguous agreement

Sometimes the agreement is ambiguous, as in the following example.

كل طرف يحاول أن ينتزع أفضل شروط.

*kull-u Taraf-in **yu-Haawil-u** ʾan ya-ntaziᶜ-a ʾafDal-a shuruuT-in.*

Every party **tries** to obtain the best conditions.

4.4 Mixing of number agreement

In the following sentences using *baᶜD*, the adjective following the plural noun is plural, but the verb is third person masculine singular, in agreement with the quantifier.

بعض النقاد الأمريكيين يعتقد أن. . .

baᶜD-u l-nuqqaad-i l-ʾamriikiyy-iina ya-ᶜtaqid-u ʾanna. . . .

some American critics believe ('believes') that . . .

In practice, the verb may optionally agree with the second term of the construct (*nuqqaad*):[3]

بعض النقاد الأمريكيين يعتقدون أن. . .

baᶜD-u l-nuqqaad-i l-ʾamriikiyy-iina ya-ᶜtaqid-uuna ʾanna. . . .

some American critics believe (m. pl.) that . . .

5 Non-quantitative specifiers

5.1 Expression of identity or reflexivity

5.1.1 *nafs* نفس 'same; self'

To express the concept of "the same" Arabic uses the word *nafs* (pl. *ʾanfus* ~ *nufuus*), either as the first term of an *ʾiDaafa*, or in apposition with the modified

---

[3] As my colleague Amin Bonnah states, the usage here depends on "a mix of grammar, style, logic, and meaning" (personal communication).

noun. Note that this word has several meanings: 'self,' 'same,' 'spirit~soul,' and 'breath.' See also its use as an appositive specifier in chapter 8, section 2.3.

5.1.1.1 IN *'iDaafa*

تعمل جميعها على نفس المنوال.

ta-ʿmal-u jamiiʿ-u-haa ʿalaa nafs-i l-minwaal-i.

They all work **the same way.**

5.1.1.2 IN APPOSITION

يردد العبارة نفسها.

yu-raddid-u l-ʿibaarat-a nafs-a-haa.

He repeats **the same expression.**

5.1.2 *dhaatiyy* ذاتيّ 'self'[4]

In certain expressions the term *dhaatiyy* is used to delineate the concept of self, e.g.,

النقد الذاتيّ

al-naqd-u l-dhaatiyy-u

self-criticism

5.2 Expression of 'any; whichever' *'ayy/ 'ayya* أيّة / أي + noun

The noun *'ayy* is used as the first term of an *'iDaafa* to express the concept of "any" or "whichever." If the noun following *'ayy* أي is feminine, *'ayy* may shift to *'ayya* أيّة , but this does not always happen. The noun following *'ayy* is **indefinite and in the genitive** case. It is normally singular, but is sometimes plural.

5.2.1 Masculine form of *'ayy* + noun
5.2.1.1 *'ayy* + MASCULINE SINGULAR NOUN

لديّ القدرة على عمل أي شيء.

laday-ya l-qudrat-u ʿalaa ʿamal-i 'ayy-i shayʾ-in.

I have the ability to do **anything.**

يعارضون أي تدخل

yu-ʿaariD-uuna 'ayy-a tadaxxul-in

they oppose **any intervention**

من أي مكان تقريبا

min 'ayy-i makaan-in taqriib-an

from almost **any place**

مثل أي شعب آخر

mithl-a 'ayy-i shaʿʾb-in 'aaxar-a

like **any other people**

---

[4] For more on the pronoun *dhaat* and its usage, see Chapter 12, section 4.

5.2.1.2 *'ayy* + FEMININE SINGULAR NOUN:

لأيّ دولة
li-'ayy-i dawlat-in
for any state

لأيّ محاولة
li-'ayy-i muHaawalat-in
for any attempt

في حالة أيّ شكوى
fii Haalat-i 'ayy-i shakwaa
in case of **any complaint**

اسأل عن معنى أيّ كلمة.
is'al'an ma'naa 'ayy-i kalimat-in.
Ask about the meaning of **any word**.

5.2.2 Feminine *'ayya* + noun

When the noun being specified is feminine, the feminine form, *'ayya* أيّة may be used:

في أية قائمة لأكابر علماء الدنيا
fii 'ayyat-i qaa'imat-in li-'akaabir-i 'ulamaa'-i l-dunyaa
on **any list** of the greatest scholars in the world

لن يجدوا أية مشاكل.
lan ya-jid-uu 'ayyat-a mashaakil-a
They will not find **any problems**.

5.2.3 *'ayy* as independent noun

The noun *'ayy* may be used independently to mean 'anything,' 'whatever,' or 'anyone.' When used with a dual noun, it indicates 'either one of'; it is normally indefinite and takes nunation.

أيّاً كان لونها
'ayy-an kaan-a lawn-u-haa
whatever its color is

أيٌّ من المرشحين
'ayy-un min-a l-murashshaH-ayni
either one of the (two) candidates

5.2.3.1 *'ayy* WITH NEGATIVE AS 'NONE':

With a negative verb, *'ayy* carries the sense of 'none':

لم يستطع أيٌّ منها.
lam ya-staTi' 'ayy-un min-haa.
None of them could.

10

Adjectives: function and form

This chapter is in two parts. The first part deals with function: adjectives in context and issues such as agreement, word order, and inflection, including inflection for comparative and superlative. The second part focuses on the derivational morphology or word structure of adjectives.

Part one: Function

1 Attributive adjectives

An **attributive adjective** is part of a noun phrase and follows the noun directly, agreeing with it in **gender, number, case, and definiteness**:

البحر الأحمر
al-baHr-u l-ʾaHmar-u
the **Red** Sea

القومية العربيّة
al-qawmiyyat-u l-ʿarabiyyat-u
Arab nationalism

الرياضيّون العرب
al-riyaaDiyy-uuna l-ʿarab-u
Arab athletes

الهلال الخصيب
al-hilaal-u l-xaSiib-u
the **Fertile** Crescent

فوز سهل
fawz-un sahl-un
an **easy** win

في دور سياسيّ
fii dawr-in siyaasiyy-in
in a **political** role

1.1 Attributive adjective modifying noun + pronoun suffix

A noun with a pronoun suffix is considered definite; therefore, an adjective that modifies that noun carries the definite article, in addition to agreeing in gender, case, and number with the noun:

في بيئاتها الطبيعيّة
fii biiʾaat-i-haa l-Tabiiʿiyyat-i
in their natural environments

هويته الثقافيّة
huwiyyat-u-hu l-thaqaafiyyat-u
its cultural identity

لدعم مرشحيهم المحليّين
li-daʿm-i murashshaH-ii-him-i l-maHalliyy-iina
to support **their local candidates**

في تاريخ فكرنا العربيّ
fii taariix-i fikr-i-naa l-ʿarabiyy-i
in the history of **our Arab thought**

2 Predicate adjectives

A predicate adjective is used in an equational (verbless) sentence to provide information about the subject of the sentence, thus completing the clause. In an Arabic equational sentence, there is usually no overt copula, or present tense form of the verb "to be," linking the subject and predicate. When acting as a predicate, the adjective agrees with the noun or pronoun subject in gender and number. It is usually in the nominative case. However, it does not normally take the definite article because it is predicating a quality or attribute to the subject.

الحصاد وفير.
al-HiSaad-u wafiir-un.
The harvest is **abundant** ('is an abundant one').

القائمة طويلة.
al-qaaʾimat-u Tawiilat-un.
The list **is long** ('is a long one').

الكرز أحمر.
al-karaz-u ʾaHmar-u.
Cherries **are red.**

القصة ظريفة.
al-qiSSat-u Zariifat-un.
The story **is charming.**

هي ذكيّة.
hiya dhakiyyat-un.
She **is intelligent.**

أنا محظوظة.
ʾanaa maHZuuZat-un.
I am **fortunate.**

نحن بعيدون عن ذلك.
naHnu baʿiid-uuna ʿan dhaalika.
We **are far** from that.

3 Adjectives as substantives

Adjectives may serve as substantives or noun substitutes, just as they sometimes do in English:

حيث القديم يختلط مع الجديد.
Hayth-u l-qadiim-u ya-xtaliT-u maʿ-a l-jadiid-i.
Where **the old** mixes with **the new.**

نزل الكبار والصغار إلى الشوارع.
nazal-a l-kibaar-u wa-l-Sighaar-u ʾilaa l-shawaariʿ-i.
The adults and children (**'the big and the little'**) descended into the streets.

بالنسبة إلى الكثيرين
bi-l-nisbat-i ʾilaa l-kathiir-iina
according to **many**

نال الفضّيّة.
naal-a l-fiDDiyyat-a.
He won ('obtained') **the silver** [medal].

قليلون من الباحثين
qaliil-uuna min-a l-baaHith-iina
few of the researchers

اجتماع كبار المسؤولين
ijtimaaʿ-u kibaar-i l-masʾuul-iina
the meeting of **senior** officials

4 Arabic adjective inflection

Adjectives in Arabic inflect for four morphological categories: **gender, number, case, and definiteness**. Many of them also inflect for a fifth category: **degree** (comparative and superlative).

As far as the first four categories are concerned, adjectives mirror the inflectional categories of the nouns that they modify, that is, they **agree** or are in **concord** with those nouns. In most cases the agreement or concord is direct or "strict," meaning that the adjective reflects exactly the categories of the noun.[1]

As noted above, Arabic adjectives normally follow the nouns they modify.

4.1 Inflectional categories: gender, number, case, definiteness

Much like nouns, Arabic adjectives have a base form, which is the singular masculine, and an inflected (marked) form for the feminine, usually marked by *taaʾ marbuuTa*. They also inflect for dual, and for plural. In the plural, they take broken or sound plural forms, or both.

In terms of case inflection, adjectives fall into the same declensions as nouns, depending on their morphological form (their lexical root and pattern structure).

4.1.1 Masculine singular adjectives

Masculine singular adjectives modify masculine singular nouns.

طقس غائم
Taqs-un ghaaʾim-un
cloudy weather

في الوقت المناسب
fii l-waqt-i l-munaasib-i
at the **proper** time

الاحترام المتبادل
al-iHtiraam-u l-mutabaadal-u
mutual respect

المفتش العام
al-mufattish-u l-ʿaamm-u
the inspector **general**

---

[1] Adjectives in general are refered to in morphological theory as "targets" rather than "controlers." That is, they are targets of the agreement requirements of nouns. As Carstairs-McCarthy (1994, 769) states: "Adjectives are gender targets, i.e., they must agree with nouns in gender as well as number and case."

البحر الأبيض المتوسّط

al-baHr-u l-ʾabyaD-u l-mutawassiT-u

the Mediterranean Sea ('the **middle white** sea')

السلك الدبلوماسيّ العربيّ والأجنبيّ

al-silk-u l-dibluumaasiyy-u l-ʿarabiyy-u wa-l-ʾajnabiyy-u

the **Arab and foreign** diplomatic corps

4.1.2 Masculine dual adjectives

Masculine dual adjectives modify masculine dual nouns.

في مجلّدين كبيرين	بين البلدين العربيّين
fii mujallad-ayni kabiir-ayni	*bayn-a l-balad-ayni l-ʿarabiyy-ayni*
in **two large** volumes	between the **two Arab** countries

4.1.3 Masculine plural adjectives

Masculine plural adjectives modify masculine plural nouns **only if the nouns refer to human beings.**

المماليك المصريّون	زوّار رسميّون
al-mamaaliik-u l-miSriyy-uuna	*zuwwaar-un rasmiyy-uuna*
the **Egyptian** Mamelukes	**official** visitors

خبراء نفطيّون	من الفنّانين اليونانيّين
xubraaʾ-u nifTiyy-uuna	*min-a l-fannaan-iina l-yuunaaniyy-iina*
oil experts	from the **Greek** artists

الأمراء الروس الآخرون	تسعة أشخاص جدد
al-ʾumaraaʾ-u l-ruus-u l-ʾaaxar-uuna	*tisʿat-u ʾashxaas-in judud-in*[2]
the **other Russian** princes	nine **new** persons

4.1.4 Feminine singular adjectives

The feminine singular adjective is used to modify **feminine singular nouns** and **also for nonhuman plural** nouns. The use of the feminine singular to modify nonhuman plural nouns is referred to as "**deflected**" agreement rather than "**strict**" agreement.

---

[2] Note that when numerals are used for counting over ten, the counted noun is grammatically singular and any **agreeing adjective is also singular**, although the meaning is plural. For example:

عشرون مهندساً جديداً

ʿishruuna muhandis-an jadiid-an

twenty **new** engineers

4.1.4.1 WITH FEMININE SINGULAR NOUNS:

الحكاية القديمة

al-Hikaayat-u l-qadiimat-u

the **old** story

نصيحة مجانيّة

naSiiHat-un **majjaaniyyat-un**

free advice

المرة القادمة

al-marrat-a l-qaadimat-a

the **next** time

الجبهة الإسلامية القومية الحاكمة

al-jabhat-u l-ʾislaamiyyat-u l-qawmiyyat-u
l-Haakimat-u

the **ruling national Islamic** front

4.1.4.2 WITH NONHUMAN PLURAL NOUNS: "DEFLECTED" AGREEMENT

Nonhuman plural nouns require feminine singular agreement.[3] Case and definiteness are in strict agreement.

الأمم المتّحدة

al-ʾumam-u **l-muttaHidat-u**

the **United** Nations

الولايات المتّحدة

al-wilaayaat-u **l-muttahidat-u**

the **United** States

نتائج أَوَليّة

nataaʾij-u **ʾawwaliyyat-un**

preliminary results

ثلاث أفكار رئيسيّة

talaath-u ʾafkaar-in **raʾiisiyyat-in**

three **main** ideas

التقاليد المسيحيّة

al-taqaaliid-u **l-masiiHiyyat-u**

the **Christian** traditions

القوات المسلحة

al-quwwaat-u **l-musallaHat-u**

the **armed** forces

4.1.5 Feminine dual adjectives

Feminine dual nouns are modified by feminine dual adjectives.

سفينتان كبيرتان

safiinat-aani **kabiirat-aani**

two big ships

خلال السنتين الماضيتين

xilaal-a l-sanat-ayni **l-maaDiyat-ayni**

during the **last two** years

المدينتان الأخريان

al-madiinat-aani **l-ʾuxray-aani**

the **other two** cities

الدولتان العظميان

al-dawlat-aani **l-ʿuZmay-aani**

the **two super** powers ('states')

4.1.6 Feminine plural adjectives

Feminine plural adjectives modify feminine plural nouns only if the nouns refer to human beings:

---

[3] See the article by Belnap and Shabeneh 1992 for discussion of the history and nature of deflected agreement in Arabic.

نساء عربيات	من سيدات مسنّات
nisaaʾ -un ʿarabiyyaat-un	*min sayyidaat-in musinnaat-in*
Arab women	from **old** ladies

من النساء المعجبات	النساء المتقدمات في السن
min-a l-nisaaʾ-i l-muʿjibaat-i	*al-nisaaʾ-u l-mutaqaddimaat-u fii l-sinn-i*
from the **admiring** women	women of advanced age ('women **advanced** in age')

الفتايات العاملات في هذا المجال
al-fataayaat-u l-ʿaamilaat-u fii haadhaa l-majaal-i
the young women **working** in this field

4.1.7 Non-gendered adjectives

There are a limited number of adjectives in MSA that do not inflect for gender. They remain in the masculine singular base form.[4]

4.1.4.1 THE ADJECTIVE *xaam* 'RAW':

مادة خام	المواد الخام
maaddat-un xaam-un	*al-mawaadd-u l-xaam-u*
raw material	the raw materials

4.1.4.2 THE ADJECTIVE *maHD* 'PURE' (WITH EXCEPTIONS):[5]

لغة عربيّة محض
lughat-un ʿarabiyyat-un maHD-un
pure Arabic language

4.1.4.3 CERTAIN ADJECTIVES THAT APPLY STRICTLY TO FEMALE ANATOMY, SUCH AS "PREGNANT":

إمرأة حامل
imraʾat-un Haamil-un
a pregnant woman

4.2 Adjective inflection for comparative and superlative (*ism al-tafDiil* اسم التفضيل)

The comparative and superlative forms of adjectives in Arabic are sometimes referred to together in grammatical descriptions of Arabic as "elative" forms

---

[4] For an interesting discussion of discrepancies in gender agreement in the Qurʾân, see Gaballa 1999.
[5] Wehr (1979, 1050) describes the adjective *maHD* as "invariable for gender and number," but I found it at least once in the feminine, in Hasan (1987, III:1) in his description of the types of *ʾiDaafa* as *maHDat-un wa-ghayr-u maHDat-in* 'pure and non-pure.'

because they signify a more intense degree of the quality described by the adjective.[6] The Arabic term *ism al-tafDiil* signifies that these are terms of preference, preeminence, or preferment. In this text, the more standard terms "comparative" and "superlative" are used to refer to these forms of adjectives.

Just as English has sequences such as *large, larger, largest,* or *nice, nicer, nicest,* to indicate increasing degrees of intensity, Arabic has equivalent sequences consisting of base form, comparative, and superlative forms.

4.2.1 Comparative adjective: *ʾafʿal* أفعل

Arabic adjectives derived from Form I triliteral roots inflect form the comparative through a pattern shift. No matter what the original or base pattern of the adjective, the comparative pattern shifts to *ʾaCCaC* (*ʾafʿal* أفعل), and it is diptote. That is, it does not take nunation or *kasra* in its indefinite form.[7] Note also that the initial *hamza* of this pattern is *hamzat al-qaTʿ*, that is, it does not elide. It is stable.

4.2.1.1 REGULAR TRILITERAL ROOTS

صغير	أصغر	بعيد	أبعد
Saghiir	*ʾaSghar*	*baʿiid*	*ʾabʿad*
small	smaller	far	farther

كثير	أكثر	حسن	أحسن
kathiir	*ʾakthar*	*Hasan*	*ʾaHsan*
many	more	good	better

كبير	أكبر	ثقيل	أثقل
kabiir	*ʾakbar*	*thaqiil*	*ʾathqal*
big	bigger	heavy	heavier

4.2.1.2 HOLLOW ROOTS: Comparative adjectives from hollow roots, where the middle radical is either *waaw* or *yaaʾ*, behave as though the *waaw* or *yaaʾ* is a regular consonant:

طويل	أطول	جيد	أجود
Tawiil	*ʾaTwal*	*jayyid*	*ʾajwad*
tall; long	taller; longer	good	better

---

[6] See, for example, Abboud and McCarus 1983, part 1:340–45. Also Blachère and Gaudefroy-Demombynes 1975, 97 "L'élatif est un aspect de l'adjectif qui en exprime une valeur supérieure, complète, en une nuance souvent délicate à exprimer en français."

[7] For more on the diptote declension see Chapter 7, section 5.4.2.2.

طيب	أطيب	سيّىء	أسوأ
Tayyib	*ʾaTyab*	*sayyiʾ*	*ʾaswaʾ*
good	better	bad	worse

4.2.1.3 ASSIMILATED ROOTS: Comparative adjectives from assimilated roots, where the initial root consonant is *waaw* or *yaaʾ*, keep that consonant:

واسع	أوسع	واضح	أوضح	وثيق	أوثق
waasiʿ	*ʾawsaʿ*	*waaDiH*	*ʾawDaH*	*wathiiq*	*ʾawthaq*
wide	wider	clear	clearer	firm	firmer

4.2.1.4 GEMINATE ROOTS: Comparative adjectives from geminate roots (where the second and third root consonants are the same) have a variant comparative form due to a rule which prevents a short vowel from occurring between two identical consonants. Thus instead of *ʾafʿal*, the form is *ʾafall* أفلّ, and the two identical consonants are together, spelled with a *shadda*:

قليل	أقلّ	هـامّ	أهـمّ
qaliil	*ʾaqall*	*haamm*	*ʾahamm*
little; few	less; fewer	important	more important

جديد	أجدّ	حارّ	أحرّ
jadiid	*ʾajadd*	*Haarr*	*ʾaHarr*
new	newer	hot	hotter

4.2.1.5 DEFECTIVE ROOTS: Comparative adjectives from defective roots have the form *ʾafʿaa* أفعى. The final root consonant (whether *waaw* or *yaaʾ*) becomes *ʾalif maqsuura*:

عالٍ	أعلى	غني	أغنى	قوي	أقوى
ʿaalin	*ʾaʿlaa*	*ghaniyy*	*ʾaghnaa*	*qawiyy*	*ʾaqwaa*
high	higher	rich	richer	strong	stronger

حلو	أحلى	ذكي	أذكى
Hilw	*ʾaHlaa*	*dhakiyy*	*ʾadhkaa*
sweet	sweeter	smart	smarter

4.2.2 Inflection and use of comparative

Note that the Arabic comparative adjective does not show difference in gender. In fact, comparative adjectives do not inflect for gender or number or definiteness. They inflect only for case. When comparing two things and contrasting them, the preposition *min* is used the way 'than' is used in English.

4.2.2.1 CASE INFLECTION FOR COMPARATIVE ADJECTIVES: The comparative adjective falls into the diptote category and therefore shows only two different case markers in the indefinite form: *Damma* and *fatHa*.

أحسن ʾaHsan 'better'
Nominative	أَحْسَنُ ʾaHsan-u
Genitive	أَحْسَنَ ʾaHsan-a
Accusative	أَحْسَنَ ʾaHsan-a

4.2.2.2 EXAMPLES OF COMPARATIVE ADJECTIVE IN CONTEXT:

تبدو أصغر من عمرها.

ta-bduu ʾaSghar-a min ʿumr-i-haa.

She appears **younger** than her age.

أكثر من خمس مئة دراسة علميّة

ʾakthar-u min xams-i miʾat-i diraasat-in ʿilmiyyat-in

more than 500 scientific studies

أكثر من نصف الأنواع المعروفة

ʾakthar-u min niSf-i l-ʾanwaaʿ-i l-maʿruufat-i

more than half the known species

أهمّ ممّا سبقه

ʾahamm-u mimmaa sabaq-a-hu

more important than what preceded it

هذا أقل ممّا نحتاج إليه.

haadhaa ʾaqall-u mimmaa na-Htaaj-u ʾilay-hi.

This is **less** than we need.

تضمّ أكثر من سبع مئة مشهد.

ta-Dumm-u ʾakthar-a min sabʿ-i miʾat-i mashhad-in.

It contains **more** than 700 scenes.

4.2.2.3 COMPARATIVE WITHOUT *min*: Sometimes the comparative is used without reference to what it is compared to, so there is no need for the preposition *min*:

صارت تأخذ دورا أكبر.

*Saar-at ta'xudh-u **dawr-an 'akbar-a.***

She started to take a **greater** role.

إلى أفق أوسع وأرحب

'ilaa 'ufuq-in 'awsa'-a wa-'arHab-a

to a **wider and more spacious** horizon

سيؤدّي إلى علاقة أوثق بينهما.

*sa-yu-'addii 'ilaa 'alaaqat-in **'awthaq-a** bayn-a-humaa.*

It will lead to a **firmer relationship** between the two of them.

4.2.2.4 COMPARATIVE IN FORM ONLY: An adjective may occasionally have the comparative form, although its meaning is not comparative. In this case, it inflects for number, gender, and definiteness, as well as case:

	m. sg.	*f. sg.*	*m. pl.*
empty	أجوف *'ajwaf*	جوفاء *jawfaa'*	جوف *juuf*
silly, stupid	أحمق *'aHmaq*	حمقاء *Hamqaa'*	حماقى حمقى حمق *Humuq~Hamqaa~Hamaaqaa*

Examples:

تبدو فكرة حمقاء.   كيس أجوف

*ta-bduu fikrat-an **Hamqaa'-a.***   *kiis-un **'ajwaf-u***

It seems [like] a **silly** idea.   an **empty** bag

(1) 'Other': *'aaxar* آخر and *'uxraa* أخرى

A special form of adjective is the word for 'other.' It has a unique inflectional paradigm that combines comparative and superlative patterns, but does not have comparative or superlative meaning. It inflects for number, gender, case, and definiteness.

	m. sg.	*f. sg.*	*m. pl.*	*f. pl.*
other; another	آخر *'aaxar*	أخرى *'uxraa*	آخرون *'aaxar-uuna*	أخريات *'uxray-aat*

Examples:

بشكل أو بآخر   مثل أي شعب آخر

*bi-shakl-in 'aw bi-**'aaxar-a***   *mithl-a 'ayy-i sha'b-in **'aaxar-a***

one way or **another**   like any **other** people

من جهة أخرى
min jihat-in ʾuxraa
from **another** perspective;
   on the **other** hand

يعتبره آخرون ضمانة.
ya-ʿtabir-u-hu ʾaaxar-uuna Damaanat-an.
Others consider it an assurance.

مرة أخرى
marrat-an ʾuxraa
another time; one more time

أما المدينتان الأخريان
ʾammaa l-madiinat-aani l-ʾuxray-aani
as for the **other two** cities

4.2.3 The periphrastic or phrasal comparative

Certain qualities, attributes, or descriptors do not fit into the pattern-change paradigm for comparative and superlative meanings. For example, *nisba* adjectives and the active and passive participles functioning as adjectives from the derived verb forms (II–X) have extra consonants or vowels as part of their essential word structure, so they cannot shift into the *ʾafʿal* pattern without losing some of their identity and meaning. Moreover, certain colors are already of the *ʾafʿal* pattern, so how does one express a quality such as "blacker," or "whiter"?

Arabic handles this using a strategy similar to using "more" in English. Intensity words such as "more" plus the adjective are used, or words such as "stronger" plus a color word in order to form a descriptive comparative phrase.

The most common intensifying words used for forming the periphrastic comparative are:

أكثر	أشدّ	أقلّ
ʾakthar	*ʾashadd*	*ʾaqall*
more	stronger	less

This intensifying word is then joined with a noun in the **indefinite accusative case**, a structure called *tamyiiz* or 'accusative of specification.'[8]

كان أكثر تعاطفاً مع العرب.
kaan-a ʾakthar-a taʿaaTuf-an maʿa l-ʿarab-i.
He was **more favorably disposed** toward the Arabs.

يمكن أن يجعله أكثر تفاهماً للموقف.
yu-mkin-u -ʾan ya-jʿal-a-hu ʾakthar-a tafaahum-an li-l-mawqif-i.
It might make him **more understanding** of the situation.

أقل سهولة منه
ʾaqall-u suhuulat-an min-hu
less easy than it ('**less in easiness**')

هي أكثر مسؤوليّة منك.
hiya ʾakthar-u masʾuuliyyat-an min-ka.
She is **more responsible** than you.

---

8 See Chapter 11, section 6 for more on the *tamyiiz* construction.

سلام أوسع وأكثر شموليّة

salaam-un ʾawsaʿ-u wa-ʾakthar-u shumuuliyyat-an

a **wider** and **more inclusive** peace

محرّك أكثر كفاءة وأكثر اعتماديّة

muHarrik-un ʾakthar-u kafaaʾat-an wa-ʾakthar-u ʿtimaadiyyat-an

a **more capable** and **more dependable** motor

هو أكثر دهاء من حسين.

huwa ʾakthar-u dahaaʾ-an min Husayn-in.

He is **more shrewd** than Hussein.

قد تكون أكثر أهميّة.

qad ta-kuun-u ʾakthar-a ʾahammiyyat-an.

They might be of **more importance.**

كان أكثر عدوانيّة وأقل سماحة.

kaan-a ʾakthar-aʿudwaaniyyat-an wa-ʾaqall-a samaaHat-an.

It was **more aggressive** and **less permissive.**

4.2.4 The superlative

The form of the Arabic superlative adjective, which indicates the highest degree of comparison, resembles the comparative form *ʾafʿal* أفعل. There are differences, however. The superlative form is always definite, defined by the definite article, a pronoun suffix, or by being the first term of an *ʾiDaafa*. Moreover, it has a feminine form as well: *fuʿlaa* فُعْلى. Because the feminine form ends with *ʾalif maqSuura*, it does not inflect for case.

Examples:	Masculine	Feminine
biggest; oldest; greatest	الأكْبَر *al-ʾakbar*	الكُبْرى *al-kubraa*
smallest	الأصْغر *al-ʾaSghar*	الصُّغْرى *al-Sughraa*
greatest	الأعْظَم *al-ʾaʿZam*	العظمى *al-ʿuZmaa*
highest; supreme	الأعْلى *al-ʾaʿlaa*	العلْيا *al-ʿulyaa*

In some instances a dual form or plural form of the superlative may be used. The plural form of the masculine superlative is either the sound masculine plural *ʾafʿal-uuna*, or CaCaaCiC (*faʿaalil* فعالل), a diptote plural pattern. The plural of the feminine superlative is CuCCayaat (*fuʿlayaat* فعْليات).

في الدولتين العظميين
fii l-dawlat-ayni l-ᶜuZmay-ayni
in the **two super** powers

في أية قائمة لأكابر علماء الدنيا
fii ʾayyat-i qaaʾimat-in li-ʾakaabir-i ᶜulamaaʾ-i l-dunyaa
on any list of **the greatest** scholars in the world

4.2.4.1 SUPERLATIVES IN CONTEXT: WORD ORDER: Superlative adjectives may follow a noun directly, may be used as the first term of an ʾiDaafa with a noun, or may have a pronoun suffix. In certain expressions, they occur alone, with the definite article.

(1) **Following a definite noun:** The superlative adjective may, like the ordinary adjective, follow the noun. In that case, it agrees with the noun in gender, number, definiteness, and case:

القوة العظمى
al-quwwat-u l-ᶜuZmaa
the greatest power/ the super power

المجلس الأعلى
al-majlis-u l-ʾaᶜlaa
the supreme council

الدب الأكبر
al-dibb-u lʾakbar-u
Ursa Major (constellation) 'the greatest bear'

الحدث الأبرز
al-Hadath-u l-ʾabraz-u
the most prominent event

ذات الأهمّية القصوى
dhaat-u l-ʾahammiyyat-i l-quSwaa
of utmost importance

السؤال الأصعب
al-suʾaal-u l-ʾaSᶜab-u
the hardest question

بعد أزمة الثلاثينات الكبرى
baᶜd-a ʾazmat-i l-thalaathiinaat-i l-kubraa
after **the major crisis** of the thirties

(1.1) **Fixed expressions with the superlative:** Sometimes, especially in set phrases, Arabic uses a superlative expression where English would use an ordinary adjective:

الشرق الأدنى
al-sharq-u l-ʾadnaa
the Near ('nearest') East

الشرق الأوسط
al-sharq-u l-ʾawsaT-u
the Middle ('middlest') East

القرون الوسطى
al-quruun-u l-wusTaa
the Middle ('middlest') Ages

الحرب الكبرى
al-Harb-u l-kubraa
the Great ('greatest') War (WWI)

أمريكا الوسطى والجنوبية	الدول الكبرى
ʾamriikaa l-wusTaa wa-l-januubiyyat-u	*al-duwal-u l-kubraa*
Central ('most central') and South America	the Great ('greatest') Powers
الإسكندر الأكبر	آسيا الصغرى
al-iskandar al-ʾakbar-u	*ʾaasiyaa l-Sughraa*
Alexander the Great ('the greatest')	Asia Minor ('the smallest')

(2) **As the first term of an *ʾiDaafa* with a singular, indefinite noun:** The superlative adjective is often used as the first term of an *ʾiDaafa* with a singular, indefinite noun as the second term. In this structure, the adjective does not inflect for gender; it remains masculine singular no matter what the gender of the noun.

أصغر سمكة في العالم	في أفضل شكل ممكن
ʾaSghar-u samakat-in fii l-ʿaalam-i	*fii ʾafDal-i shakl-in mumkin-in*
the smallest fish in the world	in the best way possible
هو أكبر مطار في كندا.	لزيارة أقدم قصر
huwa ʾakbar-u maTaar-in fii kanadaa.	*li-ziyaarat-i ʾaqdam-i qaSr-in*
It is the biggest airport in Canada.	to visit the oldest castle
على أبعد تقدير	في أقصى ساحل بحرالشمال
ʿalaa ʾabʿad-i taqdiir-in	*fii ʾaqSaa saaHil-i baHr-i l-shimaal-i*
at the furthest estimate	on the farthest shore of the North Sea
حصل على لقب أفضل لاعب عربي.	أدنى مستوى
HaSal-a ʿalaa laqab-i ʾafDal-u laaʿib-in ʿarabiyy-in.	*ʾadnaa mustawan*
He obtained the title of 'best Arab player.'	the lowest level

(3) **As first term of an *ʾiDaafa* with a plural noun:** When a superlative adjective is used as the first term of an *ʾiDaafa* with a plural noun, the noun is normally definite, but may not always be. Normally the superlative adjective is in the masculine form, although the feminine may also occur.

أجمل سنوات صباي	أقوى لاعبين في العالم
ʾajmal-u sanawaat-i Sibaaya	*ʾaqwaa laaʿib-iina fii l-ʿaalam-i*
the most beautiful years of my childhood	the strongest players in the world

بأحرّ التعازي القلبية المخلصة

bi-'aHarr-i l-ta'aazii l-qalbiyyat-i l-muxliSat-i

with **warmest**, heartfelt, sincere **condolences**

في أربع من أهمّ المدن

fii 'arba'-in min 'ahamm-i l-mudun-i

in four of **the most important cities**

باشتراك كبرى الشركات

bi-shtiraak-i kubraa l-sharikaat-i

with the participation of the **biggest companies**

في أهمّ أربع مدن

fii 'ahamm-i 'arba'-i mudun-in

in the four **most important cities**

(4) **With pronoun suffix:** A superlative adjective may occur with a pronoun suffix.

فأغلبهم من المهاجرين المسلمين.

fa-'aghlab-u-hum min-a l-muhaajir-iina l-muslim-iina.

Most of them are Muslim emigrants.

أغلبهم ليس مؤرّخا.

'aghlab-u-hum lays-a mu'arrix-an.

The majority of them are not historians.

(5) **With indefinite pronoun *maa* and following clause:** The superlative adjective may be the first term of an *'iDaafa* whose second term is a phrase starting with an indefinite pronoun.

أخطر ما في الأمر

'axTar-u maa fii l-'amr-i

the most dangerous [thing] in the affair

أغرب ما في هذا الأمر

'aghrab-u maa fii haadhaa l-'amr-i

the strangest [thing] in this affair

(6) **With definite article by itself:** In certain expressions, the superlative adjective occurs alone, with the definite article.

خمسة أشخاص على الأقل

xamsat-u 'ashxaaS-in 'alaa l-'aqall-i

five people at least

لفترة وجيزة على الأقلّ

li-fatrat-in wajiizat-in 'alaa l-'aqall-i

for a brief period at least

5 The adjective *'iDaafa*, the "false" *'iDaafa* (*'iDaafa ghayr Haqiiqiyya* إضافة غير حقيقية)

The "adjective" *'iDaafa* is a particular use of the adjective as the first term of an *'iDaafa* or annexation structure. The adjective may take the definite article if it modifies a definite noun. Since this type of construct violates the general rules (by allowing the first term of the *'iDaafa* to take a definite article), it is called "unreal" or "false."

This kind of phrase is used to describe a distinctive quality of an item, equivalent to hyphenated expressions in English such as fair-haired, long-legged, many-sided.

In this kind of 'iDaafa, the adjective agrees with the noun it modifies in case, number, and gender. The second term of the adjective 'iDaafa is a definite noun in the genitive case and refers to a particular property of the modified noun.[9]

5.1 Definite agreement
Here the adjective takes the definite article, agreeing with the noun it modifies.

اللجنة البرلمانية الواسعة النفوذ

al-lajnat-u l-barlamaaniyyat-u l-waasiʿat-u l-nafuudh-i

the **widely influential** parliamentary committee ('wide of influence')

هذا الفيلسوف العميق التفكير

haadha l-faylusuuf-u l-ʿamiiq-u l-tafkiir-i

this profound (**'deep of thought'**) philosopher

5.2 Indefinite agreement
Here the adjective 'iDaafa modifies an indefinite noun. The adjective does not therefore take a definite article but does not take nunation, either, because it is the first term of an 'iDaafa.

في ظروف بالغة الأهمية	إنكليزي بارد الأعصاب
fii Zuruuf-in baalighat-i l-ʾahammiyyat-i	*ʾinkliiziyy-un baarid-u l-ʾaʿSaab-i*
in circumstances **of extreme importance**	a **cold-blooded** ('cold-nerved') Englishman
قدر متوسط الحجم	على نار متوسطة الحرارة
qidr-un mutawassiT-u l-Hajm-i	*ʿalaa naar-in mutawassiTat-i l-Haraarat-i*
a **medium-sized** pot	on a **medium-hot** fire

5.3 Adjective 'iDaafa as predicate
When acting as a predicate adjective in an equational sentence, the adjective in the adjective 'iDaafa lacks the definite article. For example:

هو هولندي الأصل.

huwa huulandiyy-u l-ʾaSl-i.

He is **of Dutch origin.**

Part two: Adjective derivation: the structure of Arabic adjectives
Arabic adjectives are structured in two ways: through derivation from a lexical root by means of the root-and-pattern system, or by means of attaching the *nisba*

---

[9] For further discussion and examples of the adjective 'iDaafa, see Chapter 8, section 1.9.2.

suffix *-iyy* (m.) or *-iyya* (f.) to create an adjective from another word (usually a noun). Very rarely, an adjective will exist on its own, without relation to a lexical root.

In traditional Arabic grammar, adjectives and nouns both fall under the syntactic category, *ism* 'noun.' The particular designations for the *nomen adjectivum* (Wright 1967, I:105) in Arabic include *al-waSf*, الوصف, *al-Sifa* الصفة, and *al-naʕt* النعت, referring to qualities, attributes, and epithets.[10] These types of words function in ways that very closely parallel what would be termed "adjectives" in English, and many pedagogical texts refer to them simply as adjectives.

Active and passive participles may function either as adjectives or as nouns. When they function as adjectives, they follow the same inflectional and syntactic rules as adjectives, agreeing with the noun they modify in case, gender, number, and definiteness.

1 Derivation patterns from Form I triliteral roots

These adjective forms are based on particular morphological patterns derived from the base form of the verb, Form I. In some cases, an identical pattern may be used for nouns as well.[11] Some of the more commonly occurring adjectival patterns include the following.[12] Whereas the masculine plural patterns vary widely, the feminine plural, when used, is usually the sound feminine plural.

1.1 The CaCiiC or *faʕiil* فعيل pattern

This is one of the most common adjective patterns. The plural forms, used only for human beings, may be several, including sometimes both sound plurals and broken plurals. The masculine plural applies to human males and to mixed groups of males and females. The much more predictable feminine plural forms (ending in /-aat/) apply to groups of female human beings. Some of the more frequently occurring adjectives are as follows:

	m. sg.	*m. pl.*
far, distant	بعيد *baʕiid*	بعاد بعداء بعيدون *baʕiid-uuna~ buʕadaaʔ~biʕaad*
large, big	كبير *kabiir*	كبار كبيرون *kabiir-uuna~ kibaar*

[10] Beeston states: "One cannot establish for Arabic a word class of adjectives, syntactic considerations being the only identificatory criterion of an adjective" (1970, 44).

[11] For example, from the *faʕiil* pattern come nouns such as *waziir* 'minister,' *jaliid* 'ice,' and *safiir* 'ambassador.'

[12] Wright 1967, I:131–40 gives an extensive description of these adjective patterns and uses. He refers to them all as "verbal adjectives," since he considers them derived from Form I verbs. However, I prefer to reserve the term "verbal adjectives" for active and passive participles, rather than adjectives in general.

	m. sg.	*m. pl.*
small	صغير *Saghiir*	صغراء صغار *Sighaar~Sugharaaʾ*
nice; pleasant	لطيف *laTiif*	لطفاء لطاف *liTaaf~ luTafaaʾ*
great	عظيم *ʿaZiim*	عظائم عظماء عظام *ʿiZaam~ ʿuZamaaʾ~ ʿaZaaʾim*
generous	كريم *kariim*	كرام *kiraam*
poor	فقير *faqiir*	فقراء *fuqaraaʾ*
weak	ضعيف *Daʿiif*	ضعاف ضعفة ضعفاء *Duʿafaaʾ ~ Daʿafa ~Diʿaaf*
little; few	قليل *qaliil*	قلال أقلاء قلائل قليلون *qaliil-uuna ~ qalaaʾil ~ ʾaqillaa~ qilaal*
new	جديد *jadiid*	جدد *judud*

1.1.1 With passive meaning

When derived from a transitive verb root, the *faʿiil* pattern may carry the same meaning as a passive participle.

	m. sg.	*m. pl.*
wounded	جريح *jariiH (PP: majruuH)*	جرحى *jarHaa*
killed	قتيل *qatiil (PP: maqtuul)*	قتلى *qatlaa*

1.2 The CaCCiC or *faʿʿil* فعِّل pattern

Adjectives of this pattern, if applied to human beings, usually use the sound plurals. This pattern appears frequently with hollow roots.

سيّئ	جيّد	قيّم	طيّب
sayyiʾ	*jayyid*	*qayyim*	*Tayyib*
bad	good	valuable	okay; fine

1.3 The CaCiC or *faʿil* فَعِل pattern

Adjectives of this pattern also, if applied to human beings, usually use the sound plurals.

جشِع	تعِب	وسِخ	خشِن	عطِر	مرِن
jashiʿ	*taʿib*	*wasix*	*xashin*	*ʿaTir*	*marin*
greedy	tired	dirty	coarse	fragrant	flexible

Examples:

سياسيٌّ جشِع
*siyaasiyy-un **jashiʿ-un***
a **greedy** politician

سياسة مرنة
*siyaasat-un **marinat-un***
a **flexible** policy

1.4 The CaCC / CuCC or *faʿl* / *fuʿl* فَعْل/فُعْل pattern

	m. sg.	*m. pl.*
hefty, huge	ضخم *Daxm*	ضخام *Dixaam*
free	حر *Hurr*	أحرار حرائر *Haraaʾir ~ ʾaHraar*

Not usually used to refer to humans:

جمّ	سهل	صلب
jamm	*sahl*	*Sulb*
plentiful	easy	hard, firm

1.5 The CaCaC or *faʿal* فَعَل pattern

	m. sg.	*m. pl.*
good	حسن *Hasan*	حسان *Hisaan*
middle, medial	وسط *wasaT*	أوساط *ʾawsaaT*

1.6 The CaCCaan or *faʿlaan* فَعْلان pattern

This pattern is for the most part, diptote in the masculine singular.[13] It can have rather complex plural and feminine patterns, although none of these occurred in

---

[13] The MECAS grammar (1965, 44) states for instance, that *kaslaan* is diptote, but it is not noted as such in Wehr (1979, 969), although Wehr notes *zaʿlaan*, *ghaDbaan*, and *ʿaTshaan* as diptote. Wright (1967, I:133) gives both alternatives; Haywood and Nahmad (1962, 86) state that this pattern is "without nunation"; and Cowan (1964, 40) puts it in the diptote declension.

the data gathered for this book. Cowan states (1964, 40) "In Modern Arabic the pattern *faᶜlaan-u* usually takes the sound endings in the feminine and the plural."

	m. sg.	f. sg.	m. pl.
sleepy	نعسان *naᶜsaan*	نعسانة *naᶜsaana*	نعسانون *naᶜsaan-uuna*
tired	تعبان *taᶜbaan*	تعبانة *taᶜbaana*	تعبانون *taᶜbaan-uuna*
lazy	كسلان *kaslaan*	كسلانة *kaslaana*	كسلى ~ كسالى *kasaalaa ~ kaslaa*
angry	زعلان *zaᶜlaan*	زعلانة *zaᶜlaana*	زعلانون *zaᶜlaan-uuna*
angry	غضبان *ghaDbaan*	غضبى *ghaDbaa*	غضابى غضاب *ghiDaab ~ ghaDaabaa*
hungry	جوعا ن *jawᶜaan*	جوعى *jawᶜaa*	جياع *jiyaaᶜ*
thirsty	عطشان *ᶜaTshaan*	عطشى *ᶜaTshaa*	عطشى عطاش *ᶜiTaash ~ ᶜaTshaa*

1.7 The CaCCaaC or *faᶜᶜaal* فَعّال pattern

This pattern denotes intensity of a quality and takes sound plurals:

فعّال	جذّاب	مجّان	رحّال
faᶜᶜaal	*jadhdhaab*	*majjaan*	*raHHaal*
effective	attractive	free of charge	roving, roaming

2 Quadriliteral root adjective patterns

The **CaCCuuC** or *faᶜluul* pattern from quadriliteral roots:

بحبوح

baHbuuH

merry

3 Participles functioning as adjectives

Active and passive participles are verbal adjectives, that is, descriptive terms derived from a particular Form (I–X) of a verbal root. The active participle describes the doer of an action and the passive participle describes the entity that receives the action, or has the action done to it. They therefore describe or refer to entities involved in an activity, either as noun modifiers (adjectives) or as substantives (nouns) themselves. Here we are dealing with them as adjectives.[14]

3.1 Active participles as adjectives

Active participles as adjectives describe the doer of an action. In context, they agree with the modified noun in gender, number, definiteness, and case. When used as adjectives modifying nouns referring to human beings in the plural, the sound feminine or the sound masculine plural is used.[15]

AP I:	زائر	AP I:	هامّ	AP I:	عالٍ
	zaaʾir		*haamm*		*ʿaal-in*
	visiting		important		high
AP II:	مبكّر	AP III:	مماثل	AP III:	مناوب
	mukabbir		*mumaathil*		*munaawib*
	magnifying		similar		on duty
AP IV:	مشمس	AP IV:	ممطر	AP IV:	مملّ
	mushmis		*mumTir*		*mumill*
	sunny		rainy		boring
AP V:	متوفّر	AP V:	متأخّر	AP VI:	متزايد
	mutawaffir		*mutaʾaxxir*		*mutazaayid*
	abundant		late		increasing
AP VI:	متقاعد	AP VII:	منعزل	AP VII:	منكمش
	mutaqaaʿid		*munʿazil*		*munkamish*
	retired		isolated		introverted; shrunk
AP VIII:	مختلف	AP VIII:	محترم	AP X:	مستمرّ
	muxtalif		*muHtarim*		*mustamirr*
	different		respectful		continuous
		Quad.		Quad.	
AP X:	مستحيل	AP IV:	مكفهرّ	AP IV:	مطمئنّ
	mustaHiil		*mukfahirr*		*muTmaʾinn*
	impossible		dusky, gloomy		calm, serene

---

[14] See also Wright 1967, I:143–45.

[15] Form I participles may take a broken or sound plural, but usually the sound plural is used when the participle functions as an adjective. Derived participles from the Forms II–X take sound plurals.

Examples:

Form I:

المرّة القادمة
al-marrat-a l-qaadimat-a
the **next** time

الوثب العالي
al-wathab-u l-ʿaalii
the **high** jump

مهنة شاقّة
mihnat-un shaaqqat-un
a **demanding** profession

وزير الاقتصاد السابق
waziir-u l-iqtiSaad-i l-saabiq-u
the **former** Minister of the Economy

Form IV:

النسائم المنعشة
al-nasaaʾim-u l-munʿishat-u
the **refreshing** breezes

اللجنة المشرفة
al-lajnat-u l-mushrifat-u
the **supervisory** committee

Form V:

دروس متقدّمة
duruus-un mutaqaddimat-un
advanced lessons

Form X:

ساحة مستديرة
saaHat-un mustadiirat-un
a **circular** courtyard

3.2 Passive participles as adjectives

These participles usually take sound plurals when referring to human beings.

PP I:	معروف *maʿruuf* known	PP I:	مبروك *mabruuk* blessed	PP II:	معقد *muʿaqqad* complicated
PP II:	مصور *muSawwar* illustrated	PP II:	مفضل *mufaDDal* preferred; favorite	PP VI:	متداول *mutadaawal* prevailing
PP IV:	مدمج *mudmaj* compacted	PP IV:	مراد *muraad* desired	PP VIII:	منتخب *muntaxab* elected
PP VIII:	محتلّ *muHtall* occupied	PP X:	مستورد *mustawrad* imported	PP X:	مستعار *mustaʿaar* borrowed
Quad. PP I:	مُفَرْطَح *mufarTaH* flattened	Quad. PP I:	مزركش *muzarkash* embellished		

Examples:

Form II:

السلمون المدخن

al-salmuun-u **l-mudaxxan-u**

smoked salmon

بمواقعك المفضلة

bi-mawaaqiᶜ-i-ka **l-mufaDDalat-i**

in your **favorite** places

Form IV:

قرص مدمج

qurS-un **mudmaj-un**

compact disk

Form VIII:

الأراضي المحتلة

al-ʾaraaDii **l-muHtallat-u**

the **occupied** lands

Form X:

أسماء مستعارة

ʾasmaaʾ-un **mustaᶜaarat-un**

pseudonyms ('**borrowed** names')

4 Derivation through suffixation: relative adjectives (*al-nisba* النسبة)

Converting a noun, participle, or even an adjective into a relative adjective through suffixation of the derivational morpheme *-iyy* (feminine *-iyya*) is an important derivational process in MSA and is actively used to coin new terms. The words used as stems for the *nisba* suffix can be Arabic or foreign, singular or plural. For the most part, their plurals are sound, except where noted.

4.1 *Nisba* from a singular noun

تاريخي	أسبوعي	إيجابي	حالي
taariix-iyy	*ʾusbuuᶜ-iyy*	*ʾiijaab-iyy*	*Haal-iyy*
historical	weekly	positive; affirmative	current

جزئي	إسلامي	شمسي	مركزي
juzʾ-iyy	*ʾislaam-iyy*	*shams-iyy*	*markaz-iyy*
partial	Islamic	solar	central

ذهبي	تأثري	جنوبي	
dhahab-iyy	*taʾaththur-iyy*	*januub-iyy*	
golden	impressionist	southern	

Examples:

القطب الجنوبيّ

al-quTb-u **l-januub-iyy-u**

the **south** pole

حل جزئيّ

Hall-un **juzʾ-iyy-un**

a **partial** solution

العالَم الإسلامي

al-ʿaalam-u l-ʾislaam-iyy-u

the **Islamic** world

العلوم النظريّة والتطبيقيّة

al-ʿuluum-u l-naZariyyat-u wa-l-taTbiiqiyyat-u

theoretical and **applied** sciences

المكتب المركزي

al-maktab-u l-markaz-iyy-u

the **central** office

الفن الانطباعيّ

al-fann-u l-inTibaaʿ-iyy-u

impressionist art

4.1.1 *taaʾ marbuuTa* deletion

If the base noun ends in *taaʾ marbuuTa*, the *taaʾ marbuuTa* is deleted before suffix-ing the *nisba* ending:

سياسيّ political

siyaas-iyy (from *siyaasa*, سياسة 'politics, policy')

صناعيّ artificial

Sinaaʿ-iyy (from *Sinaaʿa* صناعة 'craft; industry')

ثقافيّ cultural

thaqaaf-iyy (from *thaqaafa* ثقافة 'culture')

4.1.2 *waaw* insertion

If the noun ends in a suffix consisting of *ʾalif*, or *ʾalif-hamza*, the *hamza* may be deleted and a *waaw* may be inserted as a buffer:

صحراويّ desert; desert-like

SaHraa-w-iyy (from *SaHraaʾ* صحراء 'desert' root: *s-H-r*)

مناخ صحراويّ

munaax-un **SaHraaw-iyy-un**

a **desert** climate

معنويّ semantic

maʿna-w-iyy (from *maʿnan* معنى 'meaning' root: *ʿ-n-y*)

4.1.3 Root *hamza* retention

If the *hamza* is part of the lexical root, it cannot be deleted. Thus,

استوائيّ equatorial

istiwaaʾ-iyy (from *istiwaaʾ* استواء 'equator' root: *s-w-ʾ*)

نهائيّ final

nihaaʾ-iyy (from *nihaaʾ* نهاء 'end' root: *n-h-y*)

4.1.4 Stem reduction

Sometimes the form of the base noun is reduced:

كنسيّ ecclesiastical, church-related

kanas-iyy (from *kaniisa* كنيسة 'church')

مدنيّ civic, civil

madan-iyy (from *madiina* مدينة 'city')

الطيران المدني

al-Tayaraan-u l-madan-iyy-u

civil aviation

4.2 *Nisba* from a plural noun

A plural form of the noun may occasionally be used as the stem for the *nisba* suffix. This is especially true if the singular ends in *taaʾ marbuuTa*:

ضرائبيّ tax-related

Daraaʾib-iyy (singular *Dariiba* ضريبة)

صحفيّ journalistic

SuHuf-iyy (singular *SaHiifa* صحيفة)

وثائقيّ documentary

wathaaʾiq-iyy (singular *wathiiqa* وثيقة)

دوليّ international

duwal-iyy (singular *dawla* دولة)

نسويّ، نسائيّ women's

nisaaʾ-iyy/nisaw-iyy (singular *ʾimra-a* إمرأة)

حقوقيّ legal

Huquuq-iyy (singular *Haqq* حقّ)

Examples:

في فيلم وثائقيّ

fii fiilm-in wathaaʾiq-iyy-in

in a **documentary** film

الدراسات النسويّة

al-diraasaat-u l-nisawiyyat-u

women's studies

في افتتاحيّة صحفيّة

fii ftitaaHiyyat-in SuHufiyyat-in

in a **newspaper** editorial

شبكة معلوماتيّة

shabkat-un maʿluumaatiyyat-un

information network

4.3 *Nisba* from a participle or adjective

موسوعيّ

mawsuuʿ-iyy

comprehensive

أوّليّ

ʾawwal-iyy[16]

preliminary

---

[16] A variant on the *nisba* adjective based on the stem أوّل *ʾawwal* 'first' is the additional form
ʾawwalawiyya, with an inserted /-aw/ between the stem and the *nisba* suffix, as in ضرورة أوّلويّة
Daruurat-un ʾawwalawiyyat-un 'a primary necessity.'

4.4 *Nisba* from place names

A place name is usually stripped down to its barest, simplest stem form before the *nisba* suffix is added. Definite articles, final long vowels, and final *taa' marbuuTas* are generally eliminated. It is here that one can see the origin of English adjectival terms ending in /-i/ such as 'Yemeni' and 'Iraqi,' which are modeled on the Arabic *nisba*.

4.4.1 Countries

الأردن	أردنيّ	السودان	سودانيّ
al-'urdunn	'urdunn-iyy	al-suudaan	suudaan-iyy
Jordan	Jordanian	Sudan	Sudanese

الكويت	كويتيّ	اليونان	يونانيّ
al-kuwayt	kuwayt-iyy	al-yuunaan	yuunaaan-iyy
Kuwait	Kuwaiti	Greece	Greek

الصين	صينيّ	تونس	تونسيّ
al-Siin	Siin-iyy	tunis	tunis-iyy
China	Chinese	Tunisia	Tunisian

فرنسا	فرنسيّ
faransaa	farans-iyy
France	French

4.4.2 Cities

القاهرة	قاهريّ	بغداد	بغداديّ
al-qaahira	qaahir-iyy	baghdaad	baghdaad-iyy
Cairo	Cairene	Baghdad	Baghdadi

بيروت	بيروتيّ
bayruut	bayruut-iyy
Beirut	Beiruti

4.4.3 Geographical areas

نجديّ	حجازيّ	خليجيّ
najd-iyy	Hijaaz-iyy	xaliij-iyy
from Nejd	from Hijaz	from the (Arabian) Gulf

4.4.4 Exceptions

With a few place names, a final *'alif* is retained in the *nisba*, in which case a *waaw* or *nuun* is inserted between the *'alif* and the *nisba* suffix:

نمساويّ   صنعانيّ

nimsaa-w-iyy   *Sanʿaan-iyy*

Austrian   from Sanʿaaʾ

4.5 Names of nationalities or ethnic groups

Certain terms, especially those referring to Middle Eastern groups, have non-*nisba* masculine plurals, but revert to the *nisba* form in the feminine plural. See also section 4.15.

	m. sg.	m. pl.	f. pl.
Arab	عربي *ʿarab-iyy*	عرب *ʿarab*	عربيات *ʿarabiyy-aat*
Kurdish	كردي *kurd-iyy*	أكراد *ʾakraad*	كرديات *kurdiyy-aat*
Turkish	تركي *turk-iyy*	أتراك ترك *turk ~ ʾatraak*	تركيات *turkiyy-aat*

4.6 *Nisba* from biliteral nouns

Nouns with only two root consonants usually insert a *waaw* before the affixation of the *nisba* suffix. The *waaw* is preceded by *fatHa*:

أخوي   أبوي   يدوي

ʾaxa-w-iyy   *ʾaba-w-iyy*   *yada-w-iyy*

fraternal   paternal   manual

If the biliteral noun has a *taaʾ marbuuTa* suffix, that is deleted when the *waaw* is added:

سنوي   مئوي

sana-w-iyy   *miʾa-w-iyy*

annual   centigrade; percentile

Examples:

شعور أبويّ

shuʿuur-un ʾabawiyy-un

paternal feeling

التشاور والحوار الأخويّ

al-tashaawur-u wa-l-Hiwaar-u l-ʾaxawiyy-u

consultation and **fraternal** conversation

مئة قنبلة يدويّة

miʾat-u qunbulat-in yadawiyyat-in

a hundred **hand** grenades

النسبة المئوية للمسلمين

al-nisbat-u l-miʾawiyyat-u li-l-muslimiina

the **percentage** of Muslims

4.7 *Nisbas* from quadriliteral nouns

عسكري	قرمزي	كهربائي	جمهوري
ʿaskar-iyy	*qirmiz-iyy*	*kahrabaaʾ-iyy*	*jumhuur-iyy*
military	crimson red	electrical	republican

4.8 *Nisbas* from quinquiliteral nouns

بنفسجي
banafsaj-iyy
violet; purple

4.9 *Nisbas* from borrowed nouns

Derivation of an adjective from a borrowed noun is accomplished in several ways. For example, the English word "diplomatic" is rendered in Arabic as *diibu-umaasiyy*:

هو عميد السلك الديبلوماسي.
huwa ʿamiid-u l-silk-i **l-diibluumaasiyy-i.**
He is the dean of the **diplomatic** corps.

4.9.1 Nouns ending in *-aa* or *-aaʾ*

If the borrowed noun ends in *-aa* or *-aaʾ*, the final vowel may be deleted, or the *hamza* deleted and the *-aa* buffered by a *waaw*:

كيمياويّ chemical
kiimyaa-w-iyy (from *kiimyaaʾ* كيمياء 'chemistry')

موسيقيّ musical
muusiiq-iyy (from *muusiiqaa* موسيقى 'music')

4.9.2 *hamza* insertion

The foreign noun ending in *-aa* may get an additional *hamza* as a buffer between the stem and the suffix:

سينمائيّ cinematic, film
siinamaaʾ-iyy (from *siinamaa* سينما 'movies, cinema')

4.9.3 Intact stem

The foreign noun stem may be left intact and suffixed with *-iyy*:

أرشيفيّ	برميليّ	كرنفاليّ
ʾarshiif-iyy	*barmiil-iyy*	*karnifaal-iyy*
archival	barrel-like	carnival-like

4.10 *Nisba*s from borrowed adjectives

In the following words, an English adjective ending in "-ic" or a French adjective ending in "-ique" has been borrowed and used as a stem. The *nisba* suffix is attached to it in order to convert it into an Arabic adjective:

دينامِيكيّ	أتوماتِيكيّ	كلاسِيكيّ
diinaamiik-iyy	*ʾutuumaatiik-iyy*	*kilaasiik-iyy*
dynamic	automatic	classic

4.10.1 *Nisba* ending as replacive suffix

In the following instances, the adjective stem is borrowed but the "-ic" or "-ical" suffix is **replaced** by the Arabic *nisba* suffix:

استراتِيجيّ	أكادِيميّ	سيكولوجيّ
istiraatiij-iyy	*ʾakaadiim-iyy*	*siikuuluuj-iyy*
strategic	academic	psychological

4.11 *Nisba*s from particles and pronouns

Prepositions, adverbs and other particles may also have a *nisba* suffix:

بينيّ	كميّ	كيفيّ
bayn-iyy	*kamm-iyy*	*kayf-iyy*
inter- (in compounds)	quantitative	qualitative; discretionary

أماميّ	خلفيّ	ذاتيّ
ʾamaam-iyy	*xalf-iyy*	*dhaat-iyy*
front; frontal	rear; hind	self- (in combinations)

Examples:

يجلسن في المقاعد الأماميّة.
ya-jlis-na fii l-maqaaʾid-i l-ʾamaamiyyat-i.
They (f.) sit in the **front** seats.

قدمان خلفيّتان
qadam-aani xalf-iyyat-aani
two **hind** feet

تحقيق الاكتفاء الذاتيّ
taHqiiq-u l-iktifaaʾ-i l-dhaatiyy-i
achieving **self**-sufficiency

4.12 *Nisba*s from set phrases or fixed expressions

Technically, in traditional Arabic grammar, a *nisba* adjective cannot be formed from a phrase, only from a single word. Sometimes, however, a certain phrase is used so often that it becomes a fixed expression, behaving semantically and syntactically as a morphological unit or compound noun. The following phrases and compound words with *nisba* suffixes occurred in data gathered for this study.

'Middle Eastern' شرق أوسطي
sharq ʾawsaT-iyy (from الشرق الأوسط *al-sharq-u l-ʾawsaT-u* 'the Middle East')

Examples:

النظام الشرق الأوسطي
al-niZaam-u l-sharq-u l-ʾawsaTiyy-u
the **Middle Eastern** system

إلى الأسواق الشرق الأوسطية
ʾilaa l-ʾaswaaq-i l-sharq-i l-ʾawsaTiyyat-i
to **Middle Eastern** markets

'never-ending; everlasting' لا نهائي
laa nihaaʾ-iyy (from لا نهاء *laa nihaaʾ-a* 'there is no end')

عبر تغيراته اللا نهائية
ʿabr-a taghayyuraat-i-hi l-laa nihaaʾiyyat-i
through its **never-ending** transformations

4.13 *Nisbas* from compound words

Compounding has traditionally been a very minor component of Arabic derivational morphology, but it is resorted to more often in MSA, especially when there is a requirement for coining technical terms. Relative adjectives are sometimes created from these compound stems:[17]

capitalistic رأسمالي
raʾsmaal-iyy (from رأس مال *raʾs maal* 'capital')

amphibian برمائي
barmaaʾ-iyy (through compounding from the words *barr* 'land' and *maaʾ* 'water')

Recently coined technical terms sometimes make use of the shortened forms of *qabl-a* (*qab-*) 'before' and *fawq-a* (*faw-*) 'above' to express the concepts of "pre-" and "super-." Sometimes these are combined with Arabic stems and sometimes with stems from other languages, suffixed with *-iyy*:

قبميلادي	قبتاريخي	قبكمبري	فوصوتي
qab-miilaad-iyy	*qab-taariix-iyy*	*qab-kambr-iyy*	*faw-Sawt-iyy*
Before Christ (BC)	prehistoric	Precambrian	supersonic

---

[17] For more in-depth discussion of compounding in Arabic, see Ali 1987, Emery 1988, and Shivtiel 1993.

4.14 Special use of *nisba*

Where in English one noun may be used to describe or modify another noun, in
Arabic such a phrase often uses a *nisba* adjective:

طلاب جامعيّون
Tullaab-un jaami'iyy-uuna
university students

خبراء نفطيّون
xubaraa'-u nifTiyy-uuna
oil experts

عظام حيوانية
'iZaam-un Hayawaaniyyat-un
animal bones

مناطق زمنيّة
manaaTiq-u zamaniyyat-un
time zones

4.15 *Nisba* plurals

The preponderance of *nisba* plurals are sound, using the sound masculine or sound
feminine plurals when referring to human beings. However, a few *nisbas* take broken or truncated plurals, especially when referring to ethnic or religious groups.

4.15.1 Truncated *nisba* plural

	m. sg.	*m. pl.*
Arab	عربي *'arabiyy*	عرب *'arab*
bedouin	بدوي *badawiyy*	بدو *badw*
Jewish	يهودي *yahuudiyy*	يهود *yahuud*
Berber	بربري *barbariyy*	بربر *barbar*

4.15.2 Broken *nisba* plural

	m. sg.	*m. pl.*
foreign	أجنبي *'ajnabiyy*	أجانب *'ajaanib*
Christian	نصراني *naSraaniyy*	نصارى *naSaaraa*
Kurdish	كردي *kurdiyy*	أكراد *'akraad*
Turkish	تركي *turkiyy*	ترك ، أتراك *'atraak/turk*

5 Color adjectives

Color adjectives are of three types in Arabic: pattern-derived, *nisba*, and borrowed.

5.1 Pattern-derived color adjectives

The essential colors of the spectrum have a special pattern or form *'aCCaC* or *'af'al* أفعل in the masculine singular, *CaCCaa'* or *fa'laa'*- فعلاء in the feminine singular, and *CuCC* or *fu'l* فعل in the plural. Here is a list of the most commonly occurring derived color adjectives. It includes black and white and brown as well as the primary colors: red, blue and yellow. It also includes green, but not orange or purple.

	m. sg.	*f. sg.*	*m. pl.*	*f. pl.*
black	أسود	سوداء	سود	سوداوات
	'aswad	*sawdaa'*	*suud*	*sawdaawaat*
blue	أزرق	زرقاء	زرق	زرقاوات
	'azraq	*zarqaa'*	*zurq*	*zarqaawaat*
brown	أسمر	سمراء	سمر	سمراوات
	'asmar	*samraa'*	*sumr*	*samraawaat*
green	أخضر	خضراء	خضر	خضراوات
	'axDar	*xaDraa'*	*xuDr*	*xaDraawaat*
red	أحمر	حمراء	حمر	حمراوات
	'aHmar	*Hamraa'*	*Humr*	*Hamraawaat*
white	أبيض	بيضاء	بيض	بيضاوات
	'abyaD	*bayDaa'*	*biiD*	*bayDaawaat*
yellow	أصفر	صفراء	صفر	صفراوات
	'aSfar	*Safraa'*	*Sufr*	*Safraawaat*

There are three things to note and remember about these color adjectives. First, the masculine singular pattern *'af'al* is diptote and is identical in form to the comparative adjective pattern (for example, *'akbar* 'bigger' or *'aTwal* 'longer'), which is also diptote. Second, the feminine singular pattern *fa'laa'* is also diptote. Third, the plural form is primarily used to refer to human beings, since the feminine singular would be used for modifying a nonhuman noun plural, in keeping with rules of gender and humanness agreement.[18] Examples include:

---

[18] One instance of the plural form of the adjective used with a nonhuman plural noun appeared in the corpus of data used for this text:

بطاقات «أميركان إكسبرس» الخضر

biTaaqaat-u "'amiirkaan ikisibris" l-xuDr-u
green American Express cards

5.1.1 Masculine phrases

الحوت الأزرق
al-Huut-u l-ʾazraq-u
the blue whale

البيت الأبيض
al-bayt-u l-ʾabyaD-u
the White House

البحر الأحمر
al-baHr-u l-ʾaHmar-u
the Red Sea

الصليب الأحمر
al-Saliib-u l-ʾaHmar-u
the Red Cross

5.1.2 Feminine phrases

جبنة بيضاء
jubnat-un bayDaaʾ-u
white cheese

روسيا البيضاء
ruusiyaa l-bayDaaʾ-u
White Russia

سلطة خضراء
salaTat-un xaDraaʾ-u
green salad

بدلة زرقاء
badalat-un zarqaaʾ-u
a blue suit

في القائمة السوداء
fii l-qaaʾimat-i l-sawdaaʾ-i
on the black list

في السوق السوداء
fii l-suuq-i l-sawdaaʾ-i
in the black market

5.1.3 Plural phrases

المسلمون السود
al-muslim-uuna l-suud-u
black Muslims

الخمير الحمر
al-ximiir-u l-Humr-u
the Khmer Rouge

القبعات الزرق
al-qubbaʿaat-u l-zurq-u[19]
the blue berets (UN troops)

الهنود الحمر
al-hunuud-u l-Humr-u
Red Indians

نساء سمراوات
nisaaʾ-un samraawaat-un
tawny-skinned women

5.2 Physical feature adjectives

The *ʾafʿal* pattern is used to denote not only color but also certain physical characteristics:

---

[19] Although the word *qubbaʿaat* 'berets' is technically nonhuman, the reference is to human beings.

	m. sg.	*f. sg.*	*m. pl.*
blond	أشقر ʾashqar	شقراء shaqraaʾ	شقر shuqr
blind	أعمى ʾaʿmaa	عمياء ʿamyaaʾ	عميان عمي ʿumy ~ ʿumyaan
deaf	أطرش ʾaTrash	طرشاء Tarshaaʾ	طرش Tursh
lame	أعرج ʾaʿraj	عرجاء ʿarjaaʾ	عرجان عرج ʿurj ~ ʿurjaan
dumb, mute	أخرس ʾaxras	خرساء xarsaaʾ	خرسان خرس xurs ~ xursaan
stupid	أحمق ʾaHmaq	حمقاء Hamqaaʾ	حمق Humq

مواطن سويدي أشقر
muwaaTin-un suwiidiyy-un ʾashqar-u
a **blond** Swedish citizen (m.)

الحسناء الشقراء
al-Hasnaaʾ-u l-shaqraaʾ-u
the **blonde** beauty (f.)

التعصب الأعمى
al-taʿaSSub-u l-ʾaʿmaa
blind fanaticism

5.3 *Nisba* color adjectives

Another process for deriving names of colors in Arabic is to identify the color of a
naturally occurring substance, such as ashes, roses, oranges, or coffee beans, and
then to affix the *nisba* ending *-iyy* onto that noun. Sometimes the base noun is of
Arabic origin, and sometimes it is of foreign derivation.

Item name		Color
ashes	رماد ramaad	رمادي ramaad-iyy gray
orange	برتقال burtuqaal	برتقالي burtuqaal-iyy orange

Item name		Color
rose	وردة *warda*	وردي *ward-iyy* pink
coffee beans	بنّ *bunn*	بنّي *bunn-iyy* brown
violet	بنفسج *banafsaj*	بنفسجي *banafsaj-iyy* purple; violet
bronze	برونز *buruunz*	برونزي *buruunz-iyy* bronze

Inflection of these *nisba* adjectives follows the general rules for *nisbas*: adding a *taaʾ marbuuTa* for feminine agreement (including nonhuman plurals), and adding the sound masculine or sound feminine plural for plural (human) agreement.

الكتاب البرتقالي
al-kitaab-u l-burtuqaaliyy-u
the **orange** book

الذئاب الرمادية
al-dhiʾaab-u l-ramaadiyyat-u
the **gray** wolves

الرأس البرونزي
al-raʾs-u l-buruunziyy-u
the **bronze** head

5.4 Borrowed color adjectives

In recent times, the practice has been to borrow directly names of certain colors or particular shades of colors that do not already exist in Arabic. These come mainly from European languages and do not inflect for number, gender, or case:

beige	بيج	mauve	موف	turquoise	تركواز
	biij		*muuf*		*turkwaaz*

6 Non-derived adjectives

Rarely, an Arabic adjective is non-derived and simply exists on its own, without relation to a productive lexical root:

عملاق / عمالقة
ʿamaaliqa/ ʿimlaaq
gigantic; super

فذّ / فذوذ ~ أفذاذ
ʾafdhaadh ~ fudhuudh / fadhdh
unique, extraordinary

Examples:

الزواحف العملاقة
al-zawaaHif-u l-ʕimlaaqat-u
the **giant** reptiles

نموذج فذ
*namuudhaj-un **fadhdh-un***
a **unique** example

7 Compound adjectives

In order to express complex new concepts, compound (two-word) adjectival expressions are sometimes used in MSA. They occur primarily as adjective *ʾiDaafas*, or, for negative concepts, as adjectives in construct with the noun *ghayr*.

7.1 The active participle *mutaʕaddid* متعدّد 'numerous'

To express the concept of "multi-" as the first component of an Arabic compound, the AP *mutaʕaddid* is normally used.

متعدّد الأطراف
mutaʕaddid-u l-ʾaTraaf-i
multilateral

متعدد الاستعمالات
mutaʕaddid-u l-istiʕmaalaat-i
multi-use

متعدد الأنظمة
mutaʕaddid-u l-ʾanZimat-i
multi-system

متعدد الجنسيات
mutaʕaddid-u l-jinsiyyaat-i
multinational

Examples:

لبرنامج المساعدات المتعددة الجنسيات
*li-barnaamaj-i **l-musaaʕadaat-i l-mutaʕaddidat-i l-jinsiyyaat-i***
for the program of **multinational assistance**

تتخذ الشركات المتعددة الجنسيات خطوات.
*ta-ttaxidh-u **l-sharikaat-u l-mutaʕaddidat-u l-jinsiyyaat-i** xutuwaat-in.*
The **multi-national companies** are taking steps.

في هذه القضية المتعددة الجوانب
*fii haadhihi l-qaDiyyat-i **l-mutaʕaddid-i l-jawaanib-i***
in this **multi-sided** issue

7.2 The noun *ghayr* ʕnon-; un-, in-, other than'

To express negative or privative concepts denoting absence of a quality or attribute, the noun *ghayr* is used.

The noun *ghayr* 'other than' becomes the first term of a construct phrase modifying the noun and carries the same case ending as the noun being modified. It does not, as the first term of the *ʾiDaafa*, ever have the definite article. The second term of the construct is an adjective or participle in the genitive case which agrees with the noun being modified in gender, number, and definiteness. See also Chapter 8, section 1.9.3.

غير مناسب	غير مباشر	غير إسلاميّ
ghayr-u munaasib-in	*ghayr-u mubaashir-in*	*ghayr-u -ʾislaamiyy-in*
unsuitable	indirect	non-Islamic

غير لبق	غيرعادي	غير مقدّس
ghayr-u labiq-in	*ghayr-u ʿaadiyy-in*	*ghayr-u muqaddas-in*
tactless	unusual	unholy

Examples:

المواد الخام غير المتجدّدة
al-mawaadd-u l-xaam-u ghayr-u l-mutajaddidat-i
non-renewable raw materials

بطرق غير قانونيَة
bi-turuq-in ghayr-i qaanuuniyyat-in
by illegal means

الدفعات غير المشروعة كالرشاوي مثلا
al-dafaʿaat-u ghayr-u l-mashruuʿat-i ka-l-rashaawii mathal-an
illegal payments such as bribes, for example

اتّفاقية غير مقدّسة
ittifaaqiyyat-un ghayr-u muqaddasat-in
an unholy agreement

غير قابلة للتزوير
ghayr-u qaabilat-in li-l-tazwiir-i
non-counterfeitable

11

Adverbs and adverbial expressions

A good general definition of adverbs is found in Hurford (1994, 10): "The most typical adverbs add specific information about time, manner, or place to the meanings of verbs or whole clauses." Adverbs may also add information to adjectives ("*very* easy") or even other adverbs ("*late* yesterday"). An essential characteristic of adverbs is that they are additive; that is, they are external to the core proposition in a clause or sentence. They are, as Stubbs has noted, "an optional element in clause structure" (1983, 70).

Arabic refers to this optional status as *faDla* فضلة 'extra' or 'surplus' parts of a sentence rather than part of the kernel or core predication. This optionality has meant that adverbs have traditionally received less attention from linguistic research than the major form classes (nouns and verbs), despite the fact that they are very common in both spoken and written discourse.[1]

This class of words and phrases is also very heterogeneous in terms of its composition. Adverbial modification may be accomplished with single words (*daaʾim-an* دائماً 'always,' *jidd-an* جداً 'very') or with phrases (*ʾilaa Hadd-in maa* إلى حدّ ما 'to a certain extent,' *ʿaajil-an ʾaw ʾaajil-an* عاجلاً أو آجلاً 'sooner or later'). Arabic adverbials also include grammatical structures such as the cognate accusative (*al-mafʿuul al-muTlaq* المفعول المطلق) and *Haal* حال ('circumstantial') phrases.

In Arabic, few words are adverbs in and of themselves; but there are some (such as *faqaT* فقط 'only' or *hunaa* هنا 'here').[2] Most words that function as Arabic adverbs are adjectives or nouns in the accusative case (e.g., *ʾaHyaan-an* أحياناً 'sometimes,'

---

[1] Stubbs notes that adverbs are one of three areas which have resisted traditional treatment in grammar (in addition to coordinating conjunctions and "particles") and that none of these areas "fit neatly into the syntactic and semantic categories of contemporary linguistics" (1983, 70). Furthermore, he states (1983, 77): "Adverbs then, and certain items in particular, provide problems for sentence based grammars but are of great interest in a study of discourse sequences, since their functions are largely to do with the organization of connected discourse, and with the interpretation of functional categories of speech acts."

[2] Cowan (1964, 63) starts his section on adverbs with the observation that "the Arabic language is exceedingly poor in adverbs," referring to the fact that few Arabic words are inherently and solely adverbs. Haywood and Nahmad (1962, 426) open their chapter on "adverbial usage" with the statement: "Arabic has *no Adverbs*, properly speaking" (emphasis in original). They go on to explain that "this lack is hardly felt owing to the inherent flexibility and expressiveness of the language."

ghad-an غدا 'tomorrow,' *al-yawm-a* 'today' اليوم); some adverbials occur with a *Damma* ending (e.g., *baʿd-u* بعد 'yet') and at least one ends consistently in *kasra* (*ʾams-i* أمس 'yesterday'). Still other adverbial expressions are compound words consisting of a noun and a demonstrative suffix, e.g., *yawm-a-dhaak* يومذاك 'that day.'[3]

Placement of adverbs within an Arabic sentence is flexible to a certain extent, but sometimes particular adverbs have preferred positions. Several adverbs or adverbial expressions may occur in the same sentence. In the following one, for example, are four adverbs:

هناك اليوم مثلا خلافات حول الموضوع.

hunaaka l-yawm-a mathal-an xilaafaat-un Hawl-a l-mawDuuʿ-i.

There [are] **today, for example,** disagreements **about** the subject.

The first adverb is the locative *hunaaka* هناك, 'there is/are'; the second is the time adverbial *l-yawm-a* اليوم 'today'; the third is *mathal-an* مثلا 'for example'; and the fourth is the locative adverb *Hawl-a* حول 'about.'

Most Arabic adverbials can be divided into **four major groups** according to their semantic function: **degree, manner, place,** and **time.** There are also some important categories that do not fall within these four groups, but which have key functions in Arabic, such as adverbial accusatives of cause or reason (*mafʿuul li-ʾajl-i-hi* مفعول لأجله or *mafʿuul la-hu* مفعول له) and the accusative of specification (*tamyiiz* تمييز). Within each of these categories there are several kinds of adverbial components. Given the heterogeneous and multifunctional nature of this class of expressions, the examples provided here are by no means exhaustive; but they represent a broad sample of occurrences in modern written Arabic.

1 Adverbs of degree

Adverbs of degree describe and quantify concepts such as intensity ("very," "considerably," "particularly"), measurement ("one by one"), or amount ("a little," "a great deal," "completely"). In some respects, they are a subcategory of manner adverbials, but they constitute a substantial group of their own.

1.1 Basic adverbs of degree

1.1.1 *faqaT* فقط 'only, solely'

This adverb of degree is a commonly used expression of limitation. It is invariable in form and ends with *sukuun*. In terms of its placement in a sentence, it

---

[3] In discussing the Arabic morphological category of adverb, Wright (1967, I:282) notes that "there are *three* sorts of adverbs. The first class consists of *particles* of various origins, partly inseparable, partly separable; the second class of *indeclinable nouns* ending in *u*; the third class of *nouns* in the accusative" (emphasis in original). He includes an exhaustive list of particles, including interrogatives, negatives, and tense markers in his first category. In this book these particles are discussed according to their separate functions.

tends to occur at the end of the phrase or clause it modifies, but this is not absolute.

تعلم كلمات معدودة **فقط**.   لم تكن تسجيلا **فقط**.

*ta'allam-a kalimaat-in ma'duudat-an **faqaT**.*   *lam ta-kun tasjiil-an **faqaT**.*

He **only** learned a [limited] number of words.   It was not **only** documentation.

الرحلة من جنيف إلى تونس تحتاج إلى ساعتين **فقط**.

*al-riHlat-u min jiniif 'ilaa tuunis-a ta-Htaaj-u 'ilaa saa'at-ayni **faqaT**.*

The trip from Geneva to Tunis takes **only** two hours.

استمر زواجهما سنتين **فقط**.

*istamarr-a zawaaj-u-humaa sanat-ayni **faqaT**.*

Their marriage lasted **only** two years.

كان الدور مكتوبا في ثلاثة مشاهد **فقط**.

*kaan-a l-dawr-u maktuub-an fii thalaathat-i mashaahid-a **faqaT**.*

The role was written into three scenes **only**.

رغم حصولهم **فقط** على الميدالية الفضية

*raghm-a HuSuul-i-him **faqaT** 'alaa l-miidaliyyat-i l-fiDDiyyat-i*

despite their **only** winning the silver medal

1.2 Degree nouns and adjectives in the accusative

Adverbial modification is often managed in Arabic using nouns or adjectives in the **accusative case**. Certain accusative adverbials are used so frequently that they have become idiomatic. This is especially true of degree adverbials. Note that most of them occur in the indefinite accusative.

1.2.1 *jidd-an* جدًا 'very'

This adverbial expression is of frequent occurrence in written Arabic. It follows the phrase that it modifies.

طبيعيّ **جدًا** أن نحبه.   شيء مؤسف **جدًا**

*Tabii'iyy-un **jidd-an** 'an nu-Hibb-a-hu.*   *shay'-un mu'sif-un **jidd-an***

It is **very** natural that we love it.   a **very** distressing thing

1.2.2 *kathiir-an* كثيرا 'much; a lot; greatly'

هذا أهم كثيرا مما سبقه.

*haadhaa 'ahamm-u **kathiir-an** mimmaa sabaq-a-hu.*

This is **much** more important than what preceded it.

ابني مسافر وأنا أشتاق إليه كثيرا.

*ibn-ii musaafir-un wa-ʾanaa ʾa-shtaaq-u ʾilay-hi **kathiir-an**.*

My son is traveling and I miss him **greatly**.

1.2.3 *muTlaq-an* مطلقا 'absolutely'

لا أستطيع التكلم مطلقا.

*laa ʾa-staTiiʿ-u l-takallum-a **muTlaq-an**.*

I absolutely cannot speak.

1.2.4 *qaliil-an* قليلا 'a little bit; a little'

أفهم قليلا.

*ʾa-fham-u **qaliil-an**.*

I understand **a little**.

1.2.5 *tamaam-an* تماماً 'exactly; completely'

يجب عليها أن تدعم الاتفاق تماما.

*ya-jib-u ʿalay-haa ʾan ta-dʿam-a l-ittifaaq-a **tamaam-an**.*

It must support the agreement **completely**.

1.2.6 *xuSuuS-an* خصوصا 'especially'

خصوصا في ما يتعلق بالموز

xuSuuS-an fii maa ya-taʿallaq-u bi-l-mawz-i

especially in what relates to bananas

1.2.7 *ʾajmaʿ-a* أجمع 'all; entirely; all together'

This adverbial accusative of degree is a comparative adjective. It is not nunated because the word *ʾajmaʿ* is diptote.

في أنحاء العالم أجمع

*fii ʾanHaaʾ-i l-ʿaalam-i **ʾajmaʿ-a***

in **all** parts of the world

1.2.8 Repeated noun of measurement[4]

In these expressions, a noun in the accusative is repeated in order to indicate gradual sequencing.

---

[4] ʿAbd al-Latif et al. (1997, 340) refer to this structure as *al-Haal al-jaamida* الحال الجامدة, 'solid *Haal*' or 'inflexible *Haal*.'

قام بتقبيلهم فردا فردا.

*qaam-a bi-taqbiil-i-him **fard-an fard-an**.*

He kissed ('undertook kissing') them **one by one** ('individual by individual').

أنه شيئا فشيئا يمكن أن يتدحرج

*'anna-hu **shay'-an fa-shay'-an** yu-mkin-u 'an ya-tadaHraj-a*

that it could **gradually** ('thing by thing') deteriorate

1.3 Adverbial phrases of degree

There are many of these types of phrases consisting of two or more words. These examples show some of the most frequently occurring ones.

1.3.1 *bi-l-DabT* بالضبط 'exactly, precisely'[5]

ما هو الهدف منها بالضبط؟   هذا ما أقصده بالضبط.

*maa huwa l-hadaf-u min-haa **bi-l-DabT-i**?*   *haadhaa maa 'a-qsid-u-hu **bi-l-DabT-i**.*

What is the aim of it **precisely**?   That is **exactly** what I mean.

1.3.2 *bi-kathiir-in* بكثير 'by a great amount; much'

This expression is usually used in the context of comparison or contrast.

تبدو أصغر بكثير من عمرها.

*ta-bduu 'aSghar-a **bi-kathiir-in** min ʿumr-i-haa.*

She seems **much** ('by a great amount') younger than her age.

1.3.3 *laa siyyamaa* لا سيّما 'especially; particularly'

This phrase literally means 'there is nothing similar.'[6]

لا سيّما الأيام المشمسة

laa siyyamaa l-'ayyam-a l-mushmisat-a

especially on sunny days

لا سيّما أنني لا أنتمي إلى أي جماعة

laa siyyamaa 'anna-nii laa 'a-ntamii 'ilaa 'ayy-i jamaaʿat-in

especially since I do not belong to any [particular] group

1.3.4 *li-l-ghaayat-i* للغاية 'extremely; to the utmost'

كان الوضع سيئا للغاية.

*kaan-a l-waDʿ-u sayyi'-an **li-l-ghaayat-i**.*

The situation was **extremely** bad.

---

[5] This expression is often pronounced '*bi-l-ZabT*,' as though it were spelled with a *Zaa'* instead of a *Daad*.

[6] See also Cantarino 1976, III:195–96.

1.3.5 *ʾilaa Hadd-in maa* إلى حدّ ما 'to a certain extent; kind of; sort of'
ʾilaa Hadd-in kabiir-in إلى حدّ كبير 'to a great extent'

سيساعد إلى حدّ كبير.
sa-yu-saaʿid-u ʾilaa Hadd-in kabiir-in.
It will help **to a great extent**.

1.3.6 *baʿD-a l-shayʾ-i* بعض الشيء 'somewhat'

نجحوا بعض الشيء.
najaH-uu baʿD-a l-shayʾ-i.
They succeeded **somewhat**.

1.3.7 *ʾakthar-a min-a l-laazim* أكثر من اللازم; *ʾakthar-a min-a l-luzuum-i* أكثر من اللزوم
'too; over-; too much; more than necessary'

ربما كنت واثقا من نفسي أكثر من اللزوم.
rubba-maa kun-tu waathiq-an min nafs-ii ʾakthar-a min-a l-luzuum-i.
Perhaps I was **overconfident**.

1.3.8 *ʿalaa l-ʾaqall-i* على الأقلّ 'at least'

لفترة وجيزة على الأقل
li-fatrat-in wajiizat-in ʿalaa l-ʾaqall-i
for a brief time, **at least**

قتل خمسة أشخاص على الأقل
qutil-a xamsat-u ʾashxaaS-in ʿalaa l-ʾaqall-i
at least five persons were killed

في هذه المرحلة على الأقل
fii haadhihi l-marHalat-i ʿalaa l-ʾaqall-i
at this stage, **at least**

1.3.9 *wa-Hasb-u* وحسب, *fa-Hasb-u* فحسب 'only; that's all'

لا تقتصر على حدود قطر وحسب.
laa ta-qtaSir-u ʿalaa Huduud-i qaTar-a wa-Hasb-u.
It is not limited to the borders of Qatar **only**.

2 Adverbs of manner

Manner adverbials provide a wide range of options for describing the state, condition, circumstances, manner, or way in which something is accomplished or happens.

2.1 Basic adverbs of manner

The members of this group are related to demonstrative pronouns.

2.1.1 *haakadhaa* هُكذا 'thus; and so; in such a way'

This adverb of manner indicates both comparison and consequence.

هُكذا كانت تتنقل بين مراكز الشام واليمن.

haakadhaa kaan-at ta-tanaqqal-u bayn-a maraakiz-i l-shaam-i wa-l-yaman-i.

Thus it moved between the centers of Syria and Yemen.

هُكذا يحرف الأوربيون لفظ «الجهاد» ويترجمونه خطأً.

haakadhaa yu-Harrif-u l-ʾuurubbiyy-uuna lafZ-a 'l-jihaad-u'
  wa-yu-tarjim-uuna-hu xaTT-an.

Thus do the Europeans distort the expression "*jihad*" and translate it literally.

2.1.2 *ka-dhaalika* كذلك 'likewise; as well; also'

وكذلك المقشّات التي ما زالت مستعملة

wa-ka-dhaalika l-miqashshaat-u llatii maa zaal-at mustaʿmalat-an

and **likewise** the brooms which are still used

يستعد كذلك لتصوير فيلم.

ya-staʿidd-u ka-dhaalika li-taSwiir-i fiilm-in.

He is **also** preparing to film a motion picture.

2.2 Nouns and adjectives in the accusative

Many nouns and adjectives are used in the accusative case to amplify a statement adverbially. Adverbs of manner are the most frequent, but many accusative adverbials do not fit that category precisely. In most cases, the indefinite accusative is used on the singular base form of the noun or adjective.

لن ننسى أبداً.

lan na-nsaa ʾabad-an.

We will **never** forget.

وهناك أيضاً موضوع المال.

wa-hunaaka ʾayD-an mawDuuʿ-u l-maal-i.

And there is **also** the subject of money.

أذكرها بصرياً.

ʾa-dhkur-u-haa baSriyy-an.

I remember it **visually**.

سأسافر فوراً.

sa-ʾu-saafir-u fawr-an.

I will depart **at once**.

عليه أن يدفع مئة دينار إضافةً.

ʿalay-hi ʾan ya-dfaʿ-u miʾat-a diinaar-in ʾiDaafat-an.

He has to pay 100 dinars **in addition/additionally**.

إننا جميعاً نعمل من أجل السلام

ʾanna-naa jamiiʿ-an na-ʿmal-u min ʾajl-i l-salaam-i

that we are working **together** for peace

يعرفون هذا جيّداً.	فكّر جدّياً.
*ya-ʿrif-uuna haadhaa **jayyid-an**.*	*fakkar-a **jiddiyy-an**.*
They know that **well**.	He thought **seriously**.

2.3 Manner adverbial phrases

There are four general ways to express manner adverbials in phrases: using the *Haal* structures, the cognate accusative, other accusative phrases, and prepositional phrases.

2.3.1 The circumstantial construction: *al-Haal* الحـال

The *Haal* (literally 'state' or 'condition') or circumstantial accusative structure is a way of expressing the circumstances under which an action takes place. It is often structured using an active participle in the indefinite accusative to modify or describe the circumstances of the action. The participle agrees with the doer of the action in number and gender.[7]

سأله هـامساً.	وترك المكتب مسرعاً.
*saʾal-a-hu **haamis-an**.*	*wa-tarak-a l-maktab-a **musriʿ-an**.*
He asked him, **whispering**.	He left the office **quickly/in a hurry**.

قد ارتكب هذه الجريمة منفرداً.

*qad-i rtakab-a haadhihi l-jariimat-a **munfarid-an**.*

He committed this crime **on his own/alone** ('individually').

2.3.1.1 If the *Haal* active participle is from a transitive verb, it may take a noun object in the accusative case:

وافتتح المؤتمر ممثلاً رئيس الجمهورية.

*wa-ftataH-a l-muʾtamar-a **mumaththil-an** raʾiis-a l-jumhuuriyyat-i.*

He opened the conference **representing the president of the republic**.

يكتب متهماً بعض المسؤولين.

*ya-ktub-u **muttahim-an** baʿD-a l-masʾuul-iina.*

He writes **accusing some officials**.

2.3.1.2 Occasionally, a **passive participle** is used in the *Haal* structure:

قفزت مذعورةً.

*qafaz-at **madhʿuurat-an**.*

She jumped, **frightened**.

---

[7] For more examples and discussion of the *Haal* circumstantial structure in modern written Arabic, see Abboud and McCarus (1983) Part I:535–39, and Cantarino (1975) II:186–96 and III:242–54.

2.3.1.3 An **adjective** may also be used in the circumstantial accusative structure.

فقدت أمي صغيراً.

faqad-tu ʾumm-ii ***Saghir-an.***

I lost my mother [when I was] **young.**

2.3.1.4 The circumstantial accusative is occasionally expressed with a **verbal noun** in the accusative:[8]

ألقى كلمة نيابةً عن السفير.

ʾalqaa kalimat-an ***niyaabat-an*** *ʿan-i l-safiir-i.*

He gave a speech **in place of** ('substituting for') the ambassador.

وقال رداً على سؤال ...	وتعليقاً على الحادث ...
wa-qaal-a ***radd-an*** *ʿalaa suʾaal-in* ...	*wa-***taʿliiq-an*** *ʿalaa l-Haadith-i* ...
he said, **responding to** a question ...	**commenting on** the incident ...

وكان قد أغتيل ... سيراً على القدمين ...

wa-kaan-a qad ughtiil-a ... ***sayr-an*** *ʿalaa l-qadam-ayni* ...

He had been assassinated [while] **walking** ('on two feet') ...

2.3.1.5 *Haal* EXPRESSING CAPACITY OR FUNCTION: A noun or participle may be used in the accusative to express the idea of "in the capacity of " or "as":

يعمل محرراً أدبياً.

ya-ʿmal-u ***muHarrir-an ʾadabiyy-an.***

He works **as a literary editor.**

2.3.1.6 *Haal* CLAUSE WITH *waaw* واو (*waaw al-Haal* واو الحال): Another way of expressing the circumstances under which an action takes place is to use the connecting particle *wa-* followed by a pronoun and a clause describing the circumstances.

وفوجئ وهو يقطع الحطب.

wa-fuuji-ʾa ***wa-huwa ya-qTaʿ-u l-HaTab-a.***

He was surprised **while he was cutting wood.**

دخلا وهما يرتديان زياً إسلامياً.

daxal-aa ***wa-humaa ya-rtadiy-aani*** *ziyy-an ʾislaamiyy-an.*

The two of them entered **wearing Islamic garb.**

---

[8] Cantarino (1975, II:193–96) lists five form classes that may be used with the circumstantial accusative: adjectives, active participles, passive participles, substantives, or "infinitives" (i.e., *maSdar*s; verbal nouns).

سقطت شجرة عليه وهو يحاول فتح طريقٍ.

saqaT-at shajarat-un ʿalay-hi **wa-huwa yu-Haawil-u fatH-a Tariiq-in.**

A tree fell on him **while he was trying to open a road.**

2.3.1.7 *Haal* WITH PAST TENSE: If the circumstances referred to by the *Haal* structure precede the action noted by the main verb, and especially if they form a background for the main verb, the *waaw al-Haal* is used with *qad* and a past tense verb. Abboud and McCarus state that "this construction indicates a completed action whose results are still in effect" (1985, Part I:537).

انتهى أمس المؤتمر الثاني ... وقد نظّمه النادي العربي.

intahaa ʾams-i l-muʾtamar-u l-thaanii . . . . **wa-qad naZZam-a-hu** *l-naadii l-ʿarabiyy-u.*

Yesterday the second conference ended . . . **having been organized** by the
   Arabic club ('the Arabic club having organized it').

2.3.1.8 *Haal* CLAUSES WITHOUT *waaw*: In yet another form of *Haal*, a main verb may be followed directly by another verb that gives a further description of either the agent or the object of the main verb. Most often, the main verb is past tense and the following verb in the present tense, but not always.

ومضى يقول ...	شاهدته يرش طلاء.
wa-maDaa ya-quul-u	*shaahad-at-hu ya-rushsh-u Talaaʾ-an.*
He went on, saying . . .	She saw him spattering paint.

لا تتركَك تنتظر.

laa ta-truk-u-ka ta-ntaZir-u.

It does not **leave you waiting.**

2.3.2 The cognate accusative: *al-mafʿuul al-muTlaq* المفعول المطلق

The cognate accusative is an elegant way of emphasizing or enhancing a previous statement by deriving a verbal noun from the main verb or predicate (which may also be in the form of a participle or verbal noun) and modifying the derived verbal noun with an adjective that intensifies the effect of the statement. The verbal noun and its modifying adjective are usually in the indefinite accusative.

2.3.2.1 VERBAL NOUN + ADJECTIVE:

تدرك ذلك إدراكاً كلياً.

tu-drik-u dhaalika ʾidraak-an kulliyy-an.

It **realizes** that **fully.**

يشارك فيها مشاركة فعّالةً.

*yu-shaarik-u fii-haa **mushaarakt-an faᶜᶜaalat-an**.*

He is participating **effectively** in it.

لحل الموضوع حلاً جذرياً.

*li-Hall-i l-mawDuuᶜ-i **Hall-an jidhriyy-an***

to solve the problem **fundamentally**

ففرح لذلك فرحاً شديداً.

*fa-**fariH-a** li-dhaalika **faraH-an shadiid-an**.*

He was **extremely happy** at that.

وعلى المواطنين أن يعرفوا بعضهم بعضاً معرفةً جيّدةً.

*wa-ᶜalaa l-muwaaTin-iina ʾan **ya-ᶜrif-uu** baᶜD-u-hum baᶜD-an **maᶜrifat-an jayyidat-an**.*

It is necessary for citizens to know each other **well**.

2.3.3.2 VERBAL NOUN IN *ʾiDaafa*: The cognate accusative structure may also have the verbal noun as the second term of an *ʾiDaafa* construction whose first term is a qualifier or quantifier in the accusative case:

يختلف كلَّ الاختلاف.

*ya-xtalif-u **kull-a l-ixtilaaf-i**.*

It differs **completely**.

أشكرك عميقَ الشكر على ما قدمت.

*ʾa-shkur-u-ka **ᶜamiiq-a l-shukr-i** ᶜalaa maa qaddam-ta.*

I thank you **deeply** for what you have offered.

2.3.4 Other phrasal manner adverbials

Phrases that function adverbially are of two sorts: accusative adverbials or prepositional phrases.

2.3.4.1 *waHd-a* وحْدَ + PRONOUN SUFFIX 'ALONE, BY ONE'S SELF': The adverbial expression *waHd-a* plus pronoun suffix is used in apposition with a noun to indicate or specify the meaning of 'alone,' 'on one's own,' or 'by one's self.' It is invariably in the accusative case, no matter what case its head noun is in, and is suffixed with a personal pronoun that refers back to the head noun.

للأمير العباسي وحْدَهُ

*li-l-ʾamiir-i l-ᶜabbaasiyy-i **waHd-a-hu***

for the Abbasid amir **alone**

هو وحْدَهُ المرجع الصالح.

*huwa **waHd-a-hu** l-marjiᶜ-u l-SaaliH-u.*

He **alone** is the competent authority.

النيات الحسنة وَحْدَها لا تكفي.

al-niyaat-u l-Hasanat-u **waHd-a-haa** *laa ta-kfii.*

Good intentions **alone** are not enough.

ذهب وَحْدَه إلى الدكان.

dhahab-a **waHd-a-hu** *ʾilaa l-dukkaan-i*

He went to the shop **by himself.**

2.3.4.2 PREPOSITIONAL PHRASES: A prepositional phrase may function as manner adverbial.

(1) *bi-* بـ *or fii* في: The preposition *bi-* is often used with a noun to modify a verb phrase by describing the manner in which an action takes place.

أحبّها بجنون.

ʾaHabb-a-haa **bi-junuun-in.**

He loved her **madly.**

ينظر إليها بصمت.

ya-nZur-u ʾilay-haa **bi-Samt-in.**

He looks at her **in silence/silently.**

رفضت المشروع بشدة.

rafaD-at-i l-mashruuʿ-a **bi-shiddat-in.**

It refused the plan **forcefully.**

تعال بسرعة.

taʿaal-a **bi-surʿat-in!**

Come **quickly!**

When indicating manner, *bi-* or *fii* are sometimes prefixed to a noun such as *Suura* 'manner,' *Tariiqa* 'way,' or *shakl* 'form' followed by a modifier that provides the exact description of the manner:

بهذا الشكل الواسع

bi-haadhaa l-shakl-i *l-waasiʿ-i*

in this extensive way

في شكل أساسي

fii shakl-in *ʾasaasiyy-in*

in a fundamental way

في شكل جذري

fii shakl-in *jidhriyy-in*

in a radical way

بصورة عامة

bi-Suurat-in *ʿaammat-in*

generally

بصورة حماسية

bi-Suurat-in *Hamaasiyyat-in*

enthusiastically

بصورة فورية

bi-Suurat-in *fawriyyat-in*

immediately

بطريقة غير مباشرة

bi-Tariiqat-in *ghayr-i mubaashirat-in*

indirectly

بطرق غير قانونية

bi-Turuq-in *ghayr-i qaanuuniyyat-in*

in illegal ways

(2) Other prepositions may also occur in manner adverbial phrases:

القرار سيتخذ في كلّ قضية على انفراد.

al-qaraar-u sa-yu-ttaxadh-u fii kull-i qaDiyyat-in **ʿalaa nfiraad-in.**

Decision will be made on each issue **individually.**

تدرس في المكتبة كالعادة.

ta-drus-u fii l-maktabat-i **ka-l-ʿaadat-i.**

She is studying in the library, **as usual.**

3 Place adverbials

3.1 One-word adverbs of place

3.1.1 *hunaa* هُنا and *hunaaka* هُناك 'here' and 'there'

These two adverbs are deictic locatives, that is, they indicate proximity or remoteness from the speaker. They are also considered locative pronouns. In addition to indicating relative distance, the adverb *hunaaka* هُناك 'there' is used figuratively for existential predications to indicate the concept "there is" or "there are." These adverbs are invariable; they always end with *fatHa*. A variant of *hunaaka* هُناك indicating slightly greater distance is *hunaalika* هُنالِك '(over) there.'

3.1.1.1 *hunaa* هُنا 'HERE'

هنا يبدأ الحلم.
hunaa ya-bda'-u l-Hulm-u.
Here begins the dream.

عندما جئنا إلى هنا
'ind-a-maa ji'-naa 'ilaa hunaa
when we came **here**

أعيش هنا مع أسرتي.
'a-'iish-u hunaa ma'-a 'usrat-ii.
I live **here** with my family.

فابتعد عن هنا!
fa-bta'id 'an hunaa!
So you get away from **here**!

3.1.1.2 *hunaaka* هُناك 'THERE' (SPATIAL LOCATIVE)

يريد أن يصعد إلى هناك.
yu-riid-u 'an ya-S'ad-a 'ilaa hunaaka.
He wants to go up **there**.

لن تظل هناك إلى الأبد.
lan ta-Zall-a hunaaka 'ilaa l-'abad-i.
It won't stay **there** forever.

3.1.1.3 *hunaaka* هُناك 'THERE IS; THERE ARE' (EXISTENTIAL LOCATIVE)

هناك أربعة مكاتب سياحية.
hunaaka 'arba'at-u makaatib-a siyaaHiyyat-in.
There are four tourist offices.

هناك من يقول . . .
hunaaka man ya-quul-u . . .
There are [those] who say . . .

فهناك اتفاق فلسطيني إسرائيلي.
fa-hunaaka ttifaaq-un filisTiiniyy-un-israa'iiliyy-un.
There is a Palestinian-Israeli agreement.

ينبغي أن تكون هناك علاقة حسن جوار.
ya-nbaghii 'an ta-kuun-a hunaaka 'alaaqat-u Husn-i jiwaar-in.
There ought to be a good neighbor relationship.

3.1.1.4 *hunaalika* هُنالك: This variant of *hunaaka* is very similar in meaning although sometimes it indicates a more remote distance (actual or figurative).

كانت هنالك فكرة لدخول مجلس الشعب.
kaan-at hunaalika fikrat-un li-duxuul-i majlis-i l-sha'b-i.
There was (remotely) an idea of entering the house of representatives.

3.1.2 *thammat-a* ثَمَّةَ 'there is; there are'

The word *thammat-a* ثَمَّةَ has *fatHa* as an invariable ending and predicates existence in much the same way as *hunaaka* هناك.

و ثمّة علماء يعتقدون أنّ ...
wa-thammat-a ʿulamaaʾ-u yaʿ-taqid-uuna ʾanna ...
and **there are** scholars who believe that ...

فثمّة قيم مختلفة
fa-thammat-a qiyam-un muxtalifat-un
for **there are** different values

ليس في الأمر ثمّة صقور أو حمائم.
lays-a fii l-ʾamr-i thammat-a Suquur-un ʾaw Hamaaʾim -u.
There are neither hawks nor doves in the matter.

هل ثمّة إضافات إلى ذلك؟
hal thammat-a ʾiDaafaat-un ʾilaa dhaalika?
Are **there** additions to that?

3.1.3 *Hayth-u* حيث 'where'

The connective adverb *Hayth-u* denotes the concept of 'where' or 'in which' and connects one clause with another. It has an invariable *Damma* suffix.[9]

حيث القديم يختلط مع الحديث
Hayth-u l-qadiim-u ya-xtaliT-u maʿ-a l-Hadiith-i
where the old mixes with the new

في كلية حيث تدرس
fii kulliyyat-in Hayth-u tu-darris-u
in a college **where** she teaches

حيث تشرئب الطريق
Hayth-u ta-shraʾibb-u l-Tariiq-u
where the road stretches

3.2 Accusative adverbial of place

A noun may be marked with the indefinite accusative in order to indicate direction or location.

هل سرت يميناً أو شمالاً؟
hal sir-ta yamiin-an ʾaw shimaal-an?
Did you go **right** or **left**?

3.3 Locative adverbs or semi-prepositions (*Zuruuf makaan wa-Zuruuf zamaan* ظروف مكان وظروف زمان)

These adverbs are actually nouns of location marked with the accusative case, functioning as the first term of an *ʾiDaafa*, with a following noun in the genitive, or with a pronoun suffix. The location may be spatial or temporal. Although close

---

[9] Note that the question word "where?" is different: *ʾayna* أين (see Chapter 17, section 1); see also Chapter 18, section 6.1.

to prepositions in both meaning and function, these words are of substantive (usually triliteral root) origin and may inflect for genitive case if they are preceded by a true preposition.[10]

بعد أربعة أشهور
baʿd-a ʾarbaʿat-i ʾashhur-in
after four months

قبل سنتين
qabl-a sanat-ayni
two years **ago**

تعيش تحت الماء.
*ta-ʿiish-u **taHt-a** l-maaʾ-i.*
They live **under** water.

من تحت منضدة خشبية
*min **taHt-i** minDadat-in xashabiyyat-in*
from under a wooden table

3.4 Phrasal adverbs of place
Adverbial expressions of place often occur in the form of prepositional phrases.

بدأ اجتماعاته في القدس المحتلة.
*badaʾ-a jtimaaʿaat-i-hi **fii** l-quds-i l-muHtallat-i.*
He began his meetings **in** occupied Jerusalem.

في مستشفى الملك خالد
__fii__ mustashfaa l-malik-i xaalid-in
at King Khalid **Hospital**

في مقهى على الرصيف
fii maqhan ʿalaa l-raSiif-i
at a café **on** the sidewalk

على الصعيد الدولي
__ʿalaa__ l-Saʿiid-i l-duwaliyy-i
on the international **level**

4 Time adverbials
Adverbial expressions of time fall into four categories: basic adverbs, single nouns and adjectives in the accusative, compound time demonstratives, and phrases.

4.1 Basic adverbs of time
These words denote particular points in time and tend to remain in one form without inflecting for case or definiteness.

4.1.1 *ʾams-i* أمس 'yesterday'
The invariable adverb *ʾams-i* is unusual in that it ends in *kasra*. It does not take nunation even when it lacks the definite article. According to Wright, the *kasra* is not a case ending, but an anaptyctic vowel, added to ease pronunciation.[11] In terms of placement within a sentence, it is flexible because it is a short word and it is often inserted prior to a longer phrase; the only place it does not occur is in initial position.

---

[10] See also Chapter 16 on prepositions and semi-prepositions, section 3.
[11] "The kesra is not the mark of the genitive but merely a light vowel, added to render the pronunciation easy" Wright 1967, I:290. Note that if the definite article is attached to *ʾams*, it becomes fully inflectable.

عاد إلى القاهرة أمس.

ʿaad-a ʾilaa l-qaahirat-i ʾams-i.

He returned to Cairo **yesterday.**

وصل الرئيسان إلى مسقط أمس.

waSal-a l-raʾiis-aani ʾilaa masqaT-a ʾams-i.

The two presidents arrived in Muscat **yesterday.**

ذكر راديو صوت لبنان صباح أمس . . .

dhakar-a raadyuu Sawt-u lubnaan-a SabaaH-a ʾams-i . . .

the radio [station] "The Voice of Lebanon" mentioned **yesterday morning** . . .

4.1.1.1 OCCASIONALLY, *ʾams* IS USED WITH THE DEFINITE ARTICLE.

كان ذاك بالأمس.

kaana dhaaka bi-l-ʾams-i.

That was **yesterday.**

4.1.1.2 Because it is used adverbially, *ʾams-i* is considered to be a "**virtual**" **accusative** (despite the presence of *kasra*), so that when it has a modifier, or noun in apposition, that modifier or noun is in the accusative case:

في غارة نفّذها أمس الأوّل

fii ghaarat-in naffadh-a-haa ʾams-i l-ʾawwal-a

in a raid it carried out **the day before yesterday**

4.1.2 *al-ʾaan-a* الآن 'now'

The expression *al-ʾaan-a* is invariable as an adverb, remaining in the accusative even after a preposition:

افتح الآن!

iftaH-i l-ʾaan-a!

Open **now!**

يريدان الآن جدول أعمال مشتركا.

yu-riid-aani l-ʾaan-a jadwal-a ʾaʿmaal-in mushtarik-an.

They (two) **now** want a shared agenda.

وظهر حتى الآن خمسة وخمسون عددا من المجلة.

wa-Zahar-a Hattaa l-ʾaan-a xamsat-un wa-xamsuuna ʿadad-an min-a l-majallat-i.

Up to now 55 issues of the magazine have appeared.

4.1.3 *baʿd-u* بعد 'yet; still'

The word *baʿd-u*, with the *Damma* inflection and no nunation, acts as an adverb in negative clauses to mean 'not. . . yet,' 'still . . . not.' When inflected with the *Damma*, it cannot be the first term of a genitive construct.[12]

---

[12] The *Damma* is not thought to represent the nominative case here but is rather an archaic form of Semitic locative "un ancien cas adverbial en *-u* qui n'est pas le nominatif" (Lecomte 1968, 90). Similar forms such as *qabl-u* 'before,' *fawq-u* 'above,' and *taHt-u* 'beneath' also exist, with the restriction that they may not occur as the first term of an *ʾiDaafa.* On this topic see also Fleisch 1961, I:280, and Chapter 16, section 3.4.3.

ترك جروحا لم تلتئم بعدُ.
tarak-a juruuH-an lam ta-lta'im **ba'd-u.**
It left wounds that **still** have not healed.

لم تكشف هويتهم بعدُ.
lam tu-kshaf huwiyyaat-u-hum **ba'd-u.**
Their identities have not **yet** been
revealed.

لم يحدد موعده بعدُ.
lam yu-Haddad maw'id-u-hu **ba'd-u.**
Its date has not **yet** been set.

لم يصل بعدُ سوى إلى قلة من بيوت المصريين.
lam ya-Sil **ba'd-u** siwaa 'ilaa qillat-in min buyuut-i l-miSriyy-iina.
It has **still** reached very few Egyptian households. (It still hasn't reached but a
few Egyptian households.)

4.1.3.1 *fii-maa ba'd-u* فيما بعدُ 'LATER': The idiomatic expression *fii-maa ba'd-u*
means 'later; later on.'

سأتلفن لك فيما بعدُ.
sa-'u-talfin-u la-ka **fii-maa ba'd-u.**
I will telephone ('to') you **later.**

ثم ضعها فيما بعدُ في كتابك.
thumm-a Da'-haa **fii-maa ba'd-u**
fii kitaab-i-ka.
Then put it **later** in your book.

4.1.4 *thumm-a* ثمَّ; *min thumm-a* من ثمَّ 'then; after that; subsequently'

Both of these expressions denote sequential action. Note that *thumm-a* invariably
ends with *fatHa.*

ثمَّ صعد إلى المنبر.
thumm-a Sa'ad-a 'ilaa l-minbar-i.
Then he went up onto the dais.

انتقل من ثمَّ إلى العمل في الجامعة.
intaqal-a **min thumm-a**
'ilaa l-'amal-i fii l-jaami'at-i.
After that he transferred to
work in the university.

4.2 Time nouns and adjectives in the accusative

Specific times or time nouns are marked for the accusative. They may be definite
or indefinite.

4.2.1 Indefinite accusative time nouns

هل سنتدخل أو لا نتدخل أبداً؟
hal sa-na-tadaxxal-u 'aw laa na-tadaxxal-u **'abad-an?**
Shall we interfere or **never** interfere?

كانوا دائماً على علاقة معها.
kaan-uu **daa'im-an** 'alaa 'alaaqat-in ma'-a-haa.
They were **always** in touch with her.

وأخيراً جاءت إلى القاهرة.
wa-'axiir-an jaa'-at 'ilaa l-qaahirat-i.
And **finally** she came to Cairo.

الرئيس يتفقد غداً مواقع العمل.

*al-raʾiis-u ya-tafaqqad-u **ghad-an** mawaaqiʿ-a l-ʿamal-i.*

The President inspects work sites **tomorrow.**

حصلت حديثاً على الجنسية.

*HaSal-tu **Hadiith-an** ʿalaa l-jinsiyyat-i.*

I **recently** obtained citizenship.

اللجنة ستعقد اجتماعين سنويًا.

*al-lajnat-u sa-ta-ʿqud-u jtimaaʿ-ayni **sanawiyy-an**.*

The committee will hold two meetings **yearly.**

في زيارة لإندونيسيا تستغرق أسبوعاً

*fii ziyaarat-in li-ʾinduuniisiyaa ta-staghriq-u **ʾusbuuʿ-an***

on a visit to Indonesia that lasts **a week**

الندوة تستمر يوماً واحداً.

*al-nadwat-u ta-stamirr-u **yawm-an waaHid-an**.*

The seminar lasts **one day.**

4.2.2 Definite accusative time nouns

اليومَ الخميس

al-yawm-a l-xamiis-a

today, Thursday

الليلةَ قبل الماضية

al-laylat-a qabl-a l-maaDiyat-i

the night before last

تغيّر استخدامها مطلعَ القرنِ الماضي.

*taghayyar-a stixdaam-u-haa **maTlaʿ-a** l-qarn-i l-maaDii*

Its use changed **at the onset/beginning** of the last century.

4.3 Compound time adverbials

4.3.1 -*dhaaka* ذاك– expressions

Time nouns in the accusative suffixed with the pronominal -*dhaaka* are equivalent in meaning to a locative demonstrative phrase, e.g., "that year," "that day."

4.3.1.1 ʾ*aan-a-dhaaka* آنذاك 'AT THAT TIME'

أطلق كتابه آنذاك تيّاراً من الاهتمام.

*ʾaTlaq-a kitaab-u-hu **ʾaan-a-dhaaka** tayyaar-an min-a l-ihtimaam-i.*

His book set off a wave of interest **at that time.**

قال آنذاكَ إنّهم على وشك التوصّل إلى الاتفاق.

*qaal-a **ʾaan-a-dhaaka** ʾinna-hum ʿalaa washk-i l-tawaSSul-i ʾilaa l-ittifaaq-i.*

He said **at that time** that they were on the verge of arriving at the agreement.

4.3.1.2 *yawm-a-dhaaka* يومَذاك 'THAT DAY'

انتهى الحادث يومَذاك.

*intahaa l-Hadath-u **yawm-a-dhaaka**.*

The incident ended **that day.**

تحدثوا يومَذاكَ عن الحدث.

*taHaddath-uu **yawm-a-dhaaka** ʿan-i l-Hadath-i.*

That day they spoke about the event.

4.3.1.3 *sanat-a-dhaaka* سنتَذاك AND *ʿaam-a-dhaaka* عامَذاك 'THAT YEAR'

اكتشاف أمريكا **سنتَذاك** كان الحدث الكبير.

*iktishaaf-u ʾamriikaa **sanat-a-dhaaka** kaan-a l-Hadath-a l-kabiir-a.*

The discovery of America **that year** was the great event.

حققت **عامَذاك** سبعة وعشرين بليون دولار.

*Haqqaq-at **ʿaam-a-dhaaka** sabʿat-an wa-ʿishriina bilyuun-a duulaar-in.*

It realized **that year** 27 billion dollars.

4.3.2 -ʾidhin ئذ– expressions

These are more common in literary Arabic than in day-to-day journalistic prose.

baʿd-a-ʾidhin بعدَئذ 'after that'

وبـعدَئذ انتقل إلى دار ماهر.

wa-baʿda-ʾidhin intaqal-a ʾilaa daar-i maahir-in.

And **after that** he moved to Mahir's house.

4.4 Adverbial time phrases

A noun denoting either a point in time or a period of time may occur in the accusative to denote that it is functioning adverbially. The nouns may be indefinite or definite, depending on the structure. For an expression of time in general, the indefinite accusative is used:

يسعى ليلاً ونهاراً.

ya-sʿaa layl-an wa-nahaar-an.

He hurries **night and day**.

For specific expressions of time the accusative may be used with demonstrative pronouns, the definite article, as first term of an *ʾiDaafa*, or in a prepositional phrase.

نجح هذه السنةَ في توقيع مثل هذا الاتفاق.

*najaH-a **haadhihi l-sanat-a** fii tawqiiʿ-i mithl-i haadhaa l-ittifaaq-i.*

It succeeded **this year** in signing such an agreement.

جاءوا فجرَ يوم الاقتراع.

*jaaʾ-uu **fajr-a yawm-i** l-iqtiraaʿ-i.*

They came **at dawn on the day** of balloting.

اليومَ الأحدَ الساعةَ الحاديةَ عشرةَ صباحاً

al-yawm-a l-ʾaHad-a l-saaʿat-a l-Haadiyat-a ʿashrat-a SabaaH-an

today, Sunday, at 11:00 in the morning

ألقي القبض عليه في غضونِ دقائقَ.

*ʾulqiya l-qabD-u ʿalay-hi **fii ghuDuun-i daqaaʾiq-a**.*

He was arrested **within minutes**.

إلى ندوة تعقد في مبنى البرلمان الأربعاءَ المقبلَ

*ʾilaa nadwat-in tu-ʿqad-u fii mabnaa l-barlamaan-i **l-ʾarbiʿaaʾ-a l-muqbil-a***

to a session that will be held in the parliament building **next Wednesday**

5 Numerical adverbials

For the expression of points in sequence, as in an outline, the ordinal numbers are used in the accusative indefinite. For example:

ʾawwal-an	'firstly'	أوّلاً
thaaniy-an	'secondly'	ثانياً
thaalith-an	'thirdly'	ثالثاً
ʾawwal-a l-ʾamr-i	'at first; the first thing'	أوّلَ الأمرِ

6 Adverbial accusative of specification (*al-tamyiiz* التمييز)

This form of adverbial accusative is used to label, identify, or specify something previously referred to in the sentence.[13] It specifies the nature of what has been mentioned by answering the question "in what way?" Often an equivalent English structure might include the terms "as" or "in terms of."

هذا البلد الطيب أرضاً وناساً وثقافةً

*haadhaa l-balad-u l-Tayyib-u **ʾarD-an wa-naas-an wa-thaqaafat-an***

this good country [in terms of] **land, people, and culture**

نقل ملكتها أسيرةً إلى روما.

*naqal-a malikat-a-haa **ʾasiirat-an** ʾilaa ruumaa.*

He transported its queen to Rome **[as] a prisoner**.

تحكّم الغرب اقتصادياً وعسكرياً

*taHakkum-u l-gharb-i **qtiSaadiyy-an wa-ʿaskariyy-an***

the dominance of the west **economically and militarily**

ونتيجة ذلك محرك أكثر كفاءةً.

*wa-natiijat-u dhaalika muHarrik-un ʾakthar-u **kafaaʾat-an**.*

The result of that is a **more efficient** motor.

---

[13] See also Chapter 7, section 5.3.3.7.

6.1 Other uses of *tamyiiz*

The accusative of specification is also used with the following quantifying expressions:

6.1.1 The interrogative quantifier *kam* كَمْ 'how much, how many'

The noun following *kam* كم is in the accusative **singular**.

كم طالباً في صفك؟

kam Taalib-an fii Saff-i-ka?

How many students are in your class?

كم فلماً شاهدتم؟

kam film-an shaahad-tum?

How many films did you ('all') see?

6.1.2 The counted singular noun after numerals 11-99

For more examples and discussion of this topic, see Chapter 15.[14]

عن سبعة عشر نائباً

ʿan sabʿat-a ʿashar-a **naaʾib-an**

from seventeen **representatives**

عشرون قرشاً

ʿishruuna **qirsh-an**

twenty **piasters**

أكثر من خمسة وخمسين فيلماً

ʾakthar-u min xamsat-in wa-xamsiina **fiilm-an**

more than fifty-five **films**

6.1.3 The periphrastic comparative

The expression of comparative or superlative quality with the comparative adjective *ʾakthar* allows comparison of qualities that do not fit into the comparative adjective (*ʾafʿal*) form.[15]

قد تكون أكثر أهمية.

qad ta-kuun-u ʾakthar-a
   ʾahammiyyat-an.

It might be **more important**.

   ('greater in terms of importance')

هو أكثر دهاءً بكثير.

huwa ʾakthar-u dahaaʾ-an bi-kathiir-in.

He is **more shrewd** by far.

من أجل شرق أوسط أكثر استقراراً

min ʾajl-i sharq-in ʾawsaT-a ʾakthar-a stiqraar-an

for the sake of a **more stable** Middle East

7 Adverbial accusative of cause or reason (*al-mafʿuul li-ʾajl-i-hi* المفعول لأجله, *al-mafʿuul la-hu* المفعول له)

In this adverbial structure, a **verbal noun in the indefinite accusative** is used to indicate the **motive, reason, or purpose** of the mentioned action. If the verbal

---

[14] See also Chapter 15, sections 1.4, 1.5, 1.6. For an analysis of this function of the accusative and its treatment in traditional Arabic grammar, see Carter 1972.

[15] See also Chapter 10, section 4.2.3.

noun has a preposition associated with it, that preposition remains as part of the structure.

تقديراً لـجهوده

taqdiir-an li-juhuud-i-hi

in appreciation of his efforts

تمهيداً لإحالتهم

tamhiid-an li-ʾiHaalat-i-him ...

in preparation for their transfer

نتيجةً لـلعجز الذي سيطر على الحكومة

natiijat-an li-l-ʿajz-i lladhii sayTar-a ʿalaa l-Hukuumat-i

as a result of the incapacity that dominated the government

بدأ عمليّة التمشيط بحثاً عن رجال المقاومة.

badaʾ-a ʿamaliyyat-a l-tamshiiT-i baHth-an ʿan rijaal-i l-muqaawamat-i.

It started a combing operation **to search for** ('men of') resistance.

بحث تطوير العلاقات خدمةً لمصلحتهما المشتركة.

buHith-a taTwiir-u l-ʿalaaqaat-i xidmat-an li-maSlaHat-i-himaa l-mushtarakat-i.

Development of relations was discussed **in order to serve** their [two]
  shared interest.

8 Adverbs as speech acts

A few Arabic adverbs are used both in speech and in writing to function as *performatives*, that is, to accomplish acts such as thanking, welcoming, pardoning, and so forth. A number of these are words and phrases in the indefinite accusative. These include:

'thank you'	*shukr-an*	شكراً
'pardon; you're welcome'	*ʿafw-an*	عفواً
'welcome'	*ʾahl-an wa-sahl-an*	أهلاً وسهلاً
'hello'	*marHab-an*	مرحباً

12

Personal pronouns

Personal pronouns refer to persons or entities and stand on their own as substitutes for nouns or noun phrases. This word class fills a wide range of roles in Arabic and consists of three groups: subject, object, and possessive pronouns. The first group, subject pronouns, are independent, separate words; the other two groups both take the form of suffixes.

The personal pronouns show differences in gender (masculine and feminine), number (singular, dual, plural), and person (first, second, and third). However, the number of categories of personal pronouns in Arabic is larger than in English (12 as opposed to 8) because it includes both masculine and feminine forms of the second and third person, and it also includes the dual pronouns.

1 Independent personal pronouns (*Damaaʾir munfaSila* ضمائر منفصلة)

The independent pronouns are also referred to as subject pronouns since they can serve as the subjects of verbs or of equational sentences and they correspond to the set of English subject pronouns. They are as follows:[1]

	Singular	Dual	Plural
First person	أَنا 'I' ʾanaa		نَحْنُ 'we' naHn-u
Second person Masculine	أَنْتَ 'you' ʾanta	أَنْتُما 'you two' ʾantumaa	أَنْتُمْ 'you' ʾantum
Feminine	أَنْتِ 'you' ʾanti		أَنْتُنَّ 'you' ʾantunna

[1] There is no neutral pronoun "it," since there is no neutral gender in Arabic. Everything is referred to as either masculine or feminine. Note that the third person feminine singular pronoun, in keeping with the agreement rules of Arabic, is used to refer to nonhuman plurals.

	Singular	Dual	Plural
Third person Masculine	هُوَ 'he' *huwa*	هُمَا 'they two' *humaa*	هُمْ 'they' *hum*
Feminine	هِيَ 'she' *hiya*		هُنَّ 'they' *hunna*

The masculine plural pronouns *ʾantum* أَنْتُمْ and *hum* هُمْ end with *sukuun*, which means that they require a helping vowel if they are followed directly by a cluster of two or more consonants (often the case with a following word that starts with the definite article). That helping vowel is *Damma*, based on a principle of vowel harmony with the previous vowel.

هُمُ الْمسلمون.
hum-u l-muslim-uuna.
They are the Muslims.

هُمُ الْمخترعون للشطرنج.
hum-u l-muxtariʿuuna li-l-shaTranj-i.
They are the inventors of chess.

1.1 Independent personal pronouns: functions
This form of the pronoun is used in a number of different ways, sometimes as an essential part of a clause and sometimes as a nonessential part.

1.1.1 To emphasize the subject of a verb
Because Arabic verbs incorporate the subject into their inflections, the independent personal pronoun is not necessary to mark the subject of a verb phrase.[2] However, the pronoun may be used along with the verb in order to fortify or emphasize the subject. In the following sentences, the independent pronoun could be omitted and the sentence would still be grammatically correct; however, the emphasis on the subject would be reduced.

وهو لا يبدو متفائلا.
wa-hwa laa ya-bduu mutafaaʾil-an.[3]
He does not seem optimistic.

سيكون هو المفتاح السحري.
sa-ya-kuun-u huwa l-miftaah-a l-siHriyy-a.
It will be the magic key.

أنا لا أقدر.
ʾanaa laa ʾa-qdar-u.
I cannot.

كانت هي نقطة التحول.
kaan-at hiya nuqTat-a l-taHawwal-i.
It was the turning point.

---

[2] Arabic is a "pro-drop" language; i.e., it is a language that allows a separate pronominal subject to be left unexpressed. This feature results in the verb inflectional paradigm distinguishing all persons uniquely. See Chapter 21 on verb inflection, esp. note 1.

[3] When preceded by the conjunctions *wa-* or *fa-*, the third person singular pronouns *huwa* and *hiya* may lose their first vowel, thus becoming *wa-hwa* وهُو and *wa-hya* وهِي.

أحـاول أنـا أن أدافـع عنهـا.

*ʾu-Haawil-u **ʾanaa** ʾan ʾu-daafiʿ-a ʿan-haa.*

I try to defend it.

1.1.2 Subject of an equational sentence

Equational or verbless sentences do not have an overt verb, but they may show a subject through use of a pronoun. Used in this way, the pronoun is usually the first element in the sentence.

هو خبير في شؤون الشرق الأوسط.

huwa xabiir-un fii shuʾuun-i l-sharq-i l-ʾawsaT-i.

He is an expert in Middle Eastern affairs.

أنت صديقتي.	هي ذكية.
ʾanti Sadiiqat-ii.	*hiya dhakiyyat-un.*
You (f.) are my friend.	She is intelligent.
أنا محظوظة في ذلك المجال.	نحن عاشقان.
ʾanaa maHZuuZat-un fii dhaalika l-majaal-i.	*naHnu ʿaashiq-aani.*
I am fortunate in that field.	We are lovers.

1.1.3 Predicate of equational sentence

Less common is the use of a subject pronoun as the predicate of an equational sentence; for example,

هذا هو.	أنت هي.
*haadhaa **huwa**.*	*ʾanti **hiyya**.*
This **is he**.	You are **she**.

1.1.4 As a copula

In order to clarify the relationship between the subject and predicate of an equational sentence, especially when the predicate is a definite noun or noun phrase, **a third person subject pronoun** may be inserted between the subject and predicate as a way of linking these two parts of the sentence, and as a substitute for the verb "to be." When functioning in this manner, it is said to be a **copula**.[4]

الشيء الوحيد المزعج هو الأسعار.	المهم هو العودة.
al-shayʾ-u l-waHiid-u l-muzʿij-u	*al-muhimm-u **huwa** l-ʿawdat-u.*
* **huwa** l-ʾasʿaar-u.*	The important [thing] **is to return**.
The one disturbing thing **is the prices**.	

---

[4] As Hurford puts it, "In English, a copula is any form of the verb *be* used as a 'link' or 'coupling' between its subject and a following phrase. The link either expresses identity or describes some property or attribute of the subject (*Copula* is Latin for *link*.)" 1994, 51. Because the verb "to be" in Arabic is not expressed overtly in present tense indicative sentences, an independent pronoun sometimes serves that purpose. For an excellent analysis of the Arabic pronoun copula, see Eid 1991.

المسلم هو التركي.	تلك هي الأجواء السائدة في الحزب.
*al-muslim-u **huwa** l-turkiyy-u.*	*tilka **hiya** l-ʾajwaaʾ-u l-saaʾidat-u fii l-Hizb-i.*
The Muslim **is** the Turk.	These **are** the atmospheres prevailing in the party.

2 Suffix personal pronouns (*Damaaʾir muttaSila* ضمائر متصلة)

There are two sets of suffix pronouns, one set indicates **possession** (possessive pronouns) and is suffixed to nouns, and the other set indicates the *object of a verb or object of a preposition* (object pronouns).

Although the two sets are different in their distribution and in their meanings, in form they are almost exactly alike. The only formal difference between them is in the first person singular pronoun ('my' or 'me'), which when it indicates possession and is suffixed to a noun, is /-ii/, but when it indicates the object of a verb is -nii ني.

2.1 Possessive pronoun suffixes

These suffixes are attached to nouns to show possession. They agree with the gender and number of the possessor (as in English), not the thing possessed (as in French).

	Singular	Dual	Plural
First person	ي 'my' -ii		نا 'our' -naa
Second person Masculine	ك 'your' -ka	كُما 'your' -kumaa	كُم 'your' -kum
Feminine	كِ 'your' -ki		كُنَّ 'your' -kunna
Third person Masculine	ـهُ ~ ـهِ 'his' -hu ~ -hi	ـهُما 'their' -humaa ~ -himaa	ـهُم ~ ـهِم 'their' -hum ~ -him
Feminine	ـها 'her' -haa		ـهُنَّ ~ ـهِنَّ 'their' -hunna ~ -hinna

These suffixes are attached at the end of a noun, **after the case-marking vowel**, except for the suffix -*ii* 'my' which supercedes any inflectional vowel.[5] A noun with a pronoun suffix is considered definite, the suffix acting like the second term of an annexation structure to define the noun. When a personal pronoun suffix is used, the noun cannot have the definite article (it is definite by virtue of

---

[5] Note that all the pronoun suffixes except -*ii* start with a consonant; that is why they can follow directly after a vowel. Since /-ii/ consists of a long vowel only, it cannot follow or combine with another vowel. Instead, it replaces any short inflectional vowel.

the suffix) and it does not have nunation (because it is definite rather than indefinite).

Note that words ending in *taa' marbuuTa* and pronounced with a final /-a/ in pause form shift their spelling to a regular *taa'* when they are suffixed with a personal pronoun, since the *taa'* is no longer final.

حافظوا على نظافة مدينتكُم!

*HaafiZ-uu ʿalaa naZaafat-i **madiinat-i-kum!***
Keep **your (m. pl.) city** clean ('preserve the cleanliness of your city')!

عن إذنـك	من فضلـك
ʿan ''idhn-i-ki	*min faDl-i-ka*
with **your (f.) permission**	please ('of **your kindness**') (when requesting something)
في محفظتـك	أضم صوتــي إلى صوتـك.
*fii **miHfaZat-i-ka***	*'a-Dumm-u **Sawt-ii** 'ilaa **Sawt-i-ka.***
in **your (m. sg.) wallet**	I add **my voice** to **yours** (your voice).
من شمالها إلى جنوبها	في بيئاتـها الطبيعية
*min **shimaal-i-haa** 'ilaa **junuub-i-haa***	*fii **bii'aat-i-haa** l-Tabiiʿiyyat-i*
from **its north** to **its south**	in **their** natural **environments**
كل ريال من دخلنا	علمـاؤه وجنوده
*kull-u riyaal-in min **daxl-i-naa***	*ʿulamaa'-u-hu wa-junuud-u-hu*
every riyal of **our income**	**its scholars** and **its soldiers**

2.1.1 Vowel shift pronouns

The third person suffix pronouns that include the sequence *-hu* (*-hu, -humaa, -hum, -hunna*) are affected by any front vowel (*-i* or *-ii*) or *yaa'* that precedes them. Their *-u* vowel shifts to /-i/ in vowel harmony with the preceding sound. Other vowels (*-a* or *-u*) do not affect these suffixes:

في مذكّراته	على كتفَيْه
*fii **mudhakkiraat-i-hi***	*ʿalaa **katif-ay-hi***
in **his notes/diary**	on **his [two] shoulders**
أكرما والدَيْهما	بسيّاراتـهم
*'akram-aa **waalid-ay-himaa***	*bi-**sayyaaraat-i-him***
They [two] honored **their [two] parents.**	in **their cars**

بتسويق إنتاجِهِنّ

bi-taswiiq-i ʾintaaj-i-hinna

by marketing **their** (f. pl.) **production**

من جيوبِهِم

min juyuub-i-him

from **their pockets**

2.1.2 Plural pronoun suffix helping vowel

The masculine plural pronoun suffixes, -*kum* and -*hum*/-*him*, end with a *sukuun*, which means that they need a helping vowel if followed directly by a cluster of two or more consonants. That vowel is *Damma*, based on a principle of vowel harmony with the previous vowel. If the third person plural suffix pronoun shifts from -*hum* to -*him*, the helping vowel may be either *Damma* or *kasra*.[6]

تتناول أفلامَـهُمُ الأخيرة.

ta-tanaawal-u ʾaflaam-a-hum-u l-ʾaxiirat-a.

It deals with **their** latest films.

من سياستِـهِمِ الخارجية

min siyaasat-i-him-i l-xaarijiyyat-i

from **their** foreign policy

أساتذة بلباسِـهِمِ التقليديّ

ʾasaatidhat-un bi-libaas-i-him-i l-taqliidiyy-i

professors **with** (wearing) **their** traditional **regalia** ('clothes')

2.1.3 Noun + pronoun suffix + adjective

When a noun plus pronoun suffix is modified by an attributive adjective, that adjective is definite and carries the definite article because the noun is considered definite. The adjective also agrees in number, gender, and case with the modified noun.

بدأ مؤتمره الصحافيّ.

badaʾ-a muʾtamar-a-hu l-SiHaafiyy-a.

He began **his** news conference.

في عالمِنا العربي

fii ʿaalam-i-naa l-ʿarabiyy-i

in **our** Arab world

في فيلمه الجديد

fii fiilm-i-hi l-jadiid-i

in **his** new film

في زيارته الرسميّة الأخيرة

*fii ziyaarat-i-hi l-rasmiyyat-i
l-ʾaxiirat-i*

on **his** last official visit

في محاولته الأولى

fii muHaawalat-i-hi l-ʾuulaa

on **his** first try

في جيبك الداخلي

fii jayb-i-ka l-daaxiliyy-i

in **your** inside pocket

---

[6] In this text, the principle of vowel harmony is observed.

2.1.4 Pronoun suffixes on dual and sound masculine plural nouns

Nouns with the dual suffix (-aani/-ayni) or with the sound masculine plural suffix (-uuna/-iina) drop the *nuun* when a pronoun suffix is attached:

عنواناهما	سيطلب من ناخبيه التصويت.
ʿunwaan-aa-humaa	*sa-ya-Tlub-u min **naaxib-ii-hi** l-taSwiit-i.*
their two titles	It will request **its electors** to vote.
بـيـديها	كان ملجأ لـمتعبينا.
bi-yad-ay-haa	*kaan-a malja'-an li-**mutʿab-ii-naa**.*
with **her two hands**	It was a refuge for **our weary**.
أحد مستشاريه	من أصوات مؤيديه
*'aHad-u **mustashaar-ii-hi***	*min 'aSwaat-i **mu'ayyid-ii-hi***
one of **his advisors**	from the votes of **its supporters**

2.1.4.1 SOUND MASCULINE PLURAL SUFFIX PLUS /-ii/ 'MY': The sound masculine plural (-uuna or -iina), as noted above, drops the *nuun* when a suffix pronoun is attached, leaving a long vowel /-uu/ or /-ii/. Because of restrictions on vowel combinations, adding the pronoun -ii causes a shift in these endings. They are shortened and combined into one, with a short vowel *kasra* (-i) followed by a double *yaa'* with *fatHa*: -iyya ـيّ. Note that when (-ii) 'my' is suffixed to sound masculine plural nouns it *overrides the case distinction* and the plural is reduced to only one form.[7]

معلميّ

muʿallim-iyya

my teachers (nominative and genitive/accusative)

معلميّ مصريون.	ذهبت مع معلميّ.
muʿallim-iyya miSriyy-uuna.	*dhahab-tu maʿa **muʿallim-iyya**.*
My teachers are Egyptian.	I went with **my teachers**.

2.1.4.2 DUAL SUFFIX PLUS /-ii/: The dual suffix (-aani or -ayni) drops the *nuun* when a suffix pronoun is attached, leaving a long vowel -aa or the diphthong -ay. Owing to restrictions on the combination of two long vowels in Arabic, the long vowel suffix /-ii/ is shifted to /-ya/ in both cases: nominative -aaya ـاي and genitive/accusative -ayya ـيّ.

---

[7] This is due to incompatibility between the vowels /-uu/ and /-ii/, which do not combine in MSA.

والِدايَ

waalid-aaya

my [two] parents (nominative)

والِدَيَّ

waalid-ayya

my [two] parents (genitive/accusative)

والِدايَ مِصريّان.

waalid-aaya miSriyy-aani.

My parents are Egyptian.

ذهبت مع والِدَيَّ.

dhahab-tu maʿa waalid-ayya.

I went with **my parents**.

2.1.5 The five nouns plus /-ii/: ʾab, ʾax, fuu, Ham, dhuu)

These five nouns are a special subset of semantically primitive nouns that inflect
for case with long vowels instead of short vowels whenever they have pronoun
suffixes or when they are used as the first term of an ʾiDaafa (see Chapter 5, section 10.1.3). Except for *dhuu*, which does not take pronoun suffixes, when used
with the possessive suffix /-ii/ 'my,' all three cases are neutralized into one form,
with omission of the inflectional vowel, e.g.,

my father	*ʾab-ii*	أبي
my brother	*ʾax-ii*	أخي
my father-in-law	*Ham-ii*	حمي
my mouth	*fiyya*[8]	فيَّ

2.2 Object pronoun suffixes

Object pronouns are suffixes almost identical in form with the possessive pronoun suffixes. They serve as objects of transitive verbs and of prepositions and
therefore are affixed to those word classes.

2.2.1 Pronoun objects of transitive verbs

This set of pronouns is as follows:

	Singular	Dual	Plural
First person	ـني 'me' -nii		نا 'us' -naa
Second person Masculine	كَ 'you' -ka	كُما 'you' -kumaa	كُمْ 'you' -kum

---

[8] Alternates with the variant word stem for 'mouth,' *fam*, as *fam-ii* فمي.

	Singular	Dual	Plural
Feminine	ك 'you' -ki		كُنَّ 'you' -kunna
Third person Masculine	ـهُ ~ ـه 'him' -hu ~ -hi	ـهما ~ ـهُما 'them' -humaa ~ -himaa	هُمْ ~ هِمْ 'them' -hum ~ -him
Feminine	ـها 'her' -haa		ـهُنَّ ~ ـهِنَّ 'them' -hunna ~ -hinna

These suffixes are attached at the end of a verb, after the verb inflection for person, number, gender, tense, and mood. Just as with possessive pronoun suffixes,
the third person suffix pronouns that include the sequence -hu- (-hu, -humaa, -hum,
-hunna) are affected by any front vowel (-i or -ii) or yaa' that precedes them. Their -u
vowel shifts to -i in vowel harmony with the preceding sound. Other vowels (-a or -u)
do not affect these suffixes.

أشكرَكَ.

'a-shkur-u-ka.

I thank you.

نعتبرهُم نجوماً.

na-ʿtabir-u-hum nujuum-an.

We consider them stars.

وجدتها.

wajad-tu-haa!

I found it!

اختارني.

ixtaar-a-nii.

He chose me.

اعذرني.

i-ʿdhir-nii.

Forgive me/excuse me.

لا تستخدميها !

laa ta-staxdim-ii-hi!

Don't (f. sg.) use it!

انتظرناه.

intaZar-naa-hu.

We have waited for it.

أريد أن أساعدكُما.

'u-riid-u 'an u-saaʿid-a-kumaa

I want to help you two.

2.2.1.1 SECOND PERSON PLURAL HELPING VOWEL: Whenever a pronoun suffix is
attached to the second person masculine plural form of a past tense verb (ending
in -tum), a long helping vowel -uu is inserted between the verb suffix and the
pronoun object suffix.

هل هذا ما تعلمتمـوه في المدرسة؟

hal haadhaa maa taʿallam-tum-**uu**-hu fii l-madrasat-i?

Is this what you (pl.) learned ('it') in school?

تركتمونا !

tarak-tum-**uu**-naa!

You (pl.) left us!

2.2.1.2 WORD ORDER: Because of the pronoun object attaching directly to the
verb, and the verb-initial word order in Arabic sentences, sometimes the object of
a verb in Arabic comes before the mention of the subject.

يزوره ثلاثة ملايين سائح كل عام.
ya-zuur-u-hu *thalaathat-u malaayiin-i saa'iH-in kull-a ᶜaam-in.*
Three million tourists **visit it** every year.

أعلنه اليونيسكو.	أخذها صديقك.
'aᶜlan-a-hu *l-yuuniiskuu.*	***'axadh-a-haa*** *Sadiiq-u-ka.*
UNESCO **announced it.**	Your friend **took it.**

2.2.1.3 WORD = SENTENCE: If both subject and object are in pronoun form, the verb, its subject and object can create one word which constitutes a complete predication or sentence by itself:

(1) **Past tense:**

استقبلناهم.	أقنعوها.	سمعته.	أحببناه.
istaqbal-naa-hum.	***'aqnaᶜ-uu-haa.***	***samiᶜ-tu-hu.***	***'aHbab-naa-hu.***
We met them.	**They persuaded her.**	**I heard it.**	**We loved him.**

(2) **Present tense:**

يحملها.	يقدسونه.
ya-Hmil-u-haa	***yu-qaddis-uuna-hu.***
He is carrying it.	**They venerate it.**

2.2.1.4 NOTE ABOUT WORD STRESS: Because suffix pronouns are attached to the ends of words, and because word stress is calculated by syllables from the end of a word, the suffixing of a personal pronoun lengthens a word and may cause a shift in stress when the words are spoken or pronounced out loud. (See stress rules in Chapter 2, section 7.) For example (stressed syllable is boldface):

	Pause form		Full form + pronoun suffix
policy	سياسة *siya**a**sa*	their policy	سياستهم *siyaa**sat**-u-hum*
problem	مشكلة ***mush**kila*	her problem	مشكلتها *mushki**lat**-u-haa*
world	عالم *ᶜ**aa**lam*	our world	عالمنا *ᶜaa**lam**-u-naa*
conference	مؤتمر ***mu'**tamar*	his conference	مؤتمره *mu'ta**mar**-u-hu*
we waited	انتظرنا *inta**Zar**-naa*	we waited for him	انتظرناه *intaZar-**naa**-hu*

2.2.2 Object pronoun carrier: إيّا *ʾiyyaa-*

Rarely, in MSA, a pronoun object of a verb will occur and not be attached to the verb. This may happen if the verb is one that takes a double object (direct and indirect) and both of the objects are pronouns, or it may occur as a stylistic choice. For these cases, there is a word that acts as a pronoun-carrier, *ʾiyyaa-*, and object pronouns can be attached to it.[9]

2.2.2.1 VERB THAT TAKES DOUBLE ACCUSATIVE:

أهداني إيّاها أهل صديقي.

ʾahdaa-nii ʾiyyaa-haa ʾahl-u Sadiiq-ii.

My friend's family presented **it** to me ('sent-me **it**').

أعطيني إيّاه.

ʾaʿTii-nii ʾiyyaa-hu.

Give (f.) **it** [to] me ('give me **it**').

2.2.2.2 STYLISTIC CHOICE: In the following example, the writer could have said 'taHaddath-a maʿ-a-hu,' but he chose a more classical turn of phrase, using the expression *wa-ʾiyaa-hu* instead. In this case, *wa-* is a connector which takes the accusative case (*waaw al-maʿiyya*) on a following noun, signifying concomitance or accompaniment.[10] Since a pronoun object is needed here, *wa-* is followed by *ʾiyyaa-hu*.

تحدّث وإيّاه مطولا.

taHaddath-a wa-ʾiyyaa-hu muTawwil-an.

He talked with **him** for a long time.

2.3 Pronoun objects of prepositions and semi-prepositions

Prepositions may take pronoun objects. The form of the object pronouns of prepositions is almost exactly identical to the pronoun objects of verbs.[11]

As objects of prepositions, the suffix pronouns attach directly onto the preposition itself. Sometimes a spelling change is required, however.

This subset of pronouns is as follows:

---

[9] See Wright 1967, I:103–104 for more on the use of *ʾiyyaa-*. Note also that in Classical Arabic it was possible to have both direct and indirect objects as suffixes on the verb. Lecomte states (1968, 106): "La langue ancienne, surtout poétique, admettait l'agglutination des pronoms dans l'ordre des personnes 1+2+3: *ʾaʿTay-tu-ka-hu* je te l'ai donné; depuis l'époque classique, le second pronom s'affixe toujours à une particule-outil *ʾiyyaa-*."

[10] For more on *waaw al-maʿiyya* see Baalbaki 1986 and Wright 1967, II:83–84.

[11] Note, however that the prepositions *Hattaa*, *ka-*, and *mundh-u* do not take pronoun objects.

	Singular	**Dual**	**Plural**
First person	ي ~ نِي 'me' -nii ~ -ii		نا 'us' -naa
Second person **Masculine**	كَ 'you' -ka	كُمَا 'you two' -kumaa	كُمْ 'you' -kum
Feminine	كِ 'you' -ki		كُنَّ 'you' -kunna
Third person **Masculine**	هُ ~ هِ 'him' -hu ~ -hi	هُمَا ~ هِمَا '[the two of] them' -humaa ~ -himaa	هُمْ ~ هِمْ 'them' -hum ~ -him
Feminine	هَا 'her' -haa		هُنَّ ~ هِنَّ 'them' -hunna ~ -hinna

2.3.1 One-letter prepositions: *bi* and *li*-:

2.3.1.1 *bi-* + PRONOUN SUFFIX: Pronoun suffixes with *bi-* 'with, at, to, in' are regular, except for the third person "vowel-shift" pronouns (see 2.1.1), which are affected by the *kasra* of *bi-* and shift their *-u* vowel to *-i*:

أهلاً بكَ.
'ahl-an **bi-ka**.
Welcome **to you**.

ثقتُنا بهم
thiqat-u-naa **bi-him**
our confidence **in them**

لا بأس بِه
laa ba's-a **bi-hi**
not bad
('there is no harm **in it**')

2.3.1.2 *li-* —> *la-* PLUS PRONOUN SUFFIX: The preposition *li-* 'to, for' shifts its vowel to *-a* whenever it has a pronoun suffix, except for the long vowel suffix *-ii* 'me,' which supercedes any short vowel:

الشرف لَنا.
al-sharaf-u **la-naa**
The honor is ours ('to us').

لكَ سعر خاص.
la-ka *si'r-un xaaSS-un.*
For you, a special price.

هنيئاً لَكُم.
hanii'-an **la-kum**.
Congratulations **to you** (pl.).

لا معنى لَه.ُ
laa ma'naa **la-hu**.
It is meaningless ('there is no meaning **to it**').

أرسلوا لي طرداً.
'arsal-uu **l-ii** *Tard-an.*
They sent [to] me a package.

لم يكن لَهُم أي اتصال.
lam ya-kun **la-hum** *'ayy-u ittiSaal-in.*
They did not have any contact ('there was not **to them** any contact').

2.3.2 Two-letter prepositions: *fii, min, ʿan*

2.3.2.1 *fii* + PRONOUN SUFFIX: The preposition *fii* 'in, at, into,' because it ends in a long vowel *-ii*, undergoes a slight change when suffixed with the first person object pronoun *-ii*; the two long vowels merge into each other and become a *yaaʾ* with a *shadda* on it, followed by the short vowel *fatHa: fiyya* فيّ. In writing it is sometimes hard to tell the difference between *fii* and *fiyya*, but there is often a marked *shadda* added to the *yaaʾ* when *fiyya* is intended.

Otherwise, pronouns simply follow the long *-ii*, with the "vowel shift pronouns" changing their *-u* vowel to *-i*:

أذاب الحزن فيَّ.	فيه شمس جبلية.
*ʾadhaab-a l-huzn-a **fiyya**.*	*fii-hi shams-un jabaliyyat-un.*
It dissolved the sorrow **in me**.	There's a mountain sun there ('in it').

2.3.2.2 *min* + PRONOUN SUFFIX: The preposition *min* 'of; from; than' is fairly regular in its shape when pronoun suffixes are attached, except that when suffixed with the pronoun *-ii* 'me,' the *nuun* in *min* doubles, so that instead of *min-ii, the phrase 'from me' or 'than me' becomes ***min-nii***.

أحسن منَّي	كثيرون منْهُم
*ʾaHsan-u **min-nii***	*kathiir-uuna **min-hum***
better **than I**	many **of them**
هي أكثر مسؤولية منْه.	إثنتان منْها
*hiya ʾakthar-u masʾuuliyyat-an **min-hu**.*	*ithnataani **min-haa***
She is more responsible **than he is**.	two **of them**

2.3.2.3 *ʿan* + PRONOUN SUFFIX: Like *min*, the preposition *ʿan* 'away from; from; about; of ' maintains its shape when pronoun suffixes are attached, except that when suffixed with the pronoun *-ii* 'me,' the *nuun* in *ʿan* doubles, so that instead of **ʿan-ii, the phrase 'from me' or 'away from me' becomes ***ʿan-nii***.

هل سألتم عنّي؟	الإعلان عنْهُ
*hal saʾal-tum **ʿan-nii**?*	*al-ʾiʿlaan-u **ʿan-hu**.*
Did you (pl.) ask **about me**?	the announcing **of it**

ما قيل وما سيقال عنْهُم

*maa qiil-a wa-maa sa-yu-qaal-u **ʿan-hum***

what has been said and what will be said **about them**

2.3.3 Defective three-letter prepositions: ˀilaa, ˁalaa and semi-preposition ladaa

These three words are put in one category because they all have a final ˀalif maq-Suura, and all of them shift this ˀalif to a yaaˀ preceded by fatHa whenever they receive pronoun suffixes. Thus the attachable stem for ˀilaa is ˀilay-; for ˁalaa it is ˁalay- and for ladaa, laday-.

The shift to yaaˀ has an effect on certain pronoun suffixes. The "vowel-shift" pronouns change their -u vowel to -i, and the first person singular suffix -ii 'me' merges with the yaaˀ of the preposition stem, creating a double yaaˀ, which is followed by fatHa. A model paradigm using ˁalaa is presented here.

2.3.3.1 ˁalaa + PRONOUN SUFFIX

	Singular	Dual	Plural
First person	عليَّ ˁalay-ya		علينا ˁalay-naa
Second person Masculine	عليك ˁalay-ka	عليكما ˁalay -kumaa	عليكُم ˁalay-kum
Feminine	عليك ˁalay-ki		عليكنَّ ˁalay-kunna
Third person Masculine	عليه ˁalay-hi	عليهما ˁalay -himaa	عليهم ˁalay-him
Feminine	عليها ˁalay-haa		عليهنَّ ˁalay-hinna

كان عليَّ
kaan-a ˁalay-ya
it was [incumbent] on me

السلام عليكم.
al-salaam-u ˁalay-kum.
Peace [be] upon you.

كانت الأوضاع أفضل مما هي عليه الآن.
kaan-at-i l-ˀawDaaˁ-u ˀafDal-a mimmaa hiya ˁalay-hi l-ˀaan-a.
The conditions were better than what they are ('on it') now.

2.3.3.2 ˀilaa + PRONOUN SUFFIX

ينظر إليها.
ya-nZur-u ˀilay-haa.
He looks at her.

أنا أشتاق إليه.
ˀanaa ˀa-shtaaq-u ˀilay-hi.
I miss him ('I yearn for him').

2.3.3.3 *ladaa* + PRONOUN SUFFIX

لديه المستندات الرسمية.

laday-hi l-mustanadaat-u l-rasmiyyat-u.

He has the official documents.

لا مستقبل لدي.

laa mustaqbal-a laday-ya.

I have no future ('there is no future for me').

2.3.4 Semi-prepositions + pronoun suffixes

The locative adverbs or semi-prepositions may also take pronoun suffixes.

أثار حملة من الانتقادات ضدَّه.

'athaar-a Hamlat-an min-a l-intiqaadaat-i Didd-a-hu.

It aroused a campaign of criticisms **against him**.

عندي مشكلة.

'ind-ii mushkilat-un.

I have ('at-me') a problem.

على الأرض وفوْقها

'alaa l-'arD-i wa-fawq-a-haa

on the earth and **over it**

3 Reflexive expressions with *nafs* plus pronouns

Reflexive expressions in Arabic often use the noun *nafs* 'self; same' plus a pronoun suffix, the pronoun referring back to the subject of the verb.

يجدد نفسَه.

yu-jaddid-u nafs-a-hu.

It renews **itself**.

يستطيعون أن يفرضوا أنْفُسَهُم على المستوى العالمي.

ya-staTii'-uuna 'an ya-friD-uu 'anfus-a-hum 'alaa l-mustawaa l-'aalamiyy-i.

They can impose **themselves** on the world level.

4 Independent possessive pronoun: *dhuu* + noun

This pronoun refers to the possessor or owner of something and is used for expressing descriptive concepts where English would use the word "of" plus a noun, such as "of importance" "of means." It is also used for descriptive terms such as "bald-headed" or "two-humped" when describing creatures in terms of their distinctive features. It is used chiefly in conjunction with a noun, as first term of an *'iDaafa* with that noun. Occasionally it is followed by a pronoun suffix. The masculine form, *dhuu*, is inflected as one of the "five nouns" whose final vowel is also their inflectional vowel.[12] The feminine form, *dhaat*, inflects separately. Both paradigms are presented here.[13]

---

[12] See Chapter 7, section 5.4.1.c.

[13] There are several variants of this pronoun, but only the most commonly used forms in contemporary Arabic are presented here. See Wright 1967, I:265–66 for greater detail on the Classical Arabic forms of this pronoun.

'possessor of' (masculine) ذو *dhuu*		
	Singular	Dual	Plural
Nominative	ذو *dhuu*	ذَوا *dhawaa*	ذَوو *dhawuu*
Genitive	ذي *dhii*	ذَوَي *dhaway*	ذَوي *dhawii*
Accusative	ذا *dhaa*	ذَوَي *dhaway*	ذَوي *dhawii*

'possessor of' (feminine) ذات *dhaat*		
	Singular	Dual	Plural
Nominative	ذاتُ *dhaat-u*	ذاتا ~ ذواتا *dhawaataa ~* *dhaataa*	ذواتُ *dhawaat-u*
Genitive	ذاتِ *dhaat-i*	ذاتَيْ ~ ذواتَيْ *dhawaatay ~* *dhaatay*	ذواتِ *dhawaat-i*
Accusative	ذاتَ *dhaat-a*	ذاتَيْ ~ ذواتَيْ *dhawaatay ~* *dhaatay*	ذواتِ *dhawaat-i*

4.1 Masculine

النسر ذو الرأس الأبيض
al-nasr-u dhuu l-ra's-i l-'abyaD-i
the **bald-headed** eagle ('white-headed')

لذوي الدخل المحدود
li-dhawii l-daxl-i l-maHduud-i
for those [people] of limited incomes

الجمل ذو السنامين
al-jamal-u dhuu l-sanaam-ayni
the **two-humped** camel

سافر بعيدا عن ذويه.
saafar-a ba'iid-an 'an dhawii-hi.
He traveled far from his kin ('those of his').

4.2 Feminine

The feminine singular possessive pronoun (*dhaat*) is of frequent occurrence because of its use with nonhuman plurals.[14]

---

[14] Note that this instance of *dhaat* is not the same as the demonstrative use of *dhaat* (e.g., *dhaat-a yawm-in* 'one day') (see Chapter 13, section 4.2) or the substantive *dhaat* used to express "self" or "same" (e.g., *madH-u l-dhaat-i* 'self-praise') (see Chapter 9, section 5.1.2).

وصف المحادثات بأنها ذات قيمة.

waSaf-a **l-muHaadathaat-i** *bi-ʾanna-haa* **dhaat-u qiimat-in**.

He described **the talks** as worthwhile (**'of worth'**).

مصادر ذات علاقة بالموضوع

maSaadir-u dhaat-u ʿalaaqat-in bi-l-mawDuuʿ-i

sources that have a relationship with the subject

قال إن النتائج ستكون ذات أهمية.

qaal-a ʾ inna **l-nataaʾij-a** *sa-ta-kuun-u* **dhaat-a ʾahammiyyat-in**.

He said that **the results** will be **of importance**.

13

Demonstrative pronouns

Demonstrative pronouns (*'asmaa' al-'ishaara* أسماء الإشارة) are determiners used with nouns or instead of nouns to show either distance from or proximity to the speaker, like "this" and "that" in English. English has four demonstrative pronouns: "this," "that," "these," and "those." Arabic has a richer variety of demonstratives. In fact, Classical Arabic has a complex system of sets and subsets of demonstratives,[1] but in Modern Standard Arabic, the most commonly used ones are described as follows.

1 Demonstrative of proximity: 'this; these' هذا *haadhaa*

The demonstrative pronoun meaning 'this' or 'these' shows differences in gender and number, as well as inflection for case in the dual:

	Masculine	Feminine
Singular	هذا *haadhaa*	هذه *haadhihi*
Dual Nominative	هذان *haadh-aani*	هاتان *haat-aani*
Genitive/accusative	هذين *haadh-ayni*	هاتين *haat-ayni*
Plural	هؤلاء *haa'ulaa'i*	هـؤلاء *haa'ulaa'i*

Note that the plural demonstrative has no gender distinction and is used only when referring to human beings. For referring to nonhuman plurals, the feminine singular demonstrative is used.

---

[1] More extensive paradigms of demonstrative variants are provided in Wright 1967, I:264-70; Haywood and Nahmad 1962, 80-81; Thatcher 1942, 53-55; Blachère and Gaudefroy-Demombynes 1975, 200–203.

2 Demonstrative of distance: 'that; those' ذلك *dhaalika*

The demonstrative of distance "that" and "those" inflects for gender and number but is rarely used in the dual in MSA. These forms of the demonstrative are invariable and do not inflect for case.

	Masculine	Feminine
Singular	ذلكَ *dhaalika*	تِلكَ *tilka*
Plural	أُولَئك *ʾuulaaʾika*	أُولَئك *ʾuulaaʾika*

3 Functions of demonstratives

The demonstrative pronouns can be used independently, in phrases, or in clauses.

3.1 Independent use

A demonstrative can stand by itself as a noun substitute:

نجح في ذلك.
najaH-a fii dhaalika.
He succeeded in that.

على رغم ذلك
ʿalaa raghm-i dhaalika
despite that

حدث عن ذلك كله.
Haddath-a ʿan dhaalika kull-i-hi.
He spoke about all that.

لكن هذا لا يكفي.
laakinn-a haadhaa laa ya-kfii.
But this is not enough.

معنى هذا
maʿnaa haadhaa
the meaning of this

أقول هذا عن خبرة عملية.
ʾa-quul-u haadhaa ʿan xibrat-in ʿamaliyyat-in.
I say this from practical experience.

3.2 Demonstrative phrases

In a demonstrative phrase, the demonstrative pronoun forms a syntactic unit with a definite noun in order to convey the concept of particular proximity or distance. These pronouns are considered determiners of nouns (in some ways like the definite article).

In Arabic, the demonstrative phrase consists of a demonstrative pronoun + definite article + noun, as follows:

haadhaa + l- + lawn-u   = *haadhaa l-lawn-u*   هذا اللون
'this-the-color'   = this color

haadhihi + l + ziyaarat-u	= *haadhihi l-ziyaarat-u*	هذه الزيارة
'this-the-visit'	= this visit	

haaʾulaaʾi + l + naas-u	= *haaʾulaaʾi l-naas-u*	هؤلاء الناس
'these + the + people'	= these people	

Unlike English, then, the demonstrative phrase includes the definite article with the noun. If there is a modifying adjective, it follows the noun and agrees with it in gender, number, case and definiteness.

أثار هذا الكتاب اهتماماً.
ʾathaar-a haadhaa l-kitaab-u htimaam-an.
This book aroused interest.

في هذه المرحلة
fii haadhihi l-marHalat-i
at **this stage**

في هذا الصدد
fii haadhaa l-Sadad-i
in **this connection**

من هذه المناطق
min haadhihi l-manaaTiq-i
from **these regions**

في هذه الانتخابات
fii haadhihi l-intixaabaat-i
in **these elections**

هؤلاء الأشراف
haaʾulaaʾi l-ʾashraaf-u
these distinguished people

نقد موجه إلى أولئك الوزراء
naqd-un muwajjah-un ʾilaa ʾuulaaʾika l-wuzaraaʾ-i
a criticism directed toward **those ministers**

هؤلاء المسؤولون
haaʾulaaʾ i l-masʾuul-uuna
these officials

3.3 Demonstrative with second term of *ʾiDaafa*

The bond between the demonstrative pronoun and its noun is so tight that a demonstrative phrase is allowed to be used as the second term of an *ʾiDaafa*.[2]

قيمة هذه المخدرات
qiimat-u haadhihi l-muxaddiraat-i
the value of **these drugs**

تدمير تلك الفيروسات
tadmiir-u tilka l-fiiruusaat-i
the destruction of **those viruses**

3.4 Demonstrative with first term of *ʾiDaafa*

If a demonstrative is needed for the first term of an *ʾiDaafa*, it must follow the whole *ʾiDaafa*. It cannot attach itself to the first term of the *ʾiDaafa* because it must be followed by a noun with the definite article, whereas the first term of

---

[2] Normally, an *ʾiDaafa* cannot be interrupted by any word between the two nouns joined in the annexation structure.

an *'iDaafa* is stripped of the definite article and defined through the second term.

وجهة النظر هذه
wujhat-u l-naZar-i haadhihi
this point of view

مرحلة الجمود هذه
marHalat-u l-jumuud-i haadhihi
this stage of solidity

3.5 Demonstrative with possessed noun

A noun made definite by means of a suffixed possessive pronoun cannot be preceded by a demonstrative pronoun because in order to precede the noun, the demonstrative must be followed by the definite article. Since a noun with a possessive pronoun cannot have the definite article (it is definite by virtue of the suffix), the demonstrative follows:

في كتابه هذا
fii kitaab-i-hi haadhaa
in this book of his

تجربتي الأولى هذه
tajribat-ii l-'uulaa haadhihi
this first experience of mine

في منشوراتها   هذه
fii manshuuraat-i-haa haadhihi
in these publications of hers

أهمية الاكتشافات الحديثة هذه
*'ahammiyyat-u l-iktishaafaat-i l-Hadiithat-i
   haadhihi*
the importance of **these new discoveries**

3.6 Demonstratives with proper names

Proper names are considered definite even though many of them do not have a definite article. When referring to someone's name with a demonstrative, it follows the name:

كنت أشرت إلى خالد هذا.
kun-tu 'ashar-tu 'ilaa xaalid-in haadhaa.
I had referred to **this 'Khalid.'**

3.7 Demonstrative clauses

In a demonstrative clause, the demonstrative pronoun serves as the subject of the clause, followed by a complement or predicate. There is therefore a syntactic boundary between the demonstrative and the rest of the clause.

هذا قطي.
haadhaa qiTT-ii.
This [is] my cat.

وهذا اختلاف هام.ّ
wa-haadhaa xtilaaf-un haamm-un.
('And') this [is] an important difference.

هذا رأي يناقض الحقائق.
haadhaa ra'y-un yu-naaqiD-u l-Haqaa'iq-a.
This [is] an opinion that contradicts the facts.

Most often, the predicate of a sentence or clause with a demonstrative as the subject is indefinite, or a definite noun with a pronoun suffix.

A noun with a definite article may serve as the predicate of an equational sentence, but if preceded by a demonstrative pronoun, there normally needs to be a copula or pronoun of separation between the demonstrative and the definite noun to show that there is a syntactic boundary between them, and that they do not form a phrase (see below).

3.8 Demonstrative clause with pronoun of separation (copula)

Here the predicate of the equational sentence is a noun with a definite article. In order to show clearly that there is a separation between a demonstrative pronoun subject and the definite noun, a personal pronoun is inserted at the boundary between subject and predicate to act as a copula or substitute for a verb of being.

هذا هو الكتاب.

haadhaa **huwa** l-kitaab-u.

This **is** the book.

تلك هي نقطة البداية.

tilka **hiya** nuqTat-u l-bidaayat-i.

That **is** the starting point.

تلك هي الأجواء السائدة في الحزب.

tilka **hiya** l-ʾajwaaʾ-u l-saaʾidat-u fii l-Hizb-i.

Those **are** the atmospheres prevailing
    in the party.

تلك هي الأفكار.

tilka **hiya** l-ʾafkaar-u

Those **are** the ideas.

3.8.1 Omission of copula

Occasionally, the copula pronoun or pronoun of separation is omitted in the demonstrative clause, and the separation has to be deduced from the context.

هذه المرة الأولى التي يستقبل فيها الرئيس.

haadhihi **l-marrat-u l-ʾuulaa** llatii ya-staqabil-u fii-haa l-raʾiis-a.

This is **the first time** that he met the president.

كانت تلك المرة الأولى التي غادر فيها قريته.

kaan-at **tilka** l-marrat-a l-ʾuulaa llatii ghaadar-a fii-haa qaryat-a-hu.

This **was** the first time he had left his village.

4 Other demonstratives

4.1 dhaaka ذاك

The demonstrative **dhaaka** is a variant of *dhalika* and sometimes may be used to contrast with it.

4.1.1 As an independent word

تلك الشوفينية وذلك التعصب وذاك الانغلاق

tilka l-shuufiiniyyat-u wa-dhaalika l-taʿaSSub-u wa-dhaaka l-ʾinghilaaq-u

that chauvinism, **that** tribalism, and **that** obscurity

كان ذاك بالأمس.

kaan-a dhaaka bi-l-ʾams-i.

That was yesterday.

4.1.2 As a suffix

As a suffix on an accusative noun denoting 'time when':

انتهى الحدث يومذاك.	وتحدثوا يومذاك.
intahaa l-Hadath-u yawm-a-dhaaka.	*wa-taHaddath-uu yawm-a-dhaaka.*
The event ended **that day.**	They spoke **that day.**

وأطلق كتابه آنذاك تيارا من الاهتمام.

wa-ʾaTlaq-a kitaab-u-hu ʾaan-a-dhaaka tayyaar-an min-a l-ihtimaam-i.

His book evoked a current of interest **at that time.**

اكتشاف أمريكا سنتذاك كان الحدث الكبير.

iktishaaf-u ʾamriikaa sanat-a-dhaaka kaan-a l-Hadath-a l-kabiir-a.

The discovery of America **that year** was the great event.

4.2 Demonstrative *dhaat-a* ذات

This demonstrative indicates an indefinite distance in time or space and is used as the first term of an *ʾiDaafa* with an indefinite noun:

قبل أن تعرف ذات يوم أنها وارثة

qabl-a ʾan ta-ʿrif-a dhaat-a yawm-in ʾann-a-haa waarithat-un

before she found out **one day** that she was an heiress

4.3 Use of *haa* ها 'this'

The word *haa* is sometimes used as a shortened form of *haadhaa*. It implies an immediate perception, something like English "behold."

ها هي دولتكم.

haa hiya dawlat-u-kum.

This is your country/ **Here** is your country.

4.4 Locative demonstrative pronouns: *hunaa* هنا, *hunaaka* هناك and *hunaalika* هنالك 'here', 'there' and '(over) there'

These words are considered both adverbs and locative demonstrative pronouns, since they denote a place close to, distant from, or very distant from the speaker.

They are used widely in both written and spoken Arabic. Some examples are found in Chapter 11 on adverbs. Here are some others:

4.4.1 Locative *hunaa* هنا 'here'

هنا في المدينة
hunaa fii l-madiiindat-i
here, in the city

هل أخدت المفتاح من هنا؟
hal ʾaxadh-ta l-miftaaH-a min **hunaa?**
Did you take the key from here?

مستحيل أن نجد أحدا هنا.
mustaHiil-un ʾan na-jid-a ʾaHad-an **hunaa.**
[It is] impossible to find ('that we find') anyone here.

4.4.2 Locative *hunaaka* هناك 'there'

الطائرة هناك.
al-Taaʾirat-u **hunaaka.**
The plane is [over] there.

لا بد أن أكون هناك بعد خمس دقائق.
laa budd-a ʾan ʾa-kuun-a **hunaaka** *baʿd-a xams-i daqaaʾiq-a.*
I have to be there in five minutes.

4.4.3 Existential *hunaaka* هناك and *hunaalika* هنالك: 'there is, there are'

To convey the idea of existence Arabic uses the pronoun/adverb *hunaaka* 'there' paralleling the English use of "there is, there are." Occasionally the variant *hunaalika* is also used.

فهناك أولويات أهم.
fa-hunaaka ʾawwalawiyyaat-un ʾahamm-u.
There [are] more important priorities.

هنالك مثلا القصور.
hunaalika mathal-an-i l-quSuur-u.
There [are], for example, castles.

فهناك روايات عدة عما حدث للملكة.
fa-hunaaka riwaayaat-un ʿiddat-un ʿammaa Hadath-a li-l-malikat-i.
There [are] several stories about what happened to the queen.

14

Relative pronouns and relative clauses

Relative pronouns relate an element in a subordinate relative clause (in Arabic, al-Sila الصلة) to a noun or noun phrase in the main clause of a sentence. The Arabic relative pronoun (al-ism al-mawSuul الاسم الموصول) may be definite or indefinite. MSA uses nine forms of definite relative pronoun. Only the dual form of the definite relative pronoun shows difference in case. All, however, are marked for number and gender.

Relative clauses in Arabic are either definite or indefinite; definite clauses are introduced by a relative pronoun; indefinite relative clauses do not include a relative pronoun.

1 Definite relative pronouns

	Masculine	Feminine
Singular	الَّذي alladhii	الَّتي allatii
Dual Nominative	اللَّذانِ alladhaani	اللَّتانِ allataani
Genitive/Accusative	اللَّذَيْنِ alladhayni	اللَّتَيْنِ allatayni
Plural	الَّذينَ alladhiina	اللَّواتي ~ اللّاتي allaatii ~ allawaatii

As can be seen from the above paradigm the definite relative pronouns have a component that resembles the definite article, /al-/ /الـ/. They refer only to definite nouns and noun phrases. The initial /al-/ of the relative pronoun starts with hamzat al-waSl.

2 Definite relative clauses

A relative clause referring back to a definite antecedent uses the definite relative pronouns. The relative pronoun agrees with its antecedent in number and gender.

2.1 Singular relative pronoun

هي التي أرسلت الدكتورة.

hiya **llatii** *'arsal-at-i l-duktuur-a.*

She is **the one who** sent the doctor.

وهو الذي وضع المسمار الأخير.

wa-huwa **lladhii** *waDa'-a l-mismaar-a l-'axiir-a.*

And he is **the one who** put [in] the last nail.

المركز الجديد الذي أقيم في المدينة

al-markaz-u l-jadiid-u **lladhii** *'uqiim-a fii l-madiinat-i*

the new center **which** has been established in the city

2.2 Dual relative pronoun

In the dual, the relative pronoun agrees not only in gender and number with its antecedent, but also **in case.**

البرجان اللذان لا يزالان قائمين

al-burj-aani **lladhaani** *laa ya-zaal-aani qaa'im-ayni*

the two towers **which** remain standing

للزوجين اللذين ينتظران حدثا سعيدا

li-l-zawj-ayni **lladh-ayni** *ya-ntaZir-aani Hadath-an sa'iid-an*

for **the couple who** are awaiting a happy event

في الجلستين اللتين انعقدتا أمس

fii l-jalsat-ayni **llatayni** *n'aqad-ataa 'ams-i*

in the two sessions **that** were held yesterday

2.3 Plural relative pronoun

The plural relative pronoun is used only when referring to human beings.

السياح الذين يصلون كل يوم

al-siyyaaH-u **lladhiina** *ya-Sil-uuna kull-a yawm-in*

the tourists **who** arrive every day

النسوة اللواتي أرغمن على الإخلاء بالقوة

al-niswat-u **llawaatii** *'urghim-na 'alaa l-'ixlaa'-i bi l-quwwat-i*

the women **who** were compelled to evacuate by force

3 Indefinite relative clauses

A relative clause may refer to an indefinite noun or noun phrase in the main clause, in which case the **relative pronoun is omitted.**

The indefinite relative clause follows the main clause without any relative pronoun linking them. They are like two independent sentences implicitly linked because the second refers back to the first.

في زيارة لدمشق تستغرق أسبوعا

fii ziyaarat-in li-dimashq-a ta-staghriq-u ʾusbuuʿ-an

on **a visit** to Damascus [which] lasts a week

عثرت على هيكل عظمي فقد رأسه.

ʿathar-at ʿalaa haykal-in ʿaZmiyy-in faqad-a raʾs-a-hu.

She came upon **a skeleton** [which] had lost its head.

وأخيرا يظهر كرجل يمتلك الشجاعة.

wa-ʾaxiir-an ya-Zhur-u ka-rajul-in ya-mtalik-u l-shujaaʿat-a.

Finally, he appears as **a man** [who] possesses courage.

عن مصدر فلسطيني رفض الكشف عن اسمه

ʿan maSdar-in filisTiiniyy-in rafaD-a l-kashf-a ʿan-i sm-i-hi

from **a Palestinian source** [who] refused to disclose his name

4 Resumptive pronouns in relative clauses

When a relative clause in Arabic refers back to a noun or noun phrase in the main clause which is the object of a verb or a preposition (e.g., "the book that we read," "the house that I lived in"), a pronoun must be inserted in the relative clause to serve as the object of the verb or preposition, referring back to the object noun in the main phrase ["**the book** that we read **(it)**," *al-kitaab-u lladhii qaraʾ-naa-hu* الكتاب الذي قرأناه] "**the school** I studied at **(it)**" *al-madrasat-u llatii daras-tu fii-haa* المدرسة التي درست فيها).

This substitute pronoun is called in Arabic the *ʿaaʾid* عائد or *raajiʿ* راجع 'returner' and in English it is referred to as a **resumptive** pronoun. It occurs in definite and indefinite relative clauses that contain transitive verbs or prepositions referring back to an object in the main clause.

4.1 Resumptive pronoun in definite relative clauses

المكان الذي تقصده هنا.

al-makaan-u lladhii ta-qSid-u-hu hunaa.

The place **which** you seek **(it)** is here.

هذا بيت الرجل الذي نبحث عنـه.

*haadhaa bayt-u l-rajul-i **lladhii** na-bHath-u ᶜan-hu.*

This is the house of the man **whom** we are searching for (him).

العون الذي قدمتـه لأفغانستان

*al-ᶜawn-u **lladhii** qaddam-at-hu li-ʾafghaanistaan-a*

the aid **which** it has offered (it) to Afghanistan

حافظوا على المخطوطات التي أقنعوها.

*HaafaZ-uu ᶜalaa l-maxTuuT-aat-i **llatii** ʾaqnaᶜ-uu-haa.*

They kept the manuscripts **which** they had authenticated (them).

في معظم الدوائر التي كانت النتائج فيها نهائية

*fii muᶜZam-i l-dawaaʾir-i **llatii** kaan-at-i l-nataaʾij-u **fii-haa** nihaaʾiyyat-an*

in most of the precincts **in which** the results were final

في المكان الذي سقط فيه الصاروخ

*fii l-makaan-i **lladhii** saqaT-a **fii-hi** l-Saaruux-u*

at the place **where** the rocket fell (**into it**)

4.2 Resumptive pronoun in indefinite relative clauses

Indefinite relative clauses do not include relative pronouns, but they must include a resumptive pronoun if the clause refers back to a noun or noun phrase that is the object of a preposition or a verb.

وقال في مؤتمر صحافي عقده أمس

*wa-qaal-a fii muʾtamar-in SiHaafiyy-in **ᶜaqad-a-hu** ʾams-i.*

he said in a press conference [which] he held (it) yesterday

في اجتماع مغلق عقده زعيما الحزبين . . .

*fii jtimaaᶜ-in mughlaq-in **ᶜaqad-a-hu** zaᶜiim-aa l-Hizb-ayni*

in a closed meeting [which] the two leaders of the parties held (it)

5 Indefinite or non-specific relative pronouns: *maa* ما and *man* مَنْ

These pronouns refer to non-specified entities.

whoever; he/she who; one who	من *man*
whatever; what; that which	ماذا ~ ما *maa ~ maadhaa*

5.1 Use of *man* as indefinite pronoun

The pronoun *man* is used to refer to unspecified individuals. It may denote one person or a group but is usually treated grammatically as masculine singular.

يبيعها إلى **من** يحتاجها.

*ya-biiᶜ-u-haa ʾilaa **man** ya-Htaaj-u-haa.*

He sells it to **whomever** needs it.

هناك **من** يقول . . .

*hunaaka **man** ya-quul-u . . .*

there are **those** that say . . .

كان أول **من** رأى القمر.

*kaan-a ʾawwal-a **man** raʾaa l-qamar-a.*

He was the first [person] **who** saw the moon.

5.2 Use of *maa*: 'whatever; that which'

The relative pronoun *maa* functions in a wide variety of contexts.[1] Note that this use of *maa* is distinct from its use as an interrogative or negative particle.

ما بين النهرين

maa bayn-a l-nahr-ayni

Mesopotamia ('**that which** is between two rivers')

في **ما** يتعلق بالزراعة

*fii **maa** ya-taᶜallaq-u bi-l-ziraaᶜat-i*

in **whatever** relates to agriculture

ما لا نهاية

maa laa nihaayat-a

infinity ('**that which** has no end')

وقال **ما** يلي . . .

*wa-qaal-a **maa** ya-lii . . .*

(And) he said the following . . . ('**that which** follows')

فلم يحدث **ما** حدث في الشام.

*fa-lam ya-Hdath **maa** Hadath-a fii l-shaam-i.*

What happened in Syria has not happened [here].

ما قيل و**ما** سيقال عنه.

*maa qiil-a wa-**maa** sa-yu-qaal-u ᶜan-hu.*

What has been said and **what** will be said about it.

5.3 *maa* and *man* + resumptive pronoun

The indefinite pronouns *maa* and *man*, if they refer to the object of a verb or a preposition, are usually followed by a resumptive pronoun in the relative clause.[2]

هذا **ما** أقصده بالضبط.

*haadhaa **maa** ʾaqsid-u-**hu** bi-l-DabT-i.*

This is exactly **what** I mean (it).

شكره على **ما** قدمه.

*shakar-a-hu ᶜalaa **maa** qaddam-a-**hu**.*

He thanked him for **what** he offered (it).

---

[1] Wehr lists nine different uses of *maa* (1979, 1042) and Abboud et al. (1997, 47–49) list examples of all nine uses: negative *maa*, interrogative *maa*, relative *maa*, nominalizing *maa*, durative *maa*, exclamatory *maa*, indefinite *maa*, conditional *maa*, and redundant *maa*.

[2] Technically, a resumptive pronoun is not necessary after an indefinite pronoun that refers to an object of a verb, but it was used consistently in the data gathered for this book. See Abboud and McCarus 1983, part 1:588; MECAS 1965, 97.

تحصل على ما تحتاجـه.

ta-HSul-u ʿalaa **maa** *ta-Htaaj-u-hu.*

They get **what** they need (it).

فأوضحت ما تقصده.

fa-ʾawDaH-at **maa** *ta-qSid-u-hu.*

So she explained **what** she meant (it).

5.4 *maadhaa* as relative pronoun

Sometimes the particle *maadhaa* 'what' is used instead of *maa*, especially when the use of *maa* (which also functions as a negative particle) may be confusing:

يعرف ماذا يريد حقاً.

ya-ʿrif-u **maadhaa** *yu-riid-u Haqq-an.*

He really knows **what** he wants.

5.5 Use of *maa* for approximation

Used with numbers, amounts, and times, *maa* serves as a pronoun that can link a prepositional or verbal phrase to a previous statement by indicating approximation:

يستغرق ما بين شهرين وثلاثة.

ya-staghriq-u **maa** *bayn-a shahr-ayni wa-thalaathat-in.*

It will last (**what is approximately**) between two and three months.

قد يصل إلى ما بين ثلاثمئة وأربعمئة ألف شخص.

qad ya-Sil-u ʾilaa **maa** *bayn-a thalaath-i-miʾat-i wa-ʾarbaʿ-i-miʾat-i ʾalf-i shaxS-in.*

It might reach (**what is approximately**) between 300 and 400 thousand people.

يستطيع الجمل أن يشرب ما حجمـه من الماء.

ya-staTiiʿ-u l-jamal-u ʾan ya-shrab-a **maa** *Hajam-a-hu min-a l-maaʾ-i.*

The camel can drink his weight (**what approximately** his weight is) **in water.**

يتوجب الانتظار إلى ما بعد يوم السبت.

ya-tawajjab-u l-intiZaar-u ʾilaa **maa** *baʿd-a yawm-i l-sabt-i.*

It is necessary to wait until (**approximately what is**) after Saturday.

5.6 *maa* 'a certain; some, one'

The relative pronoun *maa* is also used following a noun to emphasize its indefiniteness or non-particularity, as in the following expressions:

غيرت موقفها إلى حد ما.

ghayyar-at mawqif-a-haa ʾilaa Hadd-in **maa.**

She changed her position **to a certain extent.**

سيرجع يوما ما.

sa-ya-rjiʿ-u **yawm-an maa.**

He will come back **one day.**

لماذا تحب فناناً ما؟

li-maadhaa tu-Hibb-u **fannaan-an maa?**

Why do you like **a certain artist?**

5.7 *mimmaa* مـمّا

The contracted phrase *mimmaa (min + maa)* may be used instead of the simple *maa* when referring to a preceding situation or condition:

مما أمن له اتصالا دائما

mimmaa ʾamman-a la-hu ttiSaal-an daaʾ im-an

which guaranteed him a permanent connection

مما يؤدي إلى إعطاء المجلة طابعا أدبيًّا

mimmaa yu-ʾaddii ʾ ilaa ʾiʿTaaʾ-i l-majallat-i Taabiʿ-an ʾadabiyy-an

which leads to giving the journal a literary character

مما يعني أن كلفة المشروع

mimmaa ya-ʿnii ʾanna kalfat-a l-mashruuʿ-i

which means that the cost of the project

5.8 *bi-maa fii* بما في + pronoun 'including'

This common idiomatic expression includes the indefinite pronoun *maa*:

يجري اتصالات مع جميع الأطراف بما فيها حكومة إسرائيل.

*yu-jrii ttiSaalaat-in maʿ-a jamiiʿ-i l-ʾaTraaf-i **bi-maa fii-haa** Hukuumat-i ʾisraaʾiil-a.*

He is in communication ('conducting contacts') with all the parties **including** the government of Israel.

15

Numerals and numeral phrases

The Arabic numeral system has been described as "somewhat complicated" (Cowan 1964, 182), "assez complexe ('rather complex')" (Kouloughli 1994, 121), "one of the trickiest features of written Arabic" (Haywood and Nahmad 1962, 301), as having "a special difficulty" (Cantarino 1975, II:361), and it has been said that the numerals "do not readily lend themselves to inductive analysis" (Ziadeh and Winder 1957, 148). These observations provide an indication of the complexity of a system which is important to understand but also challenging in the diversity of its categories and rules.

Provided here is an outline of the general structure of the morphology and syntax of MSA numerals, with examples taken from various contemporary contexts.[1] The rules and examples are presented in numerical order, cardinal numerals first and then ordinal numerals.[2]

1 Cardinal numerals (al-ʾaʿdaad الأعداد)

The Arabic numerals "zero" through "ten" are listed as follows. To some extent there is resemblance with what are termed "Arabic" numbers in English, but the system is adapted from the Hindi numeral system and has significant differences.

zero	0	Sifr[3]	٠	صفر
one	1	waaHid	١	واحد
two	2	ithnaan	٢	اثنان
three	3	thalaatha	٣	ثلاثة
four	4	ʾarbaʿa	٤	أربعة
five	5	xamsa	٥	خمسة

---

[1] I am grateful to my colleague, Dr. Muhsin Esseesy, for reading, correcting, and commenting on this chapter. See also Esseesy 2000.
[2] For further reading on the morphology and syntax of Arabic numbers, see Abboud and McCarus 1983, Part 1:410–21; Cantarino 1975, II:361–98; Cowan 1964, 182–90; Haywood and Nahmad 1962, 301–26; Wright 1967, II:234–49.
[3] Cognate with English 'cipher.'

six	6	*sitta*	٦	ستّة
seven	7	*sabʿa*	٧	سبعة
eight	8	*thamaaniya*	٨	ثمانية
nine	9	*tisʿa*	٩	تسعة
ten	10	*ʿashra*	١٠	عشرة

The numerals "one" and "two" have special features. "One" has two forms: an adjectival (*waaHid*) and a noun (or pronoun) form (*ʾaHad*), used in different ways. The numeral "two" is special because of the independent and extensive nature of the dual category in Arabic morphology. The numerals three to ten, on the other hand, are all nouns.

1.1 The numeral "one"

1.1.1 *waaHid* واحد and *waaHida* واحدة

The numeral 'one' *waaHid* has the morphological pattern of an active participle of Form I (*faaʿil*). It behaves syntactically as an adjective, following the counted noun, and agreeing with it in case and gender.

في وقت واحد
fii waqt-in waaHid-in
at **one time**

بهدفين مقابل هدف واحد
bi-hadaf-ayni muqaabil-a hadaf-in waaHid-in
with two goals as opposed to **one goal**

هل لهذا البلد أكثر من اسم واحد؟
hal li-haadhaa l-balad-i ʾakthar-u min-i sm-in waaHid-in?
Does this country have more than **one name**?

قبل أن يخفف العقوبة إلى سنة واحدة فقط
qabl-a ʾan yu-xaffif-a l-ʿuquubat-a ʾilaa sanat-in waaHidat-in faqaT
before he lightened the penalty to **one year** only

1.1.2 'One of': *ʾaHad* أحد and *ʾiHdaa* إحدى

This form of "one" is usually used when expressing the notion "one of."[4] It is a noun that forms the first term of an *ʾiDaafa* or genitive construct, with the

---

[4] However, *waaHid min* is also occasionally found for the expression of "one of":

المنطقة كلها واحدة من أقلّ مناطق الجزائر سكّاناً.
al-minTaqat-u kull-u-haa waaHidat-un min ʾaqall-i manaaTiq-i l-jazaaʾir-i sukkaan-an.
The entire region is **one of the lowest-populated** in Algeria.

إلى واحد من أهمّ الفنون المعاصرة
ʾilaa waaHid-in min ʾahamm-i l-funuun-i l-muʿaaSirat-i
to **one of the most important contemporary arts**

following noun in the genitive dual or plural, or pronoun, which is dual or plural. The masculine form, ʾaHad, is triptote; the feminine form, ʾiHdaa, is invariable.

1.1.2.1 ʾaHad أحد:

أحد النوّاب المستقلّين

ʾaHad-u l-nuwwaab-i l-mustaqill-iina

one of the independent deputies

في أحد مستشفيات جدة

fii ʾaHad-i mustashfayaat-i jiddat-a

in one of the hospitals of Jidda

أحد مستشاري الرئيس

ʾaHad-u mustashaar-ii l-raʾiis-i

one of the president's counselors

أحدهم أصيب.

ʾaHad-u-hum ʾuSiib-a.

One of them was hit.

قدّم أحد أعضاء المؤتمر اقتراحاً.

qaddam-a ʾaHad-u ʾaʿDaaʾ-i l-muʾtamar-i qtiraaH-an.

One of the members of the conference offered a proposal.

1.1.2.2 ʾiHdaa إحدى: The feminine numeral ʾiHdaa is invariable in case:

في إحدى هذه المحاولات

fii ʾiHdaa haadhihi l-muHaawalaat-i

in one of these attempts

إحدى مدن المنطقة

ʾiHdaa mudun-i l-minTaqat-i

one of the cities of the region

إحدى مهام هذه اللجنة

ʾiHdaa mahaamm-i haadhihi l-lajnat-i

one of the tasks of this committee

1.1.2.3 'NO ONE, NOBODY; NEITHER ONE': Used with a negative verb, ʾaHad is equivalent to 'no one' or 'nobody':

قالت إنّ أحداً لا يستطيع أن يوقّفهم.

qaal-at ʾinna ʾaHad-an laa ya-staTiiʿ-u ʾan yu-waqqif-a-hum.

She said that no one could stop them.

لم يكن أحد من الأسرة المالكة في القصر.

lam ya-kun ʾaHad-un min-a l-ʾusrat-i l-maalikat-i fii l-qaSr-i.

No one from the royal family was in the castle.

ليس في استطاعة أحدنا أن يعيش من دون الآخر.

lays-a fii stiTaaʿat-i ʾaHad-i-naa ʾan ya-ʿiish-a min duun-i l-ʾaaxar-i.

Neither one of us can live without the other.

1.2 The numeral 'two' *ithnaan* اثنان and *ithnataan* اثنتان

The numeral "two" has both feminine and masculine forms and it also inflects for case.

	Masc.	Fem.
Nominative	اثنان *ithnaani*	اثنتان *ithnataani*
Genitive	اثنين *ithnayni*	اثنتين *ithnatayni*
Accusative	اثنين *ithnayni*	اثنتين *ithnatayni*

The genitive and accusative forms of inflection are identical, putting the numeral "two" into the two-way inflection category, just like the dual suffix on nouns and adjectives. Note that the initial vowel on *ithnaan* is a *hamzat al-waSl*, not a strong *hamza* (*hamzat al-qaT͑*).

1.2.1 The dual (*al-muthannaa* المثنّى)

The numeral "two" is rarely used for counting purposes because of the existence of the dual category in the Arabic grammatical system. Two of anything is a separate inflectional class and receives a separate inflectional suffix: *-aani* (nominative) or *-ayni* (genitive/accusative). Note that dual agreement (pronouns, verbs, adjectives) follows a dual noun. See Chapter 7, sections 3.1 and 5.4.2.1., subsection (1) for further discussion of dual inflection.

1.2.1.1 MASCULINE DUAL: The masculine dual is used to refer to masculine nouns or a mix of feminine and masculine.

دخل الملكان.
daxal-a l-malik-aani.
The **two rulers** entered.
(Here, referring to a king and queen.)

بين البلدين
bayn-a l-balad-ayni
between the **two countries**

وقد وُجد طابقان بُنيا من الحجارة.
*wa-qad wujid-a **Taabaq-aani** buniy-aa min-a l-Hijaarat-i.*
Two **floors** were found **built** of stone.

تحمل بـتوأمين.
*ta-Hmil-u **bi-taw͗am-ayni**.*
She is pregnant with **twins**.

1.2.1.2 FEMININE DUAL

أمّا المدينتـان الأخريـان
ʾammaa l-madiinat-aani l-ʾuxray-aani
as for the other two cities

الدولتـان العظميـان
al-dawlat-aani l-ʿuZmay-aani
the two super powers

خلال السنتين الماضيتين
xilaal-a l-sanat-ayni l-maaDiyat-ayni
during the past two years

1.2.1.3 DUAL OF DEMONSTRATIVE PRONOUNS: Demonstrative pronouns also have dual forms. When modifying dual nouns, they agree in duality, case, and gender:

من هذين الصحـافيَّين
min haadh-ayni l-SiHaafiyy-ayni
from these two journalists

أعضـاء هاتين اللـجنتين
ʾaʿDaaʾ-u haat-ayni l-lajnat-ayni
the members of these two committees

1.2.1.4 *nuun*-DELETION: When a dual noun is the first term of an annexation structure, or if it has a pronoun suffix, the *nuun* (and its short vowel *kasra*) of the dual suffix is deleted:

عنوانا الكتابين
ʿunwaan-aa l-kitaab-ayni
the [two] titles of the two books

في كتفي الثور
fii kitf-ay-i l-thawr-i
in the two shoulders of the bull

في وادي نهري دجلة والفرات
fii waadii nahr-ay dijlat-a wa-l-furaat-i
in the valley of the two rivers, the Tigris and the Euphrates

1.2.1.5 DUAL FOR EMPHASIS AND DISAMBIGUATION: Occasionally the number "two" is used explicitly in order to emphasize, distinguish two among others, or disambiguate.

فاثنتان منها تُعتبران معقلاً للمعارضة.
fa-thnataani min-haa tu-ʿtabar-aani maʿqil-an li-l-muʿaaraDat-i.
(For) two of them [cities] are considered a stronghold for the opposition.

تضمّ ممثّلين اثنين عن كل جانب.
ta-Dumm-u mumaththil-ayni thnayni ʿan kull-i jaanib-in.
It includes two representatives from each side.*

*Here, the word *thnayn* is added to clarify the status of the word *mumaththil-ayni* ممثّلين because in unvoweled Arabic script it looks identical to the plural, *mumaththil-iina* ممثّلين.

1.2.1.6 'BOTH' *kilaa* AND *kiltaa* The words *kilaa* (m.) and *kiltaa* (f.) are quantifiers used to express the concept of "both." These words are related to the noun *kull* 'all,' and are not part of the numeral system, but are considered to have numerative meaning. They are specifically dual and followed either by a noun in the dual or by a dual pronoun suffix.

When followed by a noun they do not inflect for case; when followed by a pronoun, they do inflect for case.

in both cases	*fii **kiltaa** l-Haalat-ayni*	في كلتا الحالتين
with both his (two) hands	*bi-**kiltaa** yad-ay-hi*	بكلتا يديه
both of them (m.)	***kilaa**-humaa*	كلاهما
with both of them	*bi-**kil-ay-himaa***	بكليهما

For further discussion of *kilaa* and *kiltaa*, see Chapter 9, section 1.3.

1.3 Numerals three to ten

Arabic numerals three to ten have two distinctive characteristics: first, they are followed by a plural noun in the genitive case, and second, they show **gender polarity**, or reverse gender agreement with the counted noun. That is, if the singular noun is masculine, the numeral will have the feminine marker *taaʾ marbuuTa*, and if the singular noun is feminine, the numeral will be in the masculine form.

The numerals three to ten are as follows:

Used for counting f. nouns		**Used for counting m. nouns**	
thalaath	ثلاث	*thalaatha*	ثلاثة
ʾarbaᶜ	أَرْبَع	*arbaᶜa*	أَرْبَعة
xams	خَمْس	*xamsa*	خَمْسَة
sitt	ستّ	*sitta*	ستّة
sabᶜ	سَبْع	*sabᶜa*	سَبْعة
thamaanin[5]	ثَمانٍ	*thamaaniya*	ثَمانية
tisᶜ	تِسْع	*tisᶜa*	تِسْعة
ᶜashr	عَشْر	*ᶜashara*	عَشْرة

---

[5] The numeral 'eight' *thamaanin*, is defective in the masculine gender (the feminine form, ending in *taaʾ marbuuTa*, is triptote, or regular in declension). As an indefinite defective noun it declines as follows: nominative and genitive have identical form: *thamaan-in*; accusative has the form *thamaaniy-an*; as a definite noun, the nominative and genitive are also identical: *thamaanii*, and the accusative definite form is *thamaaniy-a*. See the declension for defective nouns in Chapter 7, section 5.4.3

In recitation form, in counting without a counted noun, or in referring to a specific numeral alone, the form with *taa' marbuuTa* is usually used. For example:

رقم ستّة هو رقم سحريّ.

raqm-u sittat-in huwa raqm-un siHriyy-un.
The **number six** is a magic number.

واحد، إثنان، ثلاثة!

*waaHid-un, ithnaani, **thalaathat-un**!*
One, two **three**!

1.3.1 Three to ten counted nouns

Counted noun phrases from three to ten have two forms, definite ("the five houses") and indefinite ("five houses"). If an adjective follows the counted noun ("the five large houses; five large houses"), it agrees with the noun in case, gender, and definiteness. For nonhuman plural nouns, the adjective is feminine singular and for human nouns, the adjective is plural.

1.3.1.1 INDEFINITE COUNTED NOUN: With an indefinite counted item, the numeral shows reverse gender agreement and precedes the counted noun. The case marker on the numeral varies according to its role in the sentence and it is considered definite because it is in an *'iDaafa* relationship with the noun, so the case ending on the numeral is in definite form (i.e., it does not take nunation). The counted noun itself is plural, indefinite, and in the genitive case.

(1) **Feminine noun = masculine numeral form**

ثلاث مخطوطات
thalaath-u maxTuuTaat-in (singular *maxTuuTa* مخطوطة)
three manuscripts

ثلاث قصائد
thalaath-u qaSaa'id-a (singular *qaSiida* قصيدة)
three odes

نقرأ ثلاث مقابلات.
*na-qra'-u **thalaath-a** muqaabalaat-in.* (singular *muqaabala* مقابلة)
We are reading **three interviews.**

ثلاث آبار عميقة
thalaath-u 'aabaar-in 'amiiqat-in (singular *bi'r* بئر)[6]
three deep wells

---

[6] The singular of "well" (*bi'r*) looks masculine but is actually cryptofeminine.

خمس مرّات في اليوم

xams-a marraat-in fii l-yawm-i (singular *marra* مرّة)

five times a day

ضمن ستّ فرق عمل

*Dimn-a **sitt-i firaq-i** ʿamal-in* (singular *firqa* فرقة)

within **six working groups**

لمدّة ثماني ساعات

*li-muddat-i **thamaanii saaʿaat-in*** (singular *saaʿa* ساعة)

for a period of **eight hours**

سرقوا تسع سيّارات.

*saraq-uu **tisʿ-a sayyaaraat-in**.* (singular *sayyaara* سيّارة)

They stole nine cars.

(2)   **Masculine noun = feminine numeral form**

أربعة خناجر

ʾarbaʿat-u xanaajir-a (singular *xanjar* خنجر)

four daggers

خمسة دراهم

xamsat-u daraahim-a (singular *dirham* درهم)

five dirhams

بسرعة ستة كيلومترات في الثانية

*bi-surʿat-i **sittat-i kiiluumitraat-in** fii l-thaaniyat-i* (singular *kiiluumitr* كيلومتر)

at the rate of **six kilometers** per second

وأضافت أنّ سبعة أشخاص اعتقلوا.

*wa-ʾaDaaf-at ʾanna **sabʿat-a ʾashxaaS-in** uʿtuqil-uu.* (singular *shaxS* شخص)

It added that **seven persons** were detained.

إلى مسافة عشرة أمتار

*ʾilaa masaafat-i **ʿasharat-i ʾamtaar-in*** (singular *mitr* متر)

to a distance of **ten meters**

(3)   **Indefinite counted noun plus adjective:**

لنا ثلاثة احتياجات أساسية.

*la-naa **thalaathat-u Htiyaajaat-in ʾasaasiyyat-in**.* (singular *iHtiyaaj* احتياج)

We have three basic needs.

لـثلاثة مواسم متتالية

li-thalaathat-i mawaasim-a mutataaliyat-in (singular *mawsim* موسم)

for **three successive seasons**

يستقبل أربعة سفراء جدد.

ya-staqbil-u ʾarbaʿat-a sufaraaʾ-a judud-in. (singular *safiir* سفير)

He welcomes **four new ambassadors.**

خمسة مؤتمرات دولية

xamsat-u muʾtamaraat-in duwaliyyat-in (singular *muʾtamar* مؤتمر)

five international conferences

(4) **Indefinite with definite meaning:** This can occur when a numeral is used with a superlative expression, where the superlative adjective is followed by an indefinite plural noun.[7]

في أهمّ أربع مدن

fii ʾahamm-i ʾarbaʿ-i mudun-in

in the most important **four cities**

(5) **Indefinite noun with following numeral:** Rarely, an indefinite counted noun will precede the numeral. The numeral still shows reverse gender, but in this position it is in apposition with the noun and takes the same case as the noun:

من خلال جلسات ثلاث

min xilaal-i jalasaat-in thalaath-in (singular *jalsa* جلسة)

through **three sessions**

خلال عقود ثلاثة

xilaal-a ʿuquud-in thalaathat-in (singular *ʿaqd* عقد)

during **three decades**

(6) **Indefinite numeral followed by** *min* **'of':** When indicating a specific number of items among a larger number, an indefinite form of the numeral may be used followed by *min* 'of' and a definite noun or noun phrase:

يضمّ أربعة من وزراء النفط.

ya-Dumm-u ʾarbaʿat-an min wuzaraaʾ-i l-nifT-i.

It includes **four of** the petroleum ministers.

---

[7] For further discussion of this point, see Chapter 10, section 4.2.4.

1.3.1.2 DEFINITE COUNTED NOUN: In the definite form, the numeral is in apposition with the noun. It follows the noun, it agrees with the noun in case, it has the definite article, and it shows reverse gender agreement.

(1)   **Masculine noun:** With a noun that is masculine in the singular, a feminine numeral form is used:

أركان الإسلام الخمسة

ʾarkaan-u l-ʾislaam-i l-xamsat-u (singular *rukn* ركن)

the **five pillars** of Islam

طوال العقود الثلاثة الأخيرة

Tiwaal-a l-ʿuquud-i l-thalaathat-i l-ʾaxiirat-i (singular *ʿaqd* عقد)

during the last **three decades**

وزراء النفط الستة

wuzaraaʾ-u l-nifT-i l-sittat-u (singular *waziir* وزير)

the **six** oil **ministers**

(2)   **Feminine noun:** With a noun that is feminine in the singular, the masculine form of the numeral is used:

الجهات الأربع الأصلية

al-jihaat-u l-ʾarbaʿ-u l-ʾaSliyyat-u (singular *jiha* جهة)

the **four** cardinal **directions**

دقّات القلب الخمس

daqqaat-u l-qalb-i l-xams-u (singular *daqqa* دقّة).

the **five heartbeats**

في القارّات الخمس

fii l-qaarraat-i l-xams-i (singular *qaarra* قارّة)

on **the five continents**

بين ممثلي هذه الصحف السبع

bayn-a mumaththil-ii haadhihi l-SuHuf-i l-sabʿ-i (singular *SaHiifa* صحيفة)

among the representatives of **these seven newspapers**

(3)   **Definite counted noun with following adjective:** When a definite counted noun is modified by an adjective, the adjective follows the numeral and agrees with the noun in gender, case, and definiteness. For nonhuman nouns, the plural form of the adjective is feminine singular; for human nouns, the adjective is plural in form.

بين ألوان الطيف السبعة المعروفة

bayn-a ʾalwaan-i l-Tayf-i l-sabʿat-i l-maʿruufat-i (singular *lawn* لون)

among **the seven known colors** of the spectrum

أوضـح أنّ الفـائزين الخمسة الأوائل في المسابقة سوف يمثّلـون بلادهم.

ʾawDaH-a ʾanna l-faaʾiz-iina l-xamsat-a l-ʾawaaʾil-a fii l-musaabaqat-i sawfa yu-maththil-uuna bilaad-a-hum. (singular *faaʾiz* فائز)

He declared that **the first five winners** in the match would represent their country.

1.3.2 Plural numerals

The numerals taken in groups, such as "tens" are made plural with the sound feminine plural marker -*aat*:

حطموا عشرات الأرقام القياسية.

HaTam-uu ʿasharaat-i l-ʾarqaam-i l-qiyaasiyyat-i.

They broke **tens of records**.

1.4 Numerals eleven and twelve

The numerals eleven and twelve start the teens number series.[8] In this set of numerals, the numeral names are compounds, that is, they are formed of two parts, the first part referring to the first digit and the second part always some form of the word "ten" (*ʿashar* or *ʿashra*).

Eleven: The numeral eleven is **invariable in case**, being **accusative at all times**. The first component of the compound number is the word *ʾaHad* (m.) أحد or *ʾiHdaa* (f.) إحدى, rather than the word *waaHid*. Both parts of the compound numeral show the same gender.

Twelve: The numeral twelve shows **two case inflections, nominative and genitive-accusative**, along the lines of the numeral "two" and the dual. Both parts of the compound numeral show the same gender.

	Masculine	Feminine
eleven	أحد عشر *ʾaHad-a* *ʿashar-a*	إحدى عشرة *ʾiHdaa* *ʿashrat-a*
twelve nominative	اثنا عشر *ithn-aa* *ʿashar-a*	اثنتا عشرة *ʾithnat-aa* *ʿashrat-a*
twelve genitive- accusative	اثني عشر *ithn-ay* *ʿashar-a*	اثنتي عشرة *ithnat-ay* *ʿashrat-a*

---

[8] In contemporary newspaper Arabic, numerals over ten tend to be in figures rather than spelled out in words. In this chapter the numbers are converted into spelled-out numerals in order to illustrate how they are pronounced and how the numeral system works.

When used in a counted noun phrase, **both components of the compound numerals eleven and twelve agree with the counted noun in gender.** They do **not** show gender polarity. They are followed by a noun in the **accusative singular.** This accusative is a form of *tamyiiz,* or "accusative of specification."[9]

1.4.1 Indefinite counted nouns

1.4.1.1 FEMININE COUNTED NOUN = FEMININE ELEVEN OR TWELVE:

ثمنها إحدى عشرة ليرة.

thaman-u-haa 'iHdaa ʿashrat-a liirat-an.

Its price is **eleven liras/pounds.**

ثمنها اثنتا عشرة ليرة.

*thaman-u-haa **thnat-aa** ʿashrat-a liirat-an.*

Its price is **twelve liras/pounds.**

بُنيت قبل إحدى عشرة سنة.

buniy-at qabl-a 'iHdaa ʿashrat-a sanat-an.

It was built **eleven years** ago.

بُنيت قبل اثنتي عشرة سنة.

*buniy-at qabl-a **thnat-ay** ʿashrat-a sanat-an.*

It was built **twelve years** ago.

1.4.1.2 MASCULINE NOUN = MASCULINE ELEVEN OR TWELVE:

ثمنها أحد عشر درهماً.

thaman-u-haa 'aHad-a ʿashar-a dirham-an.

Its price is **eleven dirhams.**

ثمنها اثنا عشر درهماً.

*thaman-u-haa **thn-aa** ʿashar-a dirham-an.*

Its price is **twelve dirhams.**

بُنيت قبل أحد عشر عاماً.

buniy-at qabl-a 'aHad-a ʿashar-a ʿaam-an.

It was built **eleven years** ago.

بُنيت قبل اثني عشر عاماً.

*buniy-at qabl-a **thn-ay** ʿashar-a ʿaam-an.*

It was built **twelve years** ago.

1.4.2 Definite counted nouns with eleven and twelve

When the counted noun is definite, the **numeral eleven or twelve follows the plural noun** and the definite article is affixed to the first part of the numeral only. The case marker of the noun varies depending on the role of the noun in the sentence; the case marker on eleven is always accusative; the case marker on the first part of the numeral twelve varies according to the case of the noun it modifies.

---

[9] For further discussion of the *tamyiiz* structure see Chapter 7, section 5.3.3.7, and Chapter 11, section 6.

1.4.2.1 MASCULINE DEFINITE PLURAL NOUN:

حضر السفراء الأحد عشر.

HaDar-a l-sufaraaʾ-u l-ʾaHad-a ʿashar-a.

The eleven ambassadors came.

حضر السفراء الاثنا عشر.

HaDar-a l-sufaraaʾ-u l-thn-aa ʿashr-a.

The twelve ambassadors came.

يستقبل السفراء الأحد عشر.

ya-staqbil-u l-sufaraaʾ-a l-ʾaHad-a ʿashar-a.

He is welcoming the eleven ambassadors.

يستقبل السفراء الاثني عشر.

ya-staqbil-u l-sufaraaʾ-a l-thnayʿashar-a.

He is welcoming the twelve ambassadors.

1.4.2.2 FEMININE DEFINITE NOUN:

حضرت الأستاذات الإحدى عشرة.

HaDar-at-i l-ʾustaadhaat-u l-ʾiHdaa ʿashrat-a.

The eleven professors (f.) came.

حضرت الأستاذات الاثنتا عشرة.

HaDar-at-i l-ʾustaadhaat-u l-ithnat-aa ʿasharat-a.

The twelve professors (f.) came.

يستقبل الأستاذات الإحدى عشرة.

ya-staqbil-u l-ʾustaadhaat-i l-iHdaa ʿashrat-a.

He is welcoming the eleven professors (f.).

يستقبل الأستاذات الاثنتي عشرة.

ya-staqbil-u l-ʾustaadhaat-i l-ithnat-ay ʿashrat-a.

He is welcoming the twelve professors (f.).

1.5 Numbers thirteen to nineteen

The group of "teens" numerals are similar to the numeral eleven in that they are **invariably** in the **accusative case** and are followed by a **singular accusative** noun. They are unlike eleven and twelve in that the **first part of the compound number shows gender polarity** with the counted noun, while the **second part of the compound number shows direct gender agreement** with the counted noun.

That is, the first element, three to nine, behaves in gender like the cardinal numbers three to nine. The second element behaves more like an adjective, agreeing with the counted noun in gender.

With feminine counted noun:		With masculine counted noun:
thirteen	ثلاثَ عَشْرَةَ	ثلاثةَ عَشَرَ
	thalaath-a ʿashrat-a	*thalaathat-a ʿashar-a*
fourteen	أَرْبعَ عَشْرَةَ	أَرْبَعةَ عَشرَ
	ʾarbaʿ-a ʿashrat-a	*ʾarbaʿat-a ʿashar-a*
fifteen	خمْسَ عَشْرَةَ	خمْسةَ عَشرَ
	xams-a ʿashrat-a	*xamsat-a ʿashar-a*
sixteen	ستَّ عَشْرَةَ	ستةَ عَشرَ
	sitt-a ʿashrat-a	*sittat-a ʿashar-a*
seventeen	سبْعَ عَشْرَةَ	سبْعةَ عَشرَ
	sabʿ-a ʿashrat-a	*sabʿat-a ʿashar-a*
eighteen	ثمانيَ عَشْرَةَ	ثمانيةَ عَشرَ
	thamaaniy-a ʿashrat-a	*thamaaniyat-a ʿashar-a*
nineteen	تسْعَ عَشْرَةَ	تسْعةَ عَشرَ
	tisʿ-a ʿashrat-a	*tisʿat-a ʿashar-a*

1.5.1 Indefinite counted noun

يبلغ طوله ثلاثة عشر مترًا.

ya-blugh-u Tuul-u-hu **thalaathat-a ʿashar-a** *mitr-an.*

Its length reaches **thirteen meters.**

فازوا بأربع عشرة ميدالية.	على مدى خمسة عشر عامًا
faaz-uu **bi-ʾarbaʿ-a ʿashrat-a** *miidaaliyyat-an.*	*ʿalaa madaa* **xamsat-a ʿashar-a** *ʿaam-an*
They won **fourteen medals.**	over a period of **fifteen years**

ثمن الجريدة خمسة عشر ريالًا.

thaman-u l-jariidat-i **xamsat-a ʿashar-a** *riyaal-an.*

The cost of the newspaper is **fifteen rials.**

يضمّ تسع عشرة شقّة.	لمدّة ست عشرة سنة
ya-Dumm-u **tisʿ-a ʿashrat-a** *shaqqat-an.*	*li-muddat-i* **sitt-a ʿashrat-a** *sanat-an*
It contains **nineteen apartments.**	for a period of **sixteen years**

عن سبعة عشر نائباً

ʿan sabʿat-a ʿashar-a naaʾib-an

from **seventeen representatives**

عن خمسة عشر عضوا كردياً

ʿan xamsat-a ʿashar-a ʿuDw-an
kurdiyy-an

from **fifteen Kurdish members**[10]

1.5.2 Definite counted noun

A definite counted noun with a teens numeral is **in the plural, followed by the teens numeral** prefixed with the definite article. The article is on only the first part of the numeral compound, not the second part. Whereas the counted noun in this situation may be in any case that its role in the sentence requires, the **teens numeral remains invariably in the accusative** case. The first part of the compound number shows gender polarity.

في الغرف التسع عشرة

fii l-ghuraf-i l-tisʿ-a ʿasharat-a

in the **nineteen rooms**

الأعضاء الخمسة عشر

al-ʾaʿDaaʾ-u l-xamsat-a ʿashr-a

the **fifteen members**

1.5.3 In independent form

When counting or listing the numerals by themselves, the form with the feminine marker on the first element is used, i.e., *xamsat-a ʿashar-a, sittat-a ʿashar-a, sabʿat-a ʿashar-a* 'fifteen, sixteen, seventeen.'

1.6 Numerals twenty to ninety-nine

The even tens numerals are constructed as a numeral stem joined with a sound masculine plural suffix that inflects two ways for case, *-uuna* for the nominative and *-iina* for genitive-accusative.[11] These even tens numerals themselves **do not show any gender distinctions** or differences.

The numbers twenty to ninety-nine are followed by a **singular accusative counted noun**, which is a form of *tamyiiz*, or accusative of specification.

twenty	*ʿishruuna/ ʿishriina*[12]	عشرون / عشرين
thirty	*thalaathuuna/thalaathiina*	ثلاثون / ثلاثين
forty	*ʾarbaʿuuna/ ʾarbaʿiina*	أربعون / أربعين

[10] Note that the adjective agrees strictly with the counted noun and is singular, although the meaning is plural.

[11] In spoken Arabic, the tens numbers are reduced to one case, the genitive-accusative. However, in written Arabic, the case distinction is still maintained if the number is written out.

[12] The base form for this number appears to be from the lexical root for "ten," and it has been theorized that originally, it might have been something like **ʿishr-aani* 'two-tens' and that the dual suffix came subsequently to resemble the other tens suffixes by a process of analogy.

fifty	*xamsuuna/xamsiina*	خمسون/خمسين
sixty	*sittuuna/sittiina*	ستّون/ستّين
seventy	*sabʿuuna/sabʿiina*	سبعون/سبعين
eighty	*thamaanuuna/thamaaniina*	ثمـانون/ثمـانين
ninety	*tisʿuuna/tisʿiina*	تسعون/تسعين

1.6.1 Indefinite counted noun

في عشرين مجلّداً   عشرون قرشاً
fii ʿishriina mujallad-an   *ʿishruuna qirsh-an*
in twenty volumes   twenty piasters

بمشاركة أكثر من أربعين دار نشر
bi-mushaarakat-i ʾakthar-a min ʾarbaʿiina daar-a nashr-in
with the participation of more than **forty publishing houses**

بعد مرور أكثر من ستّين عاماً
baʿd-a muruur-i ʾakthar-a min sittiina ʿaam-an
after the passage of more than **sixty years**

خمسون من موظّفي المحطّة
xamsuuna min muwaZZaf-ii l-maHaTTat-i[13]
fifty of the station employees

1.6.2 Plurals of tens

The plural form of the tens numerals is the sound feminine plural, which is suffixed to the genitive-accusative form of the number:

twenties	*ʿishriinaat*	عشرينـات
thirties	*thalaathiinaat*	ثلاثينـات
forties	*ʾarbaʿiinaat*	أربعينـات
fifties	*xamsiinaat*	خمسينـات
sixties	*sittiinaat*	ستّينـات
seventies	*sabʿiinaat*	سبعينـات
eighties	*thamaaniinaat*	ثمـانينـات
nineties	*tisʿiinaat*	تسعينـات

---

[13] Because the word *xamsuuna* here is followed by the preposition *min*, the counted noun is not governed by the numeral, but is plural.

بعد أزمة الثلاثينات الكبرى

ba'd-a 'azmat-i **l-thalaathiinaat-i
l-kubraa**

after the great crisis of **the thirties**

حتّى السبعينات من القرن العشرين

Hattaa **l-sab'iinaat-i** *min-a l-qarn-i
l-'ishriina*

up to **the seventies** of the twentieth
century

1.6.3 Compound tens

To construct compound tens numerals, the first part of the compound is an indefinite number joined to the second by the conjunction *wa-* 'and.' The first digit shows case and gender as follows:

1.6.3.1 THE "ONES" AND "TWOS" The units twenty-one, thirty-one and so forth are constructed with the numeral "one" and then the tens component. The numeral "one" shows straight gender agreement with the noun. It can be either of the form *waaHid/ waaHida* or the form *'aHad/'iHdaa*.

The "twos" units inflect for case as duals and show straight gender agreement with the counted noun.

	With masculine counted noun:	**With feminine counted noun:**
twenty-one	واحدٌ وعشْرونَ	واحدةٌ وعشْرونَ
	waaHid-un wa-'ishruuna	*waaHidat-un wa-'ishruuna*
	or	or
	أحدٌ وعشْرونَ	إحْدى وعشْرونَ
	'aHad-un wa-'ishruuna	*'iHdaa wa-'ishruuna*
twenty-two	اثْنانِ وعشْرونَ	اثْنَتانِ وعشْرونَ
	ithnaani wa-'ishruuna	*ithnataani wa-'ishruuna*
	اثْنَيْنِ وعشْرونَ	اثْنَتَيْنِ وعشْرونَ
	ithnayni wa-'ishruuna	*ithnatayni wa-'ishruuna*

لمدّة واحد وعشرين يوماً

li-muddat-i **waaHid-in wa-'ishriina** *yawm-an*

for a period of **twenty-one days**

في اثنتين وعشرين صفحة

fii **thnatayni wa-'ishriina** *SafHat-an*

in **twenty-two pages**

لمدّة إحدى وعشرين سنة

li-muddat-i **'iHdaa wa-'ishriina** *sanat-an*

for a period of **twenty-one years**

لاثنين وعشرين أسبوعاً

li-thnayni wa-'ishriina 'usbuu'-an

for **twenty-two weeks**

1.6.3.2 TENS NUMERALS PLUS THREES TO NINES: Numerals such as twenty-four, seventy-six, thirty-five and so on are compounded of the single digit number linked to the tens numeral by means of the conjunction *wa-*, making combinations such as "four and twenty, six and seventy, five and thirty," and so forth. Except for the numeral eight, which belongs to the defective declension, the single digits are triptote, they take nunation, and they show **reverse gender with the counted noun**. The counted noun is singular, indefinite, and accusative. Both parts of the numeral inflect for case.

(1)   Indefinite counted noun:

بعد أربـع وعشرين ساعة
ba ʿd-a *ʾarba ʿ-in wa-ʿishriina*
   saa ʿat-an
after **twenty-four hours**

أكثر من خمسة وخمسين فيلماً
*ʾakthar-u min **xamsat-in wa-xamsiina**
   fiilm-an
more than **fifty-five films**

تنافسوا في ثمان وعشرين لـعبة.
tanaafas-uu fii **thamaan-in wa-ʿishriina la ʿbat-an.**
They competed in **twenty-eight sports.**

عمره ثلاثة وستّون عاماً.
ʿumr-u-hu **thalaathat-un wa-sittuuna** ʿaam-an.
He is sixty-three years old ('His age is **sixty-three years**').

(2)   **Definite counted noun:** With a definite counted noun from 20 to 99, the numeral comes first and has the definite article, followed by the **singular indefinite noun in the accusative case:**

عليّ بابا والأربعون لصّاً
ʿaliyy baabaa wa-**l-arba ʿuuna liSS-an**
Ali Baba and **the Forty Thieves**

طوال الثلاثين سنة الماضية
Tiwaal-a **l-thalaathiina** sanat-an-i
   l-maaDiyat-i
during **the past thirty years**

أسمـاء اللّه الحسنى التسعة وتسعون
ʾasmaaʾ-u llaah-i l-Husnaa **l-tis ʾat-u wa-tis ʾuuna**
the ninety-nine attributes of God

1.7 The even hundreds

The word for "hundred" in Arabic is *mi ʾa*, spelled both as مئة and مائة. It is a feminine noun and remains feminine at all times. When used with a counted noun, it goes into an *ʾiDaafa* relationship with the noun and that **noun is in the genitive singular**. The concept of "two hundred" is expressed by using *mi ʾa* in the dual, with the dual suffix. The dual suffix here obeys the law of *nuun*-drop when it goes into an *ʾiDaafa* with a following counted noun:

one hundred	مئة	
	mi'a	
two hundred	مئتان	(nominative)
	mi'at-aani	
	مئتين	(accusative/genitive)
	mi'at-ayni	

1.7.1 Counting in even one and two hundreds

مئة قنبلة يدوية
mi'at-u qunbulat-in yadawiyyat-in
100 hand grenades

مئة كيلومتر شرق عدن
mi'at-u kiiluumitr-in sharq-a 'adan-a
100 kilometers east of Aden

لمدّة مئة يوم
li-muddat-i mi'at-i yawm-in
for a period of **100** days

مئتا فلس
mi'at-aa fils-in
200 fils (a unit of currency)

بـمئتي دولار
bi-mi'at-ay duulaar-in
for **200** dollars

في جلساته حوالي مئة باحث.
fii jalsaat-i-hi Hawaalii mi'at-u baaHith-in.
In its sessions [are] approximately **100** researchers.

1.7.2 Definite hundreds phrases

In this case, the word mi'a has the definite article, and the counted noun is genitive singular indefinite. In these examples, the hundreds phrase serves as the second term of an 'iDaafa.

سباق المئة متر
sibaaq-u l-mi'at-i mitr-in
the **hundred-meter** race

بطل المئة متر
baTal-u l-mi'at-i mitr-in
the champion of **the hundred meters**

1.7.2.1 EXPRESSING 'PERCENT': To express the concept of percent, the term fii l-mi'at-i or bi-l-mi'at-i is used:

مئة بالمئة
mi'at-un bi-l-mi'at-i
100 percent

يملكان خمسة عشر في المئة من الشركة.
yu-mlik-aani xamsat-a 'ashar-a fii l-mi'at-i
    min-a l-sharikat-i.
The two of them own **15 percent** of the
    company.

في نحو تسعين في المئة من البلديات الريفية
fii naHw-i tis'iina fii l-mi'at-i min-a l-baladiyyaat-i l-riifiyyat-i
in approximately **90 percent** of the rural municipalities

1.7.3 Three hundred to nine hundred

When the numeral is over two hundred, the hundred noun is counted by a numeral (in the masculine form because *mi'a* is feminine) followed by the word *mi'a* in the singular genitive form. This compound numeral may be written optionally as one word.

		One word	Two words
three hundred	*thalaath-u mi'at-in*	ثلاثمئة	ثلاث مئة
four hundred	*'arbaᶜ-u mi'at-in*	أربعمئة	أربع مئة
five hundred	*xams-u mi'at-in*	خمسمئة	خمس مئة
six hundred	*sitt-u mi'at-in*	ستّمئة	ستّ مئة
seven hundred	*sabᶜ-u mi'at-in*	سبعمئة	سبع مئة
eight hundred	*thamaanii mi'at-in*	ثمانيمئة	ثماني مئة
nine hundred	*tisᶜ-u mi'at-in*	تسعمئة	تسع مئة

The following counted noun is **genitive, singular, and indefinite**:

1.7.3.1 INDEFINITE COUNTED NOUN

أربع مئة مليم
'arbaᶜ-u mi'at-i miliim-in
400 millemes

من خمس مئة متر مكعّب
min xams-i mi'at-i mitr-in mukaᶜᶜab-in
from **500 cubic meters**

في غضون خمس مئة ساعة دراسية
fii ghuDuun-i xams-i mi'at-i saaᶜat-in diraasiyyat-in
during **500 study hours**

1.8 Complex numerals with hundred

When counting in the hundreds, the word *mi'a* comes first joined to the second part of the numeral by the conjunction *wa-* 'and.' For example:

107   مئة وسبعة
mi'at-un wa-sabᶜat-un
a hundred and seven

119   مئة وتسعة عشر
mi'at-un wa-tisᶜat-a ᶜashar-a
a hundred and nineteen

150   مئة وخمسون
mi'at-un wa-xamsuuna
a hundred and fifty

275   مئتان وخمسة وسبعون
mi'at-aani wa-xamsat-un wa-sabᶜuuna
two hundred and seventy-five
('two hundred and five and seventy')

أربع مئة وأربعون   440
ʾarbaʿ-u miʾat-in wa-ʾarba-uuna
four hundred and forty

ستّ مئة وثلاثة وعشرون   623
sitt-u miʾat-in wa-thalaathat-un
wa-ʿishruuna
six hundred and twenty-three
('six hundred and three and twenty')

1.8.1 Counting with complex numerals in the hundreds

The second part of the number, being the part directly adjacent to the following
noun, is the part that determines the case and number of the counted noun.

1.8.1.1 LAST PART IS 3–10 FOLLOWED BY GENITIVE PLURAL:

بُنيت قبل مئة وسبعة أعوام.
buniy-at qabl-a miʾat-in wa-sabʿat-i ʾaʿwaam-in.
It was built **107 years ago.**

1.8.1.2 LAST PART IS 11–99 FOLLOWED BY ACCUSATIVE SINGULAR:

جاءوا من مئة وخمسين دولة.
jaaʾ-uu min miʾat-in wa-xamsiina
 dawlat-an.
They came from **150 countries.**

مئتان وسبعون مندوباً
miʾat-aani wa-sabʿuuna manduub-an
270 delegates

وصلت سرعة الرياح إلى مئة وسبعين كيلومتراً في الساعة.
waSal-at surʿat-u l-riyaaH-i ʾilaa miʾat-in wa-sabʿiina kiiluumitr-an fii l-saaʿat-i.
The wind speed reached **170 kilometers** an hour.

1.8.2 Plural "hundreds": miʾaat مئات

The word miʾa is made plural with the sound feminine plural miʾaat. When used
for counting, miʾaat is followed by either a definite noun in the genitive plural or
the preposition min to express the "hundreds of" relationship.

أُغلقت مئات المدارس.
ʾughliq-at miʾaat-u l-madaaris-i.
Hundreds of schools were closed.

أكثر من بضع مئات من الأمثلة
ʾakthar-u min biDʿ-i miʾaat-i min-a
 l-ʾamthilat-i
more than **several hundreds of**
 examples

مئات الأطفال اللبنانيّين
miʾaat-u l-ʾaTfaal-i l-lubnaaniyy-iina
hundreds of Lebanese children

ويجتمع المئات منهم.
wa-yajtimiʿ-u l-miʾaat-u min-hum.
Hundreds of them are meeting.

1.9 Thousands

The word for thousand in Arabic is ʾalf ألف, plural ʾaalaaf آلاف. It is a masculine noun and is counted as any other masculine noun:

1,000	ʾalf	ألف
2,000	ʾalf-aani/ʾalf-ayni	ألفان/ألفين
3,000	thalaathat-u ʾaalaaf-in	ثلاثة آلاف
4,000	ʾarbaʿat-u ʾaalaaf-in	أربعة آلاف
5,000	xamsat-u ʾaalaaf-in	خمسة آلاف
6,000	sittat-u ʾaalaaf-in	ستّة آلاف
7,000	sabʿat-u ʾaalaaf-in	سبعة آلاف
8,000	thamaaniyat-u ʾaalaaf-in	ثمانية آلاف
9,000	tisʿat-u ʾaalaaf-in	تسعة آلاف
10,000	ʿasharat-u ʾaalaaf-in	عشرة آلاف
11,000	ʾaHad-a ʿashar-a ʾalf-an	أحد عشر ألفاً
12,000	ithnaa ʿashar-a ʾalf-an	اثنا عشر ألفا
15,000	xamsat-a ʿashar-a ʾalf-an	خمسة عشر ألفا
20,000	ʿishruuna ʾalf-an	عشرون ألفا
25,000	xamsat-un wa-ʿishruuna ʾalf-an	خمسة وعشرون ألفا
100,000	miʾat-u ʾalf-in	مئة ألف
200,000	miʾat-aa ʾalf-in	مئتا ألف
475,000	ʾarbaʿ-u miʾat-in wa-xamsat-un wa-sabʿuuna ʾalf-an	أربع مئة وخمسة وسبعون ألفا

1.9.1 Counting in thousands

When used for counting, the numeral ʾalf / ʾaalaaf goes into an ʾiDaafa relationship with the following noun, which is in the **genitive singular**. In complex numerals over a thousand (as with *miʾa*), **it is the final component of the numeral that determines the number (singular or plural) and case of the counted noun.**

أمّا عدد الفنادق فيبلغ أربعة آلاف منشأة.

ʾammaa ʿadad-u l-fanaadiq-i fa-ya-blugh-u **ʾarbaʿat-a ʾaalaaf-i munshaʾat-in**.

As for the number of hotels, it reaches **4,000 establishments.**

أكثر من أحد عشر ألف رياضيّ جاءوا.

ʾakthar-u min ʾaHad-a ʿashar-a ʾalf-a riyaaDiyy-in jaaʾ-uu.

More than **11,000** athletes came.

أكثر من ثلاثة عشر ألف كتاب

ʾakthar-u min thalaathat-a ʿashar-a ʾalf-a kitaab-in

more than **13,000** books

مئة وثلاثة وخمسون ألف كردي

miʾat-un wa-thalaathat-un wa-xamsuuna ʾalf-a kurdiyy-in

153,000 Kurds

ثلاثة آلاف وأربع مئة واثنان وثلاثون كيلومتراً مربّعاً

*thalaathat-u ʾaalaaf-in wa-ʾarbaʿ-u miʾat-in wa-thnaani wa-thalaathuuna
kiiluumitr-an murabbaʿ-an*

3,432 square kilometers

خسرت نحو أربع مئة وخمسين ألف وظيفة.

xasar-at naHw-a ʾarbaʿ-i miʾat-in wa xamsiina ʾalf-a waZiifat-in.

It has lost approximately **450,000** jobs.

1.9.2 Special cases

For the even thousands plus "one" or "two," a special construction exists in Classical Arabic, although no instances of it were encountered in the data covered for this project.

1001 nights	ألف ليلة وليلة	
	ʾalf-u laylat-in wa-laylat-un ('a thousand nights and a night')	
2002 nights	ألفا ليلة وليلتان	
	ʾalf-aa laylat-in wa-laylat-aani ('two thousand nights and two nights')	

1.10 Reading years in dates

Because Arabic has two words for 'year,' *ʿaam* عام / *ʾaʿwaam* أعوام (masculine) and *sana* سنة / *sanawaat* سنوات (feminine), the numbers in year dates can vary in gender. When reading year dates, the word for 'year' (either *ʿaam* or *sana*) precedes the numeral expression and is in an *ʾiDaafa* with it, so that the date itself is the second term of the *ʾiDaafa* and is in the genitive case.

Because of the reverse gender rule, if the masculine noun *ʿaam* is used, then any 3–10 digit is feminine, and if the feminine noun *sana* is used, then any 3–10 digit is in the masculine.

In general, either the phrase 'in the year' *fii ʿaam-i* or *fii sanat-i* is used, or the word *ʿaam-a* or *sanat-a* is used in the accusative (time adverbial). Sometimes these phrases are understood and not explicitly mentioned.

1.10.1 'in the year 711'

1.10.1.1 USING *sana*

في سَنَة سبع مئة وإحدى عشرة

fii sanat-i sabᶜ-i miʾat-in wa-ʾiHdaa ᶜashrat-a

سنَةَ سبع مئة وإحدى عشرة

sanat-a sabᶜ-i miʾat-in wa-ʾiHdaa ᶜashrat-a

1.10.1.2 USING *ᶜaam*:

في عامٍ سبع مئة وأحد عشر

fii ᶜaam-i sabᶜ-i miʾat-in wa-ʾaHad-a ᶜashar-a

عامَ سبع مئة وأحد عشر

ᶜaam-a sabᶜ-i miʾat-in wa-ʾaHad-a ᶜashar-a

1.10.2 'in the year 1956'

1.10.2.1 USING *sana*

في سنة ألف وتسع مئة وستّ وخمسين

fii sanat-i ʾalf-in wa-tisᶜ-i miʾat-in wa-sitt-in wa-xamsiina

سنةَ ألف وتسع مئة وستّ وخمسين

sanat-a ʾalf-in wa-tisᶜ-i miʾat-in wa-sitt-in wa-xamsiina

1.10.2.2 USING *ᶜaam*:

في عامٍ ألف وتسع مئة وستّة وخمسين

fii ᶜaam-i ʾalf-in wa-tisᶜ-i miʾat-in wa-sittat-in wa-xamsiina

عامَ ألف وتسع مئة وستّة وخمسين

ᶜaam-a ʾalf-in wa-tisᶜ-i miʾat-in wa-sittat-in wa-xamsiina

1.10.3 'in the year 1998'

1.10.3.1 USING *sana*

في سنة ألف وتسع مئة وثمان وتسعين

fii sanat-i ʾalf-in wa-tisᶜ-i miʾat-in wa-thamaanin wa-tisᶜiina

سنةَ ألف وتسع مئة وثمان وتسعين

sanat-a ʾalf-in wa-tisᶜ-i miʾat-in wa-thamaanin wa-tisᶜiina

1.10.3.2 USING ʿ*aam*:

في عـام ألف وتسـع مئة وثمـانية وتسعين

fii ʿaam-i ʾalf-in wa-tisʿ-i miʾat-in wa-thamaaniyat-in wa-tisʿiina

عـام ألف وتسـع مئة وثمـانية وتسعين

ʿaam-a ʾalf-in wa-tisʿ-i miʾat-in wa-thamaaniyat-in wa-tisʿiina

1.10.4 'in the year 2001'

1.10.4.1 USING *sana*

في سنة ألفين وواحدة

fii sanat-i ʾalf-ayni wa-waaHidat-in

سنة ألفين وواحدة

sanat-a ʾalf-ayni wa-waaHidat-in

1.10.4.2 USING ʿ*aam*

في عـام ألفين وواحد

fii ʿaam-i ʾalf-ayni wa-waaHid-in

عـام ألفين وواحد

ʿaam-a ʾalf-ayni wa-waaHid-in

NB: In practice, when saying year dates out loud, short vowel case endings are often omitted.

1.11 Millions and billions

Arabic has borrowed the terms "million" (*milyuun* مليون /*malaayiin* ملايين) and "billion" (*bilyuun* بليون /*balaayiin* بلايين), using them in much the same way as the terms for hundred and thousand. The names of the numerals themselves are masculine and when counting, they form the first term of an ʾ*iDaafa* with the following noun, which is **genitive singular**.

انتـاج الولايـات المتّحدة من النفط يقـارب مليون برميل يوميًا.

ʾ*intaaj-u l-wilaayaat-i l-muttaHidat-i min-a l-nafT-i yu-qaarib-u **milyuun-a barmiil-in
yawmiyy-an**.*

The oil production of the United States approaches **a million barrels** daily.

عشرون مليون مشترك
ʿ*ishruuna milyuun-a mushtarik-in*
twenty million participants

ببليوني دولار
bi-bilyuun-ay duulaar-in
for two billion dollars

يتجـاوز ثمنهـا ثلاثة بلايين دولار.

*ya-tajaawaz-u thaman-u-haa **thalaathat-a balaayiin-i duulaar-in**.*

Their cost exceeds **three billion dollars**.

مئة مليون دولار ليست مستغربة.

miʾat-u milyuun-i duulaar-in lays-at mustaghrabat-an.

A hundred million dollars is not unusual.

2 Ordinal numerals

Ordinal numerals are essentially adjectives. They usually follow the noun that they modify and agree with it in gender, but sometimes they precede the noun as the first term of an *'iDaafa* structure. Occasionally they may also be used as independent substantives (i.e., **"the fifth of May"; "twenty seconds"**).

2.1 'First:' *'awwal* أوّل and *'uulaa* أولى

The Arabic words for "first" are *'awwal* (m.) and *'uulaa* (f.). They can either follow the noun they modify or precede it as first term of an *'iDaafa*.

2.1.1 *'awwal*

The word *'awwal* (plural *'awaa'il*) may function as the first term of an *'iDaafa* structure, as an adjective following a noun, or as an independent noun.

2.1.1.1 As first term of an *'iDaafa*, *'awwal* may be followed by either a masculine or feminine noun.

كان أوّل رجل في العالم يطبّق الفكرة.

kaan-a 'awwal-a rajul-in fii l-ʿaalam-i yu-Tabbiq-u l-fikrat-a.

He was **the first man** in the world to apply the idea.

وفقاً لأوّل إحصاء للسكّان

wafq-an li-'awwal-i 'iHSaa'-in li-l-sukkaan-i

in conformity with the **first statistics** of the population

كان أوّل من ألقى كلمة.

kaan-a 'awwal-a man 'alqaa kalimat-an.

He was **the first** to give a speech.

بدأ أوّل زيارة له لليمن.

bada'-a 'awwal-a ziyaarat-in la-hu li-l-yaman-i.

He started his **first trip** to Yemen.

وقد كانتا أوّل رياضيتين من الخليج تشاركان في الألعاب الأوليمبية.

wa-qad kaan-ataa 'awwal-a riyaaDiyyat-ayni min-a l-xaliij-i tu-shaarik-aani fii l-'alʿaab-i l-'uuliimbiyyat-i.

They were **the first two female athletes** from the Gulf to participate in the Olympic Games.

2.1.1.2 'THE FIRST': The word *'awwal* may also be used independently and followed by a preposition to convey the meaning of 'the first of; first among':

يُعتبر الأوّل من نوعه.

yu-ʿtabar-u l-'awwal-a min nawʿ-i-hi.

It is considered **the first** of its kind.

تناول الأوّل منها الوضـع السياسيّ.

tanaawal-a l-ʾawwal-u min-haa l-waDᶜ-a l-siyaasiyy-a.

The first of them dealt with the political situation.

اللقب هو الأوّل بين الألقاب الخمسة.

al-laqab-u huwa l-ʾawwal-u bayn-a l-ʾalqaab-i l-xamsat-i.

The title is **the first** of ('among') the five titles.

2.1.1.3 PLURAL OF ʾawwal: ʾawaaʾil أوائل

: The word ʾawwal has a plural, ʾawaaʾil, which can mean 'the first [ones],' the 'earliest [parts],' or the 'most prominent.'

كان من أوائل الدول العربيّة.   في أوائل الشهر الماضي

kaan-a min ʾawaaʾil-i l-duwal-i l-ᶜarabiyyat-i.	*fii ʾawaaʾil-i l-shahr-i l-maaDii*
It was among **the most prominent** Arab countries.	in **the first part** of last month

2.1.2 ʾuulaa أولى

The feminine word ʾuulaa 'first' is invariable, i.e., it does not inflect for case. It can occur in either of two structures:

2.1.2.1 AS AN ADJECTIVE FOLLOWING A NOUN:

للمرّة الأولى   أحد المشاريع الثلاثة الأولى

li-l-marrat-i l-ʾuulaa	*ʾaHad-u l-mashaariiᶜ-i l-thalaathat-i l-ʾuulaa*
for the first time	one of the first three projects

القناة الأولى   أُعطيت الأوّليّة الأولى لمياه الشرب.

al-qanaat-u l-ʾuulaa	*ʾuᶜTiy-at-i l-ʾawwaliyyat-u l-ʾuulaa li-miyaah-i l-shurb-i.*
channel one ('the first channel')	The **first priority** was given to drinking water.

الرحلة الجوّيّة الأولى   في الساعات الأولى من الصباح

al-riHlat-u l-jawwiyyat-u l-ʾuulaa	*fii l-saaᶜaat-i l-ʾuulaa min-a l-SabaaH-i*
the **first** air trip	in the **first hours** of the morning

2.1.2.2 AS THE FIRST TERM OF AN ʾiDaafa WITH A FOLLOWING FEMININE WORD: This construction is not frequent, but may occur.

كسب السعوديّون أولى مبارياتهم.

kasab-a l-saᶜuudiyy-uuna ʾuulaa mubaarayaat-i-him.

The Saudis won **the first of their matches.**

2.2 Second through tenth

The words "second" through "tenth" have the pattern of the active participle of a Form I verb: *faaᶜil* or *faaᶜila*.

Masculine/Feminine

second	*thaanin/thaaniya*[14]	ثانٍ/ثانِيَة
third	*thaalith/thaalitha*	ثالث / ثالثة
fourth	*raabiᶜ/raabiᶜa*	رابِع / رابِعة
fifth	*xaamis/xaamisa*	خامِس/خامِسة
sixth	*saadis/saadisa*[15]	سادِس/سادِسة
seventh	*saabiᶜ/saabiᶜa*	سابِع / سابِعة
eighth	*thaamin/thaamina*	ثامِن/ ثامِنة
ninth	*taasiᶜ/taasiᶜa*	تاسِع / تاسِعة
tenth	*ᶜaashir/ᶜaashira*	عاشِر/عاشِرة

These adjectival forms of the numbers usually follow the noun that they modify, agreeing with the noun in gender, definiteness, and case.

مرّة ثانية
marrat-an thaaniyat-an
a second time; another time

ثمّة مشروع ثان.
thammat-a mashruuᶜ-un thaan-in.
There is a second plan.

انتهى أمس في لندن المؤتمر الثاني.
intahaa ᵓamsi fii lundun-a l-muᵓtamar-u l-thaanii.
The second conference ended yesterday in London.

أصبح خامس أعلى ثمن.
ᵓaSbaH-a xaamis-a ᵓaᶜlaa thaman-in.
It became the fifth highest price.

في معظم القسم الثاني من الكتاب
fii muᶜZam-i l-qism-i l-thaanii min-a l-kitaab-i
in most of the second part of the book

في الذكرى الخامسة
fii l-dhikraa l-xaamisat-i
on the fifth anniversary

نجح في محاولته الثالثة.
najaH-a fii muHaawalat-i-hi l-thaalithat-i.
He succeeded on his third try.

العالم الثالث
al-ᶜaalam-u l-thaalith-u
the Third World

---

[14] The masculine form of the word for 'second' *thaanin* (pl. *thawaanin*) is a defective adjective and inflects for case and definiteness in declension six. See Chapter 7, section 5.4.3.

[15] The adjective *saadis* 'sixth' has a related but different lexical root (*s-d-s*) from the root for "six" (*s-t-t*).

تحتلّ الشركة المرتبة الرابعة عالميًا.

ta-Htall-u l-sharikat-u **l-martabat-a l-raabiᶜat-a** *ᶜaalamiyy-an.*

The company ranks fourth worldwide ('occupies **the fourth rank**').

2.2.1 Ordinal numeral as first term of *ʾiDaafa*

Occasionally, an ordinal numeral will precede the noun it modifies, as the first term of an *ʾiDaafa* structure. In this case it is usually the masculine form of the number that is used, even if the following noun is feminine:

في ثاني زيارة له

fii **thaanii ziyaarat-in** *la-hu*

on his **second visit**

ثالث المشروعات التجريبيّة مشروع ريّ.

thaalith-u l-mashruuᶜaat-i *l-tajriibiyyat-i mashruuᶜ-u rayy-in.*

The **third of the experimental projects** is an irrigation project.

يصبح ثالث عدّاء فقط يحمل اللقب العالميّ.

yu-Sbih-u **thaalith-a ᶜaddaaʾ-in** *faqaT ya-Hmil-u l-laqab-a l-ᶜaalamiyy-a.*

He becomes only **the third runner** to hold the world championship.

2.2.2 Ordinals as nouns: *thaanin/thaanii*

The ordinal "second" may be used as a substantive. In its masculine singular form, as a final-weak noun, it is in the defective declension.

في الثاني من أيّار.

fii **l-thaanii** *min ʾayyaar-a*

on **the second** of May

As a unit of time measurement, "second" in Arabic is feminine *thaaniya* ثانية with a broken defective plural, *thawaanin* ثوان.

بسرعة ستّة كيلومترات في الثانية

bi-surᶜat-i sittat-i kiiluumitraat-in **fii l-thaaniyat-i**

at the rate of six kilometers **per second**

أحرزت ذهبية مسجّلة ٧٥، ١٠ ثوان.

ʾaHraz-at dhahabiyyat-an musajjilat-an **10.75 thawaanin.**

She won a gold [medal] registering [a time of] **10.75 seconds.**

2.2.2.1 OTHER FORMS OF ORDINALS AS NOUNS: In addition to "second" as a noun, other ordinals may also be used in this way, especially when referring to days of the month:

في الثامن من تشرين الأوّل
fii **l-thaamin-i** min tishriina l-ʾawwal-i
on **the eighth** of October

في الخامس من شباط
fii **l-xaamis-i** min shubaaT-a
on **the fifth** of February

2.3 Eleventh through nineteenth

These compound adjectives consist of the tens ordinal numeral plus a masculine or feminine form of the word for "ten" ʿashar-a or ʿashrat-a. **Both parts of the compound adjective agree in gender with the noun they modify.** However, both parts of the compound teens ordinal are **always in the accusative case**, no matter what the case of the noun they are modifying. The definite article goes on the first element of the compound only.

eleventh	الحادي عشر	الحادية عشرة
	al-Haadiy-a ʿashr-a	al-Haadiyat-a ʿashrat-a
twelfth	الثاني عشر	الثانية عشرة
	al-thaaniy-a ʿashar-a	al-thaaniyat-a ʿashrat-a
thirteenth	الثالث عشر	الثالثة عشرة
	al-thaalith-a ʿashar-a	al-thaalithat-a ʿashrat-a
fourteenth	الرابع عشر	الرابعة عشرة
	al-raabiʿ-a ʿashar-a	al-raabiʿat-a ʿashrat-a
fifteenth	الخامس عشر	الخامسة عشرة
	al-xaamis-a ʿashar-a	al-xaamisat-a ʿashrat-a
sixteenth	السادس عشر	السادسة عشرة
	al-saadis-a ʿashar-a	al-saadisat-a ʿashrat-a
seventeenth	السابع عشر	السابعة عشرة
	al-saabiʿ-a ʿashar-a	al-saabiʿat-a ʿashrat-a
eighteenth	الثامن عشر	الثامنة عشرة
	al-thaamin-a ʿashar-a	al-thaaminat-a ʿashrat-a
nineteenth	التاسع عشر	التاسعة عشرة
	al-taasiʿ-a ʿashr-a	al-taasiʿat-a ʿashrat-a

المعرض السنويّ الحادي عشر
al-maʿraD-u l-sanawiyy-u l-Haadiy-a
 ʿashar-a
the eleventh annual exhibition

في دورتها الخامسة عشرة
fii dawrat-i-haa l-xaamisat-a ʿashrat-a
in its fifteenth session

يعود تاريخها إلى القرن الثاني عشر.

ya-ʿuud-u taariikh-u-haa ʾilaa l-qarn-i l-thaaniy-a ʿashar-a.

Its history goes back to **the twelfth century.**

فتى في الرابعة عشرة من العمر

fatan fii l-raabiʿat-a ʿashrat-a min-a l-ʿumr-i

a youth in his **fourteenth** year ('the **fourteenth** [year] of age')

في الذكرى الرابعة عشرة   في القرن الخامس عشر الميلاديّ

fii l-dhikraa l-raabiʿat-a ʿashrat-a   *fii l-qarn-i l-xaamis-a ʿashar-a l-miilaadiyy-i*

on the **fourteenth** anniversary   in the **fifteenth century** AD

افتتح المسابقة المحليّة السادسة عشرة.

iftataH-a l-musaabaqat-a l-maHaliyyat-a l-saadisat-a ʿashrat-a.

He opened **the sixteenth local competition.**

2.4 Twentieth to ninety-ninth

The ordinals for the group of numerals from twenty to ninety-nine are of two types: straight tens ("twentieth, fortieth, eightieth") and compound tens ("twenty-first, forty-fifth, fifty-third"). In both cases the tens component does not vary from its numeral shape. That is, twentieth (*ʿishruuna* عشرون) and twenty (*ʿishruuna*) look the same. However, as an adjective, *ʿishruuna* may take a definite article, and it agrees in case with the noun it modifies. It remains invariable in gender.

في القرن العشرين   في العيد الخمسين لاستقلالها

fii l-qarn-i l-ʿishriina   *fii l-ʿiid-i l-xamsiina l-istiqlaal-i-haa*

in the twentieth century   on the **50th anniversary** of its independence

تحتفل بيوم ميلادها الخمسين.

ta-Htafil-u bi-yawm-i miilaad-i-haa l-xamsiina.

She is celebrating her **50th birthday.**

With the compound tens ordinals, the first part of the compound has the ordinal form of the number and agrees with the following noun in gender. Both parts of the tens ordinal agree in case and definiteness with the modified noun. Note that the word *Haad-in* حاد (def. *Haadii* حادي) is used to indicate 'first' in tens compounds.

في عيد ميلادها الحادي والعشرين   في القرن الحادي والعشرين

fii ʿiid-i miilaad-i-haa l-Haadii   *fii l-qarn-i l-Haadii wa-l-ʿishriina*
   wa-l-ʿishriina   in the twenty-first century

on her **twenty-first birthday**

في المباراة الثامنة والعشرين

fii l-mubaaraat-i l-thaaminat-i wa-l-ʿishriina

in the twenty-eighth match

الذكرى الحادية والستّون

al-dhikraa l-Haadiyat-u wa-l-sittuuna

the sixty-first anniversary

2.5 Hundredth

The ordinal expression for "hundredth" looks like the word "hundred." It follows the noun it modifies and agrees in definiteness and case, but not in gender. It remains invariably feminine.

كان ترتيبه المئة.

kaan-a tartiib-u-hu l-miʾat-a.

His ranking was **hundredth**.

3 Other number-based expressions

3.1 Fractions

With the exception of the word for "half" (*niSf* نصف), fractions are of the pattern *fuʿl* فعل /*ʾafʿaal* أفعال, based on the numeral root. In syntax, the fraction word normally acts as the first term of an *ʾiDaafa* structure.

a half	*niSf/ʾanSaaf*	نصف/أنصاف
a third	*thulth/ʾathlaath*	ثُلْث / أَثْلاث
a fourth, a quarter	*rubʿ/ʾarbaaʿ*	رُبْع/أرْبـاع
a fifth	*xums/ʾaxmaas*	خُمْس / أخْمـاس
a sixth	*suds/ʾasdaas*	سدْس/ أسْداس
a seventh	*subʿ/ʾasbaaʿ*	سُبْع/ أسْباع
an eighth	*thumn/ʾathmaan*	ثُمْن / أثْمـان
a ninth	*tusʿ/ʾatsaaʿ*	تُسْع / أتْسـاع
a tenth	*ʿushr/ʾaʿshaar*	عُشْر / أعْشار

نصف الأنواع المعروفة

niSf-u l-ʾanwaaʿ-i l-maʿruufat-i

half of the known species

نصف قرن من الزمان

niSf-u qarn-in min-a l-zamaan-i

half a century of time

ربع ريال

rubʿ-u riyaal-in

a quarter of a rial

منذ ربع قرن

mundh-u rubʿ-i qarn-in

a quarter of a century ago

يحتاج إلى ثلثي الأعضاء في مجلسي الكنغرس.

*ya-Htaaj-u ʾilaa **thulth-ay-i l-aʿDaaʾ-i** fii majlis-ay-i l-kunghris.*

It requires **two-thirds of the members** of both houses of Congress.

3.1.1 Fractions as nouns

A fraction may function as a substantive or independent noun:

في النصف الثاني من القرن العشرين

*fii **l-niSf-i l-thaanii** min-a l-qarn-i l-ʿishriina*

in the **second half** of the twentieth century

كانت ثقتنا بأنفسنا أقلّ في الربع الأوّل.

*kaan-at thiqat-u-naa bi-ʾanfus-i-naa ʾaqall-a **fii l-rubʿ-i l-ʾawwal-i**.*

Our self-confidence was less in **the first quarter.**

3.1.2 Special functions of *niSf* نصف :

The term *niSf* may also function as the equivalent of "semi-" or "hemi-":

نصف الكرة الشمالي	في الاجتماع نصف السنوي
niSf-u l-kurat-i l-shimaaliyy-u	*fii l-ijtimaaʿ-i niSf-i l-sanawiyy-i*
the northern **hemisphere**	in the **semi-annual** meeting

And *niSf* also indicates the half-hour, as does English "thirty":

حتّى العاشرة والنصف صباحاً

*Hattaa l-ʿaashirat-i **wa-l-niSf-i** SabaaH-an*

until ten-**thirty** in the morning

3.2 Telling time

The ordinal numbers are used for telling time in MSA. The word "hour" (*saaʿa* ساعة) may or may not be mentioned, but the ordinal numeral is in the feminine form, agreeing with that noun.

في الساعة الثامنة

fii l-saaʿat-i l-thaaminat-i

at eight o'clock ('at the eighth hour')

اليوم الأحد الساعة الحادية عشرة صباحاً

al-yawm-a l-ʾaHad-a l-saaʿat-a l-Haadiyat-a ʿashrat-a SabaaH-an

today, Sunday, at 11:00 in the morning

Rather than expressions such as "seven-fifteen" or "seven-twenty" or "seven-thirty," Arabic usually uses fractions of the hour: *rubʿ, thulth,* and *niSf*:

في السابعة والربع من مساء غد

fii l-saabiᶜat-i wa-l-rubᶜ-i min masaaʾ-i ghad-in

at seven-fifteen ('and the quarter') tomorrow evening

في السابعة إلاّ ربعاً من مساء غد

fii l-saabiᶜat-i ʾillaa rubᵛ-an min masaaʾ-i ghad-in[16]

at 6:45 tomorrow evening (the seventh [hour] less a quarter)

في الخامسة والثلث مساء أمس

fii l-xaamisat-i wa-l-thulth-i masaaʾ-a ʾams-i

at 5:20 ('five and the third') yesterday evening

في الخامسة إلاّ ثلثاً مساء أمس

fii l-xaamisat-i illaa thulth-an masaaʾ-a ʾams-i

at 4:40 ('five less a third') yesterday evening

في العا شرة والنصف مساء اليوم

fii l-ᶜaashirat-i wa-l-niSf-i masaaʾ-a l-yawm-i

at ten-thirty ('ten and the half') this evening ('the evening of today')

The word for minute is *daqiiqa* دقيقة. In telling time, it is also used with an ordinal numeral:

الساعة الرابعة والدقيقة الخامسة

al-saaᶜat-u l-raabiᶜat-u wa-l-daqiiqat-u l-xaamisat-u

4:05 ('the fourth hour and the fifth minute')[17]

3.3 Days of the week
Most of the names of the days of the week are based on the numeral system, as follows:

Sunday	*al-ʾaHad*	الأحد
Monday	*al-ithnayn*	الاثنين
Tuesday	*al-thulaathaaʾ*	الثلاثاء
Wednesday	*al-ʾarbiᶜaaʾ*	الأربعاء
Thursday	*al-xamiis*	الخميس
Friday	*al-jumᶜa*[18]	الجمعة
Saturday	*al-sabt*[19]	السبت

---

[16] The exceptive particle *ʾillaa* ('less,' 'minus,' 'except for') takes the following noun in the accusative case. The following noun may be definite or indefinite.

[17] For further examples of telling time, see Abboud and McCarus 1985, Part 1:301-303 and Schultz et al. 2000, 212–13.

[18] The word for "Friday" is from the root *j-m-ᶜ* 'to gather together.'

[19] The root for "Saturday" is cognate with the word "Sabbath."

When used in syntax, the names of the days may occur independently, with the definite article, or as the second term of an *'iDaafa* with the word *yawm* 'day,' or they may be in apposition with a time word, such as "yesterday," "tomorrow," or "today."

3.3.1 Independent

الثلاثاء الماضي
al-thulaathaa'-a l-maaDiy-a
last **Tuesday**

الثلاثاء الجاري
al-thulaathaa'-a l-jaariy-a
next Tuesday

3.3.2 In an *'iDaafa* with the word *yawm* or *'ayyam* ('day/days')

يوم الخميس
yawm-a l-xamiis-i
on Thursday

أيّام الآحاد
'ayyaam-a l-'aaHaad-i
on Sundays

أيّام السبت وحدها
'ayyaam-a l-sabt-i waHd-a-haa
only on **Saturdays**

3.3.3 In apposition

في القاهرة صباح غد الاثنين
fii l-qaahirat-i SabaaH-a ghad-in-i l-ithnayn-i
in Cairo, **tomorrow** morning, **Monday**

اليوم الأحد
al-yawm-a l-'aHad-a
today, Sunday

3.4 Number adjectives

These are adjectival forms of numbers that attribute a numerical quality to the item being described. They fall into two categories: the *fu'aaliyy* فُعالي pattern and the *mufa''al* مُفَعَّل (PP II) pattern.

3.4.1 *thunaa'iyy* ثنائي 'bilateral; two-sided'

معاهدات ثنائيّة مع دول أخرى
mu'aahadaat-un thunaa'iyyat-un ma'-a duwal-in 'uxraa
bilateral agreements with other countries

استعرض الجانبان العلاقات الثنائيّة بين القطرين.
ista'raD-a l-jaanib-aani l-'alaaqaat-i l-thunaa'iyyat-a bayn-a l-quTr-ayni.
The two sides reviewed the **bilateral** relations between the two countries.

3.4.2 *thulaathiyy* ثلاثي 'tripartite; trilateral'; *thulaathiyya* ثلاثيّة 'trilogy'

اللجنة الثلاثيّة في جنيف
al-lajnat-u l-thulaathiyyat-u fii jiniif
the **tripartite** committee in Geneva

أفعال ثلاثيّة
'af'aal-un thulaathiyyat-un
triliteral (lexical) roots

أنّ مصر وقّعت عام ١٩٧٨ اتّفاقاً ثلاثياً

ʾanna miSr-a waqqaʿ-at ʿaam-a 1978 ittifaaq-an thulaathiyy-an

that Egypt signed in the year 1978 a **tripartite/trilateral agreement**

يعمل الآن على إنجاز ثلاثيّته.

ya-ʿmal-u l-ʾaan-a ʿalaa ʾinjaaz-i thulaathiyyat-i-hi.

He is working now to complete **his trilogy.**

3.2.3 *rubaaʿiyy* رُباعي 'quadriliteral; four-part'

أفعال رباعيّة

ʾafʿaal-un rubaaʿiyyat-un

quadriliteral verb roots

3.2.4 *mufaʿʿal* مُفَعَّل

This number adjective takes the form of a **Form II passive participle** and is used to refer to something with a characteristic number of sides or features:

مثلّث

muthallath

triangle (n.); threefold (adj.)

مربّع

murabbaʿ

square (n. and adj.)

ثلاثة آلاف وأربع مئة وثلاثون كيلومتراً مربّعا

thalaathat-u ʾaalaaf-in wa-arbaʿ-u miʾat-in wa-thalaathuuna kiiluumitr-an murabbaʿ-an

3,430 **square** kilometers

مسدّس

musaddas

six-shooter, gun, revolver; also: hexagonal

مسدّس لعبة

musaddas-un luʿbat-un

toy gun

4 Expressions of serial order: "last"

We have already seen the use of expressions for "first" and other numerical rankings. The concept of "last" or "final" is expressed by the terms *ʾaaxir* or *ʾaxiir*. They are both from the same lexical root but are different in form and distribution.

4.1 *ʾaaxir* آخِر 'last, final'

The noun *ʾaaxir* is an active participle in form, signifying the final part or the end part of something. Its plural is *ʾawaaxir* أواخر if it refers to nonhuman entities, and *ʾaaxir-uuna* آخرون (m. pl.) or *ʾaaxir-aat* آخرات (f. pl.) if it refers to humans. It is often used as the first term of an *ʾiDaafa*.

آخر كلمة
'aaxir-u kalimat-in
the last word

آخر الأنباء الواردة من الخرطوم
'aaxir-u l-'anbaa'-i l-waaridat-i min-a
l-kharTuum-i
the latest/last news ('arriving') from
Khartoum

آخر وزير للخارجيّة
'aaxir-u waziir-in li-l-xaarijiyyat-i
the last foreign minister

في أواخر آذار المقبل
fii 'awaaxir-i 'aadhaar-a l-muqbil-i
in the last [part] of next March

في آخر مقابلة له مع الصحيفة
fii 'aaxir-i muqaabalat-in la-hu
ma⁽-a l-SaHiifat-i
in his last interview with the
newspaper

عند آخر الطابور
⁽ind-a 'aaxir-i l-Taabuur-i
at the end of the line

لعب المنتخب السعوديّ آخر مبارياته في الرياض.
la⁽ib-a l-muntaxib-u l-sa⁽uudiyy-u 'aaxir-a mubaariyaat-i-hi fii l-riyaaD-i.
The Saudi team played its last match in Riyadh.

4.2 'axiir أخير 'last; final'

The word 'axiir is an adjective meaning 'final' or 'last' both in the sense of 'final'
and of 'past.' It usually follows the noun and is in concord with it in terms of gender, case, definiteness, and number.

الجملة الأخيرة
al-jumlat-u l-'axiirat-u
the last sentence

وضع المسمار الأخير.
waDa⁽-a l-mismaar-a l-'axiir-a
He put [in] the last nail.

في الأعوام الأخيرة
fii l-'a⁽waam-i l-'axiirat-i
in the last years

4.2.1 In the accusative indefinite, it is used as an adverb meaning "finally":

وأخيراً جاءت إلى القاهرة.
wa-'axiir-an jaa'-at 'ilaa l-qaahirat-i.
And finally she came to Cairo.

16

Prepositions and prepositional phrases

1 Overview

In Arabic as in English, prepositions refer to a location (e.g., 'at, in' *fii* في, *bi-* ب) or a direction (e.g., 'to, from' إلى *ʾilaa*, *min* من), and the meanings of prepositions can apply to concepts of space ('at school' *fii l-madrasat-i* في المدرسة) or time ('at five o'clock' *fii l-saaʿat-i l-xaamisat-i* في الساعة الخامسة).

Prepositions may also be used in abstract or figurative ways ('at least' *ʿalaa l-ʾaqall-i* على الأقل; 'by the way' *ʿalaa fikrat-in* على فكرة). They may occur in conjunction with verbs to convey a particular meaning (e.g., *raHHab-a bi-* رحّب ب 'to welcome' or *ʿabbar-a ʿan* عبّر عن 'to express'). Arabic has a number of these verb-preposition idioms, where the preposition used with the verb is essential for expressing a specific meaning.

1.1 Arabic preposition types
Arabic prepositional expressions fall into two groups, the first group being a relatively small number (ten) of "true" prepositions, and the other group being a more extensive collection of locative expressions.

1.2 Huruuf al-jarr حروف الجرّ
According to Arabic grammatical theory, the **non-derived prepositions** are the **true**, fundamental markers of location and direction, and are called *Huruuf al-jarr* حروف الجرّ, 'particles of attraction' because they "attract" a substantive (noun or adjective) in the genitive case or a suffix pronoun. These non-derived prepositions are a limited and invariable set of lexical items.

1.3 Zuruuf makaan wa-Zuruuf zamaan ظروف مكان وظروف زمان
The **derived prepositions**, on the other hand, usually come from triliteral lexical roots that are also the source of verbs, nouns, and other parts of speech. They are called locative adverbs, or in Arabic *Zuruuf makaan wa-Zuruuf zamaan* ظروف مكان وظروف زمان 'adverbs of place and adverbs of time.' These words denote location in much the same way as prepositions and in this work they are

referred to as **semi-prepositions.**[1] These semi-prepositions may take different case inflections or, in some cases, nunation.

Each of the two preposition types has particular attributes, but the basic rule that applies to both classes is that **the noun, noun phrase, or adjective object of the preposition is in the genitive case.**[2] If the object of the preposition or semi-preposition is a personal pronoun, it takes the form of a pronoun suffix.[3]

Prepositions and semi-prepositions are crucial elements in Arabic syntax, playing fundamental syntactic and semantic roles. However, their usage can be highly idiomatic and may not necessarily correspond to their English equivalents. Therefore, a wide selection of examples is included here.

2 True prepositions (*Huruuf al-jarr* حروف الجرّ)

This small set of lexical items contains the true Arabic prepositions, words that exist strictly as prepositions. There are only ten of them in Modern Standard Arabic, but they are of great frequency and they each have a wide range of meanings. They are: *bi- li-, ka-, fii, min, ʿan, ʾilaa, ʿalaa, Hattaa* and *mundhu*. One of the distinctive features of this word class is that a true Arabic preposition (*Harf al-jarr* حرف الجرّ) cannot be preceded by another preposition.

Another characteristic is that only this class of prepositions can combine with verbs to create verb-preposition idioms (such as *baHath-a fii* 'discuss' and *baHath-a ʿan* 'search for').

This set of items can be divided on the basis of orthography into one-letter, two-letter, and three-letter word groups. Examples are provided to illustrate both spatiotemporal and abstract uses. In certain cases, frequent idiomatic uses are noted as well.

2.1 One-letter prepositions: *bi-* بِ; *li-* لِ; and *ka-* كَ

The three members of this group consist of **one consonant plus a short vowel.** This means that they do not exist as independent orthographical items and they need to be prefixed to the noun that follows.

2.1.1 The preposition *bi-* 'at, with, in, by; by means of'

The preposition *bi-* designates contiguity in its broadest sense. It has a wide range of uses including spatiotemporal, instrumental, and manner adverbial.

---

[1] In his excellent short reference work *Grammaire de l'arabe d'aujourd' hui*, D. E. Kouloughli refers to this group of words as "quasi-prépositions" (1994, 152), which is also an appropriate label. Abboud et al. 1997, 67–68 refer to these words as "noun-prepositions."

[2] For an in-depth semantic and syntactic analysis of Arabic prepositions see Ryding-Lentzner 1977.

[3] When the object of the preposition is an invariable or non-inflected word, such as certain demonstrative pronouns or adverbs (e.g., *dhaalika* 'that' or *hunaa* 'here'), it remains invariable, e.g, *min hunaa* 'from here,' or *baʿd-a dhaalika* 'after that.'

2.1.1.1 SPATIOTEMPORAL LOCATION

(1)   **Space:** The use of *bi-* as a spatial locative ('in, at, on')

بالشمال الإفريقيّ

bi-l-shimaal-i l-ʾifriiqiyy-i

in North Africa ('the African
    north')

بشارع البركة

bi-shaariʿ-i l-barakat-i

on Baraka Street

بجدران المنازل البيضاء

bi-judraan-i l-manaazil-i l-bayDaaʾ-i

on the white **walls** of the houses

الأستاذ بجامعة القاهرة

al-ʾustaadh-u bi-jaamiʿat-i l-qaahirat-i

the professor **at the University** of Cairo

(2)   **Personal locative:** Used in this sense, *bi-* may be prefixed to a noun that
    denotes a state of being and attributes a condition to or describes the condi-
    tion of a person, or it may be prefixed to a noun that denotes an attribute or
    temporary state.

رجال بالملابس التقليدية

*rijaal-un bi-l-malaabis-i
    l-taqliidiyyat-i*

men **with (wearing)** traditional
    clothes

كلّ عامّ وأنتم بخير.

*kull-a ʿaam-in wa-ʾantum
    bi-xayr-in.*

Many happy returns.
('May you be **in wellness** every year.')

(3)   **Time:** An occasion or location in time can be marked with *bi-*:

كان ذاك بالأمس.

kaan-a dhaaka bi-l-ʾams-i.

That was **yesterday.**

بمناسبة تعيين الشيخ وزيراً للدفاع

bi-munaasabat-i taʿyiin-i l-shaykh-i waziir-an li-l-difaaʿ-i

on the occasion of the appointment of the sheikh as minister of defense

بذكرى مرور ثماني مئة سنة على وفاة صلاح الدين

bi-dhikraa muruur-i thamaanii miʾat-i sanat-in ʿalaa wafaat-i SalaaH-i l-diin-i

on the 800th anniversary of the death of Salah al-Din

2.1.1.2 INSTRUMENTAL *bi-* (*baaʾ al-ʾaala* باء الآلة; *baaʾ al-istiʿaana* باء الاستعانة):

The preposition *bi-* is used to refer to an instrument (tool, material, body part) with which an action is accomplished. The instrument can be defined as "an object that plays a role in bringing a process about, but which is not the motivating force, the cause or the instigator" (Chafe 1970, 152).

لا يستطيعون الذهاب بسيّاراتهم.
laa ya-staTiiᶜ-uuna l-dhahaab-a
  bi-sayyaaraat-i-him.
They cannot go in ('by means of')
  their cars.

بدأت بسؤال.
badaʾ-tu bi-suʾaal-in.
I began with ('by means of')
  a question.

دخلا البلد بالباخرة.
daxal-aa l-balad-a bi-l-baaxirat-i.
The two of them entered the country
  by ship.

شدّ الباب بكلتا يديه.
shadd-a l-baab-a bi-kiltaa yad-ay-hi.
He pulled the door with both
  his hands.

(1) *bi-* for substance: A related use, but not instrumental as such, is *bi-* meaning
'with' in the sense of what constitutes the nature of a filling, a substance or
an accompaniment.

أرض مليئة بالأشواك
ʾarD-un maliiʾat-un bi-l-ʾashwaak-i
ground filled with thorns

المكان المليء بالتاريخ
al-makaan-u l-maliiʾ-u bi-l-taariix-i
the place filled with history

لم يكلّل بالنجاح.
lam yu-kallal bi-l-najaaH-i.
It was not crowned with success.

شاي مثلّج بالنعناع
shaay-un muthallaj-un bi-l-naᶜnaaᶜ-i
iced tea with mint

2.1.1.3 ABSTRACT/FIGURATIVE USE: The preposition *bi-* has a wide range of
abstract/figurative uses.

بشكل أو بآخر
bi-shakl-in ʾaw bi-ʾaaxar-a
[in] one way or another

بسبب الغموض
bi-sabab-i l-ghumuuD-i
because of /on account of the mystery

بالأسلوب نفسه
bi-l-ʾusluub-i nafs-i-hi
in the same way

بهدف حلّ كلّ المشاكل
bi-hadaf-i Hall-i kull-i l-mashaakil-i
with the aim of solving all the problems

بسعر مفتوح
bi-siᶜr-in maftuuH-in
at an open price

بأرخص الأثمان
bi-ʾarxaS-i l-ʾathmaan-i
at the cheapest prices

بأحرّ التعازي
bi-ʾaHarr-i l-taᶜaazii
with warmest condolences

قرّروا مصير بلادهم بأنفسهم.
qarrar-uu maSiir-a bilaad-i-him bi-ʾanfus-i-him.
They decided the fate of their country by themselves.

2.1.1.4 MANNER ADVERBIAL: The preposition *bi-* can be used with a noun to
modify a verb phrase by describing the manner in which an action took place.

When used in this way, the *bi-* phrase answers the question "how?" and the object of the preposition is usually an abstract noun.[4]

تنموا ببطء. أن يدافع عن الموقف بشدّة مضاعفة

ta-nmuu bi-buT'-in.   *'an yu-daafi'-a 'an-i l-mawqif-i bi-shiddat-in muDaa'afat-in*

They grow slowly   to defend the position **with** redoubled **intensity**
('with slowness').

When indicating manner, *bi-* is sometimes prefixed to a noun such as *Suura* 'manner,' *Tariiqa* 'way,' or *shakl* 'form' followed by a modifier that provides the exact description of the manner:

بصورة مستمرّة   بصورة مخيّفة

bi-Suurat-in mustamirrat-in   *bi-Suurat-in muxayyifat-in*

continuously   frighteningly

بطرق غير قانونيّة   بهذا الشكل الواسع

bi-Turuq-in ghayr-i qaanuuniyyat-in   *bi-haadhaa l-shakl-i l-waasi'-i*

in illegal **ways**   **in this extensive way**

2.1.1.5 *bi-* AS PREFIX FOR THE PREDICATE OF A NEGATIVE COPULA (*al-xabar al-manfiyy* الخبر المنفي):

A negative verb of being such as *lays-a* 'is not' or *lam ya-kun* 'was not' may be followed by *bi-* as part of the predicate. This is especially the case when the predicate involves the use of a demonstrative pronoun:

لكنّ أحداً منها لم يكن بهذه الأهميّة.

laakinna 'aHad-an min-haa lam ya-kun bi-haadhihi l-'ahammiyyat-i.

But none of them was **of this importance**.

ليس في كلّ الأحيان بهذا السوء.

lays-a fii kull-i l-'aHyaan-i bi-haadhaa l-Suu'-i.

It isn't **this bad** all the time.

2.1.1.6 *bi-* 'PER; [FOR] EVERY':

The concept of 'per' meaning 'for every' may be expressed with *bi-*:

سبعة أيّام بالأسبوع   مئة بالمئة

sab'at-a 'ayyaam-in bi-l-'usbuu'-i   *mi'at-u bi-l-mi'at-i*

seven days **a week**   a hundred **percent**

تبدأ من أربعة سنتات بالدقيقة.

ta-bda'-u min 'arba'at-i sintaat-i bi-l-daqiiqat-i

It starts at four cents **a minute**.

---

[4] For more on this topic see Chapter 11 on adverbs and adverbial expressions.

2.1.2 The preposition *li-* 'to; belonging to; for; for the purpose of'

The preposition *li-* is used to express purpose, direction toward (destination), possession, the indirect object or dative concept of 'to,' and the benefactive concept of 'for' or 'on behalf of.'

There are two spelling rules to observe with *li-*.

(1) When attached to a noun with the definite article, the *'alif* of the definite article is deleted and the *laam* of *li-* attaches directly to the *laam* of the definite article (e.g., *li-l-jaamiʿat-i* للجامعة).

(2) When *li-* is followed by a pronoun suffix, it changes its short vowel to *fatHa* and becomes *la-* (*la-ka* لك, *la-ki* لك, *la-hu* له, *la-haa* لها, *la-kumaa* لكما, *la-humaa* لهما, *la-naa* لنا, *la-kum* لكم, *la-kunna* لكنّ, *la-hum* لهم, *la-hunna* لهنّ) except with the first person singular pronoun suffix, *-ii*, which is suffixed directly to the *laam* (*l-ii* لي 'to me, for me').

2.1.2.1 PURPOSE, CAUSE, REASON, OR MOTIVATION: 'IN ORDER TO, FOR THE PURPOSE OF; DUE TO, BECAUSE OF' (*laam al-taʿliil* لام التعليل): This use of *li-* includes expression of the intention for doing something as well as the reason or motivation for something. "The distinction between intention and reason is made because in English the two are expressed in different terms: the former is introduced by a phrase such as 'in order to' or 'for' whereas the latter is introduced by a phrase such as 'because of.' In Arabic these are both considered to be under the category of *taʿliil*" (Ryding-Lentzner 1977, 132).

(1) Intention:

لردم الهوّة	لدعم مرشّحيهم المحلّيين
li-radm-i l-huwwat-i	*li-daʿm-i murashshaH-ii-him-i l-maHalliyy-iina*
(in order) to fill the gap	in order to support their local candidates

(2) Reason:

لأسباب فنّيّة
li-'asbaab-in fanniyyat-in
for ('because of') technical reasons

2.1.2.2 POSSESSION (*laam al-milk* لام الملك): MSA does not normally use a verb equivalent to 'have.'[5] The preposition *li-* is usually used instead to predicate the concept of belonging in both concrete and abstract senses.[6] If the predication

---

[5] To state ownership explicitly, a verb *malak-a/ya-mlik-u* is used to mean 'own' or 'possess,' e.g., *'a-mlik-u HiSaan-an raa'iʿ-an* 'I own/possess a splendid horse.'

[6] Possession is also expressed by the semi-prepositions *ladaa* and *ʿind-a* (q.v.), although *ʿind-a* is chiefly used in spoken Arabic.

is other than present tense, an accompanying verb of being or becoming carries the tense.

(1) **Present tense:**

للحيوانات لغاتها أيضاً.

li-l-Hayawaanaat-i lughaat-u-haa ʾayD-an.

Animals have their languages too.

لك طرد في غرفة البريد.

la-ka Tard-un fii ghurfat-i l-bariid-i.

You have a package at the mail room.

لا معنى له.

laa maʿanaa *la-hu*.

It has no meaning.

للمنزل حديقة خاصّة.

li-l-manzil-i Hadiiqat-un xaaSSat-un.

The house has a private garden.

(2) **Past tense:** A past tense form of the verb *kaan-a* or sometimes another verb of being or becoming (*Saar-a, baat-a*) is used to convey the past tense of a possessive prepositional construction.

لم يكن له أيّ اتّصال بهم.

lam ya-kun la-hu ʾayy-u ttiSaal-in bi-him.

He did not have any contact with them.

كان لها منزل بديع.

kaan-a la-haa manzil-un badiiʿ-un.

She had a wonderful house.

صار للإسلام في أوروبًا تاريخ وجذور.

Saar-a li-l-ʾislaam-i fii ʾuuruubbaa taariix-un wa-judhuur-un.

Islam in Europe **has acquired** roots and history.

وبات لبعصهنّ شهرة كبيرة.

wa-baat-a li-baʿD-i-hinna shuhrat-un kabiirat-un.

Some of them (f.) came to have great fame.

2.1.2.3 'FOR': The concept of 'for' can be used in spatial or temporal time extensions. When used with persons it often expresses a benefactive or dative relationship.

نكاد لا نجد نظيراً له.

na-kaad-u laa na-jid-u naZiir-an *la-hu*.

We can almost not find a counterpart **for him**.

كانت مخزناً للتوابل.

kaan-at maxzan-an *li-l-tawaabil-i*.

It was a storehouse **for spices**.

(1) **Time:** When used with time expressions *li-* refers to an extent of time.

لمدّة ثماني ساعات	لفترة وجيزة	للمرّة الأولى
li-muddat-i thamaanii saaʿaat-in	*li-fatrat-in* wajiizat-in	*li-l-marrat-i* l-ʾuulaa
for a period of eight hours	**for a brief period**	**for the first time**

2.1.2.4 'TO': With the meaning of 'to,' *li-* may be used with persons or places. When used with places, it conveys much the same directional idea as *'ilaa;*[7] with persons it may express directionality, proximity, benefactive, or dative relationships.

من اليمين لليسار

*min-a l-yamiin-i **li-l-yasaar-i***

from right **to left**

في زيارة للبنان تستغرق أسبوعاً

*fii ziyaarat-in **li-lubnaan-a** ta-staghriq-u 'usbuu^c-an*

on a visit **to Lebanon** [that] will last a week

مبعوث الاتّحاد الأوربّي لعمليّة السلام في الشرق الأوسط

*mab^cuuth-u l-ittiHaad-i l-'uurubbiyy-i **li-^camaliyyat-i** l-salaam-i fii l-sharq-i l-'awsaT-i*

the envoy of the European Union **to the process** of peace in the Middle East

يجلس على المقعد المجاور لها.

*ya-jlis-u ^calaa l-maq^cad-i l-mujaawir-i **la-haa**.*

He is sitting on the seat next **to her**.

الحمد لله.

*al-Hamd-u **li-llaah-i**.*

Praise [be] **to God**.

هنيئاً لك.

*hanii'-an **la-ka**.*

Congratulations **to you**.

ماذا حدث لها؟

*maadhaa Hadath-a **la-haa**?*

What happened **to her**?

2.1.2.5 'OF': This is a broad category where *li-* is used in cases when an *'iDaafa* construction is avoided because of indefiniteness or definiteness of the noun prior to *li-*. It may not always translate directly into English as 'of,' but it often does.

هو انعكاس للواقع الاجتماعي.

*huwa n^cikaas-un **li-l-waaq^c-i** l-ijtimaa^ciyy-i.*

It is a reflection **of social reality**.

وقال ختماً لحديثه

*wa-qaal-a xatm-an **li-Hadiith-i-hi***

he said [in] closing **[of] his talk**

المستشار السياسيّ لرئيس الجمهوريّة

*al-mustashaar-u l-siyaasiyy-u **li-ra'iis-i** l-jumhuuriyyat-i*

the political advisor **of the president** of the republic

قال في كلمة له

*qaal-a fii kalimat-in **la-hu***

he said in a speech **of his**

الأمين العامّ لجامعة الدول العربيّة

*al-'amiin-u l-^caamm-u **li-jaami^cat-i** l-duwal-i l-^carabiyyat-i*

the secretary general **of the League** of Arab States

---

[7] William Wright (1967, II: 147–48) considers *li-* to be "etymologically connected with *'ilaa* ('to, toward') and differs from it only in . . . that *'ilaa* mostly expresses concrete relations, local or temporal, whilst *li-* generally indicates abstract or ideal relations . . . Its principal use is to show the passing on of the action to a more distant object and hence it corresponds to the Latin or German dative."

2.1.3 The preposition *ka-* ﻙ 'like, as; such as; in the capacity of'

This preposition is used for comparison and expresses similarity. It also designates capacity or function. It is restricted in occurrence because it is not used with personal (suffix) pronouns; however it can be used with demonstrative pronouns (e.g., *ka-dhaalika* ﻛﺬﻟﻚ 'like that, thus; likewise.').

2.1.3.1 DESIGNATION OF FUNCTION: The use of *ka-* in this sense specifies capacity, status or function, equivalent to 'as.'

بدا كمدافع عن الإسلام.
badaa ka-mudaafiʿ-in ʿan-i l-ʾislaam-i.
He appeared **as a defender** of Islam.

كمستشار للعاهل الأردنيّ
ka-mustashaar-in li-l-ʿaahil-i l-ʾurdunniyy-i
as counselor to the Jordanian monarch

تعمل كمترجمة.
ta-ʿmal-u ka-mutarjimat-in.
She is working **as a translator.**

كمصدر للطاقة
ka-maSdar-in li-l-Taaqat-i
as a source of energy

تحدّث عن الاستشراق كبحث علميّ.
taHaddath-a ʿan-i l-istishraaq-i ka-baHth-in ʿilmiyy-in.
He spoke of Orientalism **as scholarly research.**

2.1.3.2 SIMILARITY: The preposition *ka-* is used to denote likeness or similarity, equivalent to English 'like.'

الأمر ليس كذلك على الإطلاق.
al-ʾamr-u lays-a ka-dhaalika ʿalaa l-ʾiTlaaq-i.
The situation is not **like that** at all.

نجم كعمر الشريف
najm-un ka-ʿumar-in l-shariif-i
a star **like Omar Sharif**

ثمّ بين العرب أنفسهم كقيسيّين
thumm-a bayn-a l-ʿarab-i ʾanfus-i-him ka-qaysiyy-iina
then among the Arabs themselves **like [the] Qays** [tribe]

في بلد كتونس
fii balad-in ka-tuunis-a
in a country **like Tunisia**

This preposition does not take pronoun suffixes. If there is a need to use the concept of similarity with a personal pronoun, i.e., "like him," "like us," the semi-preposition *mithl-a* is used instead of *ka-*:

ليس هناك فنّانة مثلها.
lays-a hunaaka fannaanat-un mithl-a-haa.
There is no artist **like her.**

2.1.3.3 *ka-maa* AS ADVERBIAL 'AS': By suffixing *-maa*, the preposition *ka-* becomes an adverbial expression meaning 'as' or 'likewise, as well.' It is normally followed directly by a verb.

كما ذكر المتحدّث ...
ka-maa dhakar-a l-mutaHaddith-u ...
likewise, the spokesman mentioned ...

كما تحبّ
ka-maa tu-Hibb-u
as you like

كما تعرفون
ka-maa ta'rif-uuna
as you (pl.) know

كما فعلوا السنة الماضية
ka-maa fa'al-uu l-sanat-a l-maaDiyat-a
like they did last year

2.2 Two-letter prepositions

Prepositions that consist of two letters include: *fii, min* and *'an.*

2.2.1 *fii* في 'in; at; on'

The preposition *fii* is an essential locative preposition in Arabic. It can be used to express location in space (*fii l-jaami'at-i* الجامعة 'at the university') or in time (*fii l-SabaaH-i* الصباح 'in the morning'), as well as figuratively. It may translate as 'at,' 'in,' or 'on,' depending on the context.

2.2.1.1 SPATIAL USES OF *fii*:

في مستشفى الملك خالد
fii mustashfaa l-malik-i xaalid-in
at the King Khalid Hospital

في الحرم الجامعيّ
fii l-Haram-i l-jaami'iyy-i
on the campus ('the university grounds')

عشت في الطابق العلويّ.
'ish-tu fii l-Taabaq-i l-'ulwiyy-i.
I lived on the top floor.

جلسوا في مقهى على الرصيد.
jalas-uu fii maqhan 'alaa l-raSiid-i.
They sat in a café on the sidewalk.

في القدس المحتلة
fii l-quds-i l-muHtallat-i
in occupied Jerusalem

في مسرح الشوارع
fii masraH-i l-shawaari'-i
in the street theater

2.2.1.2 TEMPORAL USES: Used in a temporal sense, *fii* can express both punctuality and duration, i.e., points in time and extension over a span of time:

(1) Punctual use of *fii*:

في هذه المناسبة
fii haadhihi l-munaasabat-i
on this occasion

في ختام الفصل الصيفيّ
fii xitaam-i l-faSl-i l-Sayfiyy-i
at the close of the summer season

في الوقت المناسب
fii l-waqt-i l-munaasib-i
at the right time/proper time

في أوّل الأمر
fii 'awwal-i l-'amr-i
at first ('at the first of the matter')

في الساعة الثامنة   في العـاشرة مساء اليوم

fii l-saaᶜat-i l-thaaminat-i   *fii l-ᶜaashirat-i masaaʾ-a l-yawm-i*

at eight o'clock   at ten o'clock this evening

(2) **Durative:** The durative meaning of *fii* results from its use with nouns that indicate a span of time. Used in this sense it may be equivalent to English 'during.'

في هذا القرن   في حرب الخليج

fii haadhaa l-qarn-i   *fii Harb-i l-xaliij-i*

in (during) this century   in (during) the Gulf War

في الأعوام الأخيرة   في غضون دقائق

fii l-ʾaᶜwaam-i l-ʾaxiirat-i   *fii ghuDuun-i daqaaʾiq-a*

in (during) recent years   [with]in minutes

2.2.1.3 ABSTRACT/FIGURATIVE USES OF *fii*: The locative meaning of *fii* extends to nouns and noun phrases of many types.

في حالة أيّ شكوى   في زيارة لفرنسا

fii Haalat-i ʾayy-i shakwaa   *fii ziyaarat-in li-faransaa*

in case of any complaint   on a visit to France

دورهم في نشر الإسلام   في ضوء الأحداث الأخيرة

dawr-u-hum fii nashr-i l-ʾislaam-i   *fii Dawʾ-i l-ʾaHdaath-i l-ʾaxiirat-i*

their role in spreading Islam   in the light of recent events

في مجال الزراعة   يقضي لياليه في الصلاة.

fii majaal-i l-ziraaᶜat-i   *ya-qDii layaalii-hi fii l-Salaat-i.*

in the field of agriculture   He spends his nights in prayer.

2.2.1.4 AS A MANNER ADVERBIAL: In this idiomatic use, *fii* is often followed by the words *shakl* or *Suura* 'way, shape, form.'

في شكل أساسيّ   في صورة فوريّة

fii shakl-in ʾasaasiyy-in   *fii Suurat-in fawriyyat-in*

in a basic way   immediately

في شكل غريب   في أفضل شكل ممكن

fii shakl-in ghariib-in   *fii ʾafDal-i shakl-in mumkin-in*

in a strange way   in the best way possible

2.2.1.5 MEANING 'PER'

وصلت سرعة الرياح إلى مئة وسبعين كيلومتراً في الساعة.

waSal-at surʕat-u l-riyaaH-i ʔilaa miʔat-in wa-sabʕiina kiiluumitr-an fii l-saaʕat-i.

The wind velocity reached 170 kilometers **an hour/per hour.**

بسرعة ستّة كيلومترات في الثانية

bi-surʕat-i sittat-i kiiluumitraat-in fii l-thaaniyat-i

at the rate of six kilometers **per second**

خمس مرّات في اليوم

xams-a marraat-in fii l-yawm-i

five times **a day/per day**

2.2.1.6 SPECIAL FORMS OF PRONOUN SUFFIXES:

Because of its long vowel ending, *fii* has special forms for the pronoun suffixes -*ii* 'me,' -*hu* 'him,' -*humaa* 'them [two],' -*hum*, and -*hunna* 'them.' The -*ii* suffix merges with the -*ii* of *fii* and changes to -*iyya*; the vowel-shift suffixes, because they come after an -*ii* sound, change their -*u* vowel to -*i*.[8]

	fii + pronoun suffixes		
	Singular	**Dual**	**Plural**
First person:	فيّ *fiyya*		فينا *fii-naa*
Second person: Masculine	فيك *fii-ka*	فيكما *fii-kumaa*	فيكم *fii-kum*
Feminine	فيك *fii-ki*		فيكنّ *fii-kunna*
Third person: Masculine	فيه *fii-hi*	فيهما *fii-himaa*	فيهم *fii-him*
Feminine	فيها *fii-haa*		فيهنّ *fii-hinna*

لا ريب فيه.

laa rayb-a fii-hi.

There's no doubt about it ('in it').

---

[8] The vowel-shift suffixes are the personal pronoun suffixes of the third person that normally have *Damma* after *haaʔ*:-*hu*, -*humaa*, -*hum*, and -*hunna*. This *Damma* shifts to *kasra* when preceded by a front vowel or fronted semivowel (-*i*- or -*ii*- or sometimes *yaaʔ*). See also chapter 12, 2.1.1.

2.2.2 The preposition *min* مِن 'of; from; than'

The preposition *min* indicates direction away from, or point of departure when used spatiotemporally. In addition, it is used to denote source, material, or quantity. It also is used in expressions of comparison, with a comparative adjective where English would use the word "than." It can be used in figurative or abstract ways as well as concrete spatiotemporal ways. Because it ends with a *sukuun*, it sometimes needs a helping vowel. That vowel is /-a/ before the definite article and otherwise, /-i/.

2.2.2.1 *min* AS 'FROM': Used as a directional preposition, *min* indicates 'from':

من جيرانهم العرب

min jiiraan-i-him-i l-ʿarab-i

from their Arab neighbors

تتحوّل من سَيِّىء إلى أسوأ.

ta-taHawwal-u min sayyiʾ-in ʾilaa ʾaswaʾ-a.

It changes from bad to worse.

2.2.2.2 *min* AS 'OF; ONE OF': The use of *min* is especially common in expressions of quantity, measure, or constituent parts.

قصص من الحمراء

qiSaS-un min-a l-Hamraaʾ-i

stories of the Alhambra

كلّها من هذا النوع.

kull-u-haa min haadhaa l-nawʿ-i.

They are all of this type.

المادّة ١٢٥ من القانون

al-maaddat-u 125 min-a l-qaanuun-i

article 125 of the law

وصفوه بأنّه جوّ من الثقة.

waSaf-uu-hu bi-ʾanna-hu jaww-un min-a l-thiqat-i.

They described it as an atmosphere of trust.

استنبطت أنواعاً متميّزة من الصوف.

istanbaT-at ʾanwaaʿ-an mutamayyizat-an min-a l-Suuf-i.

She discovered distinctive types of wool.

ما يحتوي هذا المتحف من كنوز

maa ya-Htawii haadhaa l-mutHaf-u min kunuuz-in

what this museum contains [in terms] of treasures

2.2.2.3 *min* AS 'AMONG'

ومن هذه الفنون أيضاً السيرك

wa-min haadhihi l-funuun-i ʾayD-an-i l-siirk-u

and among these arts [is] also the circus

2.2.2.4 *min* AS 'THROUGH'

دخل من الشبّاك.

daxal-a min-a l-shubbaak-i.

He came through the window.

2.2.2.5 *min* AS 'THAN': With comparative expressions, *min* is used as the equivalent of English 'than.' For more examples, see Chapter 10 on comparative adjectives.

يمضون وقتاً أكثر من المتوقّع.
*ya-mD-uuna waqt-an ʾakthar-a **min-a** l-mutawaqqaᶜ-i.*
They are spending more time **than** expected.

أصدرت أكثر من خمس مئة دراسة علميّة.
*ʾaSdar-at ʾakthar-a **min** xams-i miʾat-i diraasat-in ᶜilmiyyat-in.*
It has published more **than** 500 scientific studies.

2.2.2.6 THE USE OF *min* WITH LOCATIVE ADVERBS: When *min* occurs before a locative adverb (or semi-preposition), it usually changes the inflectional vowel of the adverb to *kasra* if the adverb is followed by a noun or pronoun suffix.

من دون تأخير
min duun-i taʾxiir-in
without delay

من أمامهم
min ʾamaam-i-him
from in front of them

نجدها من خلال شروحه.
*na-jid-u-haa **min** xilaal-i shuruuH-i-hi.*
We find it **through** his commentaries.

(1) *min qabl-u*: Used with certain adverbs that end in *Damma* (such as *qabl-u*), *min* has no effect on the final inflectional vowel as long as the adverb is not in an *ʾiDaafa* with a following noun.[9]

> *min qabl-u* '[ever] before'
> *min Hayth-u* 'regarding, as to'

2.2.2.7 PLEONASTIC OR "DUMMY" *min*: As a way of introducing a sentence, *min* may be used with a descriptive term such as a participle or adjective expressing an introductory observation, just as in English some sentences start with "It is." This is a way to avoid mentioning the source of a judgment or evaluation and is especially common usage in media Arabic, where observations may need to be general or unattributed.

من المتوقّع أن . . .
min-a l-mutawaqqaᶜ-i ʾan . . .
It is **expected** that . . .

من الطبيعيّ أن نقوم بزيارة.
min-a l-Tabiiᶜiyy-i ʾan na-quum-a bi-ziyaarat-in.
It is **natural** that we undertake a visit.

---

[9] See Chapter 11, section 4.1.3, and Chapter 7, section 5.3.1.3.

من المؤكّد أنّ انقضاء عشرين سنة . . .

min-a l-mu'akkad-i 'anna nqiDaa'-a 'ishriina sanat-an . . .

it **is certain** that the passage of twenty years . . .

من الخطأ أن يبقى هناك استعمار.

min-a l-xaTa'-i 'an ya-bqaa hunaaka sti'maar-un.

It **is wrong** for imperialism to remain.

2.2.2.8 WITH *qariib* قريب 'NEAR': An idiomatic use of *min* occurs with the adjective *qariib* 'near, close.' English speakers think of "close to" or "near to" when using this adjective, but the correct Arabic preposition to use is *min*.

اسمه كان قريباً جدّاً من اسمها.

ism-u-hu kaan-a qariib-an jidd-an min-i sm-i-haa.

His name was very **close to** her name.

2.2.2.9 SOME SPELLING VARIATIONS: When suffixed with the pronoun *-ii* 'me,' the *nuun* in *min* doubles, so that instead of **min-ii*, the phrase 'from me' or 'than me' becomes *minnii* منّي.

When followed by the pronouns *maa* 'what, that, whatever,' or *man* 'whoever,' the *nuun* of *min* is assimilated to the *miim* of *maa*, or *man*' and doubles, yielding the contractions *mimmaa* ممّا 'of/from that, from what' and *mimman* ممّن 'of/from whom.'

أقلّ ممّا نحتاج إليه	هو أكبر منّي.
'aqall-u mimmaa na-Htaaj-u 'ilay-hi	*huwa 'akbar-u minnii.*
less **than** [that which] we need	He's older **than** I.

أهمّ كثيراً ممّا سبقه

'ahamm-u kathiir-an mimmaa sabaq-a-hu

much more important **than what** preceded it

2.2.3 The preposition *'an* 'from, away from; about'

Arabic grammars consider *'an* to be a true preposition, but its syntactic behavior under certain conditions also allows it to be classified as a noun.[10] Its original meaning, according to Wright (1967, 2:143), was as a noun meaning 'side.'[11]

---

[10] E.g., when it serves as the object of the preposition *min* (see below).

[11] Its nominal use survives in the expressions such as *min 'an yamiin-i-ka* 'from your right [side].' For discussion of this point see Ryding Lentzner 1977, 94.

This preposition has two distinct meanings, one having to do with 'distance away from,' and the other with the concept of 'concerning' or 'about.' As other prepositions, it can have spatiotemporal and abstract uses, as well as idiomatic ones.

In terms of special spelling rules, the helping vowel used with *ᶜan* is /-i/. When suffixed to a pronoun starting with *miim* (*maa, man*) the *nuun* of *ᶜan* is assimilated to the *miim*, and doubles: *ᶜammaa* عمّا, *ᶜamman* عمّن. Likewise, when suffixed with the first person singular personal pronoun *-ii*, the *nuun* doubles: *ᶜannii* عنّي.

2.2.3.1 *ᶜan* AS 'ABOUT, REGARDING, OF, CONCERNING'

أصدق تعبير عن الولاء للوطن

ʾaSdaq-u taᶜbiir-in ᶜan-i l-wilaaʾ-i li-l-waTan-i

the most sincere expression **of devotion** to the homeland

في برنامج عن دور الجامعة في الاتّصال الثقافيّ

fii barnaamaj-in ᶜan dawr-i l-jaamiᶜat-i fii l-ittiSaal-i l-thaqaafiyy-i

in a program **about the role of the university** in cultural contact

فهناك روايات عدّة عمّا حدث.

fa-hunaaka riwaayaat-un ᶜiddat-un ᶜammaa Hadath-a.

There are several stories **about what** happened.

2.2.3.2 CERTAIN VERBS REQUIRE *ᶜan*:

الكتاب صدر عن دار العلم.	تختلف عن غيرها.
al-kitaab-u Sadar-a ᶜan daar-i l-ᶜilm.	*ta-xtalif-u ᶜan ghayr-i-haa.*
The book **was published by** ('issued from') Dar al-ᶜilm.	**She differs from** others.

2.2.3.3 'ON THE RIGHT; ON THE LEFT': With directions, *ᶜan* is used as English would use 'on':

عن يمينه . . . وعن يساره

ᶜan yamiin-i-hi . . . wa-ᶜan yasaar-i-hi

on his right . . . and on his left

2.3 Three-letter prepositions: *ᶜalaa* على, *ʾilaa* إلى, and *Hattaa* حتّى

All three of these prepositions end with *ʾalif maqSuura*. A particular spelling feature of both *ᶜalaa* and *ʾilaa* is that the final *ʾalif maqSuura* converts to *yaaʾ* when a pronoun suffix is added to the word. Owing to the shift of the *ʾalif* to *yaaʾ*, the third person pronoun suffixes *-hu, -humaa, -hum,* and *-hunna* shift their vowel from /-u/ to/ -i/ and become *-hi, -himaa, -him,* and *-hinna*. For a model inflectional chart of *ᶜalay-* and *ʾilay-* plus pronoun suffixes see Chapter 12 section 2.3.

Note that *Hattaa* does not take pronoun suffixes.

2.3.1 The preposition ʿalaa على 'on, upon'

This preposition designates the concept of 'on' or 'upon' in general, whether spatio-temporal or figurative. In the abstract sense, it conveys also a sense of "incumbent upon."

2.3.1.1 ʿalaa 'ON; UPON'

(1) Spatial meaning:

عثر على هيكل عظميّ.
ʿathar-a ʿalaa haykal-in ʿaZmiyy-in.
He stumbled **upon a skeleton.**

على اليابسة
ʿalaa l-yaabisat-i
on dry land

الرجال على ظهور الخيل
al-rijaal-u ʿalaa Zuhuur-i l-xayl-i
the men **on horseback**

على الشاشة
ʿalaa l-shaashat-i
on the screen

(2) Temporal meaning: Used with a word denoting extent of time, ʿalaa has a durative sense and may indicate passage of time from a particular point in the past. This can be expressed in English in various ways.

على مدار العام
ʿalaa madaar-i l-ʿaam-i
all year round (**'on the circuit of** the year')

على مدى يومين
ʿalaa madaa yawm-ayni
for (**'during'**) two days

بعد ثلاثة أيّام على وقوع الزلزال
baʿd-a thalaathat-i ʾayyaam-in ʿalaa wuquuʿ-i l-zilzaal
after three days **since the [happening of the]** earthquake

2.3.1.2 FIGURATIVE MEANING: Used figuratively, ʿalaa can denote a range of meanings, some a direct reflection of the spatiotemporal concepts; others more abstract. Among those abstract meanings are the sense of 'according to; as for' and 'incumbent upon.'

على أساس غير عنصريّ
ʿalaa ʾasaas-in ghayr-i ʿunSuriyy-in
on a non-racist **basis**

على ما أظنّ
ʿalaa maa ʾa-Zunn-u . . .
in my opinion; as for what I think

السلام عليكم. وعليكم السلام.
al-salaam-u ʿalay-kum. wa -ʿalay-kum-u l-salaam-u.
Peace be **upon you** (pl.). And **upon you** (pl.) peace.

(1) 'up to; incumbent upon; must; have to': Used in this sense, ʿalaa denotes a required or expected action. It is therefore followed either by the particle ʾan plus a subjunctive verb, or by a verbal noun.

علينا أن نفهم معنى الرياضة.
ᶜalay-naa ᵓan na-fham-a maᶜnaa l-riyaaDat-i.
We have to understand the meaning of sport.

علينا أن نبدأ من الصفر.
ᶜalay-naa ᵓan na-bdaᵓ-a min-a l-Sifr-i
We have to begin from zero.

وعلى الدولة أن تقوم بدورها.
wa-ᶜalaa l-dawlat-i ᵓan ta-quum-a bi-dawr-i-haa.
It is up to the state to undertake its role.

عليه أن يأتي إلى هنا.
ᶜalay-hi ᵓan ya-ᵓtiy-a ᵓilaa hunaa.
He has to come here.

2.3.2 The preposition *ᵓilaa* إلى 'to, towards'

The general meaning of *ᵓilaa* is directional towards an object. It is used spatiotemporally and also in abstract and figurative ways. When used in abstract senses it often has the sense of 'addition to.'

Because its final letter is *ᵓalif maqSuura*, like *ᶜalaa*, its *ᵓalif* converts to *yaaᵓ* when pronoun suffixes are added (see Chapter 12, section 2.3).

من هناك إلى اسطنبول
min hunaaka ᵓilaa isTanbuul-a
from there to Istanbul

إلى مسافة عشرة أمتار
ᵓilaa masaafat-i ᶜasharat-i ᵓamtaar-in
to a distance of ten meters

إلى اليمين
ᵓilaa l-yamiin-i
to the right

إلى أين؟
ᵓilaa ᵓayna?
Where to?

2.3.2.1 VERBS OF MOTION PLUS *ᵓilaa*: Note that with many verbs of motion, it is necessary to use *ᵓilaa* with the point of destination.

عندما جئنا إلى هنا
ᶜinda-maa jiᵓ-naa ᵓilaa hunaa
when we came ('to') here

جئت إلى هنا لأنّني واثق من قدرتي.
jiᵓ-tu ᵓilaa hunaa liᵓanna-nii waathiq-un min qudrat-ii.
I came ('to') here because I am confident in my ability.

2.3.2.2 ABSTRACT/FIGURATIVE MEANINGS OF *ᵓilaa*:

انتهت إلى فشل ذريع.
intahat ᵓilaa fashl-in dhariiᶜ-in.
It ended **in** a devastating failure.

يترجم إلى لغته.
yu-tarjim-u ᵓilaa lughat-i-hi.
He translates **into** his language.

وما إلى ذلك
wa-maa ᵓilaa dhaalika
and **so forth**

من الألف إلى الياء
min-a l-ᵓalif-i ᵓilaa l-yaaᵓ-i
from beginning **to end**
('from the *ᵓalif* to the *yaaᵓ*')

2.3.3 The preposition *Hattaa* حَتَّى 'until, up to'

Hattaa, although it ends with *ʾalif maqSuura* like *ʾilaa* and *ʿalaa*, does not take personal pronoun objects (suffix pronouns) and therefore it does not change its shape or spelling. Its meaning as a preposition is closely related to that of *ʾilaa* 'to, towards' except that it designates direction in time rather than in space.

It is important to note that *Hattaa* has at least two other functions in Arabic syntax other than as a preposition meaning 'up to' or 'until'; it also is an adverb or preposition with the meaning of 'even' and a conjunctive particle used with verbs meaning 'in order to.'

حتّى غروب الشمس	حتّى فجر أمس
Hattaa ghuruub-i l-shams-i	*Hattaa fajr-i ʾams-i*
until sunset	**until dawn yesterday**

حتّى مساء غد	حتّى السبعينات من القرن العشرين
Hattaa masaaʾ-i ghad-in	*Hattaa l-sabʿiinaat-i min-a l-qarn-i l-ʿishriina*
until tomorrow evening	**up to the seventies of the twentieth century**

حتّى فتحها على يد المسلمين
Hattaa fatH-i-haa ʿalaa yad-i l-muslim-iina
until it was conquered ('its conquering') by the Muslims

حتّى العشرين من عمره
Hattaa l-ʿishriina min ʿumr-i-hi
until he was twenty years old ('until the twentieth [year] of his age')

2.3.4 The preposition *mundhu* مُنذُ 'since; ago; for'

This preposition has the meaning of distance or extent in time and can be translated in several ways, depending on context. Like *Hattaa* and *ka-* it does not take personal pronoun objects.

2.3.4.1 *mundhu* AS 'FOR; IN': Used to mean 'for' or 'in,' it denotes a **time span** during which something goes on. Its object is usually a noun phrase that refers to a span of time:

منذ خمس سنوات متواصلة	منذ ربع قرن
mundhu xams-i sanawaat-in mutawaaSilat-an	*mundhu rubʿ-i qarn-in*
for five continuous **years**	**for a quarter century**

يعمل منذ شهرين كمترجم.
ya-ʿmal-u mundhu shahr-ayni ka-mutarjim-in.
He has been working **for two months** as a translator.

2.3.4.2 *mundhu* AS 'SINCE; FROM': When *mundhu* means 'since,' it specifies a particular point of time in the past where the action began. It can also mean 'from' when the beginning of a time period is denoted and an end specified (often used with *Hattaa* 'until, up to').

كانت مخزّنة في صناديق منذ الحرب.

kaan-at muxazzanat-an fii Sanaadiiq-a mundhu l-Harb-i.

They had been stored in boxes **since the war.**

منذ الستّينات صارت تأخذ دوراً أكبر.

mundhu l-sittiinaat-i Saar-at ta-ʔxudh-u dawr-an ʔakbar-a.

Since the sixties she has assumed a larger role.

منذ مطلع السبعينات

mundhu maTlaᶜ-i l-sabᶜiinaat-i

since the beginning of the seventies

كانوا مصطفّين منذ الصباح الباكر.

kaan-uu muSTaff-iina mundhu l-SabaaH-i l-baakir-i.

They had been lined up **since early morning.**

2.3.4.3 'AGO': In the sense of 'ago,' *mundhu* specifies a time in the past measured from the present time:

قال منذ أكثر من قرن من الزمان

qaal-a mundhu ʔakthar-a min qarn-in min-a l-zamaan-i

he said **more than a century ('of time') ago**

كان قد بعث إليه منذ ثلاثة أسابيع برسالة.

kaan-a qad baᶜath-a ʔilay-hi mundhu thalaathat-i ʔasaabiiᶜ-a bi-risaalat-in.

He had sent him a letter **three weeks ago.**

تقديراً لجهوده . . . منذ أكثر من أربعين سنة

taqdiir-an li-juhuud-i-hi . . . mundhu ʔakthar-a min ʔarbaᶜiina sanat-in

in appreciation of his efforts . . . **more than forty years ago**

2.3.4.4 PRESENT PERFECT MEANING WITH *mundhu*: An action started in the past and continuing into the present is usually rendered by the present tense in Arabic, whereas in English, the present perfect is used. The preposition *mundhu* is used to specify at which point in the past the action started. This structure may occur with verbal predications or with equational predications.

يعمل في الإدارة منذ شهرين.

ya-ᶜmal-u fii l-ʔidaarat-i mundhu shahr-ayni.

He has been working in the administration **for two months.**

أعيش هنا منذ خمس سنوات.

*ʾaʿiish-u hunaa **mundhu** xams-i sanawaat-in.*

I have been living here **for** five years.

أهوى الغناء منذ طفولتي.

*ʾa-hwaa l-ghinaaʾ-a **mundhu** Tufuulat-ii.*

I have loved singing **since** my childhood.

2.4 Summary of true Arabic prepositions (*Huruuf al-jarr* حروف الجرّ)

One-letter prepositions:

bi-	ب	*li-*	ل	*ka-*	ك

Two-letter prepositions:

fii	في	*min*	من	*ʿan*	عن

Three-letter prepositions:

ʾilaa	إلى	*ʿalaa*	على	*Hattaa*	حتّى	*mundhu* منذ

3 Locative adverbs or semi-prepositions (*Zuruuf makaan wa-Zuruuf zamaan* ظروف مكان وظروف زمان)

These words function in many ways as prepositions but are not "true" prepositions because

(1) they are derived from triliteral lexical roots and
(2) they can be preceded by a true preposition or even another semi-preposition.

Usually they show accusative case marking with *fatHa*, to indicate their adverbial function. Under certain circumstances, that case marker can change.[12] Like true prepositions, they are normally followed by a noun in the genitive case or a pronoun suffix.

Semi-prepositions or locative adverbs are used in concrete and figurative ways, but they do not have the extensive range of abstract meanings that true prepositions have, nor are they normally used in verb-preposition idioms. Included here are examples of some of the most common ones.

3.1 *ʾamaam-a* أمام 'in front of; facing; in the face of; before; to'

The word *ʾamaam-a* refers to a position 'in front' or 'before,' both spatially and figuratively:

---

[12] The fact that the case marker may change is considered an indicator of their close relationship to nouns.

أمامنا الكثير من الفرص والكثير من التحدّيات.

'amaam-a-naa l-kathiir-u min-a l-furaS-i wa-l-kathiir-u min-a l-taHaddiyyaat-i.

Before us are many opportunities and many challenges.

أمامي الطبيعة الرائعة.

'amaam-ii l-Tabii'at-u l-raa'i'at-u.

Before me is splendid nature.

هو مَسؤول أمام المجلس.

huwa mas'uul-un 'amaam-a l-majlis-i.

He is responsible **to ('before') the council.**

3.1.1 *'amaam-a* as 'against' or 'versus'

Idiomatically, *'amaam-a* is used in the context of sports teams to express the team 'against' which another team is playing.

يلعبون مباراة أخرى أمام منتخب الصين.

ya-l'ab-uuna mubaaraat-an 'uxraa 'amaam-a muntaxab-i l-Siin-i.

They play another match **against the Chinese team.**

كسبوا أولى مبارياتهم أمام سوريا.

kasab-uu 'uulaa mubaarayaat-i-him 'amaam-a suuriyaa.

They won the first of their matches **against Syria.**

3.1.2 *'amaam* as forward position

Sometimes, *'amaam* is used as a noun referring to a forward position. When used this way it inflects for all three cases.

يمثّل خطوة كبرى إلى الأمام.

yu-maththil-u xuTwat-an kubraa 'ilaa l-'amaam-i.

It represents a great step **forward.**

من أمامهم

min 'amaam-i-him

from **in front of them**

3.2 *'athnaa'-a* أثناء and *fii 'athnaa'-i* في أثناء 'during'

The noun *'athnaa'* may be used in the accusative case to indicate 'during' or after the preposition *fii* (in the genitive case), with the same meaning.

أثناء إحدى جلسات المناقشات

'athnaa'-a 'iHdaa jalasaat-i l-munaaqashaat-i

during one of the sessions of the debates

في أثناء أزمة الخليج

fii 'athnaa'-i 'azmat-i l-xaliij-i

during the Gulf Crisis

3.3 *bayn-a* بين 'between; among'

3.3.1 Repetition of *bayn-a* with pronoun

The semi-preposition *bayn-a* means 'between' two objects and also 'among' many objects. It has the peculiarity that **when one or both of the objects are pronouns, *bayn-a* must be repeated.**

بيني وبينك
bayn-ii wa-bayn-a-ka
between me and (between) you

بينه وبينها
bayn-a-hu wa-bayn-a-haa
between him and (between) her

الخلاف بينهم وبين جزء من الجيش.
al-xilaaf-u bayn-a-hum wa-bayn-a juz'-in min-a l-jaysh-i.
The dispute is **between them and (between)** a **portion** of the army.

3.3.2 *bayn-a* plus nouns

If both of the objects of the preposition are nouns, *bayn-a* is used only once and the second noun is conjoined to the first with the conjunction *wa-* 'and.' Both nouns are considered objects of the semi-preposition and both are in the genitive case. A dual noun or a plural noun may also follow *bayn-a*.

بين البلدين
bayn-a l-balad-ayni
between the two countries

ضاع بين الزحام.
Daa°-a bayn-a l-ziHaam-i.
He got lost in (among) the crowd.

بين البنك الدوليّ وصندوق النقد الدوليّ
bayn-a l-bank-i l-duwaliyy-i wa-Sanduuq-i l-naqd-i l-duwaliyy-i
between the World **Bank** and the International Monetary **Fund**

بين الوفد الفلسطينيّ والوفد الإسرائيليّ
bayn-a l-wafd-i l-filisTiiniyy-i wa-l-wafd-i l-'israa'iiliyy-i
between the Palestinian delegation and the Israeli delegation

تبادل الآراء بين الزعماء العرب
tabaadul-u l-'aaraa'-i bayn-a l-zu°amaa'-i l-°arab-i
exchange of views **among the Arab leaders**

أفضل وسيلة لإيجاد سبل التفاهم بين الأمم
'afDal-u wasiilat-in li-'iijaad-i subul-i l-tafaahum-i bayna l-'umam-i
the best method to create ways of understanding **among nations**

3.3.3 *bayn-a* after *min*

After the preposition *min*, *bayn-a* becomes *bayn-i*, as object of the preposition:

ومن بينهم النائب اللبنانيّ
wa-min bayn-i-him-i l-naa'ib-u l-lubnaaniyy-u
and **among them** [is] the Lebanese representative

3.4 *ba°d-a* بعد 'after; in'

This function word is used as a semi-preposition and also as an adverb. As a semi-preposition, it has a *fatHa* (accusative case ending) and takes a noun or pronoun object. In some cases it might be preceded by a true preposition (usually *min* or *'ilaa*), and its case marker then changes to genitive (final *kasra*). It still is followed by a noun or pronoun in the genitive case.

3.4.1 Locative *ba'd-a*

The locative use of *ba'd-a* includes both time and place.

<table>
<tr><td dir="rtl">بعد أربعة قرون</td><td dir="rtl">بعد ولادة ابنهما</td></tr>
<tr><td>ba'd-a 'arba'at-i quruun-in</td><td>ba'd-a wilaadat-i bn-i-himaa</td></tr>
<tr><td>after four centuries</td><td>after the birth of their son</td></tr>
<tr><td dir="rtl">ماذا حدث له بعد ذلك؟</td><td dir="rtl">بعد توقيع العقد</td></tr>
<tr><td>maadhaa Hadath-a la-hu ba'd-a dhaalika?</td><td>ba'd-a tawqii'-i l-'aqd-i</td></tr>
<tr><td>What happened to him after that?</td><td>after signing the contract</td></tr>
</table>

3.4.2 *ba'd* after a preposition

Preceded by a true preposition, *ba'd* inflects in the genitive:

<table>
<tr><td dir="rtl">أكلات خفيفة لبعد منتصف الليل</td><td dir="rtl">في بعد الظهر</td></tr>
<tr><td>'akalaat-un xafiifat-un li-ba'd-i muntaSaf-i l-layl-i</td><td>fii ba'd-i l-Zuhr-i</td></tr>
<tr><td>light food for after midnight</td><td>in the afternoon</td></tr>
</table>

3.4.3 *ba'd-u* بعدُ

If there is no noun or pronoun following *ba'd*, it is considered an adverb. In this case, devoid of a noun or pronoun object, *ba'd* changes its final vowel to *Damma*.[13] In this adverbial role, the final *Damma* is invariable. The expression *ba'd-u* is used chiefly as an adverbial of time in negative clauses, meaning '[not] yet.'

لم يحدّد موعده بعد.

*lam yu-Haddad maw'id-u-hu **ba'd-u**.*

Its date has not **yet** been set.

3.4.3.1 THE EXPRESSION *fii-maa ba'd-u* فيما بعدُ 'LATER'

<table>
<tr><td dir="rtl">اعملها فيما بعد.</td><td dir="rtl">سأتلفن لك فيما بعد.</td></tr>
<tr><td>i-'mal-haa fii-maa ba'd-u.</td><td>sa-'u-talfin-u la-ka fii-maa ba'd-u.</td></tr>
<tr><td>Do it later.</td><td>I will telephone you later.</td></tr>
</table>

---

[13] The final *Damma* on *ba'd-u* and on certain other semi-prepositions (*qabl-u*, *taHt-u*) is considered to be a remnant of an old locative case. This *Damma* has two characteristics: (1) it is invariable, even after a preposition (e.g., *min qabl-u*; *min taHt-u*); (2) it cannot be on the first term of an *'iDaafa*, that is, it cannot be followed by a noun in the genitive case or by a pronoun suffix. See Chapter 11, section 4.1.3, especially note 12.

3.5 *daaxil-a* داخل 'inside, within'

The semi-preposition *daaxil-a* refers to a location inside or on the interior of something:

<table>
<tr>
<td>

لينغلقوا داخل الحدود
li-ya-nghaliq-uu daaxil-a l-Huduud-i
to be locked **inside the borders**

</td>
<td>

داخل الدولة الإسلاميّة
daaxil-a l-dawlat-i l-ʾislaamiyyat-i
inside the Islamic state

</td>
</tr>
</table>

3.5.1 After a true preposition

After a true preposition, *daaxil-* inflects for the genitive case.

في داخل الاسفنج
fii daaxil-i l-isfanj-i
on the inside of the sponge

3.6 *Didd-a* ضدّ 'against; versus'

<table>
<tr>
<td>

يشنّ حرباً ضدّ الدولة التركيّة.
ya-shunn-u Harb-an Didd-a l-dawlat-i
  l-turkiyyat-i.
He is launching a war
  against the Turkish state.

</td>
<td>

كلّ شيء ضدّي.
kull-u shayʾ-in Didd-ii.
Everything is **against me.**

</td>
</tr>
</table>

3.7 *Dimn-a* ضمنَ 'within; inside; among'

ضمن قوّات الأمم المتّحدة
Dimn-a quwwaat-i l-ʾumam-i l-muttaHidat-i
within the powers of the United Nations

أراضٍ كان يجب أن تكون ضمن حصّتهم
ʾaraaD-in kaan-a ya-jib-u an ta-kuun-a Dimn-a HiSSat-i-him
lands [which] should have been [included] **within their portion**

3.8 *duun-a* دونَ; *min duun-i* من دون; *bi-duun-i* بدون 'without'

The word *duun* by itself literally means 'below, under' and it can be used by itself marked with a *fatHa* as a semi-preposition meaning 'without.' However, it often occurs in combination with *min* or *bi-* as a compound prepositional phrase meaning 'without.'

3.8.1 *duun-a*

استخدام بعضها دون بعضها الآخر
istixdaam-u baʿD-i-haa duun-a baʿD-i-haa l-ʾaaxar-i
using some of them **without the others**

3.8.2 *min duun-i*

السلام غير ممكن من دون هذا البلد.

*al-salaam-u ghayr-u mumkin-in **min duun-i** haadha l-balad-i.*

Peace is not possible **without this country.**

من دون فرض رسم دخول

min duun-i farD-i rasm-i duxuul-in

without imposing an entrance fee

3.8.3 *bi-duun-i*

قهوة بدون كافين

*qahwat-un **bi-duun-i** kaafiin*

decaffeinated coffee ('**without caffeine**')

يبقى تعليمها بدون هدف.

*ya-bqaa taʿliim-u-haa **bi-duun-i** hadaf-in.*

Teaching it remains aimless ('**without a goal**').

3.9 *fawq-a* فوقَ 'above; upon; on top of; over'

يسير على عجلات فوقها.

*ya-siir-u ʿalaa ʿajalaat-in **fawq-a-hu.***

It goes along on wheels [which are] **above it.**

ما فوقه وما تحته

*maa **fawq-a-hu** wa-maa taHt-a-hu*

what is **above it** and below it

على الأرض وفوقها

*ʿalaa l-ʾarD-i wa-**fawq-a-haa***

on the earth and **over it**

فوق سطح منزله

fawq-a saTH-i manzal-i-hi

on [top of] the roof of his house

3.10 *fawr-a* فور 'immediately upon; immediately after; right after'

نُقل إلى مستشفى الجامعة فور إصابته.

*nuqil-a ʾilaa mustashfaa l-jaamiʿat-i **fawr-a** ʾiSaabat-i-hi.*

He was transported to the university hospital **right after being hit.**

3.11 *Hasab-a* حسبَ 'according to; in accordance with'

حسب نصّ القرار

Hasab-a naSS-i l-qaraar-i

according to the text of the resolution

3.12 *Hawl-a* حولَ 'about, regarding; around'

This semi-preposition has two distinct meanings, one being 'about' in the concrete physical sense of 'surrounding' or 'around' and the other being 'about' in the sense of 'regarding' or 'with regard to.'

التدخّل الأمريكيّ حول العالم   حول الوضع في الشرق الأوسط

al-tadaxxul-u l-ʾamriikiyy-u **Hawl-a**   **Hawl-a** l-waDᶜ-i fii l-sharq-i l-ʾawsaT-i
  l-ᶜaalam-i   **about the situation** in the Middle East
American intervention around
  the world

حول مواضيع ذات اهتمام مشترك

Hawl-a l-mawaaDiiᶜ-i dhaat-i htimaam-in mushtarak-in
about topics of common concern

3.13 *Hawaalii* حوالي 'approximately'

The word *Hawaalii* is not the typical locative adverb or semi-preposition ending in *fatHa*, yet it serves much the same function, being followed by a noun in the genitive case.

في جلساته حوالي مئة باحث.

fii jalsaat-i-hi **Hawaalii** miʾat-i baaHith-in.
In its sessions [were] **approximately** 100 researchers.

3.14 *ʾibbaan-a* إبانَ 'during'

إبان الشتاء

ʾibbaan-a l-shitaaʾ-i
during the winter

3.15 *ʾithr-a* إثرَ 'right after; immediately after'

إثر اجتماعهم

ʾithr-a jtimaaᶜ-i-him
right after their meeting

3.16 *ʾizaaʾ-a* إزاءَ 'facing; in the face of'

إزاء القضايا المصريّة

izaaʾ-a l-qaDaayaa l-miSriyyat-i
in the face of Egyptian problems

3.17 *ladaa* لدى 'at, by; upon; to; having'

This locative adverb denotes possession and proximity. Like *ʾilaa* and *ᶜalaa*, it changes its final *ʾalif maqSuura* to *yaaʾ* when it has a personal pronoun suffix. See model inflectional chart of *ᶜalaa* + pronoun suffixes, Chapter 12, section 2.3.

3.17.1 *ladaa* showing possession:

لديهما أشياء مشتركة كثيرة.

laday-himaa ʾashyaaʾ-u mushtarakat-un kathiirat-un.

They [two] have many things in common.

لا مستقبل لديَّ.

laa mustaqbal-a laday-ya.

I [would] **have** no future.

ألعاب القوى لديها نجوم بارزون.

ʾalʿaab-u l-qiwaa laday-haa nujuum-un baariz-uuna.

Track and field [sports][they] **have** prominent stars.

3.17.2 *ladaa* as 'to; at; with'

A particular use of *ladaa* is to denote the country to which an ambassador is designated.

سفير قبرص لدى مصر

safiir-u qubruS-a ladaa miSr-a

the ambassador of Cyprus to Egypt

سفير اليابان لدى السعوديّة

safiir-u l-yaabaan ladaa l-saʿuudiyyat-i

the ambassador of Japan **to Saudi Arabia**

3.17.3 *ladaa* as 'upon; at the time of'

ولدى رفضهم ذلك

wa-ladaa rafD-i-him dhaalika

and **upon their refusal** of that

لدى عودة السفير إلى تونس

ladaa ʿawdat-i l-safiir-i ʾilaa tuunis-a

upon the return of the ambassador to Tunis

3.18 *maʿ-a* مَعَ 'with'[14]

The basic meaning of *maʿ-a* has to do with accompaniment or association and is almost always equivalent to English 'with.' Note that it is not used for indicating instrumental concepts; *bi-* is used for that. It is also possible to use *maʿ-a* to express possession of something concrete that people could "have with" them, such as a wallet or keys. This expression of possession does not indicate permanency or the concept of 'belonging to.'

3.18.1 Accompaniment or association

مع الأقارب والأصدقاء

maʿ-a l-ʾaqaarib-i wa-l-ʾaSdiqaaʾ-i

with relatives and friends

مع أحرّ التمنّيات

maʿ-a ʾaHarr-i l-tamanniyaat-i

with warmest wishes

---

[14] The word *maʿ-a* may seem like a true preposition because it is a lexical primitive and is sometimes used in verb-preposition expressions (*naaqash-a maʿ-a* 'to discuss with,' *tasaawaa maʿ-a* 'to equate with,' *taʿaawan-a maʿ-a* 'to cooperate with,' *ijtamaʿ-a maʿ-a* 'to meet with'). The eighth-century Arabic grammarian Sibawayhi, however, cites the phrase *dhahab-a min maʿ-i-hi* 'he left him,' showing that *maʿ-a* can sometimes be the object of another preposition. Sibawayhi 1970, I:177.

يريدون التداول مع الأمريكيين.

*yu-riid-uuna l-tadaawul-a **ma ͨ -a l-ʾamriikiyy-iina**.*

They want to deliberate **with the Americans.**

فمع الكلّ نتقدّم من أجل الكلّ.

*fa-**ma ͨ -a l-kull-i** na-taqaddam-u min ʾajl-i l-kull-i.*

With everyone we will progress for the sake of everyone.

عندي مشكلة مع هذا الرجل.	مع كلّ قضايا الشرق الأوسط
*ͨ ind-ii mushkilat-un **ma ͨ -a haadhaa l-rajul-i.**	*ma ͨ -a kull-i qaDaayaa l-sharq-i l-ʾawsaT-i*
I have a problem **with that man.**	**with all the problems** of the Middle East

3.18.2 Possession

A sense of immediate possession (on or near a person) is conveyed by *ma ͨ -a.*

معها الكنز داخل العلبة.	معك كبريت؟
ma ͨ -a-haa l-kanz-u daaxil-a l- ͨ ulbat-i.	*ma ͨ -a-ka kibriit-un?*
She has the treasure inside the box.	**Do you have** matches?

3.18.3 Use of *ma ͨ -an* معاً as 'together'

To convey the meaning of 'together' *ma ͨ -a* takes an adverbial indefinite accusative ending *-an:*

العيش معاً في القدس

*al- ͨ aysh-u **ma ͨ -an** fii l-quds-i*

living together in Jerusalem

3.19 *mithl-a* 'like; as'

The semi-preposition *mithl-a* indicates similarity. It is close in meaning to the preposition *ka-* 'like, as.' However, it is more flexible than *ka-* because it can take suffix pronoun objects (see section 2.1.3 above).

مثل أيّ شعب آخر	مثل دواء قويّ
mithl-a ʾayy-i sha ͨ b-in ʾaaxar-a	*mithl-a dawaaʾ-in qawiyy-in*
like any other people	like a strong medicine

3.19.1 *mithl* + demonstrative + noun 'such as this/these; such a'

An idiomatic use of *mithl* occurs with a demonstrative pronoun, meaning 'such a' or 'such as this/these.'

نجح هذه السنة في توقيع مثل هذا الاتّفاق.

*najaH-a haadhihi l-sanat-a fii tawqii⁶-i **mithl-i haadhaa l-ittifaaq-i.***

This year he succeeded in signing **such an agreement.**

لا يستطيع العمل في مثل هذه الأجواء.

*laa ya-staTii⁶-u l-⁶amal-a **fii mithl-i haadhihi l-ʾajwaaʾ-i.***

He cannot work in **such an atmosphere.**

مثل هذه الأشياء لها رنينها.

***mithl-u haadhihi l-ʾashyaaʾ-i** la-haa raniin-u-haa.*

Things such as these have their resonance.

3.20 *naHw-a* نحوَ 'toward; about; approximately'

This semi-preposition has either a directional meaning of 'toward' or a figurative use of 'approximately, about.'

لتزويده نحو ثلاثين طائرة
*li-tazwiid-i-hi **naHw-a thalaathiina***
Taaʾirat-an
to equip it with **about thirty** planes

نحو غد أربح
***naHw-a** ghad-in ʾarbaH-a*
toward a more profitable tomorrow

3.20.1 *naHw* after a preposition

After a preposition or another semi-preposition, *naHw-* takes the genitive case:

بنحو ثلاثة بلايين دولار
bi-naHw-i thalaathat-i balaayiin-i duulaar-in
by approximately three billion dollars

بعد نحو تسعة قرون
ba⁶d-a naHw-i tis⁶at-i quruun-in
after about nine centuries

3.21 Words based on the root *q-b-l*

The root *q-b-l*, which denotes anteriority, is used in several forms that signify different degrees or variations on the concept.

3.21.1 *qabl-a* قبلَ 'before; prior to; ago'

ضبطت قبل أيَّام.
*DubiT-at **qabl-a ʾayyaam-in.***
It was seized **[a few] days ago.**

بعد ولادة بنتهما قبل سنة
*ba⁶d-a wilaadat-i bnat-i-himaa **qabl-a sanat-in***
after the birth of their daughter **a year ago**

قبل السباحة إلى البحر
qabl-a l-sibaaHat-i ʾilaa l-baHr-i
before swimming to the sea

الليلة قبل الماضية
*al-laylat-a **qabl-a l-maaDiyat-i***
the night **before last**

3.21.2 qubayl-a قبيلَ 'a little before, just before'

This is a diminutive form of *qabl-a* that denotes a short period of time.

قبيل الانتقال إلى مدينة صيدا

qubayl-a l-intiqaal-i ʾilaa
　　madiinat-i Saydaa
just before moving to Sidon

قبيل الـعودة إلى الكويت

qubayl-a l-ʿawadat-i ʾilaa l-kuwayt-i
just before returning to Kuwait

3.21.3 qubaalat-a قبالةَ 'opposite; facing'

في مياه المحيط الأطلسيّ قبالة إيرلندا

fii miyaah-i l-muHiit-i l-ʾaTlasiyy-i **qubaalat-a** *ʾiirlandaa*
in the waters of the Atlantic Ocean **opposite** Ireland

3.21.4 muqaabil-a مقابلَ 'opposite; in exhange for; opposed to'

كسبوا بـهدفين مقابل هدف واحد.

kasab-uu bi-hadaf-ayni **muqaabil-a** *hadaf-in waaHid-in.*
They won by two goals to one ('**as opposed to** one').

3.21.5 min qibal-i من قبل 'on the part of; by'

تلاقي إقبالاً مّن قبل المواطنات.

tulaaqii ʾiqbaal-an **min qibal-i**
　　l-muwaaTinaat-i.
It meets with acceptance **on the part of**
　　female citizens.

من قبل زملائه في الحزب

min qibal-i *zumalaaʾ-i-hi fii l-Hizb-i*
on the part of his colleagues
　　in the party

3.22 Words based on the root q-r-b

The root *q-r-b* denotes proximity and is used chiefly in two forms.

3.22.1 quraabat-a قرابة 'almost; close to'

قرابة ثلاثة عشر مليون دولار

quraabat-a thalaathat-a ʿashar-a milyuun-a duulaar-in
close to thirteen million dollars

3.22.2 qurb-a قربَ 'near; close to; in the vicinity of'

في جنوب تركيا قرب الحدود السوريّة

fii januub-i turkiyaa **qurb-a** *l-Huduud-i l-suuriyya*
in southern Turkey **near** the Syrian border[s]

3.23 *siwaa* سوى 'other than; except'

Used following a negative clause, *siwaa* indicates an exception. This use of *siwaa* after the negative is a common way to phrase restrictive expressions that would normally be expressed in English with 'only.'

لا يرى سوى سبيل واحد.

laa ya-raa siwaa sabiil-in waaHid-in.

He sees **only one way** ('he does not see **but one way**').

ليس معهما سوى مترجميهما.

lays-a maᶜ-a-humaa siwaa mutarjimay-himaa.

Only their two translators were with them.

3.24 *taHt-a* تحت 'underneath, under; below'

This semi-preposition refers to a location below, underneath or under something else.

عثر عليها تحت التراب.	تحت إشراف الأمم المتّحدة
ᶜathar-a ᶜalay-haa taHt-a l-turaab-i.	*taHt-a ʾishraaf-i l-ʾumam-i l-muttaHidat-i*
He discovered it **under the ground.**	**under the supervision** of the United Nations

3.25 *Tiwaal-a* طوال 'during; for'

طوال السنوات الماضية	طوال أكثر من أربعة عقود
Tiwaal-a l-sanawaat-i l-maaDiyat-i	*Tiwaal-a ʾakthar-a min ʾarbaᶜat-i ᶜuquud-in*
during past years; in years past	**during/for more than four decades**

3.26 *tujaah-a* تجاه 'facing, opposite, in front of; towards'

تجاه الدول النامية	سلوك الغرب تجاه الشرق
tujaah-a l-duwal-i l-naamiyat-i	*suluuk-u l-gharb-i tujaah-a l-sharq-i*
facing the developing **nations**	the behavior of the West **towards the East**

3.27 *waraaʾ-a* وراء 'behind; in back of'

تركه المسلمون وراءهم.	ظلّ يسعى وراء هدفه.
tarak-a-hu l-muslim-uuna waraaʾ-a-hum.	*Zall-a ya-sᶜaa waraaʾ-a hadaf-i-hi.*
The Muslims left it **behind (them).**	He continued to pursue/run **after his goal.**

3.28 wasT-a وسط 'in the middle of; in the midst of; among'

وسط المدينة	وسط هذه الدروب
wasT-a l-madiinat-i	*wasT-a haadhihi l-duruub-i*
in the middle of the city	among these alleyways

3.29 xalf-a خلف 'behind; in back of'

ما يكمن خلفها من حقائق	هو مختبئ خلف ستار.
maa ya-kmun-u xalf-a-haa min Haqaa'iq-a	*huwa muxtabi'-un xalf-a sitaarat-in.*
that which is hidden **behind it** of truths	He is hidden **behind a curtain.**

3.30 xaarij-a خارج 'outside; outside of'

داخل أوبيك وخارجه	إلى أسواق خارج المملكة
daaxil-a 'uubiik wa-xaarij-a-hu	*'ilaa 'aswaaq-in xaarij-a l-mamlakat-i*
inside OPEC and **outside of it**	to markets **outside the kingdom**

3.31 xilaal-a خلال 'during'; min xilaal-i من خلال 'through'

The word *xilaal-a* is used to denote an extension over a period of time; *min xilaal-i* is used in the meaning of 'via; through' or sometimes 'by means of.'

خلال العصور الوسطى	خلال دراسة مطوّلة
xilaal-a l-ʿuSuur-i l-wusTaa	*xilaal-a diraasat-in muTawwalat-in*
during the Middle Ages	during an extended study

أصبح جميلاً من خلال الفنّ.
'aSbaH-a jamiil-an min xilaal-i l-fann-i.
It was made beautiful **through art.**

3.32 ʿabr-a عبر 'across, over'

ويمتدّ عبر قارّتين.	عبر عقود من الزمن
wa ya-mtadd-u ʿabr-a qaarrat-ayni.	*ʿabr-a ʿuquud-in min-a l-zaman-i*
It extends **across two continents.**	**across decades** of time

3.33 ʿaqib- a عقب 'right after, immediately after'

عقب إعلانها	ذلك عقب تدخّل عالي المستوى
ʿaqib-a 'iʿlaan-i-haa	*dhaalika ʿaqib-a tadaxxul-in ʿaalii l-mustawaa*
immediately after her announcement	that was **right after** a high-level intervention

3.34 *ʿind-a* عَنْدَ 'on the part of'; 'in the opinion of'; 'near, by, at, upon'; *'chez'*

The semi-preposition *ʿind-a* denotes location in space or time. It can also denote temporary location at the "place" where someone lives or works (e.g., *huwa ʿind-a l-Tabiib-i* 'He's at the doctor's').

In spoken Arabic, *ʿind-a* plays a fundamental role in the expression of possession, and some of that possession role has crept into MSA, especially in the relating of conversations or interviews where people are quoted directly. The more usual preposition to use for possession in formal MSA is *li-*, or the semi-preposition *ladaa*.

3.34.1 *ʿind-a* 'on the part of; in the opinion of'

عدم الفهم عند الكثير من قرّائي

ʿadam-u l-fahm-i ʿind-a l-kathiir-i min qurraaʾ-ii

the lack of understanding **on the part of many** of my readers

الإسلام يتساوى عندهم مع التطرّف.

al-ʾislaam-u ya-tasaawaa ʿind-a-hum maʿ-a l-taTarruf-i.

Islam **for them** ('in their opinion') equates with extremism.

3.34.2 Location in time

عند إلقاء القبض عليه

ʿind-a ʾilqaaʾ-i l-qabD ʿalay-hi

at the time of his arrest

بالقرب من شاطئ البحر عند انسحاب المدّ

bi-l-qurb-i min shaaTiʾ-i l-baHr-i

ʿind-a nsiHaab-i l-madd-i

near the seashore at ebb tide

3.34.3 Location in space

يجب التوقّف عنده.

ya-jib-u l-tawaqquf-u ʿind-a-hu.

It is necessary to stop at his [place].

عند آخر الطابور

ʿind-a ʾaaxir-i l-Taabuur-i

at the end of the line

3.34.4 Possession

عندي مشكلة مع هذا الرجل.

ʿind-ii mushkilat-un maʿ-a haadhaa l-rajul-i.

I have a problem with that man.

عندهم أصدقاء.

ʿind-a-hum ʾaSdiqaaʾ-u.

They have friends.

3.34.5 Adverbial of time

ʿind-a may be suffixed with the adverbial markers *-maa* and *-idhin* to serve as an adverb denoting 'time when.' This expression is usually followed directly by a verb.

3.34.5.1 *ʿind-a-maa* 'WHEN'

كان في العشرين من عمره **عندما** وصل إلى لندن.

*kaan-a fii l-ʿishriina min ʿumr-i-hi **ʿind-a-maa** waSal-a ʾilaa landan.*

He was twenty years of age **when he arrived** in London.

عندما انخفض مستوى البحر

ʿind-a-maa nxafaD-a mustawaa l-baHr-i

when the sea level receded

عندما نزلوا إلى الشارع

ʿind-a-maa nazal-uu ʾilaa l-shaariʿ-i

when they came down into the street

3.34.5.2 *ʿind-a-idhin* عندئذ 'AT THAT POINT IN TIME; THEN'

بدأت **عندئذ** في عمل بعض الرسوم.

*badaʾ-at **ʿind-a-idhin** fii ʿamal-i baʿD-i l-rusuum-i.*

She began **at that point** to make some drawings.

4 Prepositions with clause objects

Prepositions may take entire clauses as their objects, in which case they may be followed by the subordinating conjunctions *ʾan* or *ʾanna*. For more on subordinate clauses, see Chapter 19. Here are two examples:

كأنّك تأكل السمك

ka-ʾanna-ka ta-ʾkul-u l-samak-a

as though you were eating fish

وصفوه **بأنّه** جوّ من الثقة.

*waSaf-uu-hu **bi-ʾanna-hu** jaww-un min-a l-thiqat-i.*

They described it **as** an atmosphere of trust.

17

Questions and question words

Question formation and the use of question words in Arabic are not complex. In general, the interrogative word is placed at the beginning of a sentence. There is no inversion of word order, usually just the insertion of the question word.

The most common question words in Arabic include:

ʾayn-a	'where'	أَيْنَ
ʾayy	'which; what'	أَيّ
kam	'how much; how many'	كَمْ
kayf-a	'how'	كَيْفَ
li-maadhaa	'why'	لِمَاذا
maa	'what'	مَا
maadhaa	'what'	مَاذا
man	'who/whom'	مَنْ
mataa	'when'	متى
hal	introduces yes/no question	هَلْ
ʾa-	introduces yes/no question	أ

1 ʾayn-a أَيْنَ 'where'

The question word ʾayn-a is invariable, even after a preposition. It always ends with fatHa.[1]

إلى أين، يا سيدي؟	من أين أنت؟	أين هي اللجنة الوزاريّة؟
ʾilaa ʾayn-a, yaa siidii?	min ʾayn-a ʾanta?	ʾayn-a hiya l-lajnat-u l-wizaariyyat-u?
Where to, Sir?	**Where are you from?**	**Where is it, the ministerial committee?**

[1] Note that the question word ʾayna is not used as the locative adverb 'where.' To express an idea such as "at a university where he teaches," the adverb Hayth-u is used for 'where': fii jaamiʿat-in Hayth-u yu-darris-u. See Chapter 11, section 3.1.3 for more on Hayth-u.

1.1 ʾayn-a-maa أَيْنَما 'wherever'

With the addition of the function word *maa*, interrogative *ʾayna* becomes a conditional particle with the meaning of 'wherever.'

أينما كنت

ʾayn-a-maa kunt-a

wherever you are

2 ʾayy-un أيّ 'which; what'

As a question word, *ʾayy-* can be an indefinite noun, meaning 'which one?' or as the first part of a construct phrase, it specifies 'which + noun.' It may alternatively be followed by a pronoun suffix (e.g., أيّهم *ʾayy-u-hum*? 'which of them?'). It takes the full set of three case endings, depending on its function and placement in the sentence.[2]

لأيّ دولة تذهب؟   أيّ من المرشّحيْن؟

li-ʾayy-i dawlat-in ta-dhhab-u?   *ʾayy-un min-a l-murashshaH-ayni?*

To **which country** are you going?   **Which one** of the (two) candidates?

أيّ أرنب؟

ʾayy-u ʾarnab-in?

Which rabbit?/What rabbit?

3 kam كَمْ 'how much; how many'

This question word is usually followed by **a singular indefinite noun in the accusative case.**[3]

كم نوعاً من الأسماك تعرفينه؟   كم درساً أكملتم؟

kam nawʿ-an min-a l-ʾasmaak-i ta-ʿrif-iina-hu?   *kam dars-an ʾakmal-tum?*

How many kinds of fish do you (f.) know?   **How many lessons** have you (m. pl.) completed?

3.1 kam كَمْ + nominative

When the interrogative word *kam* has the meaning of 'how much [is],' it is followed by a definite noun (either with the definite article or with a pronoun suffix) in the nominative case:[4]

---

[2] The word *ʾayy-* also has a non-interrogative use as a determiner meaning 'any.' For more on this see Chapter 9, section 5.2.

[3] The accusative case after *kam* is considered to be a form of *tamyiiz*, or accusative of specification. For more on *tamyiiz*, see Chapter 7, section 5.3.3.7 and Chapter 11, section 6.

[4] In this use of *kam*, it is actually a fronted predicate of an equational sentence; the noun is in the nominative as the subject/topic of an equational sentence.

كم الساعةُ؟

kam-i l-saaʿat-u?

What time is it? ('**How much is the hour?**')

كم عمرُه؟

kam ʿumr-u-hu?

How old is he? ('**How much is his age?**')

4 *kayf-a* كَيْفَ 'how'

The interrogative word *kayf-a* is invariable in case. It always ends with *fatHa*. It may be followed by a verb or by a noun.

كيفَ الحالُ؟

kayf-a l-Haal-u?

How are you? ('**How** is the condition?')

كيفَ عرفتِ؟

kayf-a ʿaraf-ti?

How did you (f.) know?

كيفَ وصلتَ إلى هنا؟

kayf-a waSal-ta ʾilaa hunaa?

How did you get (to) here?

كيفَ تتحرّكُ؟

kayf-a ta-taHarrak-u?

How does it move?

5 *li-maadhaa* لماذا 'why; what for'

This is a compound word consisting of the preposition *li-* 'for' and the question word *maadhaa* 'what.' Thus its meaning of 'what for' or 'why.'

لماذا تحبّ السباحةَ؟

li-maadhaa tu-Hibb-u l-sibaaHat-a?

Why do you like swimming?

لماذا اتّجهت إلى التمثيل؟

li-maadhaa ttajah-ta ʾilaa l-tamthiil-i?

Why did you turn to acting?

فلماذا لا تترك الأمور على طبيعتها؟

fa-li-maadhaa laa ta-truk-u l-ʾumuur-a ʿalaa Tabiiʿat-i-haa?

So **why** don't you leave matters as they ('naturally') are?

6 *maa* ما and *maadhaa* ماذا 'what'

The interrogatives *maa* and *maadhaa* have similar meanings but are used in different contexts. In general, *maa* is used in questions involving equational (verbless) sentences and *maadhaa* is used with verbs.[5]

6.1 *maa* 'what'

Interrogative *maa* is used with verbless predications.

ما اسمك؟

maa sm-u-ka?

What [is] your (m.) name?

ما رأيك؟

maa raʾy-u-ki?

What [is] your (f.) opinion?

---

[5] Interrogative *maa* is probably not used with verbs because it is a homonym with negative *maa*, which when used with a verb indicates negation (e.g., *maa ʾadrii* 'I don't know.').

ما الفرق؟	ما السبب؟
maa l-farq-u?	*maa l-sabab-u?*
What [is] the difference?	**What** [is] the reason?

When used to ask a question with a longer noun phrase, *maa* may be followed directly by an independent third person personal pronoun acting as a copula in the question:

ما هي المهمّة الاولى؟

maa hiya l-mahammat-u l-ʾuulaa?

What is the first task ('**What is it**, the first task')?

ما هي أهمّ مشاكل التلوّث؟

maa hiya ʾahamm-u mashaakil-i l-talawwuth-i?

What are the most important problems of pollution?

('**What are they**, the most important problems of pollution')?

6.2 *maadhaa* ماذا 'what'
The question word *maadhaa* is used mainly with verbs:

ماذا جرى؟	ماذا يفعل أهلك؟
maadhaa jaraa?	*maadhaa ya-fʿal-u ʾahl-u-ka?*
What happened?	**What** [will] your family do?

ماذا تعتقد؟	ماذا تأكل؟
maadhaa ta-ʿtaqid-u?	*maadhaa ta-ʾkul-u?*
What do you think?	**What** does it eat?

6.2.1 *maadhaa* as pronoun
Sometimes *maadhaa* is used like a relative pronoun meaning 'that which,' or 'what':

لا أفهم ماذا تقول.

laa ʾa-fham-u maadhaa ta-quul-u.

I don't understand **what** you are saying.

6.2.3 *maadhaa* ʿan 'what about'
The interrogative phrase *maadhaa* ʿan is used to express a general query about a topic.

ماذا عن القادة الآخرين؟

maadhaa ʿan-i l-qaadat-i l-ʾaaxar-iina?

What about the other leaders?

7 *man* مَنْ 'who; whom'

This word is used both as an interrogative pronoun and as an indefinite pronoun. Because it ends in *sukuun*, it needs a helping vowel, *kasra*, if it precedes a consonant cluster.

مَنْ هو؟	مَنِ الرئيس السابق؟
man huwa?	*man-i l-ra'iis-u l-saabiq-u?*
Who is he?	Who is the former president?

8 *mataa* مَتَى 'when'

The question word *mataa* is also invariable, ending in *'alif maqSuura*. Note that *mataa* is used only as an interrogative, not as a connective adverb meaning 'when.'[6]

متى وجدته؟	متى انتشرت الحياة الحضاريّة؟
mataa wajad-ta-hu?	*mataa ntashar-at-i l-Hayaat-u l-HaDaariyyat-u?*
When did you find it?	When did civilized life spread?
متى يرحل عن بيروت؟	متى وصلت؟
mataa ya-rHal-u ʿan bayruut-a?	*mataa waSal-at?*
When is he departing from Beirut?	When did she arrive?

9 *hal* and *'a-* -أ ʿinterrogative markers

Both *hal* and *'a-* are prefixed to statements in order to convert them into yes/no questions. They have equivalent functional meaning, but different distribution: *hal* is used with a wide range of constructions; *'a-* is restricted in that it is not used before a noun with the definite article or words that start with *'alif* plus *hamza*, such as *'anta* 'you.' Neither word is translatable into English, since shift in word order is the signal of yes/no question formation in English.

9.1 *hal* هَلْ

هل أنا كمبيوتر؟	هل روعي الرأي العامّ؟
hal 'anaa kumbyuutir?	*hal ruuʿiy-a l-ra'y-u l-ʿaamm-u?*
Am I a computer?	Was public opinion taken into account?
هل بالإمكان أن نبدأ؟	هل أخذت الزجاجة من هنا؟
hal bi-l-'imkaan-i 'an na-bda'-a?	*hal 'axadh-ta l-zujaajat-a min hunaa?*
May we begin?	Did you take the glass from here?

---

[6] See time adverbials in Chapter 18, and in Chapter 11, section 3.1.3.

9.2 ʾa- -أ

This ʾ*alif* plus *hamza* is prefixed to a word, but not if the word begins with ʾ*alif*:

أهذا سمير؟

ʾ*a-haadhaa samiir-un?*

Is this Samir?

أليس كذلك؟

ʾ*a-lays-a ka-dhaalika?*

Isn't that so?

9.2.1 ʾ*a-laa*

Negative yes/no interrogatives are usually prefaced with ʾ*a-laa*:

ألا يعني تقهقراً؟

ʾ*a-laa ya-ᶜnii taqahqur-an?*

Doesn't it mean regression?

ألا تعني تعصباً؟

ʾ*a-laa ta-ᶜnii taᶜaSSub-an?*

Doesn't it mean bigotry?

18

Connectives and conjunctions

Connectives – words or phrases that connect one part of discourse with another – are a pervasive feature of MSA syntax.[1] Arabic sentences and clauses within a text are connected and interconnected by means of words or phrases (such as *wa-* 'and') that coordinate, subordinate, and otherwise link them semantically and syntactically. This frequent use of connectives results in a high degree of textual cohesion in Arabic writing that contrasts significantly with the terser style of written English. Not only are parts of Arabic sentences coordinated or subordinated in various ways, but most sentences within a text actually start with a connective word that links each sentence with the previous ones.

Even paragraphs are introduced with connectives that connect them to the text as a whole. As Al-Batal remarks: "MSA seems to have a connecting constraint that requires the writer to signal continuously to the reader, through the use of connectives, the type of link that exists between different parts of the text. This gives the connectives special importance as text-building elements and renders them essential for the reader's processing of text" (1990, 256).

Connective words that link sentences within a text are referred to as "discourse markers."[2] Analysis of discourse markers in English has tended to focus on spoken conversation whereas analysis of discourse markers in Arabic (Al-Batal 1990, Johnstone 1990, Kammensjö 1993) has focused particularly on the structure of written narrative. Arabic writing has been characterized as syndetic, that is, as using conjunctions to link discourse elements; and it has also been described as formulaic, that is, relying on "fixed sets of words" (Johnstone 1990, 218) to make

---

[1] I use the term "connective" after Al-Batal 1990, whose research on Arabic connectives has been crucial to our understanding of their nature and importance. He gives the following definition: "any element in a text which indicates a linking or transitional relationship between phrases, clauses, sentences, paragraphs or larger units of discourse, exclusive of referential or lexical ties" (1994, 91). Other terms used to refer to these words include "connectors," "function words," and "particles."

[2] Schiffrin, in her work *Discourse Markers*, brings attention to the importance of cohesive elements as interpretive links that connect the "underlying propositional content" of one discourse element with another (1987, 9). She states that markers work "on the discourse level" and that they "have a sequencing function of relating syntactic units and fitting them into a textual or discourse context" (1987, 37).

semantic and syntactic links. In certain instances, short function words such as
wa- 'and,' actually function in Arabic texts as punctuation marks would function
in English texts. These connective words are therefore not always translatable
because they sometimes perform strictly grammatical functions rather than
adding semantic content. At the discourse or text level, the presence of appropriate connectives is an important feature of "acceptability," according to Al-Batal,
who notes that although "no explicit or formal rules exist," interconnection
between sentences is essential to authentic Arabic texts.[3]

Connectives are therefore an important topic in studying Arabic. However, like
the category of adverbials, the class of words and phrases used as connectives is
large and heterogeneous. Different types of words and word groups serve as connectives: conjunctions, adverbs, particles, and also certain idiomatic or set
phrases. These elements link at different discourse levels (phrase, clause, sentence, paragraph) and in different ways, some simply coordinating or introducing
text elements, and others requiring particular grammatical operations (e.g., subjunctive mood on verb, accusative case on nouns). There are therefore differences
in the form, distribution, and function of connectives.[4] Moreover, different
researchers classify members of these categories in different ways.

At the sentence level, traditional Arabic grammarians classify particles
(*Huruuf* حروف) according to whether or not they have a grammatical effect on
the following phrase or clause. For instance, the particle *kay* كَيْ 'in order that'
requires the following verb to be in the subjunctive mood; the negative particle
lam لَمْ requires the verb to be in the jussive mood; and the subordinating conjunction *'anna* أَنَّ 'that' requires the subject of the following clause to be either
a suffix pronoun or a noun in the accusative case. Thus the **operational effect**
(*'amal* عَمَل) of the function word is a primary feature in its classification. The
effects of these particles on the syntax and inflectional status of sentence
elements form a major component in the theoretical framework and analysis
of Arabic syntax.[5]

Along these lines, connectives are presented here according to whether or not
they exercise a grammatical effect on the following sentence element.

---

[3] Al-Batal points out that a lack of sentence-initial connectives in otherwise "perfectly grammatical"
Arabic texts written by nonnative speakers of Arabic reveals a stylistic gap that affects the acceptability of such texts, whose structures do not correspond with "the frequent usage of connectives
that is characteristic of Arabic written texts" (1990, 253).

[4] For further discussion of the nature of Arabic connectives, see Al-Batal 1990 and 1994 as well as
Johnstone 1990. For further description and exercises with Arabic connectives, see al-Warraki and
Hassanein, 1994.

[5] For analysis of Arabic syntactic theory in English, see Beeston 1970; Bohas, Guillaume, and
Kouloughli 1990, 49–72; Cantarino 1974–1976 (all three volumes); Holes 1995, 160–247 and
Wright II:1–349.

In one class are the many connecting words that serve linking functions only, without requiring a grammatical change, called here "**simple linking connectives.**"[6]

In the other class are the "**operative particles**" (*Huruuf ʿaamila* حروف عاملة) that require inflectional modification of the phrase or clause that they introduce. This class includes, for example, particles that require the subjunctive or the jussive on following verbs, or particles that require the accusative case on nouns, adjectives, and noun phrases. These "operative particles" are dealt with under separate headings in this book. See the sections on subjunctive, jussive, negation and exception, *ʾinna* and her sisters, and the section on cases and their functions.

In some instances, a connective may have more than one function and may fall into both classes: simple linking and operative.[7]

This chapter deals primarily with **simple linking connectives.**

1 *wa-* 'and' (*waaw al-ʿaTf* واو العطف)

This connective is of the highest frequency of all (almost 50 percent of all Arabic connectives) and occurs at all levels of text to "signal an additive relationship" (Al-Batal 1990, 245).[8]

1.1 Sentence starter *wa-*

Sentences within an expository text after the introductory sentence are often initiated with *wa-* 'and' and/or another connective expression. The following examples are beginnings of typical sentences. As a sentence-starter, *wa-* is considered good style in Arabic, but it is not usually translated into English because English style rules normally advise against starting sentences with 'and.'

وغادر القاهرة أمس مساعد وزير الدفاع ...

wa-ghaadar-a l-qaahirat-a ʾams-i musaaʿid-u waziir-i l-difaaʿ-i . . .

(**And**) the assistant minister of defense left Cairo yesterday . . .

ووصل الرئيسان إلى العاصمة أمس ...

wa-waSal-a l-raʾiis-aani ʾilaa l-ʿaaSimat-i ʾams-i . . .

(**And**) the two presidents arrived in the capital yesterday . . .

---

[6] These include what Al-Batal refers to as *Huruuf muhmala* 'inoperative particles,' *Huruuf zaaʾida* 'redundant or augmentative particles,' and *Huruuf al-ʿaTf* 'coordinating particles' (1990, 236).

[7] For example, *wa-* as a coordinating conjunction does not exercise a grammatical effect on the following phrase, but when used as the *waaw al-maʿiyya*, 'the *waaw* of accompaniment,' it requires the following noun to be in the accusative case. For more on this see Baalbaki 1986 and Wright 1967, II:83–84.

[8] According to Schiffrin (1987, 141) "and" is "a discourse coordinator; the presence of *and* signals the speaker's identification of an upcoming unit which is coordinate in structure to some prior unit."

وثمّة علماء يعتقدون أنّ . . .

wa-thammat-a ʿulamaaʾ-u ya-ʿtaqid-uuna ʾanna . . .

(**And**) there are scholars who believe that . . .

وتشير مصادر كرديّة إلى أنّ . . .

wa-tu-shiir-u maSaadir-u kurdiyyat-un ʾilaa ʾanna . . .

(**And**) Kurdish sources indicate that . . .

1.2 Coordinating conjunction *wa-*

The coordinating conjunction *wa-* 'and' functions as an additive term within sentences to link clauses, phrases, and words. In particular, Arabic uses *wa-* in lists where in English a comma would be used to separate each item. The items in the list retain the case determined by their role in the sentence.

منها مصر والأردنّ والكويت ولبنان وقطر وعمّان ودولة الإمارات العربيّة المتّحدة والمملكة العربيّة السعوديّة.

min-haa miSr-u wa-l-ʾurdunn-u wa-l-kuwayt-u wa-lubnaan-u wa-qaTar-u wa-ʿumaan-u
   wa-dawlat-u l-imaaraat-i l-ʿarabiyyat-i l-muttahidat-i wa-l-mamlakat-u l-ʿarabiyyat-u
   l-saʿuudiyyat-u.

Among them are Egypt, Jordan, Kuwait, Lebanon, Qatar, Oman, the ('State of')
   the United Arab Emirates, and the Kingdom of Saudi Arabia.

يتعلّق بقضايا العراق والسودان وليبيا والصومال والبوسنة وكشمير والشيشان.

ya-ta-ʿallaq-u bi-qaDaayaa l-ʿiraaq-i wa-l-suudaan-i wa-liibyaa wa-l-Suumaal-i
   wa-l-buusinat-i wa-kashmiir-a wa-l-shiishaan-i.

It relates to the problems of Iraq, The Sudan, Libya, Somalia, Bosnia, Kashmir,
   and Chechnia.

موادّ أدبيّة ولغويّة وتاريخيّة وفلسفيّة

mawaadd-u ʾadabiyyat-un wa-lughawiyyat-un wa-taariixiyyat-un wa-falsafiyyat-un
literary, linguistic, historical, and philosophical materials

2 *fa-* فَـ 'and so; and then; yet; and thus'

This connector implies several different kinds of relationships with the previous text elements. It can have a sequential meaning 'and then,' a resultative meaning 'and so' (*faaʾ al-sababiyya* فاء السببيّة), a contrastive meaning 'yet; but,' a slight shift in topic 'and also; moreover', or a conclusive meaning, 'and therefore; in conclusion.'[9] Beeston refers to it as "the most interesting of the ambivalent functionals" (1970, 98).

---

[9] Al-Batal refers to it as "the most complex and the most interesting" connective in his research
   because of the different functions that it has (1990, 100). Cantarino 1975, III:20–34 has an extensive
   analysis of the functions of *fa-*, with examples taken from literary contexts.

It may start a sentence in a text or it may knit elements together within a sentence.

فـهم ما زالوا مهتمّين بـأحداث الإنتفاضة.

fa-hum maa zaal-uu muhtamm-iina bi-ʾaHdaath-i l-intifaaDat-i.

Yet they are still interested in the events of the uprising.

و إذا لم يلغ الآخر، فـإنّه يتجاهله.

wa-ʾidhaa lam ya-lghi l-ʾaaxar . . . fa-ʾinna-hu ya-tajaahal-u-hu.

If he doesn't abolish the other . . . **(then)** he ignores it.

فتحت الباب فـانفتح.

fataH-tu l-baab-a fa-nfataH-a.

I opened the door **and [so]** it opened.

ما دام خـارجة من الشرعيّة ، فـإنّ المقاطعة مستمرّة.

maa daam-at xaarijat-an min-a l-sharʿiyyat-i, fa-ʾinna l-muqaaTaʿat-a mustamirrat-un.

As long as it remains outside the law, **(then)** the boycott will continue.

3 Contrastive conjunctions

These conjunctions indicate contrast in semantic content between two parts of a sentence.

3.1 *bal* بَل 'rather; but actually'

The word *bal* is termed an "adversative" by Al-Batal because it introduces a clause whose semantic content conveys the idea of something additional but also different or contrastive from the main clause.[10]

وترجمت هذه الكتب إلى اللاتينيّة بل كتب معظمها بحروف عبريّة.

*wa-turjim-at haadhihi l-kutub-u ʾilaa l-laatiiniyyat-i **bal** kutib-a muʿZam-u-haa
    bi-Huruuf-in ʿibriyyat-in.*

These books were translated into Latin, **but [actually]** they were mostly written
    in Hebrew script ('letters').

ليس في الأمر تَمّة صقور أو حمـائم بل هنـاك توزيع واسع للأدوار.

*lays-a fii l-ʾamr-i thammat-a Suquur-un ʾaw Hamaaʾim-u **bal** hunaaka tawziiʿ-un
    waasiʿ-un li-l-ʾadwaar-i.*

There are in the matter neither hawks nor doves, **but rather** there is a wide
    distribution of roles.

---

[10] See also under "negative and exceptive expressions."

3.2 *ʾinna-maa* إنَّما /*wa-ʾinna-maa* وإنَّما 'but; but moreover; but also, rather'
This connective word has both confirmational and contrastive components to its meaning.[11]

لم تكن تسجيلاً فقط و إنَّما هو انعكاس للواقع الاجتماعي.

*lam ta-kun tasjiil-an faqaT **wa-ʾinna-maa** huwa nʿikaas-un li-l-waaqʿ-i l-ijtimaaʿiyy-i.*

It was not only documentation, **but moreover** a reflection of social reality.

4 Explanatory conjunctions

4.1 *ʾay* أيْ 'that is, i.e.'
This small word (which resembles in spelling the word *ʾayy-* 'which' but is unrelated to it) is an explicative particle equivalent to the Latin abbreviation *i.e.*, for *id est* 'that is,' which is used in English texts.

أيْ كلّ ما هو واقعيّ

ʾay, kull-u maa huwa waaqiʿiyy-un

that is, everything that is real

5 Resultative conjunctions

5.1 *ʾidh* إذْ 'since,' 'inasmuch as'
This small word is a resultative particle that introduces a clause providing a rationale or reason for the main clause.

حقّق الحزب الجمهوريّ الحاكم نصراً ساحقاً على منافسيه إذ حصل على معظم المقاعد.

*Haqqaq-a l-Hizb-u l-jumhuuriyy-u l-Haakim-u naSr-an saaHiq-an ʿalaa munaafis-ii-hi **ʾidh** HaSal-a ʿalaa muʿZam-i l-maqaaʿid-i.*

The ruling republican party realized an overwhelming victory over its opponents **since** it obtained most of the seats.

5.2 *ʾidhan* إذَنْ (spelled with *nuun*) and *ʾidh-an* إذاً (spelled with nunation) 'therefore; then; so; thus; in that case'
This connective word initiates a clause or question that comes as a result or conclusion from a previous statement. In more conversational style, it may also come at the end of the clause.

إذن لماذا يتوجّب علينا ...	إذن هناك منهجان ...
ʾidhan li-maadhaa ya-tawajjab-u ʿalay-naa ...	*ʾidhan hunaaka manhaj-aani ...*
Then why do we have to ...	**Thus**, there are two methods ...

---

[11] See al-Warraki and Hassanein 1994, 59–63 for further discussion.

سيكون قطّاً كبيراً إذن!

sa-ya-kuun-u qiTT-an kabiir-an ʾidhan!

It'll be a big cat, **then**!

5.3 *Hattaa* حَتّى + past tense: 'until'

Hattaa followed by a past tense verb introduces a clause that shows the consequences or result of the previous clause. Used in this way, it refers to an event or action that has taken place in the past.[12]

ولم تزل في النموّ حتّى أصبحت من أهمّ مدن المنطقة.

wa-lam ta-zul fii l-namuww-i Hattaa ʾaSbaH-at min ʾahamm-i mudun-i l-minTaqat-i.

It kept growing **until it became** [one] of the most important cities of the region.

6 Adverbial conjunctions

Adverbial conjunctions in Arabic fill the role of subordinating conjunctions in English such as 'where,' 'when,' 'while,' and 'as.' That is, they introduce a clause subordinate to the main clause by indicating a place, time, manner, or result relation between the two.

6.1 Adverbial conjunctions of place: *Hayth-u* حَيْثُ 'where'

The connective adverb *Hayth-u* denotes the concept of 'where' or 'in which.' It has an invariable *Damma* suffix.[13] It is an extensively used conjunction of place. It also has non-locative meanings when used with other particles, such as *min Hayth-u* 'regarding; as for' or *bi-Hayth-u* 'so that; so as to.'[14]

في كلّيّة حيث تدرّس	حيث القديم يختلط مع الحديث
fii kulliyyat-in Hayth-u tu-darris-u	*Hayth-u l-qadiim-u ya-xtaliT-u maʿ-a l-Hadiith-i*
in a college **where** she teaches	**where** the old mixes with the new

في السعوديّة حيث يعمل مع شركة دوليّة

fii l-saʿuudiyyat-i Hayth-u ya-ʿmal-u maʿ-a sharikat-in duwaliyaat-in

in Saudi Arabia **where** he works for an international company

في مستشفىً حيث تقع قصص حبّ

fii mustashfan Hayth-u ta-qaʿ-u qiSaS-u Hubb-in

in a hospital **where** love stories take place

---

[12] *Hattaa* may also be an operative particle with the meaning of 'until; up to the point of,' followed by a noun in the genitive case (*Hattaa l-sanat-i l-maaDiyat-i* 'until last year'), but in that case it is considered a preposition. See Chapter 16, section 2.2.3. As a particle of purpose, it has the meaning of 'in order to' followed by a verb in the subjunctive mood (see Chapter 34, section. 2.2.6).

[13] Note that the question word 'where?' is different: *ʾayna*. See Chapter 17, section 1.

[14] For exercises on and further examples of the uses of *Hayth-u*, as well as the conjunctions *Hayth-u ʾanna* and *bi-Hayth-u*, see al-Warraki and Hassanein 1994, 93–97.

6.2 Adverbial conjunctions of time

This category includes expressions that link clauses by specifying how one clause is related to another in terms of time. These adverbials often consist of traditional *Zuruuf*, the semi-prepositions or locative adverbs, plus the indefinite relative pronoun *maa*, and sometimes the adverbial suffix *-idhin*.

The locative adverbs, as noted in the chapter on prepositions and prepositional phrases, are essentially nouns of place that act as prepositions by going into a construct relationship with another noun (e.g., بعد الحرب *baʿd-a l-Harb-i* 'after the war,' قبل سنة *qabl-a sanat-in* 'a year ago'). These nouns with the accusative marker are restricted to occurring only before other nouns or pronouns unless a buffer (such as *maa* or *ʾidhin*) is added to them. The locative adverb and buffer may be written together as one word, or they are written separately. By adding the buffer element, the semi-prepositions or locative adverbs are converted into adverbial elements that can directly precede verbs and entire clauses.

6.2.1 *bayn-a-maa* بَيْنَما 'while; whereas'

This connective word has both a temporal meaning 'while, during the time that,' and also a contrastive meaning of 'whereas.'

ضُبطوا بينما كانوا يستهلكون المخدّر.

*DubiT-uu **bayn-a-maa** kaan-uu ya-stahlik-uuna l-muxaddir-a.*

They were arrested **while** they were consuming the drug.

فكانت الثقافة العربيّة رسميّة بينما ظلّت اللاتينيّة العامّة لغة للناس.

*fa-kaan-at-i l-thaqaafat-u l-ʿarabiyyat-u rasmiyyat-an **bayn-a-maa** Zall-at-i l-laatiiniyyat-u l-ʿaammat-u lughat-an li-l-naas-i.*

Arabic culture was official **whereas** vernacular Latin remained a language of the people.

6.2.2 *baʿd-a-maa* بَعْدَما 'after'

This connective is usually followed directly by a past tense verb. Note that the preposition *baʿd-a* 'after' can be followed only by a noun or pronoun; it is necessary to use *baʿd-a-maa* before a clause beginning with a verb.

بعدما شاهده أحد المارّة
baʿd-a-maa shaahad-a-hu ʾaHad-u l-maarrat-i
after one of the passers-by saw him

بعدما وقعت على الثلج
baʿd-a-maa waqaʿ-at ʿalaa l-thalj-i
after she fell on the ice

بعدما قُدِّم للرئيس تعازيه
baʿd-a-maa quddim-a li-l-raʾiis-i taʿaazii-hi
after his condolences had been presented to the president

6.2.3 ba'd-a 'an بَعْدَ أَنْ 'after'

The expression ba'd-a 'an means essentially the same as ba'd-a maa when describing a situation that has taken place in the past. The phrase ba'd-a 'an, when referring to an event that has already taken place, is followed by a clause with a past tense verb.[15]

غادر القاهرة أمس بعد أن قابل الرئيس.

ghaadar-a l-qaahirat-a 'ams-i **ba'd-a 'an** qaabal-a l-ra'iis-a.

He left Cairo yesterday **after** he met with the President.

بعد أن شارك اللاعبون في عدّة مسابقات مختلفة

ba'd-a 'an shaarak-a l-laa'ib-uuna fii 'iddat-i musaabaqaat-in muxtalifat-in

after the players had participated in several different contests

6.2.3 ba'd-a-'idhin بَعْدَئِذٍ 'after that; then; subsequently'

This compound expression is equivalent in most situations to the adverbial conjunction thumma (see below 6.2.8):

وبعدئذٍ انتقل إلى دار كريم.

wa-**ba'd-a-'idhin**-i ntaqal-a 'ilaa daar-i kariim-in.

After that he moved to Karim's house.

6.2.4 Hiin-a-maa حينَما and Hiin-a حينَ 'when; at the time when'

لكنّ الأزمة نشبت حينما عرقلت الشرطة دخول الطلاّب

laakinna l-'azmat-a nashab-at **Hiin-a-maa** 'arqal-at-i l-shurTat-u duxuul-a l-Tullaab-i

but the crisis broke out **when** the police obstructed the entrance of students

حينما أصبحت العاصمة

Hiin-a-maa 'aSbaH-at-i l-'aaSimat-a

when it became the capital

6.2.5 'ind-a-maa عنْدَما 'when; at the time when'

عندما جئنا إلى هنا	عندما تتقدّم في الأمر
'ind-a-maa ji'naa 'ilaa hunaa	'ind-a-maa ta-taqaddam-u fii l-'umr-i
when we came here	**when** they grow older ('advance in age')

---

[15] When referring to a non-past situation, or a hypothetical situation, ba'd-a 'an is followed by a verb in the subjunctive mood. For example,

سندرس بعد أن نأكل

sa-na-drus-u ba'd-a 'an na-'kul-a.

We will study **after** we eat.

6.2.6 ‘ind-a-’idhin عندئذٍ 'then; at that point in time; at that time'

ولابدّ **عندئذٍ** من طرح قضيّة الانسحاب.

wa laa budd-a ‘inda-’idhin min TarH-i qaDiyyat-i l-insiHaab.

Rejection of the issue of withdrawal was inevitable **at that point.**

6.2.7 qabl-a ’an قَبْلَ أَنْ + subjunctive 'before'

Contrasting with *ba‘d-a ’an*, *qabl-a ’an* refers to an action anterior to the action in the main clause. The verb after *qabl-a ’an* is in the subjunctive mood, even if the main clause reference is past tense.

وصلت قوّات الأمن إلى المطار **قبل أن** يهبط.

*waSal-at quwwaat-u l-’amn-i ’ilaa l-maTaar-i **qabl-a ’an** ya-hbuT-a.*

The security forces arrived at the airport **before** he landed.

قبل أن تمزّقه الحرب

qabl-a ’an tu-mazziq-a-hu l-Harb-u

before war tears it apart

6.2.8 thumm-a ثُمَّ 'then; and then; subsequently'

The connective particle *thumm-a* is an adverb that indicates a sequential action, coming later in time than the action in the preceding sentence or clause.

ثمّ ضعها فيما بعد في صندوق.	**ثمّ** أنشدوا النشيد الوطنيّ.
thumm-a Da‘-haa fii-maa ba‘d-u fii Sanduuq-in.	*thumm-a ’anshad-uu l-nashiid-a l-waTaniyy-a.*
Then put it in a box later.	**Then** they sang the national anthem.

6.3 Adverbial conjunctions of similarity

These expressions predicate a state of similarity with something that has gone before, either in a previous statement or earlier in the same sentence.

6.3.1 ka-maa كَما 'as; just as; similarly; likewise'

The expression *ka-maa* is usually followed by a verb phrase.

كما ذكر المتحدّث	كما فعلوا السنة الماضية
ka-maa dhakar-a l-mutaHaddith-u	*ka-maa fa‘al-uu l-sanat-a l-maaDiyat-a*
the spokesman **likewise** mentioned	**just as** they did last year

6.3.2 mithl-a-maa مثْلَما 'like; just as; as'

... مثلما يقول أهلي

mithl-a-maa ya-quul-u ’ahl-ii ...

as my family says ...

6.4 Adverbial conjunction of equivalence: *qadr-a-maa* قَدْرَما 'as much as; just as; as . . . as'

إنّ أمامنا كثيراً من الفرص **قدرما** أمامنا من التحدّيّات.

*'inna 'amaam-a-naa kathiir-an min-a l-furaS-i **qadr-a-maa** 'amaam-a-naa min-a l-taHaddiyyaat-i.*

There are [**just**] **as** many opportunities before us **as** there are challenges.

6.5 Adverbial conjunction of reference or attribution: *Hasab-a-maa* حسَبَما 'according to; in accordance with; depending on'
This conjunction links one clause to another clause, expressing a relationship of reference or attribution.[16]

وحسبما تقول الأسطورة . . .

*wa-**Hasab-a-maa** ta-quul-u l-'usTuurat-u . . .*

according to what legend says . . .

حسبما جرت تسميتها آنذاك

***Hasab-a-maa** jar-at tasmiyat-u-haa 'aan-a-dhaaka*

in accordance with its naming at that time

6.6 Adverbial conjunctions of potential or possibility

6.6.1 *rubb-a-maa* رُبَّما 'perhaps; maybe; possibly' [17]

ربَّما كان كثيرون منهم مسجّلين.

rubba-maa kaan-a kathiir-uuna min-hum musajjal-iina.

Perhaps many of them were registered.

ربَّما لهذا السبب . . .

rubba-maa li-haadhaa l-sabab-i . . .

perhaps for this reason . . .

ربَّما كنت واثقاً من نفسي أكثر من اللزوم.

rubba-maa kun-tu waathiq-an min nafs-ii 'akthar-a min-a l-luzuum-i.

Perhaps I was overconfident.

7 Disjunctives
Arabic has a set of particles that indicate disjunction, that is, a distinction between one alternative and another. They include the following:

---

[16] As for the expressions *Hasab-a* and *bi-Hasab-i* 'according to,' these are not conjunctions but operative particles that are followed by a noun in the genitive case.

[17] For another word meaning 'perhaps' see *la'alla* in Chapter 19 on *'inna* and her sisters.

7.1 ʾaw أَوْ 'or'

This disjunctive indicates an option between two or more elements, but that option is **inclusive**, that is, it may include one, both, or all the elements.

عن قصد أو من غير قصد	يريدونه حيّاً أو ميّتاً.
ʿan qaSd-in ʾaw min ghayr-i qaSd-in	*yu-riid-uuna-hu Hayy-an ʾaw mayyit-an.*
on purpose **or** not on purpose	They want him dead **or** alive ('alive or dead').

لنجاح الحزب الحاكم أو فشله

li-najaaH-i l-Hizb-i l-Haakim-i ʾaw fashl-i-hi

for the success of the ruling party **or** its failure

7.2 ʾam أَمْ 'or'

This disjunctive indicates an **exclusive option**; one or the other, but not both or all. Because it ends with *sukuun*, it sometimes needs a helping vowel, *kasra*.

اللحن أم الكلمة أم الصوت؟

al-laHn-u ʾam-i l-kalimat-u ʾam-i l-Sawt-u?

the tune, **or** the words, **or** the voice?

أساتذة كانوا أم طلّاباً

ʾasaatidhat-an kaan-uu ʾam Tullaab-an

[**whether**] they were professors **or** students

7.2.1 ʾa with ʾam

Sometimes the particle ʾa- is used on the first element of the exclusive disjunction:

لم يدر أيشتم أم يضحك.

lam ya-dri ʾa -ya-shtam-u ʾam ya-DHak-u.

He didn't know **whether** to curse **or** laugh.

7.3 ʾimmaa . . . ʾaw أَو . . . . إمّا; ʾimmaa . . . wa-ʾimmaa إمّا . . . وإمّا 'either . . . or'

This two-part disjunctive conveys the idea of an exclusive choice: one or the other, but not both. Sometimes the first part of the disjunction is followed by ʾan plus a verb in the subjunctive, but not always.

هذا السلام إمّا أن يكون شاملاً أو لا يكون أبداً.

haadhaa l-salaam-u ʾimmaa ʾan ya-kuun-a shaamil-an ʾaw laa ya-kuun-u ʾabad-an.

This peace is **either** inclusive, **or** it is not at all.

إمّا أن تكونوا معنا وإمّا مع الارهاب.

ʾimmaa ʾan ta-kuun-uu maʿ-a-naa wa-ʾimmaa maʿ-a l-ʾirhaab-i.

Either you are with us **or** [you are] with terrorism.

8 Sentence-starting connectives

In addition to single words as sentence-introducers and connectors, there are also many fixed expressions or idiomatic phrases that serve to start sentences. This process of using a starting formula to introduce a sentence is especially common in journalistic and expository writing and gives it what Johnstone refers to as a certain "formulaicity." [18] Some of the more common phrasal starters are listed here.

8.1 Participle or adjective starters with *min-a l-*

A definite adjective or passive participle, often preceded by the partitive preposition *min*, is a common way of introducing a sentence, especially in journalistic prose. This use of *min* is termed "pleonastic" (superfluous or redundant). [19] It is a way of opening a statement with a generic or general observation, just as "It is . . ." may be used in English.

ومن المتوقّع أن ...

wa-min-a l-mutawaqqaᶜ-i ʾan . . .

It is expected that . . .

من الممكن أنّ ...

min-a l-mumkin-i ʾan . . .

It is possible that . . .

من المهمّ عدم تقديم الكثير من التنازلات.

min-a l-muhimm-i ᶜadam-u taqdiim-i l-kathiir-i min-a l-tanaazulaat-i.

It is important not to offer too many concessions.

من الطبيعيّ أن نقوم بزيارة ...

min-a l-Tabiiᶜiyy-i ʾan na-quum-a bi-ziyaarat-in . . .

It is natural that we undertake a visit . . .

8.1.1 Starters without *min*

Sometimes participle or adjective starters are used on their own, without *min*, but usually preceded by *wa-*.

ومعلوم أنَ ...

wa-maᶜluum-un ʾanna . . .

It is known that . . .

والمستغرب أنَ ...

wa-l-mustaghrab-u ʾanna . . .

The strange [thing] is . . .

8.2 Passive and passive-like starters

With or without *wa-* a passive verb in the third person masculine singular may initiate a sentence by introducing a general, unattributed observation. In addition to the morphological passive, a Form V or Form VII verb with passive meaning is sometimes used.

---

[18] Johnstone 1990, 223.   [19] See also pleonastic *min*, Chapter 16, section 2.2.2.7.

وعُلِم أنّ ...

wa-ʿulim-a ʾanna ...

(And) it has been learned that ...

يُشار إلى ...

yu-shaar-u ʾilaa ...

It is indicated ...

ويُذكر أنّ الأمين العام ...

wa-yu-dhkar-u ʾanna l-ʾamiin-a l-ʿaamm-a ...

(And) it is mentioned that the Secretary General ...

ويتوقّع أن يشمل التقرير اقتراحاً ...

wa-ya-tawaqqaʿ-u ʾan ya-shmul-a l-taqriir-u qtiraaH-an ...

(And) it is expected that the report will include a proposal ...

8.3 Other idiomatic starters

Some other phrases used to start sentences typically include the following.

8.3.1 Topic shift: *ʾammaa ... fa-* فَ ... أمّا 'as for ...'

This expression denotes a shift in topic from the previous sentence. It is in two parts, the first word, *ʾammaa*, signaling the new topic, and the second, *fa-*, introducing the comment on that topic. In English, the "as for" phrase is here followed by a comma, which introduces the second part of the sentence, or comment. Therefore *fa-* in this case fills the same function as the punctuation mark in English. Since *ʾammaa* introduces a new sentence and a new topic, the noun following is in the nominative case, as subject of the sentence.

أمّا القسم المترجم فمتنوّع جدّاً.

ʾammaa l-qism-u l-mutarjam-u fa-mutanawwaʿ-un jidd-an.

As for the translated part, it is very diverse.

أمّا الإسرائيليّون ... فيقولون ...

ʾammaa l-israaʾiiliyy-uuna ... fa-ya-quul-uuna ...

as for the Israelis, they say ...

أمّا المخضرمة ، فقد جاءت رابعة.

ʾammaa l-muxaDramat-u, fa-qad jaaʾ-at raabiʿat-an.

As for the old-timer, she came in fourth.

8.3.2 Addition: *ʾilaa dhaalika* إلى ذلك 'in addition to that; moreover; furthermore'

This phrase is a shortened version of *bi-l-ʾiDaafat-i ʾilaa dhaalika* 'in addition to that':

إلى ذلك أكّد الصحافيّ ...

ʾilaa dhaalika ʾakkad-a l-saHaafiyy-u ...

Moreover, the journalist affirmed ...

... إلى ذلك استمرّت قوّة الاحتلال في عمليّات

ʾilaa dhaalika stamarr-at quwwat-u l-iHtilaal-i fii ʿamaliyyaat-in . . .

In addition to that, the occupation forces continued operations . . .

8.3.3 Statement of contents: *jaaʾ-a fii* جاءَ في/*wa-jaaʾ-a fii* وَجاءَ في

The expression *jaaʾ-a fii* 'it came in' is an idiomatic way to start a sentence that reveals the contents of a letter, announcement, declaration, or other official document. The English equivalent usually omits this expression and begins with the document itself as the subject of the sentence.

... وجاء في البيان أن

wa-jaaʾ-a fii l-bayaan-i ʾanna . . .

(And) the declaration stated that . . .

('And **it came in** the declaration that . . .')

... وجاء في نصّ المشروع

wa-jaaʾ-a fii naSS-i l-mashruuʿ-i . . .

And the text of the plan stated that . . .

('And **it came in** the text of the plan . . .')

19

Subordinating conjunctions: the particle ʾ*inna* and her sisters

1 Introduction

This group of particles, referred to as ʾ*inna wa-ʾaxawaat-u-haa* وأخواتها إنّ 'ʾ*inna* and her sisters,' are part of the class of Arabic words that are referred to as *nawaasix* نواسخ, or words that cause a shift to the accusative case.[1] The members of this particular group are usually used as subordinating conjunctions, connecting two clauses, although ʾ*inna* itself may also be used at the beginning of a sentence.

These particles include:[2]

verily, indeed; that	ʾ*inna*	إنَّ
that	ʾ*anna*	أنَّ
but	*laakinna*	لكنَّ
because	*liʾanna*	لأنَّ
perhaps	*laʿalla*	لعلَّ

1.1 Grammatical effect

These particles have the grammatical effect of making the subject noun in the following clause accusative. If there is no overt subject noun in the clause, a suffix pronoun is affixed to the particle.

---

[1] For more on the *nawaasix*, see Chapter 7, section 5.3.3.8.
  Arabic grammars refer to particles that require the accusative as *Huruuf mushabbiha bi-l-fiʿl* 'particles resembling verbs' because transitive verbs require the accusative on their direct objects. There is therefore a parallel relationship between these two elements; they are both "operators" or "governors" (ʿ*awaamil*), and both have similar effects on a following noun or noun phrase. As Anghelescu states, "it must not be forgotten that ʾ*inna*, as well as other members of the *al-nawaasikh* class, resemble verbs in their capacity to 'act' (ʿ*amal*), or to govern, according to the Arab grammarians" (1999, 136).

[2] The subordinating particle ʾ*an* is also sometimes considered in this category, although it is different in that it is followed by a verb in the subjunctive mood, rather than a noun in the accusative case. For more on ʾ*an* and the subjunctive, see Chapter 34, section 2.3.

1.2 Overt noun subject

When the subject noun in the following clause is overt, it receives the accusative case and usually follows directly after the particle. Note that the form of the accusative case may vary according to the declension of the noun.

إنّ الآمالَ تحوّلت إلى أوهـام.

ʾinna l-ʾaamaal-a taHawwal-at *ʾilaa ʾawhaam-in.*

(Indeed), **the hopes** have turned into delusions.

نعتقد أنّ الزراعةَ لغة عالميّة.

na-ʿtaqid-u ʾanna l-ziraaʿat-a lughat-un *ʿaalamiyyat-un.*

We believe **that agriculture** is a world language.

ولكنّ الحـاصلَ عكس ذلك

wa-laakinna l-HaaSil-a ʿaks-u dhaalika

but the actuality is the reverse of that

رغم أنّ اتّجاهات إيجابيّةً أخذت تنبعث

raghm-a ʾanna ttijaahaat-in ʾiijaabiyyat-an ʾaxadh-at ta-nbaʿith-u

despite [the fact] **that positive trends** began to emerge

1.3 Separated subject

The accusative subject noun does not have to be immediately adjacent to the particle – it may be separated from the particle by an adverb or a prepositional phrase. It may not, however, be separated from the subordinating particle by a verb.[3]

لكنّ هناك حيوانات أخرى

laakinna hunaaka Hayawaanaat-in ʾuxraa

but there are **other animals**

لكنّ هناك بعضَ النقوش

laakinna hunaaka baʿD-a l-nuquush-i

but there are **some** inscriptions

ذكر أنّ لديه المستندات الرسميّةَ.

dhakar-a ʾanna laday-hi l-mustanadaat-i l-rasmiyyat-a.

He mentioned **that he has the official documents.**

('**that** to-him are **the official documents**')

1.4 Reduplicated pronoun subject

If the subject of the subordinated clause is shown only by the inflection of a verb, then a subject **pronoun suffix duplicating the subject of the verb** is affixed to

---

[3] "The accusative case is not necessarily immediately subsequent to the particle; e.g., it may follow the predicate in a nominal sentence. A verb, however, may never be placed between a particle and the accusative it governs" Cantarino 1975, III:117.

the particle. The subject, whether a noun or a pronoun, must at all times come before its verb in this type of subordinate clause.

إنّنا نتمنّى لكم عيداً مباركاً.

'inna-naa na-tamannaa la-kum ʿiid-an mubaarak-an.

(Indeed), **we** wish you a blessed holiday.

أدرك أنّه نسي اسمها.

'adrak-a 'anna-hu nasiy-a sm-a-haa.

He realized **that he** had forgotten her name.

1.5 Equational clause

If the clause after *'inna* or one of her sisters is an equational sentence, the subject is a pronoun or a noun in the accusative case, but the predicate (*xabar*) is in the nominative case.

إنّه ثقيلٌ جداً!

'inna-hu thaqiil-un jidd-an!

(Indeed,) **it** is very heavy!

إنّ المعلومات خاطئة.

'inna l-maʿluumaat-i xaaTi'at-un.

(Indeed,) **the information** is incorrect.

لا تهرع إلى السلالم لأنّها مكانٌ خطرٌ.

laa ta-hraʿ 'ilaa l-salaalim-i li-'anna-haa makaan-un xaTir-un.

Don't run to the stairs **because they** are a dangerous place.

1.6 With invariable pronoun or noun

Sometimes *'inna* or one of her sisters may be followed by an invariable noun or pronoun, in which case there is no overt accusative marker.[4]

إنّ هذه جريمة بشعة.

'inna haadhihi jariimat-un bashiʿat-un.

(Indeed,) **this** is a repugnant crime.

لكنّ هذا لا يكفي.

laakinna haadhaa laa ya-kfii.

But **this** is not enough.

1.7 With buffer pronoun: *Damiir al-sha'n* ضمير الشأن

Occasionally in MSA a subordinate clause may be preceded by a /-hu/ pronoun after the subordinating particle (e.g., *'anna-hu* أنّه) that does not seem to be necessary or even to agree with the subject of the verb. This pronoun refers not to the subject of the clause, but to the entire clause itself, and acts as a generic "buffer" between the subordinating particle and the following clause. In Arabic this particular use of the suffix pronoun is called *Damiir al-sha'n* 'the pronoun of the fact' or "pronoun which anticipates a whole subsequent clause."[5]

---

[4] According to traditional Arabic grammatical theory, the accusative marking is there in a "virtual" sense (*muqaddar*), even though it does not appear on the word.

[5] Definition from Cachia 1973, 57. See also Cantarino 1975, II:430–31.

كأنَّه لا توجد خلافات بيننا

ka-ʾanna-hu laa tuujad-u xilaafaat-un bayn-a-naa

as though there were no differences between us

2 The particles

2.1 Sentence-initial *ʾinna* إنَّ: 'indeed, truly, verily'

The particle *ʾinna* has a truth-intensifying function when used at the beginning of a statement. It emphasizes that what follows is true. More frequently used in Classical Arabic than MSA, it nonetheless occurs occasionally in MSA, especially when reporting an official speech.[6]

إنَّ الآمالَ تحوّلت إلى أوهام.

ʾinna l-ʾaamaal-a taHawwal-at ʾilaa ʾawhaam-in.

(Indeed,) hopes have turned into delusions.

إنَّني أُوَكّد أنّ ...

ʾinna-nii ʾuʾakkid-u ʾanna ...

(Indeed,) I affirm that ...

إنَّنا جميعاً نعمل من أجل السلام.

ʾinna-naa jamiiᶜ-an na-ᶜmal-u min ʾajl-i l-salaam-i.

Indeed, we are working all together on behalf of peace.

2.2 Subordinating *ʾinna* 'that'

The particle *ʾinna* is also used as a way of introducing reported speech. As a subordinating conjunction, it is used exclusively after the verb *qaal-a* 'to say.'[7]

وقال إنَّه ناقش هذا الموضوع.

wa-qaal-a **ʾinna-hu** naaqash-a haadha l-mawDuuᶜ-a.

He said **that he** had discussed this topic.

قال المدرّب إنَّه راضٍ.

qaal-a l-mudarrib-u **ʾinna-hu** raaD-in.

The coach said **that he** was satisfied.

قال إنّ السياسيّين يستخدمون مصطلّحات دينيّة.

qaal-a **ʾinna l-siyaasiyy-iina** ya-staxdim-uuna muSTalaHaat-in diiniyyat-an.

He said **that the politicians** use religious terminology.

2.3 *ʾanna* أنَّ 'that'

The particle *ʾanna* is used to report factual information in a subordinate clause. It is used with the meaning of 'that' after perception verbs such as *samiᶜ-a* 'hear,'

---

[6] Dahlgren, in his study of Arabic word order, reports that *ʾinna* is "a particle for marking the thematization of (mainly or exclusively) the subject by letting it precede the verb in the sentence"(1998, 217).

[7] Note that in English the word "that" may be omitted in reporting speech, but *ʾinna* may not be omitted in Arabic.

iʿtaqad-a, iftakar-a 'think' or 'believe,' and also with verbs of communicating such as *dhakar-a* 'mention,' *ʾakkad-a* 'assert, declare', or *ʾaʿlan-a* 'announce.'[8] Belnap in his study of complementation in MSA states that "*ʾanna* occurs with verbs that assume or claim that the following clause's assertion is statement of fact."[9]

The verb in the main clause is referred to in some studies as the "matrix" verb because it determines the nature of the complementizer or subordinating particle that follows it (whether it is *ʾanna* or *ʾan*).[10] Note that if the matrix verb requires a preposition, *ʾanna* follows the preposition.

لا أظنّ أنّ المسرحيات كانت رديئة.

laa ʾa-Zann-u ʾanna l-masraHiyaat-i kaan-at radiiʾat-an.

I do not think **that the plays** were bad.

ذكر أنّ العربَ أعطوها اسمها.

dhakar-a ʾanna l-ʿarab-a ʾaʿTaw-haa sm-a-haa.

He mentioned **that the Arabs** gave it its name.

ذكر أنّ هناك سياسيّاً مشهوراً . . .

dhakar-a ʾanna hunaaka siyaasiyy-an mashuur-an . . .

he mentioned **that there is a famous politician** . . .

وصفوه بأنّه جوّ من الثقة.

waSaf-uu-hu bi-ʾanna-hu jaww-un min-a l-thiqat-i.

They described it as being ('**that it is**') an atmosphere of trust.

وتشير مصادر كرديّة إلى أنّ العددَ الحقيقيَ قد يصل إلى ألف شخص.

*wa-tushiir-u maSaadir-u kurdiyyat-un ʾilaa ʾanna l-ʿadad-a l-Haqiiqiyy-a qad
   ya-Sil-u ʾilaa ʾalf-i shaxS-in.*

Kurdish sources **indicate that the true number** may reach a thousand persons.

لقد أردنا أن نثبت للجميع أنّنا فريق جيّد.

la-qad ʾarad-naa ʾan nu-thbit-a li-l-jamiiʿ-i ʾanna-naa fariiq-un jayyid-un.

We (indeed) wanted to prove to everyone **that we** are a good team.

---

[8] Note that *ʾanna* (+ noun in the accusative) and *ʾan* (+ verb in the subjunctive) are related particles which differ in their distribution. According to LeComte (1968, 120), "la subordination complétive s'exprime avec *ʾan* ou *ʾanna* (que) qui ne sont que deux formes de la même particule. Elles se distinguent toutefois par leur emploi syntaxique: *ʾan* entraîne normalement un verbe à l'inacc. subj. (subjunctive) . . . *ʾanna* ne peut être suivie que d'un nom au cas direct ou d'un pronom affixe." See also Chapter 34, section 2.3.

[9] In a personal communication to the author, summarizing his findings in Belnap 1986. Note that matrix verbs indicating attitudes such as intention, feeling, possibility, need, or desire are followed by the subordinating particle *ʾan* plus a subjunctive verb, not by *ʾanna*. See Anghelescu 1999, 138 on *ʾanna*, especially as compared with *ʾan*; and Cantarino 1975, II: 234–35 and III:106–107.

[10] See Persson 1999 for a study of matrix verbs and complement clauses in Arabic.

2.3.1 ka-ʾanna كَأَنَّ 'as though'

The preposition *ka-* may be prefixed to the subordinating conjunction *ʾanna* 'that' in order to form the expression "as though." This expression is still a sister of *ʾinna* and has the same effect on the following clause.

وكَأَنَّنا متّفقون في الواقع على كلّ شيء

wa ka-ʾanna-naa muttafiq-uuna fii l-waaqiʿ-i ʿalaa kull-i shayʾ-in

as though we actually agreed on everything

كأنه مدرّج رومانيّ

ka-ʾanna-hu mudarraj-un ruumaaniyy-un

as though it were a Roman amphitheater

2.4 laakinna 'but'

This particle introduces a clause that contrasts with the previous clause.

ليست لبنانيّة، ولكنّها سعدت في لبنان.

lays-at lubnaaniyyat-an, wa-laakinna-haa saʿid-at fii lubnaan-a.

She is not Lebanese, **but she** was happy in Lebanon.

لكنّ هذه المساجد محتلّة	ولكنّ التجربةَ تقلقني
laakinna haadhihi l-masaajid-a muHtallat-un	*wa-laakinna l-tajribat-a tu-qliq-u-nii*
but these mosques are occupied	**but the experiment** disturbs me

لكنّ البرنامجَ يبقى في الكمبيوتر

laakinna l-barnaamaj-a ya-bqaa fii l-kumbyuutir

but the program remains in the computer

2.4.1 laakin لكن / wa-laakin ولكن 'but'

This variant of *laakinna*, written without the *shadda* or *fatHa* on the *nuun*, is not a sister of *ʾinna* and can therefore be followed directly by a verb. It is not as frequent in written Arabic as *laakinna*. In written text, it is almost impossible to tell the difference between these two particles, except that *laakin* may be followed by a verb.

ولكن يجب وضع ضوابط ومراقبة

wa-laakin ya-jib-u waDʿ-u DawaabiT-a wa-muraaqabat-in

but it is necessary to put [into effect] regulations and surveillance

2.5 liʾanna لأنّ 'because'

This subordinating particle is followed by a clause that gives a rationale or reason.

لأنّها استحقاق ديموقراطيّ	لأنّها تتحدّث عن همومي
li-ʾanna-haa stiHqaaq-un diimuuqraaTiyy-un	*li-ʾanna-haa ta-taHaddath-u ʿan humuum-ii*
because it is a democratic right	**because she** speaks about my concerns

لأنّ السنتين الأخيرتين كانتا من أفضل السنوات

li-ʾanna l-sanat-ayni l-ʾaxiirat-ayni kaan-ataa min ʾafDal-i l-sanawaat-i

because the last two years were among the best years

2.6 *laʿalla* لَعَلَّ / *wa-laʿalla* ولَعَلَّ 'perhaps, maybe'

This particle is similar in meaning to *rubba-maa* 'perhaps,' but is a sister of *ʾinna*. Like *ʾinna*, it may start a sentence as well as a clause. If it is followed by a verbal sentence, the subject of the verb must reduplicate itself in the form of a pronoun prefix attached to *laʿalla*. Abboud and McCarus state that *laʿalla* "often has the implication of hopeful expectation" (1983, Part 1:519).

ولعلّنا رأينا فعلاً أوّل عناصر مخطّة.

wa-laʿalla-naa raʾay-naa fiʿl-an ʾawwal-a ʿanaaSir-i muxaTTat-in.

Perhaps we have really seen the first elements of a plan.

ولعلّه مات قبل ذلك.

wa-laʿalla-hu maat-a qabl-a dhaalika.

Perhaps he died before that.

ولعلّ ذلك يعود إلى أنّ أغلبهم أجانب.

wa-laʿalla dhaalika ya-ʿuud-u ʾilaa ʾanna ʾaghlab-a-hum ʾajaanib-u.

Perhaps that is because ('goes back to that') the majority of them are foreigners.

20

Verb classes

Arabic verbs fall into two major groups, those with three-consonant roots (triliteral) and those with four-consonant roots (quadriliteral). Around each lexical root is structured a set of possible stem classes or verb forms (normally ten for triliteral roots and four for quadriliteral).[1] Moreover, each Arabic verb has a corresponding verbal noun (*maSdar* مصدر), an active participle (*ism faaʿil* اسم فاعل), and often, a passive participle (*ism mafʿuul* اسم مفعول). Thus verbs and their derivatives form the foundation for substantial amounts of Arabic vocabulary and can be considered in some ways as the core of the Arabic lexicon.[2]

1 Verb roots

Every Arabic verb has a lexical root, that is, a set of consonants or phonemes in a specific order that embody a broad lexical meaning, such as k-t-b 'write'; h-n-d-s 'engineer'; d-r-s 'study'; ʿ-l-m 'know'. These roots may consist of three or four consonants, with three being the most common. Within these two different root types, there are phonological variations according to the nature of the consonant phonemes occurring in the root.

This is mainly to do with the fact that the semivowels /w/ (*waaw*) and /y/ (*yaaʾ*) are not full-fledged consonants; they are weak in the sense that there are restrictions on how they combine with and interact with vowels. Sometimes when these semi-consonants are root phonemes, they behave as regular consonants, sometimes, however, they shift into long vowels, or they may become short vowels, or they turn into *hamza*, or in some cases, they disappear altogether. This can be confusing when learners need to identify the consonantal root of a word in order to look it up in a dictionary, so it is important for learners to have a basic understanding of how root types interact with rules for word formation.

---

[1] These stem classes are sometimes referred to in current literature on morphological theory as *binyanim* (singular *binyan*), using the Hebrew term. See Aronoff 1994, especially Chapter 5: 123–164. Note also that there are in fact fifteen (rather then ten) potential verb forms for triliteral verb roots. But Forms XI–XV are rare in MSA. For more on Forms XI–XV see Chapter 32.

[2] Kouloughli (1994, 215) gives the following description of the "deverbal" derivatives: "Tout verbe a dans son sillage des formes déverbales qui lui sont associées et avec lesquelles il entretient des relations morphologiques, syntaxiques et sémantiques stables."

There are phonotactic rules — rules of sound distribution — for Arabic words, many of which were deduced by Arabic grammarians as long ago as the eighth century (AD), and which remain valid today for MSA.[3] Whenever possible here, these rules are described and applied in order to explain variations in word structure.

Arabic verb roots are classified into two major classes: *SaHiiH* 'sound' and *muʿtall* 'weak.' Sound roots are ones that do not contain either *waaw* or *yaaʾ*; "weak" roots contain *waaw* or *yaaʾ* as one or more of the root phonemes. It is essential to know these classes because verb inflection affects the phonological structure of the verb root in all cases except the regular or sound triliteral root.

Within the two major classes of verbal roots, further classification occurs in several subcategories. Each of the subcategories manifests particular variation in the root. This variation is rule-governed, but complex.[4]

1.1 Regular (sound) triliteral root (*al-fiʿl al-SaHiiH al-saalim* الفعل الصحيح السالم)

Sound or regular verbal roots consist of three consonants, all of which are different and none of which are *waaw*, *yaaʾ*, or *hamza*. For example:

General meaning	Root consonants	
hear	*s-m-ʿ*	س - م - ع
reveal	*k-sh-f*	ك - ش - ف
work	*ʿ-m-l*	ع - م - ل

1.2 Geminate verb root (*al-fiʿl al-muDaʿʿaf* الفعل المضعّف)

Geminate or doubled verbal roots are ones *where the second and third consonant of the root are the same.* They show an alternation between repetition of the geminate consonant, with a vowel between, and doubling of the consonant, under specific phonological conditions.[5]

respond, reply	*r-d-d*	ر - د - د
cause	*s-b-b*	س - ب - ب
solve	*H-l-l*	ح - ل - ل

---

[3] Al-Khalil ibn Ahmad (d. ca. 791) pioneered Arabic phonological theory and developed the theory of root phonotactics in his introduction to the first Arabic dictionary, the *Kitaab al-ʿayn*. For more on this, see Sara 1991.

[4] See Killean 1978 for mnemonic aids to weak verb inflection and Timothy Mitchell 1981 for description of phonological rules in hollow and defective verbs. Extensive and useful descriptions of the morphophonemic rules for geminate, assimilated, hollow, and defective verbs are found in Abboud and McCarus 1983, Part 2: 1-173.

[5] For an analysis of the nature of geminate root morphology, see Moore 1990.

1.3 Hamzated verb root (*al-fiᶜl al-mahmuuz* الفعل المهموز)

A hamzated verb root is one where *hamza* (the glottal stop) occurs as the first, second, or third consonant. These verbs are considered a separate category because of morphophonemic rules that govern the occurrence and distribution of *hamza*, and also because of *hamza* spelling rules.

take	ᵓ-x-dh	ء - خ - ذ
eat	ᵓ-k-l	ء - ك - ل
ask	s-ᵓ-l	س - أ - ل
begin	b-d-ᵓ	ب - د - أ
read	q-r-ᵓ	ق - ر - ء

1.4 Roots with semi-consonants

1.4.1 Assimilated verb root (*al-fiᶜl al-mithaal* الفعل المثال)

"Assimilated" verb roots begin with a semi-consonant (*waaw* or *yaaᵓ*), most often *waaw*. They are termed "assimilated" because this *waaw*, even though it is part of the root, often disappears in the present tense and in certain other situations.

arrive	w-S-l	و - ص - ل
be abundant	w-f-r	و - ف - ر
find	w-j-d	و - ج - د
be dry	y-b-s	ي - ب - س

1.4.2 Hollow verb root (*al-fiᶜl al-ᵓajwaf* الفعل الأجوف)

"Hollow" verbs are ones in which the second or middle root consonant is either *waaw* or *yaaᵓ*. These two consonants undergo various mutations, turning into *ᵓalif*, a short vowel, a *hamza*, or a long vowel depending on the word structure. In the past tense citation form, for example, the *waaw* or *yaaᵓ* is not present and is replaced by *ᵓalif*. However, to look up one of these words or its derivation in a dictionary, one must know what the middle root consonant is. The root consonant often recurs in the present tense verb stem (as a vowel) and elsewhere, as will be shown. There are essentially three variations on the hollow verb, determined by which long vowel is present in the present-tense or imperfective stem: *waaw*, *yaaᵓ* or *ᵓalif*.

say	q-w-l	ق - و - ل
be	k-w-n	ك - و - ن
sell	b-y-ᶜ	ب - ي - ع
live	ᶜ-y-sh	ع - ي - ش

1.4.3 Defective verb root (*al-fiᶜl al-naaqiS* الفعل الناقص)

"Defective" verb roots are ones where the final consonant is either *waaw* or *yaa'*. These semi-consonants may assume various forms and even seem to disappear in certain circumstances.

be sufficient	*k-f-y*	ك - ف - ي
forget	*n-s-y*	ن - س - ي
complain	*sh-k-w*	ش - ك - و
appear	*b-d-w*	ب - د - و
build	*b-n-y*	ب - ن - ي

1.4.4 Doubly weak or "mixed" verb roots

Doubly weak verb roots have semi-consonants and/or *hamza* in two places, sometimes as the first and third consonants, and sometimes as the second and third. They are not many in number, but some of them are frequently used:

come	*j-y-'*	ج - ي - ء
come	*'-t-y*	ء - ت - ي
see	*r-'-y*	ر - أ - ي
follow	*w-l-y*	و - ل - ي
intend	*n-w-y*	ن - و - ي

1.5 Quadriliteral verb root (*al-fiᶜl al-rubaaᶜiyy* الفعل الرباعيّ)

Quadriliteral verb roots contain four consonants. Sometimes the four consonants are all different and sometimes they are reduplicated, that is, the first two consonants are repeated. Reduplicated quadriliteral roots are often considered to be onomatopoeic, that is, derived from particular sounds or repeated motions.

crystalize	*b-l-w-r*	ب - ل - و - ر
dominate	*s-y-T-r*	س - ي - ط - ر
obstruct	*ᶜ-r-q-l*	ع - ر - ق - ل
flutter	*r-f-r-f*	ر - ف - ر - ف
whisper	*w-s-w-s*	و - س - و - س
hum	*h-m-h-m*	ه - م - ه - م
shake, quake	*z-l-z-l*	ز - ل - ز - ل

1.6 Denominal verb roots

Normally, the verb is considered the most basic or elemental form of a lexical entry, but in a few instances, the verb is ultimately derived from a noun, and sometimes the concept is borrowed from another language. These denominals tend to exist chiefly in Forms II and V and rarely in other forms. They can be triliteral or quadriliteral. Some examples of denominal verbs include:

Form II:

| to unite | *waHHada* | وحّد | *w-H-d* | و - ح - د |
| to appoint | *ʿayyana* | عيّن | *ʿ -y-n* | ع - ي - ن |

Form V:

| to adopt | *tabannaa* | تبنّى | *b-n* | ب - ن |

Form II quadriliteral:

| to center | *tamarkaza* | تمركز | *m-r-k-z*[6] | م - ر - ك - ز |

2 Verb derivation patterns: *ʾawzaan al-fiʿl* أوزان الفعل

2.1 Comparison with English

In English, it is possible to modify verb meanings or even create verbs from other parts of speech through several morphological procedures, for example, prefixing the morpheme /un-/ as in *undo, unfasten, unlock, unpack*, indicating the reversal of an action. Nouns and adjectives can be converted into verbs by adding the suffix /-en/, as in *strengthen* or *widen* indicating an increase of that quality. Or one can, for example, create verbs by using the suffix /-ize/ as in *standardize, mechanize, minimize, maximize, formalize*, or *trivialize*, to indicate the act of adding that quality to something. And there are many more such procedures. Other parts of speech, such as prepositions, adverbs, and nouns are converted to verbs just by inflecting them as verbs: "to *down* a glass of water," "to *up* the price," "to *impact* a situation."

Arabic verb derivation is much more restricted; Arabic verbs fall into a limited number of stem classes. It is much rarer for new verbs to be created in Modern Standard Arabic than in English because each Arabic verb belongs to a particular derivational and inflectional class. That is, it has a particular internal shape, or pattern.

---

[6] In this instance, the word *markaz*, 'center,' a noun of place from the triliteral root *r-k-z*, has taken on such a lexical identity of its own that a denominal verb form has emerged based on the four consonants, *m-r-k-z*.

2.2 The ten-form template: *ʾafʿaal mujarrada wa-ʾafʿaal maziida*

أفعال مجرّدة وأفعال مزيدة

Arabic has a verb grid, or template of ten derived "forms" into which any triliteral verb root may theoretically fit.[7] That is, the lexical root of three consonants can theoretically interlock with ten different patterns to produce ten lexical variants on the same root. These variants all have a central, related lexical meaning, but each verb form has a different semantic slant on that meaning. For example, different forms of the lexical root *ʿ-l-m* produce verbs having to do with knowledge: Form I *ʿalim-a* means 'to know, to be informed' Form II *ʿallam-a* means 'to teach' (cause someone to know), Form IV *ʾaʿlama* means 'to inform' (cause someone to be informed), Form V *taʿallama* means 'to learn, to study' (cause one's self to know). The triconsonantal sequence *ʿ-l-m* is common to all these lexical items.

The base form, or Form I is referred to in Arabic as *fiʿl mujarrad* فعل مجرّد, literally the 'stripped' form; meaning the morphologically simplest form. All other forms (II–X) are referred to as *ʾafʿaal maziida* أفعال مزيدة, literally, 'increased' or 'augmented' forms, i.e., more morphologically complex.

In practice, not every lexical root occurs in all ten forms of the verb; some occur in very few forms, while others occur in four, five, or six forms. Dictionaries normally list all the forms in which a lexical root regularly appears.

The interlocking of the lexical root with the various verb form templates creates actual verbs whose meanings can often be analyzed or deduced through the use of compositional semantics. That is, the lexical meaning of the consonantal root plus the grammatical meaning of the particular template combine to yield an actual word. This two-part formula sometimes yields a very clear meaning derivable from the component parts, but other times, the meaning is not as clear because of its evolution over time.[8]

Quadriliteral verbs have a more restricted grid of four possible templates or forms into which they fall.

---

[7] As mentioned in note 1, there are a possible five more forms, XI–XV, but they are much rarer.

[8] As a concise summary of the interrelationships of the Arabic verb forms, Lecomte (1968, 34) writes: "Si l'on met à part la forme dérivée IX, qui est nettement en marge du système, et la forme VII, commune à tout le domaine sémitique et de constitution claire, on peut expliquer comme suit la formation des autres formes dérivées: les formes I, II, III et IV sont les quatre formes de base, auxquelles correspondent respectivement les formes VIII, V, VI et X, obtenues en principe par préfixation d'un *t-*, qui leur confère une valeur réfléchie-passive. Le principe est appliqué sans altération dans les formes dérivées V et VI. Dans la forme dérivée VIII, on observe une métathèse immédiatement perceptible. La forme dérivée X est issue non de la forme dérivée IV à préfixe *hamza*, mais d'une forme dérivée IV à préfixe *s-* qui a existé dans d'autres langues sémitiques (ex. assyrien tardif)."

2.2.1 Conventions

2.2.1.1 FORMS AND MEASURES (*'awzaan* أوزان): The derivations or verb templates are identified by the morphological pattern that characterizes them and are often referred to in western grammars of Arabic as "forms" or "measures" of the verb. They are usually identified in English by a roman numeral, i.e., Form II or Form VI. In this convention, when the word "form" refers to a specific verb template, it is capitalized, e.g., Form II. Since this is a widespread convention in the United States and Europe, and because it is the way that verbs are identified in the most widely used Arabic-English dictionary, Hans Wehr's *Dictionary of Modern Written Arabic*, it is used in this reference grammar.

Arabic grammars term the verb forms *'awzaan* 'weights' or 'measures' (sg. *wazn* وزن), and refer to them via the medium of a model root (traditionally *f-ʿ-l* فعل) keyed into particular morphological patterns. The base form is *mujarrad* 'stripped, bare' and the derived forms are *maziid* 'augmented' on the model of a particular pattern, for example,

«انتخب» على وزن افتعل

"*intaxab*" *ʿalaa wazn-i ftaʿal;*
i.e., *intaxab* 'he elected' is on the model of *iftaʿal;*

«تجنّب» على وزن تفعّل

"*tajannab*" *ʿalaa wazn-i tafaʿʿal;*
tajannab 'he avoided' is on the model of *tafaʿʿal.*

2.2.1.2 CITATION FORM FOR VERBS: The conventional way of citing Arabic verbal roots is to refer to them using the shortest verb inflection, **the third person masculine singular, past tense**. This is considered equivalent to using the English citation form, the infinitive (there is no infinitive verb form in Arabic[9]). It is helpful to cite the verb in its past and present forms together, and that is how they are presented in this book. For example:

to discuss	*baHath-a/ya-bHath-u*	بَحَثَ / يَبْحَثُ
to reveal	*kashaf-a/ya-kshif-u*	كَشَفَ / يَكْشِفُ

---

[9] The verbal noun, or *maSdar*, is considered equivalent to the infinitive for several reasons: first, it is an abstraction of the action of a verb, and second, it does not possess a time reference (i.e., tense marking) and is therefore non-finite. Moreover, in certain syntactic constructions it functions as an infinitive does in English. However, it is not used as a citation form for the verb.

2.3 The model root: *f-ʿ -l* (*faaʾ - ʿayn - laam* ف - ع - ل)

In order to exemplify patterns or prosodic templates in Arabic, a **model root** *f-ʿ -l* is used so that any pattern can be referred to or expressed by fitting into it.[10] This procedure was established centuries ago when Arabic grammarians first started extracting and analyzing the rules and structures of the language, and it is still the practice today. Any initial root consonant is represented by *faaʾ*, any medial consonant by *ʿayn*, and any final root consonant by *laam*.[11] The Form IV verb *ʾarsala* ('to send') would be said to be on the pattern of *ʾafʿala* (*ʿalaa wazn ʾafʿal-a* على وزن أَفْعَلَ); the verb *katab-a* ('to write') is on the pattern of *faʿal-a* (*ʿalaa wazn faʿal-a* على وزن فَعَلَ), and so forth.

If a root or stem has four consonants instead of three, then another *laam* is added to illustrate the pattern. Thus the verb *tarjam-a* ('to translate') would be said to be on the pattern of *faʿlal-a* (*ʿalaa wazn faʿlal-a* على وزن فَعْلَلَ).

The use of the root *f-ʿ -l* as the prime exemplar for all Arabic words is a powerful symbolic formalization that provides a model of any morphological template or word pattern. This procedure is used not only to refer to verb forms but also to refer to any lexical item based on the root and pattern system. It is an efficient way of illustrating paradigmatic contrasts, and in keeping with this practice, this reference grammar uses the root *f-ʿ -l* for points of reference and examples.

2.4 Morphological shifts

When a non-sound root interlocks with a particular pattern, a situation arises where rules of phonology intersect and may clash with rules of morphology, so a modification of the word-structure occurs. When this happens, the rules of phonology are primary. These instances result, therefore, in what are called morphophonemic processes, i.e., rule-governed changes in word structure. These rules generate particular inflectional classes (e.g., Form VIII hollow verbs) which are illustrated in paradigms.

Although it may seem that there are many exceptions to rules in Arabic, the fact is that Arabic phonological structure and rules of phonotactics are primary, and they determine the sequences of morphological alternations that occur. The phonological rules of Arabic and how they interact with the morphology result in morphological structures of Arabic being coherent and rule-governed.

---

[10] The lexical root *f-ʿ-l* has the base meaning of 'doing' or 'making.'

[11] The letters/phonemes of the model root are referred to in Arabic as *Huruuf al-miizaan al-Sarfiyy* 'the letters of the morphological measure.' As described by Abd al-Latif et al., "*bi-Hayth-u ta-kuun-a haad-hihi l-Huruuf-u l-thalaathat-u mushakkalat-an bi-Harakaat-i ʾaHruf-i l-kalimat-i l-muraad-i wazn-u-haa wazn-an Sarfiyy-an*" (1997, 141). "In order that these three letters be vowelized with the vowels of the word whose pattern is desired."

This reference grammar defines and describes some basic MSA morphophonemic processes in order to make clear the systematization in the language. However, learners who would prefer to focus on forms rather than rules can consult the paradigms without examining the morphophonemic processes.

2.5 The verb forms: patterns, meanings, deverbal substantives

Verb patterns are traditionally given in their citation forms, the third person masculine singular active past tense, as well as the third person masculine singular present tense. This is a standard procedure for citing Arabic verbs, since there is a stem change between past and present tense.

It is traditional to refer to the short vowel which follows the second root consonant of a verb as the **"stem" vowel**. Therefore in a present tense verb such as *ya-rfuD-u* 'he refuses,' the stem vowel is *Damma*. In a derived verb form such as Form VIII *ya-HtafiZ-u* 'he maintains,' the stem vowel is *kasra*.

Verb citations are provided in Arabic script and in transcription; for discussion of consonant–vowel patterning, consonant-vowel structures are also sometimes given, using the convention:

C = Consonant;   V = short vowel

C₁ represents the first root consonant,   VV = long vowel

C₂ represents the second and

C₃ represents the third.

C₄ represents the fourth consonant (if any)

In the following chapters, each verb form is described, with its particular patterns and meanings. Inflectional characteristics are noted, and examples are provided.

As mentioned at the start of this section, each verb form has in its wake a set of three deverbal substantives: a **verbal noun** (the name of the action, e.g., 'defense,' or 'defending'), an **active participle** (describing the doer of the action: 'defender' or '[person] defending') and a **passive participle** (describing the item which undergoes the action, e.g., 'defended'). Whereas the verbal noun is used strictly as a noun, the participles, being descriptors, may function either as nouns or as adjectives. Different sections of this book describe the form and function of verbal nouns and participles, but because they form such an integral part of the lexical repository of each verb, they are also listed in the context of their deverbal derivations.

21

Verb inflection: a summary

1 Verb inflection

Arabic verbs inflect for six morphological categories: gender, number, person, tense, mood, and voice. These inflections are marked by means of prefixes, suffixes, changes in vowel pattern, and stem changes. The first three categories, gender, number, and person, are determined by the subject of the verb. That is, the verb agrees with the subject in all those respects.

1.1 Agreement markers: gender, number, and person

Agreement markers ensure that the verb inflects in accordance with the nature of its subject. Arabic verbs inflect by means of **affixes** attached to a verb stem. In the past tense, the inflectional marker is a **suffix** that carries all the agreement markers: gender, number, and person. For example: the suffix /-at/ on a past tense stem such as *katab-* (*katab-at* كَتَبَتْ) carries the information: third person, feminine, singular: i.e., "she wrote."

In the present tense, the verb stem has a **prefix** as well as a suffix. For example, **prefix** *ya-* on a present tense stem such as *-ktub-* carries partial information: third person. The **suffix** on the present tense stem carries more information: therefore the suffix *-uuna* (as in *ya-ktub-uuna* يَكْتُبُونَ 'they write') gives information on number (plural) and gender (masculine), as well as mood (indicative). This combination of information is uniquely marked on each member in a verb paradigm.[1]

1.1.1 Gender: masculine or feminine

Arabic verbs are marked for masculine or feminine gender in the second and third persons. The first person (I, we) is gender-neutral.

---

[1] In technical linguistic terms, Arabic is a "pro-drop" (i.e., "pronoun-drop") language. That is, every inflection in a verb paradigm is specified uniquely and does not need to use independent pronouns to differentiate the person, number, and gender of the verb. For Modern Standard Arabic that means that there are thirteen different inflections in every verb paradigm. Consult Haegeman 1994, 19–25 and 454–57 for more on pro-drop languages and the pro-drop parameter in general.

1.1.2 Number: singular, dual, plural

Arabic verbs are inflected for three number categories: singular, dual, or plural. The dual in Arabic verbs is used in the second person ("you two") and in the third person ("they two"), but not the first person.

1.1.3 Person: first, second, third

The concept of "person" refers to the individual/s involved in the speech act: the one/s speaking (first person), the one/s spoken to (second person), and one/s spoken about (third person). Arabic verbs inflect for: first person (I, we), second person (you), and third person (she, he, they).

1.2 Tense

The two basic Arabic verb tenses differ in terms of stems as well as inflectional markers.

1.2.1 Verb stems

Each Arabic verb has two stems, one used for the perfect/past tense and one for the imperfect/present. The past tense stem takes suffixes in order to inflect, and the present tense stem takes both prefixes and suffixes. Because of the salience of the prefix in the present tense and of the suffix in the past tense, certain scholars refer to these tenses as "the prefix set" and "the suffix set," respectively.[2]

In Form I verbs, the present tense inflectional stem is not usually predictable from the past tense stem, but in the derived forms and quadriliteral verbs, the present stem is *predictable*. In this text, stems are usually written with a hyphen where they would connect with inflectional formatives,[3] e.g.

	Past tense stem		**Present tense stem**	
write	*katab-*	كَتَبـ	*-ktub-*	ـكْتُبـ
complete	*ʾakmal-*	أَكْمَلـ	*-kmil-*	ـكْمِلـ
meet	*ijtamaʿ-*	ـاجتَمَعـ	*-jtamiʿ-*	ـجتَمِعـ
use	*istaxdam-*	ـاستَخدَمـ	*-staxdim-*	ـستَخدِمـ

1.2.2 Tense/Aspect

Arabic verbs show a range of tenses, but two of them are basic: **past** and **present**. These tenses are also often referred to as **perfect** and **imperfect**, or **perfective** and

---

[2] For example, see Holes 1995, 86–90 and Beeston 1970, 71–86.
[3] Where the prefix or suffix merges with the verb stem (as in the past tense of defective verbs or the present tense of passive assimilated verbs) the morpheme boundary is blurred and therefore not indicated.

imperfective, but those latter terms are more accurately labels of aspect rather than tense.

Tense and aspect can be described as two different ways of looking at time. Tense usually deals with linear points in time that stretch from the far past into the future, in relation to the speaker. Aspect, on the other hand deals with the degree of completeness of an action or state: is the action completed, partial, ongoing, or yet to occur? So the perspectives of tense and aspect are different: tense focuses on the point on the timeline at which the action occurs, whereas aspect is focused on the action itself – whether it is complete or not.[4]

The difference between tense and aspect can be subtle, and the two categories may overlap to a significant extent. It is theorized that Classical Arabic was more aspect-specific than tense-specific, but in dealing with the modern written language, some linguists and teachers find it more pragmatic to describe Arabic verbs in terms of tense.[5]

In this work, I often use the term "past tense" to refer to what is also called the perfect, or the perfective aspect; and I use the term "present tense" to refer to what is also called the imperfect tense or the imperfective aspect. In general, I prefer to stick with timeline terms ("past" and "present") when using the term "tense" because I have found this to be less confusing to learners.[6]

---

[4] "Tense involves the basic location in time of an event or state of affairs, in relation to the time of speaking (or writing), while aspect relates more to the internal nature of events and states of affairs, such as whether they are (or were) finished, long-lasting, instantaneous, repetitive, the beginning of something, the end of something, and so on" (Hurford 1994, 240). Abboud and McCarus use the terms "perfect tense" and "imperfect tense" (1983, part 1:263): "The perfect tense denotes completed actions; the imperfect tense denotes actions which have not taken place or have not been completed."

Likewise, Haywood and Nahmad state (1962, 95–96): "Arabic, in common with other Semitic languages, is deficient in tenses, and this does not make for ease in learning. Moreover the tenses do not have accurate time-significances as in Indo-European languages. There are two main tenses, the Perfect الماضي *al-maaDii*, denoting actions completed at the time to which reference is being made; and the Imperfect المضارع *al-muDaari*[c], for incompleted actions."

[5] For a thorough and lucid discussion of Arabic verb aspect and tense see Blachère and Gaudefroy-Demombynes 1975, 245–56. More concisely, Wright states the following: "A Semitic Perfect or Imperfect has, in and of itself, no reference to the temporal relations of the speaker (thinker or writer) and of other actions which are brought into juxtaposition with it. It is precisely these relations which determine in what sphere of time (past, present, or future) a Semitic Perfect or Imperfect lies, and by which of our tenses it is to be expressed – whether by our Past, Perfect, Pluperfect, or Future-perfect; by our Present, Imperfect, or Future. The Arabian Grammarians themselves have not, however, succeeded in keeping this important point distinctly in view, but have given an undue importance to the idea of time" (1967, I:51).

[6] The terms "perfect" and "imperfect" are sometimes misleading for English-speaking learners of Arabic because they often compare the terms to European languages they have studied, such as French, for example, where "*imparfait*" refers to a continuing state or action in the past. Note the definition of "imperfect" in Webster's Third (unabridged: 1986, q.v.): "of or relating to or being a verb tense used to designate a continuing state or action *esp. in the past*" (my italics).

1.2.3 The present tense (the imperfect): *al-muDaari*ᶜ المضارع

1.2.3.1 FORM: The present tense is formed from the present tense stem of a verb, to which both a prefix and a suffix are added. The stem by itself is not an independent word; it needs the prefixes and suffixes to convey a complete meaning. The prefixes are subject markers of person while the suffixes show mood and number.[7] In MSA, thirteen present tense inflectional forms are used.

		Present tense stem -*ktub*- 'write' Present tense indicative conjugation	
	Singular	Dual	Plural
First person	أَكْتُبُ *ʾa-ktub-u*		نَكْتُبُ *na-ktub-u*
Second person m.	تَكْتُبُ *ta-ktub-u*	تَكْتُبَانِ *ta-ktub-aani*	تَكْتُبُونَ *ta-ktub-uuna*
f.	تَكْتُبِينَ *ta-ktub-iina*	تَكْتُبَانِ *ta-ktub-aani*	تَكْتُبْنَ *ta-ktub-na*
Third person m.	يَكْتُبُ *ya-ktub-u*	يَكْتُبَانِ *ya-ktub-aani*	يَكْتُبُونَ *ya-ktub-uuna*
f.	تَكْتُبُ *ta-ktub-u*	تَكْتُبَانِ *ta-ktub-aani*	يَكْتُبْنَ *ya-ktub-na*

The prefix and suffix together give the full meaning of the verb. They are sometimes referred to together as a "circumfix" because they surround the stem on both sides.[8]

---

[7] The term *muDaari*ᶜ literally means 'resembling.' This term was adopted because of the fact that the present tense mood markers on the verb (the suffixed *Damma* of the indicative and the *fatHa* of the subjunctive) resemble the case markers on nouns (especially the nominative and accusative). In other words, whereas the past tense verb has only one mood (the indicative) the present tense verb shifts its mood depending on the syntactic context, just as a noun shifts its case depending on its role in the sentence. The present tense therefore "resembles" a noun in this ability to shift its desinence.

[8] The term "circumfix" refers to a combination of prefix and suffix used with a stem to create a lexical item, such as the English word "enlighten." As Anderson states, they "involve simultaneous prefixation and suffixation that correspond to a single unit of morphological form" (1992, 53). The discontinuous inflectional affixes on Arabic present tense verbs may be considered circumfixes, but the concept of circumfix as a separate morphological category is disputed. See Golston 1996, 731, esp. note 8, as well as Anderson 1992, 53, 59, and 389.

1.2.3.2 MEANING: The present tense, or imperfect, refers in a general way to incomplete, ongoing actions or ongoing states. It corresponds to both the English present and present continuous tenses. There is no distinction between these in Arabic.

I write; I am writing	*ʾa-ktub-u*	أكتبُ
we study; we are studying	*na-drus-u*	ندرسُ
they (m.) translate, are translating	*yu-tarjim-uuna*	يترجمون
they (f.) meet; they are meeting	*ya-jtamiᶜ-na*	يجتمعْنَ

Examples:

يعمل في الإدارة.
ya-ᶜmal-u fii l-ʾidaarat-i.
He works in the administration.

يلعبون مباراة.
ya-lᶜab-uuna mubaaraat-an.
They are playing a match.

تختلف عن غيرها.
ta-xtalif-u ᶜan ghayr-i-haa.
She differs from others.

يجلس على المقعد.
ya-jlis-u ᶜalaa l-maqᶜad-i.
He is sitting on the seat.

1.2.4 Future tense: *al-mustaqbal* المستقبل

1.2.4.1 FORM: The future tense is formed by prefixing either the morpheme *sa-* or the particle *sawfa* to a present tense indicative verb. The verb may be active or passive. The particle *sa-* is identified by some grammarians as an abbreviation of *sawfa*.

1.2.4.2 MEANING: This procedure conveys an explicitly future action.

سأفكّرُ في ذلك.
sa-ʾu-fakkir-u fii dhaalika.
I'll think about that.

سيساعدُ إلى حدّ كبير.
sa-yu-saaᶜid-u ʾilaa Hadd-in kabiir-in.
It will help to a great extent.

سوف يمثّلونَ بلادهم.
sawfa yu-maththil-uuna bilaad-a-hum.
They will represent their country.

القرار سيُتّخذُ.
al-qaraar-u sa-yu-ttaxadh-u.
The decision will be taken.

1.2.5 Past tense: *al-maaDii* الماضي

1.2.5.1 FORM: The past tense in Arabic is formed by suffixing person-markers to the past tense verb stem. The person markers in the past tense also denote number (singular, dual, plural) and gender. In MSA, thirteen person markers are used in the past tense paradigm:

Past tense stem *katab-* 'wrote'			
	Singular	**Dual**	**Plural**
First person	كَتَبْتُ *katab-tu*		كَتَبْنا *katab-naa*
Second person **m.**	كَتَبْتَ *katab-ta*	كَتَبْتُما *katab-tumaa*	كَتَبْتُم *katab-tum*
f.	كَتَبْتِ *katab-ti*	كَتَبْتُما *katab-tumaa*	كَتَبْتُنَّ *katab-tunna*
Third person **m.**	كَتَب *katab-a*	كَتَبا *katab-aa*	كَتَبوا *katab-uu*
f.	كَتَبْت *katab-at*	كَتَبَتا *katab-ataa*	كَتَبْنَ *katab-na*

1.2.5.2 SPELLING: The third person masculine plural suffix, /-uu/ is spelled with a final 'alif, which is not pronounced, sometimes called "otiose" 'alif.[9] It is simply a traditional spelling convention. It is deleted if the verb has a pronoun object suffix, e.g.,

كتبوا	كتبوها.	استخدموا	استخدموه.
katab-uu	*katab-uu-haa.*	*istaxdam-uu*	*istaxdam-uu-hu.*
they wrote	They wrote it.	they used	They used it.

وصفوه.
waSaf-uu-hu.
They described it.

1.2.5.3 MEANING

(1) **Action in the past:** The Arabic past tense refers to a completed action and thus equates in most respects with English past tense and past perfect.[10]

---

[9] See Chapter 2, section 4.2.1.3, subsection (3.3).
[10] See Wright 1967, II:1–4 for further analysis of the past tense.

حاول انقاذ حياة رجل.

Haawal-a ʾinqaadh-a Hayaat-i rajul-in

He tried to save a man's life.

عادت من إجازة.

ʿaad-at min ʾijaazat-in.

She returned from a vacation.

سلّموا بياناً.

sallam-uu bayaan-an.

They (m.) delivered a statement.

شكراً لكلّ ما فعلتموه.

shukr-an li-kull-i maa faʿal-tum-uu-hu.[11]

Thank you for everything **you (m.pl.) have done.**

(2) **Non-past action:** Depending on the context, the Arabic past tense may also be used to convey other meanings.[12] For example:

وصلنا تقريباً.

waSal-naa taqriib-an.

We are almost there (lit. 'we **have** almost **arrived**').

بارك الله فيك.

baarak-a llaah-u fii-ka.

God bless you (lit. 'God **has blessed** you').

1.3 Moods of the verb

Mood or "mode" refers to the Arabic verb properties **indicative, subjunctive, jussive, and imperative.** These categories, or morphosyntactic properties, reflect contextual modalities that condition the action of the verb. For example, the indicative mood is characteristic of straightforward, factual statements or questions, while the subjunctive mood reflects an attitude toward the action such as doubt, desire, intent, wishing, or necessity, and the jussive mood, when used for the imperative, indicates an attitude of command, request, or need-for-action on the part of the speaker.

In Arabic, mood marking is done only on the present tense or imperfective stem; there are no mood variants for the past tense. The Arabic moods are therefore nonfinite; that is, they do not refer to specific points in time and are not differentiated by tense. Tense is inferred from context and other parts of the clause.[13] For more extensive description of the moods and their uses, see Chapters 34 and 35.

---

[11] The second person plural masculine suffix *-tum* requires a long vowel *-uu* as a helping vowel before a suffixed personal pronoun.

[12] For example, the past tense is used in conditional sentences, as well as in optative (wishing) expressions. For more on this function of the past tense, see Chapter 39.

[13] The question of mood marking (on verbs) is a central one in Arabic grammar, along with case marking (on nouns and adjectives). Moods fall under the topic of morphology because they are reflected in Arabic word structure, that is, they are usually indicated by suffixes or modifications of suffixes attached to the present tense verb stem, and the phonological nature of the verb stem determines what form the suffix will take. Moods also, however, fall under the topic of syntax because their use is determined either by particles which govern their occurrence, or by the narrative context in general, including attitude of the speaker and intended meaning. They are therefore referred to in some reference works and theoretical discussions as "morphosyntactic" categories.

1.3.1 Indicative mood

نرحّب بزبائننا.

nu-raHHib-u bi-zabaaʾin-i-naa.

We **welcome** our customers.

يغادر القاهرة اليوم.

yu-ghaadir-u l-qaahirat-a l-yawm-a.

He **leaves** Cairo today.

1.3.2 Subjunctive mood

يجب أن نقوم بزيارة.

ya-jib-u ʿan **na-quum-a** bi-ziyaarat-in.

It is necessary that **we undertake** a visit.

1.3.3 Jussive mood

The jussive mood in MSA is used most often with the negative particle *lam* to negate the past tense, and as a basis for forming the imperative.

لم نأت.

lam na-ʾti.

We did not **come**.

إصلاحات لم تكتمل منذ عامين

*ʾiSlaaH-aat-un lam **ta-ktamil** mundh-u ʿaam-ayni*

renovations that **haven't been completed** for two years

1.3.4 Imperative

افتحْ يا سمسم!

iftaH yaa simsim-u!

Open, Sesame!

اسمح لي.

ismaH lii.

Permit me.

لا تنسَ !

laa ta-nsa!

Don't **forget**!

1.4 Voice: active or passive

Whereas the tense of a verb conveys temporal or time-related information, the "voice" of a verb conveys information on the topical focus of a sentence. The active voice is used when the doer of the action is the subject of the verb ("I ate the cake"), and the passive voice is used when the object of the verbal action is the subject ("The cake was eaten.").

Generally speaking, the passive voice is used in Arabic only if the agent or doer of the action is unknown or not to be mentioned for some reason. This contrasts with English where one may mention the agent in a passive construction through use of the preposition "by" ("The cake was eaten by me.") Rarely is the agent mentioned when the passive is used in Arabic.

The Arabic passive may be internal, through a change in the nature of the internal vowels (e.g., *ʿuqid-a* 'it was held') or derivational (e.g., *inʿaqad-a* 'it was held').

For example, the following sentence is in the active voice:

عقَدَ الملكُ الاجتماعَ.

ʿaqad-a l-malik-u l-ijitmaaʿ-a.

The king held the meeting.

where *al-malik-u* 'the king' is the subject of the verb as well as the agent or doer of the action, *ʿaqad-a*, and the object of the verb is *al- ijtimaaʿ-a* 'the meeting.'

If the sentence were re-phrased as a passive construction, the object of the verb becomes the subject of the sentence, and the verb is marked for passive. The internal morphological change that signals the Arabic passive is a change in the vowel pattern of the verb:

عُقِدَ الاجتماعُ.

ʿuqid-a l-ijtimaaʿ-u.
The meeting was held.

where *al-ijtimaaʿ-u* is now the subject, and the verb is inflected for passive voice through the vowel sequence /-u-i-/ instead of /-a-a-/.

Another way of expressing the passive is to use another form of the verb which is passive or reflexive in meaning, usually the Form VII verb, if it exists, or Form V:

انْعَقَدَ الاجتماعُ.

inʿaqad-a l-ijtimaaʿ-u.
The meeting was held.

where the Form VII verb is active in form, but passive in meaning, and the subject of the Form VII verb is *al-ijtimaaʿ-u*. Passive and passive-like structures are described at greater length in Chapter 38.

2 Complex predicates: compound verbs, *qad*, and verb strings
Arabic verbal expressions may consist of more than the main verb. Auxiliary verbs may be used in conjunction with a main verb to express variations of tense and aspect, and the verbal particle *qad* is also used to convey information about aspect.

2.1 Compound verbs
Compound verbs are tenses that consist of the verb **kaan-a** plus a **main verb**. They are as follows:

2.1.1 The past progressive
To convey the idea of continued or habitual action in the past, the verb *kaan-a* is used in the past tense in conjunction with the present tense of the main verb. Both parts of this compound verb are inflected for person, gender, and number. The main verb always comes after *kaan-a*; if there is a specific subject mentioned, it comes between the two parts of the verb.

This tense of the verb is used for expressing what in English would be "used to," or "was _____ ing." Sometimes, with certain verbs in certain contexts it is used to express a concept of an action that took place in the past, but extended or endured over a period of time, rather than taking place at a discrete moment in time. This is especially true of experiential verbs that denote states of mind, such as knowing, feeling, liking. In those cases, the English equivalent is often just a simple past tense.

كانت ترتدي قميصاً أزرق.
kaan-at ta-rtadii qamiiS-an ʾazraq-a.
She **was wearing** a blue shirt.

كان يعمل في المطبخ.
kaan-a ya-ʿmal-u fii l-maTbax-i.
He **used to work** in the kitchen.

كانوا يستيقظونَ يومياً في الساعة السادسة.
kaan-uu ya-stayqiZ-uuna yawmiyy-an fii al-saaʿat-i al-saadisat-i.
They **used to wake up** daily at 6:00.

كنّا نأمل
kun-naa na-ʾmal-u
we were hoping

2.1.1.1 PAST PROGRESSIVE WITH EXPERIENTIAL VERBS: A state of knowing, feeling, or understanding is one that is considered to extend over a period of time in the past, and therefore such verbs are often expressed with the past continuous tense rather than the simple past in Arabic. English does not usually express these concepts with the past progressive tense, but with the simple past.

كانوا يعرفون الشعوب الإيبيرية.
kaan-uu ya-ʿrif-uuna l-shuʿuub-a l-ʾiibiiriyyat-a.
They **knew** [over a period of time] the Iberian peoples.

كانا يعلمان بالغارة.
kaan-aa ya-ʿlam-aani bi-l-ghaarat-i
They (two) **knew about / had knowledge about** the raid.

2.1.1.2 PAST PERFECT PROGRESSIVE MEANING WITH PRESENT TENSE AND *mundhu*: When a state or action begins in the past and continues into the present, with specific reference to the length of time that the state or action continued, the present tense is used in Arabic although the past perfect progressive is used in English. In equational sentences the present tense is expressed without a verb. This meaning occurs most frequently with the particle *mundh-u* 'since; for; ago.' (See also Chapter 16, section 2.3.4.)

(1) Verbal sentences:

أعيش هنا منذ خمس سنوات.
ʾa-ʿiish-u hunaa mundhu xams-i sanawaat-in
I have been living here for five years.

يـعمل في دائراة البلديّة منذ شهرين.

ya-ʿmal-u fii daaʾirat-i l-baladiyyat-i mundhu shahr-ayni.

He has been working in the county administration for two months.

(2)   **Equational sentences:** In these two sentences, an active participle is used instead of a verb with past perfect progressive meaning.

تجارتها قائمة على التصدير والاستيراد منذ زمن طويل.

tijaarat-u-haa qaaʾimat-un ʿalaa l-taSdiir-i wa-l-istiiraad-i mundh-u zaman-in Tawiil-in.

Its trade has been based on export and import for a long time.

هذا الزحف مستمرّ منذ ملايين السنين.

haadhaa l-zaHf-u mustamirr-un mundh-u malaayiin-i l-saniina.

This reptile has been [in] continuous [existence] for millions of years.

2.2 Pluperfect or past perfect: anteriority

To express an anterior action, i.e., an action in the past that is over with and which serves as a background action for the present, the past tense of *kaan-a* is used with a past tense of the main verb[14]. The particle *qad* may be optionally inserted just before the main verb. Note that the subject of the verb, if mentioned as a separate noun, goes between the auxiliary verb and the main verb. If the subject noun is human and plural, the main verb inflects for plural, although the auxiliary verb remains singular because it precedes the subject.

2.2.1 With subject noun

كان السفير قد وصل مساء الجمعة.

kaan-a l-safiir-u (qad) waSal-a masaaʾ-a l-jumʿat-i.

The ambassador had arrived Friday evening.

وكان العلماء توافدوا إلى مدينة بغداد.

wa-kaan-a l-ʿulamaaʾ-u tawaafad-uu ʾ ilaa madiinat-i baghdaad-a.

The scholars had flocked to the city of Baghdad.

كان محامون أمريكيّون شاركوا.

kaan-a muHaam-uuna ʾamriikiyy-uuna shaarak-uu.

American lawyers had participated.

---

[14] An alternative but less frequently used way of expressing the pluperfect in MSA is to use the expression *sabaq-a ʾan* 'it preceded that' before the main verb:

سبق أن التقى مراراً قادة الأكراد.

sabaq-a ʾan-i ltaqaa maraar-an qaadat-a l-ʾakraad-i.

He had [already] met with the leaders of the Kurds many times.

وكان المسجد قد بُني قبل ثلاثة عشر قرناً.

wa-kaan-a l-masjid-u qad buniy-a qabl-a thalaathat-a ʿashar-a qarn-an.

The mosque **had been built** thirteen centuries ago.

2.2.2 Without subject noun

كان اتّهمهم بالتحرّش به.

kaan-a ttaham-a-hum bi-l-taHarrush-i bi-hi.

He **had accused them** of provoking him.

كانوا عملوا مع عمّان.

kaan-uu ʿamil-uu maʿ-a ʿammaan-a.

They **had been working** with Amman.

لم تكن طلبت حماية.

lam ta-kun Talab-at Himaayat-an.

She **had not requested** protection.

2.3 Future perfect

To indicate a state or action expected to be completed in the future, **the present or future tense of *kaan-a* is used with a past tense main verb:**

وإلا، فستكون فشلت في دورها . . .

wa-ʾillaa, fa-sa-ta-kuun-u fashil-at fii dawr-i-haa . . .

and if not, **it will have failed** in its role . . .

2.4 Unreal condition

To describe an action that would or could have taken place, but actually did not, the **past tense of *kaan-a* is used with the future tense of the main verb.** This is called an unreal condition or a contrary-to-fact condition.

ما كانت ستعرف القراءة والكتابة.

maa kaan-at sa-ta-ʿrif-u l-qiraaʾat-a wa-l-kitaabat-a.

She **would not have known** [how] to read and write ('reading and writing').

كنت سأستخدم شيئاً آخر.

kun-tu sa-ʾa-staxdim-u shayʾ-an ʾaaxar-a.

I **was going to use** something else.

كان الفريق سيفوز بالمسابقات إذا كانت اللجنة قد سمحت لهم بالتسابق.

*kaan-a l-fariiq-u sa-ya-fuuz-u bi-l-musaabaqaat-i ʾidhaa kaan-at-i l-lajnat-u qad
    samaH-at la-hum bi-l-tasaabuq-i.*

The team **would have won** in the competitions if the committee had permitted
    them to participate.

2.5 The particle *qad*

The particle **qad** is used with verbs. It has no exact lexical equivalent in English and various theories have been put forth as to its function.[15] One theory is that it is used to emphasize or confirm aspect; that is, whether or not an action has been completed, and to what degree. Used with the past (or "perfect") tense, *qad* emphasizes and asserts that the action has indeed happened. In this context it may be translated as 'indeed,' 'already,' or 'really' but sometimes it is not translatable.[16]

With the imperfect or present tense, it emphasizes the possibility of the action or its potentiality rather than its actual achievement. In this case it is usually translated as 'may,' 'might,' or 'perhaps.'

Used in conjunction with the compound pluperfect tense verb (*kaana qad* كان قد), it is part of the compound verb structure, coming after the auxiliary verb *kaan-a* and before the past tense main verb.[17] Rarely is *qad* used when the verb is negative.

As with other words that end in *sukuun*, *qad* needs a helping vowel *kasra* if it occurs before a consonant cluster.

2.5.1 *qad* with past (perfect) tense

Used with the past tense, *qad* may occur on its own, but it may also be prefixed with the particles *wa-* و, *fa-* ف or *la-* ل. These particles do not change the meaning of *qad* although they may imply a temporal sequence such as "and then." Depending on context, the past tense verb with *qad* may be equivalent either to the simple past or to the past perfect. The use of *qad* here serves to confirm the meaning of the past tense by emphasizing that the action did indeed happen. Sometimes the insertion of the word "indeed" in English is appropriate.

قد تحققت أخيراً.

qad taHaqqaq-at ʾaxiir-an.

It was finally / has finally been realized.

ولقد وجدته في الصندوق.

wa-la-qad wajad-tu-hu fii l-Sanduuq-i.

And (then) I found it in the box.

قد ارتكب هذه الجريمة منفرداً.

qad-i rtakab-a haadhihi l-jariimat-a munfarid-an.

(Indeed) He committed / has committed this crime on his own.

ولذلك فقد حافظوا على المخطوطات.

wa-li-dhaalika fa-qad HaafaZ-uu ʿalaa l-maxTuuTaat-i.

And therefore they (**indeed**) kept the manuscripts.

---

[15] See Bahloul 1996 for an in-depth analysis of the nature and uses of *qad*.

[16] ʿAbd al-Latif et al. (1997, 233) state that *qad* "is a particle of affirmation if it comes before a past tense verb, and a particle of diminution if it comes before a present tense verb." *qad Harf-u taHqiiq-in ʾidhaa daxal-at ʿalaa l-maaDii, wa-Harf-u taqliil-in ʾidhaa daxal-at ʿalaa l-muDaariʿ.*

[17] "The modal particle *qad* tends quite often to occur inside the verbal complex, that is, between the auxiliary verb and the thematic verb" (Bahloul 1996, 37).

قـال « **لقد** اتّفقنـا مـع الإسـرائيليّيـن.»

*qaal-a "***la-qad***-i ttafaq-naa maʿ-a l-ʾisraaʾiiliyy-iina."*

He said "(**Indeed**) we have agreed with the Israelis."

لقد أردنـا أن نثبت للجميـع أنّنـا فـريـق جيّـدٌ.

la-qad ʾarad-naa ʾan nu-thbit-a li-l-jamiiʿ-i ʾanna-naa fariiq-un jayyid-un.

We (**indeed**) wanted to prove to everyone that we are a good team.

2.5.1.1 *fa-qad* + PAST TENSE: This conjunction introduces a clause in the past tense that acts as circumstance or background to the previous clause, stating an action or state that precedes the action in the previous clause chronologically or logically.[18] As Abboud and McCarus state (1983, part 1:537), "this construction indicates a completed action whose results are still in effect" with regard to the previous clause. This is considered a type of *Haal* or circumstantial structure.

لم يجب شيئاً. **فقد** غرق في نوم عميقٍ.

*lam ya-jib shayʾ-an. ***fa-qad*** *ghariq-a fii nawm-in ʿamiiq-in.*

He did not answer anything, **having fallen** into a deep sleep.

    (Kouloughli 1994, 274)

2.5.2 *qad* with present (imperfect) tense = possibility

Used with the indicative present tense, *qad* implies possibility.

بل **قد** يكون هناك ثلج.

*bal ***qad*** *ya-kuun-u hunaaka thalj-un.*

There **might** even be snow.

قد يتبـادر إلى ذهنك.

qad ya-tabaadar-u ʾilaa dhihn-i-ka.

It **might cross** your mind.

قد تتّخذ أشكالاً مختلفة.

qad ta-ttaxidh-u ʾashkaal-an muxtalifat-an.

They **may adopt** different shapes.

قد تكون أكثر أهمية.

qad ta-kuun-u ʾakthar-a ʾahamiyyat-an.

It **might be** of greater importance.

2.6 Verb strings or serial verb constructions

Certain verbs can directly precede others, thereby modifying the meaning of the main verb and acting as auxiliary verbs. Whenever the verb phrase consists of two or more verbs, the subject, if mentioned, is usually put between them. These verbs fall into several classes.

---

[18]Haywood and Nahmad state: "The particle *qad* is sometimes used before the Perfect verb. It is a confirmatory particle, which may make the verb definitely Past perfect ... However, this particle may also make the verb Pluperfect ... according to context" (1962, 100).

2.6.1 Verbs of appropinquation

These verbs indicate proximity or nearness to an action, but not quite the achievement of it, referred to by Wright as verbs of "appropinquation" (1967, II:106).[19] These include verbs such as *kaad-a/ya-kaad-u* 'to almost [do something]; be on the point of [doing something]' and *ʾawshaka/yuushik-u* 'to be on the verge' of doing something.

وكاد الموضوع يُمحى من الذاكرة العربية.

wa-kaad-a l-mawDuuʿ-u yu-mHaa min-a l-dhaakirat-i l-ʿarabiyyat-i.

The subject **was almost erased** from Arab memory.

كادت الشمس تشرق.	نكاد لا نجد نظيراً له.
kaad-at-i l-shams-u tu-shriq-u.	*na-kaad-u laa na-jid-u naZiir-an la-hu.*
The sun **had almost risen.**	**We can almost not find** a counterpart to it.

كادت تتحوّل إلى اشتباك بالأيدي.

kaad-at ta-taHawwal-u ʾilaa shtibaak-in bi-l-ʾaydii.

It almost changed into hand-to-hand combat.

Sometimes, *kaad-a* or *ʾawshak-a* are followed by the subjunctivizing particle *ʾan*, in which case the following verb is in the subjunctive:

كادت الملاحة الجويّة أن تتوقّف تماماً.

kaad-at-i l-milaaHat-u l-jawwiyyat-u ʾan ta-tawaqqaf-a tamaam-an.

Air traffic **almost stopped** totally.

أوشكنا أن نسقط.	أوشك أن يسأل عن اسمها.
ʾawshak-naa ʾan na-squt-a.	*ʾawshak-a ʾan ya-sʾal-a ʿan-i sm-i-haa.*
We almost fell (were on the verge of falling).	**He almost asked** about her name.

Sometimes, with *ʾawshak-a*, a verbal noun may be used instead of a following verb:

أوشك الاعتقاد بوجود مؤامرة.

ʾawshak-a l-iʿtiqaad-u bi-wujuud-i muʾaamarat-in.

They almost believed in the existence of a conspiracy ('belief verged').

Used in the negative, the implication of *kaad-a* is that an action has just barely taken place, usually translatable as 'hardly,' or 'scarcely.'

لم يكد يسدل الستار.

lam ya-kad yu-sdal-u l-sitaar-u.

The curtain **had hardly been dropped.**

---

[19] Blachère and Goudefroy Demombynes refer to them as "verbes d'imminence" (1975, 268).

2.6.2 Inceptive verbs

Another set of helping verbs is inceptive or inchoative. They convey the idea of starting or setting about an action and are usually used in the past with a present tense main verb. In MSA these verbs include:

to set about	*ja͑al-a* (literally 'to make')	جعل
to start	*'axadh-a* (literally, 'to take')	أخذ
to start	*bada'-a* (literally, 'to begin')	بدأ
to set about	*Saar-a* (literally, 'to become')	صار
	'aSbaH-a	أصبح

بدأ يلفت النظر.
bada'-a yu-lfit-u l-naZar-a.
It started to attract attention.

منذ الستّينات صارت تأخذ دوراً أكبر.
mundhu l-sittiinaat-i Saar-at ta-'xudh-u dawr-an 'akbar-a.
Since the sixties **it has started to assume** a larger role.

2.6.3 Verbs of continuation

These verbs, when used as auxiliaries, convey the concept of continuing an action or a state:

baat-a بات

باتت البلاد تُعرف به اليوم.
baat-at-i l-bilaad-u tu-͑raf-u bi-hi l-yawm-a.
The country is still known by it today.

Zall-a ظلّ

ظلّ يردّد العبارة.
Zall-a yu-raddid-u l-͑ibaarat-a.
He kept repeating the expression.

ظلّ يسعى وراء هدفه.
Zall-a ya-s͑aa waraa'-a hadaf-i-hi
He continued to pursue ('after') his goal.

maa zaal-a ما زال

الأمور لا تزال تحتاج إلى كثير من الجهد.
al-'umuur-u laa ta-zaal-u ta-Htaaj-u 'ilaa kathiir-in min-a l-jahd-i.
Matters **still require** much effort.

maDaa مضى

ومضى يشتري الخضار.
wa-maDaa ya-shtirii l-xuDaar-a.
He went on to buy vegetables.

baqiya بقي

بقيت القضية تتفاقم وتهدأ.

baqiy-at-i l-*qaDiyyat-u* *ta-tafaaqam-u* *wa-ta-hda'-u*.

The problem **kept getting** dangerous and [then] subsiding.

2.6.4 Simultaneous verbal action (*al-Haal* الحال)

Certain concepts are conveyed by verbs describing simultaneous states or actions. The subject may remain the same for both verbs, or it may be different. This structure is a form of *Haal*, or adverbial expression that describes what someone was doing at the time of the action of the main verb.[20]

With same subject:

ومضى يقول . . .

wa-maDaa ya-quul-u . . .

He **continued**, saying . . .

With different subject:

شاهدها ترشّ طلاءً.   لا تتركك تنتظر.

shaahad-a-haa ta-rushsh-u Tilaa'-an.   *laa ta-truk-u-ka ta-ntaZir-u.*

He saw her spattering paint.   It doesn't **leave** you waiting.

---

[20] On the *Haal* حال construction, see Chapter 11, section 2.3.1, and also Chapter 7, section 5.3.3.3.

22

Form I: The base form triliteral verb

1 Basic characteristics

1.1 Pattern

Form I is considered the base form because of its fundamental structure. In Arabic, this form is termed *mujarrad* مُجَرَّد: 'bare; stripped' because it is the simplest stem of all. The base pattern for Form I past tense is **CaCVC**, that is, consonant-*fatHa*-consonant-short vowel-consonant. Although the first short vowel is consistently *fatHa*, the second, or **stem vowel**, may be *fatHa*, *kasra* or *Damma*: *faʿal-a* فَعَلَ, *faʿil-a* فَعِلَ, *faʿul-a* فَعُلَ.

The present tense stem vowel (the vowel that follows the second root consonant) is also variable in Form I. It may be /a/, /u/, or /i/.

1.2 Meaning

Form I is the closest indicator of the meaning of the lexical root. There are shades of meaning associated with the **stem vowel** differences in the past tense citation forms, but these semantic differences are very subtle. Note that every verb and verbal noun has a range of meanings, sometimes extensive. Glosses or English equivalents provided here are not exclusive or exact meanings but represent common standard usage.

1.3 Transitivity

Form I covers a wide semantic range and may be either intransitive or transitive. Occasionally it is doubly transitive.

1.4 Inflection

A particular inflectional characteristic of Form I verbs is that the present tense subject-marker vowel is *fatHa* (e.g., *ya-drus-u*, *ya-wadd-u*, *ya-ʿnii*).

1.5 Root types

The nature of the three root consonants determines the root type. Phonological and morphophonemic rules apply to various kinds of sound and irregular roots, as follows.[1] Paradigm charts for all Form I root types are located at the end of this chapter.

2 Regular (sound) triliteral root (*al-fiᶜl al-SaHiiH al-saalim* الفعل الصحيح السالم)

Sound or regular verbal roots consist of three consonants, all of which are different and none of which are *waaw*, *yaa'*, or *hamza*. The Form I verbs are presented here by their stem types, which fall into three groups.[2]

2.1 Past tense stem vowel is *fatHa*

When the past tense stem vowel is *fatHa*, the present tense stem vowel may be /a/, /u/, or /i/, so there are three subgroups within this class. Occasionally, the present tense may show two different stem vowels.

2.1.1 *faᶜal-a/ ya-fᶜal-u*

Here *fatHa* is the stem vowel in both the past and present tenses. There is some indication that the present tense medial vowel in this verb form is conditioned by the nature of its contiguous consonants, which would be the second and third root consonants. The general theory is that a *fatHa* in the present tense is associated with a back (pharyngeal or glottal) consonant.[3]

to gather, to collect	*jamaᶜ-a/ya-jmaᶜ-u*	جمع/يجمعُ
to open; to conquer	*fataH-a/ya-ftaH-u*	فتح/يفتحُ
to go	*dhahab-a/ya-dhhab-u*	ذهب/يذهبُ
to grant	*manaH-a/ya-mnaH-u*	منع/يمنعُ
to remove, take off	*xalaᶜ-a/ya-xlaᶜ-u*	خلع/يخلعُ

2.1.2 *faᶜal-a / ya-fᶜil-u*

This type of Form I verb has *fatHa* in the past tense stem and *kasra* as the medial vowel in the present tense.

to return, to go back	*rajaᶜ-a/ya-rjiᶜ-u*	رجع/يرجعُ
to dig	*Hafar-a/ya-Hfir-u*	حفَر/يَحْفرُ

---

[1] Traditional Arabic grammar divides verb roots into two major classes: (1) SaHiiH صحيح 'sound' and (2) *muᶜtall* معتل 'weak.' Sound roots are ones that do not contain either *waaw* or *yaa'*; weak roots contain *waaw* or *yaa'* as one or more of the root phonemes. In this text, I have allotted separate categories for doubled and hamzated verbs because they sometimes involve stem changes when inflected, even though they are considered SaHiiH, or 'sound,' in Arabic grammatical terms.

[2] Certain roots may have more than one stem in the past. Sometimes this indicates a meaning difference, sometimes not. For example, *shamal-a/ya-shmal-u* 'to contain, include' and also *shamil-a/ ya-shmal-u* with the same meaning.

[3] For more analysis of the Form I stem-vowel alternation see McCarthy 1991, esp. pp. 69–70, and see also McOmber 1995, 178–85.

to carry	Hamal-a/ya-Hmil-u	حَمَلَ / يَحْمِلُ
to know	ʿaraf-a/ya-ʿrif-u	عَرَفَ / يَعْرِفُ
to acquire, possess	malak-a/ya-mlik-u	مَلَكَ / يَمْلِكُ

2.1.3 *faʿal-a/ ya-fʿul-u*

The past tense stem vowel is *fatHa*, the present tense stem vowel is *Damma*.

to rub	farak-a/ya-fruk-u	فَرَكَ / يَفْرُكُ
to leave	tarak-a/ya-truk-u	تَرَكَ / يَتْرُكُ
to request, ask for	Talab-a/ya-Tlub-u	طَلَبَ / يَطْلُبُ
to study	daras-a/ya-drus-u	دَرَسَ / يَدْرُسُ
to transfer	naqal-a/ya-nqul-u	نَقَلَ / يَنْقُلُ

2.2 Past tense stem vowel is *kasra*: *faʿil-a/ ya-fʿal-u*

When the past tense stem vowel is *kasra*, the present tense stem vowel is normally *fatHa*.

to drink	sharib-a/ya-shrab-u	شَرِبَ / يَشْرَبُ
to do, make; to work	ʿamil-a/ya-ʿmal-u	عَمِلَ / يَعْمَلُ
to know	ʿalim-a/ya-ʿlam-u	عَلِمَ / يَعْلَمُ
to hear	samiʿ-a/ya-smaʿ-u	سَمِعَ / يَسْمَعُ

2.3 Past tense stem vowel is *Damma*: *faʿul-a/ ya-fʿul-u*

This Form I stem has *Dammas* as both stem vowels. This stem class generally denotes states of being, or the acquisition or increase of a certain quality. These roots therefore also are the roots of many adjectives. This type of Form I verb is usually intransitive.

to be heavy (adjective: 'heavy' *thaqiil* ثقيل)	thaqul-a/ya-thqul-u	ثَقُلَ / يَثْقُلُ
to grow or be big; grow older (adjective: 'big, great' *kabiir* كبير)	kabur-a/ya-kbur-u	كَبُرَ / يَكْبُرُ
to be good (adjective: 'good' Hasan حسن)	Hasun-a/ya-Hsun-u	حَسُنَ / يَحْسُنُ

2.4 Examples of Form I sound verbs in context

يَهْطِل الثلج على الجبال.
ya-hTil-u l-thalj-u ʿalaa l-jibaal-i.
Snow **falls** on the mountains.

يدفعون الثمن.
ya-dfaʿ-uuna l-thaman-a.
They are paying the price.

حضر اللقاء عدد من الممثّلين.	فتح الباب.
HaDar-a l-liqaaɔ-a ʕadad-un min-a l-mumaththil-iina.	*fataH-a l-baab-a.*
A number of representatives **attended** the meeting.	**It opened** the door.

3 Geminate verb root (*al-fiʕl al-muDaʕʕaf* الفعل المضعَّف)[4]

Geminate or doubled verbal roots are ones where the second and third consonant of the root are the same. In the citation form of Form I, the doubled or geminate consonant is written only once, with a *shadda* above it to show that it is double.

3.1 Stem shifts

Geminate verbs have two stems in the past and also two in the present. This is because of a phonological rule that prevents two identical consonants from being in sequence with a short vowel between them when they are directly followed by a vowel, e.g., instead of *ɔradad-a* it is *radd-a* ('he replied'), instead of *ɔya-HTuT-uuna*, it is *ya-HuTT-uuna* ('they put').

However, if the second identical stem consonant is followed by another consonant, the identical consonants remain separated, e.g., *radad-tu* ('I replied'), *ya-HTuT-na* ('they (f.) put').[5] This second type of stem, where the identical consonants are split, is referred to here as the "split stem."

In the past tense conjugation, many of the inflectional suffixes start with consonants (*-tu, -ta, -ti, -tumaa, -naa, -tunna, -tum, -na*), so the split stem in the past tense is fairly common; in the present tense, however, the only suffix that starts with a consonant is the *-na* of the second and third persons feminine plural (e.g., *ya-rdud-na* 'they (f.) reply').

3.2 Stem types

Doubled Form I verbs fall into three stem types, according to their stem vowels. The citation forms of the past tense third person singular all look alike, so in order to know the stem type, it is necessary to know the stem vowel in the present tense. The first person singular past tense and the third person feminine plural present tense are given as examples for these verbs to illustrate the stem vowels.

3.2.1 *faʕal-a /ya-fʕul-u (a/u) –> faʕl-a/ya-fuʕl-u*

to show, indicate	*dall-a/ya-dull-u*	دلَّ / يدلُّ
past tense split stem:	*dalal-tu*	دلَلْت
present tense split stem:	*ya-dlul-na*	يدللْن

---

[4] The technical Arabic term for "doubled" is given as *muDaʕʕaf* مضعَّف in ʕAbd al-Latif et al. (1997, 140) and as *muDaaʕaf* مضاعف by Wright 1967 (I:69).

[5] Abboud and McCarus 1983 (Part 2:81–88) have a detailed description of the phonological rules and the forms of the doubled Form I verb.

to put, place	HaTT-a/ya-HuTT-u	حطَّ / يَحُطُّ
past tense split stem:	HaTaT-tu	حَطَطْتُ
present tense split stem:	ya-HTuT-na	يَحْطُطْنَ

3.2.2 *fa ʿal-a/ya-f ʿil-u* (a/i) –> *fa ʿl-a/ya-fi ʿl-u*

be small, few; diminish	qall-a/ya-qill-u	قَلَّ / يَقِلُّ
past tense split stem:	qalal-tu	قَلَلْتُ
present tense split stem:	ya-qlil-na	يَقْلِلْنَ
to be complete	tamm-a/ya-timm-u	تَمَّ / يَتِمُّ
past tense split stem:	tamam-tu	تَمَمْتُ
present tense split stem:	ya-tmim-na	يَتِمِمْنَ

3.2.3 *fa ʿil-a/ya-f ʿa-lu* (i/a) –> *fa ʿl-a/ya-fa ʿl-u*

In this stem type, the past tense **stem vowel *kasra*** shows up only in the split stem, when the verb has a suffix that starts with a consonant. In the citation form, it has been deleted because of phonological restrictions.[6]

to want; to like	wadd-a/ya-wadd-u	وَدَّ / يودُّ
past tense split stem:	wadid-tu	وَدِدْتُ
present tense split stem:	ya-wdad-na	يودَدْنَ
to continue, keep doing (s.th.)	Zall-a/ya-Zall-u	ظَلَّ / يَظَلُّ
past tense split stem:	Zalil-tu	ظَلِلْتُ
present tense split stem:	ya-Zlal-na	يَظْلَلْنَ

3.1 Examples of Form I geminate verbs in context

تمَّ الاتّفاق.
tamm-a l-ittifaaq-u.
The agreement **was completed.**

سيّارة تمرّ في الشارع
sayyaarat-un ta-murr-u fii l-shaari ʿ-i
a car **passing by** in the street

ردّت على سؤال.
radd-at ʿalaa suʾaal-in.
She responded to a question.

كيف تتمّ عمليات الإخلاء؟
kayf-a ta-timm-u ʿamaliyyaat-u l-ʾixlaaʾ-i?
How **are** the evacuation operations **accomplished?**

---

[6] Wehr (1979) gives both the citation form and the split-stem form for this stem type of doubled verb.

4 Hamzated verb root (*al-fiʿl al-mahmuuz* الفعل المهموز)

A hamzated verb is one where any one of the root consonants is *hamza*. It may occur as the first, second, or third consonant. These verbs are considered a separate category because of rules that govern the occurrence and distribution of *hamza*, and also because of *hamza* spelling rules. As the verbal roots inflect within conjugations or as they shift into derived forms, the seat of *hamza* may change.

4.1 *Hamza*-initial Form I verbs

to eat   *ʾakal-a/ya-ʾkul-u*   أَكَلَ / يَأْكُلُ   to take   *ʾaxadh-a/ya-ʾxudh-u*   أَخَذَ / يَأْخُذُ

4.2 *Hamza*-medial Form I verbs

to ask (s.o. s.th.)   *saʾal-a/ya-sʾal-u*   سَأَلَ / يَسْأَلُ

to repair, to bandage   *laʾam-a/ya-lʾam-u*   لأَمَ / يَلأَمُ

4.3 *Hamza*-final Form I verbs

to begin   *badaʾ-a/ya-bdaʾ-u*   بَدَأَ / يَبْدَأُ   to read   *qaraʾ-a/ya-qraʾ-u*   قَرَأَ / يَقْرَأُ

Examples of Form I hamzated verbs in context:

علينا أن نبدأ من الصفر.   في بيروت يبدأ سحر الشرق.
*ʿalay-naa ʾan **na-bdaʾ-a** min-a l-Sifr-i.*   *fii bayruut-a **ya-bdaʾ-u** siHr-u l-sharq-i.*
We have to **begin** from zero.   In Beirut **starts** the magic of the East.

5 Assimilated verb root (*al-fiʿl al-mithaal* الفعل المثال)

Assimilated verb roots begin with a semi-consonant (*waaw* or *yaaʾ*), most often *waaw*. They are called **assimilated** in English because the initial *waaw*, even though it is part of the root, often disappears in the present tense, deleted or assimilated to the subject-marker prefix. The *yaaʾ* does not normally get assimilated.[7]

5.1 First root consonant deleted in present tense

This group consists of a number of frequently occurring verbs in MSA. They fall into two groups: those with *fatHa* in the past tense stem and *kasra* in the present tense, and those with *fatHa* as the stem vowel in both tenses.

5.1.1 *fatHa/kasra*

to arrive   *waSal-a/ya-Sil-u*   وَصَلَ / يَصِلُ   to be
necessary   *wajab-a/ya-jib-u*   وَجَبَ / يَجِبُ

to find   *wajad-a/ya-jid-u*   وَجَدَ / يَجِدُ   to weigh   *wazan-a/ya-zin-u*   وَزَنَ / يَزِنُ

---

[7] Wright 1967 (I:78–81) provides an extensive analysis of this verb type in Classical Arabic.

5.1.2 *fatHa/fatHa*

to fall waqaᶜ-a/ya-qaᶜ-u وَقَعَ / يَقَعُ   to put waDaᶜ-a/ya-Daᶜ-u وَضَعَ / يَضَعُ

5.2 First root consonant not deleted in present tense

This group consists of *waaw*-initial verbs whose stem vowel in the past is *kasra* or *Damma*, and of verbs whose initial root consonant is *yaaʾ*. They behave as regular or sound verbs.

5.2.1 *kasra/fatHa*

to ache, hurt wajiᶜ-a/ya-wjaᶜ-u وَجِعَ / يَوْجَعُ

to like, love wadd-a/ya-wadd-u[8] وَدَّ / يَوَدُّ

5.2.2 *Damma/Damma*

to be wide wasuᶜ-a/ya-wsuᶜ-u وَسُعَ / يَوْسُعُ

5.2.3 *yaaʾ*-initial

to be easy yasir-a/ya-ysir-u[9] يَسِرَ / يَيْسِرُ

to wake up yaqiZ-a/ya-yqaZ-u[10] يَقِظَ / يَيْقَظُ

Examples of Form I assimilated verbs in context:

يَجِبُ أَن تَتَوَقَّفَ.
***ya-jib-u* ʾ*an ta-tawaqqaf-a*.**
They **must** stop ('it is necessary that they stop').

وَصَفُوهَا.
***waSaf-uu*-haa.**
They **described** her.

وَصَلَ الرَّئِيسُ إِلَى تُونِسَ أَمْسِ.
***waSal-a* l-raʾiis-u ʾilaa tuunis-a ʾams-i.**
The president **arrived** in Tunis yesterday.

6 Hollow root (*al-fiᶜl al-ʾajwaf* الفعل الأجوف)

Hollow verbs are ones in which the second root consonant is actually a semi-consonant: either *waaw* or *yaaʾ*. These two semi-consonants undergo various mutations, turning into *ʾalif*, a short vowel, or a long vowel depending on the word structure and derivation. In the past tense citation form, for example, the *waaw* or *yaaʾ* is not present and is replaced by *ʾalif*. However, to look up one of these words

---

[8] This verb is geminate as well as assimilated. Phonotactic rules prevent the initial *waaw* from becoming assimilated in this case.
[9] Also *ya-sur-a/ya-ysur-u* 'to be small; to be easy.'   [10] Also *ya-quZ-a/ya-yquZ-u.*

in a dictionary, one must know what the medial root consonant is, either *waaw* or
yaaʾ. The medial root consonant often shows itself in the present tense verb stem
(as a long or short vowel) and elsewhere, as in the verbal nouns or participles.

There are essentially three variations on the hollow verb root, determined by
which long vowel is in the present tense or imperfective stem: *waaw, yaaʾ,* or *ʾalif.*

6.1 Hollow-*waaw*

These verbs have *waaw* as their medial radical. The stem vowel in the past tense is
ʾalif when it is long and *Damma* when it is short. Examples of both stems are given.
The first person singular is used to exemplify the short stem. The stem vowel in
the present tense is *waaw* when long and *Damma* when short. The third person
feminine plural is used to exemplify the short stem.

to say	*qaal-a (qul-tu)/ya-quul-u (ya-qul-na)*	قالَ (قُلْتُ) / يَقولُ (يَقُلْنَ)
to visit	*zaar-a (zur-tu)/ya-zuur-u (ya-zur-na)*	زارَ (زُرْتُ) / يَزورُ (يَزُرْنَ)

6.2 Hollow *yaaʾ*

These verbs have *yaaʾ* as the medial radical. The stem vowel in the past tense is *ʾalif*
when it is long and *kasra* when it is short. Examples of both stems are given. The
first person singular is used to exemplify the short stem. The stem vowel in the
present tense is *yaaʾ* when long and *kasra* when short. The third person feminine
plural is used to exemplify the short stem.

to live	*ʿaash-a (ʿish-tu) /ya-ʿiish-u (ya-ʿish-na)*	عاشَ (عِشْتُ) / يَعيشُ (يَعِشْنَ)
to sell	*baaʿ-a (biʿ-tu)/ya-biiʿ-u (ya-biʿ-na)*	باعَ (بِعْتُ) / يَبيعُ (يَبِعْنَ)

6.3 Hollow *ʾalif*

These verb roots have either medial *waaw* or *yaaʾ* but do not show it in the present
tense, using *ʾalif* instead. The stem vowel in the past tense is *ʾalif* when it is long
and *kasra* when it is short. Examples of both stems are given. The first person singular is used to exemplify the short stem. The stem vowel in the present tense is
ʾalif when long and *fatHa* when short. The third person feminine plural is used to
exemplify the short stem.

to sleep	*naam-a (nim-tu)/ya-naam-u (ya-nam-na)* (root: n-w-m)	نامَ (نِمْتُ) / يَنامُ (يَنَمْنَ)
to fear	*xaaf-a (xif-tu)/ya-xaaf-u (ya-xaf-na)* (root: x-w-f)	خافَ (خِفْتُ) / يَخافُ (يَخَفْنَ)
to obtain	*naal-a (nil-tu)/ya-naal-u (ya-nal-na)* (root: n-y-l)	نالَ (نِلْتُ) / يَنالُ (يَنَلْنَ)

6.3.3 Examples of Form I hollow verbs in context

يعيش مرحلة انتقالية.

ya-ʿiish-u marHalat-an-i ntiqaaliyyat-an.

It is living [through] a transitional stage.

عادوا إليها.

ʿaad-uu ʾilay-haa.

They returned to it.

لا أفهم ماذا تقول.

laa ʾa-fham-u maadhaa ta-quul-u.

I don't understand what **you are saying.**

وعلى الدولة أن تقوم بدورها.

wa-ʿalaa l-dawlat-i ʾan ta-quum-a bi-dawr-i-haa.

It is up to the state **to undertake** its role.

7 Defective verb root (*al-fiʿl al-naaqiS* الفعل الناقص)

Defective verb roots are ones where the final consonant is either *waaw* or *yaaʾ*. These final semi-consonants may take on various forms and even seem to disappear under certain circumstances. In the past tense citation form, these roots all have final *ʾalif*. Roots where *yaaʾ* is the final consonant appear with *ʾalif maqSuura* or *yaaʾ*; roots where *waaw* is the final consonant are written with *ʾalif Tawiila*.[11]

7.1 *waaw*-defective roots

to appear, to seem	*badaa/ya-bduu*	بَدَا / يَبْدو
to hope; wish; request	*rajaa/ya-rjuu*	رجا / يَرجو
to call, invite	*daʿaa/ya-dʿuu*	دعا / يَدْعو

7.2 *yaaʾ* defective roots

Yaaʾ defective Form I verbs fall into two main categories: ones that end in *-aa* (*ʾalif maqSuura*) and ones that end with *yaaʾ*. The ones ending in *-aa* usually inflect in the present tense with *-ii*; the ones that end with *yaaʾ* in the past tense usually take *-aa* in the present tense. A few verbs take *-aa* in both the past and the present.

7.2.1 *-aa/-ii* verbs

to build	*banaa/ya-bnii*	بَنى / يَبْني
to be sufficient	*kafaa/ya-kfii*	كَفى / يَكْفي
to walk	*mashaa/ya-mshii*	مَشى / يمشي

7.2.2 *-ya/-aa* verbs

to remain	*baqiy-a/ya-bqaa*	بَقِيَ / يَبْقى
to forget	*nasiy-a/ya-nsaa*	نَسِيَ / يَنْسى
to encounter	*laqiy-a/ya-lqaa*	لَقِيَ / يَلْقى

---

[11] For a concise phonological analysis of hollow and defective verbs, see Timothy Mitchell 1981.

7.2.3 -aa/-aa verbs

to move forward; to strive   sa'aa/ya-s'aa   سَعى / يَسْعى

7.2.4 -ya/-ii verb

to be near; to follow; to govern   waliy-a/ya-lii   وَلِيَ / يَلِي

7.3 Examples of Form I defective verbs in context

هذا لا يكفي.
haadhaa laa ya-kfii.
This **is not enough.**

يقضون لياليهم في الصلاة.
ya-qDuuna layaalii-him fii l-Salaat-i.
They **spend** their nights in prayer.

تنمو ببطء.
ta-nmuu bi-buT'-in.
They grow slowly.

ستبقى طويلاً في ذاكرة العالم.
sa-ta-bqaa Tawiil-an fii dhaakirat-i l-'aalam-i
It will remain long in the world's memory.

نرجو الاتّصال بالإدارة.
na-rjuu l-ittiSaal-a bi-l-'idaarat-i.
We would like to contact the management.

شكا عدد من الناخبين.
shakaa 'adad-un min-a l-naaxib-iina.
A number of voters **complained.**

8 Doubly weak or "mixed" verb root

Doubly weak verb roots have semi-consonants and/or *hamza* in two places, sometimes as the first and third consonants, and sometimes as the second and third. They are not many in number, but some of them are frequently used:

8.1 Hollow and hamzated

to come   jaa'-a (ji'-tu)/ya-jii'-u (ya-ji'-na)   جاءَ (جِئْتُ) / يَجيئُ (يَجِئْنَ)
(root: *j-y-'*)

8.2 Hamzated and defective

to come   'ataa/ya-'tii   أتى / يَأتي   to see   ra'aa/ya-raa   رأى / يَرى
(root: *'-t-y*)   (root: *r-'-y*)

8.3 Assimilated and defective (*al-fi'l al-lafiif al-mafruuq* الفعل اللفيف المفروق)

These roots have *waaw* or *yaa'* in the first and third root consonants.

to perceive, be aware of   wa'aa/ya-'ii   وَعى / يَعي
(root: *w-'-y*)

to be near; to follow; to govern   waliya/yalii   وَلِيَ / يَلي
(root: *w-l-y*)

8.4 Hollow and defective (*al-fiʿl al-lafiif al-maqruun* الفعل اللفيف المقرون)

Where a root is both hollow and defective, the medial root semi-consonant (usually *waaw*) appears as a regular consonant:

to intend   *nawaa/ya-nwii* نَوى / يَنْوِي   to narrate   *rawaa/ya-rwii* رَوى / يَرْوِي
(root: *n-w-y*)   (root: *r-w-y*)

8.5 Examples of Form I doubly weak verbs in context

ستری!	لأنّي أهوي ركوب الخيل	عليه أن يأتي إلى هنا.
sa-taraa!	*liʾann-ii ʾa-hwii rukuub-a*	*ʿalay-hi ʾan ya-ʾtiy-a ʾilaa hunaa.*
You'll see!	*l-xayl-i*	He has **to come** here.
	because **I am fond of** riding horses	

9 Verbal nouns of Form I

Form I verbal nouns have many variations of pattern.[12] Wright lists forty-four possible verbal noun patterns for Form I or as he terms it, "the ground form" of the ordinary triliteral verb (1967, I:110–112); Ziadeh and Winder (1957, 71–72) list eighteen of the most commonly used ones in MSA. ʿAbd al-Latif, ʿUmar and Zahran give an extensive list (in Arabic) with examples and some explanations (1997, 83–86). To some extent, particular verbal noun patterns may be associated with particular Form I verb stem types. For a discussion of this, see Blachère and Demombynes 1975, 78–84. See also Bateson 2003, 15–21 for a general discussion of Arabic noun derivation. The most common forms of Form I verbal nouns are listed here by root type. Sometimes the meaning of the verbal noun is abstract and sometimes it has acquired a specific, concrete denotation.

Note that many verbs have more than one verbal noun. In this case, the nouns usually have different connotations. Owing to space restrictions, I have not listed all verbal noun options for Form I, only typical examples.

9.1 Form I sound root verbal nouns

The most common verbal noun patterns of Form I regular or sound verbs are:
faʿl

support   *daʿm* دَعم   jumping   *qafz* قَفْز

---

[12] Beeston states (1970, 35): "Morphologically, the verbal abstracts which match primary verbs have unpredictable word-patterns, and constitute lexical items." ʿAbd al-Latif, ʿUmar and Zahran declare that "The verbal nouns of the base form are many and varied and cannot be known except by resorting to language [reference] books" *maSaadir-u l-thulaathiyy-i kathiirat-un wa-mutanawwaʿ-at-un laa tuʿ-raf-u ʾillaa bi-l-rujuuʿ-i ʾilaa kutub-i l-lughat-i* (1997, 83).

faⁿal

danger	*xaTar*	خَطَر	honor	*sharaf*	شَرَف

fuⁿl

distance	*buⁿd*	بُعْد	life-span, age	*ⁿumr*	عُمْر

fiⁿl

thinking	*fikr*	فكْر	root	*jidhr~jadhr*	جِذْر

fiⁿla ~ fuⁿla ~ faⁿla

error, mistake	*ghalTa*	غَلْطَة	expertise	*xibra*	خِبْرَة
wisdom	*Hikma*	حِكْمَة	license, permit	*ruxSa*	رُخْصَة

fuⁿuul

attendance	*HuDuur*	حُضور	feeling	*shuⁿuur*	شُعور

fuⁿuula

heroism	*buTuula*	بُطولَة	flexibility	*muruuna*	مُرونَة

fiⁿaal

mixture	*mizaaj*	مِزاج	scope, sphere	*niTaaq*	نِطاق

fiⁿaala ~ faⁿaala

writing	*kitaaba*	كتابَة	studying	*diraasa*	دِراسَة
splendor	*faxaama*	فَخامَة	happiness	*saⁿaada*	سَعادَة

fuⁿlaan ~ fiⁿlaan

forgiveness	*ghufraan*	غُفْران	loss; losing	*fiqdaan*	فقْدان

mafⁿil ~ mafⁿila

logic	*manTiq*	مَنطِق	knowledge; knowing	*maⁿrifa*	مَعْرِفَة

9.2 Form I geminate root verbal nouns

Common verbal noun patterns for Form I geminate verbs include:

faⁿl ~ fuⁿl

pilgrimage	*Hajj*	حَجّ	response	*radd*	رَدّ
solution	*Hall*	حَلّ	friendship	*wudd*	وُدّ

*fa*ʿ*al*

| number | ʿadad | عَدَد | reason | sabab | سَبَب |

*fa*ʿ*uula*

| necessity | Daruura | ضَرورة | | | |

*fa*ʿ*aala*

| indication | dalaala | دَلالَة | | | |

*fi*ʿ*la*

| paucity | qilla | قِلّة | | | |

9.3 Form I hamzated verbal nouns

*fa*ʾ*l, fu*ʾ*l, fi*ʾ*l*

| command | ʾamr | أَمْر | part | juzʾ | جُزْء |
| light; brightness | Dawʾ | ضَوْء | burden | ʿibʾ | عِبْء |

*fu*ʿ*aal*

| question | suʾaal | سُؤال | | | |

*fi*ʿ*aala , fa*ʿ*aala*

| reading | qiraaʾa | قِراءة | beginning | badaaʾa/bidaaya | بِداية |

*fu*ʿ*uul*

| growth | nushuuʾ | نُشوء | refuge | lujuuʾ | لُجوء |

9.4 Form I Assimilated root verbal nouns

ʿila: In this form of verbal noun, assimilated roots delete the first root semi-consonant.

| direction | jiha | جِهة | trust | thiqa | ثِقة |

*fa*ʾ*l*

| promise | waʿd | وَعْد | delegation | wafd | وَفْد |

*fu*ʿ*uul*

| arrival | wuSuul | وُصول | clarity | wuDuuH | وُضوح |

*fi*ʿ*aala*

| agency | wikaala | وِكالة | sovereignty; province | wilaaya | وِلايَة |

fiᶜlaan

   feeling; ecstasy   *wijdaan*   وِجْدان

mafaᶜla

   wishing, wanting   *mawadda*   مَوَدّة

9.5 Form I hollow root verbal nouns
Common hollow verb verbal noun patterns include:

faᶜl

   victory   *fawz*   فَوْز   shame   *ᶜayb*   عَيْب

   sleep   *nawm*   نَوْم   living; life   *ᶜaysh*   عَيْش

faᶜla

   revolution   *thawra*   ثَوْرَة   return   *ᶜawda*   عَوْدَة

fuᶜl: This pattern in combination with a hollow root yields a long vowel /uu/ in the middle of the word.

   length   *Tuul*   طول   intensity; lute   *ᶜuud*   عود

fiᶜaal and *fiᶜaala*: When hollow verbs use this pattern for the verbal noun, the medial semi-consonant often takes the form of *yaaʾ* even if the root consonant is *waaw*.[13]

   establishing,   *qiyaam*   قِيام   mathematics;   *riyaaDa*   رِياضَة
   setting up   sports
   (root: *q-w-m*)   (root: *r-w-D*)

   visit   *ziyaara*   زِيارَة   increase   *ziyaada*   زِيادَة
   (root: *z-w-r*)   (root: *z-y-d*)

faᶜlaa

   chaos; disorder   *fawDaa*   فوضى

faᶜalaan

   flying   *Tayaraan*   طَيَران   flooding   *fayaDaan*   فَيَضان

mafaal ~ mafiil ~ mafiila: These are *miimii maSdar*s.

   destiny   *maSiir*   مَصير   obtaining   *manaal*   مَنال

   livelihood   *maᶜiisha*   مَعيشَة   procession   *masiira*   مَسيرة

---

[13] The phonological sequence /-iw-/ is usually avoided in Arabic. Therefore hypothetical forms like *ziwaara and *qiwaam shift to become *ziyaara* 'visit' or *qiyaam* 'establishing.'

9.6 Form I defective root verbal nouns

faʕl

pardon; kindness	ʕafw	عَفو	negation	nafy	نَفي

faʕaal ~ fiʕaal; In this verbal noun pattern, the final root semi-consonant shifts to *hamza.*

building	binaaʾ	بِناء	space	faDaaʾ	فَضـاء
singing	ghinaaʾ	غِنـاء	meeting	liqaaʾ	لِقاء

fiʕaala

building	binaaya	بِنايَة	protection	Himaaya	حِمـايَة

fuʕuul: This pattern is often found with final-*waaw* verbs. The combination of the long /uu/ vowel in this pattern with the final *waaw* consonant yields a doubled *waaw:*

height, altitude	ʕuluww	عُلُوّ	growth	numuww	نمُوّ

faʕlaa: Because these nouns terminate with an added /-aa/ suffix, they are feminine in gender.

piety	taqwaa	تَقوى	complaint	shakwaa	شَكوى

fiʕlaan ~ fuʕlaan

aggression; hostility	ʕudwaan	عُدوان	forgetting; oblivion	nisyaan	نِسـيـان

mafʕan (mafʕal مفعل)

meaning	maʕnan	مَعـنـى	effort; striving	masʕan	مَسـعـى

9.7 Form I doubly weak or 'mixed' verb roots

9.7.1 Hollow and hamzated

mafʕil:

coming	majiiʾ	مَجيء

9.7.2 Defective and hamzated

faʕl

opinion	raʾy	رَأي

fuʕla

seeing	ruʾya	رُؤيَة

9.7.3 Hollow and defective

fiʿla and *faʿl*: In these verbal noun patterns, the medial *waaw* assimilates to the *yaaʾ*, yielding a double *yaaʾ*:

intent	*niyya*	نِيَّة	ironing	*kayy*	كَيّ

When a hollow root combines with a defective root, the medial *waaw* is maintained in these verbal noun patterns:

fiʿaala:

narrative	*riwaaya*	رِوايَة	hobby; amateurism	*hiwaaya*	هِوايَة

faʿaal

medicine, remedy	*dawaaʾ*	دَواء

9.8 Form I verbal nouns in context

قَبلَ السِباحَة إلى البَحر
qabl-a l-sibaaHat-i ʾilaa l-baHr-i
before **swimming** to the sea

نَحتاج إلى مِجهَر لِرؤيَتِه.
*na-Htaaj-u ʾilaa mijhar-in li-**ruʾyat**-i-hi*
We need a microscope **to see** it.

قِيام دَولة القانون
qiyaam-u dawlat-i l-qaanuun-i
establishing a state of law

ما مَعنى هذا؟
*maa **maʿnaa** haadhaa?*
What is **the meaning** of this?

10 Form I participles

10.1 Form I active participle (AP): *faaʿil* فاعِل

APs that refer to living beings take the natural gender of the referent; APs that refer to non-living things may be either masculine or feminine. For more detail on AP morphology and syntax see Chapter 6 on participles. Examples are provided here of how the various root types fit into the pattern. The items are categorized as either noun or adjective, but many have both noun and adjective functions.

10.1.1 Strong/regular root

Nouns:

writer	*kaatib/ kuttaab*	كاتِب / كُتّاب	rule; base	*qaaʿida/ qawaaʿid*	قاعِدة / قَواعِد
researcher	*baaHith/ -uuna*	باحِث / باحِثون	university	*jaamiʿa/ -aat*	جامِعة / جامِعات

Adjectives:

former	*saabiq*	سابِق	empty	*faarigh*	فارِغ

10.1.2 Geminate root: *faa*ᶜᶜ

In the active participle of the geminate root, the usual form of the AP is *faa*ᶜᶜ, that is, the second and third radicals are together (written with *shadda*), with no vowel between them.

Noun:

commodity; material	*maadda/mawaadd*[14]	مادَّة / مَواد

Adjective:

dry	*jaaff*	جافّ	hot	*Haarr*	حارّ
important	*haamm*	هامّ	urgent, pressing	*maass*	ماسّ

10.1.3 Hamzated root

Certain spelling rules for the *hamza* apply in the AP *hamzated* root, depending where in the word the *hamza* occurs.

Noun:

reader	*qaari'/qurraa'*	قارِئ / قُرّاء
accident; emergency	*Taari'a/Tawaari'*	طارِئَة / طَوارِئ
refugee	*laaji' / laaji'uuna*	لاجِئ / لاجِئُون

Adjective:

final; last	*'aaxir*[15]*/'awaaxir~'aaxir-uuna*	آخِر /أُواخِر ~ آخِرون
calm, peaceful	*haadi'*	هادِئ

10.1.4 Assimilated root: *faa*ᶜ*il*

Assimilated roots are regular in Form I active participle formation.

Noun:

mother	*waalida/-aat*	والِدة / والِدات	import/s	*waarid/-aat*	وارِد / وارِدات

---

[14] The plural *mawaadd* is the form that the plural pattern *fawaaᶜil* takes in geminate nouns because of the phonological restriction on sequences that include a vowel between identical consonants. **mawaadid -> mawaadd*. It is diptote (CaCaaCiC pattern).

[15] From the hamzated root *'-x-r*; the initial *hamza* followed by the long /aa/ of the *faaᶜil* pattern creates /'aa/, spelled with *'alif madda*.

father *waalid/-uuna* والِد / والِدونْ   duty; homework *waajib/-aat* واجِب / واجِبات

Adjective:

wide, broad   *waasi^c*   واسِع   dry; arid   *yaabis*   يابِس

10.1.5 Hollow root: *faa^ʾil*

Hollow roots of Form I have *hamza* between the long /aa/ and the short /i/ of the AP pattern.

Noun:

visitor/s	*zaa^ʾir/zuwwaar*	زائِر / زُوّار
fluid; liquid/s	*saa^ʾil/sawaa^ʾil*	سائِل / سَوائِل
being/s	*kaa^ʾin/-aat*	كائِن / كائِنات
circle/s; department/s	*daa^ʾira/dawaa^ʾir*	دائِرة / دَوائِر

Adjective:

visiting *zaa^ʾir/zaa^ʾir-uuna* زائِر / زائِرونْ   dreadful *haa^ʾil* هائِل

10.1.6 Defective root: *faa^c-in* فاع

The defective root shows its weakness in the AP form by having its final *waaw* or *yaa^ʾ* in the form of *kasrataan* on the base masculine form, putting it into the defective declension. In feminine APs the weakness is regularized into an /-iya / ending.

Noun:

judge/s	*qaaDin/quDaah*	قاضٍ / قُضاة
corner/s	*zaawiya/zawaayaa*	زاوِية / زَوايا
club/s	*naadin/ ^ʾandiya ~ nawaad-in*	نادٍ / أنْدِية ~ نوادٍ
pedestrian/s; infantry	*maashin/mushaat*	ماشٍ / مُشاة

Adjective:

walking	*maashin*	ماشٍ	last; past *maaDin*	ماضٍ
remaining	*baaqin*	باقٍ	adequate *kaafin*	كافٍ

10.1.7 Examples of Form I AP in context

المَشاريع الباقِية
al-mashaarii^c-u l-baaqiyat-u
the **remaining** projects

في حاجةٍ ماسّةٍ إلى المُساعَدة
*fii Haajat-in **maassat-in** ^ʾilaa l-musaa^cadat-i*
in **urgent** need of help

الثلاثاء الجاري
al-thulaathaa'-u l-jaarii
this ('current') Tuesday

قوافل أيّام زمان
qawaafil-u 'ayyam-i zamaan-in
the caravans of yesteryear

في جلسة طارئة
fii jalsat-in Taari'at-in
at an **emergency** session

ظلّت في غيبوبة تامّة.
Zall-at fii ghaybuubat-in taammat-in.
She remained in a **complete** coma.

10.2 Form I passive participle (PP): *maf'uul* مَفْعول

The *maf'uul* pattern is maintained in most root types except for the hollow and defective:

10.2.1 Strong/regular root

Noun:

concept/s	*mafhuum/mafaahiim*	مفْهوم / مفَاهيم
plan/s	*mashruu'/aat~mashaarii'*	مَشْروع / مشروعات ~ مَشاريع
prisoner/s	*masjuun/-uuna*	مَسْجون / مَسْجونون
group/s	*majmuu'a/-aat*	مَجْموعة / مَجْموعات

Adjective:

famous	*mashhuur*	مشهور	reserved	*maHjuuz*	مَحْجوز
blessed	*mabruuk*	مَبْروك	audible	*masmuu'*	مسموع

10.2.2 Geminate root

Noun:

yield; return	*marduud*	مَرْدود	manuscript/s	*maxTuuT/ aat*	مَخْطوط/ مخطوطات

Adjective:

lucky	*maHZuuZ*	محظوظ	beloved	*maHbuub*	مَحْبوب

10.2.3 Hamzated root

Noun:

official	*mas'uul*	مَسْؤول	readable	*maqruu'*	مقْروء

Adjective:

taken	*ma'xuudh*	مَأْخوذ	peopled	*ma'huul*	مَأْهول

10.2.4 Assimilated root

Noun:

topic, subject	*mawDuuᶜ*	مَوْضوع

Adjective:

present; found	*mawjuud*	مَوْجود	inherited	*mawruuth*	مَوْروث

10.2.5 Hollow root

In the hollow root, the *mafᶜuul* pattern becomes **mafuul** for roots whose middle radical is *waaw*, and **mafiil** for roots whose middle radical is *yaaʾ*:

blamed	*maluum (l-w-m)*	مَلوم	sold	*mabiiᶜ (b-y-ᶜ)*	مَبيع

10.2.6 Defective root

In the defective root, the *mafᶜuul* PP pattern becomes **mafᶜuww** for roots whose final radical is *waaw* and **mafᶜiyy** for roots whose final radical is *yaaʾ*:

Adjective:

invited	*madᶜuww (d-ᶜ-w)*	مدعوّ	stuffed	*maHshuww (H-sh-w)*[16]	محشوّ
forgotten	*mansiyy (n-s-y)*	منسيّ	spoken	*maHkiyy (H-k-y)*	محكيّ

10.2.7 Examples of Form I PP's in context

طاولة مَحجوزة
Taawilat-un **maHjuuzat-un**
a **reserved** table

من مصادر موثوق بها
min maSaadir-a **mawthuuq-in** *bi-haa*
from **trusted** sources

تمور مكبوسة
tumuur-un **makbuusat-un**
pressed dates

خطها مقروء.
xaTT-u-haa **maqruuʾ-un**.
Her handwriting is **legible**.

محشوّ بالقشّ
maHshuww-un bi-l-qashsh-i
stuffed with straw

العربيّة المحكيّة
al-ᶜarabiyyat-u l-**maHkiyyat-u**
spoken Arabic

---

[16] In spoken Arabic this PP is often converted to *maHshiyy*, used especially when referring to stuffed meat or other food items.

Form I Sound root: فَعَلَ ، يَفْعَلُ AP: فَاعِل PP: مَفْعُول VN: فِعْل 'to do; to make'

	Active	Active	Active	Active	Active	Passive	Passive
	Perfect	Imperfect	Imperfect	Imperfect	Imperfect	Perfect	Imperfect
		Indicative	Subjunctive	Jussive	Imperative		
أنا	فَعَلْتُ	أَفْعَلُ	أَفْعَلَ	أَفْعَلْ		فُعِلْتُ	أُفْعَلُ
أنْتَ	فَعَلْتَ	تَفْعَلُ	تَفْعَلَ	تَفْعَلْ	افْعَلْ	فُعِلْتَ	تُفْعَلُ
أنْتِ	فَعَلْتِ	تَفْعَلِينَ	تَفْعَلِي	تَفْعَلِي	افْعَلِي	فُعِلْتِ	تُفْعَلِينَ
أنْتُما—m/f	فَعَلْتُما	تَفْعَلانِ	تَفْعَلا	تَفْعَلا	افْعَلا	فُعِلْتُما	تُفْعَلانِ
هُوَ	فَعَلَ	يَفْعَلُ	يَفْعَلَ	يَفْعَلْ		فُعِلَ	يُفْعَلُ
هِيَ	فَعَلَتْ	تَفْعَلُ	تَفْعَلَ	تَفْعَلْ		فُعِلَتْ	تُفْعَلُ
هُما—m	فَعَلا	يَفْعَلانِ	يَفْعَلا	يَفْعَلا		فُعِلا	يُفْعَلانِ
هُما—f	فَعَلَتا	تَفْعَلانِ	تَفْعَلا	تَفْعَلا		فُعِلَتا	تُفْعَلانِ
نَحْنُ	فَعَلْنا	نَفْعَلُ	نَفْعَلَ	نَفْعَلْ		فُعِلْنا	نُفْعَلُ
أنْتُم	فَعَلْتُم	تَفْعَلُونَ	تَفْعَلوا	تَفْعَلوا	افْعَلوا	فُعِلْتُم	تُفْعَلُونَ
أنْتُنَّ	فَعَلْتُنَّ	تَفْعَلْنَ	تَفْعَلْنَ	تَفْعَلْنَ	افْعَلْنَ	فُعِلْتُنَّ	تُفْعَلْنَ
هُم	فَعَلوا	يَفْعَلُونَ	يَفْعَلوا	يَفْعَلوا		فُعِلوا	يُفْعَلُونَ
هُنَّ	فَعَلْنَ	يَفْعَلْنَ	يَفْعَلْنَ	يَفْعَلْنَ		فُعِلْنَ	يُفْعَلْنَ

Form I Geminate root: دَلَّ، يَدُلُّ   AP: دالّ   PP: مَدْلُول   VN: دَلالَة   'to indicate'

	Active	Active	Active	Active	Active	Passive	Passive
	Perfect	Imperfect	Imperfect	Imperfect	Imperfect	Perfect	Imperfect
		Indicative	Subjunctive	Jussive	Imperative		
أنا	دَلَلْتُ	أَدُلُّ	أَدُلَّ	أَدُلَّ		دُلِلْتُ	أُدَلُّ
أنْتَ	دَلَلْتَ	تَدُلُّ	تَدُلَّ	تَدُلَّ	دُلَّ/أُدْلُلْ	دُلِلْتَ	تُدَلُّ
أنْتِ	دَلَلْتِ	تَدُلِّين	تَدُلِّي	تَدُلِّي	دُلِّي	دُلِلْتِ	تُدَلِّين
أنْتُما—m/f	دَلَلْتُما	تَدُلّانِ	تَدُلّا	تَدُلّا	دُلّا	دُلِلْتُما	تُدَلّانِ
هُوَ	دَلَّ	يَدُلُّ	يَدُلَّ	يَدُلَّ		دُلَّ	يُدَلُّ
هِيَ	دَلَّتْ	تَدُلُّ	تَدُلَّ	تَدُلَّ		دُلَّتْ	تُدَلُّ
هُما—m	دَلّا	يَدُلّانِ	يَدُلّا	يَدُلّا		دُلّا	يُدَلّانِ
هُما—f	دَلَّتا	تَدُلّانِ	تَدُلّا	تَدُلّا		دُلَّتا	تُدَلّانِ
نَحْنُ	دَلَلْنا	نَدُلُّ	نَدُلَّ	نَدُلَّ		دُلِلْنا	نُدَلُّ
أنْتُم	دَلَلْتُم	تَدُلّون	تَدُلّوا	تَدُلّوا	دُلّوا	دُلِلْتُم	تُدَلّون
أنْتُنَّ	دَلَلْتُنَّ	تَدْلُلْنَ	تَدْلُلْنَ	تَدْلُلْنَ	أُدْلُلْنَ	دُلِلْتُنَّ	تُدْلَلْنَ
هُم	دَلّوا	يَدُلّون	يَدُلّوا	يَدُلّوا		دُلّوا	يُدَلّون
هُنَّ	دَلَلْنَ	يَدْلُلْنَ	يَدْلُلْنَ	يَدْلُلْنَ		دُلِلْنَ	يُدْلَلْنَ

Form I hamza-initial root: أَكَلَ ، يَأْكُلُ   AP: آكِل   PP: مَأْكُول   VN: أَكْل   'to eat'

	Active	Active	Active	Active	Active	Passive	Passive
	Perfect	Imperfect	Imperfect	Imperfect	Imperfect	Perfect	Imperfect
		Indicative	Subjunctive	Jussive	Imperative		
أنا	أَكَلْتُ	آكُلُ	آكُلَ	آكُلْ		أُكِلْتُ	أُوكَلُ
أنْتَ	أَكَلْتَ	تَأْكُلُ	تَأْكُلَ	تَأْكُلْ	كُلْ	أُكِلْتَ	تُوكَلُ
أنْتِ	أَكَلْتِ	تَأْكُلِينَ	تَأْكُلِي	تَأْكُلِي	كُلِي	أُكِلْتِ	تُوكَلِينَ
أنْتُما—m/f	أَكَلْتُما	تَأْكُلانِ	تَأْكُلا	تَأْكُلا	كُلا	أُكِلْتُما	تُوكَلانِ
هُوَ	أَكَلَ	يَأْكُلُ	يَأْكُلَ	يَأْكُلْ		أُكِلَ	يُوكَلُ
هِيَ	أَكَلَتْ	تَأْكُلُ	تَأْكُلَ	تَأْكُلْ		أُكِلَتْ	تُوكَلُ
هُما—m	أَكَلا	يَأْكُلانِ	يَأْكُلا	يَأْكُلا		أُكِلا	يُوكَلونَ
هُما—f	أَكَلَتا	تَأْكُلانِ	تَأْكُلا	تَأْكُلا		أُكِلَتا	تُوكَلانِ
نَحْنُ	أَكَلْنا	نَأْكُلُ	نَأْكُلَ	نَأْكُلْ		أُكِلْنا	نُوكَلُ
أنْتُم	أَكَلْتُم	تَأْكُلونَ	تَأْكُلوا	تَأْكُلوا	كُلوا	أُكِلْتُم	تُوكَلونَ
أنْتُنَّ	أَكَلْتُنَّ	تَأْكُلْنَ	تَأْكُلْنَ	تَأْكُلْنَ	كُلْنَ	أُكِلْتُنَّ	تُوكَلْنَ
هُم	أَكَلوا	يَأْكُلونَ	يَأْكُلوا	يَأْكُلوا		أُكِلوا	يُوكَلونَ
هُنَّ	أَكَلْنَ	يَأْكُلْنَ	يَأْكُلْنَ	يَأْكُلْنَ		أُكِلْنَ	يُوكَلْنَ

Form I hamza-medial root: سَأَلَ ، يَسْأَلُ AP: سائل PP: مَسْؤُول VN: سُؤَال *'to ask'*

	Active	Active	Active	Active	Active	Passive	Passive
	Perfect	Imperfect	Imperfect	Imperfect	Imperfect	Perfect	Imperfect
		Indicative	Subjunctive	Jussive	Imperative		
أنا	سَأَلْتُ	أَسْأَلُ	أَسْأَلَ	أَسْأَلْ		سُئِلْتُ	أُسْأَلُ
أنْتَ	سَأَلْتَ	تَسْأَلُ	تَسْأَلَ	تَسْأَلْ	اسْأَلْ	سُئِلْتَ	تُسْأَلُ
أنْتِ	سَأَلْتِ	تَسْأَلين	تَسْأَلي	تَسْأَلي	اسْأَلي	سُئِلْتِ	تُسْأَلين
أنتُما—m/f	سَأَلْتُما	تَسْأَلان	تَسْأَلا	تَسْأَلا	اسْأَلا	سُئِلْتُما	تُسْأَلان
هُوَ	سَأَلَ	يَسْأَلُ	يَسْأَلَ	يَسْأَلْ		سُئِلَ	يُسْأَلُ
هِيَ	سَأَلَتْ	تَسْأَلُ	تَسْأَلَ	تَسْأَلْ		سُئِلَتْ	تُسْأَلان
هُما—m	سَأَلا	يَسْأَلانِ	يَسْأَلا	يَسْأَلا		سُئِلا	يُسْأَلانِ
هُما—f	سَأَلَتا	تَسْأَلانِ	تَسْأَلا	تَسْأَلا		سُئِلَتا	تُسْأَلان
نَحْنُ	سَأَلْنا	نَسْأَلُ	نَسْأَلَ	نَسْأَلْ		سُئِلْنا	نُسْأَلُ
أنْتُم	سَأَلْتُم	تَسْأَلون	تَسْأَلوا	تَسْأَلوا	اسْأَلوا	سُئِلْتُم	تُسْأَلون
أنْتُنَّ	سَأَلْتُنَّ	تَسْأَلْنَ	تَسْأَلْنَ	تَسْأَلْنَ		سُئِلْتُنَّ	تُسْأَلْنَ
هُم	سَأَلوا	يَسْأَلون	يَسْأَلوا	يَسْأَلوا		سُئِلوا	يُسْأَلون
هُنَّ	سَأَلْنَ	يَسْأَلْنَ	يَسْأَلْنَ	يَسْأَلْنَ	اسْأَلْنَ	سُئِلْنَ	يُسْأَلْنَ

Form I hamza-final root: قَرَأَ ، يَقْرَأُ   AP: قارِئ   PP: مَقْروء   VN: قِراءة   *'to read'*

	Active	Active	Active	Active	Active	Passive	Passive
	Perfect	Imperfect	Imperfect	Imperfect	Imperfect	Perfect	Imperfect
		Indicative	Subjunctive	Jussive	Imperative		
أنا	قَرَأْتُ	أَقْرَأُ	أَقْرَأَ	أَقْرَأْ		قُرِئْتُ	أُقْرَأُ
أنتَ	قَرَأْتَ	تَقْرَأُ	تَقْرَأَ	تَقْرَأْ	اِقْرَأْ	قُرِئْتَ	تُقْرَأُ
أنتِ	قَرَأْتِ	تَقْرَئِين	تَقْرَئِي	تَقْرَئِي	اِقْرَئِي	قُرِئْتِ	تُقْرَئِين
أنتُما—m/f	قَرَأْتُما	تَقْرَآن	تَقْرَآ	تَقْرَآ	اِقْرَآ	قُرِئْتُما	تُقْرَآن
هُوَ	قَرَأَ	يَقْرَأُ	يَقْرَأَ	يَقْرَأْ		قُرِئَ	يُقْرَأُ
هيَ	قَرَأَتْ	تَقْرَأُ	تَقْرَأَ	تَقْرَأْ		قُرِئَتْ	تُقْرَأُ
هُما—m	قَرَآ	يَقْرَآن	يَقْرَآ	يَقْرَآ		قُرِئا	يُقْرَآن
هُما—f	قَرَأَتا	تَقْرَآن	تَقْرَآ	تَقْرَآ		قُرِئَتا	تُقْرَآن
نَحْنُ	قَرَأْنا	نَقْرَأُ	نَقْرَأَ	نَقْرَأْ		قُرِئْنا	نُقْرَأُ
أنتُم	قَرَأْتُما	تَقْرَؤُون	تَقْرَؤُوا	تَقْرَؤُوا	اِقْرَؤُوا	قُرِئْتُم	تُقْرَؤُون
أنتنَّ	قَرَأْتُنَّ	تَقْرَأْنَ	تَقْرَأْنَ	تَقْرَأْنَ	اِقْرَأْنَ	قُرِئْتُنَّ	تُقْرَأْنَ
هُم	قَرَؤُوا	يَقْرَؤُون	يَقْرَؤُوا	يَقْرَؤُوا		قُرِئوا	يُقْرَؤُون
هنَّ	قَرَأْنَ	يَقْرَأْنَ	يَقْرَأْنَ	يَقْرَأْنَ		قُرِئْنَ	يُقْرَأْنَ

Form I Assimilated root: وَضَعَ ، يَضَعُ   AP: واضِع   PP: مَوْضوع   VN: وَضْع   'to put, to place'

	Active	Active	Active	Active	Active	Passive	Passive
	Perfect	Imperfect	Imperfect	Imperfect	Imperfect	Perfect	Imperfect
		Indicative	Subjunctive	Jussive	Imperative		
أنا	وَضَعْتُ	أَضَعُ	أَضَعَ	أَضَعْ		وُضِعْتُ	أُوضَعُ
أنْتَ	وَضَعْتَ	تَضَعُ	تَضَعَ	تَضَعْ	ضَعْ	وُضِعْتَ	تُوضَعُ
أنْتِ	وَضَعْتِ	تَضَعينَ	تَضَعي	تَضَعي	ضَعي	وُضِعْتِ	توضَعينَ
أنْتُما—m/f	وَضَعْتُما	تَضَعانِ	تَضَعا	تَضَعا	ضَعا	وُضِعْتُما	توضَعانِ
هُوَ	وَضَعَ	يَضَعُ	يَضَعَ	يَضَعْ		وُضِعَ	يوضَعُ
هِيَ	وَضَعَتْ	تَضَعُ	تَضَعَ	تَضَعْ		وُضِعَتْ	توضَعُ
هُما—m	وَضَعا	يَضَعانِ	يَضَعا	يَضَعا		وُضِعا	يوضَعانِ
هُما—f	وَضَعَتا	تَضَعانِ	تَضَعا	تَضَعا		وُضِعَتا	توضَعانِ
نَحْنُ	وَضَعْنا	نَضَعُ	نَضَعَ	نَضَعْ		وُضِعْنا	نوضَعُ
أنْتُم	وَضَعْتُم	تَضَعونَ	تَضَعوا	تَضَعوا	ضَعوا	وُضِعْتُم	توضَعونَ
أنْتُنَّ	وَضَعْتُنَّ	تَضَعْنَ	تَضَعْنَ	تَضَعْنَ	ضَعْنَ	وُضِعْتُنَّ	توضَعْنَ
هُم	وَضَعوا	يَضَعونَ	يَضَعوا	يَضَعوا		وُضِعوا	يوضَعونَ
هُنَّ	وَضَعْنَ	يَضَعْنَ	يَضَعْنَ	يَضَعْنَ		وُضِعْنَ	يوضَعْنَ

Form I Hollow, Medial waaw root: زار، يَزور AP: زائِر PP: مَزور VN: زِيارة 'to visit'

	Active	Active	Active	Active	Active	Passive	Passive
	Perfect	Imperfect	Imperfect	Imperfect	Imperfect	Perfect	Imperfect
		Indicative	Subjunctive	Jussive	Imperative		
أنا	زُرْتُ	أزورُ	أزورَ	أزُرْ		زِرْتُ	أزارُ
أنتَ	زُرْتَ	تزورُ	تزورَ	تزُرْ	زُرْ	زِرْتَ	تُزارُ
أنتِ	زُرْتِ	تزورينَ	تزوري	تزوري	زوري	زِرْتِ	تُزارين
أنتُما m/f	زُرْتُما	تزورانِ	تزورا	تزورا	زورا	زِرْتُما	تُزاران
هوَ	زارَ	يزورُ	يزورَ	يزُرْ		زِيرَ	يُزارُ
هيَ	زارتْ	تزورُ	تزورَ	تزُرْ		زِيرتْ	تُزارُ
هما—m	زارا	يزورانِ	يزورا	يزورا		زِيرا	يُزاران
هما—f	زارتا	تزورانِ	تزورا	تزورا		زِيرتا	تُزاران
نحنُ	زُرْنا	نزورُ	نزورَ	نزُرْ		زِرْنا	نُزارُ
أنتُم	زُرْتُم	تزورونَ	تزوروا	تزوروا	زوروا	زِرْتُم	تُزارون
أنتنَّ	زُرْتنَّ	تزُرْنَ	تزُرْنَ	تزُرْنَ	زُرْنَ	زِرْتنَّ	تُزَرْنَ
هم	زاروا	يزورونَ	يزوروا	يزوروا		زِيروا	يُزارون
هنَّ	زُرْنَ	يزُرْنَ	يزُرْنَ	يزُرْنَ		زِرْنَ	يُزَرْنَ

Form I Hollow Medial yaa' root: باع، يبيع   AP: بائع   PP: مبيع   VN: بَيْع   'to sell'

	Active	Active	Active	Active	Active	Passive	Passive
	Perfect	Imperfect	Imperfect	Imperfect	Imperfect	Perfect	Imperfect
		Indicative	Subjunctive	Jussive	Imperative		
أنا	بِعْتُ	أبيعُ	أبيعَ	أبِعْ		بِعْتُ	أُباعُ
أنْتَ	بِعْتَ	تبيعُ	تبيعَ	تبِعْ	بِعْ	بِعْتَ	تُباعُ
أنْتِ	بِعْتِ	تبيعينَ	تبيعي	تبيعي	بيعي	بِعْتِ	تُباعينَ
أنْتُما—m/f	بِعْتُما	تبيعانِ	تبيعا	تبيعا	بيعا	بِعْتُما	تُباعانِ
هوَ	باعَ	يبيعُ	يبيعَ	يبِعْ		بيعَ	يُباعُ
هيَ	باعَتْ	تبيعُ	تبيعَ	تبِعْ		بيعَتْ	تُباعُ
هُما—m	باعا	يبيعانِ	يبيعا	يبيعا		بيعا	يُباعانِ
هُما—f	باعَتا	تبيعانِ	تبيعا	تبيعا		بيعَتا	تُباعانِ
نحْنُ	بِعْنا	نبيعُ	نبيعَ	نبِعْ		بِعْنا	نُباعُ
أنْتُمْ	بِعْتُمْ	تبيعونَ	تبيعوا	تبيعوا	بيعوا	بِعْتُمْ	تُباعونَ
أنْتُنَّ	بِعْتُنَّ	تبِعْنَ	تبِعْنَ	تبِعْنَ	بِعْنَ	بِعْتُنَّ	تُبَعْنَ
هُمْ	باعوا	يبيعونَ	يبيعوا	يبيعوا		بيعوا	يُباعونَ
هُنَّ	بِعْنَ	يبِعْنَ	يبِعْنَ	يبِعْنَ		بِعْنَ	يُبَعْنَ

Form I Hollow, Medial ʾalif root: خَافَ ، يَخاف   AP: خَائِف   PP: مَخوف   VN: خَوْف   *'to fear'*

	Active Perfect	Active Imperfect Indicative	Active Imperfect Subjunctive	Active Imperfect Jussive	Active Imperfect Imperative	Passive Perfect	Passive Imperfect
أنا	خِفْتُ	أَخافُ	أَخافَ	أَخَفْ		خِفْتُ	أُخافُ
أَنْتَ	خِفْتَ	تَخافُ	تَخافَ	تَخَفْ	خَفْ	خِفْتَ	تُخافُ
أَنْتِ	خِفْتِ	تَخافينَ	تَخافي	تَخافي	خافي	خِفْتِ	تُخافينَ
أَنْتُما—m/f	خِفْتُما	تَخافانِ	تَخافا	تَخافا	خافا	خِفْتُما	تُخافانِ
هُوَ	خافَ	يَخافُ	يَخافَ	يَخَفْ		خيفَ	يُخافُ
هِيَ	خافَتْ	تَخافُ	تَخافَ	تَخَفْ		خيفَتْ	تُخافُ
هُما—m	خافا	يَخافانِ	يَخافا	يَخافا		خيفا	يُخافانِ
هُما—f	خافَتا	تَخافانِ	تَخافا	تَخافا		خيفَتا	تُخافانِ
نَحْنُ	خِفْنا	نَخافُ	نَخافَ	نَخَفْ		خِفْنا	نُخافُ
أَنْتُم	خِفْتُمْ	تَخافونَ	تَخافوا	تَخافوا	خافوا	خِفْتُمْ	تُخافونَ
أَنْتُنَّ	خِفْتُنَّ	تَخَفْنَ	تَخَفْنَ	تَخَفْنَ	خَفْنَ	خِفْتُنَّ	تُخَفْنَ
هُم	خافوا	يَخافونَ	يَخافوا	يَخافوا		خيفوا	يُخافونَ
هُنَّ	خِفْنَ	يَخَفْنَ	يَخَفْنَ	يَخَفْنَ		خِفْنَ	يُخَفْنَ

Form I Defective root (waaw): دعا ، يَدْعو   AP: داعٍ   PP: مَدْعوّ   VN: دَعْوة / دُعاء   'to call, invite'

	Active	Active	Active	Active	Active	Passive	Passive
	Perfect	Imperfect	Imperfect	Imperfect	Imperfect	Perfect	Imperfect
		Indicative	Subjunctive	Jussive	Imperative		
أنا	دَعَوْتُ	أَدْعو	أَدْعوَ	أَدْعُ		دُعيتُ	أُدْعى
أنتَ	دَعَوْتَ	تَدْعو	تَدْعوَ	تَدْعُ	اُدْعُ	دُعيتَ	تُدْعى
أنتِ	دَعَوْتِ	تَدْعينَ	تَدْعي	تَدْعي	اُدْعي	دُعيتِ	تُدْعينَ
أنتما—m/f	دَعَوْتُما	تَدْعوانِ	تَدْعوا	تَدْعوا	اُدْعوا	دُعيتُما	تُدْعوانِ
هو	دَعا	يَدْعو	يَدْعوَ	يَدْعُ		دُعِيَ	يُدْعى
هي	دَعَتْ	تَدْعو	تَدْعوَ	تَدْعُ		دُعيتْ	تُدْعى
هما—m	دَعَوا	يَدْعوانِ	يَدْعوا	يَدْعوا		دُعِيا	يُدْعوانِ
هما—f	دَعَتا	تَدْعوانِ	تَدْعوا	تَدْعوا		دُعِيَتا	تُدْعوانِ
نحن	دَعَوْنا	نَدْعو	نَدْعوَ	نَدْعُ		دُعينا	نُدْعى
أنتم	دَعَوْتُم	تَدْعونَ	تَدْعوا	تَدْعوا	اُدْعوا	دُعيتُم	تُدْعونَ
أنتنَّ	دَعَوْتُنَّ	تَدْعونَ	تَدْعونَ	تَدْعونَ	اُدْعونَ	دُعيتُنَّ	تُدْعونَ
هم	دَعَوا	يَدْعونَ	يَدْعوا	يَدْعوا		دُعوا	يُدْعونَ
هنَّ	دَعَوْنَ	يَدْعونَ	يَدْعونَ	يَدْعونَ		دُعينَ	يُدْعونَ

Form I Defective root (-aa/-ii): بَنَى ، يَبْنِي AP: بانٍ PP: مبنيّ VN: بِناء 'to build'

	Active	Active	Active	Active	Active	Passive	Passive
	Perfect	Imperfect	Imperfect	Imperfect	Imperfect	Perfect	Imperfect
		Indicative	Subjunctive	Jussive	Imperative		
أنا	بَنَيْتُ	أَبْنِي	أَبْنِيَ	أَبْنِ		بُنِيتُ	أُبْنَى
أنْتَ	بَنَيْتَ	تَبْنِي	تَبْنِيَ	تَبْنِ	اِبْنِ	بُنِيتَ	تُبْنَى
أنْتِ	بَنَيْتِ	تَبْنِينَ	تَبْنِي	تَبْنِي	اِبْنِي	بُنِيتِ	تُبْنَيْنَ
أنتُما—m/f	بَنَيْتُما	تَبْنِيانِ	تَبْنِيا	تَبْنِيا	اِبْنِيا	بُنِيتُما	تُبْنَيانِ
هُوَ	بَنَى	يَبْنِي	يَبْنِيَ	يَبْنِ		بُنِيَ	يُبْنَى
هِيَ	بَنَتْ	تَبْنِي	تَبْنِيَ	تَبْنِ		بُنِيَتْ	تُبْنَى
هُما—m	بَنَيا	يَبْنِيانِ	يَبْنِيا	يَبْنِيا		بُنِيا	يُبْنَيانِ
هُما—f	بَنَتا	تَبْنِيانِ	تَبْنِيا	تَبْنِيا		بُنِيَتا	تُبْنَيانِ
نَحْنُ	بَنَيْنا	نَبْنِي	نَبْنِيَ	نَبْنِ		بُنِينا	نُبْنَى
أنتُم	بَنَيْتُم	تَبْنُونَ	تَبْنُوا	تَبْنُوا	اِبْنُوا	بُنِيتُم	تُبْنَوْنَ
أنتنَّ	بَنَيْتُنَّ	تَبْنِينَ	تَبْنِينَ	تَبْنِينَ	اِبْنِينَ	بُنِيتُنَّ	تُبْنَيْنَ
هُم	بَنَوْا	يَبْنُونَ	يَبْنُوا	يَبْنُوا		بُنُوا	يُبْنَوْنَ
هُنَّ	بَنَيْنَ	يَبْنِينَ	يَبْنِينَ	يَبْنِينَ		بُنِينَ	يُبْنَيْنَ

Form I Defective (-iy/-aa): نَسِيَ ، يَنْسَى AP: ناسٍ PP: مَنْسِيّ VN: نِسْيَان *'to forget'*

	Active	Active	Active	Active	Active	Passive	Passive
	Perfect	Imperfect	Imperfect	Imperfect	Imperfect	Perfect	Imperfect
		Indicative	Subjunctive	Jussive	Imperative		
أنا	نَسِيتُ	أَنْسَى	أَنْسَى	أَنْسَ		نُسِيتُ	أُنْسَى
أَنْتَ	نَسِيتَ	تَنْسَى	تَنْسَى	تَنْسَ	انْسَ	نُسِيتَ	تُنْسَى
أَنْتِ	نَسِيتِ	تَنْسِينَ	تَنْسَي	تَنْسَي	انْسَي	نُسِيتِ	تُنْسَيْنَ
أَنْتُما –m/f	نَسِيتُما	تَنْسِيانِ	تَنْسِيا	تَنْسِيا	انْسِيا	نُسِيتُما	تُنْسِيانِ
هُوَ	نَسِيَ	يَنْسَى	يَنْسَى	يَنْسَ		نُسِيَ	يُنْسَى
هِيَ	نَسِيَتْ	تَنْسَى	تَنْسَى	تَنْسَ		نُسِيَتْ	تُنْسَى
هُما –m	نَسِيا	يَنْسِيانِ	يَنْسِيا	يَنْسِيا		نُسِيا	يُنْسِيانِ
هُما –f	نَسِيَتا	تَنْسِيانِ	تَنْسِيا	تَنْسِيا		نُسِيَتا	تُنْسِيانِ
نَحْنُ	نَسِينا	نَنْسَى	نَنْسَى	نَنْسَ		نُسِينا	نُنْسَى
أَنْتُم	نَسِيتُم	تَنْسَوْنَ	تَنْسَوْا	تَنْسَوْا	انْسَوْا	نُسِيتُم	تُنْسَوْنَ
أَنْتُنَّ	نَسِيتُنَّ	تَنْسَيْنَ	تَنْسَيْنَ	تَنْسَيْنَ	انْسَيْنَ	نُسِيتُنَّ	تُنْسَيْنَ
هُم	نَسُوا	يَنْسَوْنَ	يَنْسَوْا	يَنْسَوْا		نُسُوا	يُنْسَوْنَ
هُنَّ	نَسِينَ	يَنْسَيْنَ	يَنْسَيْنَ	يَنْسَيْنَ		نُسِينَ	يُنْسَوْنَ

Form I Hollow and hamzated root: جاءَ ، يَجِيءُ   AP: جاءٍ   PP: مَجِيءٌ   VN: مَجِيء   *'to come'*

	Active	Active	Active	Active	Active	Passive	Passive
	Perfect	Imperfect	Imperfect	Imperfect	Imperfect	Perfect	Imperfect
		Indicative	Subjunctive	Jussive	Imperative		
أنا	جِئْتُ	أَجِيءُ	أَجِيءَ	أَجِئْ		جِئْتُ	أُجاءُ
أَنْتَ	جِئْتَ	تَجِيءُ	تَجِيءَ	تَجِئْ	تَعالَ	جِئْتَ	تُجاءُ
أَنْتِ	جِئْتِ	تَجِيئِينَ	تَجِيئِي	تَجِيئِي	تَعالَيْ	جِئْتِ	تُجائِينَ
أنتُما—m/f	جِئْتُما	تَجِيئانِ	تَجِيئا	تَجِيئا	تَعالِيا	جِئْتُما	تُجاءانِ
هُوَ	جاءَ	يَجِيءُ	يَجِيءَ	يَجِئْ		جِيئَ	يُجاءُ
هِيَ	جاءَتْ	تَجِيءُ	تَجِيءَ	تَجِئْ		جِيئَتْ	تُجاءُ
هُما—m	جاءا	يَجِيئانِ	يَجِيئا	يَجِيئا		جِيئا	يُجاءانِ
هُما—f	جاءَتا	تَجِيئانِ	تَجِيئا	تَجِيئا		جِيئَتا	تُجاءانِ
نَحْنُ	جِئْنا	نَجِيءُ	نَجِيءَ	نَجِئْ		جِئْنا	نُجاءُ
أنتُم	جِئْتُمْ	تَجِيئُونَ	تَجِيئُوا	تَجِيئُوا	تَعالَوْا	جِئْتُمْ	تُجاؤُونَ
أَنْتُنَّ	جِئْتُنَّ	تَجِئْنَ	تَجِئْنَ	تَجِئْنَ	تَعالَيْنَ	جِئْتُنَّ	تُجَأْنَ
هُم	جاءُوا	يَجِيئُونَ	يَجِيئُوا	يَجِيئُوا		جِيئُوا	يُجاؤُونَ
هُنَّ	جِئْنَ	يَجِئْنَ	يَجِئْنَ	يَجِئْنَ		جِئْنَ	يُجَأْنَ

This verb has a replacive form for the imperative.

Form I Doubly weak root: يَرى ، رَأى AP: راءٍ PP: مَرئِيّ VN: رَأْي *'to see'*

	Active	Active	Active	Active	Active	Passive	Passive
	Perfect	Imperfect	Imperfect	Imperfect	Imperfect	Perfect	Imperfect
		Indicative	Subjunctive	Jussive	Imperative		
أنا	رَأَيْتُ	أرى	أرى	أرَ		رُئِيتُ	أرى
أنْتَ	رَأَيْتَ	تَرى	تَرى	تَرَ	رَ	رُئِيتَ	تُرى
أنْتِ	رَأَيْتِ	تَرَيْنَ	تَرَيْ	تَرَيْ	رَيْ	رُئِيتِ	تُرَيْنَ
أنْتُما—m/f	رَأَيْتُما	تَرَيانِ	تَرَيا	تَرَيا	رَيا	رُئِيتُما	تُرَيانِ
هُوَ	رَأى	يَرى	يَرى	يَرَ		رُئِيَ	يُرى
هِيَ	رَأَتْ	تَرى	تَرى	تَرَ		رُئِيَتْ	تُرى
هُما—m	رَأَيا	يَرَيانِ	يَرَيا	يَرَيا		رُئِيا	يُرَيانِ
هُما—f	رَأَتا	تَرَيانِ	تَرَيا	تَرَيا		رُئِيَتا	تُرَيانِ
نَحْنُ	رَأَيْنا	نَرى	نَرى	نَرَ		رُئِينا	نُرى
أنْتُم	رَأَيْتُمْ	تَرَوْنَ	تَرَوْا	تَرَوْا	رَوْا	رُئِيتُمْ	تُرَوْنَ
أنْتُنَّ	رَأَيْتُنَّ	تَرَيْنَ	تَرَيْنَ	تَرَيْنَ	رَيْنَ	رُئِيتُنَّ	تُرَيْنَ
هُم	رَأَوْا	يَرَوْنَ	يَرَوْا	يَرَوْا		رُؤُوا	يُرَوْنَ
هُنَّ	رَأَيْنَ	يَرَيْنَ	يَرَيْنَ	يَرَيْنَ	رَيْنَ	رُئِينَ	يُرَيْنَ

Form I Doubly weak: وَعَى ، يَعِي   AP: واعٍ   PP: مَوْعِيّ   VN: وَعْي   'to perceive'

	Active	Active	Active	Active	Active	Passive	Passive
	Perfect	Imperfect	Imperfect	Imperfect	Imperfect	Perfect	Imperfect
		Indicative	Subjunctive	Jussive	Imperative		
أنا	وَعَيْتُ	أَعِي	أَعِيَ	أَعِ		وُعِيتُ	أُوعَى
أَنْت	وَعَيْتَ	تَعِي	تَعِيَ	تَعِ	عِ	وُعِيتَ	تُوعَى
أَنْت	وَعَيْتِ	تَعِينَ	تَعِي	تَعِي	عِي	وُعِيتِ	تُوعَيْنَ
أَنْتُما—m/f	وَعَيْتُما	تَعِيانِ	تَعِيا	تَعِيا	عِيا	وُعِيتُما	تُوعَيانِ
هُوَ	وَعَى	يَعِيانِ	يَعِيَ	يَعِ		وُعِيَ	يُوعَى
هِيَ	وَعَتْ	تَعِي	تَعِيَ	تَعِ		وُعِيَتْ	تُوعَى
هُما—m	وَعَيا	يَعِيانِ	يَعِيا	يَعِيا		وُعِيا	يُوعَيانِ
هُما—f	وَعَتا	تَعِيانِ	تَعِيا	تَعِيا		وُعِيَتا	تُوعَيانِ
نَحْنُ	وَعَيْنا	نَعِي	نَعِيَ	نَعِ		وُعِينا	نُوعَى
أَنْتُم	وَعَيْتُمْ	تَعُونَ	تَعُوا	تَعُوا	عُوا	وُعِيتُمْ	تُوعَوْنَ
أَنْتُنَّ	وَعَيْتُنَّ	تَعِينَ	تَعِينَ	تَعِينَ	عِينَ	وُعِيتُنَّ	تُوعَيْنَ
هُم	وَعَوْا	يَعُونَ	يَعُوا	يَعُوا		وُعُوا	يُوعَوْنَ
هُنَّ	وَعَيْنَ	يَعِينَ	يَعِينَ	يَعِينَ		وُعِينَ	يُوعَيْنَ

Form I Hollow, defective root: نَوَى ، يَنْوِي AP: ناوٍ PP: مَنْوِيّ VN: نِيَّة 'to intend'

	Active	Active	Active	Active	Active	Passive	Passive
	Perfect	Imperfect	Imperfect	Imperfect	Imperfect	Perfect	Imperfect
		Indicative	Subjunctive	Jussive	Imperative		
أنا	نَوَيْتُ	أَنْوِي	أَنْوِيَ	أَنْوِ		نُوِيتُ	أُنْوَى
أَنْتَ	نَوَيْتَ	تَنْوِي	تَنْوِيَ	تَنْوِ	اِنْ	نُوِيتَ	تُنْوَى
أَنْتِ	نَوَيْتِ	تَنْوِينَ	تَنْوِي	تَنْوِي	اِنْي	نُوِيتِ	تُنْوَيْنَ
أنتُما—m/f	نَوَيْتُما	تَنْوِيانِ	تَنْوِيا	تَنْوِيا	اِنْيا	نُوِيتُما	تُنْوَيانِ
هُوَ	نَوَى	يَنْوِي	يَنْوِيَ	يَنْوِ		نُوِيَ	يُنْوَى
هِيَ	نَوَتْ	تَنْوِي	تَنْوِيَ	تَنْوِ		نُوِيَتْ	تُنْوَى
هُما—m	نَوَيا	يَنْوِيانِ	يَنْوِيا	يَنْوِيا		نُوِيا	يُنْوَيانِ
هُما—f	نَوَتا	تَنْوِيانِ	تَنْوِيا	تَنْوِيا		نُوِيَتا	تُنْوَيانِ
نَحْنُ	نَوَيْنا	نَنْوِي	نَنْوِيَ	نَنْوِ		نُوِينا	نُنْوَى
أنْتُم	نَوَيْتُم	تَنْوُونَ	تَنْوُوا	تَنْوُوا	اِنْوُوا	نُوِيتُم	تُنْوَوْنَ
أنْتُنَّ	نَوَيْتُنَّ	تَنْوِينَ	تَنْوِينَ	تَنْوِينَ	اِنْوِينَ	نُوِيتُنَّ	تُنْوَيْنَ
هُم	نَوَوْا	يَنْوُونَ	يَنْوُوا	يَنْوُوا		نُوُوا	يُنْوَوْنَ
هُنَّ	نَوَيْنَ	يَنْوِينَ	يَنْوِينَ	يَنْوِينَ		نُوِينَ	يُنْوَيْنَ

23

Form II

1 Basic characteristics

1.1 Pattern: *fa*ᶜᶜ*al-a* فَعَّلَ / *yu-fa*ᶜᶜ*il-u* يُفَعِّلُ

Form II verbs are augmented with respect to Form I in that the medial consonant is doubled. They have the stem patterns $C_1aC_2C_2aC_3$- in the past tense and yu-$C_1aC_2C_2iC_3$- in the present. The medial root consonant retains its doubled status throughout the past and present tense conjugations.

1.2 Meaning

Form II verbs are often causative of transitive Form I verbs, or, if Form I is intransitive, Form II may have transitive meaning. Another shade of meaning that is said to be conveyed by Form II is intensive or repeated action (*kassar-a* 'to smash, to shatter'). Form II may also be denominative, used to form verbs out of nouns (e.g., *Sawwar-a* 'to photograph' from *Suura*, 'picture').[1]

1.3 Transitivity

Form II is normally transitive but may sometimes be intransitive.[2] It may also be doubly transitive, taking two direct objects (e.g., *darras-a* 'to teach (s.o. s.th.)').

1.4 Inflection

A particular inflectional characteristic of Form II verbs is that the present tense subject-marker vowel is *Damma* and the present tense stem vowel is *kasra* (*yu-darris-u*).

---

[1] In Arabic, the verb is usually considered the most elemental form of a lexical entry, but in a few instances, the verb is derived from a noun. These "denominal" verbs tend to exist in Forms II and V and rarely in other forms. They can be triliteral or quadriliteral. Denominal verbs rarely have a Form I. Some examples of Form II denominal verbs include:

to unite	*waHHad-a/yu-waHHid-u* وحّد | يوحّد (from 'one' *waaHid* واحد)	
to head	*ra''as-a/yu-ra''is-u* رأّس | يرئّس (from 'head' *ra's* رأس)	
to name	*sammaa/yu-sammii* سمّى | يسمّي (from 'name' *ism* اسم)	

[2] Kouloughli 1994, 201 states that Form II is transitive 95 percent of the time. Likewise he states that Form II is "l'une des plus vivaces de l'arabe moderne" (ibid.).

Paradigm charts for Form II verbs of various root types are located at the end of this chapter.

2 Regular (sound) triliteral root

These are examples of verbs that have sound triliteral roots:

to prefer	faDDal-a/yu-faDDil-u	فَضَّلَ / يُفَضِّلُ
to arrange	rattab-a/yu-rattib-u	رتَّبَ / يرتِّب
to clean	naZZaf-a/yu-naZZif-u	نظَّفَ / يُنظِّفُ
to appreciate	qaddar-a/yu-qaddir-u	قدَّرَ / يُقدِّر

3 Geminate (doubled) root Form II

Geminate roots in Form II have the following stem patterns: $C_1aC_2C_2aC_2$- in the past tense and $yuC_1aC_2C_2iC_2$- in the present. The doubling of the medial consonant changes the geminate root in Form II so that it inflects as a regular Form II, that is, there is no stem shift as there is in Form I geminates. For example:

to cause	sabbab-a/yu-sabbib-u	سبَّبَ / يسبِّب
to decide, determine	qarrar-a/ yu-qarrir-u	قرَّر / يُقرِّر
to criticize	naddad-a/yu-naddid-u	ندَّد / يندِّد
to analyze	Hallal-a/yu-Hallil-u	حلَّلَ / يُحلِّل

4 Hamzated roots in Form II

A *hamza* may occur in the first, second, or third position in the triliteral root. Depending on its position, and the surrounding vowels, the *hamza* may have to change its "seat" when the verb inflects for person and tense in Form II.

4.1 Initial *hamza*

Hamza-initial verbs in Form II have *'alif* as the *hamza* seat in the past tense, and *waaw* as the *hamza* seat in the present tense. The *hamza* seat is determined by its position in the word, according to the orthographical rules for *hamza* described in Chapter 2, section 3.3. In Form II verbs, initial *hamza* shifts from word-initial position in the past tense stem to word-medial position in the present tense stem and is influenced by the *Damma* of the present tense subject-marking prefix so that its seat shifts from *'alif* to *waaw*.

to delay	'ajjal-a/yu-'ajjil-u	أجَّلَ / يُؤجِّلُ
to establish, found	'assas-a/yu-'assis-u	أسَّسَ / يُؤسِّسُ
to affirm	'akkad-a/yu-'akkid-u	أكَّدَ / يُؤكِّد
to affect	'aththar-a/yu-'aththir-u	أثَّر / يُؤثِّر

4.2 Medial *hamza*

The seat for medial *hamza* shifts from *ʾalif* in the past tense to *yaaʾ* in the present tense (because of the shift of stem vowel from *fatHa* to *kasra*).

to appoint as head   *raʾʾas-a/ yu-raʾʾis-u*   رأَّس / يُرَئِّس

4.3 Final *hamza*

The seat for final *hamza* in Form II, as in other forms, shifts according to the rules for word-final *hamza*; note that certain inflectional suffixes extend the word length, and therefore the seat for *hamza* is affected (e.g., *hannaʾ-uu-haa* هنّؤوها 'they congratulated her').

to free	*barraʾ-a/yu-barriʾ-u*	برّأ / يبرّئ
to congratulate	*hannaʾ-a/yu-hanniʾ-u*	هنّأ / يهنّئ
to hide	*xabbaʾ-a/yu-xabbiʾ-u*	خبّأ / يخبّئ
to heat, warm	*daffaʾ-a/yu-daffiʾ-u*	دفّأ / يدفّئ

5 Assimilated roots in Form II

Assimilated roots, where the first radical is either *waaw* or *yaaʾ*, are inflected as sound roots in Form II; the *waaw* or *yaaʾ* remains stable in both tenses.

to sign, endorse	*waqqaʿ-a/yu-waqqiʿ-u*	وقّع / يوقّع
to stop, halt	*waqqaf-a/yu-waqqif-u*	وقّف / يوقّف

6 Hollow roots in Form II

Hollow roots behave as sound roots in Form II, the *waaw* or *yaaʾ* that is the second radical functions as a stable consonant.

to create	*kawwan-a/yu-kawwin-u*	كوّن / يكوّن
to change	*ghayyar-a/yu-ghayyir-u*	غيّر / يغيّر
to photograph	*Sawwar-a/yu-Sawwir-u*	صوّر / يصوّر
to appoint	*ʿayyan-a/yu-ʿayyin-u*	عيّن / يعيّن

7 Defective roots in Form II

Defective roots, where the final radical is either *waaw* or *yaaʾ*, behave as *-aa/-ii* verbs in Form II. They depend on the stem vowel for the nature of the final radical, and the stem vowel is consistently /a/ in the past tense and /i/ in the present tense.

to cover	ghaTTaa/yu-ghaTTii	غطّى / يُغَطّي
to pray	Sallaa/yu-Sallii	صلّى / يُصَلّي
to sing	ghannaa/yu-ghannii	غنّى / يُغَنّي
to sacrifice	DaHHaa/yu-DaHHii	ضحّى / يُضَحّي

8 Doubly weak roots in Form II

These roots have two forms of weakness which may occur at any point in the root.

8.1 Hamzated and defective

| to carry out; to perform (s.th.) | 'addaa/yu-'addii | أدّى / يُؤَدّي |

8.2 Hamzated and hollow

| to help, aid (s.o. or s.th.) | 'ayyad-a/yu-'ayyid-u | أيّد / يُؤَيِّد |

8.3 Hollow and defective

| to greet; keep alive; grant long life | Hayyaa/yu-Hayyii | حيّى / يُحَيّي |

9 Examples of Form II verbs in context

الله يسلّمك.
allaah-u **yu-sallim-u-ka**.
(May) God **keep you safe**.

يهنّئ الرئيس الجديد.	نرحّب بكم.	ضحّيتم كثيراً.
yu-hanni'-u l-ra'iis-a l-jadiid-a.	*nu-raHHib-u* bi-kum.	*DaHHay-tum* kathiir-an.
He **congratulates** the new president.	We **welcome** you.	You (pl.) **have sacrificed** much.

أصدر بياناً ندّد فيه باستمرار الاحتلال.
'aSdar-a bayaan-an **naddad-a** fii-hi bi-stimraar-i l-iHtilaal-i.
He issued a statement in which **he criticized** the continuation of occupation.

10 Form II verbal nouns

Verbal nouns from Form II most often have the form *taf'iil* تفعيل; occasionally *taf'iila* تفعيلة.[3] Variations on Form II verbal nouns also include *taf'aal* تفعال or *tif'aal* تفعال and *taf'ila* تَفعِلة.

---

[3] For an extensive list of Form II verbal noun variants in Classical Arabic see Wright 1967, I:115–16.

10.1 Sound/regular root

arrangement	*tartiib*	تَرْتيب			
reminder; souvenir	*tadhkaar*	تَذْكار	experiment	*tajriba*	تَجْرِبَة

10.2 Geminate root

repetition	*takraar*	تَكْرار	renewal	*tajdiid*	تَجْديد

10.3 Hamzated root

founding	*ta'siis*	تَأْسيس	visa	*ta'shiira*	تَأْشيرة
congratulating	*tahni'a*	تَهْنِئَة	heating	*tadfi'a*	تَدْفِئَة

10.4 Assimilated root

unification	*tawHiid*	تَوْحيد	clarification	*tawDiiH*	تَوْضيح

10.5 Hollow root

creation	*takwiin*	تَكْوين	appointing	*ta'yiin*	تَعْيين
photographing	*taSwiir*	تَصْوير	change	*taghyiir*	تَغْيير

10.6 Defective root

naming	*tasmiya*	تَسْمِيَة	covering	*taghtiya*	تَغْطِيَة

10.7 Doubly weak

Here are a few examples of doubly weak Form II verbal nouns.

10.7.1 Hamzated and defective

carrying out; performing	*ta'diya*	تَأْدِيَة

10.7.2 Hamzated and hollow

assistance	*ta'yiid*	تَأْييد

10.7.3 Hollow and defective

greeting, salutation	*taHiyya*	تَحِيَّة

10.8 Borrowing from Form I

Occasionally a Form II verb uses a verbal noun derived from Form I:

singing	*ghinaa'*	غِناء	praying, prayer	*Salaat*	صَلاة

10.9 Examples of Form II verbal nouns in context

تدفئة مركزيّة
tadfiʾat-un markaziyyat-un
central **heating**

تقرير مصيره
taqriir-u maSiir-i-hi
self-determination ('**deciding** its
  future')

تعيين اللواء مديراً للدائرة
taʿyiin-u l-liwaaʾ-i mudiir-an li-l-daaʾirat-i
appointing the general as director of the
  department

التغييرات السياسيّة
al-taghyiiraat-u l-siyaasiiyyat-u
political **changes**

11 Form II participles

Form II participles occur as nouns and as adjectives. Examples are provided wherever possible.

11.1 Form II active participle (AP): *mufaʿʿil* مُفَعِّل

11.1.1 Sound/regular root

coordinator;	*munassiq*	مُنَسِّق	smuggler	*muharrib*	مُهَرِّب
organizer					
inspector	*mufattish*	مُفَتِّش	drug/s	*muxaddir/-aat*	مُخَدِّر / مُخَدِّرات

11.1.2 Geminate root

| editor | *muHarrir* | مُحَرِّر | analyst | *muHallil* | مُحَلِّل |

11.1.3 Hamzated root

| muezzin | *muʾadhdhin* | مُؤَذِّن | congratulating | *muhanniʾ* | مُهَنِّئ |

11.1.4 Assimilated root

| connecting | *muwaSSil* | مُوَصِّل |

11.1.5 Hollow root

| distinctive | *mumayyiz* | مُمَيِّز | creator; | *mukawwin* | مُكَوِّن |
| | | | component | | |

11.1.6 Defective root

The active participle of defective roots is inflected as a defective noun or adjective (declension six) and ends with the defective marker of *kasratayn*:

| praying[4] | *muSall-in* | مُصَلٍّ | singer/singing | *mughann-in* | مُغَنٍّ |

[4] Also, 'person in prayer.'

11.1.7 Examples of Form II active participles in context

في عمر مبكّر   منسّق نشاطات الأمم المتّحدة

*fii ʿumr-in **mubakkir-in***   ***munassiq-u** nashaaTaat-i l-ʾumam-i*
at an **early** age   *l-muttaHidat-i*
                      the coordinator of UN activities

مهرّبو المخدّرات   محلّل الشؤون السياسيّة العسكريّة

***muharrib-uu** l-mukhaddir-aat*   ***muHallil-u** l-shuʾuun-i l-siyaasiyyat-i*
drug smugglers   *l-ʿaskariyyat-i*
  (smugglers of drugs)   political-military affairs **analyst**

منظّمة الأقطار العربيّة المصدّرة للنفط

*munaZZamat-u l-ʾaqTaar-i l-ʿarabiyyat-i **l-muSaddirat-i** li-l-nafT-i*
the organization of Arab oil-**exporting** countries

11.2 Form II passive participle (PP): *mufaʿʿal* مُفَعَّل

11.2.1 Sound/regular root

volume; tome	*mujallad*	مُجَلَّد	complicated	*muʿaqqad*	مُعَقَّد
triangle	*muthallath*	مُثَلَّث	cubic; cubed	*mukaʿʿab*	مُكَعَّب
square	*murabbaʿ*	مُرَبَّع	armed	*musallaH*	مُسَلَّح

12.2 Assimilated root

employee	*muwaZZaf*	مُوَظَّف	successful; lucky	*muwaffaq*	مُوَفَّق

12.3 Geminate root

shattered	*mufakkak*	مُفَكَّك	set, delineated	*muHaddad*	مُحَدَّد

12.4 Hamzated root

nationalized	*muʾammam*	مُؤَمَّم	foundation	*muʾassassa*	مُؤَسَّسَة

12.5 Hollow root

illustrated	*muSawwar*	مُصَوَّر	appointed, designated	*muʿayyan*	مُعَيَّن

12.6 Defective root

The passive participle of defective roots ends with *ʾalif maqSuura* and is inflected as an indeclinable noun or adjective (declension seven).

educated, raised; preserves, jam	*murabban*	مُرَبَّى	covered	*mughaTTan*	مُغَطَّى

11.2.7 Examples of Form II passive participles in context

مُعجَم مُفَصَّل	القوّات المسلّحة
*muˤjam-un **mufaSSal-un***	*al-quwwaat-u **l-musallaHat-u***
a **detailed** lexicon	the **armed** forces
في موعد مُحدَّد	مصالح مؤمَّمة
*fii mawˤid-in **muHaddad-in***	*maSaaliH-u **muˀammamat-un***
at a **set** time	**nationalized** interests/assets
قاموس مصوَّر	السفير المعيَّن
*qaamuus-un **muSawwar-un***	*al-safiir-u **l-muˤayyan-u***
an **illustrated** dictionary	the ambassador-**designate**

Form II   Sound root: رتَّب ، يُرتِّب   *AP:* مُرتِّب   *PP:* مُرتَّب   *VN:* تَرتيب   'to arrange'

	Active	Active	Active	Active	Active	Passive	Passive
	Perfect	Imperfect	Imperfect	Imperfect	Imperfect	Perfect	Imperfect
		Indicative	Subjunctive	Jussive	Imperative		
أنا	رتَّبتُ	أُرتِّبُ	أُرتِّبَ	أُرتِّبْ		رُتِّبتُ	أُرتَّبُ
أنتَ	رتَّبتَ	تُرتِّبُ	تُرتِّبَ	تُرتِّبْ	رتِّبْ	رُتِّبتَ	تُرتَّبُ
أنتِ	رتَّبتِ	تُرتِّبين	تُرتِّبي	تُرتِّبي	رتِّبي	رُتِّبتِ	تُرتَّبين
أنتما—m/f	رتَّبتُما	تُرتِّبان	تُرتِّبا	تُرتِّبا	رتِّبا	رُتِّبتُما	تُرتَّبان
هو	رتَّبَ	يُرتِّبُ	يُرتِّبَ	يُرتِّبْ		رُتِّبَ	يُرتَّبُ
هي	رتَّبتْ	تُرتِّبُ	تُرتِّبَ	تُرتِّبْ		رُتِّبتْ	تُرتَّبُ
هما—m	رتَّبا	يُرتِّبان	يُرتِّبا	يُرتِّبا		رُتِّبا	يُرتَّبان
هما—f	رتَّبتا	تُرتِّبان	تُرتِّبا	تُرتِّبا		رُتِّبتا	تُرتَّبان
نحن	رتَّبنا	نُرتِّبُ	نُرتِّبَ	نُرتِّبْ		رُتِّبنا	نُرتَّبُ
أنتم	رتَّبتُم	تُرتِّبون	تُرتِّبوا	تُرتِّبوا	رتِّبوا	رُتِّبتُم	تُرتَّبون
أنتن	رتَّبتُنَّ	تُرتِّبنَ	تُرتِّبنَ	تُرتِّبنَ	رتِّبنَ	رُتِّبتُنَّ	تُرتَّبنَ
هم	رتَّبوا	يُرتِّبون	يُرتِّبوا	يُرتِّبوا		رُتِّبوا	يُرتَّبون
هن	رتَّبنَ	يُرتِّبنَ	يُرتِّبنَ	يُرتِّبنَ		رُتِّبنَ	يُرتَّبنَ

Form II Geminate root: قرر ، يقرر AP: مقرِّر PP: مقرَّر VN: تقرير ، قرار 'to decide'

	Active	Active	Active	Active	Active	Passive	Passive
	Perfect	Imperfect	Imperfect	Imperfect	Imperfect	Perfect	Imperfect
		Indicative	Subjunctive	Jussive	Imperative		
أنا	قرّرت	أقرِّر	أقرِّر	أقرِّر		قرِّرت	أقرَّر
أنتَ	قرّرت	تقرِّر	تقرِّر	تقرِّر	قرِّر	قرِّرت	تقرَّر
أنتِ	قرّرت	تقرِّرين	تقرِّري	تقرِّري	قرِّري	قرِّرت	تقرَّرين
أنتُما—m/f	قرّرتما	تقرِّرانِ	تقرِّرا	تقرِّرا	قرِّرا	قرِّرتما	تقرَّرانِ
هو	قرّر	يقرِّر	يقرِّر	يقرِّر		قرِّر	يقرَّر
هي	قرّرت	تقرِّر	تقرِّر	تقرِّر		قرِّرت	تقرَّر
هما—m	قرّرا	يقرِّرانِ	يقرِّرا	يقرِّرا		قرِّرا	يقرَّرانِ
هما—f	قرّرتا	تقرِّرانِ	تقرِّرا	تقرِّرا		قرِّرتا	تقرَّرانِ
نحن	قرّرنا	نقرِّر	نقرِّر	نقرِّر		قرِّرنا	نقرَّر
أنتم	قرّرتم	تقرِّرون	تقرِّروا	تقرِّروا	قرِّروا	قرِّرتم	تقرَّرون
أنتن	قرّرتن	تقرِّرن	تقرِّرن	تقرِّرن	قرِّرن	قرِّرتن	تقرَّرن
هم	قرّروا	يقرِّرون	يقرِّروا	يقرِّروا		قرِّروا	يقرَّرون
هن	قرّرن	يقرِّرن	يقرِّرن	يقرِّرن		قرِّرن	يقرَّرن

Form II **hamza**-initial root: أجَّل ، يُؤَجِّل   AP: مُؤَجِّل   PP: مُؤَجَّل   VN: تَأْجيل 'to delay'

	Active	Active	Active	Active	Active	Passive	Passive
	Perfect	Imperfect	Imperfect	Imperfect	Imperfect	Perfect	Imperfect
		Indicative	Subjunctive	Jussive	Imperative		
أنا	أجَّلْتُ	أُوَجِّلُ	أُوَجِّلَ	أُوَجِّلْ		أُجِّلْتُ	أُوَجَّلُ
أنْتَ	أجَّلْتَ	تُوَجِّلُ	تُوَجِّلَ	تُوَجِّلْ	أجِّلْ	أُجِّلْتَ	تُوَجَّلُ
أنْتِ	أجَّلْتِ	تُوَجِّلينَ	تُوَجِّلي	تُوَجِّلي	أجِّلي	أُجِّلْتِ	تُوَجَّلينَ
أنْتُما—m/f	أجَّلْتُما	تُوَجِّلانِ	تُوَجِّلا	تُوَجِّلا	أجِّلا	أُجِّلْتُما	تُوَجَّلانِ
هُوَ	أجَّلَ	يُوَجِّلُ	يُوَجِّلَ	يُوَجِّلْ		أُجِّلَ	يُوَجَّلُ
هِيَ	أجَّلَتْ	تُوَجِّلُ	تُوَجِّلَ	تُوَجِّلْ		أُجِّلَتْ	تُوَجَّلُ
هُما—m	أجَّلا	يُوَجِّلانِ	يُوَجِّلا	يُوَجِّلا		أُجِّلا	يُوَجَّلانِ
هُما—f	أجَّلَتا	تُوَجِّلانِ	تُوَجِّلا	تُوَجِّلا		أُجِّلَتا	تُوَجَّلانِ
نَحْنُ	أجَّلْنا	نُوَجِّلُ	نُوَجِّلَ	نُوَجِّلْ		أُجِّلْنا	نُوَجَّلُ
أنْتُم	أجَّلْتُمْ	تُوَجِّلونَ	تُوَجِّلوا	تُوَجِّلوا	أجِّلوا	أُجِّلْتُمْ	تُوَجَّلونَ
أنْتُنَّ	أجَّلْتُنَّ	تُوَجِّلْنَ	تُوَجِّلْنَ	تُوَجِّلْنَ	أجِّلْنَ	أُجِّلْتُنَّ	تُوَجَّلْنَ
هُم	أجَّلوا	يُوَجِّلونَ	يُوَجِّلوا	يُوَجِّلوا		أُجِّلوا	يُوَجَّلونَ
هُنَّ	أجَّلْنَ	يُوَجِّلْنَ	يُوَجِّلْنَ	يُوَجِّلْنَ		أُجِّلْنَ	يُوَجَّلْنَ

*Form II **hamza**-final root:* هنّأ ، يهنّئ AP: مُهنّئ PP: مُهنّأ VN: تَهنِئَة *'to congratulate'*

	Active	Active	Active	Active	Active	Passive	Passive
	Perfect	Imperfect	Imperfect	Imperfect	Imperfect	Perfect	Imperfect
		Indicative	Subjunctive	Jussive	Imperative		
أنا	هنّأتُ	أُهنّئُ	أُهنّئَ	أُهنّئْ		هُنّئتُ	أُهنّأُ
أنتَ	هنّأتَ	تُهنّئُ	تُهنّئَ	تُهنّئْ	هنّئْ	هُنّئتَ	تُهنّأُ
أنتِ	هنّأتِ	تُهنّئينَ	تُهنّئي	تُهنّئي	هنّئي	هُنّئتِ	تُهنّئينَ
أنتُما–m/f	هنّأتُما	تُهنّئانِ	تُهنّئا	تُهنّئا	هنّئا	هُنّئتُما	تُهنّآنِ
هو	هنّأ	يُهنّئُ	يُهنّئَ	يُهنّئْ		هُنّئَ	يُهنّأُ
هي	هنّأتْ	تُهنّئُ	تُهنّئَ	تُهنّئْ		هُنّئتْ	تُهنّأُ
هما–m	هنّآ	يُهنّئانِ	يُهنّئا	يُهنّئا		هُنّئا	يُهنّآنِ
هما–f	هنّأتا	تُهنّئانِ	تُهنّئا	تُهنّئا		هُنّئتا	تُهنّآنِ
نحن	هنّأنا	نُهنّئُ	نُهنّئَ	نُهنّئْ		هُنّئنا	نُهنّأُ
أنتم	هنّأتُمْ	تُهنّئونَ	تُهنّئوا	تُهنّئوا	هنّئوا	هُنّئتمْ	تُهنّؤونَ
أنتنّ	هنّأتنّ	تُهنّئنَ	تُهنّئنَ	تُهنّئنَ	هنّئنَ	هُنّئتنّ	تُهنّأنَ
هم	هنّؤوا	يُهنّئونَ	يُهنّئوا	يُهنّئوا		هُنّئوا	يُهنّؤونَ
هنّ	هنّأنَ	يُهنّئنَ	يُهنّئنَ	يُهنّئنَ		هُنّئنَ	يُهنّأنَ

Form II Defective root: غطَّى ، يُغَطِّي AP: مُغَطٍّ PP: مُغَطًى VN: تَغْطِية 'to cover'

	Active	Active	Active	Active	Active	Passive	Passive
	Perfect	Imperfect	Imperfect	Imperfect	Imperfect	Perfect	Imperfect
		Indicative	Subjunctive	Jussive	Imperative		
أنا	غَطَّيْتُ	أُغَطِّي	أُغَطِّيَ	أُغَطِّ		غُطِّيتُ	أُغَطَّى
أنْتَ	غَطَّيْتَ	تُغَطِّي	تُغَطِّيَ	تُغَطِّ	غَطِّ	غُطِّيتَ	تُغَطَّى
أنْتِ	غَطَّيْتِ	تُغَطِّينَ	تُغَطِّي	تُغَطِّي	غَطِّي	غُطِّيتِ	تُغَطَّيْنَ
أنْتُما–m/f	غَطَّيْتُما	تُغَطِّيانِ	تُغَطِّيا	تُغَطِّيا	غَطِّيا	غُطِّيتُما	تُغَطَّيانِ
هُوَ	غَطَّى	يُغَطِّي	يُغَطِّيَ	يُغَطِّ		غُطِّيَ	يُغَطَّى
هِيَ	غَطَّتْ	تُغَطِّي	تُغَطِّيَ	تُغَطِّ		غُطِّيتْ	تُغَطَّى
هُما–m	غَطَّيا	يُغَطِّيانِ	يُغَطِّيا	يُغَطِّيا		غُطِّيا	يُغَطَّيانِ
هُما–f	غَطَّتا	تُغَطِّيانِ	تُغَطِّيا	تُغَطِّيا		غُطِّيتا	تُغَطَّيانِ
نَحْنُ	غَطَّيْنا	نُغَطِّي	نُغَطِّيَ	نُغَطِّ		غُطِّيْنا	نُغَطَّى
أنْتُمْ	غَطَّيْتُمْ	تُغَطُّونَ	تُغَطُّوا	تُغَطُّوا	غَطُّوا	غُطِّيتُمْ	تُغَطَّوْنَ
أنْتُنَّ	غَطَّيْتُنَّ	تُغَطِّينَ	تُغَطِّينَ	تُغَطِّينَ	غَطِّينَ	غُطِّيتُنَّ	تُغَطَّيْنَ
هُمْ	غَطَّوْا	يُغَطُّونَ	يُغَطُّوا	يُغَطُّوا		غُطُّوا	يُغَطَّوْنَ
هُنَّ	غَطَّيْنَ	يُغَطِّينَ	يُغَطِّينَ	يُغَطِّينَ		غُطِّينَ	يُغَطَّيْنَ

24

Form III triliteral verb

1 Basic characteristics

1.1 Pattern: *faaᶜal-a* فاعَلَ / *yu-faaᶜil-u* يُفاعِل

Form III is augmented from Form I by insertion of the long vowel /aa/ after the first radical of the root. It has the basic stem patterns $C_1aaC_2aC_3$- in the past tense and -$C_1aaC_2iC_3$- in the present tense, maintaining the long vowel in both tenses.

1.2 Meaning

In terms of meaning, Form III often has the meaning of involving another person in the action. For this reason it is termed "associative." Related semantic modifications conveyed by this inflectional class include reciprocal action, repeated action, and attempted action.[1]

1.3 Transitivity

Form III verbs are usually transitive, but may occasionally be intransitive.

1.4 Inflection

A distinctive inflectional characteristic of Form III verbs is that the present tense subject-marker vowel is *Damma* and the present tense stem vowel is *kasra* (*yu-saaᶜid-u*).

2 Regular (sound) triliteral root

These verbs are examples of Form III sound triliteral roots:

to experience	*maaras-a/yu-maaris-u*	مارَسَ / يُمارِسُ
to defend	*daafaᶜ-a/yu-daafiᶜ-u*	دافَعَ / يُدافِعُ
to assist, help	*saaᶜad-a/yu-saaᶜid-u*	ساعَدَ / يُساعِدُ
to observe	*raaqab-a/yu-raaqib-u*	راقَبَ / يُراقِبُ

---

[1] For an extensive analysis of Form III and its semantic implications, see Fleisch 1979, II:288–301.

2.1 Associative meaning

Arabic Form III associative verbal concepts are often directly transitive whereas English would need to use the word "with" to indicate reciprocality or associativeness:

to correspond with (s.o.)	*raasal-a/yu-raasil-u*	راسَلَ / يُراسِلُ
to share with (s.o.)	*shaarak-a/yu-shaarik-u*	شارَكَ / يُشارِكُ
to deal with (s.o., s.th.)	*ʿaalaj-a/yu-ʿaalij-u*	عالَجَ / يُعالِجُ
to compete with (s.o.)	*saabaq-a/yu-saabiq-u*	سابَقَ / يُسابِقُ

3 Geminate (doubled) root Form III

It is rare to find geminate roots in Form III. The ones that do exist have two variant patterns: one where the identical consonants are written together with a *shadda* and one where they are written separately, with an intervening *fatHa*. The following stem patterns occur: $C_1aaC_2C_2$-a (*faaᶜᶜ-*) and $C_1aaC_2aC_2$-a (*faaᶜaᶜ-*) in the past tense, and yu-$C_1aaC_2C_2$- (*yu-faaᶜᶜ-* or yu-$C_1aaC_2iC_2$- (*yu-faaᶜiᶜ-*) in the present.[2]

to punish	*qaaSaS-a/yu-qaaSiS-u*	قاصَصَ / يُقاصِصُ

4 Hamzated roots in Form III

The *hamza* may occur in the first, second, or third position in the triliteral root. Depending on its position, and the surrounding vowels, the *hamza* may have to change its seat when the verb inflects for person and tense.

4.1 Initial *hamza*

In Form III, initial *hamza* merges with the long vowel *-aa* of the first syllable in the past tense and it written as one *ʾalif* with *madda*. In the present tense, initial *hamza* sits on a *waaw* seat because it is preceded by the *Damma* of the person-marking prefix:

to censure, to blame	*ʾaaxadh-a/yu-ʾaaxidh-u*	آخَذَ / يُؤاخِذُ
to consult	*ʾaamar-a/yu-ʾaamir-u*	آمَرَ / يُؤامِرُ

4.2 Medial *hamza*

The medial *hamza* sits aloof in the past tense of Form III.[3] In the present tense it sits on a *yaaʾ* seat because it is followed by a *kasra*.

---

[2] See Wright 1967, I:71 for further discussion of this variation.
[3] This is because it is situated after a long vowel /aa/ and before a short vowel /a/. It would have an *ʾalif* seat, but the general rule is that two *ʾalifs* cannot follow each other in Arabic script, so the *hamza* here floats aloof.

to match; to be suitable for	laaʾam-a/yu-laaʾim-u	لاءَمَ / يُلائِمُ
to question, interrogate	saaʾal-a/yu-saaʾil-u	ساءَلَ / يُسائِلُ

4.3 Final *hamza*

Final *hamza* sits on an *ʾalif* seat in the past tense and on a *yaaʾ* seat in the present tense, but because it is the final consonant in the stem, the seat of the *hamza* may shift with inflectional suffixes.

to surprise	faajaʾ-a/yu-faajiʾ-u	فاجَأَ / يُفاجِئُ
to reward; to be commensurate with	kaafaʾ-a/yu-kaafiʾ-u	كافَأَ / يُكافِئُ

5 Assimilated roots in Form III

Assimilated roots, where the first radical is either *waaw* or *yaaʾ*, are inflected as sound roots in Form III; the *waaw* or *yaaʾ* is stable.

to agree with	waafaq-a/yu-waafiq-u	وافَقَ / يُوافِقُ
to face, confront	waajah-a/yu-waajih-u	واجَهَ / يُواجِهُ

6 Hollow roots in Form III

Hollow roots behave as strong roots in Form III, the *waaw* or *yaaʾ* that is the second radical functions as a consonant.

to answer	jaawab-a/yu-jaawib-u	جاوَبَ / يُجاوِبُ
to try, attempt	Haawal-a/yu-Haawil-u	حاوَلَ / يُحاوِلُ
to consult with	shaawar-a/yu-shaawir-u	شاوَرَ / يُشاوِرُ
to be gentle with	laayan-a/yu-laayin-u	لايَنَ / يُلايِنُ

7 Defective roots in Form III

Defective roots, where the final radical is either *waaw* or *yaaʾ*, behave as -aa/-ii verbs in Form III. They depend on the stem vowel for the nature of the final radical, and the stem vowel is consistently /a/ in the past tense and /i/ in the present tense.

to call; summon; invite	naadaa/yu-naadii	نادى / يُنادي
to compete (with)	baaraa/yu-baarii	بارى / يُباري
to endure, to suffer (s.th.)	ʿaanaa/yu-ʿaanii	عانى / يُعاني

8 Doubly weak roots in Form III

Hollow and defective:

to be equivalent to; to equalize	*saawaa/yu-saawii*	ساوى / يُساوي

9 Examples of Form III verbs in context

تحاضر في جامعات مختلفة.
tu-HaaDir-u fii jaamiʿaat-in muxtalifat-in.
She lectures at different universities.

سيسافر غداً.
sa-yu-saafir-u ghad-an.
He will travel tomorrow.

في كتبه يعالج الأوضاع السياسيّة في الشرق الأوسط.
fii kutub-i-hi *yu-ʿaalij-u* l-ʾawDaaʿ-a l-siyaasiyyat-a fii l-sharq-i l-ʾawsaT-i.
In his books **he deals with** political conditions in the Middle East.

سيقاصصونه
sa-yu-qaaSiS-uuna-hu.
They will punish him.

يعاني من التمزّق.
yu-ʿaanii min-a l-tamazzuq-i.
It suffers from fragmentation.

10 Form III verbal noun

The verbal noun of Form III verbs takes two basic forms: *mufaaʿala* and *fiʿaal*. Usually, one of these verbal nouns is used for a particular Form III verb, but occasionally, a verb may use both of these Form III verbal nouns, with either equivalent or slightly different meanings. For example:

Form: Form III *Haawar-a* 'talk, debate, argue'

argument, dispute	*muHaawara*	مُحاوَرة	conversation, dialogue	*Hiwaar*	حِوار

Form: Form III *kaafaH-a* 'to combat, fight, struggle'

confrontation, battle	*mukaafaHa*	مُكافَحة	fight, battle, strife	*kifaaH*	كِفاح

For the most part, however, one of these two verbal nouns suffices for a Form III verb. Both of these verbal noun patterns take the sound feminine plural.

10.1 Sound/regular root

mufaaʿala مُفاعَلَة

lecture	*muHaaDara*	مُحاضَرة	debate	*munaaqasha*	مُناقَشة
boycott	*muqaaTaʿa*	مُقاطَعة	initiative	*mubaadara*	مُبادَرة
review	*muraajaʿa*	مُراجَعة	conversation	*mukaalama*	مُكالَمة

fiʿaal فِعال

struggle	*niDaal*	نِضال	struggle	*jihaad*	جِهاد
combat	*kifaaH*	كِفاح	defense	*difaaʿ*	دِفاع

10.2 Hamzated root

10.2.1 *Hamza* initial
The *hamza* sits on a *waaw* seat.

censure, blame	*muʾaaxadha*	مُؤاخَذَة	consultation; plotting	*muʾaamara*	مُؤامَرَة

10.2.2 *Hamza* medial
In these verbal nouns, the *hamza* "floats" aloof by itself and has no chair.

suitability; appropriateness	*mulaaʾama*	مُلاءَمَة
questioning, interrogation	*musaaʾala*	مُساءَلَة

10.2.3 *Hamza* final
In these verbal nouns, *hamza* sits on ʾ*alif*.

surprise	*mufaajaʾa*	مُفاجَأة	reward	*mukaafaʾa*	مُكافَأة

10.3 Assimilated root
The assimilated root behaves as a sound root in the Form III verbal noun.

agreement	*muwaafaqa*	مُوافَقَة	balance	*muwaazana*	مُوازَنَة

10.4 Hollow root
The hollow root behaves as a sound root in the Form III verbal noun.

attempt	*muHaawala*	مُحاوَلَة	vicinity	*jiwaar*	جِوار
negotiation	*mufaawaDa*	مُفاوَضَة	dialogue; conversation	*Hiwaar*	حِوار

10.5 Defective root
In verbal nouns of defective Form III verbs, the second radical is followed by an ʾ*alif* and *taaʾ marbuuTa*.

legal defense	*muHaamaat*	مُحاماة	suffering, enduring	*muʿaanaat*	مُعاناة
equality	*musaawaat*	مُساواة	competition, match	*mubaaraat*	مُباراة

10.6 Examples of Form III verbal nouns in context

مكالمة تليفونيّة
mukaalamat-un tiliifuuniyyat-un
a telephone **conversation**

محافظة صنعاء
muHaafaZat-u Sanʿaaʾ-a
the **province** of Sanaa

بمناسبة إعادة تعيين الشيخ
bi-munaasabat-i ʾiʿaadat-i taʿyiin-i l-shaykh-i
on the **occasion** of the re-appointment of
  the sheikh

سباق الخيل
sibaaq-u l-xayl-i
horse **racing**

وزارة الدفاع
wizaarat-u l-difaaʿ-i
ministry of **defense**

لا مؤاخذة !
laa muʾaaxadhat-a!
No **offense** [intended]!

بعد محاولات عدّة فاشلة
baʿd-a muHaawalaat-in ʿiddat-in faashilat-in
after several failed **attempts**

صراع الحضارات
Siraaʿ-u l-HaDaaraat-i
culture wars
  ('**the struggle** of cultures')

11 Form III participles
Form III participles occur as nouns and as adjectives. In some cases they occur in both functions.

11.1 Form III active participle (AP): *mufaaʿil* مُفاعِل

11.1.1 Sound/regular root

lecturer	*muHaaDir*	مُحاضِر	similar	*mumaathil*	مُماثِل
assistant	*musaaʿid*	مُساعِد	contemporary	*muʿaaSir*	مُعاصِر
farmer	*muzaariʿ*	مُزارِع	adjacent	*mutaaxim*	مُتاخِم
observer	*muraaqib*	مُراقِب	appropriate	*munaasib*	مُناسِب

11.1.2 Hamzated root
The final root *hamza* sits on a *yaaʾ* because it is preceded by *kasra*.

| surprising | *mufaajiʾ* | مُفاجِئ |

11.1.3 Assimilated root
Assimilated roots behave as sound roots in the Form III AP.

| citizen | *muwaaTin* | مُواطِن |

11.1.4 Hollow root

Hollow roots also behave as sound roots in the Form III AP.

on duty	*munaawib*	مُناوِب
neutral	*muHaayid*	مُحايِد
neighboring, adjacent	*mujaawir*	مُجاوِر

11.1.5 Defective root

The Form III defective root AP falls into declension six, the defective declension, where the indefinite form of the noun shows the final root consonant as two kasras in the nominative and genitive cases. See Chapter 7, section 5.4.3.

lawyer	*muHaamin*	مُحامٍ

11.1.6 Examples of Form III APs in context

الفُنون المُعاصِرة
al-funuun-u l-muʿaaSirat-u
contemporary arts

الدُوَل المُعارِضة
al-duwal-u l-muʿaariDat-u
the **opposing** states

الضابِط المُناوِب
al-DaabiT-u l-munaawib-u
the officer **on duty**

دولة مُحايِدة
dawlat-un muHaayidat-un
a **neutral** country

على المَقعَد المُجاوِر
ʿalaa l-maqʿad-i l-mujaawir-i.
on the **adjacent** seat

مُحامون أمريكيّون
muHaam-uuna ʾamriikiyy-uuna
American **lawyers**

11.2 Form III passive participle (PP): *mufaaʿal* مُفاعَل

This particular type of passive participle is infrequent, but does exist:

blessed	*mubaarak*	مُبارَك

شهر رمضان المبارك
shahr-u ramaDaan-a l-mubaarak-u
the **blessed** month of Ramadan

Form III Sound root: ساعَدَ ، يُساعِدُ AP: مُساعِد PP: مُساعَد VN: مُساعَدة 'to help'

	Active Perfect	Active Imperfect Indicative	Active Imperfect Subjunctive	Active Imperfect Jussive	Active Imperfect Imperative	Passive Perfect	Passive Imperfect
أنا	ساعَدْتُ	أُساعِدُ	أُساعِدَ	أُساعِدْ		سوعِدْتُ	أُساعَدُ
أنتَ	ساعَدْتَ	تُساعِدُ	تُساعِدَ	تُساعِدْ	ساعِدْ	سوعِدْتَ	تُساعَدُ
أنتِ	ساعَدْتِ	تُساعِدينَ	تُساعِدي	تُساعِدي	ساعِدي	سوعِدْتِ	تُساعَدينَ
أنتُما m/f	ساعَدْتُما	تُساعِدانِ	تُساعِدا	تُساعِدا	ساعِدا	سوعِدْتُما	تُساعَدانِ
هو	ساعَدَ	يُساعِدُ	يُساعِدَ	يُساعِدْ		سوعِدَ	يُساعَدُ
هي	ساعَدَتْ	تُساعِدُ	تُساعِدَ	تُساعِدْ		سوعِدَتْ	تُساعَدُ
هما m	ساعَدا	يُساعِدانِ	يُساعِدا	يُساعِدا		سوعِدا	يُساعَدانِ
هما f	ساعَدَتا	تُساعِدانِ	تُساعِدا	تُساعِدا		سوعِدَتا	تُساعَدانِ
نحن	ساعَدْنا	نُساعِدُ	نُساعِدَ	نُساعِدْ		سوعِدْنا	نُساعَدُ
أنتم	ساعَدْتُمْ	تُساعِدونَ	تُساعِدوا	تُساعِدوا	ساعِدوا	سوعِدْتُمْ	تُساعَدونَ
أنتنّ	ساعَدْتُنَّ	تُساعِدْنَ	تُساعِدْنَ	تُساعِدْنَ	ساعِدْنَ	سوعِدْتُنَّ	تُساعَدْنَ
هم	ساعَدوا	يُساعِدونَ	يُساعِدوا	يُساعِدوا		سوعِدوا	يُساعَدونَ
هنّ	ساعَدْنَ	يُساعِدْنَ	يُساعِدْنَ	يُساعِدْنَ		سوعِدْنَ	يُساعَدْنَ

Form III hamza-final root: فاجَأَ، يُفاجِئُ AP: مُفاجِئٌ PP: مُفاجَأٌ VN: مُفاجَأَة 'to surprise'

	Active	Active	Active	Active	Active	Passive	Passive
	Perfect	Imperfect	Imperfect	Imperfect	Imperfect	Perfect	Imperfect
		Indicative	Subjunctive	Jussive	Imperative		
أنا	فاجَأْتُ	أُفاجِئُ	أُفاجِئَ	أُفاجِئْ		فوجِئْتُ	أُفاجَأُ
أنْتَ	فاجَأْتَ	تُفاجِئُ	تُفاجِئَ	تُفاجِئْ	فاجِئْ	فوجِئْتَ	تُفاجَأُ
أنْتِ	فاجَأْتِ	تُفاجِئِينَ	تُفاجِئِي	تُفاجِئِي	فاجِئِي	فوجِئْتِ	تُفاجَئِينَ
أنْتُما—m/f	فاجَأْتُما	تُفاجِئانِ	تُفاجِئا	تُفاجِئا	فاجِئا	فوجِئْتُما	تُفاجَآنِ
هُوَ	فاجَأَ	يُفاجِئُ	يُفاجِئَ	يُفاجِئْ		فوجِئَ	يُفاجَأُ
هِيَ	فاجَأَتْ	تُفاجِئُ	تُفاجِئَ	تُفاجِئْ		فوجِئَتْ	تُفاجَأُ
هُما—m	فاجَآ	يُفاجِئانِ	يُفاجِئا	يُفاجِئا		فوجِئا	يُفاجَآنِ
هُما—f	فاجَأَتا	تُفاجِئانِ	تُفاجِئا	تُفاجِئا		فوجِئَتا	تُفاجَآنِ
نَحْنُ	فاجَأْنا	نُفاجِئُ	نُفاجِئَ	نُفاجِئْ		فوجِئْنا	نُفاجَأُ
أنْتُم	فاجَأْتُمْ	تُفاجِئُونَ	تُفاجِئُوا	تُفاجِئُوا	فاجِئُوا	فوجِئْتُمْ	تُفاجَؤُونَ
أنْتُنَّ	فاجَأْتُنَّ	تُفاجِئْنَ	تُفاجِئْنَ	تُفاجِئْنَ	فاجِئْنَ	فوجِئْتُنَّ	تُفاجَأْنَ
هُم	فاجَؤُوا	يُفاجِئُونَ	يُفاجِئُوا	يُفاجِئُوا		فوجِئُوا	يُفاجَؤُونَ
هُنَّ	فاجَأْنَ	يُفاجِئْنَ	يُفاجِئْنَ	يُفاجِئْنَ		فوجِئْنَ	يُفاجَأْنَ

Form III Assimilated root: واجَهَ ، يُواجِه AP: مُواجِه PP: مُواجَه VN: مُواجَهَة *'to face, confront'*

	Active	Active	Active	Active	Active	Passive	Passive
	Perfect	Imperfect	Imperfect	Imperfect	Imperfect	Perfect	Imperfect
		Indicative	Subjunctive	Jussive	Imperative		
أنا	واجَهْتُ	أُواجِهُ	أُواجِهَ	أُواجِهْ		وُوجِهْتُ	أُواجَهُ
أنْتَ	واجَهْتَ	تُواجِهُ	تُواجِهَ	تُواجِهْ	واجِهْ	وُوجِهْتَ	تُواجَهُ
أنْتِ	واجَهْتِ	تُواجِهِين	تُواجِهِي	تُواجِهِي	واجِهِي	وُوجِهْتِ	تُواجَهِين
أنْتُما—m/f	واجَهْتُما	تُواجِهانِ	تُواجِها	تُواجِها	واجِها	وُوجِهْتُما	تُواجَهانِ
هُوَ	واجَهَ	يُواجِهُ	يُواجِهَ	يُواجِهْ		وُوجِهَ	يُواجَهُ
هِيَ	واجَهَتْ	تُواجِهُ	تُواجِهَ	تُواجِهْ		وُوجِهَتْ	تُواجَهُ
هُما—m	واجَها	يُواجِهانِ	يُواجِها	يُواجِها		وُوجِها	يُواجَهانِ
هُما—f	واجَهَتا	تُواجِهانِ	تُواجِها	تُواجِها		وُوجِهَتا	تُواجَهانِ
نَحْنُ	واجَهْنا	نُواجِهُ	نُواجِهَ	نُواجِهْ		وُوجِهْنا	نُواجَهُ
أنْتُم	واجَهْتُم	تُواجِهُون	تُواجِهُوا	تُواجِهُوا	واجِهُوا	وُوجِهْتُم	تُواجَهُون
أنْتُنَّ	واجَهْتُنَّ	تُواجِهْنَ	تُواجِهْنَ	تُواجِهْنَ	واجِهْنَ	وُوجِهْتُنَّ	تُواجَهْنَ
هُم	واجَهُوا	يُواجِهُون	يُواجِهُوا	يُواجِهُوا		وُوجِهُوا	يُواجَهُون
هُنَّ	واجَهْنَ	يُواجِهْنَ	يُواجِهْنَ	يُواجِهْنَ		وُوجِهْنَ	يُواجَهْنَ

Form III Hollow root: حاوَلَ ، يُحاوِلُ   AP: مُحاوِل   PP: مُحاوَل   VN: مُحاوَلَة   *'to try'*

	Active	Active	Active	Active	Active	Passive	Passive
	Perfect	Imperfect	Imperfect	Imperfect	Imperfect	Perfect	Imperfect
		Indicative	Subjunctive	Jussive	Imperative		
أنا	حاوَلْتُ	أُحاوِلُ	أُحاوِلَ	أُحاوِلْ			
أنْتَ	حاوَلْتَ	تُحاوِلُ	تُحاوِلَ	تُحاوِلْ	حاوِلْ		
أنْتِ	حاوَلْتِ	تُحاوِلين	تُحاوِلي	تُحاوِلي	حاوِلي		
أنْتُما–m/f	حاوَلْتُما	تُحاوِلان	تُحاوِلا	تُحاوِلا	حاوِلا		
هُوَ	حاوَلَ	يُحاوِلُ	يُحاوِلَ	يُحاوِلْ		حوولَ	يُحاوَلُ
هِيَ	حاوَلَتْ	تُحاوِلُ	تُحاوِلَ	تُحاوِلْ		حوولَتْ	تُحاوَلُ
هُما–m	حاوَلا	يُحاوِلان	يُحاوِلا	يُحاوِلا			
هُما–f	حاوَلَتا	تُحاوِلان	تُحاوِلا	تُحاوِلا			
نَحْنُ	حاوَلنا	نُحاوِلُ	نُحاوِلَ	نُحاوِلْ			
أنْتُم	حاوَلْتُم	تُحاوِلونَ	تُحاوِلوا	تُحاوِلوا	حاوِلوا		
أنْتُنَّ	حاوَلْتُنَّ	تُحاوِلْنَ	تُحاوِلْنَ	تُحاوِلْنَ	حاوِلْنَ		
هُم	حاوَلوا	يُحاوِلونَ	يُحاوِلوا	يُحاوِلوا			
هُنَّ	حاوَلْنَ	يُحاوِلْنَ	يُحاوِلْنَ	يُحاوِلْنَ			

Form III Defective root: يُنادي ، نادى AP: مُنادٍ PP: مُنادى VN: مُناداة 'to call'

	Active	Active	Active	Active	Active	Passive	Passive
	Perfect	Imperfect	Imperfect	Imperfect	Imperfect	Perfect	Imperfect
		Indicative	Subjunctive	Jussive	Imperative		
أنا	نادَيْتُ	أُنادي	أُناديَ	أُنادِ		نوديتُ	أُنادى
أنْتَ	نادَيْتَ	تُنادي	تُناديَ	تُنادِ	نادِ	نوديتَ	تُنادى
أنْتِ	نادَيْتِ	تُنادين	تُنادي	تُنادي	نادي	نوديتِ	تُنادَيْنَ
أنْتُما—m/f	نادَيتُما	تُناديان	تُناديا	تُناديا	ناديا	نوديتُما	تُنادَيان
هُوَ	نادى	يُنادي	يُناديَ	يُنادِ		نودِيَ	يُنادى
هِيَ	نادَت	تُنادي	تُناديَ	تُنادِ		نودِيَتْ	تُنادى
هُما—m	ناديا	يُناديان	يُناديا	يُناديا		نودِيا	يُنادَيان
هُما—f	نادَتا	تُناديان	تُناديا	تُناديا		نودِيَتا	تُنادَيان
نَحْنُ	نادَيْنا	نُنادي	نُناديَ	نُنادِ		نودِينا	نُنادى
أنْتُم	نادَيتُمْ	تُنادون	تُنادوا	تُنادوا	نادوا	نوديتُمْ	تُنادَوْنَ
أنْتُنَّ	نادَيتُنَّ	تُنادين	تُنادين	تُنادين	نادين	نوديتُنَّ	تُنادَيْنَ
هُم	نادَوْا	يُنادون	يُنادوا	يُنادوا		نودوا	يُنادَوْنَ
هُنَّ	نادَيْنَ	يُنادين	يُنادين	يُنادين		نودينَ	يُنادَيْنَ

25

Form IV triliteral verb

1 Basic characteristics

1.1 Pattern: ʾafʿal-a أَفْعَلَ / yu-fʿil-u يُفْعِل

Form IV is augmented from Form I by the prefixing of *hamza* plus *fatHa* on the past tense stem. It has the stem pattern ʾaC₁C₂aC₃- in the past tense and the stem pattern yu-C₁aC₂iC₃- in the present tense.

1.2 Meaning

Form IV verbs are often causative of Form I. If the Form I verb is intransitive, Form IV is transitive; if the Form I verb is transitive, Form IV may be doubly transitive, taking two objects. Form IV verbs may have meanings similar to Form II verbs. For example, *xabbar-a* and ʾ*axbar-a*, both mean 'to inform'; *waqqaf-a* and ʾ*awqaf-a* both mean 'to halt, to stop.' Sometimes the meanings of Form II and Form IV verbs are close but not exactly the same. For example, *ʿallam-a* means 'to teach' whereas ʾ*aʿlam-a* means 'to inform.'[1]

1.3 Transitivity

Form IV verbs are usually transitive and sometimes doubly transitive.[2] Intransitive Form IV is rare.[3]

A doubly transitive Form IV verb may take two objects. It often has the option of marking the indirect object (or beneficiary) with a dative-marking preposition such as *li-*.[4]

سيعطيــها التذكرة.

sa-yu-ʿTii-haa l-tadhkarat-a.

He will give her the ticket.

---

[1] Sterling 1904, 51–53 lists four other less common semantic modifications of Form IV: "finding [estimative]," "change," "motion to," and "to be in season," with examples from Classical Arabic. Wright 1967, I:34–36 gives also a denominative meaning for Form IV.

[2] Kouloughli 1994, 203 estimates 80 percent of Form IV verbs are transitive.

[3] One example is: "to grow dark" ʾ*aZlam-a/yu-Zlim-u* أَظْلَمَ / يُظْلِم.

[4] For more on double accusatives and use of dative-marking prepositions, see Chapter 4, section 2.5.

1.4 Inflection

Inflectional characteristics of Form IV verbs include:

(1)   the present tense subject-marker vowel is *Damma* and the present tense stem vowel is **kasra** (*ʾakmal-a/yu-kmil-u*).
(2)   the prefixed *hamza* plus *fatHa* in the past tense **disappears** in the present tense, replaced by the subject markers.[5]
(3)   the prefixed *hamza* in the past tense is stable (*hamzat al-qaTᶜ*) and is not deleted when pronounced after a vowel.

2 Regular (sound) triliteral root: *ʾafᶜal-a* أَفْعَلَ / *yu-fᶜil-u* يُفْعِلُ

These verbs are examples of Form IV sound triliteral roots:

to include, insert	*ʾadraj-a/yu-drij-u*	أَدْرَجَ / يُدْرِجُ
to disturb, bother	*ʾazᶜaj-a/yu-zᶜij-u*	أَزْعَجَ / يُزْعِجُ
to announce	*ʾaᶜlan-a/yu-ᶜlin-u*	أَعْلَنَ / يُعْلِنُ
to supervise	*ʾashraf-a/yu-shrif-u*	أَشْرَفَ / يُشْرِفُ
to send	*ʾarsal-a/yu-rsil-u*	أَرْسَلَ / يُرْسِلُ
to please	*ʾaᶜjab-a/yu-ᶜjib-u*	أَعْجَبَ / يُعْجِبُ

3 Geminate (doubled) root Form IV: *ʾafaᶜᶜ-a* أَفَعَّ / *yu-fᶜᶜ-i* يُفِعَّ

The geminate root in Form IV behaves very much as Form I geminates. The geminate or doubled consonant is doubled and written with *shadda* when followed by a vowel suffix and it separates into two separate consonants when followed by a suffix that begins with a consonant.

to feel, perceive, sense	*ʾaHass-a/yu-Hiss-u*	أَحَسَّ / يُحِصُّ
to like, to love	*ʾaHabb-a/yu-Hibb-u*	أَحَبَّ / يُحِبُّ
to persist in, insist on	*ʾaSarr-a/yu-Sirr-u ᶜalaa*	أَصَرَّ / يُصِرُّ على
to prepare	*ʾaᶜadd-a/yu-ᶜidd-u*	أَعَدَّ / يُعِدُّ

---

[5] This has the effect of making unvoweled Form IV verbs resemble Form I verbs in written Arabic. For verbs which exist in both forms (for example, *Sadar-a/ ya-Sdur-u* صَدَرَ / يَصْدُرُ 'to emanate, come out' and *ʾaSdar-a/yu-Sdir-u* أَصْدَرَ / يُصْدِرُ 'to publish'), context is used to disambiguate form as well as meaning.

4 Hamzated roots in Form IV

4.1 Initial *hamza*

In Form IV, initial root *hamza* merges with the prefix *hamza* in the past tense and they are written as one *'alif* with a *madda* over it. In the present tense, initial *hamza* sits on a *waaw* seat because it is preceded by the *Damma* of the person-marking prefix:

to believe, have faith	*'aaman-a/yu-'min-u*	آمَنَ / يُؤْمِنُ
to rent out, to lease	*'aajar-a/yu-'jir-u*	آجَرَ / يُؤْجِرُ

4.2 Medial *hamza*

The medial *hamza* sits on an *'alif* seat in the past tense. In the present tense it sits on a *yaa'* seat because it is followed by a *kasra*.

to comply with someone's request	*'as'al-a/yu-s'il-u*	أَسْأَلَ / يُسْئِلُ

4.3 Final *hamza*

Final *hamza* may sit on an *'alif* seat in the past tense, but because it is the final consonant in the stem, the seat of *hamza* may shift with certain suffixes:

to set up, establish	*'ansha'-a / yu-nshi'-u*	أَنْشَأَ / يُنْشِئُ
to extinguish	*'aTfa'-a/yu-Tfi'-u*	أَطْفَأَ / يُطْفِئُ

5 Assimilated roots in Form IV: *'af'al-a* أَفْعَلَ / *yuu-'il-u* يوعِلُ

In the past tense of Form IV, the initial *waaw* or *yaa'* of the assimilated root behaves as a regular consonant. In the present tense, however, it assimilates to the vowel /u/ of the subject-marking prefix and becomes long /uu/.

to explain, clarify	*'awDaH-a/yuuDiH-u*	أَوْضَحَ / يوضِحُ
to halt, stop	*'awqaf-a/yuuqif-u*	أَوْقَفَ / يوقِفُ
to awaken	*'ayqaZ-a/yuuqiZ-u*	أَيْقَظَ / يوقِظُ
to bring, convey 'to cause to arrive'	*'awSal-a/yuuSil-u*	أَوْصَلَ / يوصِلُ

6 Hollow roots in Form IV: *'afaal-a/ yu-fiil-u* أَفالَ / يُفيلُ

The semi-consonants *waaw* and *yaa'* of hollow roots in Form IV show up as *'alif* (long stem) and *fatHa* (short stem) in the past tense and *yaa'* and *kasra* in the present tense stem. The pattern is *'afaal-a/ yu-fiil-u*. Examples of both stems are given in both tenses: in addition to the standard citation form of third person masculine singular, first person singular (in the past), and third person feminine plural (in the present).

to broadcast	ʾadhaaʿ-a (ʾadhaʿ-tu)	(أَذَعْتُ) أذاعَ
	/yu-dhiiʿ-u (yudhiʿ-na)	(يُذِعْنَ) يُذيعُ/
to manage, administer	ʾadaar-a (ʾadar-tu)	(أَدَرْتُ) أدارَ
	/yu-diir-u (yu-dir-na)	(يُدِرْنَ) يُديرُ/

7 Defective roots in Form IV: ʾafʿaa أَفْعَى / yu-fʿii يُفْعِي

Defective roots, where the final radical is either *waaw* or *yaaʾ*, behave as -*aa*/-*ii* verbs in Form IV. They depend on the stem vowel for the nature of the final radical, and the stem vowel is consistently /a/ in the past tense and /i/ in the present tense.

to eliminate	ʾalghaa/yu-lghi	أَلْغَى / يُلْغِي
to conduct, to run	ʾajraa/yu-jrii	أَجْرَى / يُجْري
to throw; to deliver (a speech)	ʾalqaa/yu-lqii	أَلْقَى / يُلْقي
to give	ʾaʿTaa/yu-ʿTii	أَعْطَى / يُعْطي

8 Doubly weak roots in Form IV

8.1 *Hamza*-initial, hollow, and defective

to shelter, accommodate (from ʾ-w-y 'to seek refuge')	ʾaawaa/yu-ʾwii[6]	آوَى / يُؤْوي

8.2 *Hamza*-medial and defective

to show (s.o. s.th.) ('to cause to see')	ʾaraa/yu-rii[7] (from r-ʾ-y 'to see')	أرَى / يُري

8.3 *Hamza*-final and hollow

to harm, to hurt	ʾasaaʾ-a/yu-siiʾ-u	أساءَ / يُسيءُ

9. Exclamatory Form IV (*fiʿl al-taʿajjub* فعل التعجّب)

A Form IV verb in the citation form (3 m.sg. past tense) may be used in written Arabic preceded by the function word *maa* to indicate surprise, wonder, or astonishment

---

[6] The initial root *hamza* merges with the prefix *hamza* in the past tense and the initial vowel /a/ lengthens to /aa/.

[7] This verb in Form IV has lost its root *hamza* completely and inflects as a defective -*aa*/-*ii* verb.

at a certain quality or characteristic of something or someone. It is followed by a noun in the accusative, or a pronoun suffix that denotes the possessor of the quality. The occurrence of this construction in media Arabic is rare, but it is found in literary contexts.

The verbs used in this type of construction are usually related to adjectival roots and are sometimes referred to as "adjectival verbs."[8] They are also termed "verbs of surprise or admiration" (Cowan 1964, 177). Cantarino describes the word following *maa* as "an elative in the accusative of exclamation" (1974–76, II:210), that is, as a comparative adjective. See also in this book Chapter 7, section 5.3.3.12 on "less frequent accusatives."

ما أَجمل البيتَ !

maa ᵓajmal-a l-bint-a!

How beautiful the girl is!

ما أَلطفـهم !

maa ᵓalTaf-a-hum![9]

How nice they are!

10 Examples of Form IV verbs in context

فـأوضحت ما تقصده.

fa-ᵓawDaH-at maa ta-qSid-u-hu.

She clarified what she meant.

أجرى محادثات مع بعض المسؤولين.

ᵓajraa muHaadathaat-in maᶜ-a baᶜD-i l-masᵓuul-iina.

He conducted talks with some officials.

لا يضيف أشياء جديدة.

laa yu-Diif-u ᵓashyaaᵓ-a jadiidat-an.

It does not **add** anything new ('new things').

أهداني كتاباً قيّماً.

ᵓahdaa-nii kitaab-an qayyim-an.

He gave me a valuable book.

هناك أفضلية لمن يجيد اللغة الإنكليزيّة.

hunaaka ᵓafDaliyyat-un li-man yu-jiid-u l-lughat-a l-ᵓinkliiziyyat-a.

There is a preference for whomever **is proficient** in English.

أعربت عن أسفها.

ᵓaᶜrab-at ᶜan ᵓasaf-i-haa.

She expressed her sorrow.

11 Verbal noun of Form IV: *ᵓifᶜaal* إفْعال

The verbal noun of Form IV normally has the pattern *ᵓifᶜaal*.

11.1 Sound/regular root

announcement	*ᵓiᶜlaan*	إعْلان	sending	*ᵓirsaal*	إرْسال
disturbance, bother	*ᵓizᶜaaj*	إزْعاج	bankruptcy	*ᵓiflaas*	إفْلاس

---

[8] See Abboud and McCarus 1976, Part 2:272.
[9] These examples are taken from *The MECAS Grammar* 1965, 239. See also Fischer 2002, 80.

11.2 Geminate root

The geminate root maintains the *ʾiʿfaal* pattern, splitting the doubled consonant:

perception, sensation	*ʾiHsaas*	إحْساس	preparation	*ʾiʿdaad*	إعْداد
injury, harm	*ʾiDraar*	إضْرار	insistence, persistence	*ʾiSraar*	إصْرار

11.3 Hamzated root

11.3.1 *Hamza*-initial root

The verbal noun of *hamza*-initial roots in Form IV lengthens the *kasra* of the initial syllable into long /ii/ and deletes the root *hamza*:

faith	*ʾiimaan* (*instead of ʾiʾmaan)	إيمان	rent, renting	*ʾiijaar* (*instead of ʾiʾjaar)	إيجار

11.3.2 *Hamza*-final root

In this verbal noun, the *hamza* sits aloof after the *ʾalif*.

establishment, setting up	*ʾinshaaʾ*	إنْشاء	extinguishing	*ʾiTfaaʾ*	إطْفاء

11.4 Assimilated root: *ʾiiʿaal* إيعال

In the verbal nouns of Form IV assimilated verbs, the initial *waaw* or *yaaʾ* of the root is assimilated to the *kasra* /i/ of the initial *hamza*, and it lengthens to /ii/, i.e., *ʾifʿaal* becomes *ʾiiʿaal*.

clarification	*ʾiiDaaH*	إيضاح	bringing, conveying	*ʾiiSaal*	إيصال
stopping, halting	*ʾiiqaaf*	إيقاف	awakening	*ʾiiqaaZ*	إيقاظ

11.5 Hollow root: *ʾifaala* إفالة

The verbal noun of Form IV hollow roots is *ʾifaala* إفالة, ending with *taaʾ marbuuTa*.

inflicting	*ʾiSaaba*	إصابة	administration	*ʾidaara*	إدارة
broadcasting	*ʾidhaaʿa*	إذاعة	repetition	*ʾiʿaada*	إعادة

11.6 Defective root: *ʾifʿaaʾ* إفْعاء

In the Form IV verbal noun of defective verbs, the defective semi-consonant (*waaw* or *yaaʾ*) disappears and is replaced by *hamza*, i.e., *ʾifʿaal* becomes *ʾifʿaaʾ* إفْعاء.

elimination	*ʾilghaaʾ*	إلغاء	conducting	*ʾijraaʾ*	إجراء
giving	*ʾiʿTaaʾ*	إعطاء	delivery (of a speech)	*ʾilqaaʾ*	إلقاء

11.7 Examples of Form IV verbal nouns in context

إنعاش الاقتصاد
'in°aash-u l-iqtiSaad-i
reviving the economy

إسعاف الدفاع المدنيّ الفوريّ
'is°aaf-u l-difaa°-i l-madaniyy-i l-fawriyy-u
emergency civil defense aid

لا يريد إرسال قوّات أمريكيّة إلى الخارج.
laa yu-riid-u 'irsaal-a quwwaat-in 'amriikiyyat-in 'ilaa l-xaarij-i.
He doesn't want **to send** American forces abroad.

حاول إنقاذ حياة رجل.
Haawal-a ' **inqaadh-a** Hayaat-i rajul-in.
He tried **to save** a man's life.

مشكلة إدمان المخدّرات
mushkilat-u ' **idmaan-i** l-mukhaddir-aat-i
the problem of drug **addiction**

بيت للإيجار
bayt-un li-**l-iijaar-i**
a house for **rent**

إيقاظ الاهتمام
'**iiqaaZ-u** l-ihtimaam-i
the **awakening** of interest

12 Form IV participles

Form IV participles occur as nouns and as adjectives. In some cases they occur in both functions.

12.1 Form IV active participle (AP): *muf°il* مُفْعِل

12.1.1 Sound/regular root

Muslim	*muslim*	مُسْلِم	possible	*mumkin*	مُمْكِن
supervisor; supervising	*mushrif*	مُشْرِف	rainy	*mumTir*	مُمْطِر
director (stage or screen)	*muxrij*	مُخْرِج	snowy	*muthlij*	مُثْلِج

12.1.2 Geminate root: *mufi°°* مُفِعّ

The final two consonants of the geminate root are written together, with no intervening vowel. Thus instead of being in the pattern *mufi°l*, they are of the pattern *mufi°°* مُفِعّ

tedious, boring	*mumill*	مُمِلّ	injurious, harmful	*muDirr*	مُضِرّ
insistent, determined	*muSirr*	مُصِرّ	preparing, preparer	*mu°idd*	مُعِدّ

12.1.3 Hamzated root

12.1.3.1 *Hamza*-INITIAL

faithful	*mu'min*	مُؤْمِن	regrettable	*mu'sif*	مُؤْسِف

12.1.3.2 *Hamza*-FINAL:

| founder | *munshi'* | مُنْشِئ | mistaken | *muxTi'* | مُخْطِئ |

12.1.4 Assimilated root: *muu'il* مُوعِل

In this root type, the initial *waaw* assimilates to the *Damma* of the *miim*-prefix and yields a long /-uu-/ as the first vowel.

| clarifying | *muuDiH* | مُوضِح | consignor, depositor | *muudi'* | مُودِع |
| originator | *muujid* | مُوجِد | deep-reaching | *muughil* | مُوغِل |

12.1.5 Hollow root: *mufiil* مُفِيل

| ocean | *muHiiT* | مُحِيط | manager; director | *mudiir* | مُدِير |
| broadcaster | *mudhii'* | مُذِيع | beneficial | *mufiid* | مُفِيد |

12.1.6 Defective root: *muf'in* مُفْعِ

| giver; giving | *mu'Tin* | مُعْطٍ | mufti, giver of formal legal opinions | *muftin* | مُفْتٍ |

12.1.7 Examples of Form IV APs in context

اللجنة المشرفة
al-lajnat-u l-mushrifat-u
the **supervising** committee

بتقديم كل المساعدة الممكنة
bi-taqdiim-i kull-i l-musaa'adat-i l-mumkinat-i
by offering all **possible** aid

بسرعة مذهلة
bi-sur'at-in mudhhilat-in
with **amazing** speed

شيء مؤسف جداً
shay'-un mu'sif-un jidd-an
a very **regrettable** thing

المحيط الأطلسي
al-muHiiT-u l-'aTlasiyy-u
the Atlantic **Ocean**

سماحة المفتي
samaaHat-u l-muftii
His Eminence the **Mufti**

12.2 Form IV passive participle (PP): *muf'al* مُفْعَل

12.2.1 Sound/regular root

| lexicon | *mu'jam* | مُعْجَم | compacted | *mudmaj* | مُدْمَج |
| singular word مُلْحَق | *mufrad* | مُفْرَد | attaché, officer | *mulHaq* | |

12.2.2 Geminate root: *mufa''* مُفَعّ

The final two consonants of the root fall together, with no intervening vowel.

ready, prepared   *muʿadd*   مُعَدّ

12.2.3 Hamzated root

foundation, establishment;   *munshaʾa*   مُنْشَأة
installation

12.2.4 Assimilated root: *muuʿal* موعَل

summary   *muujaz*   موجَز

12.2.5 Hollow root: *mufaal* مُفال

melted, dissolved   *mudhaab* مُذاب   injured, afflicted   *muSaab* مُصاب

12.2.6 Defective root: *mufʿan* مُفْعَى

abolished; abrogated   *mulghan* مُلْغَى   cast off; discarded   *mulqan* مُلْقَى

12.2.7 Examples of Form IV PPs in context

ملحق الشؤون الثقافيّة
mulHaq-u l-shuʾuun-i l-thaqaafiyyat-i
cultural affairs **attaché**

حلقة مفرغة
Halqat-un **mufraghat-un**
a vicious circle ('a **seamless** circle')

معجم مفصّل
muʿjam-un mufaSSal-un
a detailed **lexicon**

قرص مدمج
qurS-un **mudmaj-un**
a **compact** disk

موجز الأخبار
muujaz-u l-ʾaxbaar-i
summary of the news

الأكسجين المذاب في الماء
al-ʾuuksijiin-u **l-mudhaab-u** fii l-maaʾ-i
oxygen **dissolved** in water

Form IV Sound root: أُرْسِلَ ، يُرْسِلُ ‏ AP: مُرْسِل ‏ PP: مُرْسَل ‏ VN: إِرْسال ‏ *'to send'*

	Active	Active	Active	Active	Active	Active	Passive
	Perfect	Imperfect	Imperfect	Imperfect	Imperfect	Perfect	Imperfect
		Indicative	Subjunctive	Jussive	Imperative		
أنا	أَرْسَلْتُ	أُرْسِلُ	أُرْسِلَ	أُرْسِلْ		أُرْسِلْتُ	أُرْسَلُ
أنتَ	أَرْسَلْتَ	تُرْسِلُ	تُرْسِلَ	تُرْسِلْ	أَرْسِلْ	أُرْسِلْتَ	تُرْسَلُ
أنتِ	أَرْسَلْتِ	تُرْسِلين	تُرْسِلي	تُرْسِلي	أَرْسِلي	أُرْسِلْتِ	تُرْسَلين
أنتُما—m/f	أَرْسَلْتُما	تُرْسِلان	تُرْسِلا	تُرْسِلا	أَرْسِلا	أُرْسِلْتُما	تُرْسَلان
هُوَ	أَرْسَلَ	يُرْسِلُ	يُرْسِلَ	يُرْسِلْ		أُرْسِلَ	يُرْسَلُ
هِيَ	أَرْسَلَتْ	تُرْسِلُ	تُرْسِلَ	تُرْسِلْ		أُرْسِلَتْ	تُرْسَلُ
هُما—m	أَرْسَلا	يُرْسِلان	يُرْسِلا	يُرْسِلا		أُرْسِلا	يُرْسَلان
هُما—f	أَرْسَلَتا	تُرْسِلان	تُرْسِلا	تُرْسِلا		أُرْسِلَتا	تُرْسَلان
نَحْنُ	أَرْسَلْنا	نُرْسِلُ	نُرْسِلَ	نُرْسِلْ		أُرْسِلْنا	نُرْسَلُ
أنتُم	أَرْسَلْتُمْ	تُرْسِلون	تُرْسِلوا	تُرْسِلوا	أَرْسِلوا	أُرْسِلْتُمْ	تُرْسَلون
أنتُنَّ	أَرْسَلْتُنَّ	تُرْسِلْنَ	تُرْسِلْنَ	تُرْسِلْنَ	أَرْسِلْنَ	أُرْسِلْتُنَّ	تُرْسَلْنَ
هُم	أَرْسَلوا	يُرْسِلون	يُرْسِلوا	يُرْسِلوا		أُرْسِلوا	يُرْسَلون
هُنَّ	أَرْسَلْنَ	يُرْسِلْنَ	يُرْسِلْنَ	يُرْسِلْنَ		أُرْسِلْنَ	يُرْسَلْنَ

Form IV Geminate root: أَعَدَّ ، يُعِدُّ   AP: مُعِدّ   PP: مُعَدّ   VN: إِعْداد   *'to prepare'*

	Active	Active	Active	Active	Active	Passive	Passive
	Perfect	Imperfect	Imperfect	Imperfect	Imperfect	Perfect	Imperfect
		Indicative	Subjunctive	Jussive*	Imperative**		
أنا	أَعْدَدْتُ	أُعِدُّ	أُعِدَّ	أُعِدَّ		أُعْدِدْتُ	أُعَدُّ
أنْتَ	أَعْدَدْتَ	تُعِدُّ	تُعِدَّ	تُعِدَّ	أَعِدَّ	أُعْدِدْتَ	تُعَدُّ
أنْتِ	أَعْدَدْتِ	تُعِدِّين	تُعِدِّي	تُعِدِّي	أَعِدِّي	أُعْدِدْتِ	تُعَدِّين
أنْتُما—m/f	أَعْدَدْتُما	تُعِدّان	تُعِدّا	تُعِدّا	أَعِدّا	أُعْدِدْتُما	تُعَدّان
هُوَ	أَعَدَّ	يُعِدُّ	يُعِدَّ	يُعِدَّ		أُعِدَّ	يُعَدُّ
هِيَ	أَعَدَّتْ	تُعِدُّ	تُعِدَّ	تُعِدَّ		أُعِدَّتْ	تُعَدُّ
هُما—m	أَعَدّا	يُعِدّان	يُعِدّا	يُعِدّا		أُعِدّا	يُعَدّان
هُما—f	أَعَدَّتا	تُعِدّان	تُعِدّا	تُعِدّا		أُعِدَّتا	تُعَدّان
نَحْنُ	أَعْدَدْنا	نُعِدُّ	نُعِدَّ	نُعِدَّ		أُعْدِدْنا	نُعَدُّ
أنْتُمْ	أَعْدَدْتُمْ	تُعِدّون	تُعِدّوا	تُعِدّوا	أَعِدّوا	أُعْدِدْتُمْ	تُعَدّون
أنْتُنَّ	أَعْدَدْتُنَّ	تُعْدِدْنَ	تُعْدِدْنَ	تُعْدِدْنَ	أَعْدِدْنَ	أُعْدِدْتُنَّ	تُعَدَدْنَ
هُمْ	أَعَدّوا	يُعِدّون	يُعِدّوا	يُعِدّوا		أُعِدّوا	يُعَدّون
هُنَّ	أَعْدَدْنَ	يُعْدِدْنَ	يُعْدِدْنَ	يُعْدِدْنَ		أُعْدِدْنَ	يُعْدَدْنَ

*Also أَعْدِدْ ؛ تُعْدِدْ ؛ تُعْدِدي ؛ تُعْدِدا ؛ يُعْدِدْ ؛ تُعْدِدْ ؛ نُعْدِدْ ؛ تُعْدِدوا ؛ يُعْدِدوا

**Also أَعْدِدْ ؛ أَعْدِدي ؛ أَعْدِدا ؛ أَعْدِدوا

Form IV hamza-final: أَنْشَأَ ، يُنْشِئُ   AP: مُنْشِئ   PP: مُنْشَأ   VN: إِنْشاء   '*to establish*'

	Active Perfect	Active Imperfect Indicative	Active Imperfect Subjunctive	Active Imperfect Jussive	Active Imperfect Imperative	Passive Perfect	Passive Imperfect
أنا	أَنْشَأْتُ	أُنْشِئُ	أُنْشِئَ	أُنْشِئْ		أُنْشِئْتُ	أُنْشَأ
أَنْتَ	أَنْشَأْتَ	تُنْشِئُ	تُنْشِئَ	تُنْشِئْ	أَنْشِئْ	أُنْشِئْتَ	تُنْشَأ
أَنْتِ	أَنْشَأْتِ	تُنْشِئِين	تُنْشِئِي	تُنْشِئِي	أَنْشِئِي	أُنْشِئْتِ	تُنْشَئِين
أَنْتُما m/f	أَنْشَأْتُما	تُنْشِئان	تُنْشِئا	تُنْشِئا	أَنْشِئا	أُنْشِئْتُما	تُنْشَآن
هُوَ	أَنْشَأَ	يُنْشِئُ	يُنْشِئَ	يُنْشِئْ		أُنْشِئَ	يُنْشَأ
هِيَ	أَنْشَأَتْ	تُنْشِئُ	تُنْشِئَ	تُنْشِئْ		أُنْشِئَتْ	تُنْشَأ
هُما m	أَنْشَآ	يُنْشِئان	يُنْشِئا	يُنْشِئا		أُنْشِئا	يُنْشَآن
هُما f	أَنْشَأَتا	تُنْشِئان	تُنْشِئا	تُنْشِئا		أُنْشِئَتا	تُنْشَآن
نَحْنُ	أَنْشَأْنا	نُنْشِئُ	نُنْشِئَ	نُنْشِئْ		أُنْشِئْنا	نُنْشَأ
أنتم	أَنْشَأْتُم	تُنْشِئُون	تُنْشِئُوا	تُنْشِئُوا	أَنْشِئُوا	أُنْشِئْتُم	تُنْشَؤُون
أَنْتُنَّ	أَنْشَأْتُنَّ	تُنْشِئْنَ	تُنْشِئْنَ	تُنْشِئْنَ	أَنْشِئْنَ	أُنْشِئْتُنَّ	تُنْشَأْن
هُم	أَنْشَؤُوا	يُنْشِئُون	يُنْشِئُوا	يُنْشِئُوا		أُنْشِئُوا	يُنْشَؤُون
هُنَّ	أَنْشَأْنَ	يُنْشِئْنَ	يُنْشِئْنَ	يُنْشِئْنَ		أُنْشِئْنَ	يُنْشَأْن

Form IV Assimilated root: أَوْضَحَ ، يُوضِحُ AP: مُوضِح PP: مُوضَح VN: إيضاح *'to clarify'*

	Active	Active	Active	Active	Active	Passive	Passive
	Perfect	Imperfect	Imperfect	Imperfect	Imperfect	Perfect	Imperfect
		Indicative	Subjunctive	Jussive	Imperative		
أنا	أَوْضَحْتُ	أُوضِحُ	أُوضِحَ	أُوضِحْ			
أَنْتَ	أَوْضَحْتَ	تُوضِحُ	تُوضِحَ	تُوضِحْ	أَوْضِحْ		
أَنْتِ	أَوْضَحْتِ	تُوضِحين	تُوضِحي	تُوضِحي	أَوْضِحي		
أَنْتُما–m/f	أَوْضَحْتُما	تُوضِحان	تُوضِحا	تُوضِحا	أَوْضِحا		
هُوَ	أَوْضَحَ	يُوضِحُ	يُوضِحَ	يُوضِحْ		أُوضِحَ	يُوضَحُ
هِيَ	أَوْضَحَتْ	تُوضِحُ	تُوضِحَ	تُوضِحْ		أُوضِحَتْ	تُوضَحُ
هُما–m	أَوْضَحا	يُوضِحان	يُوضِحا	يُوضِحا			
هُما–f	أَوْضَحَتا	تُوضِحان	تُوضِحا	تُوضِحا			
نَحْنُ	أَوْضَحْنا	نُوضِحُ	نُوضِحَ	نُوضِحْ			
أَنْتُم	أَوْضَحْتُمْ	تُوضِحون	تُوضِحوا	تُوضِحوا	أَوْضِحوا		
أَنْتُنَّ	أَوْضَحْتُنَّ	تُوضِحْنَ	تُوضِحْنَ	تُوضِحْنَ	أَوْضِحْنَ		
هُم	أَوْضَحوا	يُوضِحون	يُوضِحوا	يُوضِحوا			
هُنَّ	أَوْضَحْنَ	يُوضِحْنَ	يُوضِحْنَ	يُوضِحْنَ			

Form IV Hollow root: أذاعَ ، يُذيعُ AP: مُذيع PP: مُذاع VN: إذاعة *'to broadcast'*

	Active	Active	Active	Active	Active	Passive	Passive
	Perfect	Imperfect	Imperfect	Imperfect	Imperfect	Perfect	Imperfect
		Indicative	Subjunctive	Jussive	Imperative		
أنا	أذَعْتُ	أُذيعُ	أُذيعَ	أُذِعْ		أُذِعْتُ	أُذاعُ
أنْتَ	أذَعْتَ	تُذيعُ	تُذيعَ	تُذِعْ	أذِعْ	أُذِعْتَ	تُذاعُ
أنْتِ	أذَعْتِ	تُذيعينَ	تُذيعي	تُذيعي	أذيعي	أُذِعْتِ	تُذاعين
أنتُما—m/f	أذَعْتُما	تُذيعانِ	تُذيعا	تُذيعا	أذيعا	أُذِعْتُما	تُذاعانِ
هُوَ	أذاعَ	يُذيعُ	يُذيعَ	يُذِعْ		أُذيعَ	يُذاعُ
هِيَ	أذاعَتْ	تُذيعُ	تُذيعَ	تُذِعْ		أُذيعَتْ	تُذاعُ
هُما—m	أذاعا	يُذيعانِ	يُذيعا	يُذيعا		أُذيعا	يُذاعانِ
هُما—f	أذاعَتا	تُذيعانِ	تُذيعا	تُذيعا		أُذيعَتا	تُذاعانِ
نَحْنُ	أذَعْنا	نُذيعُ	نُذيعَ	نُذِعْ		أُذِعْنا	نُذاعُ
أنتُم	أذَعْتُم	تُذيعونَ	تُذيعوا	تُذيعوا	أذيعوا	أُذِعْتُم	تُذاعونَ
أنتُنَّ	أذَعْتُنَّ	تُذِعْنَ	تُذِعْنَ	تُذِعْنَ	أذِعْنَ	أُذِعْتُنَّ	تُذَعْنَ
هُم	أذاعوا	يُذيعونَ	يُذيعوا	يُذيعوا		أُذيعوا	يُذاعونَ
هُنَّ	أذَعْنَ	يُذِعْنَ	يُذِعْنَ	يُذِعْنَ		أُذِعْنَ	يُذَعْنَ

Form IV Defective: أَلْغَى ، يُلْغِي AP: مُلْغٍ PP: مُلْغىً VN: إِلْغاء *'to abolish'*

	Active	Active	Active	Active	Active	Passive	Passive
	Perfect	Imperfect	Imperfect	Imperfect	Imperfect	Perfect	Imperfect
		Indicative	Subjunctive	Jussive	Imperative		
أَنا	أَلْغَيْتُ	أُلْغِي	أُلْغِيَ	أُلْغِ		أُلْغيتُ	أُلْغَى
أَنْتَ	أَلْغَيْتَ	تُلْغِي	تُلْغِيَ	تُلْغِ	أَلْغِ	أُلْغيتَ	تُلْغَى
أَنْتِ	أَلْغَيْتِ	تُلْغِينَ	تُلْغِي	تُلْغِي	أَلْغِي	أُلْغيتِ	تُلْغَيْنَ
أَنْتُما—m/f	أَلْغَيْتُما	تُلْغِيانِ	تُلْغِيا	تُلْغِيا	أَلْغِيا	أُلْغيتُما	تُلْغَيانِ
هُوَ	أَلْغَى	يُلْغِي	يُلْغِيَ	يُلْغِ		أُلْغِيَ	يُلْغَى
هِيَ	أَلْغَتْ	تُلْغِي	تُلْغِيَ	تُلْغِ		أُلْغيتْ	تُلْغَى
هُما—m	أَلْغَيا	يُلْغِيانِ	يُلْغِيا	يُلْغِيا		أُلْغِيا	يُلْغَيانِ
هُما—f	أَلْغَتا	تُلْغِيانِ	تُلْغِيا	تُلْغِيا		أُلْغِيَتا	تُلْغَيانِ
نَحْنُ	أَلْغَيْنا	نُلْغِي	نُلْغِيَ	نُلْغِ		أُلْغِينا	نُلْغَى
أَنْتُمْ	أَلْغَيْتُمْ	تُلْغُونَ	تُلْغُوا	تُلْغُوا	أَلْغُوا	أُلْغيتُمْ	تُلْغَوْنَ
أَنْتُنَّ	أَلْغَيْتُنَّ	تُلْغِينَ	تُلْغِينَ	تُلْغِينَ	أَلْغِينَ	أُلْغيتُنَّ	تُلْغَيْنَ
هُم	أَلْغَوْا	يُلْغُونَ	يُلْغُوا	يُلْغُوا		أُلْغُوا	يُلْغَوْنَ
هُنَّ	أَلْغَيْنَ	يُلْغِينَ	يُلْغِينَ	يُلْغِينَ		أُلْغِينَ	يُلْغَيْنَ

26

Form V triliteral verb

1 Basic characteristics

1.1 Pattern: tafaᶜᶜal-a تَفَعَّلَ/ya-tafaᶜᶜal-u يَتَفَعَّلُ

Form V verbs are augmented with respect to Form I in that the medial consonant of the triliteral root is doubled (as in Form II) and a prefix ta- is added to the stem.[1] In the present tense, the subject-marking prefix vowel is fatHa and the two stem vowels are fatHa. Form V verbs thus have the stem patterns $taC_1aC_2C_2aC_3$- in the past tense and ya-$taC_1aC_2C_2aC_3$- in the present.[2]

1.2 Meaning

In many cases Form V is the reflexive of the Form II verb, meaning that the action expressed in Form II is done to or happens to one's self. This is sometimes referred to by grammarians as mediopassive.[3] Form V may also be resultative of Form II, showing the result of the Form II action, e.g., kassar-tu-haa fa-takassar-at 'I broke it (Form II) and it broke (Form V).'[4] Other semantic modifications embodied in this form include gradual progress in an activity or state (e.g., taHassan-a 'to improve,' tadaxxal-a 'to meddle, to interfere,' tamazzaq-a 'to be ripped apart, fragmented') and acquisition or imitation of a quality (e.g., taʾassaf-a 'to be or act sorry'; taʾaddab-a 'to behave courteously').

---

[1] The prefixed ta-, used as a derivational affix is often characterized as a marker of reflexive action or even of the passive. "Its main derivational function is that of the passive" (Cowell 1964, 85). In more recent studies of this form, it is said often to represent "unaccusative" constructions in Arabic. See Mahmoud 1991 for further discussion of both Form V and Form VII as Arabic counterparts for unaccusative structures.

[2] Note that in the present tense, there is both an inflectional prefix (the subject marker) and a derivational prefix (the ta- of Form V).

[3] "No grammatical distinction is made in Arabic verbs between 'reflexive' acts and spontaneous developments – what one does to one's self and what simply happens to one are equally accommodated by the mediopassive" (Cowell 1964, 238).

[4] The Arabic term used to refer to the resultative meaning of derived forms (especially V, VII, and VIII) is muTaawaᶜa مطاوعة 'obedience, conformity' or muTaawiᶜ مطاوع 'obedient, conforming' – that is, conforming with a particular, lexically related action. Fleisch 1979 states (II:305) "Ce muTaawiᶜ exprime l'état dans lequel se trouve un sujet, sous l'action ... [d'un verbe] précédente."

1.3 Transitivity

Form V verbs are often reflexive or intransitive, but they may be transitive as well.

1.4 Inflection

Inflectional characteristics of Form V verbs:

The present tense subject-marker vowel is *fatHa* and the present tense stem vowel is *fatHa* (*taqaddam-a/ya-taqaddam-u*).

2 Regular (sound) triliteral root

These verbs are examples of Form V sound triliteral roots:

to breathe	*tanaffas-a/ya-tanaffas-u*	تنفّس / يتنفّس
to move, be in motion	*taHarrak-a/ya-taHarrak-u*	تحرّك / يتحرّك
to require	*taTallab-a/ya-taTallab-u*	تطلّب / يتطلّب
to speak	*takallam-a/ya-takallam-u*	تكلّم / يتكلّم
to get, to receive	*tasallam-a/ya-tasallam-u*	تسلّم / يتسلّم
to avoid	*tajannab-a/ya-tajannab-u*	تجنّب / يتجنّب

3 Geminate (doubled) root Form V

Geminate roots in Form V have the following stem patterns: $taC_1aC_2C_2aC_2$- in the past tense and $yataC_1aC_2C_2aC_2$- in the present. For example;

to hesitate	*taraddad-a/ya-taraddad-u*	تردّد / يتردّد
to feel (s.th.); handle, touch (s.th.)	*taHassas-a/ya-taHassas-u*	تحسّس / يتحسّس

4 Hamzated roots in Form V

The *hamza* may occur in the first, second, or third position in the triliteral root. Depending on its position, and the surrounding vowels, the *hamza* may have to change its "seat" when the verb inflects for person and tense.

4.1 Initial *hamza*

In *hamza*-initial Form V verbs, the *hamza* sits on *'alif* in both tenses:

to be late	*ta'axxar-a/ya-ta'axxar-u*	تأخّر / يتأخّر
to be affected (by)	*ta'aththar-a/ya-ta'aththar-u bi-*	تأثّر / يتأثّر
to be sorry	*ta'assaf-a/ya-ta'assaf-u*	تأسّف / يتأسّف

| to be composed (of) | ta'allaf-a/ya-ta'allaf-u min | تَأَلَّفَ / يَتَأَلَّفُ مِن |
| to contemplate (s.th.) | ta'ammal-a/ya-ta'ammal-u | تَأَمَّلَ / يَتَأَمَّلُ |

4.2 Medial *hamza*

| to be at the head; to chair | tara''as-a/ ya-tara''as-u | تَرَأَّسَ / يَتَرَأَّسُ |

4.3 Final *hamza*

| to get prepared | tahayya'-a/ya-tahayya'-u | تَهَيَّأَ / يَتَهَيَّأُ |
| to predict, forecast | tanabba'-a/ya-tanabba'-u | تَنَبَّأَ / يَتَنَبَّأُ |

5 Assimilated roots in Form V

Assimilated roots, where the first radical is either *waaw* or *yaa'*, are inflected as sound roots in Form V; the *waaw* or *yaa'* remain in both tenses.

to be extended, spread out	tawassa'-a/ya-tawassa'-u	تَوَسَّعَ / يَتَوَسَّعُ
to be abundant, plentiful	tawaffar-a/ya-tawaffar-u	تَوَفَّرَ / يَتَوَفَّرُ
to expect, anticipate	tawaqqa'-a/ya-tawaqqa'-u	تَوَقَّعَ / يَتَوَقَّعُ
to stop; stand still	tawaqqaf-a/ya-tawaqqaf-u	تَوَقَّفَ / يَتَوَقَّفُ

6 Hollow roots in Form V

Hollow roots behave as sound roots in Form V, the *waaw* or *yaa'* that is the second radical functions as a normal consonant, with *shadda*.

| to change (intr.) | taghayyar-a/ya-taghayyar-u | تَغَيَّرَ / يَتَغَيَّرُ |
| to volunteer | taTawwa'-a/ya-taTawwa'-u | تَطَوَّعَ / يَتَطَوَّعُ |

7 Defective roots in Form V: *tafa''aa* تَفَعَّى/تَفَعَّى *ya-tafa''aa* يَتَفَعَّى

Defective roots, where the final radical is either *waaw* or *yaa'*, behave as *-aa/-aa* verbs in Form V.[5]

to receive, accept	talaqqaa/ya-talaqqaa	تَلَقَّى / يَتَلَقَّى
to wish	tamannaa/ya-tamannaa	تَمَنَّى / يَتَمَنَّى
to trespass, to transcend	ta'addaa/ya-ta'addaa	تَعَدَّى / يَتَعَدَّى
to challenge	taHaddaa/ya-taHaddaa	تَحَدَّى / يَتَحَدَّى

---

[5] They depend on the stem vowel for the nature of the final radical, and the stem vowel is consistently /a/ in the past tense and also /a/ in the present tense.

8 Doubly weak roots in Form V

These roots have two forms of weakness which may occur at any point in the root. For example:

8.1 Assimilated and defective

to take charge of ;   *tawallaa/ya-tawallaa*   تَوَلَّى / يَتَوَلَّى
be entrusted with   (root: w-l-y)

9 Examples of Form V verbs in context

تَبَنَّى العِراقُ استراتيجيّة عسكريّة جديدة.

tabannaa l-ʿiraaq-u straatijiyyat-an ʿaskariyyat-an jadiidat-an.

Iraq **has adopted** a new military strategy.

والرجلُ تَصَرَّفَ ببرودة.

wa-l-rajul-u taSarraf-a bi-buruudat-in.

(And) the man **behaved** coldly.

تحدَّثَ عن الاستشراق.

taHaddath-a ʿan-i l-istishraaq-i.

He **spoke** of orientalism.

تَتحوّل من سيّءٍ إلى أسوأ.

*ta-taHawwal-u min sayyiʾ-in
ʾilaa ʾaswaʾ-a.*

It **changes** from bad to worse.

نَتمنّى لكم عيداً مباركاً.

*na-tamannaa la-kum ʿiid-an
mubaarak-an.*

We wish you a blessed holiday.

سيَتولّى منصبه غداً.

sa-ya-tawallaa manSib-a-hu ghad-an.

He **will assume** his office tomorrow.

سوف يَتحسّن.

sawfa ya-taHassan-u.

It will get better.

10 Form V verbal nouns: *tafaʿʿul* تَفَعُّل

10.1 Sound roots

Form V verbal nouns of regular or sound verbs have the pattern **taC₁aC₂C₂uC₃**.

breathing	*tanaffus*	تَنَفُّس	progress	*taqaddum*	تَقَدُّم
avoidance	*tajannub*	تَجَنُّب	interference	*tadaxxul*	تَدَخُّل

10.2 Geminate roots

hesitation	*taraddud*	تَرَدُّد	feeling, touching	*taHassus*	تَحَسُّس

10.3 Hamzated roots

The placement of *hamza* on a particular seat is determined by contiguous vowels.

lateness	*taʾaxxur*	تَأَخُّر	prediction	*tanabbuʾ*	تَنَبُّؤ
being affected	*taʾaththur*	تَأَثُّر	chairmanship	*taraʾʾus*	تَرَؤُّس

10.4 Assimilated roots

being extended, spreading out	*tawassuᶜ*	توسُّع	penetration, absorption	*tawaghghul*	توغُّل
abundance, availability	*tawaffur*	توفُّر	tension	*tawattur*	توتُّر

10.5 Hollow roots

change	*taghayyur*	تغيُّر	development	*taTawwur*	تطوُّر
volunteering	*taTawwuᶜ*	تطوُّع	pollution	*talawwuth*	تلوُّث

10.6 Defective roots: *tafaᶜᶜin* تَفَعٍّ

The verbal nouns of defective verbs in Form V inflect as defective nouns (declension six in this book).

accepting	*talaqqin*	تلقٍّ	wishing	*tamannin*	تمنٍّ
transcending, overtaking	*taᶜaddin*	تعدٍّ	challenge	*taHaddin*	تحدٍّ

10.7 Examples of Form V verbal nouns in context

يعاني من التمزُّق.
yu-ᶜaanii min-a l-tamazzuq-i.
It suffers from **fragmentation**.

منذ تسلُّمه الرئاسة
mundhu tasallum-i-hi l-riʾaasat-a
since his **assumption** of the presidency

حالة التأهُّب
Haalat-u l-taʾahhub-i
state of alert

عدم التدخُّل
ᶜadam-u l-tadaxxul-i
non-**interference**

11 Form V participles

The great majority of Form V participles occur as active participles. The Form V AP may have active, passive, or reflexive meaning. Few occur as passive participles.

11.1 Form V active participle (AP): *mutafaᶜᶜil* مُتَفَعِّل

The Form V active participle may have an active meaning but it may also have a passive or reflexive sense because of the reflexive or resultative meaning of many verbs of this form.

11.1.1 Strong/regular root

spokesperson	*mutakallim*	متكلِّم	frozen	*mutajammid*	متجمِّد
extremist	*mutaTarrif*	متطرِّف	married	*mutazawwij*	متزوِّج

11.1.2 Geminate root

specialist   *mutaxaSSiS*   مُتَخَصِّص   renewed   *mutajaddid*   مُتَجَدِّد

11.2.3 Hamzated root

sorry, regretful   *muta'assif*   مُتَأَسِّف   late   *muta'axxir*   مُتَأَخِّر

11.2.4 Assimilated root

abundant   *mutawaffir*   مُتَوفِّر   middle   *mutawassiT*   مُتَوسِّط

11.2.5 Hollow root

volunteer   *mutaTawwi^c*   مُتَطوِّع

11.2.6 Defective root: *mutafa^c^cin* مُتَفَعٍّ

These participles inflect as defective nouns (declension six).

challenger;   *mutaHaddin*   مُتَحَدٍّ   wishing   *mutamannin*   مُتَمَنٍّ
  challenging

11.2 Form V passive participle (PP): *mutafa^c^cal* مُتَفَعَّل

Occurrences of these are few due to the passive-like or reflexive meaning of the many Form V verbs. A few examples include:

forced, feigned   *mutakallaf*   مُتَكَلَّف

requirement/s   *mutaTallab/aat*   مُتَطَلَّب / ات

expected   *mutawaqqa^c*   مُتَوقَّع

11.3 Form V participles in context

11.3.1 Active participle

المحيط المتجمّد الشمالـيّ
*al-muHiiT-u l-**mutajammid**-u
  l-shimaaliyy-u*
the Arctic Ocean (the '**frozen**
  northern' ocean)

البحر الأبيض المتوسّط
*al-baHr-u l-'abyaD-u l-**mutawassiT**-u*
the Mediterranean Sea ('the **middle** white sea')

يغادر القاهرة اليوم متوجّهاً إلى باريس.
*yu-ghaadir-u l-qaahirat-a l-yawm-a **mutawajjih**-an 'ilaa baariis.*
He leaves Cairo today **heading** for Paris.

11.3.2 Passive participle

من المتوقّع أن...

*min-a **l-mutawaqqaʿ-i ʾan** ...*

it is **expected** that

Form V Sound root: تكلّم ، يتكلّم   *AP:* متكلّم   *PP:* متكلّم   *VN:* تكلّم   *'to speak'*

	Active	Active	Active	Active	Active	Passive	Passive
	Perfect	Imperfect	Imperfect	Imperfect	Imperfect	Perfect	Imperfect
		Indicative	Subjunctive	Jussive	Imperative		
أنا	تكلمت	أتكلم	أتكلم	أتكلم		تكلمت	أتكلم
أنْت	تكلمت	تتكلم	تتكلم	تتكلم	تكلم	تكلمت	تتكلم
أنْت	تكلمت	تتكلمين	تتكلمي	تتكلمي	تكلمي	تكلمت	تتكلمين
أنتما—m/f	تكلمتما	تتكلمان	تتكلما	تتكلما	تكلما	تكلمتما	تتكلمان
هو	تكلم	يتكلم	يتكلم	يتكلم		تكلم	يتكلم
هي	تكلمت	تتكلم	تتكلم	تتكلم		تكلمت	تتكلم
هما—m	تكلما	يتكلمان	يتكلما	يتكلما		تكلما	يتكلمان
هما—f	تكلمتا	تتكلمان	تتكلما	تتكلما		تكلمتا	تتكلمان
نحن	تكلمنا	نتكلم	نتكلم	نتكلم		تكلمنا	نتكلم
أنتم	تكلمتم	تتكلمون	تتكلموا	تتكلموا	تكلموا	تكلمتم	تتكلمون
أنتنّ	تكلمتن	تتكلمن	تتكلمن	تتكلمن	تكلمن	تكلمتن	تتكلمن
هم	تكلموا	يتكلمون	يتكلموا	يتكلموا		تكلموا	يتكلمون
هنّ	تكلمن	يتكلمن	يتكلمن	يتكلمن		تكلمن	يتكلمن

Form V Geminate root: تردَّد ، يتردَّد   AP: مُتردِّد   PP: VN: تردُّد   *'to hesitate'*

	Active Perfect	Active Imperfect Indicative	Active Imperfect Subjunctive	Active Imperfect Jussive	Active Imperfect Imperative	Passive Perfect	Passive Imperfect
أنا	تردَّدتُ	أتردَّد	أتردَّد	أتردَّد			
أنتَ	تردَّدتَ	تتردَّد	تتردَّد	تتردَّد	تردَّد		
أنتِ	تردَّدتِ	تتردَّدين	تتردَّدي	تتردَّدي	تردَّدي		
أنتُما m/f	تردَّدتُما	تتردَّدان	تتردَّدا	تتردَّدا	تردَّدا		
هو	تردَّد	يتردَّد	يتردَّد	يتردَّد			
هي	تردَّدت	تتردَّد	تتردَّد	تتردَّد			
هما—m	تردَّدا	يتردَّدان	يتردَّدا	يتردَّدا			
هما—f	تردَّدتا	تتردَّدان	تتردَّدا	تتردَّدا			
نحن	تردَّدنا	نتردَّد	نتردَّد	نتردَّد			
أنتم	تردَّدتم	تتردَّدون	تتردَّدوا	تتردَّدوا	تردَّدوا		
أنتنَّ	تردَّدتن	تتردَّدن	تتردَّدن	تتردَّدن	تردَّدن		
هم	تردَّدوا	يتردَّدون	يتردَّدوا	يتردَّدوا			
هنَّ	تردَّدن	يتردَّدن	يتردَّدن	يتردَّدن			

Form V hamza-initial root: يَتَأَخَّر ، تَأَخَّر AP: مُتَأَخِّر PP: VN: تَأَخُّر *'to be late, delayed'*

	Active	Active	Active	Active	Active	Passive	Passive
	Perfect	Imperfect	Imperfect	Imperfect	Imperfect	Perfect	Imperfect
		Indicative	Subjunctive	Jussive	Imperative		
أنا	تَأَخَّرْتُ	أَتَأَخَّرُ	أَتَأَخَّرَ	أَتَأَخَّرْ			
أنْتَ	تَأَخَّرْتَ	تَتَأَخَّرُ	تَتَأَخَّرَ	تَتَأَخَّرْ	تَأَخَّرْ		
أنْتِ	تَأَخَّرْتِ	تَتَأَخَّرِينَ	تَتَأَخَّرِي	تَتَأَخَّرِي	تَأَخَّرِي		
أنْتُما—m/f	تَأَخَّرْتُما	تَتَأَخَّرانِ	تَتَأَخَّرا	تَتَأَخَّرا	تَأَخَّرا		
هُوَ	تَأَخَّرَ	يَتَأَخَّرُ	يَتَأَخَّرَ	يَتَأَخَّرْ			
هِيَ	تَأَخَّرَتْ	تَتَأَخَّرُ	تَتَأَخَّرَ	تَتَأَخَّرْ			
هُما—m	تَأَخَّرا	يَتَأَخَّرانِ	يَتَأَخَّرا	يَتَأَخَّرا			
هُما—f	تَأَخَّرَتا	تَتَأَخَّرانِ	تَتَأَخَّرا	تَتَأَخَّرا			
نَحْنُ	تَأَخَّرْنا	نَتَأَخَّرُ	نَتَأَخَّرَ	نَتَأَخَّرْ			
أنْتُم	تَأَخَّرْتُم	تَتَأَخَّرُونَ	تَتَأَخَّرُوا	تَتَأَخَّرُوا	تَأَخَّرُوا		
أنْتُنَّ	تَأَخَّرْتُنَّ	تَتَأَخَّرْنَ	تَتَأَخَّرْنَ	تَتَأَخَّرْنَ	تَأَخَّرْنَ		
هُم	تَأَخَّرُوا	يَتَأَخَّرُونَ	يَتَأَخَّرُوا	يَتَأَخَّرُوا			
هُنَّ	تَأَخَّرْنَ	يَتَأَخَّرْنَ	يَتَأَخَّرْنَ	يَتَأَخَّرْنَ			

Form V hamza-final root: تنبّأ ، يتنبّأ AP: مُتنبّئ PP: مُتنبّأ VN: تنبّؤ 'to predict'

	Active	Active	Active	Active	Active	Passive	Passive
	Perfect	Imperfect	Imperfect	Imperfect	Imperfect	Perfect	Imperfect
		Indicative	Subjunctive	Jussive	Imperative		
أنا	تنبّأْتُ	أتنبّأُ	أتنبّأَ	أتنبّأْ		تُنبِّئْتُ	أتنبّأُ
أنتَ	تنبّأْتَ	تتنبّأُ	تتنبّأَ	تتنبّأْ	تنبّأْ	تُنبِّئْتَ	تتنبّأُ
أنتِ	تنبّأْتِ	تتنبّئين	تتنبّئي	تتنبّئي	تنبّئي	تُنبِّئْتِ	تتنبّئين
أنتما–m/f	تنبّأْتما	تتنبّآن	تتنبّآ	تتنبّآ	تنبّآ	تُنبِّئْتما	تتنبّآن
هو	تنبّأ	يتنبّأُ	يتنبّأَ	يتنبّأْ		تُنبِّئ	يتنبّأُ
هي	تنبّأتْ	تتنبّأُ	تتنبّأَ	تتنبّأْ		تُنبِّئتْ	تتنبّأُ
هما–m	تنبّآ	يتنبّآن	يتنبّآ	يتنبّآ		تُنبِّئا	يتنبّآن
هما–f	تنبّأتا	تتنبّآن	تتنبّآ	تتنبّآ		تُنبِّئتا	تتنبّآن
نحن	تنبّأْنا	نتنبّأُ	نتنبّأَ	نتنبّأْ		تُنبِّئْنا	نتنبّأُ
أنتم	تنبّأْتم	تتنبّؤون	تتنبّؤوا	تتنبّؤوا	تنبّؤوا	تُنبِّئْتم	تتنبّؤون
أنتنّ	تنبّأْتنّ	تتنبّأن	تتنبّأن	تتنبّأن	تنبّأن	تُنبِّئْتنّ	تتنبّأن
هم	تنبّؤوا	يتنبّؤون	يتنبّؤوا	يتنبّؤوا		تُنبِّئوا	يتنبّؤون
هنّ	تنبّأن	يتنبّأن	يتنبّأن	يتنبّأن		تُنبِّئن	يتنبّأن

Form V Hollow root: تطوَّع ، يتطوَّع   AP: مُتطوِّع   PP: VN: تطوُّع   *'to volunteer'*

	Active	Active	Active	Active	Active	Passive	Passive
	Perfect	Imperfect	Imperfect	Imperfect	Imperfect	Perfect	Imperfect
		Indicative	Subjunctive	Jussive	Imperative		
أنا	تطوَّعتُ	أتطوَّعُ	أتطوَّعَ	أتطوَّعْ			
أنْت	تطوَّعتَ	تتطوَّعُ	تتطوَّعَ	تتطوَّعْ	تطوَّعْ		
أنْت	تطوَّعتِ	تتطوَّعين	تتطوَّعي	تتطوَّعي	تطوَّعي		
أنتُما—m/f	تطوَّعتُما	تتطوَّعان	تتطوَّعا	تتطوَّعا	تطوَّعا		
هُو	تطوَّع	يتطوَّعُ	يتطوَّعَ	يتطوَّعْ			
هِي	تطوَّعت	تتطوَّعُ	تتطوَّعَ	تتطوَّعْ			
هُما—m	تطوَّعا	يتطوَّعان	يتطوَّعا	يتطوَّعا			
هُما—f	تطوَّعتا	تتطوَّعان	تتطوَّعا	تتطوَّعا			
نحْنُ	تطوَّعنا	نتطوَّعُ	نتطوَّعَ	نتطوَّعْ			
أنتُم	تطوَّعتم	تتطوَّعون	تتطوَّعوا	تتطوَّعوا	تطوَّعوا		
أنتنَّ	تطوَّعتنَّ	تتطوَّعن	تتطوَّعن	تتطوَّعن	تطوَّعن		
هُم	تطوَّعوا	يتطوَّعون	يتطوَّعوا	يتطوَّعوا			
هنَّ	تطوَّعن	يتطوَّعن	يتطوَّعن	يتطوَّعن			

Form V Assimilated root: توقّع ، يتوقّع AP: مُتوقِّع PP: مُتوقَّع VN: توقُّع 'to expect'

	Active Perfect	Active Imperfect Indicative	Active Imperfect Subjunctive	Active Imperfect Jussive	Active Imperfect Imperative	Passive Perfect	Passive Imperfect
أنا	توقّعت	أتوقّع	أتوقّع	أتوقّع		توقّعت	أتوقّع
أنتَ	توقّعت	تتوقّع	تتوقّع	تتوقّع	توقّع	توقّعت	تتوقّع
أنتِ	توقّعت	تتوقّعين	تتوقّعي	تتوقّعي	توقّعي	توقّعت	تتوقّعين
أنتما—m/f	توقّعتما	تتوقّعان	تتوقّعا	تتوقّعا	توقّعا	توقّعتما	تتوقّعان
هو	توقّع	يتوقّع	يتوقّع	يتوقّع		توقّع	يتوقّع
هي	توقّعت	تتوقّع	تتوقّع	تتوقّع		توقّعت	تتوقّع
هما—m	توقّعا	يتوقّعان	يتوقّعا	يتوقّعا		توقّعا	يتوقّعان
هما—f	توقّعتا	تتوقّعان	تتوقّعا	تتوقّعا		توقّعتا	تتوقّعان
نحن	توقّعنا	نتوقّع	نتوقّع	نتوقّع			نتوقّع
أنتم	توقّعتم	تتوقّعون	تتوقّعوا	تتوقّعوا	توقّعوا	توقّعتم	تتوقّعون
أنتنّ	توقّعتنّ	تتوقّعن	تتوقّعن	تتوقّعن	توقّعن	توقّعتنّ	تتوقّعن
هم	توقّعوا	يتوقّعون	يتوقّعوا	يتوقّعوا		توقّعوا	يتوقّعون
هنّ	توقّعن	يتوقّعن	يتوقّعن	يتوقّعن		توقّعن	يتوقّعن

Form V Defective root: تحدّى ، يتحدّى   AP: مُتحدٍّ   PP: مُتحدًّى   VN: تحدٍّ   'to challenge'

	Active	Active	Active	Active	Active	Passive	Passive
	Perfect	Imperfect	Imperfect	Imperfect	Imperfect	Perfect	Imperfect
		Indicative	Subjunctive	Jussive	Imperative		
أنا	تحدّيتُ	أتحدّى	أتحدّى	أتحدَّ		تُحُدّيتُ	أتحدّى
أنتَ	تحدّيتَ	تتحدّى	تتحدّى	تتحدَّ	تحدَّ	تُحُدّيتَ	تتحدّى
أنتِ	تحدّيتِ	تتحدّين	تتحدّي	تتحدّي	تحدّي	تُحُدّيتِ	تتحدّين
أنتما—m/f	تحدّيتما	تتحدّيان	تتحدّيا	تتحدّيا	تحدّيا	تُحُدّيتما	تتحدّيان
هو	تحدّى	يتحدّى	يتحدّى	يتحدَّ		تُحُدّي	يتحدّى
هي	تحدّت	تتحدّى	تتحدّى	تتحدَّ		تُحُدّيت	تتحدّى
هما—m	تحدّيا	يتحدّيان	يتحدّيا	يتحدّيا		تُحُدّيا	يتحدّيان
هما—f	تحدّتا	تتحدّيان	تتحدّيا	تتحدّيا		تُحُدّيتا	تتحدّيان
نحن	تحدّينا	نتحدّى	نتحدّى	نتحدَّ		تُحُدّينا	نتحدّى
أنتم	تحدّيتم	تتحدّون	تتحدّوا	تتحدّوا	تحدّوا	تُحُدّيتم	تتحدّون
أنتنّ	تحدّيتنّ	تتحدّين	تتحدّين	تتحدّين	تحدّين	تُحُدّيتنّ	تتحدّين
هم	تحدّوا	يتحدّون	يتحدّوا	يتحدّوا		تُحُدّوا	يتحدّون
هنّ	تحدّين	يتحدّين	يتحدّين	يتحدّين		تُحُدّين	يتحدّين

27

Form VI triliteral verb

1 Basic characteristics

1.1 Pattern: *tafaaᶜal-a* تَفاعَلَ /*ya-tafaaᶜal-u* يَتَفاعَلُ

Form VI verbs are augmented with respect to Form I in that there is a prefixed /ta-/ and a long vowel /-aa-/ inserted after the first consonant of the triliteral root. It looks like a Form III verb with a /ta-/ prefix. In the present tense, the subject-marking prefix vowel is *fatHa* and the two stem vowels are *fatHa*. Form VI verbs thus have the stem patterns $taC_1aaC_2C_2aC_3$- in the past tense and $ya-taC_1aaC_2aC_3$- in the present.

1.2 Meaning

In many cases Form VI is the **reciprocal** of the Form III verb, meaning that the action expressed in Form VI is mutual and happens to two (or more) parties (e.g., 'to embrace one another' *taᶜaanaq-a* تَعانق/*ya-taᶜaanaq-u* يَتَعانق).[1] Other meanings of this form of the verb include gradual, continuous movement or increase in a quality (e.g., 'to diminish, grow smaller' *taDaaʾal-a* تَضاءَل/*ya-taDaaʾal-u* يَتَضاءَل), and also pretending or feigning something (e.g., 'to feign ignorance' *tajaahal-a* تَجاهَل/*ya-tajaahal-u* يَتَجاهَل).

1.3 Transitivity

Form VI verbs are often reciprocal or intransitive, but sometimes they are transitive.

1.4 Inflection

The present tense subject-marker vowel is *fatHa* and both the past and present tense stem vowels are *fatHa* (e.g., *tabaadal-a*/*ya-tabaadal-u* 'to exchange').

2 Regular (sound) triliteral root

These verbs are examples of Form VI sound triliteral roots:

---

[1] See LeTourneau 1998 for discussion of Form VI reciprocality.

to retire, be pensioned	*taqaaʿad-a/ya-taqaaʿad-u*	تَقاعَد / يَتَقاعَد
to correlate (with)	*taraafaq-a/ya-taraafaq-u (maʿ-a)*	تَرافَق / يَتَرافَق (مع)
to understand each other	*tafaaham-a/ya-tafaaham-u*	تَفاهَم / يَتَفاهَم

3 Geminate (doubled) root Form VI

Geminate roots in Form VI have the following stem patterns: **taC_1aaC_2C_2aC_2-** in the past tense and **ya-taC_1aaC_2C_2aC_2-** in the present. These are very rare. No examples occurred in the corpus.

4 Hamzated roots in Form VI

The *hamza* may occur in the first, second, or third position in the triliteral root. Depending on its position, and the surrounding vowels, the *hamza* may have to change its "seat" when the verb inflects for person and tense:

4.1 Initial *hamza*

When an initial root *hamza* meets the ʾ*alif* infix of Form VI, they are written together as ʾ*alif madda*:

| to deliberate; to conspire | *taʾaamar-a/ya-taʾaamar-u* | تَآمَر / يَتَآمَر |
| to harmonize (with each other) | *taʾaallaf-a/ya-taʾaallaf-u (maʿa)* | تَآلَف / يَتَآلَف (مع) |

4.2 Medial *hamza*

The medial *hamza* in Form VI sits aloof, after the long *vowel* ʾ*alif* in the past tense. In the present tense it also sits aloof after the ʾ*alif*.[2]

to be optimistic	*tafaaʾal-a/ya-tafaaʾal-u*	تَفاءَل / يَتَفاءَل
to be pessimistic	*tashaaʾam-a/ya-tashaaʾam-u*	تَشاءَم / يَتَشاءَم
to be mended; be in harmony	*talaaʾam-a/ya-talaaʾam-u*	تَلاءَم / يَتَلاءَم
to diminish	*taDaaʾal-a/ ya-taDaaʾal-u*	تَضاءَل / يَتَضاءَل

4.3 Final *hamza*

Final *hamza* may sit on an ʾ*alif* seat in the past tense, but because it is the final consonant in the stem, the seat of *hamza* may shift with certain suffixes.

---

[2] This is because it is situated after a long vowel /aa/ and before a short vowel /a/. It would have an ʾ*alif* seat, but two ʾ*alifs* cannot follow each other in Arabic script, so it floats aloof.

| be equal to; to counterbalance | takaafaʾ-a/ya-takaafaʾ-u | تَكافَأَ / يَتَكافَأَ |

5 Assimilated roots in Form VI

Assimilated roots, where the first radical is either *waaw* or *yaaʾ*, are inflected as sound roots in Form VI; the *waaw* or *yaaʾ* remains.

| to coincide; agree with each other | tawaafaq-a/ya-tawaafaq-u | تَوافَقَ / يَتَوافَقُ |
| to be in equilibrium | tawaazan-a/ya-tawaazan-u | تَوازَنَ / يَتَوازَنُ |

6 Hollow roots in Form VI

Hollow roots behave as sound roots in Form VI, the *waaw* or *yaaʾ* that is the second radical functions as a normal consonant.

to deliberate; consult one another	tashaawar-a/ya-tashaawar-u	تَشاوَرَ / يَتَشاوَرُ
to cooperate with one another	taˁaawan-a/ya-taˁaawan-u	تَعاوَنَ / يَتَعاوَنُ
to coexist	taˁaayash-a/ya-taˁaayash-u	تَعايَشَ / يَتَعايَشُ
to deal with; treat	tanaawal-a/ya-tanaawal-u	تَناوَلَ / يَتَناوَلُ

7 Defective roots in Form VI

Defective roots, where the final radical is either *waaw* or *yaaʾ*, behave as -aa/-aa verbs in Form VI. They depend on the stem vowel for the nature of the final radical, and the stem vowel is consistently /a/ in the past tense and /a/ in the present tense.

to take, undertake, pursue (a task)	taˁaaTaa/ya-taˁaaTaa	تَعاطى / يَتَعاطى
to meet each other, come together	talaaqaa/ya-talaaqaa	تَلاقى / يَتَلاقى
to be equivalent to; be in balance	tasaawaa/ya-tasaawaa	تَساوى / يَتساوى

8 Examples of Form VI verbs in context

يَتَضاءَل تدريجيًّا.
ya-taDaaʾal-u tadriijiyy-an.
It **diminishes** gradually.

قد يتبادر إلى ذهنك.
*qad **ya-tabaadar-u** ʾilaa dhihn-i-ka.*
It might **cross** your mind.

وترافق ذلك مع شكاوى من بعض الناخبين.

wa-taraafaq-a dhaalika ma°-a shakaawaa min ba°D-i l-naaxib-iina.

This **correlated with** complaints of some of the voters.

أنَّ الإسلام يتساوى عندهم مع التطرُّف...

'anna l-'islaam-a ya-tasaawaa °ind-a-hum ma°-a l-taTarruf-i ...

that for them, Islam **equates with** extremism ...

9 Form VI verbal noun: *tafaa°ul* تَفاعُل

The verbal noun from Form VI has the pattern **CaCaaCuC**:

9.1 Strong/regular root

embracing	*ta°aanuq*	تَعانُق	partition	*taqaasum*	تَقاسُم
retirement	*taqaa°ud*	تَقاعُد	mutual understanding	*tafaahum*	تَفاهُم

9.2 Geminate root

This is rare in Form VI.

9.3 Hamzated root

9.3.1 *Hamza*-initial

Here the root *hamza* combines with the infixed *'alif* of Form VI to result in *'alif madda*:

harmony; camaraderie	*ta'aaluf*	تَآلُف	conspiracy	*ta'aamur*	تَآمُر

9.3.2 *Hamza*-medial

In these verbal nouns, the *hamza* sits on a *waaw* seat because it is followed by *Damma*.

optimism	*tafaa'ul*	تَفاؤُل	pessimism	*tashaa'um*	تَشاؤُم

9.3.3 *Hamza*-final

In these verbal nouns, *hamza* sits on *waaw* because it is preceded by *Damma*:

equivalence, sameness	*takaafu'*	تَكافُؤ

9.4 Assimilated root

Assimilated roots preserve their initial root consonant and behave as regular roots in the Form VI verbal noun.

congruity; coinciding	*tawaafuq*	تَوافُق

9.5 Hollow root

The hollow roots behave as regular roots in the Form VI verbal noun.

cooperation	*ta'aawun*	تَعَاوُن	increase, increment	*tazaayud*	تَزَايُد
joint consultation	*tashaawur*	تَشَاوُر	alternation	*tanaawub*	تَنَاوُب

9.6 Defective root

In verbal nouns of defective Form VI verbs, the noun is defective:

meeting, encounter	*talaaq-in*	تَلاق	equivalence, sameness	*tasaaw-in*	تَسَاوٍ

9.7 Examples of Form VI verbal nouns in context

الترابط بين قوّة النظام وشرعيّته

al-taraabuT-u bayn-a quwwat-i l-niZaam-i wa-shar'iyyat-i-hi

the **interconnection** between the power of the system and its legitimacy

قيام التسامح والتعايش السلميّ بين الشعوب

qiyaam-u l-tasaamuH-i wa-l-ta'aayush-i l-silmiyy-i bayn-a l-shu'uub-i

establishing **mutual tolerance** and **coexistence** among peoples

قد يقود إلى تقاسم ثنائيّ.

qad ya-quud-u 'ilaa taqaasum-in thunaa'iyy-in.

It might lead to a bilateral **partition**.

مجلس تعزيز التفاهم العربي البريطاني

majlis-u ta'ziiz-i l-tafaahum-i l-'arabiyy-i l-bariiTaaniyy-i

the council for strengthening Arab-British (**mutual**) **understanding**

بعد أن اتّهمهم بالتآمر مع الحكومة

ba'd-a 'an-i ttaham-a-hum bi-l-ta'aamur-i ma'-a l-Hukuumat-i

after it accused them of **conspiracy** with the government

صدر الكتاب بالتعاون مع مجلس السفراء العرب.

Sadar-a l-kitaab-i bi-l-ta'aawun-i ma'-a majlis-i l-sufaraa'-i l-'arab-i.

The book was published with **the cooperation of** the council of Arab ambassadors.

10 Form VI participles

As with other participle forms, Form VI active and passive participles occur both as nouns and as adjectives. The active participle is much more frequent in occurrence.

10.1 Form VI active participle (AP): *mutafaaᶜil* مُتَفاعِل

10.1.1 sound/regular root

| synonym | *mutaraadif* | مُتَرادِف | scattered | *mutanaathir* | مُتَناثِر |
| retired | *mutaqaaᶜid* | مُتَقاعِد | mutual, reciprocal | *mutaDaamin* | مُتَضامِن |

10.1.2 Geminate root
This is rare in Form VI.

10.1.3 Hamzated root

10.1.3.1 *Hamza*-INITIAL

| harmonious | *mutaʾaalif* | مُتآلِف | corroded | *mutaʾaakil* | مُتآكِل |

10.1.3.2 *Hamza*-MEDIAL

| optimistic | *mutafaaʾil* | مُتَفائِل | pessimistic | *mutashaaʾim* | مُتَشائِم |

10.1.3.3 *Hamza*-FINAL

| commensurate, alike | *mutakaafiʾ* | مُتَكافِئ |

10.1.4 Assimilated root

| balanced | *mutawaazin* | مُتَوازِن | continuous | *mutawaaSil* | مُتَواصِل |

10.1.5 Hollow root

| increasing | *mutazaayid* | مُتَزايِد | alternating, rotating | *mutanaawib* | مُتَناوِب |

10.1.6 Defective root

| successive, following | *mutataalin* | مُتَتالٍ |

10.1.7 Examples of Form VI APs in context

الاهتمام المتزايد بالإسلام
al-ihtimaam-u **l-mutazaayid-u** *bi-l-ʾislaam-i*
the **increasing** interest in Islam

مباراة متكافئة
mubaaraat-un **mutakaafiʾat-un**
an **equal** match

في سنوات متتالية
fii sanawaat-in **mutataaliyat-in**
in **successive** years

علب متناثرة
ᶜilab-un **mutanaathirat-un**
scattered containers

10.2 Form VI passive participle (PP): *mutafaaᶜal* متفاعَل

This participle form is not frequent in MSA, but a few examples are provided here.

10.2.1 Sound/regular root

mutual, reciprocal   *mutabaadal*   مُتَبادَل

10.2.2 Hollow root

prevailing, *mutadaawal* مُتَداوَل   availability; reach; *mutanaawal* مُتَناوَل
current   available

10.2.3 Examples of Form VI PPs in context

بالمعنى المتداول
bi-l-maᶜnaa **l-mutadaawal-i**
in the **current** meaning

الاحترام المتبادل
al-iHtiraam-u **l-mutabaadal-u**
mutual respect

Form VI Sound root: تَقاعَدَ / يَتَقاعَدُ AP: مُتَقاعِد PP: VN: تَقاعُد *'to retire'*

	Active	Active	Active	Active	Active	Passive	Passive
	Perfect	Imperfect	Imperfect	Imperfect	Imperfect	Perfect	Imperfect
		Indicative	Subjunctive	Jussive	Imperative		
أنا	تَقاعَدْتُ	أتَقاعَدُ	أتَقاعَدَ	أتَقاعَدْ			
أنْتَ	تَقاعَدْتَ	تَتَقاعَدُ	تَتَقاعَدَ	تَتَقاعَدْ	تَقاعَدْ		
أنْتِ	تَقاعَدْتِ	تَتَقاعَدينَ	تَتَقاعَدي	تَتَقاعَدي	تَقاعَدي		
أنْتُما—m/f	تَقاعَدْتُما	تَتَقاعَدانِ	تَتَقاعَدا	تَتَقاعَدا	تَقاعَدا		
هُوَ	تَقاعَدَ	يَتَقاعَدُ	يَتَقاعَدَ	يَتَقاعَدْ			
هِيَ	تَقاعَدَتْ	تَتَقاعَدُ	تَتَقاعَدَ	تَتَقاعَدْ			
هُما—m	تَقاعَدا	يَتَقاعَدانِ	يَتَقاعَدا	يَتَقاعَدا			
هُما—f	تَقاعَدَتا	تَتَقاعَدانِ	تَتَقاعَدا	تَتَقاعَدا			
نَحْنُ	تَقاعَدْنا	نَتَقاعَدُ	نَتَقاعَدَ	نَتَقاعَدْ			
أنْتُم	تَقاعَدْتُمْ	تَتَقاعَدونَ	تَتَقاعَدوا	تَتَقاعَدوا	تَقاعَدوا		
أنْتُنَّ	تَقاعَدْتُنَّ	تَتَقاعَدْنَ	تَتَقاعَدْنَ	تَتَقاعَدْنَ	تَقاعَدْنَ		
هُم	تَقاعَدوا	يَتَقاعَدونَ	يَتَقاعَدوا	يَتَقاعَدوا			
هُنَّ	تَقاعَدْنَ	يَتَقاعَدْنَ	يَتَقاعَدْنَ	يَتَقاعَدْنَ			

Form VI hamza-initial root: يَتَآمَرُ / تَآمَرَ AP: مُتَآمِر PP: VN: تَآمُر *'to conspire'*

	Active	Active	Active	Active	Active	Passive	Passive
	Perfect	Imperfect	Imperfect	Imperfect	Imperfect	Perfect	Imperfect
		Indicative	Subjunctive	Jussive	Imperative		
أنا	تَآمَرْتُ	أتَآمَرُ	أتَآمَرَ	أتَآمَرْ			
أنْتَ	تَآمَرْتَ	تتَآمَرُ	تتَآمَرَ	تتَآمَرْ	تآمَرْ		
أنْتِ	تَآمَرْتِ	تتَآمَرينَ	تتَآمَري	تتَآمَري	تآمَري		
أنْتُما—m/f	تَآمَرْتُما	تتَآمَرانِ	تتَآمَرا	تتَآمَرا	تآمَرا		
هُوَ	تَآمَرَ	يتَآمَرُ	يتَآمَرَ	يتَآمَرْ			
هِيَ	تَآمَرَتْ	تتَآمَرُ	تتَآمَرَ	تتَآمَرْ			
هُما—m	تآمَرا	يتَآمَرانِ	يتَآمَرا	يتَآمَرا			
هُما—f	تآمَرَتا	تتَآمَرانِ	تتَآمَرا	تتَآمَرا			
نَحْنُ	تَآمَرْنا	نتَآمَرُ	نتَآمَرَ	نتَآمَرْ			
أنْتُم	تَآمَرْتُمْ	تتَآمَرونَ	تتَآمَروا	تتَآمَروا	تآمَروا		
أنْتُنَّ	تَآمَرْتُنَّ	تتَآمَرْنَ	تتَآمَرْنَ	تتَآمَرْنَ	تآمَرْنَ		
هُم	تآمَروا	يتَآمَرونَ	يتَآمَروا	يتَآمَروا			
هُنَّ	تآمَرْنَ	يتَآمَرْنَ	يتَآمَرْنَ	يتَآمَرْنَ			

Form VI hamza-medial root: تَفاءَلَ /يَتَفاءَلُ   AP: مُتَفائِل   PP: VN: تَفاؤُل   'to be optimistic'

	Active	Active	Active	Active	Active	Passive	Passive
	Perfect	Imperfect	Imperfect	Imperfect	Imperfect	Perfect	Imperfect
			Indicative	Subjunctive	Jussive	Imperative	
أنا	تَفاءَلْتُ	أتَفاءَلُ	أتَفاءَلَ	أتَفاءَلْ			
أنْتَ	تَفاءَلْتَ	تَتَفاءَلُ	تَتَفاءَلَ	تَتَفاءَلْ	تَفاءَلْ		
أنْتِ	تَفاءَلْتِ	تَتَفاءَلينَ	تَتَفاءَلي	تَتَفاءَلي	تَفاءَلي		
أنْتُما—m/f	تَفاءَلْتُما	تَتَفاءَلانِ	تَتَفاءَلا	تَتَفاءَلا	تَفاءَلا		
هُوَ	تَفاءَلَ	يَتَفاءَلُ	يَتَفاءَلَ	يَتَفاءَلْ			
هِيَ	تَفاءَلَتْ	تَتَفاءَلُ	تَتَفاءَلَ	تَتَفاءَلْ			
هُما—m	تَفاءَلا	يَتَفاءَلانِ	يَتَفاءَلا	يَتَفاءَلا			
هُما—f	تَفاءَلَتا	تَتَفاءَلانِ	تَتَفاءَلا	تَتَفاءَلا			
نَحْنُ	تَفاءَلْنا	نَتَفاءَلُ	نَتَفاءَلَ	نَتَفاءَلْ			
أنتُم	تَفاءَلْتُمْ	تَتَفاءَلونَ	تَتَفاءَلوا	تَتَفاءَلوا	تَفاءَلوا		
أنتنَّ	تَفاءَلْتنَّ	تَتَفاءَلْنَ	تَتَفاءَلْنَ	تَتَفاءَلْنَ	تَفاءَلْنَ		
هُم	تَفاءَلوا	يَتَفاءَلونَ	يَتَفاءَلوا	يَتَفاءَلوا			
هُنَّ	تَفاءَلْنَ	يَتَفاءَلْنَ	يَتَفاءَلْنَ	يَتَفاءَلْنَ			

Form VI hamza-final root: تَكَافَأُ ، يَتَكَافَأُ   AP: مُتَكَافِئٍ   PP: VN: تَكَافُوٌ   *'to be equal'*

	Active	Active	Active	Active	Active	Passive	Passive
	Perfect	Imperfect	Imperfect	Imperfect	Imperfect	Perfect	Imperfect
		Indicative	Subjunctive	Jussive	Imperative		
أنا	تَكَافَأْتُ	أَتَكَافَأُ	أَتَكَافَأَ	أَتَكَافَأْ			
أَنْتَ	تَكَافَأْتَ	تَتَكَافَأُ	تَتَكَافَأَ	تَتَكَافَأْ	تَكَافَأْ		
أنْتِ	تَكَافَأْتِ	تتَكَافَئِينَ	تتَكَافَئِي	تتَكَافَئِي	تَكَافَئِي		
أنْتُما m/f–	تَكَافَأْتُما	تَتَكَافَآنِ	تَتَكَافَآ	تَتَكَافَآ	تَكَافَآ		
هُوَ	تَكَافَأَ	يَتَكَافَأُ	يَتَكَافَأَ	يَتَكَافَأْ			
هِيَ	تَكَافَأَتْ	تَتَكَافَأُ	تَتَكَافَأَ	تَتَكَافَأْ			
هُما m–	تَكَافَآ	يَتَكَافَآنِ	يَتَكَافَآ	يَتَكَافَآ			
هُما f–	تَكَافَأَتا	تَتَكَافَآنِ	تَتَكَافَآ	تَتَكَافَآ			
نَحْنُ	تَكَافَأْنا	نَتَكَافَأُ	نَتَكَافَأَ	نَتَكَافَأْ			
أنْتُمُ	تَكَافَأْتُمْ	تتَكَافَؤُونَ	تتَكَافَؤُوا	تتَكَافَؤُوا	تَكَافَؤُوا		
أنْتُنَّ	تَكَافَأْتُنَّ	تتَكَافَأْنَ	تتَكَافَأْنَ	تتَكَافَأْنَ	تَكَافَأْنَ		
هُم	تَكَافَؤُوا	يتَكَافَؤُونَ	يتَكَافَؤُوا	يتَكَافَؤُوا			
هُنَّ	تَكَافَأْنَ	يتَكَافَأْنَ	يتَكَافَأْنَ	يتَكَافَأْنَ			

Form VI Defective root: تَداعى ، يَتَداعى   AP: مُتَداعٍ   PP: VN: تَداعٍ   *'to decline, subside'*

	Active	Active	Active	Active	Active	Passive	Passive
	Perfect	Imperfect	Imperfect	Imperfect	Imperfect	Perfect	Imperfect
		Indicative	Subjunctive	Jussive	Imperative		
أَنا	تَداعَيْتُ	أَتَداعى	أَتَداعى	أَتَداعَ			
أَنْتَ	تَداعَيْتَ	تَتَداعى	تَتَداعى	تَتَداعَ	تَداعَ		
أَنْتِ	تَداعَيْتِ	تَتَداعَيْنَ	تَتَداعَيْ	تَتَداعَيْ	تَداعَيْ		
أَنْتُما—m/f	تَداعَيْتُما	تَتَداعَيانِ	تَتَداعَيا	تَتَداعَيا	تَداعَيا		
هُوَ	تَداعى	يَتَداعى	يَتَداعى	يَتَداعَ			
هِيَ	تَداعَت	تَتَداعى	تَتَداعى	تَتَداعَ			
هُما—m	تَداعَيا	يَتَداعَيانِ	يَتَداعَيا	يَتَداعَيا			
هُما—f	تَداعَتا	تَتَداعَيانِ	تَتَداعَيا	تَتَداعَيا			
نَحْنُ	تَداعَيْنا	نَتَداعى	نَتَداعى	نَتَداعَ			
أَنْتُم	تَداعَيْتُم	تَتَداعَوْنَ	تَتَداعَوْا	تَتَداعَوْا	تَداعَوْا		
أَنْتُنَّ	تَداعَيْتُنَّ	تَتَداعَيْنَ	تَتَداعَيْنَ	تَتَداعَيْنَ	تَداعَيْنَ		
هُم	تَداعَوْا	يَتَداعَوْنَ	يَتَداعَوْا	يَتَداعَوْا			
هُنَّ	تَداعَيْنَ	يَتَداعَيْنَ	يَتَداعَيْنَ	يَتَداعَيْنَ			

28

Form VII triliteral verb

1 Basic characteristics

1.1 Pattern: *infaᶜal-a* اِنْفَعَلَ /*ya-nfaᶜil-u* يَنْفَعِل

Form VII verbs are augmented with respect to Form I in that a prefix /n/ is added to the Form I stem. Form VII has the past tense stem **inC$_1$aC$_2$aC$_3$-** and the present tense stem **-nC$_1$aC$_2$iC$_3$-**. A prefixed elidable *hamza* with *kasra* is added to the past tense stem of Form VII; this *hamza* and its vowel are deleted in the present tense, replaced by the present tense subject markers. There is a restriction on the roots that can be used in Form VII: roots beginning with the consonants *hamza, waaw, yaaʾ, raaʾ, laam*, or *nuun* do not have a Form VII.[1] In these instances, either Form V or Form VIII is used instead.

1.2 Meaning

Form VII verbs may be reflexive, resultative, passive, or mediopassive in meaning. They may express the consequences of a Form I verb action and have been classified also as verbs that express ergative and "unaccusative" constructions in Arabic.[2] The Arabic term for referring to their meaning is *muTaawiᶜ* 'obeying, corresponding with' – that is, Form VII verbs show the result of Form I action, e.g., *fataH-tu l-baab-a fa-nfataH-a* 'I opened (Form I) the door and it opened (Form VII).'[3]

1.3 Transitivity

Form VII verbs are intransitive.

1.4 Inflection

The prefixed *hamzat al-waSl* with *kasra* in the past tense stem is deleted in the present tense and replaced by the subject-marker prefix. The vowel of the present

---

[1] The prefixed /n/ of Form VII is considered phonologically incompatible with these consonants. In addition, roots whose initial consonant is *miim* are relatively rare in Form VII in MSA.

[2] See Mahmoud 1991 for further discussion and definition of Arabic unaccusatives.

[3] For more on *muTaawiᶜ* see Chapter 26 on Form V, note 4.

tense subject-marker prefix is *fatHa* and the stem vowel in the present tense is *kasra* (e.g., *inSaraf-a/ya-nSarif-u* 'to leave, go out').

2 Regular (sound) triliteral root

2.1 Intransitive

to explode	*infajar-a/ya-nfajir-u*	انْفَجَرَ / يَنْفَجِرُ
to be at ease, be happy[4]	*inbasaT-a/ya-nbasiT-u*	انْبَسَطَ / يَنْبَسِطُ
to sink, decline	*inxafaD-a/ya-nxafiD-u*	انْخَفَضَ / يَنْخَفِضُ
to withdraw; be withdrawn	*insaHab-a/ya-nsaHib-u*	انْسَحَبَ / يَنْسَحِبُ

2.2 Passive/reflexive
Form VII is often the passive, resultative, or reflexive of Form I:

to be separated, divided	*inqasam-a/ya-nqasim-u*	انْقَسَمَ / يَنْقَسِمُ
to be cut off	*inqaTa^c-a/ya-nqaTi^c-u*	انْقَطَعَ / يَنْقَطِعُ
to be reflected	*in^cakas-a/ya-n^cakis-u*	انْعَكَسَ / يَنْعَكِسُ
to be held, convened	*in^caqad-a/ya-n^caqid-u*	انْعَقَدَ / يَنْعَقِدُ

3 Geminate (doubled) root Form VII
Geminate roots in Form VII have the following stem patterns: **inC₁aC₂C₂-** in the past tense and **ya-nC₁aC₂C₂ -** in the present.

to affiliate; join (with)	*inDamm-a/ya-nDamm-u (ʾilaa)*	انْضَمَّ / يَنْضَمُّ
to disintegrate	*inHall-a/ya-nHall-u*	انْحَلَّ / يَنْحَلُّ
to split, crack	*inshaqq-a/ya-nshaqq-u*	انْشَقَّ / يَنْشَقُّ

4 Hamzated roots in Form VII
The *hamza* may occur in the second or third position of the triliteral root in Form VII, but not in root-initial position. Depending on its position and the surrounding vowels, the *hamza* may have to change its "seat" when the verb inflects for person and tense:

Medial *hamza*: rare
Final *hamza*:

to be extinguished	*inTafa^ʾ-a/ya-nTafi^ʾ-u*	انْطَفَأَ / يَنْطَفِئُ

---

[4] Also, 'to be spread out;' *s.v. basaT-a* in Wehr 1979.

5 Assimilated roots in Form VII

These do not occur (see 1.1).

6 Hollow roots in Form VII *infaal-a* انْفَال /*ya-nfaal-u* يَنْفَال

Hollow roots in Form VII are inflected with ʾ*alif* as the long vowel and *fatHa* as the short vowel in the present and in the past: inC_1aaC_3-a /$ya-nC_1aaC_3-u$.

| to take sides, align | inHaaz-a/ya-nHaaz-u | انْحَاز / يَنْحَازُ |
| to decline, collapse | inhaar-a/ya-nhaar-u | انْهَار / يَنْهَار |

7 Defective roots in Form VII

Defective roots in Form VII inflect as *-aa/-ii* defectives.

to be necessary; ought to	inbaghaa/ya-nbaghii	انْبَغَى / يَنْبَغِي
to elapse; expire	inqaDaa/ya-nqaDii	انْقَضَى / يَنْقَضِي
to be folded; be absorbed[5]	inTawaa/ya-nTawii	انْطَوَى / يَنْطَوِي

8 Examples of Form VII verbs in context

انْفَجَرَ الوَضْعُ في الشوارع.
infajar-a l-waDᶜ-u fii l-shawaariᶜ-i.
The situation **exploded** in the streets.

اندَمَجَتْ في حياتها الجديدة بسهولة.
indamaj-at fii Hayaat-i-haa l-jadiidat-i bi-suhuulat-in.
She easily **got involved** in her new life.

انْقَطَعَ التيّارُ الكهربائيَّ.
inqaTaᶜ-a l-tayyaar-u l-kahrabaaʾiyy-u.
The electric current **was cut off.**

انْخَرَطوا في جدل عنيف.
inxaraT-uu fii jadal-in ᶜaniif-in.
They plunged into violent debate.

9 Form VII verbal noun: *infiᶜaal* انْفِعَال

9.1 Strong/regular root

| reflection | inᶜikaas | انْعِكَاس | coup d'état | inqilaab | انْقِلاب |
| explosion | infijaar | انْفِجَار | isolation | inᶜizaal | انْعِزَال |

9.2 Geminate root

The Form VII verbal noun of geminate roots has the regular pattern *infiᶜaal*, the *alif* coming between the identical second and third root consonants:

| affiliating | inDimaam | انْضِمَام | disintegration | inHilaal | انْحِلال |

---

[5] Used with the preposition ᶜ*alaa*, *inTawaa* means 'to contain.'

9.3 Hamzated root

extinguishing   *inTifaa'*   انْطِفاء

9.4 Assimilated root
These do not occur.

9.5 Hollow root: *infiyaal* انْفِيال
The verbal noun for Form VII hollow verbs has a *yaa'* as the medial consonant, no matter what the root of origin.

alignment   *inHiyaaz*   انْحِياز   collapse; decline   *inhiyaar*   انْهِيار

9.6 Defective root: *infiᶜaa'* انْفِعاء
The verbal noun of defective Form VII verbs is of the pattern *infiᶜaa'* انفعاء, with *hamza* after the long /-aa-/.[6]

expiration, elapsing   *inqiDaa'*   انْقِضاء   introversion   *inTiwaa'*   انْطِواء

9.7 Examples of Form VII verbal nouns in context

الانحِلال السِياسِيّ
al-inHilaal-u l-siyaasiyy-u
political **disintegration**

بِسَبَب انشِغال المسؤولين
bi-sabab-i nshighaal-i l-mas'uul-iina
because of the **preoccupation** of the officials

قَبل انقِضاء عام على ذلك
qabl-a nqiDaa'-i ᶜaam-in ᶜalaa dhaalika
before **the elapsing** of a year after that

هو انعِكاس للواقع الاجتماعيّ.
huwa nᶜikaas-un li-l-waaqᶜ-i l-ijtimaaᶜiyy-i.
It is **a reflection** of social reality.

10 Form VII participles

10.1 Form VII active participle (AP): *munfaᶜil* مُنْفَعِل

10.1.1 Sound/regular root

isolated   *munᶜazil*   مُنْعَزِل   sloping   *munHadir*   مُنْحَدِر

introverted; shrunk   *munkamish*   مُنْكَمِش   sliding   *munzaliq*   مُنْزَلِق

10.1.2 Geminate root: *munfaᶜᶜ* مُنْفَعّ
The active and passive participles for geminate roots in Form VII have the same pattern; *munfaᶜᶜ*. If the verb itself has a passive, reflexive, or intransitive meaning,

---

[6] Because of the shift of the semi-consonant (*waaw* or *yaa'*) to *hamza*, this verbal noun winds up looking like the verbal noun for *hamza*-final roots.

the AP will carry that passive or reflexive meaning. It is therefore sometimes difficult to tell the Form VII AP and PP apart.

closely packed;   *munDamm*   مُنْضَمّ   separatist   *munshaqq*   مُنْشقّ
affiliated with

10.1.3 Hamzated root

extinguished   *munTafiʾ*   مُنْطَفِئ

10.1.4 Assimilated root

These do not occur.

10.1.5 Hollow root: *munfaal* مُنْفَال

The active and passive participles for hollow roots in Form VII have the same pattern; *munfaal*. If the verb itself has a passive, reflexive, or intransitive meaning, the AP will carry that passive or reflexive meaning. It is often difficult to distinguish between the Form VII AP and PP.

aligned   *munHaaz*   مُنْحَاز

10.1.6 Defective root

introverted   *munTawin*   مُنْطَوٍ

10.2 Form VII passive participle (PP): *munfaʿal* مُنْفَعَل

These are not frequent in occurrence because of the intransitivity or reflexivity of the meaning of this form. Form VII PPs that do occur tend to be used as **nouns of place**.

10.2.1 Sound/regular root

slope, incline   *munHadar*   مُنْحَدَر   starting point   *munTalaq*   مُنْطَلَق
lowland   *munxafaD*   مُنْخَفَض

10.2.2 Geminate root: *munfaʿʿ* مُنْفَعّ

As noted in 10.1.2, the passive participle and active participle are indistinguishable in form.

10.2.3 Hamzated root

This does not occur.

10.2.4 Assimilated root

This does not occur.

10.2.5 Hollow root: *munfaal* مُنْفَال

As noted in 10.1.5, the passive participles and active participles of hollow roots in this form are identical.

10.2.6 Defective root: *munfaʿan* مُنْفَعًى

enclosed, folded in   *munTawan*   مُنْطَوًى

10.3 Examples of Form VII participles in context

باب منزلق
*baab-un **munzaliq-un***
a **sliding** door

الدول غير المنحازة
*al-duwal-u ghayr-u **l-munHaazat-i***
non-**aligned** states

تطوّق منحدراته الأشجار.
*tu-Tawwiq-u **munHadaraat-i-hi** l-ʾashjaar-u.*
Trees encircle **its slopes**.

Form VII Sound root: اِنْبَسَطَ ، يَنْبَسِطُ AP: مُنْبَسِط PP: VN: اِنْبِساط *'to be glad, happy'*

	Active	Active	Active	Active	Active	Passive	Passive
	Perfect	Imperfect	Imperfect	Imperfect	Imperfect	Perfect	Imperfect
		Indicative	Subjunctive	Jussive	Imperative		
أنا	اِنْبَسَطْتُ	أَنْبَسِطُ	أَنْبَسِطَ	أَنْبَسِطْ			
أنْتَ	اِنْبَسَطْتَ	تَنْبَسِطُ	تَنْبَسِطَ	تَنْبَسِطْ	اِنْبَسِطْ		
أنْتِ	اِنْبَسَطْتِ	تَنْبَسِطين	تَنْبَسِطي	تَنْبَسِطي	اِنْبَسِطي		
أنْتُما–m/f	اِنْبَسَطْتُما	تَنْبَسِطان	تَنْبَسِطا	تَنْبَسِطا	اِنْبَسِطا		
هُوَ	اِنْبَسَطَ	يَنْبَسِطُ	يَنْبَسِطَ	يَنْبَسِطْ			
هِيَ	اِنْبَسَطَتْ	تَنْبَسِطُ	تَنْبَسِطَ	تَنْبَسِطْ			
هُما–m	اِنْبَسَطا	يَنْبَسِطان	يَنْبَسِطا	يَنْبَسِطا			
هُما–f	اِنْبَسَطَتا	تَنْبَسِطان	تَنْبَسِطا	تَنْبَسِطا			
نحْنُ	اِنْبَسَطْنا	نَنْبَسِطُ	نَنْبَسِطَ	نَنْبَسِطْ			
أنْتُم	اِنْبَسَطْتُم	تَنْبَسِطون	تَنْبَسِطوا	تَنْبَسِطوا	اِنْبَسِطوا		
أنْتُنَّ	اِنْبَسَطْتنَّ	تَنْبَسِطْنَ	تَنْبَسِطْنَ	تَنْبَسِطْنَ	اِنْبَسِطْنَ		
هُم	اِنْبَسَطوا	يَنْبَسِطون	يَنْبَسِطوا	يَنْبَسِطوا			
هُنَّ	اِنْبَسَطْنَ	يَنْبَسِطْنَ	يَنْبَسِطْنَ	يَنْبَسِطْنَ			

Form VII Geminate root: انْضَمَّ / يَنْضَمُّ AP: مُنْضَمّ PP: VN: انْضِمام *'to join with, affiliate with'*

	Active	Active	Active	Active	Active	Passive	Passive
	Perfect	Imperfect	Imperfect	Imperfect	Imperfect	Perfect	Imperfect
		Indicative	Subjunctive	Jussive	Imperative		
أنا	انْضَمَمْتُ	أنْضَمُّ	أنْضَمَّ	أنْضَمَّ			
أنْت	انْضَمَمْتَ	تنْضَمُّ	تنْضَمَّ	تنْضَمَّ	انْضَمَّ		
أنْتِ	انْضَمَمْتِ	تنْضَمِّين	تنْضَمِّي	تنْضَمِّي	انْضَمِّي		
أنْتُما—m/f	انْضَمَمْتُم	تنْضَمَّان	تنْضَمَّا	تنْضَمَّا	انْضَمَّا		
هو	انْضَمَّ	ينْضَمُّ	ينْضَمَّ	ينْضَمَّ			
هي	انْضَمَّتْ	تنْضَمُّ	تنْضَمَّ	تنْضَمَّ			
هُما—m	انْضَمَّا	ينْضَمَّان	ينْضَمَّا	ينْضَمَّا			
هُما—f	انْضَمَّتا	تنْضَمَّان	تنْضَمَّا	تنْضَمَّا			
نَحْنُ	انْضَمَمْنا	ننْضَمُّ	ننْضَمَّ	ننْضَمَّ			
أنْتُم	انْضَمَمْتُم	تنْضَمُّون	تنْضَمُّوا	تنْضَمُّوا	انْضَمُّوا		
أنْتُنّ	انْضَمَمْتُنّ	تنْضَمِمْن	تنْضَمِمْن	تنْضَمِمْن	انْضَمِمْن		
هُم	انْضَمُّوا	ينْضَمُّون	ينْضَمُّوا	ينْضَمُّوا			
هُنّ	انْضَمَمْن	ينْضَمِمْن	ينْضَمِمْن	ينْضَمِمْن			

Form VII Hollow root: انْحَازَ/يَنْحَازُ   *AP:* مُنْحَازٌ   *PP:*   *VN:* انْحِيازٌ   *'to take sides'*

	Active	Active	Active	Active	Active	Passive	Passive
	Perfect	Imperfect	Imperfect	Imperfect	Imperfect	Perfect	Imperfect
		Indicative	Subjunctive	Jussive	Imperative		
أنا	انْحَزْتُ	أنْحَازُ	أنْحَازَ	أنْحَزْ			
أنتَ	انْحَزْتَ	تَنْحَازُ	تَنْحَازَ	تَنْحَزْ	انْحَزْ		
أنتِ	انْحَزْتِ	تَنْحازينَ	تَنْحازي	تَنْحازي	انْحازي		
أنتُما—m/f	انْحَزْتُما	تَنْحازانِ	تَنْحازا	تَنْحازا	انْحازا		
هُوَ	انْحازَ	يَنْحازُ	يَنْحازَ	يَنْحَزْ			
هِيَ	انْحازَتْ	تَنْحازُ	تَنْحازَ	تَنْحَزْ			
هُما—m	انْحازا	يَنْحازانِ	يَنْحازا	يَنْحازا			
هُما—f	انْحازَتا	تَنْحازانِ	تَنْحازا	تَنْحازا			
نَحْنُ	انْحَزْنا	نَنْحازُ	نَنْحازَ	نَنْحَزْ			
أنْتُم	انْحَزْتُمْ	تَنْحازونَ	تَنْحازوا	تَنْحازوا	انْحازوا		
أنتنَّ	انْحَزْتنَّ	تَنْحَزْنَ	تَنْحَزْنَ	تَنْحَزْنَ	انْحَزْنَ		
هُمْ	انْحازوا	يَنْحازونَ	يَنْحازوا	يَنْحازوا			
هُنَّ	انْحَزْنَ	يَنْحَزْنَ	يَنْحَزْنَ	يَنْحَزْنَ			

Form VII Defective root: انْقَضَى / يَنْقَضِي　AP: مُنْقَضٍ　PP:　VN: انْقِضاء　*'to elapse, expire'*

	Active	Active	Active	Active	Active	Passive	Passive
	Perfect	Imperfect	Imperfect	Imperfect	Imperfect	Perfect	Imperfect
		Indicative	Subjunctive	Jussive	Imperative		
أنا	انْقَضَيْتُ	أنْقَضِي	أنْقَضِيَ	أنْقَضِ			
أنْت	انْقَضَيْتَ	تَنْقَضِي	تَنْقَضِيَ	تَنْقَضِ	انْقَضِ		
أنْت	انْقَضَيْتِ	تَنْقَضِين	تَنْقَضِي	تَنْقَضِي	انْقَضِي		
أنْتُما—m/f	انْقَضَيْتُما	تَنْقَضِيان	تَنْقَضِيا	تَنْقَضِيا	انْقَضِيا		
هُوَ	انْقَضَى	يَنْقَضِي	يَنْقَضِيَ	يَنْقَضِ			
هِي	انْقَضَتْ	تَنْقَضِي	تَنْقَضِيَ	تَنْقَضِ			
هُما—m	انْقَضَيا	يَنْقَضِيان	يَنْقَضِيا	يَنْقَضِيا			
هُما—f	انْقَضَتا	تَنْقَضِيان	تَنْقَضِيا	تَنْقَضِيا			
نَحْنُ	انْقَضَيْنا	نَنْقَضِي	نَنْقَضِيَ	نَنْقَضِ			
أنْتُم	انْقَضَيْتُمْ	تَنْقَضُون	تَنْقَضُوا	تَنْقَضُوا	انْقَضُوا		
أنْتُنَّ	انْقَضَيْتُنَّ	تَنْقَضِين	تَنْقَضِين	تَنْقَضِين	انْقَضِين		
هُم	انْقَضَوْا	يَنْقَضُون	يَنْقَضُوا	يَنْقَضُوا			
هُنَّ	انْقَضَيْنَ	يَنْقَضِين	يَنْقَضِين	يَنْقَضِين			

29

Form VIII triliteral verb

1 Basic characteristics

1.1 Pattern: *iftaʿal-a* اِفْتَعَلَ / *ya-ftaʿil-u* يَفْتَعِلُ

Form VIII verbs are augmented with respect to Form I in that an infix /t/ is added to the Form I stem after the first radical. Thus Form VIII has the past tense stem $iC_1taC_2aC_3$- and the present tense stem $-C_1taC_2iC_3$-. A prefixed elidable *hamza* with *kasra* is added to the past tense stem of Form VIII in order to make it pronounceable; this *hamza* and its vowel are deleted in the present tense, replaced by the present tense subject markers.

1.2 Meaning

Form VIII verbs may be reflexive or medio-passive in meaning, but they also express a wide range of meanings that are difficult to predict. They may express the consequences of a Form I verb action and are sometimes considered resultative (*muTaawiʿ* مطاوع), in the same way that Form VII verbs may be resultative of the action of a Form I verb. This is especially true for verb roots starting with the consonants *hamza, waaw, yaaʾ, raaʾ, laam* or *nuun*, because these roots do not occur in Form VII and often use Form VIII instead to express the resultative (e.g., Form I *rafaʿ-a/ya-rfaʿ-u* 'to raise' and Form VIII *irtafaʿ-a* اِرْتَفَعَ /*ya-rtafiʿ-u* يَرْتَفِعُ 'to be raised, to rise'). Form VIII is distinguished from Form VII by the ability to have a reciprocal meaning, that is, the action takes place mutually among several entities, e.g., Form I *jamaʿ-a/ya-jmaʿ-u* 'to collect, gather (s.th.)' and Form VIII *ijtamaʿ-a* اِجْتَمَعَ / *ya-jtamiʿ-u* يَجْتَمِعُ to meet with each other; collect together.'[1]

1.3 Transitivity

Form VIII verbs may be transitive or intransitive. Some are doubly transitive, such as *iʿtabar-a* اِعْتَبَرَ /*ya-ʿtabir-u* يَعْتَبِرُ 'to consider (s.o.) (s.th.).'

---

[1] On this point see Fleisch 1979, II: 311.

1.4 Inflection

The prefixed *hamzat al-waSl* with *kasra* in the past tense stem is deleted in the present tense and replaced by the subject-marker prefix. The vowel of the present tense subject-marker prefix is *fatHa* and the stem vowel in the present tense is *kasra* (e.g., *intaxab-a* انْتَخَبَ /*ya-ntaxib-u* يَنْتَخِبُ 'to elect').

1.5 Special phonological characteristics of Form VIII

The insertion of the extraneous consonant /t/ within the root sometimes affects the spelling and pronunciation of Form VIII verbs. Various forms of **assimilation** of the infixed *taaʾ* to the initial root consonant occur, and with assimilated verb roots the *taaʾ* itself assimilates the initial *waaw* or *yaaʾ* completely.

1.5.1 Progressive assimilation

In progressive assimilation, the *taaʾ* is influenced by the preceding sound in the word.

1.5.1.1 VELARIZATION: **Where the initial root consonant is velarized (S, D, T, Z)** and the infixed *taaʾ* acquires the velarization feature. This results in a spelling change from *taaʾ* to **Taaʾ**.

to crash (into); collide with	*iSTadam-a/ya-STadim-u (bi-)* (root: S-d-m)	اِصْطَدَمَ / يَصْطَدِمُ
to be disturbed, agitated	*iDTarab-a/ya-DTarib-u* (root: D-r-b)	اِضْطَرَبَ / يَضْطَرِبُ
to be aware; examine, look into	*iTTalaᶜ-a/ya-TTaliᶜ-u (ᶜalaa)* (root: T-l-ᶜ)	اِطَّلَعَ / يَطَّلِعُ (على)

1.5.1.2 VOICED ALVEOLARS: **Where the initial root consonant is voiced and alveolar (d or z)**

(1)   *daal*-**initial root:** The *taaʾ* assimilates totally to the *daal*.

to be inserted; to assimilate	*iddagham-a/ya-ddaghim-u* (root: d-gh-m)	اِدَّغَمَ / يَدَّغِمُ
to allege, claim	*iddaᶜaa/ya-ddaᶜii* (root: d-ᶜ-w)	اِدَّعى / يَدَّعي

(2)   *zaay*-**initial root:** In the *zaay*-initial root, the infixed *taaʾ* partially assimilates to the /z/ sound by becoming a voiced dental stop (*daal*) instead of a voiceless dental stop (/t/). That is, instead of *iftaᶜal-a* it becomes *ifdaᶜal-a*.

to flourish	*izdahar-a/ya-zdahir-u* (root: z-h-r)	اِزْدَهَرَ / يَزْدَهِرُ
to be crowded	*izdaHam-a/ya-zdaHim-u* (root: z-H-m)	اِزْدَحَمَ / يَزْدَحِمُ
to be doubled, be paired	*izdawaj-a/ya-zdawij-u* (root: z-w-j)	اِزْدَوَجَ / يَزْدَوِجُ
to increase	*izdaad-a/ya-zdaad-u* (root: z-w-d)	اِزْدَادَ / يَزْدَادُ

1.5.1.3 INTERDENTALS: Where the initial root consonant is interdental (*th*, *dh*, *Z*)

The infixed *taa'* assimilates completely to the interdental root consonant.

(1) ***thaa'*-initial root**

| to avenge, get revenge | *iththa'ar-a/ya-ththa'ir-u* | اِثَّأَرَ / يَثَّئِرُ |

(2) ***dhaal*-initial root:** In *dhaal*-initial roots, the *dhaal* and infixed *taa'* mutually influence one another, assimilating together as two **daals** (the *dhaal* loses its interdental quality, the *taa'* acquires voicing):

| to amass, save | *iddaxar-a/ya-ddaxir-u* (root: dh-x-r) | اِدَّخَرَ / يَدَّخِرُ |

(3) ***Zaa'*-initial root:**

| to be wronged, suffer injustice | *iZZalam-a/ya-ZZalim-u* (root: Z-l-m) | اِظَّلَمَ / يَظَّلِمُ |

1.5.2 Form VIII regressive assimilation

In regressive assimilation, the initial root consonant *waaw* or *yaa'* is affected by the infixed *taa'* and is assimilated into it. That is, for example, instead of the shape **iwtaHad-a* (from the root w-H-d) the actual Form VIII verb is *ittaHad-a*.

to be united	*ittaHad-a/ya-ttaHid-u* (root w-H-d)	اِتَّحَدَ / يَتَّحِدُ
to expand	*ittasaᶜ-a/ya-ttasiᶜ-u* (root: w-s-ᶜ)	اِتَّسَعَ / يَتَّسِعُ
to face, take the direction of	*ittajah-a/ya-ttajih-u* (root: w-j-h)	اِتَّجَهَ / يَتَّجِهُ
to accuse	*ittaham-a/ya-ttahim-u* (root w-h-m)	اِتَّهَمَ / يَتَّهِمُ

2 Regular or sound roots

to celebrate, have a party	iHtafal-a/ya-Htafil-u	اِحْتَفَلَ / يَحْتَفِلُ
to respect	iHtaram-a/ya-Htarim-u	اِحْتَرَمَ / يَحْتَرِمُ
to earn	iktasab-a/ya-ktasib-u	اِكْتَسَبَ / يَكْتَسِبُ
to be different; to differ	ixtalaf-a/ya-xtalif-u	اِخْتَلَفَ / يَخْتَلِفُ

2.1 Initial-*nuun* roots

A number of intransitive Form VIII verbs are from roots whose initial consonant is /n/, since these do not assume Form VII.

to move, be transferred	intaqal-a/ya-ntaqil-u	اِنْتَقَلَ / يَنْتَقِلُ
to spread out	intashar-a/ya-ntashir-u	اِنْتَشَرَ / يَنْتَشِرُ
to elect	intaxab-a/ya-ntaxib-u	اِنْتَخَبَ / يَنْتَخِبُ

3 Geminate (doubled) root Form VIII

to be interested, concerned (with)	ihtamm-a/ya-htamm-u (bi-)	اِهْتَمَّ / يَهْتَمُّ بـ
to be spread, extended	imtadd-a/ya-mtadd-u	اِمْتَدَّ / يَمْتَدُّ
to occupy	iHtall-a/ya-Htall-u	اِحْتَلَّ / يَحْتَلُّ

4 Hamzated roots in Form VIII

4.1 *Hamza*-initial

to deliberate; to plot	i'tamar-a/ya-'tamir-u	اِئْتَمَرَ / يَأْتَمِرُ
to go well together; form a coalition	i'talaf-a/ya-'talif-u	اِئْتَلَفَ / يَأْتَلِفُ

4.2 *Hamza*-medial

to be healed, to heal	ilta'am-a/ya-lta'im-u	اِلْتَأَمَ / يَلْتَئِمُ

4.3 *Hamza*-final

to begin	ibtada'-a/ya-btadi'-u	اِبْتَدَأَ / يَبْتَدِئُ
to be filled	imtala'-a/ya-mtali'-u	اِمْتَلَأَ / يَمْتَلِئُ

5 Assimilated roots in Form VIII

In Form VIII, the inflixed *taa'* assimilates the initial semi-consonant *waaw* or *yaa'*, and doubles in strength (see above 1.5.2).

6 Hollow roots in Form VIII *iftaal-a* اِفْتَال / *ya-ftaal-u* يَفْتَال

Hollow roots in Form VIII are usually inflected with *'alif* as the long vowel and *fatHa* as the short vowel in the present and in the past iC₁CaaC₃-a /ya-C₁CaaC₃-u.

to need	iHtaaj-a/ya-Htaaj-u	اِحْتَاج / يَحْتَاج
to assassinate	ightaal-a/ya-ghtaal-u	اِغْتَال / يَغْتَال
to choose	ixtaar-a/ya-xtaar-u	اِخْتَار / يَخْتَار

6.1 Retention of medial semivowel

In some cases, a hollow root in Form VIII keeps its medial semi-consonant, as follows:

| to be doubled, paired | izdawaj-a/ya-zdawij-u | اِزْدَوَج / يَزْدَوِج |
| to contain | iHtawaa/ya-Htawii | اِحْتَوى / يَحْتَوِي |

7 Defective roots in Form VIII

Defective roots in Form VIII inflect as -aa/-ii defectives:

to meet, encounter (s.o.)	iltaqaa/ya-ltaqii	اِلْتَقَى / يَلْتَقِي
to be content, satisfied	iktafaa/ya-ktafii	اِكْتَفَى / يَكْتَفِي
to wear, be dressed (in)	irtadaa/ya-rtadii	اِرْتَدَى / يَرْتَدِي

7.1 Hollow and defective

The hollow-defective Form VIII verb keeps its medial semi-consonant (usually *waaw*) as a strong consonant:

| to contain (s.th.) | iHtawaa/ya-Htawii | اِحْتَوى / يَحْتَوِي |

8 Examples of Form VIII verbs in context

واكتشف أيضاً أخطاءً

wa-ktashaf-a 'ayD-an 'axTaa'-an
and he also **discovered** mistakes

ما يحتوي هذا المتحف

maa *ya-Htawii* haadhaa l-matHaf-u
what this museum **contains**

تجتذب الطلاب الجيّدين.

ta-jtadhib-u l-Tullaab-a l-jayyid-iina.
It **attracts** good students.

يترك لكلّ إنسان أن يختار.

ya-truk-u li-kull-i insaan-in 'an *ya-xtaar-a*.
He leaves [it] to every person **to choose**.

9 Verbal nouns of Form VIII

9.1 Sound/regular root: *ifti°aal* افْتِعال

respect	iHtiraam	احْتِرام	meeting	ijtimaa°	اجْتِماع
election	intixaab	انْتِخاب	difference	ixtilaaf	اخْتِلاف

9.1.1 With assimilation of *taa°*

collision, crash	iSTidaam	اصْطِدام	flourishing, bloom	izdihaar	ازْدِهار
disturbance, unrest	iDTiraab	اضْطِراب	crowd, jam, crush	izdiHaam	ازْدِحام

9.2 Geminate root

interest, concern	ihtimaam	اهْتِمام	occupation	iHtilaal	احْتِلال
spreading	imtidaad	امْتِداد	gratitude	imtinaan	امْتِنان

9.3 Hamzated root

coalition	i°tilaaf	ائْتِلاف	beginning	ibtidaa°	ابْتِداء

9.4 Assimilated root

union	ittiHaad	اتّحاد	accusation	ittihaam	اتّهام

9.5 Hollow root

reserve; precaution	iHtiyaaT	احْتِياط	increase	izdiyaad	ازْدِياد
pleasure, delight	irtiyaaH	ارْتِياح	doubling, pairing	izdiwaaj[2]	ازْدِواج

9.6 Defective root

In the defective root Form VIII verbal noun, the final defective root consonant is represented by a *hamza*.

membership; belonging	intimaa°	انْتِماء	disappearance	ixtifaa°	اخْتِفاء

---

[2] In this particular root, the *waaw* behaves as a strong consonant. See section 6 above.

9.7 Form VIII verbal nouns in context

عدم ارتياح الجانبين
ᶜadam-u rtiyaaH-i l-jaanib-ayni
the discomfort of both sides

اجتماع كبار المسؤولين
ijtimaaᶜ-u kibaar-i l-masᵓuul-iina
the meeting of senior officials

لا احترام للحقوق الشخصيّة للإنسان.
laa Htiraam-a li-l-Huquuq-i l-shaxSiyyat-i li-l-insaan-i.
There is no **respect** for the personal rights
of humans.

اكتشاف رسائل حبّ
iktishaaf-u rasaaᵓil-i Hubb-in
the **discovery** of love letters

10 Form VIII participles

10.1 Form VIII active participle (AP): *muftaᶜil* مُفْتَعِل

In addition to carrying the meaning of doer of the action, the AP of Form VIII may
sometimes convey a passive or resultative meaning, especially when derived from
a resultative verb, e.g., *muqtaniᶜ* 'convinced' or *muttaHid* 'united.'

10.1.1 Sound/regular root: *muftaᶜil* مُفْتَعِل

respecting	*muHtarim*	مُحْتَرِم	convinced	*muqtaniᶜ*	مُقْتَنِع
listener	*mustamiᶜ*	مُسْتَمِع	objecting	*muᶜtariD*	مُعْتَرِض
different, differing	*muxtalif*	مُخْتَلِف	spreading	*muntashir*	مُنْتَشِر

10.1.2 Geminate root: *muftaᶜᶜ* مُفْتَعّ

Because of the sequence of identical second and third root consonants, the stem
vowel *kasra* is deleted from this AP form. That is, instead of **muftaᶜiᶜ*, the form is
muftaᶜᶜ.[3] As a result of the deletion of the stem vowel in this AP form, the AP and
PP are identical.

occupying	*muHtall*	مُحْتَلّ	concerned (with)	*muhtamm (bi-)*	مُهْتَمّ بـ

10.1.3 Hamzated root
Hamza-final: *muftaᶜiᵓ* مُفْتَعِئ

beginning	*mubtadiᵓ*	مُبْتَدِئ	filled	*mumtaliᵓ*	مُمْتَلِئ

---

[3] This stems from phonological restrictions on identical consonants separated by a short vowel.

10.1.4 Assimilated root: *mutta*ᶜ*il* مُتَّعِل

united	*muttaHid*	مُتَّحِد	facing	*muttajih*	مُتَّجِه
contacting	*muttaSil*	مُتَّصِل	accusing; accuser	*muttahim*	مُتَّهِم

10.1.5 Hollow root: *muftaal* مُفْتال

relaxing; satisfied	*murtaaH*	مُرْتاح	double	*muzdawij*[4]	مُزْدَوِج
accustomed (to); usual	*muᶜtaad* (ᶜalaa)	مُعْتاد على	needing	*muHtaaj*	مُحْتاج

10.1.6 Defective root: *mufta*ᶜ*in* مُفْتَعِ

belonging	*muntam-in*	مُنْتَمِ	containing	*muHtaw-in*	مُحْتَوِ

10.1.7 Form VIII APs in context

الوِلايات المُتَّحِدة
al-wilaayaat-u l-muttaHidat-u
the **United** States

الأُمَم المُتَّحِدة
al-ʾumam-u l-muttaHidat-u
the **United** Nations

مازِق مزدوج
maaziq-un muzdawij-un
a **double** bind

في مكانه المعتاد
fii makaan-i-hi l-muᶜtaad-i
in its **usual** place

باتوا مقتنعين.
baat-uu muqtaniᶜ-iina.
They have become **convinced**.

10.2 Form VIII passive participle (PP): *mufta*ᶜ*al* مُفْتَعَل

In addition to acting as an adjective, in many cases the Form VIII passive participle acts as a noun of place, denoting the location where the Form VIII verbal activity takes place.

10.2.1 Strong/regular root: *mufta*ᶜ*al* مُفْتَعَل

respected	*muHtaram*	مُحْتَرَم	shared, common	*mushtarak*	مُشْتَرَك
society	*mujtamaᶜ*	مُجْتَمَع	document	*mustanad*	مُسْتَنَد
elected	*muntaxab*	مُنْتَخَب	informed	*muTTalaᶜ*	مُطَّلَع

---

[4] See note 2.

10.2.2 Geminate root: *mufta*ᶜᶜ مُفْتَعّ

The AP and PP of geminate Form VIII verbs are identical. Context is often needed to differentiate the meaning.

occupied   *muHtall*   مُحْتَلّ

10.2.2 Hamzated root
Hamza- initial: *mu*ʾ*ta*ᶜ*al* مُؤْتَعَل

conference   *mu*ʾ*tamar*   مُؤْتَمَر

10.2.3 Assimilated root: *mutta*ᶜ*al* مُتَّعَل

accused; suspected   *muttaham*   مُتَّهَم

10.2.4 Hollow root: *muftaal*

The AP and PP of hollow Form VIII verbs are identical. Context is needed to differentiate the meaning.

excellent,   *mumtaaz*   مُمْتاز   chosen   *muxtaar*   مُختار
  distinguished

10.2.5 Defective root: *mufta*ᶜ*an* مُفْتَعَى

required   *muqtaD-an* مُقْتَدَى   level   *mustaw-an*   مُسْتَوَى

10.2.6 Examples of Form VIII PPs in context

مصادر مطّلعة | لديه المستندات الرسميّة
maSaadir-u muTTalaᶜt-un | *laday-hi l-mustanadaat-u l-rasmiyyat-u.*
informed sources | He has the official **documents**.

بـمقتضى الحقوق | الرئيس المنتخب
bi-muqtaDaa l-Huquuq-i | *al-ra*ʾ*iis-u l-muntaxab-u*
in **accordance** with the laws | the president-**elect**

جدول أعمال مشترك | في الأراضي المحتلّة
jadwal-u ʾ*a*ᶜ*maal-in mushtarak-un* | *fii l-*ʾ*araaDii l-muHtallat-i*
a **shared** agenda | in the **occupied** territories

Form VIII Sound root: اِحْتَرَمَ ، يَحْتَرِمُ   AP: مُحْتَرِم   PP: مُحْتَرَم   VN: اِحْتِرام   'to respect'

	Active	Active	Active	Active	Active	Passive	Passive
	Perfect	Imperfect	Imperfect	Imperfect	Imperfect	Perfect	Imperfect
		Indicative	Subjunctive	Jussive	Imperative		
أنا	اِحْتَرَمْتُ	أَحْتَرِمُ	أَحْتَرِمَ	أَحْتَرِمْ		اُحْتُرِمْتُ	أُحْتَرَمُ
أَنْتَ	اِحْتَرَمْتَ	تَحْتَرِمُ	تَحْتَرِمَ	تَحْتَرِمْ	اِحْتَرِمْ	اُحْتُرِمْتَ	تُحْتَرَمُ
أَنْتِ	اِحْتَرَمْتِ	تَحْتَرِمِينَ	تَحْتَرِمِي	تَحْتَرِمِي	اِحْتَرِمِي	اُحْتُرِمْتِ	تُحْتَرَمِينَ
أَنْتُما—m/f	اِحْتَرَمْتُما	تَحْتَرِمانِ	تَحْتَرِما	تَحْتَرِما	اِحْتَرِما	اُحْتُرِمْتُم	تُحْتَرَمانِ
هُوَ	اِحْتَرَمَ	يَحْتَرِمُ	يَحْتَرِمَ	يَحْتَرِمْ		اُحْتُرِمَ	يُحْتَرَمُ
هِيَ	اِحْتَرَمَتْ	تَحْتَرِمُ	تَحْتَرِمَ	تَحْتَرِمْ		اُحْتُرِمَتْ	تُحْتَرَمُ
هُما—m	اِحْتَرَما	يَحْتَرِمانِ	يَحْتَرِما	يَحْتَرِما		اُحْتُرِما	يُحْتَرَمانِ
هُما—f	اِحْتَرَمَتا	تَحْتَرِمانِ	تَحْتَرِما	تَحْتَرِما		اُحْتُرِمَتا	تُحْتَرَمانِ
نَحْنُ	اِحْتَرَمْنا	نَحْتَرِمُ	نَحْتَرِمَ	نَحْتَرِمْ		اُحْتُرِمْنا	نُحْتَرَمُ
أَنْتُم	اِحْتَرَمْتُم	تَحْتَرِمُونَ	تَحْتَرِموا	تَحْتَرِموا	اِحْتَرِموا	اُحْتُرِمْتُم	تُحْتَرَمُونَ
أَنْتُنَّ	اِحْتَرَمْتُنَّ	تَحْتَرِمْنَ	تَحْتَرِمْنَ	تَحْتَرِمْنَ	اِحْتَرِمْنَ	اُحْتُرِمْتُنَّ	تُحْتَرَمْنَ
هُم	اِحْتَرَموا	يَحْتَرِمُونَ	يَحْتَرِموا	يَحْتَرِموا		اُحْتُرِموا	يُحْتَرَمُونَ
هُنَّ	اِحْتَرَمْنَ	يَحْتَرِمْنَ	يَحْتَرِمْنَ	يَحْتَرِمْنَ		اُحْتُرِمْنَ	يُحْتَرَمْنَ

Form VIII Geminate root: اِحْتَلَّ ، يَحْتَلُّ   AP: مُحْتَلّ   PP: مُحْتَلّ   VN: اِحْتِلال   *'to occupy'*

	Active Perfect	Active Imperfect Indicative	Active Imperfect Subjunctive	Active Imperfect Jussive	Active Imperfect Imperative	Passive Perfect	Passive Imperfect
أنا	اِحْتَلَلْتُ	أَحْتَلُّ	أَحْتَلَّ	أَحْتَلِلْ or أَحْتَلَّ		اُحْتُلِلْتُ	أُحْتَلُّ
أنْت	اِحْتَلَلْتَ	تَحْتَلُّ	تَحْتَلَّ	تَحْتَلِلْ or تَحْتَلَّ	اِحْتَلِلْ or اِحْتَلَّ	اُحْتُلِلْتَ	تُحْتَلُّ
أنْت	اِحْتَلَلْتِ	تَحْتَلّين	تَحْتَلّي	تَحْتَلّي	اِحْتَلّي	اُحْتُلِلْتِ	تُحْتَلّين
أنْتُما—m/f	اِحْتَلَلْتُما	تَحْتَلّان	تَحْتَلّا	تَحْتَلّا	اِحْتَلّا	اُحْتُلِلْتُما	تُحْتَلّان
هُوَ	اِحْتَلَّ	يَحْتَلُّ	يَحْتَلَّ	يَحْتَلِلْ or يَحْتَلَّ		اُحْتُلَّ	يُحْتَلُّ
هِي	اِحْتَلّت	تَحْتَلُّ	تَحْتَلَّ	تَحْتَلِلْ or تَحْتَلَّ		اُحْتُلّت	تُحْتَلُّ
هُما—m	اِحْتَلّا	يَحْتَلّان	يَحْتَلّا	يَحْتَلّا		اُحْتُلّا	يُحْتَلّان
هُما—f	اِحْتَلّتا	تَحْتَلّان	تَحْتَلّا	تَحْتَلّا		اُحْتُلّتا	تُحْتَلّان
نَحْنُ	اِحْتَلَلْنا	نَحْتَلُّ	نَحْتَلَّ	نَحْتَلِلْ or نَحْتَلَّ		اُحْتُلِلْنا	نُحْتَلُّ
أنْتُم	اِحْتَلَلْتُم	تَحْتَلّون	تَحْتَلّوا	تَحْتَلّوا	اِحْتَلّوا	اُحْتُلِلْتُم	تُحْتَلّون
أنْتُنَّ	اِحْتَلَلْتُنَّ	تَحْتَلِلْن	تَحْتَلِلْن	تَحْتَلِلْن	اِحْتَلِلْن	اُحْتُلِلْتُنَّ	تُحْتَلِلْن
هُم	اِحْتَلّوا	يَحْتَلّون	يَحْتَلّوا	يَحْتَلّوا		اُحْتُلّوا	يُحْتَلّون
هُنَّ	اِحْتَلَلْن	يَحْتَلِلْن	يَحْتَلِلْن	يَحْتَلِلْن		اُحْتُلِلْن	يُحْتَلِلْن

Form VIII hamza-final root: اِبْتَدَأَ ، يَبْتَدِئ ، اِبْتَدَأْ   AP: مُبْتَدِئ   PP: مُبْتَدَأ   VN: اِبْتِداء   *'to begin'*

	Active	Active	Active	Active	Active	Passive	Passive
	Perfect	Imperfect	Imperfect	Imperfect	Imperfect	Perfect	Imperfect
		Indicative	Subjunctive	Jussive	Imperative		
أنا	اِبْتَدَأْتُ	أَبْتَدِئ	أَبْتَدِئ	أَبْتَدِئْ			
أنت	اِبْتَدَأْتَ	تَبْتَدِئ	تَبْتَدِئ	تَبْتَدِئْ	اِبْتَدِئْ		
أنت	اِبْتَدَأْتِ	تَبْتَدِئين	تَبْتَدِئي	تَبْتَدِئي	اِبْتَدِئي		
أنتما—m/f	اِبْتَدَأْتُما	تَبْتَدِئان	تَبْتَدِئا	تَبْتَدِئا	اِبْتَدِئا		
هُو	اِبْتَدَأَ	يَبْتَدِئ	يَبْتَدِئ	يَبْتَدِئْ			
هي	اِبْتَدَأَتْ	تَبْتَدِئ	تَبْتَدِئ	تَبْتَدِئْ			
هما—m	اِبْتَدَآ	يَبْتَدِئان	يَبْتَدِئا	يَبْتَدِئا			
هما—f	اِبْتَدَأَتا	تَبْتَدِئان	تَبْتَدِئا	تَبْتَدِئا			
نَحْنُ	اِبْتَدَأْنا	نَبْتَدِئ	نَبْتَدِئ	نَبْتَدِئْ			
أنتُمْ	اِبْتَدَأْتُمْ	تَبْتَدِئون	تَبْتَدِئوا	تَبْتَدِئوا	اِبْتَدِئوا		
أنتنّ	اِبْتَدَأْتُنَّ	تَبْتَدِئْن	تَبْتَدِئْن	تَبْتَدِئْن	اِبْتَدِئْن		
هُم	اِبْتَدَؤُوا	يَبْتَدِئون	يَبْتَدِئوا	يَبْتَدِئوا			
هُنَّ	اِبْتَدَأْن	يَبْتَدِئْن	يَبْتَدِئْن	يَبْتَدِئْن			

Form VIII Hollow root: اِخْتَارَ، يَخْتَارُ AP: مُخْتَار PP: مُخْتَار VN: اِخْتِيار 'to choose'

	Active	Active	Active	Active	Active	Passive	Passive
	Perfect	Imperfect	Imperfect	Imperfect	Imperfect	Perfect	Imperfect
		Indicative	Subjunctive	Jussive	Imperative		
أنا	اِخْتَرْتُ	أَخْتَارُ	أَخْتَارَ	أَخْتَرْ		أُخْتِرْتُ	أُخْتَارُ
أَنْتَ	اِخْتَرْتَ	تَخْتَارُ	تَخْتَارَ	تَخْتَرْ	اِخْتَرْ	أُخْتِرْتَ	تُخْتَارُ
أنتِ	اِخْتَرْتِ	تَخْتَارِينَ	تَخْتَارِي	تَخْتَارِي	اِخْتَارِي	أُخْتِرْتِ	تُخْتَارِينَ
أَنْتُما–m/f	اِخْتَرْتُما	تَخْتَارانِ	تَخْتَارا	تَخْتَارا	اِخْتَارا	أُخْتِرْتُما	تُخْتَارانِ
هُوَ	اِخْتَارَ	يَخْتَارُ	يَخْتَارَ	يَخْتَرْ		أُخْتِيرَ	يُخْتَارُ
هِي	اِخْتَارَتْ	تَخْتَارُ	تَخْتَارَ	تَخْتَرْ		أُخْتِيرَتْ	تُخْتَارُ
هُما–m	اِخْتَارا	يَخْتَارانِ	يَخْتَارا	يَخْتَارا		أُخْتِيرا	يُخْتَارانِ
هُما–f	اِخْتَارَتا	تَخْتَارانِ	تَخْتَارا	تَخْتَارا		أُخْتِيرَتا	تُخْتَارانِ
نَحْنُ	اِخْتَرْنا	نَخْتَارُ	نَخْتَارَ	نَخْتَرْ		أُخْتِرْنا	نُخْتَارُ
أنتُم	اِخْتَرْتُمْ	تَخْتَارونَ	تَخْتَاروا	تَخْتَاروا	اِخْتَاروا	أُخْتِرْتُمْ	تُخْتَارونَ
أنْتُنَّ	اِخْتَرْتُنَّ	تَخْتَرْنَ	تَخْتَرْنَ	تَخْتَرْنَ	اِخْتَرْنَ	أُخْتِرْتُنَّ	تُخْتَرْنَ
هُم	اِخْتَاروا	يَخْتَارونَ	يَخْتَاروا	يَخْتَاروا		أُخْتِيروا	يُخْتَارونَ
هُنَّ	اِخْتَرْنَ	يَخْتَرْنَ	يَخْتَرْنَ	يَخْتَرْنَ		أُخْتِرْنَ	يُخْتَرْنَ

Form VIII Defective root: التْقى ، يلتْقي   AP: مُلتْقٍ   PP: مُلتْقىً   VN: الالتْقاء   'to encounter, meet'

	Active	Active	Active	Active	Active	Passive	Passive
	Perfect	Imperfect	Imperfect	Imperfect	Imperfect	Perfect	Imperfect
		Indicative	Subjunctive	Jussive	Imperative		
أنا	التْقيتُ	ألتْقي	ألتْقي	ألتْقِ		أُلتْقيتُ	أُلتْقى
أنت	التْقيتَ	تلتْقي	تلتْقي	تلتْقِ	التْقِ	أُلتْقيتَ	تُلتْقى
أنت	التْقيتِ	تلتْقين	تلتْقي	تلتْقي	التْقي	أُلتْقيتِ	تُلتْقين
أنتُما—m/f	التْقيتُما	تلتْقيان	تلتْقيا	تلتْقيا	التْقيا	أُلتْقيتُما	تُلتْقيان
هو	التْقى	يلتْقي	يلتْقي	يلتْقِ		أُلتْقي	يُلتْقى
هي	التْقت	تلتْقي	تلتْقي	تلتْقِ		أُلتْقيتْ	تُلتْقى
هُما—m	التْقيا	يلتْقيان	يلتْقيا	يلتْقيا		أُلتْقيا	يُلتْقيان
هُما—f	التْقتا	تلتْقيان	تلتْقيا	تلتْقيا		أُلتْقيتا	تُلتْقيان
نحن	التْقينا	نلتْقي	نلتْقي	نلتْقِ		أُلتْقينا	نُلتْقى
أنتم	التْقيتم	تلتْقون	تلتْقوا	تلتْقوا	التْقوا	أُلتْقيتم	تُلتْقون
أنتنّ	التْقيتنّ	تلتْقين	تلتْقين	تلتْقين	التْقين	أُلتْقيتنّ	تُلتْقين
هم	التْقوا	يلتْقون	يلتْقوا	يلتْقوا		أُلتْقوا	يُلتْقون
هنّ	التْقين	يلتْقين	يلتْقين	يلتْقين		أُلتْقين	يُلتْقين

30

Form IX triliteral verb

1 Basic characteristics

1.1 Pattern: *ifʿall-a* اِفْعَلَّ / *ya-fʿall-u* يَفْعَلُّ

Form IX verbs are augmented with respect to Form I in that the final root consonant is doubled and the first and second root consonants are not separated by
a vowel. Form IX has the past tense stem $iC_1C_2aC_3C_3$ - and the present tense
stem $-C_1C_2aC_3C_3$-. A prefixed elidable *hamza* with *kasra* is added to the past
tense stem of Form IX to make it pronounceable; this *hamza* and its vowel are
deleted in the present tense, replaced by the present tense subject markers. The
vowel of the present tense subject marker in Form IX is *fatHa*.

1.2 Meaning

Form IX verbs generally denote the acquisition of a color or a physical trait. They
are normally based on roots occurring in the *ʾafʿal* adjectival pattern, as the
colors, e.g., *ʾaswad* 'black,' *ʾaHmar* 'red,' or adjectives that describe physical
defects. These verbs are infrequent in MSA.[1]

1.3 Transitivity

Form IX verbs are intransitive.

1.4 Inflection

The prefixed *hamzat al-waSl* with *kasra* in the past tense stem is deleted in the present tense and replaced by the subject-marker prefix. The vowel of the present tense
subject-marker prefix is *fatHa* and the stem vowel in the present tense is *fatHa*.

2 Sound/regular roots in Form IX: *ifʿall-a* اِفْعَلَّ / *ya-fʿall-u* يَفْعَلُّ

to be or become green   *ixDarr-a/ya-xDarr-u*   اِخْضَرَّ / يَخْضَرُّ

---

[1] Kouloughli (1994, 207) reports their occurrence as 0.5 percent of all the augmented forms of the
verb (II–X).

to be or become red; to blush	*iHmarr-a/ya-Hmarr-u*	اِحْمَرَّ / يَحْمَرُّ
to be or become yellow; to become pale	*iSfarr-a/ya-Sfarr-u*	اِصْفَرَّ / يَصْفَرُّ

3 Geminate (doubled) roots in Form IX

These roots are rare in Form IX.

4 Hamzated roots in Form IX

These roots are rare in Form IX.

5 Assimilated roots in Form IX

These roots are rare in Form IX.

6 Hollow roots in Form IX

The semi-consonant of the hollow root stabilizes in Form IX and acts as a strong consonant (*waaw* or *yaa'*):

to become black	*iswadd-a/ya-swadd-u*	اِسْوَدَّ / يَسْوَدُّ
to be or become white	*ibyaDD-a/ya-byaDD-u*	اِبْيَضَّ / يَبْيَضُّ
to squint; be cross-eyed	*iHwall-a/ya-Hwall-u*	اِحْوَلَّ / يَحْوَلُّ
to become crooked	*iʿwajj-a/ya-ʿwajj-u*	اِعْوَجَّ / يَعْوَجُّ

7 Defective roots in Form IX: rare

8 Form IX verbs in context

اعوجّت الشجرة.

iʿwajj-at-i l-shajarat-u.

The tree **became crooked.**

9 Verbal nouns of Form IX

9.1 Sound/regular root: *ifʿilaal* اِفْعِلال

greenness	*ixDiraar*	اِخْضِرار
blushing	*iHmiraar*	اِحْمِرار
yellowness; pallor	*iSfiraar*	اِصْفِرار

9.2 Hollow root: *if⁽ilaal*

squinting	*iHwilaal*	اِحْوِلال
crookedness	*i⁽wijaaj*	اِعْوِجاج

10 Form IX participles

10.1 Form IX participles (AP and PP): *muf⁽all* مُفْعَلّ

Form IX active participles and passive participles have the same pattern. However, passive participles in this form are exceedingly rare, since the verbs are intransitive.

Strong/regular root:

blushing	*muHmarr*	مُحْمَرّ

Hollow root:

blackening	*muswadd*	مُسْوَدّ

Form IX Sound root: احْمَرَّ، يَحْمَرُّ AP: مُحْمَرّ PP: VN: اِحْمِرار 'to become red'

	Active	Active	Active	Active	Active	Passive	Passive
	Perfect	Imperfect	Imperfect	Imperfect	Imperfect	Perfect	Imperfect
		Indicative	Subjunctive	Jussive	Imperative		
أنا	اِحْمَرَرْتُ	أحْمَرُّ	أحْمَرَّ	أحْمَرَّ or أحْمَرِرْ			
أنْت	اِحْمَرَرْتَ	تَحْمَرُّ	تَحْمَرَّ	تَحْمَرَّ or تَحْمَرِرْ	اِحْمَرَّ or اِحْمَرِرْ		
أنْت	اِحْمَرَرْتِ	تَحْمَرِّينَ	تَحْمَرِّي	تَحْمَرِّي	اِحْمَرِّي		
أنتُما–m/f	اِحْمَرَرْتُمْ	تَحْمَرّانِ	تَحْمَرّا	تَحْمَرّا	اِحْمَرّا		
هو	اِحْمَرَّ	يَحْمَرُّ	يَحْمَرَّ	يَحْمَرَّ or يَحْمَرِرْ			
هي	اِحْمَرَّتْ	تَحْمَرُّ	تَحْمَرَّ	تَحْمَرَّ or تَحْمَرِرْ			
هُما–m	اِحْمَرّا	يَحْمَرّانِ	يَحْمَرّا	يَحْمَرّا			
هُما–f	اِحْمَرَّتا	تَحْمَرّانِ	تَحْمَرّا	تَحْمَرّا			
نحْنُ	اِحْمَرَرْنا	نَحْمَرُّ	نَحْمَرَّ	نَحْمَرَّ or نَحْمَرِرْ			
أنتُم	اِحْمَرَرْتُمْ	تَحْمَرّونَ	تَحْمَرّوا	تَحْمَرّوا	اِحْمَرّوا		
أنتنّ	اِحْمَرَرْتنّ	تَحْمَرِرْنَ	تَحْمَرِرْنَ	تَحْمَرِرْنَ	اِحْمَرِرْنَ		
هُم	اِحْمَرّوا	يَحْمَرّونَ	يَحْمَرّوا	يَحْمَرّوا			
هُنّ	اِحْمَرَرْنَ	يَحْمَرِرْنَ	يَحْمَرِرْنَ	يَحْمَرِرْنَ			

Form IX Hollow root: اسوَدَّ ، يَسوَدُّ   *AP:* مُسوَدّ   *PP:*   *VN:* اسوِداد   '*to turn black*'

	Active	Active	Active	Active	Active	Passive	Passive
	Perfect	Imperfect	Imperfect	Imperfect	Imperfect	Perfect	Imperfect
		Indicative	Subjunctive	Jussive	Imperative		
أنا	اسوَدَدتُ	أسوَدُّ	أسوَدَّ	أسوَدِد or أسوَدَّ			
أنت	اسوَدَدتَ	تَسوَدُّ	تَسوَدَّ	تَسوَدِد or تَسوَدَّ	اسوَدِد or اسوَدَّ		
أنت	اسوَدَدتِ	تَسوَدّينَ	تَسوَدّي	تَسوَدّي	اسوَدّي		
m/f–أنتما	اسوَدَدتُما	تَسوَدّانِ	تَسوَدّا	تَسوَدّا	اسوَدّا		
هو	اسوَدَّ	يَسوَدُّ	يَسوَدَّ	يَسوَدِد or يَسوَدَّ			
هي	اسوَدَّت	تَسوَدُّ	تَسوَدَّ	تَسوَدِد or تَسوَدَّ			
m–هما	اسوَدّا	يَسوَدّانِ	يَسوَدّا	يَسوَدّا			
f–هما	اسوَدَّتا	تَسوَدّانِ	تَسوَدّا	تَسوَدّا			
نحن	اسوَدَدنا	نَسوَدُّ	نَسوَدَّ	نَسوَدِد or نَسوَدَّ			
أنتم	اسوَدَدتُم	تَسوَدّونَ	تَسوَدّوا	تَسوَدّوا	اسوَدّوا		
أنتن	اسوَدَدتُنَّ	تَسوَدِدنَ	تَسوَدِدنَ	تَسوَدِدنَ	اسوَدِدنَ		
هم	اسوَدّوا	يَسوَدّونَ	يَسوَدّوا	يَسوَدّوا			
هن	اسوَدَدنَ	يَسوَدِدنَ	يَسوَدِدنَ	يَسوَدِدنَ			

31

Form X triliteral verb

1 Basic characteristics

1.1 Pattern: *istafᶜal-a* اِسْتَفْعَل/*ya-stafᶜil-u* يَسْتَفْعِل

Form X verbs are augmented with respect to Form I in that a prefixed /-st-/ is added and the first and second root consonants are not separated by a vowel. Form X has the past tense stem **istaC₁C₂aC₃-** and the present tense stem **-staC₁C₂iC₃-**. A prefixed elidable *hamza* with *kasra* is added to the past tense stem of Form X to make it pronounceable; this *hamza* and its vowel are deleted in the present tense, replaced by the present tense subject markers. The vowel of the present tense subject marker in Form X is *fatHa*.

1.2 Meaning

Form X verbs may be requestative or estimative but may also reflect other semantic modifications of the base form. Examples of requestatives include:

to request guidance (from s.o.)	*istarshad-a/ya-starshid-u*	اِسْتَرْشَد / يَسْتَرْشِد
to request or seek explanation (from s.o.)	*istafsar-a/ya-stafsir-u*	اِسْتَفْسَر / يَسْتَفْسِر

Examples of estimatives include:

to consider (s.th.) good	*istaHsan-a/ya-staHsin-u*	اِسْتَحْسَن / يَسْتَحْسِن
to consider (s.th.) strange	*istaghrab-a/ya-staghrib-u*	اِسْتَغْرَب / يَسْتَغْرِب

Form X may be the reflexive of Form IV: Wright writes (1967, I:44) : "Form X converts the factitive signification of Form IV into the reflexive or middle." For example, Form IV *ʾaᶜadd-a* أَعَدّ /*yu-ᶜidd-u* يِعِدّ 'to prepare (s.th.)' and Form X *istaᶜadd-a* اِسْتَعَدّ /*ya-staᶜidd-u* يَسْتَعِدّ 'to prepare one's self, get ready.'

1.3 Transitivity

Form X verbs may be transitive or intransitive.[1]

---

[1] Kouloughli (1994, 208) reports that Form X is transitive more than 75 percent of the time.

1.4 Inflection

The prefixed *hamzat al-waSl* with *kasra* in the past tense stem is deleted in the present tense and replaced by the subject-marker prefix. The vowel of the present tense subject-marker prefix is *fatHa* and the stem vowel in the present tense is *kasra* (e.g., *istaqbal-a* اِسْتَقْبَلَ /*ya-staqbil-u* يَسْتَقْبِلُ 'to receive (s.o.)').

2 Sound/regular root

to consume	*istahlak-a/ya-stahlik-u*	اِسْتَهْلَكَ / يَسْتَهْلِكُ
to discover; invent	*istanbaT-a/ya-stanbiT-u*	اِسْتَنْبَطَ / يَسْتَنْبِطُ
to disdain; detest	*istankar-a/ya-stankir-u*	اِسْتَنْكَرَ / يَسْتَنْكِرُ
to invest	*istathmar-a/ya-stathmir-u*	اِسْتَثْمَرَ / يَسْتَثْمِرُ

3 Geminate (doubled) roots in Form X

to continue, to last	*istamarr-a/ya-stamirr-u*	اِسْتَمَرَّ / يَسْتَمِرُّ
to be independent	*istaqall-a/ya-staqill-u*	اِسْتَقَلَّ / يَسْتَقِلُّ

4 Hamzated roots in Form X

to rent, to hire	*ista'jar-a/ya-sta'jir-u*	اِسْتَأْجَرَ / يَسْتَأْجِرُ
to resume	*ista'naf-a/ya-sta'nif-u*	اِسْتَأْنَفَ / يَسْتَأْنِفُ

5 Assimilated roots in Form X

The root-initial semi-consonant *waaw* or *yaa'* acts as a regular consonant in the inflected verb forms.

to import	*istawrad-a/ya-stawrid-u*	اِسْتَوْرَدَ / يَسْتَوْرِدُ
to colonize, settle	*istawTan-a/ya-stawTin-u*	اِسْتَوْطَنَ / يَسْتَوْطِنُ
to awaken, wake up	*istayqaZ-a/ya-stayqiZ-u*	اِسْتَيْقَظَ / يَسْتَيْقِظُ

6 Hollow roots in Form X

Hollow roots in Form X, whether based on roots with *waaw* or *yaa'* as the medial semi-consonant, inflect with long /ii/ in the present tense stem.

to benefit (from or by) (root: *f-y-d* / ف – ي – د)	*istafaad-a/ya-stafiid-u (min)*	اِسْتَفَادَ / يَسْتَفِيدُ من
to be able (to do s.th.) (root: *T-w-ᶜ*/ط – و – ع)	*istaTaaᶜ-a/ya-staTiiᶜ-u*	اِسْتَطَاعَ / يَسْتَطِيعُ

to resign	istaqaal-a/ya-staqiil-u	اِسْتَقَالَ / يَسْتَقِيلُ
(root: q-y-l / ل – ي – ق)		

7 Defective roots in Form X

Defective roots in Form X inflect as *-aa/-ii* defectives.

to except, exclude	istathnaa/ya-stathnii	اِسْتَثْنَى / يَسْتَثْنِي
to seek an opinion	istaftaa/ya-staftii	اِسْتَفْتَى / يَسْتَفْتِي
to appropriate	istawlaa/ya-stawlii	اِسْتَوْلَى / يَسْتَوْلِي

8 Examples of Form X verbs in context

حتّى عندما **استضافت** القمّة

*Hattaa ʿind-a-maa **staDaafat-i** l-qimmat-a*

even when **it hosted** the summit [conference]

لا **يستطيعون** الذهاب.

*laa **ya-staTiiʿ-uuna** l-dhahaab-a.*

They are not **able** to go.

في زيارة لفرنسا **تستغرق** أسبوعا

*fii ziyaarat-in li-faransaa **ta-staghriq-u** ʾusbuuʿ-an*

on a visit to France that **lasts** a week

تستمرّ فترة الثلوج من تشرين الثاني حتّى آذار.

***ta-stamirr-u** fatrat-u l-thuluuj-i min tishriin-a l-thaanii Hattaa ʾaadhaar-a.*

The snow season **lasts** from November until March.

9 Form X verbal nouns: *istifʿaal* اِسْتِفْعال

9.1 Sound/regular root

inquiry	istixbaar	اِسْتِخْبار	use	istixdaam	اِسْتِخْدام
investment	istithmaar	اِسْتِثْمار	disdain	istinkaar	اِسْتِنْكار

9.2 Geminate root

The verbal noun of the geminate Form X verb is regular, using the *istifʿaal* pattern and splitting the identical second and third root consonants:

continuation	istimraar	اِسْتِمْرار	merit, worthiness, claim	istiHqaaq	اِسْتِحْقاق
preparation	istiʿdaad	اِسْتِعْداد	independence	istiqlaal	اِسْتِقْلال

9.3 Hamzated root

The verbal noun of hamzated roots of Form X is usually regular in formation. The *hamza* takes a seat appropriate to its phonetic context.

renting	istiʾjaar	اِسْتِئْجار	resumption	istiʾnaaf	اِسْتِئْناف

9.4 Assimilated root: اِسْتِيعَال

In the verbal noun of assimilated-root Form X, the root-initial *waaw* assimilates to the preceding *kasra* and becomes long /ii/:

importation	*istiiraad*[2]	اِسْتِيرَاد	colonizing	*istiiTaan*	اِسْتِيطَان
awakening	*istiiqaaZ*	اِسْتِيقَاظ			

9.5 Hollow root: اِسْتِفَالَة

The verbal noun of Form X hollow verbs has the form *istifaala* اِسْتِفَالَة spelled with *taa' marbuuTa*.

benefit	*istifaada*	اِسْتِفَادَة	ability	*istiTaaʕa*	اِسْتِطَاعَة
response	*istijaaba*	اِسْتِجَابَة	resignation	*istiqaala*	اِسْتِقَالَة

9.6 Defective root: اِسْتِفْعَاء

The verbal noun of defective roots in From X has the pattern *istifʕaa'* اِسْتِفْعَاء. The weakness of the final root element converts into *hamza*:

exception	*istithnaa'*	اِسْتِثْنَاء	renunciation	*istighnaa'*	اِسْتِغْنَاء
plebiscite, referendum	*istiftaa'*	اِسْتِفْتَاء	appropriation	*istiilaa'*	اِسْتِيلَاء

9.7 Form X verbal nouns in context

لِأَنَّهَا اسْتِحْقَاق دِيمُوقرَاطِيّ
li-'anna-haa **stiHqaaq-un** *diimuuqraaTiyy-un*
because it is a democratic **claim**

إلى اسْتِثْمَار بِلَايِين الدُّولَارَات
'ilaa **stithmaar-i** *balaayiin-i l-duulaaraat-i*
to **the investment** of billions of dollars

فِي العِيد الخَمْسِين لِاسْتِقْلَال لُبنَان
fii l-ʕiid-i l-xamsiina **l-istiqlaal-i** *lubnaan-a*
on the 50th [anniversary] celebration of **the independence** of Lebanon

10 Form X participles

10.1 Form X active participle (AP): *mustafʕil* مُسْتَفْعِل

10.1.1 Sound/regular root

consumer	*mustahlik*	مُسْتَهْلِك	orientalist	*mustashriq*	مُسْتَشْرِق

---

[2] Instead of *istiwraad* or *istiwTaan*. The sequence /-iw-/ is usually avoided in Arabic.

10.1.2 Geminate root: *mustafi⁽ᶜᶜ⁾* مُسْتَفِعّ

| continuous | mustamirr | مُسْتَمِرّ | independent | mustaqill | مُسْتَقِلّ |
| ready | musta⁽c⁾idd | مُسْتَعِدّ | entitled; worthy | mustaHiqq | مُسْتَحِقّ |

10.1.3 Hamzated root

| tenant, renter | musta'jir | مُسْتَأْجِر |

10.1.4 Assimilated root

| importer | mustawrid | مُسْتَوْرِد | colonizer | mustawTin | مُسْتَوْطِن |

10.1.5 Hollow root: *mustafiil* مُسْتَفِيل

| circular | mustadiir | مُسْتَدِير | impossible | mustaHiil | مُسْتَحِيل |

10.1.6 Defective root: *mustaf⁽c⁾in* مُسْتَفْعٍ

| doing without | mustaghnin | مُسْتَغْنٍ |

10.1.7 Form X APs in context

ساحة مستديرة
saaHat-un **mustadiirat-un**
a **circular** courtyard

أحد النوّاب المستقلّين
'aHad-u l-nuwwaab-i **l-mustaqill-iina**
one of the **independent** deputies

10.2 Form X passive participle (PP): *mustaf⁽c⁾al* مُسْتَفْعَل

In addition to acting as an adjective, the Form X passive participle may also serve as a noun of place, denoting the location where the Form X activity takes place.

10.2.1 Sound/regular root: *mustaf⁽c⁾al* مُسْتَفْعَل

laboratory	mustaxbar	مُسْتَخْبَر	colony	musta⁽c⁾mara	مُسْتَعْمَرة
future	mustaqbal	مُسْتَقْبَل	strange	mustaghrab	مُسْتَغْرَب
swamp	mustanqa⁽c⁾	مُسْتَنْقَع	used	musta⁽c⁾mal	مُسْتَعْمَل

10.2.2 Geminate root

This root type is rare in the passive participle.

10.2.3 Hamzated root

resumed	musta'naf	مُسْتَأْنَف	rented	musta'jar	مُسْتَأْجَر

10.2.4 Assimilated root: *mustafʿal* مُسْتَفْعَل

settlement	mustawTana	مُسْتَوْطَنَة	imported	mustawrad	مُسْتَوْرَد

10.2.5 Hollow root: *mustafaal* مُسْتَفال

borrowed; false; artificial	mustaʿaar	مُسْتَعار	counsellor	mustashaar	مُسْتَشار

10.2.6 Defective root: *mustafʿan*

hospital	mustashfan	مُسْتَشْفىً	excepted	mustathnan	مُسْتَثْنىً

10.2.7 Form X PPs in context

أَسْماءٌ مُسْتَعارةٌ
'asmaa'-un mustaʿaarat-un
pseudonyms ('**borrowed** names')

وضع حجر الأساس للمستشفى
waDʿ-u Hajr-i l-'asaas-i li-**l-mustashfaa**
setting the foundation stone for **the
hospital**

في المستقبل القريب
fii **l-mustaqbal-i** l-qariib-i
in the near **future**

مئة مليون دولار ليست مستغربة.
mi'at-u milyuun-i duulaar-in lays-at
mustaghrabat-an.
A hundred million dollars is not **unusual.**

Form X Sound root: اِسْتَخْدَم ، يَسْتَخْدِمُ AP: مُسْتَخْدِم PP: مُسْتَخْدَم VN: اِسْتِخْدام 'to use'

	Active	Active	Active	Active	Active	Passive	Passive
	Perfect	Imperfect	Imperfect	Imperfect	Imperfect	Perfect	Imperfect
		Indicative	Subjunctive	Jussive	Imperative		
أنا	اِسْتَخْدَمْتُ	أَسْتَخْدِمُ	أَسْتَخْدِمَ	أَسْتَخْدِمْ		اُسْتُخْدِمْتُ	أُسْتَخْدَمُ
أنْتَ	اِسْتَخْدَمْتَ	تَسْتَخْدِمُ	تَسْتَخْدِمَ	تَسْتَخْدِمْ	اِسْتَخْدِمْ	اُسْتُخْدِمْتَ	تُسْتَخْدَمُ
أنْتِ	اِسْتَخْدَمْتِ	تَسْتَخْدِمِين	تَسْتَخْدِمِي	تَسْتَخْدِمِي	اِسْتَخْدِمِي	اُسْتُخْدِمْتِ	تُسْتَخْدَمِين
أنتُما—m/f	اِسْتَخْدَمْتُما	تَسْتَخْدِمان	تَسْتَخْدِما	تَسْتَخْدِما	اِسْتَخْدِما	اُسْتُخْدِمْتُما	تُسْتَخْدَمان
هُوَ	اِسْتَخْدَمَ	يَسْتَخْدِمُ	يَسْتَخْدِمَ	يَسْتَخْدِمْ		اُسْتُخْدِمَ	يُسْتَخْدَمُ
هِيَ	اِسْتَخْدَمَتْ	تَسْتَخْدِمُ	تَسْتَخْدِمَ	تَسْتَخْدِمْ		اُسْتُخْدِمَتْ	تُسْتَخْدَمُ
هُما—m	اِسْتَخْدَما	يَسْتَخْدِمان	يَسْتَخْدِما	يَسْتَخْدِما		اُسْتُخْدِما	يُسْتَخْدَمان
هُما—f	اِسْتَخْدَمَتا	تَسْتَخْدِمان	تَسْتَخْدِما	تَسْتَخْدِما		اُسْتُخْدِمَتا	تُسْتَخْدَمان
نَحْنُ	اِسْتَخْدَمْنا	نَسْتَخْدِمُ	نَسْتَخْدِمَ	نَسْتَخْدِمْ		اُسْتُخْدِمْنا	نُسْتَخْدَمُ
أنتُم	اِسْتَخْدَمْتُم	تَسْتَخْدِمون	تَسْتَخْدِموا	تَسْتَخْدِموا	اِسْتَخْدِموا	اُسْتُخْدِمْتُم	تُسْتَخْدَمون
أنتُنَّ	اِسْتَخْدَمْتُنَّ	تَسْتَخْدِمْنَ	تَسْتَخْدِمْنَ	تَسْتَخْدِمْنَ	اِسْتَخْدِمْنَ	اُسْتُخْدِمْتُنَّ	تُسْتَخْدَمْنَ
هُم	اِسْتَخْدَموا	يَسْتَخْدِمون	يَسْتَخْدِموا	يَسْتَخْدِموا		اُسْتُخْدِموا	يُسْتَخْدَمون
هُنَّ	اِسْتَخْدَمْنَ	يَسْتَخْدِمْنَ	يَسْتَخْدِمْنَ	يَسْتَخْدِمْنَ		اُسْتُخْدِمْنَ	يُسْتَخْدَمْنَ

Form X Geminate root: اِسْتَمَرَّ ، يَسْتَمِرُّ   AP: مُسْتَمِرّ   PP: VN: اِسْتِمْرار   'to last'

	Active	Active	Active	Active	Active	Passive	Passive
	Perfect	Imperfect	Imperfect	Imperfect	Imperfect	Perfect	Imperfect
		Indicative	Subjunctive	Jussive	Imperative		
أنا	اِسْتَمْرَرْتُ	أَسْتَمِرُّ	أَسْتَمِرَّ	أَسْتَمْرِرْ or أَسْتَمِرَّ			
أنْتَ	اِسْتَمْرَرْتَ	تَسْتَمِرُّ	تَسْتَمِرَّ	تَسْتَمْرِرْ or تَسْتَمِرَّ	اِسْتَمْرِرْ or اِسْتَمِرَّ		
أنْتِ	اِسْتَمْرَرْتِ	تَسْتَمِرِّينَ	تَسْتَمِرِّي	تَسْتَمِرِّي	اِسْتَمِرِّي		
أنْتُما—m/f	اِسْتَمْرَرْتُما	تَسْتَمِرّانِ	تَسْتَمِرّا	تَسْتَمِرّا	اِسْتَمِرّا		
هو	اِسْتَمَرَّ	يَسْتَمِرُّ	يَسْتَمِرَّ	يَسْتَمْرِرْ or يَسْتَمِرَّ			
هي	اِسْتَمَرَّت	تَسْتَمِرُّ	تَسْتَمِرَّ	تَسْتَمْرِرْ or تَسْتَمِرَّ			
هُما—m	اِسْتَمَرّا	يَسْتَمِرّانِ	يَسْتَمِرّا	يَسْتَمِرّا			
هُما—f	اِسْتَمَرَّتا	تَسْتَمِرّانِ	تَسْتَمِرّا	تَسْتَمِرّا			
نَحْنُ	اِسْتَمْرَرْنا	نَسْتَمِرُّ	نَسْتَمِرَّ	نَسْتَمْرِرْ or نَسْتَمِرَّ			
أنْتُم	اِسْتَمْرَرْتُم	تَسْتَمِرّونَ	تَسْتَمِرّوا	تَسْتَمِرّوا	اِسْتَمِرّوا		
أنْتُنَّ	اِسْتَمْرَرْتُنَّ	تَسْتَمْرِرْنَ	تَسْتَمْرِرْنَ	تَسْتَمْرِرْنَ	اِسْتَمْرِرْنَ		
هُم	اِسْتَمَرّوا	يَسْتَمِرّونَ	يَسْتَمِرّوا	يَسْتَمِرّوا			
هُنَّ	اِسْتَمْرَرْنَ	يَسْتَمْرِرْنَ	يَسْتَمْرِرْنَ	يَسْتَمْرِرْنَ			

Form X hamza-initial root: اِسْتَأْجَرَ، يَسْتَأْجِرُ AP: مُسْتَأْجِر PP: مُسْتَأْجَر VN: اِسْتِئْجار   'to rent'

	Active Perfect	Active Imperfect Indicative	Active Imperfect Subjunctive	Active Imperfect Jussive	Active Imperfect Imperative	Passive Perfect	Passive Imperfect
أنا	اِسْتَأْجَرْتُ	أَسْتَأْجِرُ	أَسْتَأْجِرَ	أَسْتَأْجِرْ		اُسْتُؤْجِرْتُ	أُسْتَأْجَرُ
أنْتَ	اِسْتَأْجَرْتَ	تَسْتَأْجِرُ	تَسْتَأْجِرَ	تَسْتَأْجِرْ	اِسْتَأْجِرْ	اُسْتُؤْجِرْتَ	تُسْتَأْجَرُ
أنْتِ	اِسْتَأْجَرْتِ	تَسْتَأْجِرينَ	تَسْتَأْجِري	تَسْتَأْجِري	اِسْتَأْجِري	اُسْتُؤْجِرْتِ	تُسْتَأْجَرانِ
أنْتُما—m/f	اِسْتَأْجَرْتُما	تَسْتَأْجِرانِ	تَسْتَأْجِرا	تَسْتَأْجِرا	اِسْتَأْجِرا	اُسْتُؤْجِرْتُما	تُسْتَأْجَرانِ
هُوَ	اِسْتَأْجَرَ	يَسْتَأْجِرُ	يَسْتَأْجِرَ	يَسْتَأْجِرْ		اُسْتُؤْجِرَ	يُسْتَأْجَرُ
هِيَ	اِسْتَأْجَرَتْ	تَسْتَأْجِرُ	تَسْتَأْجِرَ	تَسْتَأْجِرْ		اُسْتُؤْجِرَتْ	تُسْتَأْجَرُ
هُما—m	اِسْتَأْجَرا	يَسْتَأْجِرانِ	يَسْتَأْجِرا	يَسْتَأْجِرا		اُسْتُؤْجِرا	يُسْتَأْجَرانِ
هُما—f	اِسْتَأْجَرَتا	تَسْتَأْجِرانِ	تَسْتَأْجِرا	تَسْتَأْجِرا		اُسْتُؤْجِرَتا	تُسْتَأْجَرانِ
نَحْنُ	اِسْتَأْجَرْنا	نَسْتَأْجِرُ	نَسْتَأْجِرَ	نَسْتَأْجِرْ		اُسْتُؤْجِرْنا	نُسْتَأْجَرُ
أنْتُمْ	اِسْتَأْجَرْتُمْ	تَسْتَأْجِرونَ	تَسْتَأْجِروا	تَسْتَأْجِروا	اِسْتَأْجِروا	اُسْتُؤْجِرْتُمْ	تُسْتَأْجَرونَ
أنْتُنَّ	اِسْتَأْجَرْتُنَّ	تَسْتَأْجِرْنَ	تَسْتَأْجِرْنَ	تَسْتَأْجِرْنَ	اِسْتَأْجِرْنَ	اُسْتُؤْجِرْتُنَّ	تُسْتَأْجَرْنَ
هُمْ	اِسْتَأْجَروا	يَسْتَأْجِرونَ	يَسْتَأْجِروا	يَسْتَأْجِروا		اُسْتُؤْجِروا	يُسْتَأْجَرونَ
هُنَّ	اِسْتَأْجَرْنَ	يَسْتَأْجِرْنَ	يَسْتَأْجِرْنَ	يَسْتَأْجِرْنَ		اُسْتُؤْجِرْنَ	يُسْتَأْجَرْنَ

Form X Assimilated root: اِسْتَوْرَدَ ، يَسْتَوْرِدُ AP: مُسْتَوْرِد PP: مُسْتَوْرَد VN: اِسْتيراد *'to import'*

	Active	Active	Active	Active	Active	Passive	Passive
	Perfect	Imperfect	Imperfect	Imperfect	Imperfect	Perfect	Imperfect
		Indicative	Subjunctive	Jussive	Imperative		
أنا	اِسْتَوْرَدْتُ	أَسْتَوْرِدُ	أَسْتَوْرِدَ	أَسْتَوْرِدْ		اُسْتُورِدْتُ	أُسْتَوْرَدُ
أنْتَ	اِسْتَوْرَدْتَ	تَسْتَوْرِدُ	تَسْتَوْرِدَ	تَسْتَوْرِدْ	اِسْتَوْرِدْ	اُسْتُورِدْتَ	تُسْتَوْرَدُ
أنْتِ	اِسْتَوْرَدْتِ	تَسْتَوْرِدين	تَسْتَوْرِدي	تَسْتَوْرِدي	اِسْتَوْرِدي	اُسْتُورِدْتِ	تُسْتَوْرَدين
أنْتُما—m/f	اِسْتَوْرَدْتُما	تَسْتَوْرِدان	تَسْتَوْرِدا	تَسْتَوْرِدا	اِسْتَوْرِدا	اُسْتُورِدْتُما	تُسْتَوْرَدان
هُوَ	اِسْتَوْرَدَ	يَسْتَوْرِدُ	يَسْتَوْرِدَ	يَسْتَوْرِدْ		اُسْتُورِدَ	يُسْتَوْرَدُ
هِيَ	اِسْتَوْرَدَتْ	تَسْتَوْرِدُ	تَسْتَوْرِدَ	تَسْتَوْرِدْ		اُسْتُورِدَتْ	تُسْتَوْرَدُ
هُما—m	اِسْتَوْرَدا	يَسْتَوْرِدان	يَسْتَوْرِدا	يَسْتَوْرِدا		اُسْتُورِدا	يُسْتَوْرَدان
هُما—f	اِسْتَوْرَدَتا	تَسْتَوْرِدان	تَسْتَوْرِدا	تَسْتَوْرِدا		اُسْتُورِدَتا	تُسْتَوْرَدان
نَحْنُ	اِسْتَوْرَدْنا	نَسْتَوْرِدُ	نَسْتَوْرِدَ	نَسْتَوْرِدْ		اُسْتُورِدْنا	نُسْتَوْرَدُ
أنْتُمْ	اِسْتَوْرَدْتُمْ	تَسْتَوْرِدون	تَسْتَوْرِدوا	تَسْتَوْرِدوا	اِسْتَوْرِدوا	اُسْتُورِدْتُمْ	تُسْتَوْرَدون
أنْتُنَّ	اِسْتَوْرَدْتُنَّ	تَسْتَوْرِدْنَ	تَسْتَوْرِدْنَ	تَسْتَوْرِدْنَ	اِسْتَوْرِدْنَ	اُسْتُورِدْتُنَّ	تُسْتَوْرَدْنَ
هُمْ	اِسْتَوْرَدوا	يَسْتَوْرِدون	يَسْتَوْرِدوا	يَسْتَوْرِدوا		اُسْتُورِدوا	يُسْتَوْرَدون
هُنَّ	اِسْتَوْرَدْنَ	يَسْتَوْرِدْنَ	يَسْتَوْرِدْنَ	يَسْتَوْرِدْنَ		اُسْتُورِدْنَ	يُسْتَوْرَدْنَ

Form X Hollow root: يَسْتَطِيعُ ، اِسْتَطَاعَ AP: مُسْتَطِيع PP: مُسْتَطَاع VN: اِسْتِطَاعة *'to be able'*

	Active	Active	Active	Active	Active	Passive	Passive
	Perfect	Imperfect	Imperfect	Imperfect	Imperfect	Perfect	Imperfect
		Indicative	Subjunctive	Jussive	Imperative		
أنا	اِسْتَطَعْتُ	أَسْتَطِيعُ	أَسْتَطِيعَ	أَسْتَطِعْ		أُسْتُطِعْتُ	أُسْتَطَاعُ
أنْتَ	اِسْتَطَعْتَ	تَسْتَطِيعُ	تَسْتَطِيعَ	تَسْتَطِعْ	اِسْتَطِعْ	أُسْتُطِعْتَ	تُسْتَطَاعُ
أنْتِ	اِسْتَطَعْتِ	تَسْتَطِيعِينَ	تَسْتَطِيعِي	تَسْتَطِيعِي	اِسْتَطِيعِي	أُسْتُطِعْتِ	تُسْتَطَاعِينَ
أنتُما—m/f	اِسْتَطَعْتُما	تَسْتَطِيعانِ	تَسْتَطِيعا	تَسْتَطِيعا	اِسْتَطِيعا	أُسْتُطِعْتُما	تُسْتَطَاعانِ
هُوَ	اِسْتَطَاعَ	يَسْتَطِيعُ	يَسْتَطِيعَ	يَسْتَطِعْ		أُسْتُطِيعَ	يُسْتَطَاعُ
هِيَ	اِسْتَطَاعَتْ	تَسْتَطِيعُ	تَسْتَطِيعَ	تَسْتَطِعْ		أُسْتُطِيعَتْ	تُسْتَطَاعُ
هُما—m	اِسْتَطَاعا	يَسْتَطِيعانِ	يَسْتَطِيعا	يَسْتَطِيعا		أُسْتُطِيعا	يُسْتَطَاعانِ
هُما—f	اِسْتَطَاعَتا	تَسْتَطِيعانِ	تَسْتَطِيعا	تَسْتَطِيعا		أُسْتُطِيعَتا	تُسْتَطَاعانِ
نَحْنُ	اِسْتَطَعْنا	نَسْتَطِيعُ	نَسْتَطِيعَ	نَسْتَطِعْ		أُسْتُطِعْنا	نُسْتَطَاعُ
أنتُمْ	اِسْتَطَعْتُمْ	تَسْتَطِيعونَ	تَسْتَطِيعوا	تَسْتَطِيعوا	اِسْتَطِيعوا	أُسْتُطِعْتُمْ	تُسْتَطَاعونَ
أنتُنَّ	اِسْتَطَعْتُنَّ	تَسْتَطِعْنَ	تَسْتَطِعْنَ	تَسْتَطِعْنَ	اِسْتَطِعْنَ	أُسْتُطِعْتُنَّ	تُسْتَطَعْنَ
هُمْ	اِسْتَطَاعوا	يَسْتَطِيعونَ	يَسْتَطِيعوا	يَسْتَطِيعوا		أُسْتُطِيعوا	يُسْتَطَاعونَ
هُنَّ	اِسْتَطَعْنَ	يَسْتَطِعْنَ	يَسْتَطِعْنَ	يَسْتَطِعْنَ		أُسْتُطِعْنَ	يُسْتَطَعْنَ

Form X Defective root: اسْتَثْنَى ، يَسْتَثْنِي   AP: مُسْتَثْنٍ   PP: مُسْتَثْنًى   VN: اِسْتِثْنَاء   'to except'

	Active	Active	Active	Active	Active	Passive	Passive
	Perfect	Imperfect	Imperfect	Imperfect	Imperfect	Perfect	Imperfect
			Indicative	Subjunctive	Jussive	Imperative		
أنا	اسْتَثْنَيْتُ	أَسْتَثْنِي	أَسْتَثْنِيَ	أَسْتَثْنِ		اُسْتُثْنِيتُ	أُسْتَثْنَى
أنْت	اسْتَثْنَيْتَ	تَسْتَثْنِي	تَسْتَثْنِيَ	تَسْتَثْنِ	اسْتَثْنِ	اُسْتُثْنِيتَ	تُسْتَثْنَى
أنْت	اسْتَثْنَيْتِ	تَسْتَثْنِينَ	تَسْتَثْنِي	تَسْتَثْنِي	اسْتَثْنِي	اُسْتُثْنِيتِ	تُسْتَثْنَيْنَ
أنْتما—m/f	اسْتَثْنَيْتُما	تَسْتَثْنِيانِ	تَسْتَثْنِيا	تَسْتَثْنِيا	اسْتَثْنِيا	اُسْتُثْنِيتُما	تُسْتَثْنَيانِ
هو	اسْتَثْنَى	يَسْتَثْنِي	يَسْتَثْنِيَ	يَسْتَثْنِ		اُسْتُثْنِيَ	يُسْتَثْنَى
هي	اسْتَثْنَتْ	تَسْتَثْنِي	تَسْتَثْنِيَ	تَسْتَثْنِ		اُسْتُثْنِيَتْ	تُسْتَثْنَى
هُما—m	اسْتَثْنَيا	يَسْتَثْنِيانِ	يَسْتَثْنِيا	يَسْتَثْنِيا		اُسْتُثْنِيا	يُسْتَثْنَيانِ
هُما—f	اسْتَثْنَتا	تَسْتَثْنِيانِ	تَسْتَثْنِيا	تَسْتَثْنِيا		اُسْتُثْنِيَتا	تُسْتَثْنَيانِ
نَحْن	اسْتَثْنَيْنا	نَسْتَثْنِي	نَسْتَثْنِيَ	نَسْتَثْنِ		اُسْتُثْنِينا	نُسْتَثْنَى
أنْتُم	اسْتَثْنَيْتُم	تَسْتَثْنُونَ	تَسْتَثْنُوا	تَسْتَثْنُوا	اسْتَثْنُوا	اُسْتُثْنِيتُم	تُسْتَثْنَوْنَ
أنْتُنّ	اسْتَثْنَيْتُنَّ	تَسْتَثْنِينَ	تَسْتَثْنِينَ	تَسْتَثْنِينَ	اسْتَثْنِينَ	اُسْتُثْنِيتُنَّ	تُسْتَثْنَيْنَ
هُم	اسْتَثْنَوْا	يَسْتَثْنُونَ	يَسْتَثْنُوا	يَسْتَثْنُوا		اُسْتُثْنُوا	يُسْتَثْنَوْنَ
هُنّ	اسْتَثْنَيْنَ	يَسْتَثْنِينَ	يَسْتَثْنِينَ	يَسْتَثْنِينَ		اُسْتُثْنِينَ	يُسْتَثْنَيْنَ

32

Forms XI–XV triliteral verb

These forms of the triliteral verb are chiefly archaic and/or poetic in use. For the sake of completeness, they are described briefly here, but few examples occurred in the corpus, and even in Classical Arabic, they are rare. Examples are taken from Wright 1967, I:43–47 or Fleisch 1979, II: 330–40.[1]

1 Form XI: *ifʿaall-a* افْعَالَّ / *ya-fʿaall-u* يَفْعَالُّ

This form is related to Form IX and usually denotes a similar concept: the acquisition or existence of a color or physical trait.[2] It is prefixed with *hamzat al-waSl* and is distinguished by the lengthening of the stem vowel from *fatHa* to *ʾalif*, and the doubling of the final consonant, giving the pattern $iC_1C_2aaC_3C_3$-a/ya-$C_1C_2aaC_3C_3$-u. It is intransitive.

to become temporarily red	*iHmaarr-a/ya-Hmaarr-u*	احْمَارٌّ / يَحْمَارٌّ
to become temporarily yellow	*iSfaarr-a/ya-Sfaarr-u*	اصْفَارٌّ / يَصْفَارٌّ
to be dark brown	*ismaarr-a/ya-smaarr-u*	اسْمَارٌّ / يَسْمَارٌّ

1.1 Verbal noun: *ifʿiilaal* افْعِيلال

turning temporarily red	*iHmiiraar*	احْمِيرار

2 Form XII: *ifʿawʿal-a* افْعَوْعَلَ / *ya-fʿawʿil-u* يَفْعَوْعِلُ

Form XII has the pattern $iC_1C_2awC_2C_3$ -a/ya-$C_1C_2awC_2iC_3$ -u, with doubling of the medial radical and insertion of a *waaw* between the two doubled radicals. It is

---

[1] Fleisch (1979, II:330–35) provides examples and discussion of the etymology of these forms. Haywood and Nahmad (1962, 152–53) have a comprehensive verb form chart that includes Forms XI–XV. Although some grammars include the verbal nouns of these forms, most do not include the participles, so I have omitted these, except where they are found in Wehr 1979.

[2] See Haywood and Nahmad 1962, 185. Wright (1967, I:43–44) states: "According to some grammarians, the distinction between the ninth and the eleventh forms is, that the ninth indicates permanent colours or qualities, the eleventh those that are transitory or mutable . . . Others hold that Form XI indicates a higher degree of the quality than IX."

prefixed with *hamzat al-waSl*. In meaning it, like Form IX, usually indicates color or physical quality.

to be convex; be humpbacked	iHdawdab-a/ya-Hdawdib-u	اِحْدَوْدَبَ / يَحْدَوْدِبُ

2.1 Verbal noun: *if⁽ii⁾aal*

becoming humpbacked	iHdiidaab	اِحْدِيداب

2.2 Active participle: *muf⁽aw⁾il*

mounded; humpbacked	muHdawdib	مُحْدَوْدِب

3 Form XIII: *if⁽awwal-a* افْعَوَّلَ / *ya-f⁽awwil-u* يَفْعَوِّلُ

Form XIII inserts a doubled *waaw* between the second and third root consonants, yielding the pattern iC₁C₂awwaC₃ -a/ya-C₁C₂awwiC₃ -u. It, too, usually denotes color or quality but may also denote an action.

to last long	ixrawwaT-a/ya-xrawwiT-u	اخْرَوَّطَ / يَخْرَوِّطُ
to mount a camel without a saddle	i⁽lawwaT-a/ ya-⁽lawwiT-u	اعْلَوَّطَ / يَعْلَوِّطُ

3.1 Verbal noun: *if⁽iwwaal* افْعِوّال

lasting long	ixriwwaaT	اخْرِوّاط

4 Form XIV: *if⁽anlal-a* افْعَنْلَلَ / *ya-f⁽anlil-u* يَفْعَنْلِلُ

Form XIV has the pattern iC₁C₂anC₃aC₃ -a/ya-C₁C₂anC₃iC₃-u, with doubling of the third radical and insertion of a *nuun*[3] between the second and third radicals. It is prefixed with *hamzat al-waSl*. In meaning it, like Form IX, usually indicates color or physical quality.

to be dark	isHankak-a	اسْحَنْكَكَ

4.1 Verbal noun: *if⁽inlaal* افْعِنْلال

being dark	isHinkaak	اسْحِنْكاك

5 Form XV: *if⁽anlaa* افْعَنْلى /*ya-f⁽anlii* يَفْعَنْلي

Form XV resembles Form XIV in that there is an inserted *nuun* between the second and third radicals of the root. However, there is an added suffix /-aa/ which turns

---

[3] Note that this form with its inserted *nuun* correlates closely with Form III of quadriliteral verbs (also very rare): e.g., *ibranshaq-a* ابرنشق / *ya-branshiq-u* يبرنشق 'to bloom.' The difference is that in the quadriliteral, the third and fourth root consonants are different. See Chapter 33, section 4.

the verb into a defective of the *-aa/-ii* type. It has the pattern iC₁C₂anC₃aa/ya-C₁C₂anC₃ii.

to be stout and strong	*iʿlandaa/ya-ʿlandii*	اِعْلَنْدى / يَعْلَنْدي
to conquer, vanquish	*israndaa/ya-srandii*	اِسْرَنْدى / يَسْرَنْدي

5.1 Verbal noun: *ifʿinlaaʾ* افْعِنْلاء

conquering	*isrindaaʾ*	اِسْرِنْداء

33

Quadriliteral verbs

1 Basic characteristics of quadriliteral verb roots (ʾafʿaal rubaaʿiyya أفعال رباعيّة)
Quadriliteral verb roots contain four consonants instead of three (e.g., zaxraf-a
زَخْرَف / yu-zaxrif-u يُزَخْرِف 'to embellish, adorn' or fahras-a فَهْرَس / yu-fahris-u يُفَهْرِس
'to compile an index, to index'). Sometimes the four consonants are all different
and sometimes they are reduplicated.

1.1 Reduplicated quadriliteral verbs
In reduplicated quadriliteral verbs the first two consonants repeat themselves
(somewhat like English words such as chitchat, zigzag, or mishmash). These verbs
usually refer to repeated motion or sound. When referring to a sound, they are
onomatopoeic; that is, they reflect or mimic the sound itself (e.g., rafraf-a رَفْرَف /
yu-rafrif-u يُرَفْرِف 'to flutter,' waswas-a وَسْوَس / yu-waswis-u يُوَسْوِس 'to whisper').

1.2 Complex roots
Complex roots combine elements from more than one root into a quadriliteral verb
(e.g., basmala) بَسْمَل / yu-basmil-u يُبَسْمِل 'to say bi-sm-i llaah-i بِسْم اللّٰه 'in the name of God.'

1.3 Borrowed roots
Quadriliteral verb patterns are sometimes used to borrow verbal concepts from
another language (e.g., talfan-a تَلْفَن /yu-talfin-u يَتَلْفِن 'to telephone').

1.4 Forms
Quadriliteral roots occur in four different forms or stem classes, labeled with
roman numerals I-IV, along the same lines as the labeling system for the ten forms
of the triliteral verb. Forms I and II of the quadriliterals are by far the most common in MSA.

2 Form I: faʿlal-a فَعْلَلَ /yu-faʿlil-u يُفَعْلِل

2.1 Pattern
The consonant-vowel distribution pattern for Form I of the quadriliteral verb mirrors Form II of the triliteral: $C_1aC_2C_3aC_4$-/yu-$C_1aC_2C_3iC_4$-. This is possible because

599

the triliteral Form II is increased by one consonant by virtue of the doubling of its second radical. The difference between them is that in a quadriliteral verb Form I, the two middle consonants are different, whereas in a Form II triliteral, they are the same.

2.2 Transitivity
Form I quadriliterals may be transitive or intransitive.

2.3 Regular quadriliterals
In regular or sound quadriliteral roots, all the consonants are different. Most quadriliterals of this type contain a "liquid" consonant: /r/, /l/, /n/.[1]

to obstruct	*ʿarqal-a/yu-ʿarqil-u*	عَرْقَلَ / يُعَرْقِلُ
to translate	*tarjam-a/yu-tarjim-u*	تَرْجَمَ / يُتَرْجِمُ
to dominate	*sayTar-a/yu-sayTir-u*	سَيْطَرَ / يُسَيْطِرُ
to prove	*barhan-a/yu-barhin-u*	بَرْهَنَ / يُبَرْهِنُ

2.4 Reduplicated quadriliterals
In these roots the first two consonants are repeated, either in imitation of a sound or to refer to a movement, especially a repeated movement.[2]

to gargle	*gharghar-a/yu-gharghir-u*	غَرْغَرَ / يُغَرْغِرُ
to flutter	*rafraf-a/yu-rafrif-u*	رَفْرَفَ / يُرَفْرِفُ
to move, to budge	*zaHzaH-a/yu-zaHziH-u*	زَحْزَحَ / يُزَحْزِحُ
to ruin, demolish	*DaʿDaʿ-a/yu-DaʿDiʿ-u*	ضَعْضَعَ / يُضَعْضِعُ
to shake	*zalzal-a/yu-zalzil-u*	زَلْزَلَ / يُزَلْزِلُ
to chatter	*tharthar-a/yu-tharthir-u*	ثَرْثَرَ / يُثَرْثِرُ

2.5 Complex roots

2.5.1 Acronymic roots
This involves taking the initial letters of a string of words in a traditional, formulaic saying, or an often-repeated phrase, and turning them into a lexical root. It is

---

[1] Certain quadriliteral verbs appear to be expanded triliterals, with liquid or continuant phonemes /r/, /n/, /m/, /l/, or /w/ added to the root. They are called *mulHaqaat bi-l-rubaaʿiyy* ملحقات بالرباعي، for example: *zaHlaf-a* زَحْلَفَ */yu-zaHlif-u* يُزَحْلِفُ 'to roll along' from z-H-f ز – ح – ف 'advance slowly.' See Roochnik, n.d.; Sterling 1904, 26–27; Wright 1967, I:47–48.

[2] For a semantic analysis of reduplicated quadriliteral verbs see Procházka 1993.

somewhat like creating an acronym, but in Arabic this particular usage creates verbs that denote saying a set phrase.

basmal-a/yu-basiml-u   بَسْمَلَ / يُبَسْمِلُ

to say: *bi-ism-i llaah-i* بسم اللّه ('in the name of God')

Hawqal-a/yu-Hawqil-u   حَوْقَلَ / يُحَوْقِلُ

to say: لا حَوْلَ ولا قُوَّةَ إلاّ بِاللّه

laa Hawl-a wa laa quwwat-a ʾillaa bi-llaah-i
('There is no power and no strength save in God')

fadhlak-a/yu-fadhlik-u   فَذْلَكَ / يُفَذْلِكُ

to say   فَذلكَ كَذَا وكَذَا

fa-dhaalika kadhaa wa-kadhaa ...
('And that is thus and so ...')

2.5.2 Compound roots

These verbs combine consonants from two roots. They are mostly of older usage.

to worship the sun   *ʿabsham-a/yu-ʿabshim-u*   عَبْشَمَ / يُعَبْشِمُ

(from roots: ع – ب – د *ʿ-b-d* 'to serve, to worship' and ش – م – س *sh-m-s* 'sun')

to be petrified   *jalmad-a/yu-jalmid-u*   جَلْمَدَ / يُجَلْمِدُ

(from roots: ج – ل – د *j-l-d* 'freeze' and ج – م – د *j-m-d* 'harden')

2.6 Borrowed quadriliterals

Verbal concepts from foreign languages can sometimes be transferred into Arabic through use of the quadriliteral verb pattern.

to telephone   *talfan-a/yu-talfin-u*   تَلْفَنَ / يُتَلْفِنُ

to televise   *talfaz-a/yu-talfiz-u*   تَلْفَزَ / يُتَلْفِزُ

to philosophize   *falsaf-a/yu-falsif-u*   فَلْسَفَ / يُفَلْسِفُ

3 Form II quadriliterals: *tafaʿlal-a* تَفَعْلَلَ / *ya-tafaʿlal-u* يَتَفَعْلَلُ

3.1 Pattern

The consonant-vowel distribution pattern for Form II quadriliterals mirrors Form V of the triliteral verb: **taCaCCaC-a /ya-taCaCCaC-u**.

3.2 Meaning

In meaning, this form is often the reflexive, resultative, or passive of the Form I quadriliteral.

become electrified	*takahrab-a/ya-takahrab-u*	تَكَهْرَبَ / يَتَكَهْرَبُ
to decline, go down	*tadahwar-a/ya-tadahwar-u*	تَدَهْوَرَ / يَتَدَهْوَرُ
to be crystallized	*tabalwar-a/ya-tabalwar-u*	تَبَلْوَرَ / يَتَبَلْوَرُ
to adorn one's self, dress up	*tabahraj-a/ya-tabahraj-u*	تَبَهْرَجَ / يَتَبَهْرَجُ
to acclimatize (o.s.)	*ta'aqlam-a/ya-ta'aqlam-u*	تَأَقْلَمَ / يَتَأَقْلَمُ
to become dilapidated	*taDaʿDaʿ-a/ya-taDaʿDaʿ-u*	تَضَعْضَعَ / يَتَضَعْضَعُ

3.3 Denominals

Form II quadriliterals may be denominalizations, as in the following verb:

to concentrate, be centered, concentrated	*tamarkaz-a/ya-tamarkaz-u*	تَمَرْكَزَ / يَتَمَرْكَزُ

(from the noun of place, *markaz* مَرْكَز 'center' from the root ر – ك – ز *r-k-z*)

3.4 Verbs of comportment

Form II quadriliterals may also have a meaning of acting or behaving in a certain way, e.g.,

to play the philosopher, act like a philosopher	*tafalsaf-a/ya-tafalsaf-u*	تَفَلْسَفَ / يَتَفَلْسَفُ
to act American	*ta'amrak-a/ya-ta'amrak-u*	تَأَمْرَكَ / يَتَأَمْرَكُ

4 Form III: *ifʿanlal-a* اِفْعَنْلَلَ / *ya-fʿanlil-u*[3] يَفْعَنْلِلُ

This form of the quadriliteral verb is rare in MSA. It has an infixed /-n-/ inserted between the second and third radicals of the root and corresponds in meaning to form VII of the triliteral roots. It is normally intransitive. No occurrences of this form of the verb occurred in the data covered for this book. Examples include:

to bloom, to flourish (Wright 1967, I:49)	*ibranshaq-a/ya-branshiq-u*	اِبْرَنْشَقَ / يَبْرَنْشِقُ
to be proud, raise the nose (Haywood and Nahmad 1962, 263)	*ixranTam-a/ya-xranTim-u*	اِخْرَنْطَمَ / يَخْرَنْطِمُ

---

[3] Whereas Wright (1967) as well as Haywood and Nahmad (1962) give this Form as III, other authors, including the MECAS grammar (1965, 225) and Sterling (1904, 26) give it as Form IV of the quadriliteral, and Form IV as Form III.

5 Form IV: *if·alall-a* اِفْعَلَلَّ / *ya-f·alill-u* يَفْعَلِلُّ

Form IV of the quadriliteral corresponds in meaning to Form IX of the triliteral verb. The final radical is doubled, giving the pattern **iCCaCaCC-a, ya-CCaCiCC-u**. It denotes an intensity of quality or degree and is intransitive.

to be calm, serene, reassured	*iTma'ann-a/ya-Tma'inn-u*	اِطْمَأَنَّ / يَطْمَئِنُّ
to vanish away, disappear	*iDmaHall-a/ya-DmaHill-u*	اِضْمَحَلَّ / يَضْمَحِلُّ
to shudder	*iqsha·arr-a/ya-qsha·irr-u*	اِقْشَعَرَّ / يَقْشَعِرُّ
to stretch	*ishra'abb-a/ya-shra'ibb-u*	اِشْرَأَبَّ / يَشْرَئِبُّ
to shrink, shudder, recoil	*ishma'azz-a/ya-shma'izz-u*	اِشْمَأَزَّ / يَشْمَئِزُّ
to become dark, gloomy	*ikfaharr-a/ya-kfahirr-u*	اِكْفَهَرَّ / يَكْفَهِرُّ

6 Examples of quadriliteral verbs in context

Form I:

بحلق في عينيها.
baHlaq-a fii ʿayn-ay-haa.
He **stared** into her eyes.

الكتب الّتي لم تُفَهْرَس
al-kutub-u llatii lam tu-fahras
the books which have not **been indexed**

يترجم إلى لغته.
yu-tarjim-u ʾilaa lughat-i-hi.
He **translates** into his language.

ويترجمونه خطأً.
wa-yu-tarjim-uuna-hu xaTT-an.
And **they translate it** literally.

Form II:

تزحزحت الصخرة.
tazaHzaH-at-i l-Saxrat-u.
The rock **moved**.

شيئاً فشيئاً يمكن أن يتدحرج.
shay'-an fa-shay'-an yu-mkin-u ʾan *ya-tadaHraj-a.*
It can **deteriorate** ('it is possible that **it deteriorate**') bit by bit.

Form IV:

وضع يطمئنّ فيه جميع المواطنين
waDʿ-un ya-Tma'inn-u fii-hi jamiiʿ-u
l-muwaaTin-iina
a situation in which all citizens can
be reassured

حيث تشرئبّ الطريق
Hayth-u ta-shra'ibb-u l-Tariiq-u
where the road **stretches**

7 Quadriliteral verbal nouns

7.1 Form I quadriliteral verbal nouns

7.1.1 *faʿlala* فَعْلَلَة ~ *fiʿlila* فِعْلِلَة

translation	*tarjama*	تَرْجَمَة	obstacle; obstruction	*ʿarqala*	عَرْقَلَة
chattering	*tharthara*	ثَرْثَرَة	link, chain	*silsila*	سِلْسِلَة

7.1.2 *fuʿlaal* فُعْلال ~ *faʿlaal* فَعْلال ~ *fiʿlaal* فِعْلال

proof, evidence	*burhaan*	بُرْهان	earthquake	*zilzaal*	زِلْزال

7.2 Form II quadriliteral verbal nouns: *tafaʿlul* تَفَعْلُل

deterioration	*tadahwur*	تَدَهْوُر	sequence; continuity	*tasalsul*	تَسَلْسُل

7.3 Form III quadriliteral verbal nouns: *ifʿinlaal* افْعِنْلال

flourishing	*ibrinshaaq*	اِبْرِنْشاق

7.4 Form IV quadriliteral verbal nouns: *ifʿillaal* افْعِلّال

serenity	*iTmiʾnaan*	اِطْمِئْنان	vanishing	*iDmiHlaal*	اِضْمِحْلال

7.5 Quadriliteral verbal nouns in context

سلسلة جبال   لوقف تدهور الدينار
silsilat-u jibaal-in   *li-waqf-i **tadahwur-i** l-diinaar*
a **chain** of mountains   to stop **the decline** of the dinar

8 Form I quadriliteral participles

Quadriliteral verb participles are formed on the same basis as participles of triliteral verb roots. There are active and passive participles, all prefixed with /mu-/ and differentiated by a stem vowel /-i-/ for the active participle and stem vowel /-a-/ for the passive participle. They occur both as nouns and as adjectives.

8.1 Quadriliteral active participle (QAP)

8.1.1 Form I QAP: *mufaʿlil* مُفَعْلِل

engineer	*muhandis*	مُهَنْدِس	explosive	*mufarqiʿ*	مُفَرْقِع

8.1.2 Form II QAP: *mutafaʿlil* مُتَفَعْلِل

deteriorating   *mutadahwir*   مُتَدَهْوِر   crystalline   *mutabalwir*   مُتَبَلْوِر

8.1.3 Form III QAP: rare

8.1.4 Form IV QAP: *mufʿalill* مُفْعَلِلّ

serene, calm   *muTmaʾinn*   مُطْمَئِنّ   dusky, gloomy   *mukfahirr*   مُكْفَهِرّ

8.1.5 QAPs in context

هم في حال صحّة متدهورة.

*hum fii Haal-i SiHHat-in **mutadahwirat-in**.*

They are in a **deteriorating** state of health.

بنايات حيّ المهندسين

*binaayaat-u Hayy-i **l-muhandis-iina***

the buildings of the **Muhandisin** ('engineers') quarter

8.2 Quadriliteral passive participle (QPP)

8.2.1 Form I passive participle: *mufaʿlal* مُفَعْلَل

camp	*muʿaskar*	مُعَسْكَر	embellished	*muzarkash*	مُزَرْكَش
series	*musalsal*	مُسَلْسَل	crystallized	*mubalwar*	مُبَلْوَر
old-timer	*muxaDram*	مُخَضْرَم	electrified	*mukahrab*	مُكَهْرَب

8.2.2 Form II QPP: *mutafaʿlal* مُتَفَعْلَل

This form is rare.

8.2.3 Form III and Form IV QPP

These are rare.

8.2.4 Quadriliteral PPs in context

مسلسل جديد

musalsal-un jadiid-un

a new **series**

مقالات مترجمة من العربية

maqaalaat-un mutarjamat-un min-a l-ʿarabiyyat-i

articles translated from Arabic

34

Moods of the verb I: indicative and subjunctive

Mood or "mode" refers to the Arabic verb properties **indicative, subjunctive, and jussive**.[1] These categories reflect or are caused by contextual modalities that condition the action of the verb. For example, the indicative mood tends to be characteristic of straightforward, factual statements or questions, while the subjunctive mood reflects an attitude toward the action such as doubt, desire, intent, wishing, or necessity, and the jussive mood, when used for the imperative, indicates an attitude of command, request, or need for action on the part of the speaker.

In Arabic, mood marking is only done on the present tense or imperfective stem; there are no mood variants for the past tense. The Arabic moods are therefore non-finite; that is, they do not refer to points in time and are not differentiated by tense. Tense is inferred from context and other parts of the clause.[2]

1 The indicative mood: *al-muDaari͑ al-marfuu͑* المضارع المرفوع

The indicative mood is considered the basic mood; it is used in factual statements or straightforward questions. It is also used in statements about the future, either with the future markers *sa-* ـس or *sawfa* سوْف, or in a context that refers to a future action. A full paradigm of the indicative mood for a regular Form I verb is as follows:

---

[1] An additional mood, the "energetic" exists in Classical Arabic but not in MSA. It denotes an intensified affirmation of action. See Wright 1967, I:61ff. and Fischer 2002, 110 and 118 for more on the energetic mood.

[2] The question of mood marking (on verbs) is a central one in traditional Arabic grammar, along with case marking (on nouns and adjectives). Moods fall under the topic of morphology because they are indicated in Arabic word structure, that is, they are usually marked by suffixes or modifications of suffixes attached to the present tense verb stem. Moods also, however, fall under the topic of syntax because their use is determined either by particles which govern their occurrence, or by the narrative context in general, including attitude of the speaker and intended meaning. They are therefore referred to in some reference works and theoretical discussions as "morphosyntactic" categories, combining features of morphology and syntax.

1.2 Indicative mood paradigm

Present tense stem -ᶜrif- - عرِف - 'know'

	Singular	Dual	Plural
First person	أَعْرِفُ ʾa-ᶜrif-u		نَعْرِفُ na-ᶜrif-u
Second person m.	تَعْرِفُ ta-ᶜrif-u	تَعْرِفَانِ ta-ᶜrif-aani	تَعْرِفُونَ ta-ᶜrif-uuna
f.	تَعْرِفِينَ ta-ᶜrif-iina	تَعْرِفَانِ ta-ᶜrif-aani	تَعْرِفْنَ ta-ᶜrif-na
Third person m.	يَعْرِفُ ya-ᶜrif-u	يَعْرِفَانِ ya-ᶜrif-aani	يَعْرِفُونَ ya-ᶜrif-uuna
f.	تَعْرِفُ ta-ᶜrif-u	تَعْرِفَانِ ta-ᶜrif-aani	يَعْرِفْنَ ya-ᶜrif-na

It is the **suffix on the verb that indicates the mood**. The indicative mood shows the full form of the suffixes, and that is one reason why it is considered the base form. Particular indicators of the indicative are:

1. the short vowel *Damma* (-*u*-) suffix on five of the persons (I, we, you m.sg., he and she);[3]
2. the /-na/ suffix after the long vowel /-uu- / in the second and third persons masculine plural and after /-ii-/ in the second person feminine singular;
3. the /-ni/ suffix after the long vowel /-aa-/ in the dual.

1.3 Examples of indicative in context

1.3.1 Statements

تَعْرِفُ كلّ شيءٍ.
ta-ᶜrif-u kull-a shayʾ-in.
She knows everything.

نرحّبُ بزبائنِنا.
nu-raHHib-u bi-zabaaʾin-i-naa.
We welcome our customers.

---

[3] It is this *Damma* suffix that leads to the name of the mood, because the *Damma* mood marker resembles the *Damma* case marker on nouns. Both the indicative mood and the nominative case are called *marfuuᶜ* in Arabic.

يغادرُ القاهرة اليوم.
yu-ghaadir-u l-qaahirat-a l-yawm-a.
He leaves Cairo today.

يدرجونَها في البرامـج.
yu-drij-uuna-haa fii l-baraamij-i.
They include it in the programs.

نتشرَّفُ.
na-tasharraf-u.
We are honored.

تستمرّ ساعتين.
ta-stamirr-u saaᶜat-ayni.
It lasts two hours.

1.3.2 Questions

ماذا تفعل؟
maadhaa ta-fᶜal-u?
What does it (f.) **do?**

لماذا تحبّه؟
li-maadhaa tu-Hibb-u-hu?
Why do you **like** it (m.)?

1.3.3 Future tense

1.3.3.1 WITH FUTURE MARKER

سوف يتحسَّن.
sawfa ya-taHassan-u.
It will get better.

سيعقدون اجتماعاً.
sa-ya-ᶜqud-uuna jtimaaᶜ-an.
They will hold a meeting.

1.3.3.2 BY CONTEXT

يغادر العاصمة غدا.
yu-ghaadir-u l-ᶜaaSimat-a ghad-an.
He leaves (will leave) the capital tomorrow.

1.3.4 Passive indicative

The indicative may occur in the passive voice, for example:

أسعار لا تُصدَّق!
ʾasᶜaar-un laa tu-Saddaq-u!
Unbelievable prices!
('prices that **are not believed**')

تُستخدم لصنع الأوراق.
tu-staxdam-u li-Sanᶜ-i l-ʾawraaq-i
It is used to make papers.

2 The subjunctive mood: *al-muDaariᶜ al-manSuub* المضارع المنصوب

The subjunctive mood is a form of the present tense, or imperfect, that occurs under specific circumstances in Arabic, taking the form of a distinct subset of inflectional endings on the imperfect verb stem, in other words, a separate conjugation. It has the following features: the short inflectional vowel suffix is *fatHa* (instead of the *Damma* of the indicative). For the longer verb suffixes, such as

/-uuna/, /-iina/, and /-aani/, the *nuun* and its short vowel are dropped, so the suffixes are left as long vowels /-uu/, /-ii/, /-aa/.[4]

Because of the use of *fatHa* instead of *Damma* as the short vowel suffix, the subjunctive mood is referred to in Arabic as **al-muDaariᶜ al-manSuub** المضارع المنصوب, using the same term for the subjunctive as for the accusative case on nouns and adjectives (*al-manSuub* المنصوب).

Subjuctive mood paradigm
Present tense stem -ᶜrif- عرِف *- 'know'*

	Singular	**Dual**	**Plural**
First person	أَعْرِف		نَعْرِف
	ʾa-ᶜrif-a		*na-ᶜrif-a*
Second person **m.**	تَعْرِف	تَعْرِفا	تَعْرِفوا
	ta-ᶜrif-a	*ta-ᶜrif-aa*	*ta-ᶜrif-uu*
f.	تَعْرِفي	تَعْرِفا	تَعْرِفْنَ
	ta-ᶜrif-ii	*ta-ᶜrif-aa*	*ta-ᶜrif-na*
Third person **m.**	يَعْرِف	يَعْرِفا	يَعْرِفوا
	ya-ᶜrif-a	*ya-ᶜrif-aa*	*ya-ᶜrif-uu*
f.	تَعْرِف	تَعْرِفا	يَعْرِفْنَ
	ta-ᶜrif-a	*ta-ᶜrif-aa*	*ya-ᶜrif-na*

In general, the subjunctive mood is determined by an attitude toward the verbal action such as volition, intent, purpose, doubt, attempting, expectation, permission, hope, ability, or necessity. In Arabic, the subjunctive is **also syntactically determined by the presence of particular 'subjunctivizing' particles**. Those particles include *lan* لَنْ, which negates the future; a series of particles that express purpose (*li-* لِ, *kay* كَيْ, *li-kay* لِكَيْ, *Hattaa* حتّى), and the subordinating conjunction particle *ʾan*, which links a subordinate clause to a main clause. The subjunctive mood may also occur in the passive voice.

2.1 Negative particle: *lan* لَنْ 'will not; shall not'
After the negative particle *lan* the subjunctive is used. This combination of *lan* + subjunctive yields a future negative.

---

[4] For the history and development of the Arabic subjunctive, see Testen 1994.

لن ننسى.

lan na-nsaa.

We will not forget.

لنْ يمنعوهم من أن يكونوا عرباً.

lan ya-mnaᶜ-uu-hum min ʾan ya-kuun-uu ᶜarab-an.

They will not prevent them from being Arabs.

2.2 Particles of purpose

These particles are subordinating conjunctions that denote the sense of 'in order to' or 'in order that.' With certain particles a verbal noun may be substituted for the subjunctive verb.

2.2.1 *li-* ـل 'for; to; in order to, in order that'

The purpose particle *li-* ـل may be followed by a verb in the subjunctive, or by a verbal noun in the genitive case.

2.2.1.1 WITH SUBJUNCTIVE

لينغلقوا داخل الحدود

li-ya-nghaliq-uu daaxil-a l-Huduud-i

in order that they be closed inside the borders

لآخذه في نزهة

li-ʾaaxudh-a-hu fii nuzhat-in

in order that I take him for a walk

2.2.1.2 WITH VERBAL NOUN

للدفاع عن نفسه

li-l-difaaᶜ-i ᶜan nafs-i-hi

in order to defend himself

2.2.2 *kay* كَيْ 'in order that, in order to'

كي نستعدّ للامتحان

kay na-staᶜidd-a li-l-imtiHaan-i

in order for us to get ready for the exam

2.2.3 *kay laa* كَيْ لا 'in order not to'

كي لا يَبْقى قويّاً

kay laa ya-bqaa qawiyy-an

so that it not remain strong

كي لا أقولَ ...

kay laa ʾa-quul-a ...

in order that I not say ...

2.2.4 *li-kay* لكَيْ 'in order to; in order that'

لكي يحافظ على موقعه

li-kay yu-HaafiZ-a ᶜalaa mawqiᶜ-i-hi

in order to maintain his position

لكي يعودَ إلى بلاده

li-kay ya-ᶜuud-a ʾilaa bilaad-i-hi

in order to return to his country

لكي يغيّروا العالم

li-kay yu-ghayyir-uu l-ʿaalam-a

in order to change ('that they change') the world

2.2.5 *li-kay-laa* لكَيلا 'in order not to'

لكيلا تدخلَ المكتب

li-kay-laa ta-dxul-a l-maktab-a

in order that she not enter the office

2.2.6 *Hattaa* حتّى 'in order that'

The particle *Hattaa* has other meanings, as well ('until' or 'even'), but when used with a verb in the subjunctive it indicates purpose.

حتّى ندركَ صعوبة هذا العمل

Hattaa nu-drik-a Suʿuubat-a haadhaa l-ʿamal-i

in order that we realize the difficulty of this work

2.2.7 *Hattaa laa* حتّى لا 'in order not to; so that . . . not'

حتّى لا يشطَّ في تأييد الانسحاب

Hattaa laa ya-shuTT-a fii taʾyiid-i l-insiHaab-i

so that it does not go too far in supporting withdrawal

2.3 Subordinating conjunction: *ʾan* أنْ + subjunctive

The particle / ʾan/ أنْ follows certain types of verbs in order to conjoin a complement clause to the verb. These verbs (sometimes called "matrix" verbs) usually denote attitudes or feelings toward the action such as liking, disliking, expecting, deciding, intending, wanting, wishing, requesting, possibility, attempting, needing.[5] For example:

to like, love	ʾaHabb-a ʾan	أحبَّ أنْ	to be possible	ʾamkan-a ʾan	أمكن أنْ
to decide	qarrar-a ʾan	قرّر أنْ	to be able	istaTaaʿ-a ʾan	استطاع أنْ
to want	ʾaraad-a ʾan	أراد أنْ	to be able	qadar-a ʾan	قدر أنْ
to be on the verge of	ʾawshak-a ʾan	أوشك أنْ	to be able	tamakkan-a min ʾan	تمكّن من أنْ
to try to	Haawal-a ʾan	حاول أنْ	to intend	qaSad-a ʾan	قصد أنْ

---

[5] Cantarino states: "after verbs that present their objects as something striven for or simply as a possibility or capability of a future action, only ʾan will be used" (1975, III:107). See his extensive section on ʾan 1975, III: 107–16. Compare these verbs to verbs followed by the particle ʾanna, which is used to report factual information in a subordinate clause (see Chapter 19, section 2.3).

In most cases, the *'an* أنْ + **subjunctive** structure is replaceable with a verbal noun. Thus it is possible to have sentences such as:

نحبُ أنْ نقرأَ.

nu-Hibb-u 'an na-qra'-a.
We like **to read** (lit. 'we like that we read').[6]

or

نحبُ القراءةَ.

nu-Hibb-u l-qiraa'at-a.
We like **to read** (lit. 'we like reading').

Sentences in English may use the infinitive (e.g., "to read") as the equivalent of either structure. For example:

لا نريدُ أنْ ننسى.

laa nu-riid-u 'an na-nsaa.
We don't want to forget ('that we forget').

نستطيعُ أنْ نفعلَه.

na-staTii^c-u 'an na-f^cal-a-hu.
We are able to do it ('we are able that we do it').

ثمَّ طلبت أنْ يكونَ الموعد بعد غد.

thumm-a Talab-at 'an ya-kuun-a l-maw^cid-u ba^cd-a ghad-in.
Then it requested that the appointment **be** [the day] after tomorrow.

2.3.1 *qabl-a 'an* قبل أنْ 'before' and *ba^cd-a 'an* بعد أنْ 'after'

The particle *'an* also follows certain semi-prepositions so that they may be followed by a verb phrase or entire clause.[7]

2.3.1.1 *qabl-a 'an* قبل أن 'BEFORE': The semi-preposition *qabl-a* قبل by itself must be directly followed by a noun or a pronoun suffix. Using *'an* as a buffer, *qabl-a* may be followed by a verb in the subjunctive mood. Tense is inferred from context.

(1)   Present tense meaning:

قبل أن نفكّرَ بذلك	قبل أن تمزّقَه الحرب
qabl-a 'an nu-fakkir-a bi-dhaalika	*qabl-a 'an tu-mazziq-a-hu l-Harb-u*
before we think of that	before war rips it apart

---

[6] For more detailed description of the use of the verbal noun in such structures, see Chapter 5, section 1.3.

[7] Normally, prepositions and semi-prepositions are followed by a noun in the genitive case or by a pronoun.

(2) **Past tense meaning:**

قال ذلك قبل أن يخفّفَ العقوبة.

*qaal-a dhaalika **qabl-a ʾan yu-xaffif-a** l-ʿuquubat-a.*

He said that **before he lightened** the penalty.

2.3.1.2 *baʿd-a ʾan* بعد أن 'AFTER': The phrase *baʿd-a ʾan* بعد أن may be followed either by a verb in the subjunctive mood or by a past tense verb. It requires a verb in the subjunctive if the situation is not yet an actual fact, that is, if the situation is in the future or is still a possibility.

However, if the situation is in the past and has already taken place, *baʿd-a ʾan* بعد أن is followed by a past tense verb. The latter case is one of the few situations where the particle *ʾan* أن is followed by anything other than a subjunctive.[8]

(1) **Describing the past:**

بعد أن اتّهمهم بالتآمر

baʿd-a ʾan-i ttaham-a-hum bi-l-taʾaamur-i

after he accused them of conspiracy

(2) **Discussing the future:**

سنأكلُ بعد أن ندرسَ.

sa-na-ʾkul-u baʿd-a ʾan na-drus-a.

We will eat **after we study.**

2.3.2 Impersonal verbs + subjunctive

Certain **impersonal verbal expressions** followed by /ʾan/ أن plus a verb in the subjunctive indicate necessity or possibility:

it is necessary that	*ya-jib-u ʾan*[9]	يجب أن
it ought to be that	*ya-nbaghii ʾan*	ينبغي أن
it is possible that	*yu-mkin-u ʾan*	يمكن أن
	min-a l-mumkin-i ʾan	من الممكن أن

---

[8] Al-Warraki and Hassanein (1994, 51) state it clearly: "If *baʿd-a ʾan* is preceded by a perfect [verb] in the main clause, it is also followed by a perfect; if it is preceded by imperfect or future in the main clause, it is followed by a subjunctive." They devote an entire chapter to *baʿd-a ʾan* and *qabl-a ʾan*.

[9] The phrase *ya-jib-u an* may include the use of the preposition *ʿalaa* to specify for whom the action is necessary, e.g., *ya-jib-u ʿalay-naa ʾan nu-faawiD-a* يجب علينا أن نفاوض 'We have to negotiate (it is necessary/ incumbent **upon us** that we negotiate').

يمكن أن تتحوّل إلى فخّ.

yu-mkin-u ʾan ta-taHawwal-a ʾilaa faxx-in.

It could turn into a trap.

يجب أن نقوم بزيارة.

ya-jib-u ʾan na-quum-a bi-ziyaarat-in.

It is necessary that we undertake
a visit.

يجب على الولايات المتّحدة أن تدعم الاتّفاق.

ya-jib-u ʿalaa l-wilaayaat-i l-muttaHidat-i ʾan ta-dʿam-a l-ittifaaq-a.

It is necessary for the US to support the agreement.

وينبغي أن يصبح جزءاً لا يتجزأ من سياستهم.

ya-nbaghii ʾan yu-SbiH-a juzʾ-an laa ya-tajazzaʾ-u min siyaasat-i-him.

It ought to become an indivisible part of their policy.

2.3.2.1 NEGATION OF NECESSITY involves prefixing the negative particle *laa* before the verb of necessity:

ألا يجب علينا أن ندافع عن أنفسنا؟

ʾa-laa ya-jib-u ʿalay-naa ʾan nu-daafiʿ-a ʿan ʾanfus-i-naa?

Isn't it necessary ('for us') that we defend ourselves?

2.3.2.2 NEGATION OF ACTION involves prefixing the negative particle *laa* before the subjunctive verb. Sometimes ʾan + laa لا + أنْ is contracted into one word: ʾallaa ألّا:

ينبغي أن لا يشعر بقلق.

ya-nbaghii ʾan laa ya-shʿar-a bi-qalaq-in

He must not feel anxious.

يجب أنْ لا تُدفع نقداً.

ya-jib-u ʾan laa tu-dfaʿ-a naqd-an.

It must not be paid in cash.

يجب ألّا يغضّ النظر عنه.

ya-jib-u ʾallaa ya-ghiDD-a l-naZar-a ʿan-hu.

It is necessary that he not disregard it.

2.3.2.3 PAST TENSE OF IMPERSONAL VERBS: These impersonal verbs are put into the past tense through the use of the past tense verb *kaan-a* as an auxiliary verb:

[أراضٍ] كان يجب أن تكون ضمن حصّتهم

[ʾaraaDin] kaan-a ya-jib-u ʾan ta-kuun-a Dimn-a HiSSat-i-him

[lands which] should have been [included] within their portion

2.3.3 ʿalaa + ʾan على + أنْ + subjunctive

The preposition *ʿalaa* may indicate necessity or incumbence "upon" someone to do something. It may be used with a pronoun suffix or with a noun in the genitive, followed by ʾan and a verb in the subjunctive.

وعلينا أن نبدأ من الصفر.

wa-ʿalay-naa ʾan na-bdaʾ-a min-a l-Sifr-i.

We must begin from zero.

وعلى الدولة أن تقوم بدورها.

wa-ʿalaa l-dawlat-i ʾan ta-quum-a bi-dawr-i-haa.

It is incumbent upon the state to assume its role.

2.3.4 Adjective + *ʾan* أن + subjunctive

The particle *ʾan* may be used with an adjective or participle used to express a feeling, expectation, or opinion.

طبيعيّ جدًا أن نحبّ بلادنا.

Tabiiʿiyy-un jidd-an ʾan nu-Hibb-a bilaad-a-naa.

[It is] very natural that we love our country.

المستغرب أن نتأخّر.

al-mustaghrab-u ʾan na-taʾaxxar-a.

[It is] strange that we delay.

ومن المقرّر أن يفجّر خبراء المفرقعات القنابل.

wa-min-a l-muqarrar-i ʾan yu-fajjir-a xubaraaʾ-u l-mufarqiʿaat-i l-qanaabil-a.

It has been determined that explosives experts **will detonate** the bombs.

35

Moods of the verb II: jussive and imperative

1 The jussive: *al-jazm* الجزم

The jussive mood is restricted in occurrence. It does not carry a particular semantic content; rather, it is a mood of the verb required in written Arabic under specific circumstances. The distinctive feature of jussive inflection is the absence of a final short inflectional vowel. Where the indicative mood inflects with *Damma* and the subjunctive mood inflects with *fatHa*, the jussive mood inflects with *sukuun*.

Like the subjunctive, the jussive shortens the longer verb suffixes, such as /-uuna/, /-iina/, and /-aani/, by deleting the *nuun* and its short vowel, so those suffixes are left as long vowels /-uu/, /-ii/, /-aa/. Again, as with the subjunctive and indicative, the /-na/ of the second and third persons feminine plural is retained.

1.1 Jussive mood paradigm: sound Form I verb

عرِف - *ʿrif* - 'know'			
	Singular	Dual	Plural
First person	أَعْرِفْ *ʾa-ʿrif*		نَعْرِفْ *na-ʿrif*
Second person m.	تَعْرِفْ *ta-ʿrif*	تَعْرِفا *ta-ʿrif-aa*	تَعْرِفوا *ta-ʿrif-uu*
f.	تَعْرِفي *ta-ʿrif-ii*	تَعْرِفا *ta-ʿrif-aa*	تَعْرِفْنَ *ta-ʿrif-na*
Third person m.	يعرِفْ *ya-ʿrif*	يعرِفا *ya-ʿrif-aa*	يعرِفوا *ya-ʿrif-uu*
f.	تَعْرِفْ *ta-ʿrif*	تَعْرِفا *ta-ʿrif-aa*	يَعْرِفْنَ *ya-ʿrif-na*

The absence of an inflectional vowel in the first person singular and plural, the second person masculine singular and the third persons feminine and masculine singular causes certain pronunciation and spelling changes in geminate, hollow, and defective verbs.

1.2 Jussive mood paradigm: geminate Form I verb

When the jussive mood is used with geminate verbs, the deletion of the inflectional short vowel in the first person singular and plural, the second person masculine singular, and the third persons feminine and masculine singular causes a consonant cluster to occur at the end of the inflected verb, and this violates the phonological rule against word-final consonant clusters in MSA. To counteract this, a short vowel /-a/ is added to these persons of the verb in order to make them pronounceable. However, the addition of the short vowel /-a/ has the effect of making the jussive of geminate verbs look exactly like the subjunctive.

رَدَّ - *rudd* - 'return; reply'			
	Singular	**Dual**	**Plural**
First person	أَرُدَّ *ʾa-rudd-a*		نَرُدَّ *na-rudd-a*
Second person m.	تَرُدَّ *ta-rudd-a*	تَرُدَّا *ta-rudd-aa*	تَرُدُّوا *ta-rudd-uu*
f.	تَرُدِّي *ta-rudd-ii*	تَرُدَّا *ta-rudd-aa*	تَرْدُدْنَ *ta-rdud-na*
Third person m.	يَرُدَّ *ya-rudd-a*	يَرُدَّا *ya-rudd-aa*	يَرُدُّوا *ya-rudd-uu*
f.	تَرُدَّ *ta-rudd-a*	تَرُدَّا *ta-rudd-aa*	يَرْدُدْنَ *ya-rdud-na*

1.3 Jussive mood paradigm: hollow Form I verb

Hollow verbs inflected in the jussive mood have both a long vowel stem and a short vowel stem. The long vowel stem is only used when the inflectional suffix is a vowel, as follows:

1.3.1 Hollow-*waaw* verb

<table>
<tr><td colspan="4" align="center">-qul / quul - 'say'</td></tr>
<tr><td></td><td>Singular</td><td>Dual</td><td>Plural</td></tr>
<tr><td>First person</td><td>أَقُلْ
ʾa-qul</td><td></td><td>نَقُلْ
na-qul</td></tr>
<tr><td>Second person
m.</td><td>تَقُلْ
ta-qul</td><td>تَقُولَا
ta-quul-aa</td><td>تَقُولُوا
ta-quul-uu</td></tr>
<tr><td>f.</td><td>تَقُولِي
ta-quul-ii</td><td>تَقُولَا
ta-quul-aa</td><td>تَقُلْنَ
ta-qul-na</td></tr>
<tr><td>Third person
m.</td><td>يَقُلْ
ya-qul</td><td>يَقُولَا
ya-quul-aa</td><td>يَقُولُوا
ya-quul-uu</td></tr>
<tr><td>f.</td><td>تَقُلْ
ta-qul</td><td>تَقُولَا
ta-quul-aa</td><td>يَقُلْنَ
ya-qul-na</td></tr>
</table>

1.3.2 Hollow *yaaʾ* verb

<table>
<tr><td colspan="4" align="center">- biᶜ- / - biiᶜ- 'buy'</td></tr>
<tr><td></td><td>Singular</td><td>Dual</td><td>Plural</td></tr>
<tr><td>First person</td><td>أَبِعْ
ʾa-biᶜ</td><td></td><td>نَبِعْ
na-biᶜ</td></tr>
<tr><td>Second person
m.</td><td>تَبِعْ
ta-biᶜ</td><td>تَبِيعَا
ta-biiᶜ-aa</td><td>تَبِيعُوا
ta-biiᶜ-uu</td></tr>
<tr><td>f.</td><td>تَبِيعِي
ta-biiᶜ-ii</td><td>تَبِيعَا
ta-biiᶜ-aa</td><td>تَبِعْنَ
ta-biᶜ-na</td></tr>
<tr><td>Third person
m.</td><td>يَبِعْ
ya-biᶜ</td><td>يَبِيعَا
ya-biiᶜ-aa</td><td>يَبِيعُوا
ya-biiᶜ-uu</td></tr>
<tr><td>f.</td><td>تَبِعْ
ta-biᶜ</td><td>تَبِيعَا
ta-biiᶜ-aa</td><td>يَبِعْنَ
ya-biᶜ-na</td></tr>
</table>

1.3.3 Hollow ʾalif verb

<table>
<tr><td colspan="4" align="center">-nam- / -naam- 'sleep'</td></tr>
<tr><td></td><td>Singular</td><td>Dual</td><td>Plural</td></tr>
<tr>
<td>First person</td>
<td>أَنَمْ
ʾa-nam</td>
<td></td>
<td>نَنَمْ
na-nam</td>
</tr>
<tr>
<td>Second person
m.</td>
<td>تَنَمْ
ta-nam</td>
<td>تَنَامَا
ta-naam-aa</td>
<td>تَنَامُوا
ta-naam-uu</td>
</tr>
<tr>
<td>f.</td>
<td>تَنَامِي
ta-naam-ii</td>
<td>تَنَامَا
ta-naam-aa</td>
<td>تَنَمْنَ
ta-nam-na</td>
</tr>
<tr>
<td>Third person
m.</td>
<td>يَنَمْ
ya-nam</td>
<td>يَنَامَا
ya-naam-aa</td>
<td>يَنَامُوا
ya-naam-uu</td>
</tr>
<tr>
<td>f.</td>
<td>تَنَمْ
ta-nam</td>
<td>تَنَامَا
ta-naam-aa</td>
<td>يَنَمْنَ
ya-nam-na</td>
</tr>
</table>

1.4 Jussive mood paradigm: Defective Form I verb

The effect of the *sukuun* of the jussive on certain inflectional forms of defective verbs is to shorten the long vowel ending to a short vowel. As a short vowel it usually does not appear in written text.

1.4.1 Jussive of *yaaʾ*-defective verb (-aa/-ii)

<table>
<tr><td colspan="4" align="center">- bni- / -bniy- 'build'</td></tr>
<tr><td></td><td>Singular</td><td>Dual</td><td>Plural</td></tr>
<tr>
<td>First person</td>
<td>أَبْنِ
ʾa-bni</td>
<td></td>
<td>نَبْنِ
na-bni</td>
</tr>
<tr>
<td>Second person
m.</td>
<td>تَبْنِ
ta-bni</td>
<td>تَبْنِيَا
ta-bniy-aa</td>
<td>تَبْنُوا
ta-bnuu</td>
</tr>
<tr>
<td>f.</td>
<td>تَبْنِي
ta-bn-ii</td>
<td>تَبْنِيَا
ta-bniy-aa</td>
<td>تَبْنِينَ
ta-bnii-na</td>
</tr>
</table>

- bni- / -bniy- 'build'			
	Singular	**Dual**	**Plural**
Third person m.	يَبْنِ ya-bni	يَبْنِيَا ya-bniy-aa	يَبْنُوا ya-bnuu
f.	تَبْنِ ta-bni	تَبْنِيَا ta-bniy-aa	يَبْنِينَ ya-bnii-na

1.4.2 Jussive of *yaaʾ*-defective verb (-*ii*/-*aa*)

-nsa- / -nsay- 'forget'			
	Singular	**Dual**	**Plural**
First person	أَنْسَ ʾa-nsa		نَنْسَ na-nsa
Second person m.	تَنْسَ ta-nsa	تَنْسَيَا ta-nsay-aa	تَنْسَوْا ta-nsaw
f.	تَنْسَي ta-nsay	تَنْسَيَا ta-nsay-aa	تَنْسَيْنَ ta-nsay-na
Third person m.	يَنْسَ ya-nsa	يَنْسَيَا ya-nsay-aa	يَنْسَوْا ya-nsaw
f.	تَنْسَ ta-nsa	تَنْسَيَا ta-nsay-aa	يَنْسَيْنَ ya-nsay–na

1.4.3 Jussive of *waaw*-defective verb

-bdu- / -bduw- 'seem, appear'			
	Singular	**Dual**	**Plural**
First person	أَبْدُ ʾa-bdu		نَبْدُ na-bdu

-bdu- / -bduw- 'seem, appear'			
	Singular	**Dual**	**Plural**
Second person **m.**	تَبْدُ *ta-bdu*	تَبْدُوا *ta-bduw-aa*	تَبْدُوا *ta-bduu*
f.	تَبْدِي *ta-bdii*	تَبْدُوا *ta-bduw-aa*	تَبْدُونَ *ta-bduu-na*
Third person **m.**	يَبْدُ *ya-bdu*	يَبْدُوا *ya-bduw-aa*	يَبْدُوا *ya-bduu*
f.	تَبْدُ *ta-bdu*	تَبْدُوا *ta-bduw-aa*	يَبْدُونَ *ya-bduu–na*

Full paradigms of verbs in all moods are found in chapters on the respective verb forms (I–X).

1.5 Use of the jussive

The jussive is used in essentially five ways: with conditional sentences, with the negative particle *lam* لَمْ; with the negative imperative particle *laa* لا, the indirect imperative particle /li/ لِ, and as a basis for forming the imperative.

Most often, the jussive mood in MSA is used with the negative particle *lam* to negate the past tense, and with the imperative.

1.5.1 In conditional sentences

The jussive in conditional sentences occurred rarely in the MSA database covered for this analysis. This particular function of the jussive is more common in literary and classical texts.[1] For discussion of this use of the jussive see Chapter 39 on conditional and optative expressions.

إنْ تَذْهَبِي، أَذْهَبْ مَعَكِ.

'in ta-dhhab-ii, 'a-dhhab maᶜ-a-ki.

If you (f.) go, I'll go with you.

---

[1] See, for example, Cantarino's extensive description of conditional clauses in literary Arabic, Cantarino 1975, III:311–71, and Haywood and Nahmad 1962, 290–300.

إنْ يكسرْ إنسانٌ سنّ آخر، فسنّه تُكسرُ.

'in ya-ksir 'insaan-un sinn-a 'aaxar-a, fa-sinn-u-hu tu-ksar-u.[2]

If a person **breaks** the tooth of another, (then) his tooth shall be broken.

1.5.2 With *lam* لم

The negative particle *lam* is used to negate the past tense. However, it is not used with a past tense verb. Instead, it is used with the jussive form of the verb, conveying a **meaning** of past tense. In Arabic grammatical terms if is said to "transform the [meaning of] the verb following it to the past."[3]

لم نأتِ.

lam na-'ti.

We did not come.

لم أنَمْ.

lam 'a-nam.

I didn't sleep.

لم تكُنْ تدفعُ الإيجارَ.

lam ta-kun ta-dfaᶜ-u l-'iijaar-a.

She didn't used to pay the rent.

لم تنجحْ حتّى الآنَ.

lam ta-njaH Hattaa l-'aan-a

She has **not yet succeeded**.

إصلاحاتٌ لم تكتملْ منذ عامين

'iSlaaH-aat-un lam ta-ktamil mundh-u ᶜaam-ayni

renovations that **haven't been completed** in two years

لم يُبلغوا زملاءَهم.

lam yu-bligh-uu zumalaa'-a-hum.

They did **not notify** their colleagues.

For further examples of *lam* لم plus the jussive, see Chapter 37 on negation and exception, section 2.2.1.

2 The imperative: *al-'amr* الأمر

The imperative or command form of the verb in Arabic is based upon the imperfect/present tense verb in the jussive mood. It occurs in the second person (all forms of "you"), for the most part, although it occasionally occurs in the first person plural ("let's") and the third person ("let him/her/them").

2.1 To form the imperative

The general rule for forming the imperative is to take the second person form of the jussive verb and remove the subject marker (the *ta-* or *tu-* prefix). If the remaining

---

[2] From Ziadeh and Winder 1957, 160.

[3] ᶜAbd al-Latif et al. 1997, 307: "*wa-ta-dull-u [lam] ᶜalaa l-nafii, wa-tu-qallib-u l-muDaariᶜ-a baᶜd-a-haa 'ilaa l-maaDii wa-li-dhaalik-a yu-Tliq-u ᶜalay-haa l-muᶜrib-uuna: "Harf-u nafii wa-jazm-in wa-qalb-in.*" [The particle] *lam* indicates negation, and it transforms the present-tense verb after it into the past tense and therefore grammarians call it the particle of negation, jussive, and transformation."

verb stem starts with a consonant-vowel (CV) sequence, then the stem is left as it is because it is easily pronounceable. If the remaining stem starts with a consonant cluster, then it needs a helping vowel prefix. The nature of the helping vowel depends on the verb form and (in Form I) the nature of the stem vowel.

For example, the verb *katab-a* 'to write' in the **present tense, jussive mood, second person** is:

you (m. sg.) write	*ta-ktub*	تَكْتُبْ
you (f. sg.) write	*ta-ktub-ii*	تَكْتُبِي
you two write	*ta-ktub-aa*	تَكْتُبَا
you (m. pl.) write	*ta-ktub-uu*	تَكْتُبُوا
you (f. pl.) write	*ta-ktub-na*	تَكْتُبْنَ

To create the imperative, the *ta-* prefix is dropped, leaving:

*ktub	كْتُبْ
*ktub-ii	كْتُبِي
*ktub-aa	كْتُبَا
*ktub-uu	كْتُبُوا
*ktub-na	كْتُبْنَ

Because these forms start with consonant clusters, they violate a phonological rule in Arabic that prohibits word-initial consonant clusters. They therefore need a helping vowel to be pronounceable. The helping vowel selected in this case is /u/ because the stem vowel of the verb is /u/. However, another rule in Arabic prohibits words from starting with vowels, so the /u/ vowel is preceded by *hamza*, and the *hamza* plus short vowel sit on an *'alif* seat. This yields the pronounceable forms:

Write!	*u-ktub!*	أُكْتُبْ !
	u-ktub-ii!	أُكْتُبِي!
	u-ktub-aa!	أُكْتُبَا !
	u-ktub-uu!	أُكْتُبُوا !
	u-ktub-na!	أُكْتُبْنَ !

This helping vowel is used with **hamzat al-waSl**, that is, elidable *hamza*, which is normally not written and drops out if it is preceded by another vowel, as in:

| Read and write! | *i-qra' wa-ktub!* | اقْرَأْ وَاكْتُبْ ! |

Note that although the prefix *hamza* drops out in pronunciation, the ʾ*alif* seat remains in the spelling of the word.

The deletion of the subject-marker prefix (*ta-* or *tu-*) does not always leave a stem that starts with two consonants. For example, in the Form II verb *fassar-a* فَسَّرَ 'to explain':

you (m. sg.) explain	*tu-fassir*	تفسّر
you (f. sg.) explain	*tu-fassir-ii*	تفسّري
you two explain	*tu-fassir-aa*	تفسّرا
you (m. pl.) explain	*tu-fassir-uu*	تفسّروا
you (f. pl.) explain	*tu-fassir-na*	تفسّرن

The imperative forms stripped of the subject marker are:

Explain!	*fassir!*	فسّر!
	fassir-ii!	فسّري !
	fassir-aa!	فسّرا!
	fassir-uu!	فسّروا!
	fassir-na!	فسّرن !

These are pronounceable just as they are, so they need no initial helping vowel and are left as they are in the imperative.

2.1.1 Summary

The word-initial helping vowel is needed in the imperative of **Forms I, IV, VII, VIII, and X** of the verb. Forms II, III, V, and VI do not need helping vowels in the imperative. The specifics of the Forms are summarized here.

2.2 Form I imperatives

Form I imperatives usually require initial helping vowels, either /*i*/ or /*u*/. The nature of the helping vowel is determined by the stem vowel of the present tense. **If the stem vowel is *fatHa* or *kasra*, the helping vowel is *kasra*; if the stem vowel is *Damma*, the helping vowel is *Damma*.**

2.2.1 Sound verbs

2.2.1.1 STEM VOWEL *fatHa*

افْتَحْ يا سمسم!	ارْفَعْ يديك!	اسْمَحي لي.
i-ftaH yaa simsim-u!	*i-rfaʿ yad-ay-ka!*	*i-smaH-ii lii!*
Open, Sesame!	**Raise** your (two) hands!	**Permit** (f. sg.) me!

2.2.1.2 STEM VOWEL *kasra*

احْفِرْ هنا!   اعْذِرْني.

i-Hfir hunaa!   *i-ʿdhir*-nii.

Dig here!   **Forgive** me/**Excuse** me.

2.2.1.3 STEM VOWEL *Damma*

اُدْخُلْ!   اُنْظُرْ جيّداً!

u-dxul!   *u-nZur* jayyid-an!

Enter!   **Look** well/ **look** closely!

2.2.2 Hamzated verbs

Form I verbs with **initial hamza** tend to drop the *hamza* entirely in the imperative in order to avoid less acceptable phonological sequences that involve two *hamzas* in sequence such as **ʾuʾ kul* or **ʾuʾxudh*:

كُلِ الجزرَ.   خُذْ هذه!

kul-i l-jazar-a.   *xudh* haadhihi!

Eat the carrots.   **Take** this!

Verbs with **medial hamza** may behave as regular verbs or may drop the initial *hamza*:

سَلْ! ~ اسْأَلْ!   اسْأَلْ عن معنى أيّ كلمة.

i-sʾal! ~ *sal!*   *isʾal* ʿan maʿnaa ʾayy-i kalimat-in.

Ask!   **Ask** about the meaning of any word.

Verbs with **final hamza** behave regularly in the imperative:

اقْرَأْ!   ابْدَئِي!

i-qraʾ!   *i-bdaʾ-ii!*

Read!   **Begin**(f. sg.)!

2.2.3 Geminate verbs

Form I geminate verbs are mixed as to whether or not they take a helping vowel prefix. They do not take the *hamza* prefix in the forms that end with a long vowel, but they may or may not take the *hamza* in the second person masculine singular. If the *hamza* is omitted, the imperative in this person takes a final *fatHa* in order for it to be pronounceable. A *hamza* prefix is used in the second person feminine plural.

Respond!	*rudd-a ~ u-rdud!*	اُرْدُدْ ~ رُدَّ
	rudd-ii	رُدّي
	rudd-aa	رُدَّا

rudd-uu	رُدّوا
u-rdud-na!	اُرْدُدْنَ

2.2.4 Assimilated verbs

Most verbs whose initial root consonant is *waaw* or *yaaʾ* (such as *waDaʿ-a/ ya-Daʿ-u* 'to put, place') delete that consonant in all moods of the present tense. Therefore when the subject prefix is deleted from the jussive mood in order to form the imperative, it leaves a very short but pronounceable stem. For example:

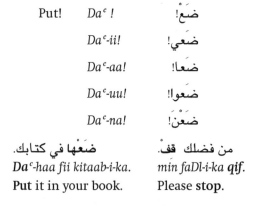

Put!	*Daʿ !*	ضَعْ!
	Daʿ-ii!	ضَعِي!
	Daʿ-aa!	ضَعَا!
	Daʿ-uu!	ضَعوا!
	Daʿ-na!	ضَعْنَ!

ضَعْها في كتابك.	من فضلك قفْ.
Daʿ-haa fii kitaab-i-ka.	*min faDl-i-ka qif.*
Put it in your book.	Please **stop.**

2.2.5 Hollow verbs

Form I hollow verbs, just as regular verbs, make the imperative based on the jussive forms without the subject-marker prefix. There are two stem variants in the jussive of hollow verbs, short-vowel and long-vowel. Both stems are pronounceable without the need for a helping vowel prefix. For example:

2.2.5.1 HOLLOW *waaw* VERB: *qaal-a* قَالَ/*ya-quul-u* يَقولُ 'TO SAY'

Say!	*qul!*	قُلْ !
	quul-ii!	قولي!
	quul-aa!	قولا !
	quul-uu!	قولوا !
	qul-na!	قُلْنَ !

2.2.5.2 HOLLOW *yaaʾ* VERB: *baaʿ-a* بَاعَ/*ya-biiʿ-u* يَبيعُ 'TO SELL'

Sell!	*biʿ !*	بِعْ !
	biiʿ-ii!	بيعي !

biiᶜ-aa!	بيعا !
biiᶜ-uu!	بيعوا !
biᶜ-na!	بِعْنَ !

سيروا بمحاذاة السور.

siir-uu bi-muHaadhaat-i l-suur-i.

Go (m. pl.) alongside the wall.

2.2.5.3 HOLLOW ʾalif VERB: *naam-a* نامَ/*ya-naam-u* يَنامُ 'TO SLEEP'

Sleep!	nam!	نَمْ !
	naam-ii!	نامي !
	naam-aa!	ناما !
	naaam-uu!	ناموا !
	nam-na!	نَمْنَ !

2.2.6 Defective verbs

Defective verbs have either *waaw* or *yaaʾ* as their final root consonant. In the jussive mood, this consonant undergoes shifts in length and quality. The imperative of defectives is based on the jussive form, with no changes except the deletion of the subject marker and the addition of the helping vowel prefix. As with regular verbs, the nature of the short helping vowel prefix depends on the stem vowel of the verb.

2.2.6.1 Yaaʾ-DEFECTIVE VERBS: The *yaaʾ*-defective verbs are of two types: ones that end in *-aa* (ʾalif maqSuura ألف مقصورة) and ones that end with *yaaʾ* in the past tense. The ones ending in *-aa* usually inflect the present tense with *-ii*; the ones that end with *yaaʾ* in the past tense take *-aa* in the present tense. These verbs take *kasra* as their imperative prefix helping vowel.

(1) /-aa-ii/ verb: *ramaa* رمى /*ya-rmii* يَرمي 'to throw'

Throw!	i-rmi!	اِرْمِ !
	i-rm-ii!	اِرمي !
	i-rmiy-aa!	اِرميا !
	i-rm-uu!	اِرموا !
	i-rmii-na!	اِرمينَ !

(2)   /-*ii-aa*/ verb: *nasiy-a* نَسِيَ / *ya-nsaa* يَنْسى 'to forget'

Forget!	*i-nsa!*	اِنْسَ !
	i-ns-ay!	اِنْسَيْ !
	i-nsay-aa!	اِنْسَيا !
	i-ns-aw!	اِنْسَوْا!
	i-nsay-na!	اِنْسَيْنَ !

2.2.6.2 *Waaw*-DEFECTIVE VERBS: The *waaw*-defective verbs end in -*aa* ('*alif Tawiila* ألف طويلة) in the past tense citation form, and in *waaw* in the present tense. In the jussive mood, the *waaw* shifts and sometimes shortens. The prefix helping vowel for these imperative forms is *Damma*.

(1)   /-*aa-uu*/ verb: *shakaa* شكَا/ *ya-shkuu* يَشْكو 'to complain'

Complain!	*u-shku!*	أُشْكُ !
	u-shk-ii!	أُشْكِي !
	u-shkuw-aa!	أُشْكُوا !
	u-shk-uu!	أُشْكوا !
	u-shkuu-na!	أُشْكونَ !

2.2.7 Doubly defective verbs

Doubly defective verbs have semi-consonants and/or *hamza* in two places, sometimes as the first and third consonants, and sometimes as the second and third. Their imperatives are defective in more ways than one. Two examples are given here, the verb *ra'aa* رأَى / *ya-raa* يرى 'to see' and the verb *wa'aa* وعى / *ya-'ii* يعي 'to heed, pay attention.'

2.2.7.1 IMPERATIVE OF *ra'aa* رأَى / *ya-raa* يَرى [4]

See!	*ra~ rah!*	رَه ~ رَ !
	ray!	رَيْ !
	ray-aa!	رَيا !
	raw!	رَوْا!
	ray-na!	رَيْنَ !

---

[4]   Taken from Wright 1967, I:93. Note that the verb *ra'aa* is used primarily in written Arabic and is not normally used in the vernacular forms of the language.

2.2.7.2 IMPERATIVE OF *waʿaa* وَعى / *ya-ʿii* يَعي

Pay attention!	*ʿi!*	ع !
	ʿii!	عي !
	ʿiy-aa!	عيا !
	ʿ-uu!	عوا !
	ʿii-na!	عينَ !

2.2.8 Replacive imperative verb: *taʿaal* تَعال 'come!'

The verb *jaaʾa* جاءَ / *ya-jiiʾ-u* يَجيءُ 'to come' has a different form in the imperative, based on another root entirely:[5]

Come!	*taʿaal-a!*	تَعالَ !
	taʿaal-ay!	تَعالَيْ!
	taʿaal-aa!	تَعالا !
	taʿaal-aw!	تَعالَوْا !
	taʿaalay-na!	تَعالَيْنَ!

تعالَ هنا !
taʿaal-a hunaa !
Come here!

2.3 Form II imperative

Form II imperatives do not require the addition of an initial helping vowel. Examples include:

خبِّرْني!	فكِّر فيما تأكلُه.
xabbir-nii!	*fakkir fii-maa ta-ʾkul-u-hu.*
Tell me!	**Think about what you eat.**

سلِّمْ لي عليه.	سكِّروا كتبكم.
sallim lii ʿalay-hi.	*sakkir-uu kutub-a-kum.*
Greet him for me.	**Close (m. pl.) your books.**

2.4 Form III

Form III imperatives do not require the addition of an initial helping vowel. Examples include:

---

[5] Based on the Form VI defective verb *taʿaalaa/ya-taʿaalaa* 'to rise, ascend, be sublime.' For discussion of this "suppletive imperative" see Testen 1997.

حافظوا على نظافة مدينتكم.
HaafiZ-uu ʿalaa naZaafat-i madiinat-i-kum!
Preserve the cleanliness of your city!

قاطع البضائع اليابانيّة !
qaaTiʿ-i l-baDaaʾiʿ-a l-yaabaaniyyat-a!
Boycott Japanese goods!

شاركوني في الترحيب به.
shaarik-uu-nii fii l-tarHiib-i bi-hi.
Join me in welcoming him.

سارع إلى إغلاقها.
saariʿ ʾilaa ʾighlaaq-i-haa.
Hasten to turn it off.

2.5 Form IV

Form IV verbs are prefixed by the vowel /a/ (fatHa) and a non-elidable *hamza* (*hamzat al-qaTʿ*):

أعطوني الواجبات.
ʾaʿT-uu-nii l-waajibaat-i.
Give (m. pl.) me the homework.

أغلقْ يا سمسم!
ʾaghliq yaa simsim!
Close, Sesame!

أعيدي السؤال.
ʾaʿiid-ii l-suʾaal-a.
Repeat (f. sg.) the question.

أجب عن سؤالي !
ʾajib ʿan suʾaal-ii!
Answer my question!

2.6 Form V

Form V imperative verbs do not require a prefix vowel.

تصوّرْ !
taSawwar!
Imagine!

تفضّل بالدخول.
tafaDDal bi-l-duxuul-i.
Please come in.

2.7 Form VI

Form VI imperative verbs do not require a prefix vowel.

تعاونّوا !
taʿaawan-uu!
Cooperate (m. pl.)!

2.8 Form VII

Form VII verbs require a prefixed /i/ vowel (*kasra*) and *hamzat al-waSl*.

انصرفْ من هنا.
inSarif min hunaa.
Leave here.

2.9 Form VIII

Form VIII verbs require a prefixed /i/ vowel (*kasra*) and *hamzat al-waSl*.

ابتعدوا عن هنا !	انتظرْ دقيقة !
ibta⁣ᶜid-uu ᶜan hunaa!	*intaZir daqiiqat-an!*
Get away (m. pl.) from here!	**Wait a minute!**

2.10 Form IX

This form is rarely used in the imperative.

2.11 Form X

Form X verbs require a prefixed /i/ vowel (*kasra*) and *hamzat al-waSl*.

استعملْ هذا المفتاح.	إسترحْ !	استعجلْ !
istaᶜmil haadhaa l-miftaaH-a.	*istariH!*	*istaᶜjil!*
Use this key.	**Relax!**	**Hurry up!**

2.12 Quadriliteral imperatives

Using the identical process of stripping the subject prefix from the second person jussive verb forms, one gets, for example, in the Form I quadriliteral verb *tarjam-a* ترجم 'to translate':

Base form jussive:

you (m. sg.) translate	*tu-tarjim*	تترجمْ
you (f. sg.) translate	*tu-tarjim-ii*	تترجمي
you two translate	*tu-tarjim-aa*	تترجما
you (m. pl.) translate	*tu-tarjim-uu*	تترجموا
you (f. pl.) translate	*tu-tarjim-na*	تترجمْنَ

The imperative forms stripped of the subject marker are:

Translate!	*tarjim!*	ترجمْ !
	tarjim-ii!	ترجمي !
	tarjim-aa!	ترجما !
	tarjim-uu!	ترجموا !
	tarjim-na!	ترجمْنَ !

These are pronounceable so they need no initial helping vowel and are left as they are in the imperative. Form I is by far the most frequent in usage, since the quadriliteral Form II (for example, *tabalwar-a* تَبَلْوَرَ 'to be crystallized') is often reflexive or passive in meaning.

تلفنْ لي غدا.	ترجمي هذه الجملة.
talfin lii ghad-an.	*tarjim-ii haadhihi l-jumlat-a.*
Phone me tomorrow.	**Translate** (f. sg.) this sentence.

3 The permissive or hortative imperative: *laam al-ʾamr* لام الأمر

An "indirect" type of imperative may be used to exhort or enjoin someone to do something. This may occur in the first (I, we) or third (he, she, they) persons. In this type of imperative structure, the jussive verb is used (no deletion of subject marker), preceded by the particle /li-/ لِ, implying the idea of permission or encouragement to do something:

لننظرْ في السلّة.
li-na-nZur fii l-sallat-i.
Let's look in the basket.

Sometimes the / *li-*/ لِ particle is preceded by the particle /*fa-*/ فَ, in which case the vowel is dropped from /li-/ making it just /l-/.

فَلْنذهبْ	فَلْنسرعْ.
fa-l-na-dhhab.	*fa-l-na-sri^c^.*
(So) let's go.	Let's hurry.

4 The negative imperative: *laa* لا + jussive

The negative imperative is formed by using the negative particle *laa* plus the jussive form of the (second person) verb. Note that in the negative imperative, the jussive verb form preserves its prefix.

Don't go back!

m. sg.	*laa ta-rji^c^ !*	لا تَرْجِعْ !
f. sg.	*laa ta-rji^c^-ii!*	لا تَرْجِعي !
dual	*laa ta-rji^c^-aa!*	لا تَرْجِعا !
m. pl.	*laa ta-rji^c^-uu!*	لا تَرْجِعوا !
f. pl.	*laa ta-rji^c^-na!*	لا تَرْجِعْنَ !

Examples:

لا تفتحي الشبّاك.	لا تنسَ !	لا تدخّن.
laa ta-ftaH-ii l-shubbaak-a.	*laa ta-nsa!*	*laa tu-daxxin.*
Don't (f. sg.) open the window.	Don't forget!	Don't smoke.

لا تخافوا !

laa ta-xaaf-uu!

Don't (m. pl.) be afraid!

لا تنتظروا.

laa ta-ntaZir-uu.

Don't (m.pl.) wait.

لا تستعجل.

laa ta-staʿjil.

Don't hurry.

لا تؤجّل عمل اليوم إلى الغد.

laa tu-ʾajjil ʿamal-a l-yawm-i ʾilaa l-ghad-i.

Don't postpone today's work to tomorrow.

لا تزعج نفسك.

laa tu-zʿij nafs-a-ka.

Don't disturb yourself/don't bother.

36

Verbs of being, becoming, remaining, seeming (*kaan-a wa-ʾaxawaat-u-haa*)

Verbs of being, becoming, and remaining have special status in Arabic. Because these verbs resemble each other in meaning and in syntactic effect, they are referred to as "sisters" of the verb 'to be,' *kaan-a* كان (*ʾaxawaat-u kaan-a* أخوات كان). All of them describe states of existence (e.g., being, inception, duration, continuation) and each of them requires the accusative marker on the predicate or complement (*xabar kaan-a* خبر كان), e.g., *kaan-a zaʿiim-an* كان زعيماً 'He was **a leader**.' The subject of *kaan-a* (*ism kaan-a* اسم كان) and her sisters, if mentioned specifically, is in the nominative case (e.g., *kaan-a l-rajul-u zaʿiim-an,* كان الرجلُ زعيماً '**The man** was a leader'.[1]

Another special characteristic of *kaan-a* and her sisters is that they function as auxiliary verbs. In particular, *kaan-a* is used for forming compound tenses such as past progressive and future perfect. Some examples of this are offered here, but the topic is presented in detail in Chapter 21.

Verbs of seeming or appearing also mark their complements with the accusative case, but they are not usually classified among the "sisters" of *kaan-a*.

1 The verb *kaan-a* كان /*ya-kuun-u* يَكونُ 'to be'
This verb is unusual in that it is not generally used in the present tense indicative. It is omitted from the syntax of a simple predication.

1.1 Omission of *kaan-a* in simple present tense predication
These verbless sentences are usually termed "equational" sentences in English descriptions of Arabic syntax; in Arabic they are called "nominal sentences" (*jumal ismiyya* جمل اسمية).[2] For more on equational sentences, see Chapter 4, section 2.

أنا متأكّدٌ.	هي محظوظةٌ.
ʾanaa mutaʾakkid-un.	*hiya maHZuuZat-un.*
I [am] certain.	She [is] fortunate.

---

[1] For more extensive discussion of *kaan-a wa-ʾaxawaat-u-haa* in Classical Arabic, see Wright 1967, II:99–109.

[2] Arab grammarians actually term any sentence that starts with a noun a "nominal sentence" even if it includes a verb. Following the practice of Cantarino (1974, I:2), I use the terms "nominal sentence" and "equational sentence" as equivalents.

هو الملك.
huwa l-malik-u.
He [is] the king.

هم متأخّرونَ.
hum muta'axxir-uuna.
They [are] late.

1.2 Use of *kaan-a* كانَ

The verb *kaan-a* enters when the predication is anything but present tense indicative. It takes a subject in the nominative and it requires that the complement be in the accusative case.

1.2.1 Past tense

كُنْتُ متأكّداً.
kun-tu muta'akkid-an.
I was certain.

كانَتْ محظوظةً.
kaan-at maHZuuZat-an.
She was fortunate.

كانوا متأخّرينَ.
kaan-uu muta'axxir-iina.
They were late.

كانَ الملكَ.
kaan-a l-malik-a.
He was the king.

1.2.2 Future tense

سأكونُ متأكّداً.
sa-'a-kuun-u muta'akkid-an.
I will be certain.

ستكونُ محظوظةً.
sa-ta-kuun-u maHZuuZat-an.
She will be fortunate.

سيَكونونَ متأخّرينَ.
sa-ya-kuun-uuna muta'axxir-iina.
They will be late.

سيَكونُ الملكَ.
sa-ya-kuun-u l-malik-a.
He will be the king.

1.2.3 Further examples

Here are some examples of **kaan-a** in various tenses and moods:

1.2.3.1 PAST TENSE

كان جاسوساً.
kaan-a jaasuus-an.
He was a spy.

كان كثيرون منهم مسجّلين.
kaan-a kathiir-uuna min-hum musajjal-iina.
Many of them were registered.

هذه كانت منازلَنا.
haadhihi kaan-at manaazil-a-naa.
These were our homes.

كان مخزناً للتوابل.
kaan-a maxzan-an li-l-tawaabil-i.
It was a storehouse for spices.

1.2.3.2 NEGATIVE PAST WITH *lam* لَمْ + JUSSIVE MOOD OF *kaan-a* كانَ

يمكن القول إنّ هذا الاجتماع لم يَكُنْ ضروريّاً.

yu-mkin-u l-qawl-u ʾinna haadhaa l-ijtimaaʿ-a **lam ya-kun** *Daruuriyy-an.*

It could be said that this meeting **was not** necessary.

لم يَكُنْ حلماً عاديّاً.

lam ya-kun Hulm-an ʿaadiyy-an.

It was not a regular dream.

1.2.3.3 PAST TENSE FOR OPTATIVE/CONDITIONAL

كم كُنّا سعداء!

kam **kun-naa** *suʿadaaʾ-a !*

How happy **we would be!**

1.2.3.4 FUTURE TENSE

لبنان سَيَكونُ غائباً عن القمّة.

lubnaan-u **sa-ya-kuun-u** *ghaaʾib-an ʿan-i l-qimmat-i.*

Lebanon **will be** absent from the summit [meeting].

1.2.3.5 SUBJUNCTIVE MOOD

لا يمكن أن يَكونَ عربيّاً.

laa yu-mkin-u **ʾan ya-kuun-a** *ʿarabiyy-an.*

It is not possible **that he is** an Arab.

1.3 The use of *kaan-a* as auxiliary verb

An important function of *kaan-a* is as an auxiliary verb in conjunction with main verbs to construct compound verb forms that convey different temporal meanings. Compound verbs are discussed at greater length in Chapter 21, section 2.

1.3.1 Past progressive

For habitual or continual action in the past, the past tense of *kaan-a* is used with the present tense of the main verb. Both the main verb and the auxiliary are inflected for person, number, and gender.

كُنّا نَأْمُلُ	أنا من عائلة كانتْ تعملُ في المدينة.
kun-naa na-ʾmul-u	*ʾanaa min ʿaaʾilat-in* **kaan-at ta-ʿmal-u** *fii l-madiinat-i.*
we were hoping	I am from a family that **used to work** in the city.

1.3.2 Pluperfect or past perfect

To express an action in the past that is over with and which serves as a background action for the present, the past tense of *kaan-a* is used with a past tense of the main verb. The particle *qad* قَدْ may be optionally inserted just before the main verb.

كانوا (قَدْ) عَمِلوا معهم على إعادة فتح السفارة.

kaan-uu (qad) ʿamil-uu maʿ-a-hum ʿalaa ʾiʿaadat-i fatH-i l-sifaarat-i.

They had **worked** with them on re-opening the embassy.

كانَ السفيرُ (قَدْ) وَصَلَ مساء الجمعة.

kaana l-safiir-u (qad) waSal-a masaaʾ-a l-jumʿat-i.

The ambassador **had arrived** Friday evening.

كُنْتُ (قَدْ) أَيَّدْتُ وضع مصر على القائمة.

kun-tu (qad) ʾayyad-tu waDʿ-a miSr-a ʿalaa l-qaaʾimat-i.

I **had supported** putting Egypt on the list.

2 The verb *lays-a* لَيْسَ 'to not be'

This irregular verb negates the present tense. It is discussed in detail in Chapter 37, section 1. It is noted here because it is a sister of *kaan-a* and requires a complement in the accusative case. Although it is inflected as a past tense verb, it conveys negation of the present tense.

هذا لَيْسَ صديقنا.

*haadhaa **lays-a** Sadiiq-a-naa.*

This **is not** our friend.

لَيْسَ محامياً.

lays-a muHaamiy-an.

He **is not** a lawyer.

3 Verbs of becoming: *baat-a* بات, *ʾaSbaH-a* أَصْبَحَ, *Saar-a* صارَ

Verbs that indicate a change of state or condition are also sisters of *kaan-a*.

3.1 *baat-a* بات 'to become; come to be'

The verb *baat-a/ya-biit-u* indicates a change of state (or sometimes the continuation of a state) and is used chiefly in the past tense. It may be used as a main verb or as an auxiliary verb.

باتوا مقتنعينَ.

baat-uu muqtaniʿ-iina.

They **have become** convinced.

باتَ من الضروريِّ.

baat-a min-a l-Daruuriyy-i.

It **has become** necessary.

باتَت البلادُ تُعرف به اليومَ.

baat-at-i l-bilaad-u tu-ʿraf-u bi-hi l-yawm-a.

The country **has come** to be known for it today.

3.2 ʾaSbaH-a /yu-SbiH-u أَصْبَحَ / يُصْبِحُ 'to become'

This is a Form IV verb that has an inceptive meaning: 'to start to be,' or 'to become.'

قَدْ أَصْبَحَ أَمْراً ضَرُورِيّاً.

qad ʾaSbaH-a ʾamr-an Daruuriyy-an.

It has become an essential matter.

أَصْبَحَ هَمَّهُمُ اليَوْمِيّ.

ʾaSbaH-a hamm-a-hum-u l-yawmiyy-a.

It became their daily concern.

وَسَيُصْبِحُ جُزْءاً أَكْثَرَ أَهَمِّيّة.

wa-sa-yu-SbiH-u juzʾ-an ʾakthar-a
ʾahammiyyat-an.

And **it will become** a more
important part.

أَصْبَحَ مشكلةً.

ʾaSbaH-a mushkilat-an.

It became a problem.

3.3 Saar-a /ya-Siir-u صَارَ / يَصِيرُ 'to become; to come to be'

The verb *Saar-a* was not found to be very frequent in the material covered for this work. When used as the main verb it has the same meaning and effect as *ʾaSbaH-a*.

صارت ثقافتها أطلسية عالميّة.

Saar-at thaqaafat-u-haa ʿaalamiyyat-an.

Its culture **became** global.

3.3.1 As an auxiliary verb

When used as an **auxiliary verb**, *Saar-a* denotes inception and continuation:

منذ السّتّينات صارت تأخذ دوراً أكبر.

mundhu l-sittiinaat-i *Saar-at* ta-ʾxudh-u dawr-an ʾakbar-a.

Since the sixties it **has come to play** a greater role.

3.3.2 *Saar li-*

When used with the preposition *li-* expressing possession, it conveys the idea of 'come to have' or 'come to possess':

صار الولاء للعثمانيّين شكليّاً.

Saar-a l-wilaaʾ-u li-l-ʿuthmaaniyy-iina shakliyy-an.

The Ottomans **came to have** allegiance in form.

('Allegiance came to be to the Ottomans in form').

4 Verbs of remaining: *baqiy-a* بَقِيَ, *Zall-a* ظَلَّ, *maa zaal-a* ما زال, *maa daam-a* ما دامَ

Several verbs and verbal expressions that are sisters of *kaan-a* denote the concept of remaining in a particular state or condition. They may be used independently or as auxiliary verbs. These include:

4.1 baqiy-a / ya-bqaa بَقِيَ / يَبْقَى 'to stay; remain'

سَيَبْقَى سِرِّيّاً.
sa-ya-bqaa sirriyy-an.
It will remain secret.

سَتَبْقَى طويلاً في ذاكرة العالم.
*sa-ta-bqaa Tawiil-an fii dhaakirat-i
l-ʿaalam-i.*
It will remain long in the world's
memory.

4.2 Zall-a / ya-Zall-u ظلَّ / يَظَلُّ 'to keep, keep on, to remain'

ظَلَّ في غيبوبة تامّة.
Zall-a fii ghaybuubat-in taamat-in.
He **remained** in a complete coma.

سَيَظَلُّ أفضلُ.
sa-ya-Zall-u ʾafDal-a.
It will remain better.

ظَلَّتْ موجودةً تحت رماد العلاقات الجيّدة.
Zall-at mawjuudat-an taHt-a ramaad-i l-ʿalaqaat-i l-jayyidat-i.
It **remained present** under the ashes of good relations.

4.3 maa zaal-a / laa ya-zaal-u ما زالَ / لا يَزالُ 'to remain; to continue to be; to still be'

This expression consists of a negative particle (*maa* plus the past tense; *lam* plus
the jussive; or *laa* plus the imperfect) plus the verb *zaal-a* 'to cease,' thus it
means literally 'to not cease to be.' In terms of tense, both the past tense form
and the present tense usually have present tense meaning. Sometimes in context, however, they may refer to the past, or be equivalent to an English past
tense.

الصناعات الشعبيّة ما زالتْ حيَّةً.
*al-Sinaaʿaat-u l-shaʿbiyyat-u maa
zaal-at Hayyat-an.*
Handicrafts **continue to be** lively.

ما زالَ قائماً.
maa zaal-a qaaʾim-an.
It **still exists**.

ما زالَ انهيارُه مستمرّاً.
maa zaal-a nhiyaar-u-hu mustamirr-an.
Its decline **is still** continuous.

ما زالَتْ مستعملةً.
maa zaal-at mustaʿmalat-an.
They **are still** used.

4.3.1 maa zaal-a As an auxiliary verb

As an auxiliary verb *maa zaal-a* conveys the idea of continuation of a state or
action. It is followed by a present tense main verb.

أسوارٌ لا تزالُ تقفُ
ʾaswaar-un laa ta-zaal-u ta-qif-u
walls that **are still** standing

ما زلْنا نُحبُّه.
maa zil-naa nu-Hibb-u-hu
We **still** love it.

4.3.1.1 WITH EQUATIONAL SENTENCES

ما زِلْتُ في مرحلة التحضير.

maa zil-tu *fii marHalat-i l-taHDiir-i.*

I am still in the preparation stage.

لا يَزالُ عندنا وقت.

laa ya-zaal-u *'ind-a-naa waqt-un.*

We still have time
('there is still time to-us').

4.4 *maa daam-a* 'as long as'

The expression *maa daam-a* ما دام consists of the pronoun *maa* 'that which' or
'what' and the verb *daam-a* دام 'to continue,' 'to remain,' or 'to last.'

ما دامَتْ خارجةً من الشرعية ، فإنّ المقاطعة مستمرّة.

maa daam-at *xaarijat-an min-a l-shar'iyyat-i, fa-'inna l-muqaaTa'at-a*
mustamirrat-un.

As long as **it remains** outside legality, the boycott will continue.

5 Verbs of seeming or appearing

These verbs are not considered sisters of *kaan-a* but are similar in that they take an
object complement in the accusative case even though they are not transitive.

5.1 *badaa / ya-bduu* بدا /يَبْدو 'to seem; to appear'

يَبْدو عتيقاً جداً.

ya-bduu 'atiiq-an jidd-an.

It looks very ancient/antique.

لا يَبْدو متفائلاً.

laa ya-bduu mutafaa'il-an

He does not seem optimistic.

5.2 *Zahar-a/ya-Zhar-u* ظهر / يظْهَرُ 'to seem; to appear'

يظْهَرُ ضعيفاً.

ya-Zhar-u Da'iif-an.

He seems weak.

37

Negation and exception

Arabic uses a variety of means to express negation and exception. This is accomplished primarily through the use of negative or exceptive **particles**, which often affect the following phrase by requiring a particular case on a noun or noun phrase, or a particular mood of the verb. There is also a verb, *lays-a* لَيْسَ, which has a negative meaning 'to not be.' Each of these negative or exceptive expressions could be the topic for extensive grammatical analysis, but here their description is limited to their basic functions in MSA.

1 The verb *lays-a* لَيْسَ 'to not be'

This verb is exceptional in two ways:

(1) it is inflected only as a past tense verb but it negates the present tense of "be"[1];

(2) it is a sister of *kaan-a* كانَ and therefore requires its complement to be in the accusative case.

1.1 Chart: conjugation of *lays-a* لَيْسَ 'to not be'

The verb *lays-a* لَيْسَ has only one type of conjugation. It appears on the surface to resemble a past tense verb because it is inflected with the past tense suffixes, but in terms of meaning, it negates the present tense. Like a hollow verb, *lays-a* لَيْسَ has two stems; a short one, *las-* لَسْ, used when the suffix starts with a consonant, and a longer stem, *lays-* لَيْسَ, used when the suffix starts with a vowel or is only a vowel.[2]

---

[1] Negation of the perfect or past tense of "be" is not done with *lays-a*, but with the use of the negative particle *lam* plus the jussive form of *kaan-a* 'to be.' Similarly, the future tense of "be" is negated through the use of the future negative particle *lan* plus the subjunctive of *kaan-a*. The verb *lays-a*, therefore, is specialized and limited to negating the present tense of "be."

[2] Lecomte (1968, 87) states that *lays-a* "est une curieuse particule pseudo-verbale dotée d'une conjugaison d'allure concave."

	Singular	Dual	Plural
First person	لَسْتُ las-tu		لَسْنا las-naa
Second person: m.	لَسْتَ las-ta	لَسْتُما las-tumaa	لَسْتُم las-tum
f.	لَسْتِ las-ti	لَسْتُما las-tumaa	لَسْتُنَّ las-tunna
Third person: m.	لَيْسَ lays-a	لَيْسا lays-aa	لَيْسوا lays-uu
f.	لَيْسَتْ lays-at	لَيْسَتا lays-ataa	لَسْنَ las-na

1.2 Discussion and examples of *lays-a* لَيْسَ

لَيْسَ الأَستاذُ مؤرّخاً.

lays-a l-ʾustaadh-u muʾarrix-**an**.

The professor **is not** a historian.

In the above example, the verb *lays-a* لَيْسَ starts the sentence, followed by the subject noun *al-ʾustaadh-u* الأستاذ in the nominative case. The predicate or complement of the verb *lays-a* لَيْسَ (*muʾarrix-an* مؤرّخاً) is in the accusative case because *lays-a* لَيْسَ is a "sister" of the verb *kaan-a* كان and thus belongs to a group of verbs that (although intransitive in the traditional sense of the term) take their complements in the accusative case.[3]

If the sentence were not negative, it would be equational and verbless. The subject would be *al-ʾustaadh-u* الأستاذ and the predicate *muʾarrix-un* مؤرّخ, both in the nominative case, as is the rule with equational sentences:

الأستاذُ مؤرّخٌ.

al-ʾustaadh-u muʾarrix-un.

The professor is a historian.

In another example,

لَسْتُ لبنانيّةً.

las-tu lubnaaniyyat-an.

I am not Lebanese.

---

[3] See Chapter 36, on verbs of being, becoming, remaining, seeming (*kaan-a wa-ʾaxawaat-u-haa* كان وأخواتها).

The verb is inflected for the first person ("I") and the predicate or complement consists of just one word, an adjective, in the accusative case: *lubnaaniyyat-an* لبنانيّة. It is feminine because the writer is feminine and speaking of herself. If the sentence were not negative it would be:

أنا لبنانيةٌ.

ʾanaa lubnaaniyyat-un.

I [am] Lebanese (f.).

with a pronoun subject (*ʾanaa* أنا 'I'), no overt verb, and the adjective as predicate, in the nominative case. For more extensive discussion of equational sentences, see Chapter 4, section 2.

1.3 Further examples

Here are a few more examples of *lays-a* لَيْسَ in context:

1.3.1 Predicate of *lays-a* لَيْسَ is a noun or adjective in the accusative case

لَيْسَتْ منقّبةَ آثارٍ.

lays-at munaqqibat-a ʾaathaar-in.

She is not an archaeologist.

هذا لَيْسَ رجلاً شريفاً.

haadhaa lays-a rajul-an shariif-an.

This **is not** a noble man.

هذا لَيْسَ السببَ.

haadhaa lays-a l-sabab-a.

This **is not** the reason.

سمعتك لَيْسَتْ جيّدةً.

sumʿat-u-ka lays-at jayyidat-an.

Your reputation **is not** good.

1.3.2 Predicate of *lays-a* لَيْسَ is a prepositional phrase

The predicate or complement of *lays-a* may be a prepositional phrase rather than a noun, noun phrase, or adjective. In this case, the preposition causes the following noun to be in the genitive case.

لَيْسَ من الضروريّ.

lays-a min-a l-Daruuriyy-i.

It is not necessary.

أَلَيْسَ كذلك؟

ʾa-lays-a ka-dhaalika?

Isn't it so ('like that')?

لَسْتُ على اطّلاعٍ كافٍ على الموضوع.

las-tu ʿalaa TTilaaʿ-in kaaf-in ʿalaa l-mawDuuʿ-i.

I am not informed enough about the subject.

1.3.3 Predicate of *lays-a* لَيْسَ is an adverb

The predicate of *lays-a* may also be an invariable adverb that does not take case inflections. In the following sentence, the adverb *hunaaka* هناك is the predicate and *Siraaʿ-un* صراع 'struggle' is the subject of *lays-a* لَيْسَ.

لَيْسَ هُناكَ صِراعٌ.

lays-a hunaaka Siraaᶜ-un.

There is **no** struggle ('There **is not** a struggle').

2 Negative particles and their effects

2.1 *laa* لا 'no; not; there is no'

The negative particle *laa* has five functions: (1) by itself, it can mean simply 'no' in response to a statement, question, or a request; (2) it negates the present tense of verbs; (3) it is used for the negative imperative; (4) to indicate categorical negation; and (5) when repeated, indicates 'neither . . . nor.'

2.1.1 *laa* = 'no'

هلْ أنتَ مصريٌّ؟

hal ʾanta miSriyy-un?

Are you Egyptian?

لا. لَسْتُ مصريّاً.

laa. las-tu miSriyy-an.

No. I am not Egyptian.

2.1.2 *laa* لا = not; negation of present tense verb

The negative particle *laa* is used to negate present tense verbs. The verb remains in the indicative mood.[4]

لا أَفْهَمُ ماذا تقولُ.

laa ʾa-fham-u maadhaa ta-quul-u.

I do not understand what you are saying.

لا أُدَخِّنُ.

laa ʾu-daxxin-u.

I do not smoke.

لا يُحاولُ الخروجَ.

laa yu-Haawil-u l-xuruuj-a.

He is not trying to leave.

لا أُحبُّ الجزرَ.

laa ʾu-Hibb-u l-jazar-a.

I do not like carrots.

لا يُشَكّلُ ضمانةً.

laa yu-shakkil-u Damaanat-an.

It does not constitute a guarantee.

لا يَجوزُ.

laa ya-juuz-u.

It is not possible/permissible.

2.1.3 *laa* لا with the subjunctive

2.1.3.1 *ʾallaa* ألّا = *ʾan* أنْ + *laa* لا: The negative particle *laa* may negate a verb in the subjunctive if there is a subjunctivizing element present. In the following

---

[4] In his 1996 article "Negative polarity and presupposition in Arabic" Elabbas Benmamoun proposes that "negative *laa* has three different suppletive forms that correlate with different temporal interpretations: *laa* which occurs in the present tense . . . , *lam* which carries past tense . . . , and *lan* which carries future tense" (Benmamoun 1996, 51). While all three particles are negations, and all start with the letter *laam*, they have different effects on the following verb and are presented separately here.

sentences, the subjunctivizing phrase *ya-jib-u ʾan* ('it is necessary that') is followed by *laa* plus a verb in the subjunctive, and the subjunctivizing verb phrase, *qarrar-a ʾan* 'to decide to' is also followed by *laa* plus a verb in the subjunctive. The particles *ʾan* and *laa* are joined together in a contraction, *ʾallaa*:

قرّرتُ أَلَّا أَعْمَلَ فيه.

qarrar-tu ʾallaa ʾa-ʿmal-a fii-hi.
I decided **not to work** in it.

2.1.3.2 *laa* لا **AFTER** *Hattaa* حتّى: The subjunctivizing particle *Hattaa* حتّى 'in order that, so that' may be followed by *laa* لا plus a verb in the subjunctive:

حتّى لا يَشُطَّ في تأييدِ سياستهم

Hattaa laa ya-shuTT-a fii taʾyiid-i siyaasat-i-him
so that it does not go too far in supporting their policy

2.1.4 *laa* لا + verb as modifier

A negative verb phrase is occasionally used to express a negative adjectival or adverbial concept in Arabic. This phrase usually takes the form of an indefinite relative clause:

حركة لا تَهْدأُ قربَ المسجدِ

Harakat-un laa-ta-hdaʾ-u qurb-a l- masjid-i
non-stop motion/movement near the mosque

تعطي للسياحةِ معنىً خاصّاً لا يُمْكِنُ إنْكارُهُ.

tu-ʿTii li-l-siyaaHat-i maʿnan xaaSS-an laa yu-mkin-u ʾinkaar-u-hu.
It gives to tourism an **undeniably** special meaning.

2.1.5 The negative imperative with *laa* لا

The negative imperative is formed by using *laa* **plus the jussive** form of the verb in the second person ("you").[5]

لا تُزْعِجْ نفسكَ.

laa tu-zʿij nafs-a-ka.
Don't disturb yourself/don't bother.

لا تَسْتَخْدِم المصعدَ.

laa ta-staxdim-i l-miSʿad-a.
Don't use the elevator.

2.1.6 The *laa* لا of categorical or absolute negation: (*laa al-naafiya li-l-jins* لا النافية للجنس)

This is a special use of *laa* that negates the existence of something absolutely. The particle *laa* precedes a noun which is in the accusative, but with no nunation

---

[5] For further discussion of the imperative, see Chapter 35.

and no definite article. This type of negation is used in a number of idiomatic
expressions.

لا جَديدَ تحتَ الشمسِ.
laa jadiid-a taHt-a l-shams-i.
There is no[thing] new under the sun.

لا سبيلَ لدفعِه.
laa sabiil-a li-dafʿ-i-hi
There is no way to defend it.

لا رَيْبَ فيه.
laa rayb-a fii-hi.
There is no doubt about it.

لا قَلْبَ لها.
laa qalb-a la-haa.
She is heartless ('there is no heart
   to her').

لا فائدةَ.
laa faaʾidat-a.
It is useless. It is no use.

لا شَكَّ فيه.
laa shakk-a fii-hi.
There's no doubt about it.

لا شُكْرَ على الواجبِ.
laa shukr-a ʿalaa l-waajib-i.
'There is no thanking for a duty'
   (used as a polite response to an
   expression of thanks). = 'Don't
   mention it.'

لا بَأْسَ به.
laa baʾs-a bi-hi.
It's not bad ('There is no harm in it').

2.1.6.1 RELIGIOUS EXPRESSIONS WITH *laa* لا OF ABSOLUTE NEGATION

لا حَوْلَ ولا قُوَّةَ إلّا بِاللّه.
laa Hawl-a wa-laa quwwat-a ʾillaa
   bi-llaah-i.
There is no power and no strength but
   in God.

لا إلهَ إلّا اللّه.
laa ʾilaah-a ʾillaa llaah-u.
There is no god but God.

2.1.7 *laa . . . wa-laa* لا . . . ولا 'neither . . . nor'

The two-part formation of *laa . . . wa-laa* لا . . . ولا is used for the coordinate negative
'neither . . . nor' or 'don't . . . even . . .'. In response to a negative statement, the
wa-laa ولا part may be used at the start of the response.

لا في فاسَ ولا في مرّاكشَ
laa fii faas-a wa-laa fii marraakash-a
neither in Fez nor in Marrakesh

ولا أنا.
wa-laa ʾanaa.
Me either/me neither
   (depending on context)

لا الولاياتِ المتّحدةُ ولا الاتّحادُ السوفياتيُّ
laa l-wilaayaat-u l-muttaHidat-u wa-laa l-ittiHaad-u l-suufiyaatiyy-u
neither the United States nor the Soviet Union

2.1.8 *laa* لا as component of compound

Because of its ability to negate a noun or adjective directly, *laa* enters actively into the formation of compound words that include concepts of negation. They include both adjectives and nouns. For example,

invertebrate	*laa-faqaariyy*	لا فقاريّ
never-ending	*laa -nihaaʾiyy*	لا نهائيّ
decentralization	*al-laa-markaziyya*	اللامركزيّة
the unconscious	*al-laa-waᶜy*	اللاوعي

نقطةُ اللا رجوع

nuqTat-u l-laa-rujuuᶜ-i

the point of **no return**

2.2 Negation of the past

2.2.1 *lam* لَم + jussive

The most common way to negate a past tense verb in written Arabic is to use the negative particle *lam* followed by the verb in the jussive mood.

لم نَأت.	لم تَكْشِفِ الشرطةُ هويّتَهُ.
lam na-ʾti.	*lam ta-kshuf-i l-shurTat-u huwiyyat-a-hu.*
We did not come.	**The police did not reveal his identity.**
لم يَقَعْ حادثٌ.	لم يَسْبِقْ لَهُ مثيلٌ.
lam ya-qaᶜ Haadith-un.	*lam ya-sbiq la-hu mathiil-un.*
No accident happened.	It is unprecedented.
('an accident **did not happen**')	('an equivalent **has not preceded it**')
لم يَمُتْ أحدٌ.	فلم يَحْدُثْ ما حدث في الشام.
lam ya-mut ʾaHad-un.	*fa-lam ya-Hdath maa Hadath-a fii l-shaam-i.*
No one died.	What happened in Syria **did not happen** [here].
('[some]one **did not die**')	

2.2.2 *maa* ما + past tense verb

This way of negating the past is rare in written Arabic, although it is widely used in spoken Arabic vernaculars. The only instance of it that occurred in the database was in a negation of a future perfect verb:

ما كانَتْ سَتَعْرِفُ القراءةَ والكتابةَ.

maa kaan-at sa-ta-ᶜrif-u l-qiraaʾat-a wa-l-kitaabat-a.

She **would not have known** how to read and write ('reading and writing').

2.2.3 *lan* لَنْ plus subjunctive to negate the future tense

To negate a proposition in the future the particle *lan* لَنْ is used followed by the verb in the subjunctive mood.

لَنْ أَنْسى.

lan 'a-nsaa.

I won't forget.

لَنْ يَكونَ الأخيرَ مِن نوعِه.

lan ya-kuun-a l-'axiir-a min naw'-i-hi.

It will not be the last of its kind.

لَنْ يَتوَقَّفَ.

lan ya-tawaqqaf-a.

He will not stop.

لَن تُعرْقِلَ الاتّفاقَ.

lan tu-'arqil-a l-ttifaaq-a.

It will not obstruct the agreement.

2.2.4 Use of *ghayr* غَيْر 'other than; non-'

The noun *ghayr* is used in three ways: as a noun plus pronoun suffix, as the first term of a construct phrase with another noun, and as the first term of a descriptive construct phrase whose second term is an adjective.

It conveys the idea of "otherness" or that something is different from something else.[6]

2.2.4.1 USE OF *ghayr* غَيْر PLUS PRONOUN SUFFIX: The pronoun suffix on *ghayr* غَيْر reflects the number and gender of the noun or pronoun antecedent.

تختلف عن غَيْرِها.

ta-xtalif-u 'an ghayr-i-haa.

She differs from others
   ('other than she').

مثلَ غَيْرِها مِن المنظَّمات

mithl-a ghayr-i-haa min-a l-munaZZamaat-i

like other ('other than it') organizations

مصرُ وغَيْرُها مِن البلاد العربيّة

miSr-u wa-ghayr-u-haa min-a l-bilaad-i l-'arabiyyat-i

Egypt and other Arab countries

2.2.4.2 USE OF *ghayr* غَيْر AS FIRST TERM OF NOUN CONSTRUCT: Used as the first term of a construct phrase or *'iDaafa* إضافة, *ghayr* غَيْر carries the meaning of 'other than.'

لا يأكلُ غَيْرَ اللّحمِ والبطاطا.

laa ya-'kul-u ghayr-a l-laHm-i wa-l-baTaaTaa.

He doesn't eat [anything] other than meat and potatoes.

---

[6] Cantarino 1975 (II:147–53) provides an extensive analysis of *ghayr* غَيْر and its usage in literary Arabic. See also Wright 1967, II:208–209.

2.2.4.3 *ghayr* غَيْر **+ ADJECTIVE: 'NON-; IN-; UN-; OTHER THAN; -LESS':** In this construction, the noun *ghayr* 'non-; un-, in-, other than' is used as the first term of a construct phrase or *'iDaafa* إضافة in order to express negative or privative concepts denoting absence of a quality or attribute. The second term of this kind of construct phrase is an adjective. **As the first term of a construct,** *ghayr* غَيْر **carries the same case as the noun it modifies. As a noun which is the first term of an *'iDaafa*, it cannot have the definite article.**

The second term of the *'iDaafa* construction is an adjective or participle in the genitive case which agrees with the noun being modified in gender, number, and definiteness. Therefore, it is the second term of this descriptive construct that shows agreement with the modified noun.[7] Here are some examples:[8]

non-Islamic	*ghayr-u 'islaamiyy-in*	غَيْرُ إسلامي
unusual	*ghayr-u ʿaadiyy-in*	غَيْرُ عادي
non-oil-exporting	*ghayr-u muSaddir-in li-l-nafT-i*	غَيْرُ مصدرٍ للنفط
unsuitable	*ghayr-u munaasib-in*	غَيْرُ مناسب
indirect	*ghayr-u mubaashir-in*	غَيْرُ مباشر
unofficial	*ghayr-u rasmiyy-in*	غَيْرُ رسمي

(1) **Modifying definite noun:** To modify a definite noun, *ghayr* غَيْر is followed by an adjective with the definite article.

الدولُ غَيْرُ الإسلاميَّة
al-bilaad-u ghayr-u l-'islamiyyat-i
the **non-Islamic** countries

الدولُ غَيْرُ المنحازة
al-duwal-u ghayr-u l-munHaazat-i
non-aligned states

الدولُ الإسلاميَّةُ غَيْرُ العربيَّة
al-duwal-u l-'islaamiyyat-u ghayr-u l-ʿarabiyyat-i
the **non-Arab** Muslim countries

القارئُ غَيْرُ المسلم
al-qaari'-u ghayr-u l-muslim-i
the **non-Muslim** reader

(2) **Modifying indefinite noun:** To modify an indefinite noun, *ghayr* غَيْر is followed by an indefinite adjective.

كلبٌ غَيْرُ أصيل
kalb-un ghayr-u 'aSiil-in
a **non-pedigreed** dog

غَيْرُ صحيحٍ ما يقولُهُ.
ghayr-u SaHiiH-in maa ya-quul-u-hu.
It is **untrue** what he says.

---

[7] For more examples, see *ghayr* غَيْر in Chapter 10, section 7.2.

[8] For further discussion of *ghayr* غَيْر see Beeston 1970, 101–102; Kouloughli 1994, 105 and 277–78; Wright 1967, II:208–209.

بطرق غَيْرِ قانونيّة
بشكلٍ غَيْرِ منتظمٍ

bi-turuq-in **ghayr-i qaanuuniyyat-in**
bi-shakl-in **ghayr-i muntaZam-in**

in **illegal** ways
in **a disorganized** manner

2.2.4.3 *ghayr* غَيْر FOLLOWING NEGATIVE VERB: Following a negative verb, *ghayr* غَيْر has the meaning of 'only' or 'merely.'

لم يقدّمْ غَيْرَ القليلِ من الأموال.

lam yu-qaddim **ghayr-a** *l-qaliil-i min-a l-ʾamwaal-i.*

It offered only a little money ('It did not offer **other than** a little money').

2.2.5 ʿadam عَدَم + noun 'non-'

The noun *ʿadam* 'lack; absence; nonexistence' may be annexed to another noun as the first term of a genitive construct to create a compound lexical item equivalent to various kinds of privative or negative expressions. Although the annexation structure or *ʾiDaafa* is a two-word expression in Arabic, it may carry a non-compositional meaning.[9]

non-interference	*ʿadam-u tadaxxul-in*	عَدَمُ تدخلٍ
nonexistence	*ʿadam-u wujuud-in*	عَدَمُ وجودٍ
neutrality; non-alignment	*ʿadam-u nHiyaaz-in*	عَدَمُ انحيازٍ
instability	*ʿadam-u stiqraar-in*	عَدَمُ استقرارٍ

عَدَمُ دعمِ أيٍّ حركةٍ كرديّةٍ
عدمُ تحقيقٍ تقدّمٍ

ʿadam-u daʿm-i ʾayy-i Harakat-in kurdiyyat-in
ʿadam-u taHqiiq-i taqaddum-in

the **non-support** of any Kurdish movement
the **non-realization** of progress

من المهمِّ عَدَمُ تقديمِ الكثيرِ من التنازلاتِ.

min-a l-muhimm-i **ʿadam-u taqdiim-i** *l-kathiir-i min-a l-tanaazulaat-i.*

It is important **not to offer** [too] many concessions.

3 Exceptive expressions

This category of expressions includes connectives and adverbs with meanings that contrast with previous propositional content. It includes items that have meanings such as "except for," "however," "nevertheless'" and "despite; in spite of." Sometimes these items consist of one word, other times they are phrases. They are also referred to as "adversative" expressions.

---

[9] See also Chapter 8, section 1.7.1.

3.1 *bal* بَلْ : 'but; rather; but rather'

This word introduces a subordinate clause that contrasts in meaning with the main clause.[10] The verb in the main clause is normally negative, with *bal* introducing a contrary affirmation.

ليست زائدةً بَلْ من أصل الكلمة.

lays-at zaaʾidat-an bal min ʾaSl-i l-kalimat-i.

It is not an affix; **rather**, it is [part] of the root of the word.

ليس فقط في الشرق الأدنى بَلْ في العالم كلّه.

lays-a faqaT fii l-sharq-i l-ʾadnaa bal fii l-ʿaalam-i kull-i-hi.

Not only in the Near East, **but [also]** in the whole world.

3.2 *ʾillaa* إلّا: 'except; but; but for'

This is a frequently used exceptive word in modern written Arabic. Its effect on the following phrase varies depending on whether the main clause is a negative or positive assertion.

3.2.1 Affirmative clause + *ʾillaa* إلّا

When the **main clause is affirmative** and *ʾillaa* introduces an exception to that statement, it is **followed by a noun in the accusative.**

الساعة الخامسةَ إلّا ربعاً

al-saaʿat-a l-xaamisat-a ʾillaa rubʿ-an

at a quarter to five ('the fifth hour **except for a quarter**')

جاءَ كلُّ الطلابِ إلّا نجيباً.

jaaʾ-a kull-u l-Tullab-i ʾillaa najiib-an.

All the students came **except Najib.**

3.2.2 Negative clause + *ʾillaa* إلّا

When the **main clause is negative**, *ʾillaa* إلّا is followed by a noun that takes **whatever case its role in the sentence requires.** That is, *ʾillaa* إلّا has no grammatical effect on the noun. In the following sentences, for example, the noun phrase after *ʾillaa* إلّا fills the logical role of subject of the verb and is therefore in the nominative case.[11]

لا يوجد إلّا أقلّيّةٌ صغيرةٌ.

laa yuujad-u ʾillaa ʾaqalliyyat-un Saghiirat-un.

There is only a small minority. ('There is not **but a small minority**.')

---

[10] See al-Warraki and Hassanein 1994, 62. In this book, see also Chapter 18, section 3.1.

[11] It is interesting to note that verb-subject gender agreement does not extend across *ʾillaa* back to the verb. Although the logical subject in all these cases is feminine singular, the verb is masculine singular.

لا يفصلُ المغربَ عَنْ إسبـانيا إلاّ بضعةُ كيلومترات.

laa ya-fSil-u l-maghrib-a ʿan isbaanyaa ʾillaa biD ʿat-u kiiluumitiraat-in.

Only a few kilometers separate Morocco from Spain ('there does not separate Morocco from Spain **but a few kilometers**').

لا يفصلُ نشأةَ الإسلام عن نشأة المسيحيّة إلاّ قرونٌ قليلةٌ.

laa ya-fSil-u nash ʾat-a l-ʾislaam-i ʿan nash ʾat-i l-masiiHiyyat-i ʾillaa quruun-un
  qaliilat-un.

Only a few centuries separate the birth of Islam from the birth of Christianity ('there does not separate the birth of Islam from the birth of Christianity **but a few centuries**').

3.2.3 ʾillaa إلاّ + prepositional phrase

A prepositional phrase may follow ʾillaa, especially after a negative main clause.

لا عودةَ للمهجرين إلاّ من خلال الوزير.

laa ʿawdat-a li-l-mahjar-iina ʾillaa min xilaal-i l-waziir-i.

There is no return for exiles **except through the minister**.

هذه الفرصةُ لا نجدُها إلاّ في القاهرة.

haadhihi l-furSat-u laa na-jid-u-haa ʾillaa fii l-qaahirat-i.

This opportunity is found only in Cairo.

  ('We do not find this opportunity **except in Cairo**.')

لا يخرجُ من مخابئه إلاّ خلالَ الليل.

laa ya-xruj-u min maxaabi ʾ-i-hi ʾillaa xilaal-a l-layl-i.

He doesn't leave his hiding places **except at night**.

3.2.4 ʾillaa ʾanna إلاّ أنَّ : 'however; nonetheless; but'

This exceptive phrase introduces a clause or a sentence which contrasts with or balances out the previous one. Following the subordinating particle ʾanna is either a noun in the accusative case, or else a suffixed pronoun. In the following sentences, ʾillaa ʾanna is the initial element, relating the sentence to one that came just prior to it.

إلاّ أنَّ تطوّراً أكثرَ إثارةً بدأ يلفتُ النظرَ.

ʾillaa ʾanna taTawwur-an ʾakthar-a ʾithaarat-an bada ʾ-a yu-lfit-u l-naZar-a.

However, a more exciting development has started to redirect attention.

إلاّ أنّه لم يُنجزْ حتّى موعدٍ قريب.

ʾillaa ʾanna-hu lam yu-njaz Hattaa maw ʿid-in qariib-in.

However, it wasn't completed until recently.

إلاّ أنّ العدالةَ ستأخذُ مجراها.

ʾillaa ʾanna l-ʿadaalat-a sa-ta-ʾxudh-u majraa-haa.

However, justice will take its course.

In the following sentences, *ʾillaa ʾanna* إلاّ أنّ introduces an exceptive clause that contrasts with the main clause. In this situation, it does not always have a lexical equivalent in English. Note that the main clause may start with an exceptive expression.

كادَ يُمحى إلاّ أنّ الأستاذَ أقامَ مؤتمراتٍ.

kaad-a yu-mHaa ʾilla ʾanna l-ʾustaadh-a ʾaqaam-a muʾtamaraat-in.

It would have disappeared, **except that** the professor held conferences.

وإنْ كانَتْ بدايتي تأخّرتْ إلاّ أنّها جاءتْ.

wa-ʾin kaan-at bidaayat-ii taʾaxxar-at ʾillaa ʾanna-haa jaaʾ-at.

Although my start was delayed, [**however**] it did come.

ورَغْمَ بلوغي الستّين تقريباً إلاّ أنّني سريعُ التعلّمِ.

wa-raghm-a buluugh-ii l-sittiina taqriib-an ʾillaa ʾanna-nii sariiʿ-u l-taʿallum-i.

Despite my reaching almost sixty [years old], [**however**] I'm quick to learn.

ومع أنّني لم أعرف التفاصيلَ إلاّ أنّ إدراكي هو أنّ المفاوضاتِ تجري.

wa-maʿ-a ʾanna-nii lam ʾa-ʿrif-i l-tafaaSiil-a ʾillaa ʾanna ʾidraak-ii huwa
  ʾanna l-mufaawaDaat-i ta-jrii.

Although I didn't know the details, [**however**] it was my understanding that the negotiations were being held.

3.3 maa ʿadaa: 'except; except for'

This exceptive phrase is followed by an accusative noun:

ضحك الطلاّبُ جميعُهُم ما عدا أحمدَ.

DaHik-a l-Tullaab-u jamiiʿ-u-hum maa ʿadaa ʾaHmad-a.

All the students laughed **except Ahmad.**

وما عدا هذه الملاحظات	كلّ يوم ما عدا الإثنين
wa-maa ʿadaa haadhihi l-mulaaHaZaat-i	*kull-a yawm-in maa ʿadaa l-ithnayn-a*
except for these observations	every day **except Monday**

3.4 siwaa سوى: 'except; except for'

This word is an indeclinable noun which normally goes into an *ʾiDaafa* إضافة structure with the following noun, very much as does *ghayr* غير. The following noun or noun phrase is therefore in the genitive case. Usually, *siwaa* سوى introduces an exception to a negative statement.

لم يبقَ سوى أشهرٍ قليلة.

*lam ya-bqa **siwaa** ʾashhur-in qaliilat-in.*

There remained only a few months ('there did not remain **but a few months**').

لم يكنْ في الصندوقِ سوى جواهرَ نفيسة.

*lam ya-kun fii l-Sanduuq-i **siwaa** jawaahir-a nafiisat-in.*

In the box were only precious jewels

  ('There was not in the box **but precious jewels**').

حتّى لو لم تشاهدْ في السنةِ سوى فلمٍ واحدٍ فقط

*Hattaa law lam tu-shaahid fii l-sanat-i **siwaa** film-in waaHid-in faqaT*

even if you don't see **but one film** a year

3.5 *maᶜ-a dhaalika* مَعَ ذلك: 'nevertheless; in spite of that' *maᶜ-a ʾanna* مَعَ أنَّ: 'although, despite'

The semi-preposition *maᶜ-a* مع means 'with' but it may also convey a sense of con-trast or exception, as in these two expressions.

ومَعَ ذلكَ فإنّ الكتابَ على مستوى عالٍ.

wa-maᶜ-a dhaalika fa-ʾinna l-kitaab-a ᶜalaa mustaw-an ᶜaal-in.

Nevertheless, the book is on a high level.

ومَعَ أنَّني لم أعرف التفاصيل

wa-maᶜ-a ʾanna-nii lam ʾa-ᶜrif-i l-tafaaSiil-a

although I do not know the details

3.6 *raghm-a* رَغْمَ, *bi-l-raghm-i* بالرَّغْمِ, *ᶜalaa l-raghm-i* على الرَّغْمِ: 'despite; in spite of'

The word *raghm* is a noun which goes into an ʾiDaafa relationship with the fol-lowing noun or noun phrase, which is thus in the genitive case. It may be used by itself, or with *bi-* or with *ᶜalaa*.

رَغْمَ إنكارِها ذلك	ورَغْمَ الاحتجاجاتِ
raghm-a ʾinkaar-i-haa dhaalika	*wa-**raghm-a** l-iHtijaajaat-i*
despite her denying that	**despite** excuses
رَغْمَ الضغوطِ كلِّها	بالرّغْمِ من مرور عشرين عاماً
raghm-a l-DughuuT-i kull-i-haa	*bi-l-**raghm**-i min muruur-i ᶜishriina ᶜaam-an*
despite all the pressures	**despite** the passage of twenty years
وعَلى رغْمِ هذه العودةِ القويّة	على رغْمِ عدم انتظامِها
*wa-ᶜalaa **raghm**-i haadhihi l-ᶜawdat-i l-qawwiyyat-i*	*ᶜalaa **raghm**-i ᶜadam-i ntiZaam-i-haa*
despite this strong comeback	**despite** its lack of organization

3.7 ʿalaa raghm-i ʾanna أَنْ رَغْمِ عَلَى: 'despite [the fact] that'

The phrase ʿalaa raghm-i رَغْمِ عَلَى may be directly followed by the subordinating conjunction ʾanna and a subordinate clause. In this case, the entire clause acts as the second term of an ʾiDaafa after raghm. It is often followed by another exceptive clause introduced by ʾillaa ʾanna 'nevertheless.'

وَعَلَى رَغْمِ أَنَّ مَسْؤُولِين فِي الوِزَارَة قَالُوا ... إِلاَّ أَنَّه يُعتقد أَنَّ ...

wa-ʿalaa raghm-i ʾanna masʾuul-iina fii l-wizaarat-i qaal-uu . . . ʾillaa ʾanna-hu
 yu-ʿtaqad-u ʾanna . . .

despite the fact that ministry officials said . . . it is **nevertheless** considered
 that . . .

وَعَلَى رَغْمِ أَنَّ الشَّرِكَة لم تعلن كلفة المشروع، إِلاَّ أَنَّ مَصادِر صناعة الغَاز الطبيعيّ

wa-ʿalaa raghm-i ʾanna l-sharikat-a lam tu-ʿlin kalfat-a l-mashruuʿ-i, ʾillaa ʾanna
 maSaadir-a Sinaaʿat-i l-ghaaz-i l-Tabiiʿiyy-i

despite the fact that the company did not announce the cost of the plan,
 nevertheless, natural gas industry sources . . .

فَعَلَى رَغْمِ أَنَّ الخِلافَةَ العبّاسِيّة كانت المرجعَ

fa-ʿalaa raghm-i ʾanna l-xalaafat-a l-ʿabbaasiyy-a kaan-at l-marjiʿ-a

despite the fact that the Abbasid Caliphate was the authority

3.8 wa-ʾin وَإِنْ: 'even though; even if; despite the fact that'

This phrase is a combination of the conjunction wa- and the conditional marker,
ʾin.

وَإِنْ كانَ هناك محافظون يرفضون الإذعان لهذا التغيير

wa-ʾin kaan-a hunaaka muHaafiZ-uuna ya-rfuD-uuna l-ʾidhʿaan-a li-haadhaa l-taghyiir-i

even though there were conservatives who refused to comply with this change

3.9 law-laa لَوْلا: 'had it not been for; if it were not for'

This word is a conjunction with exceptive meaning created through the contraction
of two particles, law لَوْ (contrary to fact conditional) + laa لا (negative), resulting in
the meaning of hypothetical negation: 'had it not been for.' It is generally followed
by a noun in the nominative case but may also be followed by a suffix pronoun.[12]

لَوْلا السبعون ملماً التي انهمرت على البلاد

law-laa l-sabʿuuna milim-an-i llatii nhamar-at ʿalaa l-bilaad-i

had it not been for the 70 millimeters [of rain] that poured on the country

---

[12] No instances of law-laa لَوْلا followed by a suffix pronoun were encountered in the data. For
 further discussion and examples, including suffix pronouns, see Cantarino 1975, III:326–30.

لَوْ لا احتكاكُها بالشعوبِ اليونانيّة

law-laa Htikaak-u-haa bi-l-shuʿuub-i l-yuunaaniyyat-i

had it not been for their close contact with the Greek peoples

كاد المسرح يُنسى لَوْ لا الأوبرا.

kaad-a l-masraH-u yu-nsaa law-laa l-ʾuubiraa.

The theater would have almost been forgotten **had it not been for the opera.**

38

Passive and passive-type expressions

1 Introduction

The concept of passive meaning contrasted with active meaning is referred to as **voice** in Western grammatical terms. That is, a verb is either in the active voice or the passive voice. In general, when in the active voice, the doer of the action is the subject of the verb ('**We studied** the problem' *daras-naa l-mushkilat-a* المشكلة دَرَسْنا); when a verb is in the passive, the entity affected by the action (the direct object of the verb) becomes the subject ('The problem **was studied**' *duris-at-i l-mushkilat-u* المشكلة دُرِسَت). The voice of a verb therefore conveys information on the topical focus of a sentence.

1.1 Two types of Arabic passive: inflectional and derivational

There are two basic ways to convey a passive meaning in Arabic, the first being an **inflectional (or internal) passive**, involving a shift of vowel pattern within the verb: e.g., *ʿuqid-a* عُقِد 'it was held' from *ʿaqad-a* عَقَد 'he held,' and the second a **derivational passive**, where a derivational verb form (typically V, VII, or VIII) is used to convey a passive, reflexive, or mediopassive sense of the action involved in the verb (e.g., Form VII *inʿaqad-a* انعَقَد 'it was held').[1] The type of action denoted by the derivational passive is referred to in Arabic as *muTaawaʿa* مطاوعة 'obedience, conformity' because it reflects a **resultative** state of the object (*fataH-tu l-baab-a fa-nfataH-a* فَتَحْتُ البابَ فانفَتَح 'I opened the door and it opened').[2]

---

[1] As Wright notes (1967, I:51): "The idea of the passive voice must not be thought to be absolutely identical with that of the fifth, seventh, and eighth forms. These are, strictly speaking *effective* [or resultative-KCR] . . . whilst the other is *purely passive*" (Italics in original). In English, however, it is sometimes necessary to render the equivalent meaning of these derived forms in the passive.

[2] Terminology for the passive: The passive voice, especially the inflectional passive (*fuʿil-a* فُعِل), is referred to in Arabic as the "unknown" *al-majhuul* المجهول, indicating that the agent or doer of the action is not known. When a passive-like or mediopassive meaning is conveyed by a derived form of the verb, it is characterized as *muTaawiʿ* مطاوع or, literally, 'obedient' to an action that has occurred (e.g., *infataH-a* انفَتَح 'it opened').

1.2 Use of the inflectional passive

Generally speaking, the inflectional passive is used in Arabic only if the agent or doer of the action is non-designated, unknown, or not to be mentioned for some reason. This contrasts with English where one may readily mention the agent in a passive construction through use of the preposition 'by' ('The problem was studied **by us**').[3]

1.3 Contrast between active and passive voice

When the Arabic passive voice is used **the object of the action is the subject of the verb**. The object of the action in the passive is therefore in the nominative case. Note that an essential requirement for a verb to take a passive form is that it **must be a transitive verb**, i.e., one that takes an object.[4]

If active-verb sentences are rephrased as passive constructions, the object of the verb becomes the subject of the sentence, and the verb is marked for passive by virtue of a change in the internal vowels. The doer of the action is normally not mentioned.

Active:	Passive:
فَتَحْتُ البابَ.	فُتِحَ البابُ
fataH-tu l-baab-a.	*futiH-a l-baab-u.*
I **opened** the door.	The door **was opened**.
فَتَحْتُهُ.	فُتِحَ.
fataH-tu-hu.	*futiH-a.*
I **opened** it.	It **was opened**.

In the derivational passive, or resultative, a particular form of the verb is used to convey passive meaning. Here, it is Form VII:

انْفَتَحَ البابُ.	انْفَتَحَ.
infataH-a l-baab-u.	*infataH-a.*
The door **opened**.	It **opened**.

---

[3] Wright states: "the passive is especially used in four cases; namely (a) when God or some higher being, is indicated as the author of the act; (b) when the author is unknown, or at least not known for certain; (c) when the speaker or writer does not wish to name him; (d) when the attention of the hearer or reader is directed more to the person affected by the act (*patiens*, the patient), than to the doer of it (*agens*, the agent)" 1967, I:50.

[4] The term that Arab grammarians use for "transitive verbs" is ʾafʿaal mutaʿaddiya أفعال متعدية, derived from the Form V verb taʿaddaa 'to go beyond, exceed.' That is, the action of the verb extends beyond the agent and all the way to the object. For intransitive verbs, the Arabic term is either ʾafʿaal ghayr mutaʿaddiya أفعال غير متعدية or ʾafʿaal laazima أفعال لازمة, verbs whose action does not extend beyond the subject.

Sometimes Arabic inflectional and derivational passives exist side by side; other times one is preferred. Moreover, they may carry slightly different implications about how the action was accomplished (see below).

1.4 Syntax: Restriction on mention of agent

When a passive verb is used in Arabic, mention of the identity of the agent or doer of the action is usually omitted.[5] It may be unknown or simply unnecessary. For this reason, a term used to refer to the passive in Arabic is *al-majhuul* المجهول 'the unknown.' In fact, if the agent is to be mentioned, the passive is not normally used; the active verb is then the preferred option.[6]

However, **instruments** or other inanimate causative factors (such as the weather) may be mentioned by means of prepositional phrases, e.g.,

فُتِحَ البابُ بهذا المفتاح.

futiH-a l-baab-u bi-haadhaa l-miftaaH-i.
The door was opened **by/with this key.**

When the subject of the passive verb is mentioned as a separate noun, it is in the nominative case (as in the sentence above, *al-baab-u* البابُ). The technical Arabic term for the subject of a passive verb is *naa'ib al-faa'il* نائب الفاعل 'the deputy doer; the representative of the doer.'[7]

Note that the passive verb may occur in the present or past tense, and in the indicative, jussive or subjunctive moods, depending on context.

2 The internal or inflectional passive

The internal passive is formed by changing the vowel sequence of the verb in the following ways:

2.1 Past tense

In the past or perfect tense, the vowel sequence is /*-u -i-*/. That is, within the stem, all vowels previous to the stem vowel are /*u*/ and the stem vowel itself is /*i*/. This is true for all verb forms (derivations), and for quadriliteral verbs as well as triliteral verbs. Aside from the internal vowel change, the past tense verb in the passive conjugates as usual, with the normal suffixes:

---

[5] Another term used to describe the passive verb in Arabic is *maa lam yu-samma faa'il-u-hu* 'that whose agent is not named.' See Wright 1967, I:50–51 for more on terminology and section 2.5 in this chapter.

[6] As Cowan notes (1964, 59): "If the agent is mentioned in the sentence one *cannot use the passive*" (emphasis in original). This rule is occasionally, but only rarely, broken in MSA.

[7] On the syntax of passive verbs in literary Arabic, see Cantarino 1974, I:52–58.

Paradigm: wulid-a وُلِدَ *'was/were born'*

	Singular	Dual	Plural
First person:	وُلِدْتُ wulid-tu		وُلِدْنا wulid-naa
Second person: m.	وُلِدْتَ wulid-ta	وُلِدْتُما wulid-tumaa	وُلِدْتُمْ wulid-tum
f.	وُلِدْتِ wulid-ti	وُلِدْتُما wulid-tumaa	وُلِدْتُنَّ wulid-tunna
Third person: m.	وُلِدَ wulid-a	وُلِدا wulid-aa	وُلِدوا wulid-uu
f.	وُلِدَتْ wulid-at	وُلِدَتا wulid-ataa	وُلِدْنَ wulid-na

2.1.1 Examples of the Form I past tense passive in context

2.1.1.1 STRONG/REGULAR ROOT

نُقِلَ إلى المستشفى.
nuqil-a ʾilaa l-mustashfaa.
He **was transported** to the hospital.

مُنِعوا من دخول المدينة.
muniᶜ-uu min duxuul-i l-madiinat-i.
They **were prevented** from entering
    the city.

كُتِبَ بحروف عبريّة.
kutib-a bi-Huruuf-in ᶜibriyyat-in.
It **was written** in Hebrew characters.

فُرِضَ رسمُ دخولٍ.
furiD-a rasm-u dukhuul-in.
An entry fee **was imposed**.

2.1.1.2 ASSIMILATED ROOT

سوريا وُضِعَتْ على القائمة.
suuriyaa **wuDiᶜ-at** ᶜalaa l-qaaʾimat-i.
Syria **was placed** on the list.

وُجِدَ في الإسطبل.
wujid-a fii l-isTabil-i.
It **was found** in the stable.

2.1.1.3 GEMINATE ROOT

عُدَّتِ الأصوات.
ᶜudd-at-i l-ʾaSwaaT-u.
The votes **were counted**.

2.1.1.4 HAMZATED ROOT

سُئِلَ الوزير عن الجريمة.

su'il-a l-waziir-u *'an-i* l-jariimat-i.

The minister **was asked** about the crime.

2.1.1.5 HOLLOW ROOT: In the past tense passive of hollow roots, the long medial vowel is /-ii-/. This applies to Forms I, IV, VII, VIII, and X.

و بِيعَتْ لأحد المتاحف

wa-bii'at li-'aHad-i l-mataaHif-i

and **it was sold** to one of the museums

قيلَ له.

qiil-a la-hu.

It was said to him.

2.1.1.6 DEFECTIVE ROOT: In the past tense passive of defective verbs, the final radical is *yaa'*. This applies to the derived forms as well.

وجدوا برجين بُنِيا من الحجارة.

wajad-uu burj-ayni **buniy-aa** *min-a* l-Hijaarat-i.

They found two towers [which] **were built** of stone.

ولذلك سُمِّيَت القرى هناك بأسمائهم.

wa-li-dhaalika **summiy-at-i** *l-quraa hunaaka bi-'asmaa'-i-him.*

Therefore, the villages there **were named** after them.

وقد دُعِيَ الصحفيّون إلى الحضور.

wa-qad **du'iy-a** *l-SuHufiyy-uuna 'ilaa* l-HuDuur-i.

The journalists **were invited** to attend.

2.1.2 The past passive in derived forms of the verb

2.1.2.1 FORM II: *fu''il-a* فُعِّلَ

عُيِّنَ طبيباً للملك.

'uyyin-a Tabiib-an li-l-malik-i.

He **was appointed** physician to the king.

أُجِّلَت الاجتماعاتُ.

'ujjil-at-i l-ijtimaa'aat-u.

The meetings **were delayed**.

2.1.2.2 FORM III: *fuu'il-a* فوعل: The long vowel *-aa-* characteristic of Form III verbs changes to long *-uu-* in the passive.

بورك الاتّفاقُ.

buurik-a l-ittifaaq-u.

The agreement **was blessed**.

فوجئَت بالاتّفاق.

fuuji'-at bi-l-ittifaaq-i.

She **was surprised** at the agreement.

2.1.2.3 FORM IV: *ʾuf'il-a* أُفْعِلَ; HOLLOW FORM IV *ʾufiil-a* أُفيلَ; DEFECTIVE
FORM IV *ʾuf'iy-a* أُفْعِي

أُرسِلَتِ الرسالةُ من أمريكا.
ʾursil-at-i l-risaalat-u min ʾamriikaa.
The letter **was sent** from America.

أُغْلِقَ المطارُ.
ʾughliq-a l-maTaar-u.
The airport **was closed**.

أُدخِلَتْ إلى المستشفى.
ʾudxil-at ʾilaa l-mustashfaa.
She **was admitted** to the hospital.

أحدهم أُصيبَ بجروح خطرة.
ʾaHad-u-hum ʾuSiib-a bi-juruuH-in xaTirat-in.
One of them **was afflicted** with serious wounds.

أُقيمَ في الفندق عشاءٌ.
ʾuqiim-a fii l-funduq-i 'ashaaʾ-un.
A dinner **was given** at the hotel.

خلال الانتخابات التي أُجرِيَتْ قبل سنة
xilaal-a l-intixaabaat-i llatii ʾujriy-at qabl-a sanat-in
during the elections that **were held** ('were run') a year ago

2.1.2.4 FORM V: *tufu''il-a* (rare) تُفُعِّلَ

تُوُفِّيَ.
tuwuffiy-a.
He passed away.

2.1.2.5 FORM VI: *tufuu'il-a* تُفوعِلَ (rare)

2.1.2.6 FORM VII: none.[8]

2.1.2.7 FORM VIII: *uftu'il-a* اُفْتُعِلَ, FORM VIII HOLLOW *uftiil-a* اُفْتيلَ, FORM VIII DEFECTIVE *uftu'iy-a* اُفْتُعِي

سبعةُ أشخاصٍ اعْتُقِلوا.
sab'at-u ʾashxaaS-in u'tuqil-uu.
Seven persons **were arrested**.

اتُّهِمَ بالجريمة.
uttuhim-a bi-l-jariimat-i.
He **was accused** of the crime.

وكانَ قد اُغْتيلَ .
wa-kaan-a qad ughtiil-a.
He **had been assassinated**.

اقْتُضِيَ الحضورُ.
uqtuDiy-a l-HuDuur-u.
Attendance **was required**.

---

[8] Note that although the Form VII passive verb does not occur, some Form VII passive participles do exist, e.g., *munHadar* منحدر 'slope.'

2.1.2.8 FORM IX: none.

2.1.2.9 FORM X: *ustufʿil-a* اُسْتُفْعِلَ, FORM X HOLLOW *ustufiil-a* اُسْتُفِيلَ, FORM X DEFECTIVE *ustufʿiy-a* اُسْتُفْعِيَ

اُسْتُخْدِمَ.	اُسْتُفِيدَ مِنْهُ.	اُسْتُدْعِيَ بَعْضُ المُراسِلِينَ.
ustuxdim-a.	*ustafiid-a min-hu.*	*ustudʿiy-a baʿD-u l muraasil-iina.*
It was used.	It was beneficial ('it was benefitted from').	Some correspondents **were invited**.

2.1.3 Quadriliteral verbs in the past passive

Quadriliteral verbs have the same vowel sequence (*-u-i-*) as triliteral verbs in the passive.

2.1.3.1 FORM I: *fuʿlil-a* فُعْلِلَ

تُرْجِمَتْ هذه الشروحُ إلى اللاتينيّة.

turjim-at haadhihi l-shuruuH-u ʾilaa l-laatiiniyyat-i

These commentaries **were translated** into Latin.

2.1.3.2 FORMS II, III, IV: rare.

2.2 Inflectional passive: present tense stem

In the present tense, the vowel sequence in the passive is /u/ on the subject marker and, subsequently, /a/ within the verb stem. Note that the present tense stem is used for the subjunctive and jussive, as well.

Present tense passive indicative: yu-dhkar-u يُذْكَرُ *'he/it is mentioned'*

	Singular	Dual	Plural
First person:	أُذْكَرُ *ʾu-dhkar-u*		نُذْكَرُ *nu-dhkar-u*
Second person: m.	تُذْكَرُ *tu-dhkar-u*	تُذْكَرانِ *tu-dhkar-aani*	تُذْكَرونَ *tu-dhkar-uuna*
f.	تُذْكَرِينَ *tu-dhkar-iina*	تُذْكَرانِ *tu-dhkar-aani*	تُذْكَرْنَ *tu-dhkar-na*
Third person: m.	يُذْكَرُ *yu-dhkar-u*	يُذْكَرانِ *yu-dhkar-aani*	يُذْكَرونَ *yu-dhkar-uuna*
f.	تُذْكَرُ *tu-dhkar-u*	تُذْكَرانِ *tu-dhkar-aani*	يُذْكَرْنَ *yu-dhkar-na*

2.2.1 Examples of the Form I present tense passive in context

2.2.1.1 STRONG/REGULAR ROOT: *yu-fʿal-u* يُفْعَل

تُعْقَدُ في القاهرة صباح غد.
tu-ʿqad-u fii l-qaahirat-i SabaH-a ghad-in.
It will be held tomorrow morning
  in Cairo.

و يُذكَرُ أنّ الأمينَ العامَّ
*wa-yu-dhkar-u ʾanna l-ʾamiin-a
  l-ʿaamm-a*
it is mentioned that the secretary
  general

2.2.1.2 ASSIMILATED ROOTS: *yuuʿal-u* يُوعَل: In assimilated verbs, the present tense passive shows a long vowel /-uu-/ after the subject marker because of the merging of the /-u-/ of the passive with the underlying verb-initial semivowel (usually *waaw*).

السلالُ التي يوضَعُ فيها الخبزُ
*al-silaal-u llatii **yuuDaʿ-u** fii-haa l-xubz-u*
baskets in which bread **is put**

يوجدُ حلٌّ للمشكلة.
yuujad-u Hall-un li-l-mushkilat-i.
There is (**'is found'**) an answer to
  the problem.

2.2.1.3 GEMINATE ROOTS: *yu-faʿʿ-u* يُفَعُّ

تُعَدُّ أديبةً موهوبةً.
tu-ʿadd-u ʾadiibat-an mawhuubat-an.
She is **considered** a gifted writer.

2.2.1.4 HAMZATED ROOTS: *hamza*-INITIAL: *yu-ʾʿal-u* يُؤْعَل; *hamza*-MEDIAL: *yu-fʾal-u* يُفْأَل; *hamza*-FINAL: *yu-fʿaʾ-u* يُفْعَأ

تُؤكَلُ المقبّلاتُ.
tu-ʾkal-u l-muqabbilaat-u.
The hors d'oeuvres **are being eaten.**

يُسأَلُ عن السياسة.
yu-sʾal-u ʿan-i l-siyaasat-i.
He **is being asked** about the policy.

تُقْرَأُ المقالةُ.
tu-qraʾ-u l-maqaalat-u.
The article **is being read.**

2.2.1.5 HOLLOW ROOTS: *yu-faal-u* يُفال

تُباعُ فيها الهدايا.
tu-baaʿ-u fii-haa l-hadaayaa.
Gifts **are sold** in it.

ما قيل وما سيُقالُ عنه
maa qiil-a wa-maa sa-yu-qaal-u ʿan-hu
what has been said and what **will be
  said** about it

2.2.1.6 DEFECTIVE ROOTS: *yu-fᶜaa* يُفْعى

وكادَ الموضوعُ يُمْحى.

wa-kaad-a l-mawDuuᶜ-u yu-mHaa.

The topic **was almost erased**.

2.2.2 Derived forms of the verb in the present tense passive

Following are examples of the present passive in derived forms of the verb. Note that certain forms (V, VI, VII, VIII, IX) occur less frequently in the inflectional passive because they are intransitive or have passive or mediopassive meaning.[9]

2.2.2.1 FORM II: *yu-faᶜᶜal-u* يُفَعَّلُ; DEFECTIVE: *yu-faᶜᶜaa* يُفَعّى

أسعارٌ لا تُصدَّق

ᵓasᶜaar-un laa tu-Saddaq-u

unbelievable ('not believed') prices

لَمْ يُكَلَّلْ بالنجاحِ.

lam yu-kallal bi-l-najaaH-i.

It was not crowned with success.

يُسَمّى أحمدُ.

yu-sammaa ᵓaHmad-u.

He is called/named Ahmad.

2.2.2.2 FORM III: *yu-faaᶜal-u* يُفاعَلُ: rare.

2.2.2.3 FORM IV: *yu-fᶜal-u* يُفْعَلُ; HOLLOW: *yu-faal-u* يُفال; DEFECTIVE: *yu-fᶜaa* يُفْعى

سيُعْلَنُ غدا.

sa-yu-ᶜlan-u ghad-an.

It will be announced tomorrow.

تُجرى محادثاتٌ مهمّةٌ.

tu-jraa muHaadathaat-un muhimmat-un.

Important talks **are being conducted**.

يُضافُ إليها عشرون بالمئة ضريبة حكوميّة.

yu-Daaf-u ᵓilay-haa ᶜishruuna bi-l-miᵓat-i Dariibat-an Hukuumiyyat-an.

Added to it is twenty percent government tax.

2.2.2.4 FORM V: *yu-tafaᶜᶜal-u* يُتَفَعَّلُ: rare.

2.2.2.5 FORM VI: *yu-faaᶜal-u* يُفاعَلُ: rare.

2.2.2.6 FORM VII: *yu-nfaᶜal-u* يُنفَعَلُ: rare.

---

[9] See section 3.

2.2.2.7 FORM VIII: *yu-fta^cal-u* يُفْتَعَلُ; HOLLOW: *yu-ftaal-u* يُفْتَالُ; DEFECTIVE: *yu-fta^caa* يُفْتَعَى

يُعْتَبَرُ من أشهر الرسّامين في العصر الحديث.

yu-^ctabar-u min ʾashhar-i l-rassaam-iina fii l-^caSr-i l-Hadiith-i.

He is considered one of the most famous artists of the modern era.

فـكان الخليفة يُنْتَخَبُ في المسجد.

fa-kaan-a l-xaliifat-u yu-ntaxab-u fii l-masjid-i.

The Caliph **used to be elected** at the mosque.

يُنْتَظَرُ أن تعلن الحكومة ...

yu-ntaZar-u ʾan tu-^clin-a l-Hukuumat-u ...

it is expected that the government will announce ...

2.2.2.8 FORM IX: none.

2.2.2.9 FORM X: *yu-staf^cal-u* يُسْتَفْعَلُ: HOLLOW: *yu-stafaal-u* يُسْتَفَالُ; DEFECTIVE: *yu-staf^caa* يُسْتَفْعَى

تُسْتَخْدَمُ لصنع الأوراق.

tu-staxdam-u li-Sanaa^c-i l-ʾawraaq-i.

It is used to make papers.

2.2.3 Quadriliteral present tense passive

Form I: *yu-fa^clal-u* يُفَعْلَلُ

The passive of quadriliterals occurs most often in Form I.

الكتب التي لَمْ تُفَهْرَسْ	الكتب التي تُتَرْجَمُ
al-kutub-u llatii lam tu-fahras	*al-kutub-u llatii tu-tarjam-u*
the books which **have not been indexed**	the books which **are being translated**

2.3 Passive with verb-preposition idioms

When a concept is conveyed by a verb-preposition idiom, the **verb remains in the third person masculine singular in the passive**. It does not inflect for agreement in number or gender. If a passive participle is used, it also remains in the masculine singular. In the following illustrations, an active sentence using a verb-preposition idiom is changed to passive.

Verb-preposition idiom: *baHath-a ʿan* بَحَثَ عَنْ 'to search for, to look for'

Active:

Passive:

بَحَثْنا عن الأولاد.

baHath-naa ʿan-i l-ʾawlaad-i.

We looked for the children.

بُحِثَ عن الأولاد.

buHith-a ʿan-i l-ʾawlaad-i.

The children **were looked for.**

بَحَثْنا عن المقالة.

baHath-naa ʿan-i l-maqaalat-i.

We looked for the article.

بُحِثَ عن المقالة.

buHith-a ʿan-i l-maqaalat-i.

The article **was looked for.**

Further examples:

حُكِمَ على الرجال بالحبس لمدّة مئة يوم.

Hukim-a ʿalaa l-rijaal-i bi-l-Habs-i li-muddat-i miʾat-i yawm-in.

The men **were sentenced** to imprisonment for 100 days.

من مَصادِرَ مَوْثوقٍ بها

min maSaadir-a mawthuuq-in bi-haa

from **trusted** sources

ألواحٌ طينيّةٌ عُثِرَ عليها في الهلال الخصيب

ʾalwaaH-un Tiiniyyat-un ʿuthir-a ʿalay-haa fii l-hilaal-i l-xaSiib-i

clay tablets **discovered** in the Fertile Crescent

2.4 Passive with doubly transitive verbs

With verbs that are doubly transitive, taking two objects, only one of the objects switches to be the subject of the passive sentence. The other remains in the accusative case:

لأنّه يُعْتَبَرُ انتقالاً نوعيّاً بين النصر والهزيمة.

li-ʾanna-hu yu-ʿtabar-u ntiqaal-an nawʿiyy-an bayn-a l-naSr-i wa-l-haziimat-i.

Because **it is considered** a characteristic transition between victory and defeat.

يُعْتَبَرُ أحدَ أروعِ الآثارِ الفنّيّة.

yu-ʿtabar-u ʾaHad-a ʾarwaʿ-i l-ʾaathaar-i l-fanniyyat-i.

It is considered one of the most splendid artifacts.

عُيِّنَ طبيباً للملك.

ʿuyyin-a Tabiib-an li-l-malik-i.

He was appointed physician to the king.

أودعوا السجن.

ʾuudiʿ-uu l-sijn-a.

They were thrown [into] prison.

2.5 Mention of agent: ʿalaa yad-i يَد على, min qibal-i مِنْ قِبَل

Rarely, an agent or doer of the action may be mentioned in an Arabic passive sentence. When this is the case, certain phrases tend to be used, just as English would use the term "by." These are ʿalaa yad-i يَد على + noun 'by the hand of' or *min qibal-i* قِبَل مِنْ + noun 'on the part of.'

لكنّ هذه المساجد محتلّة مِنْ قِبَل المسلمين.

laakinna haadhihi l-masaajid-a muHtallat-un min qibal-i l-muslim-iina.

But these mosques are occupied **by Muslims.**

أُغتيل عَلى يَد علمانيَّين.

ughtiil-a ʿalaa yad-i ʿalmaaniyy-iina.

He was assassinated **by laymen.**

حتّى فتحها عَلى يَد المسلمين

Hattaa fatH-i-haa ʿalaa yad-i l-muslim-iina

until it was conquered ('its conquering') **by the Muslims**

2.5.1 *bi-qalam-i* بقَلَم

With authors of books, the phrase *bi-qalam-i* + noun 'by the pen of' is often used instead of 'by':

بقلم العالم والشاعر المعروف

bi-qalam-i l-ʿaalim-i wa-l-shaaʿir-i l-maʿruuf-i

by the famous scholar and poet

2.6 Passive with potential meaning

The Arabic passive is sometimes used to indicate possibility, worth, or potential. The passive participle in particular may have a meaning equivalent to an English adjective ending in "-able."

فلم يكن للمعارضة وجودٌ يُذْكَرُ.

fa-lam ya-kun li-l-muʿaaraDat-i wujuud-un yu-dhkar-u.

The opposition did not have a presence [**worth**] mentioning.

المأكولات	المشروبات
al-maʾkuulaat-u	*al-mashruubaat-u*
edibles, foods	refreshments ('drinkables')

3 Passive with derived forms of the verb

Derived forms of the verb, especially V, VII, VIII, and IX may indicate a passive or passive-like meaning, and may sometimes be used in this way. However, this is not always the case. These derivational verbs need to be learned as separate lexical items in order to know if their meaning is equivalent to a passive expression in English. For more detailed analysis of these verb forms, see the separate chapters on each derivational form.

3.1 The Form V verb: *tafaᶜᶜal-a / ya-tafaᶜᶜal-u* تَفَعَّلَ / يَتَفَعَّلُ

Form V verbs may function as the reflexive of the Form II verb. This is sometimes referred to by grammarians as "mediopassive."[10] Form V may also be resultative of Form II, showing the result of the Form II action, e.g., *kassar-tu-haa fa-takassar-at* كَسَّرْتُهَا فَتَكَسَّرْت 'I broke it (Form II) and it broke (Form V).'[11]

to disintegrate, break apart	*tafakkak-a/ya-tafakkak-u*	تَفَكَّكَ / يَتَفَكَّكُ
be fragmented	*tamazzaq-a/ya-tamazzaq-u*	تَمَزَّق / يَتَمَزَّقُ

3.2 The Form VII verb: *infaᶜal-a/ya-nfaᶜil-u* اِنْفَعَلَ / يَنْفَعِلُ

The **Form VII verb** may be analyzed as **ergative**, that is, the subject of the Form VII verb is the same as the object of the transitive Form I verb.[12] Form VII verbs are also referred to as reflexive, resultative, passive or mediopassive in meaning. In Arabic they are described as *muTaawiᶜ* 'obeying, corresponding with' – that is, Form VII verbs show the result of Form I action.[13]

اِنْقَطَعَ التِيَّارُ الكهربائيّ.   اِنْعَقَدَ الاجتماعُ أمسِ.

inqaTaᶜ-a l-tayyaar-u l-kahrabaaʾiyy-u.   *inᶜaqad-a l-ijtimaaᶜ-u ʾams-i.*

The electric current **was cut off.**   The meeting **was held** yesterday.

تَنْقَسِمُ البلاد إلى خمس عشرة منطقة.

ta-nqasim-u l-bilaad-u ʾilaa xams-a ᶜashrat-a minTaqat-an.

The country **is divided** into fifteen regions.

3.3 Form VIII

Form VIII may also have mediopassive meaning.[14] Some examples include:

be spread out	*intashar-a/ya-ntashir-u*	اِنْتَشَر / يَنْتَشِرُ
to be related, linked	*intasab-a/ya-ntasib-u*	اِنْتَسَب / يَنْتَسِبُ

---

[10] "No grammatical distinction is made in Arabic verbs between "reflexive" acts and spontaneous developments – what one does to one's self and what simply happens to one are equally accommodated by the mediopassive" (Cowell 1964, 238).

[11] For more on the Form V verb and its meanings, see Chapter 26.

[12] Ergative verbs are sometimes referred to as "unaccusative" verbs, especially in relational grammar. See Crystal 1997, 138–39 and Mahmoud 1991.

[13] For more on *muTaawiᶜ* مطاوع see section 1.1 in this chapter and also Chapter 26, note 4.

[14] One reason for the existence of mediopassive verbs in Form VIII is the phonological restriction in Form VII against lexical roots beginning with the consonants *hamza, waaw, yaaʾ, raaʾ, laam,* or *nuun.* Form VIII or Form V take over the mediopassive function for those roots.

to rise, be raised	*irtafaʿ-a/ya-rtafiʿ-u*	اِرْتَفَعَ / يَرْتَفِعُ
to be healed	*ilta'am-a/ya-lta'im-u*	اِلْتَأَمَ / يَلْتَئِمُ
to be completed	*iktamal-a/ya-ktamil-u*	اِكْتَمَلَ / يَكْتَمِلُ

إِصْلاحاتٌ لَمْ تَكْتَمِلْ منذ عامين

*'iSlaaHaat-un lam **ta-ktamil** mundh-u ʿaam-ayni*

renovations that **haven't been completed** in two years

جروحٌ لَمْ تَلْتَئِمْ بعد

*juruuH-un lam **ta-lta'im** baʿd-u*

wounds that **have not been healed yet**

39

Conditional and optative expressions

Conditional propositions are ones in which hypothetical conditions are specified in order for something else to take place. Usually there are two clauses, one that specifies the condition (typically starting with "if . . .") and one that specifies the consequences or result of those conditions (typically starting with "then . . ."). In traditional English grammar the clause that specifies the conditions (the "if-clause") is termed the **protasis** and the second clause (the "then-clause") is termed the **apodosis**. In Arabic the equivalent terms are *sharT* شرط (for the condition clause) and *jawaab* جواب (for the consequence clause).

Arabic often uses a **past tense verb in the conditional clause or protasis (*sharT* شرط)**. However, **the jussive mood** of the present tense verb may also be used in the protasis. The apodosis or consequence clause (*jawaab* جواب) may be in the same tense as the previous one, or it may be different. If there is a tense switch between clauses, the particle *fa-* normally precedes the apodosis; in practice in current MSA, however, it is often omitted.[1]

Some conditions are reasonably realizable ("If you wait, I'll go with you"), but others are simply expressions of impossible or "contrary to fact" conditions ("If I were your fairy godmother, I would grant your wish"). Arabic uses **different particles** to express possible conditions and impossible conditions.[2]

1 Possible conditions: *idhaa* إذا and *ʾin* إنْ

To express possible conditions, Arabic uses two conditional particles: *ʾidhaa* or *ʾin* to start the protasis or *sharT* conditional clause. In the texts covered for this study, *ʾidhaa* occurred much more frequently than *ʾin*.[3] The use of *ʾidhaa* is considered to imply probable conditions.[4]

---

[1] See Taha 1995, 180–82 on this topic.

[2] For a book-length description of conditional structures in Arabic, see Peled 1992, which contains an extensive bibliography on the topic as well. See also Cantarino 1975, III: 311–69, Blachère and Gaudefroy-Demombynes 1975, 450–68, and Fischer 2002, 227–36 for discussion of conditional structures in classical and literary Arabic.

[3] Note that *ʾidhaa* does not always translate as 'if.' Sometimes it is used in the adverbial sense of 'when.' See Cantarino 1975, III:297–302.

[4] "*ʾin* is a straight hypothesis – 'if, if it is the case that . . ., if it should be that . . .' while *ʾidhaa* 'if ' implies some degree of probability and sometimes implies 'when, whenever.'" Abboud and McCarus 1983, Part 2:176.

1.1 ʾidhaa إذا 'if' + past tense

When ʾidhaa is used as the conditional particle in the *sharT* clause, the verb is in the past tense. In the *jawaab*, a tense switch may or may not happen. This type of conditional is the most frequent in MSA.

إذا كنتَ في الطوابق العلويّة، لا تهرع إلى الأسفل.

ʾidhaa kun-ta fii l-Tawaabiq-i l-ʿulawiyyat-i, laa ta-hraʿ ʾilaa l-ʾasfal-i.

If you are on the upper floors, **do not rush** to the lower [floors].

إذا كانت الشبابيك مفتوحة ، سارع إلى إغلاقها.

ʾidhaa kaan-at-i l-shabaabiik-u maftuuHat-an, saariʿ ʾilaa ʾighlaaq-i-haa.

If the windows **are** open, **hasten** to close them.

إذا رغبتَ في حجز تذكرة، فعليك أن تدفع مسبّقاً.

ʾidhaa raghib-ta fii Hajz-i tadhkarat-in, fa-ʿalay-ka ʾan ta-dfaʿ-a musabbaq-an.

If you want to reserve a ticket, **(then) you must** pay in advance.

1.1.1 Negative conditional: ʾidhaa lam إذا لمْ

A negative condition may be expressed with *lam* + jussive verb.

إذا لم يلغ القانون...فإنّه يتجاهله.

idhaa lam ya-lghi l-qaanuun-a . . . fa-ʾinna-hu ya-tajaahal-u-hu.

[Even] if he hasn't abolished the law . . . **he ignores** it.

1.1.2 Negative conditional wa-ʾillaa . . . fa- 'if not; or else'

Another type of negative condition is expressed through the used of **wa-ʾillaa** (a contraction of **wa-ʾin-laa**), which introduces a consequence clause. Sometimes it is accompanied by *fa-* :

و إلا، فـستكون فشلت في دورها

wa-ʾillaa, fa-sa-ta-kuun-u fashal-at fii dawr-i-haa

and **if not**, it will have failed in its role

كل الخضر و إلاّ قاصصوك.

kul-i l-xuDar-a wa-ʾillaa qaaSaS-uu-ka.

Eat the vegetables **or else** they [will] punish you.

1.1.3 Reversal of clause order

Most of the time, the *sharT* clause comes first, before the *jawaab* or apodosis, but sometimes the order is reversed. This is referred to as a "postposed condition," and the normal rules for the result clause do not apply. The particle *fa-* is omitted and the verb in the first clause may vary as to tense.

كان الفريق سيفوز إذا كانت اللجنة قد سمحت لهم بالتسابق.

kaan-a l-fariiq-u sa-ya-fuuz-u ʾidhaa kaan-at-i l-lajnat-u qad samaH-at la-hum
   bi-l-tasaabuq-i.

The team would have won **if** the committee **had permitted them** to
   participate.

1.2 Conditional with ʾ*in* + perfect or ʾ*in* + jussive

The conditional particle /ʾ*in*/ may be followed by either verbs in the perfect or
verbs in the jussive in both the condition and the result clauses. If the jussive
is used in the conditional clause, then the verb in the result clause may also be
jussive.[5] For this reason, the particle /ʾ*in*/ is called in Arabic grammar one of the
"particles that require the jussive on two verbs": *al-ʾadawaat-u llatii ta-jzim-u*
fiˤl-ayni الأدوات التي تجزم فعلين. If, however, the verb in the result clause is part
of a nominal clause (i.e., a clause that starts with a noun), then it is in the
imperfect indicative.[6] The verb in the result clause may also be in the past
tense.

The use of ʾ*in* with conditional clauses is less frequent in Modern Standard Arabic than in literary and classical Arabic.

سيمرضون إن أكلوا كلّ هذا الآن.

sa-ya-mraD-uuna ʾ*in* ʾ*akal-uu* kull haadhaa l-ʾaan-a.

They will get sick **if they eat** all that now.

إن زرتموني أكرمتكم.	إن شاء اللّه.
ʾ*in zur-tum-uu-nii* ʾakram-tu-kum.[7]	ʾ*in shaaʾ-a* llaah-u.
If you (pl.) visit me I shall honor you.	**If God wills.**

---

[5] See Abboud and McCarus 1983, Part 2:178: "If the verb in the condition clause is jussive, the verb
   in the result clause must also be jussive." See also ˤAbd al-Latif et al., 1997, 307ff. for more examples. But note that in Haywood and Nahmad 1962, 291, they list under possibilities for the conditional sentence: "The Jussive is used in the Protasis, the Perfect in the Apodosis:

إن يذهب زيدٌ ذهبتُ معه.

   ʾ*in ya-dhhab zayd-un dhahab-tu maˤ-a-hu.*
   'If Zayd goes I will go.' (their example)

   The condition clause may also be in the imperative, without a conditional particle, and followed
   immediately by a verb in the jussive in the result clause. Abboud and McCarus 1983 give the following example (Part 2:178):

أُدرُسْ تَنجَحْ.

   u-drus ta-njaH.
   Study [and] you [will] succeed.

[6] See Ziadeh and Winder 1957, 162.

[7] From Abboud & McCarus 1983, Part 2:182.

إن يكسر إنسان سنّ آخر، فسنّه تُكسر.

'in ya-ksir 'insaan-un sinn-a 'aaxar-a, fa-sinn-u-hu tu-ksar-u.[8]

If a person **breaks** the tooth of another, (then) his tooth **shall be broken.**

إن تنتظرني في المطار وقت وصولي، عددتُ ذلك كرماً منك.

*'in ta-ntaZir-nii fii l-maTaar-i waqt-a wuSuul-ii, **'adad-tu** dhaalika karam-an min-ka.*[9]

If you **would wait** for me at the airport at the time of my arrival, **I would consider** that a kindness from you.

1.2.1 *wa-'in* وَإِنْ 'although; even though'

وإن كانت بدايته تأخّرت إلاّ أنّها جاءت.

wa-'in kaan-at bidaayat-u-hu ta'axxar-at 'illaa 'anna-haa jaa'-at.

Although his start **was late,** nevertheless it came.

حقّق الحلم في ميداليّة وإن كانت برونزيّة.

*Haqqaq-a l-Hulm-a fii miidaaliyyat-in **wa-'in** kaan-at biruunziyyat-an.*

He realized the dream of a medal **although** it was bronze.

2 Conditional expressed with *-maa* ما 'ever'

The adverbial suffix *-maa* can be suffixed to an adverb or a noun to shift its meaning to '-ever,' such as "whenever" or "wherever." These expressions are considered conditionals in Arabic and follow the rules for conditional sentences. Cowell 1964 refers to clauses using these particles as "quasi-conditional" clauses.[10]

2.1 *mahmaa* مَهْما 'whatever'

لا أعتقد أنّها ستتوقّف، مهما قالت الولايات المتّحدة.

*laa 'a-ctaqid-u 'anna-haa sa-ta-tawaqqaf-u, **mahmaa** qaal-at-i l-wilaayaat-u l-muttaHidat-u.*

I don't think it will stop, **whatever** the United States **says.**

2.2 *'ayn-a-maa* أيْنَما 'wherever'

أينما كنتَ، يمكنك أن تستمع.

'ayn-a-maa kun-ta, yu-mkin-u-ka 'an ta-stamic-a.

Wherever you are, you can listen.

---

[8] From Ziadeh and Winder 1957, 160.

[9] Ibid., 164.

[10] Cowell 1964, 337–38. Cowell is describing types of conditional clauses in Syrian Arabic but deals with similar particles.

2.3 *kull-a-maa* كلّما 'whenever'

This connective also specifies a condition and therefore requires the use of the past tense verb in the clause that it introduces.

يمكن تكرارها كلّما تجدّد الخطر.

*yu-mkin-u takraar-u-haa **kull-a-maa tajaddad-a** l-xaTar-u.*

It can be repeated **whenever** danger **recurs**.

2.4 *ʾidhaa + maa* إذا ما 'if ever'

Occasionally, even *ʾidhaa* will be followed by the particle *-maa*. In this sense, *-maa* is **not used as a negative** particle but implies 'if ever' or 'if and when.'

إذا ما فُتح باب الحوار

ʾidhaa-maa futiH-a baab-u l-Hiwaar-i

if the door of discussion is **ever opened**

2.5 *man* مَنْ 'whoever'

The pronoun *man*, meaning 'who' or 'whoever' may be followed by a conditional clause in the jussive. This kind of conditional is often found in proverbs.

من يزرع شوكاً يحصد شوكاً.

man ya-zraʕ shawk-an ya-HSid shawk-an.[11]

He who sows thorns [will] **reap** thorns.

من يقتل يُقتل.

man ya-qtul yu-qtal.[12]

He who kills, shall be killed.

3. Contrary-to-fact conditionals: *la-* لـ *law* لَوْ

Some conditional sentences express impossible or unreasonable conditions. The conditional particle used to introduce contrary-to-fact conditions is *law* لَوْ, followed by either a past tense verb or *lam* plus the jussive for the negative. The contrary-to-fact condition is usually followed by a result clause (*jawaab*) that is preceded by the particle *la-* لـ; there are some exceptions, however. The *la-* لـ is omitted when the result clause precedes the condition clause as in:

عنزة ولو طارت.

*ʕanzat-un **wa-law** Taar-at.*

It is [still] a goat **even if** it flies.[13]

---

[11] Cited in ʕAbd al-Latif et. al., 1997, 308.
[12] From Ziadeh and Winder 1957, 160.
[13] This Arabic saying is cited in McLaughlin 1988, 82.

اطلبوا العلم ولو في الصين.

*uTlub-uu l-ᶜilm-a **wa-law** fii l-Siin.*

Seek knowledge **even if** it be in China.

or if the result clause is understood or implied, and therefore not specified:

لو سمحت.

law samaH-ta.

If you permit.

3.1 'even if' حتّى لو *Hattaa law* and *Hattaa wa-law* حتّى ولو

The addition of *Hattaa* to *law*, yields the meaning of 'even if.' It is usually followed by a past tense verb or negated past tense through the use of *lam* plus the jussive.

حتّى ولو عثرت الحكومة على وسائل أخرى

Hattaa wa-law ᶜathar-at-i l-Hukuumat-u ᶜalaa wasaaʾil-a ʾuxraa

even if the government discovers other means

حتّى لو لم نعترف بذلك

Hattaa law lam na-ᶜtarif bi-dhaalika

even if we don't acknowledge that

4 Optative constructions

Wishes, blessings, and curses are often expressed in the past tense in Arabic, just as the past tense is used in many hypothetical expressions. There is no need for a particular particle, just the expression phrased in the past tense.

بارك اللّه فيك.

baarak-a llaah-u fii-ka.

May God **bless** you.

حفظه اللّه.

HafiZ-a-hu llaah-u.

May God **preserve him.**

رحمه اللّه.

raHam-a-hu llaah-u.

May God **have mercy on him.**

أيّدك اللّه.

ʾayyad-a-ka llaah-u.

May God **help you.**

عاش الملك!

ᶜaash-a l-malik-u!

[**Long**] **live** the king!

طال عمرك.

Taal-a ᶜumr-u-ka.

May you **live long.**

('May [God] **lengthen** your life.')

4.1 Optatives in the present tense

The past tense is not always used in optatives. Some of them are in the **present tense**:

اللّه يسلّمك.

allaah-u yu-sallim-u-ka.

May God **keep you safe.**

يحيى الملك!

ya-Hyaa l-malik-u!

[**Long**] **live** the king!

السلام عليكم.

al-salaam-u ᶜalay-kum.

Peace **be** upon you.

Appendix I: How to use an Arabic dictionary

Using an Arabic dictionary

The organization of Arabic dictionaries is based on word roots and not word spelling. Word roots are listed alphabetically according to the order of letters in the Arabic alphabet. For example, the root *k-t-f* comes after *k-t-b* because /f / comes after /b / in the Arabic alphabet. Therefore, in order to find the root, one has to know the order of the alphabet. This system applies to genuinely Arabic words or words that have been thoroughly Arabized.

Loanwords, however, — words borrowed from other languages — are listed in an Arabic dictionary according to their spelling (e.g., *haliikubtar* هليكبتر 'helicopter').

Instead of relying on the exact orthography of a word, therefore, Arabic dictionaries are organized by the root or consonant core of a word, providing under that initial entry every word derived from that particular root. The root is therefore often called a "lexical root" because it is the actual foundation for the lexicon, or dictionary. The lexical root provides a semantic field within which actual vocabulary items can be located. In this respect, an Arabic dictionary might be seen as closer to a thesaurus than a dictionary, locating all possible variations of meaning in one referential domain or semantic field under one entry.

Most often, Arabic words can be reduced to three radicals or root consonants (e.g., *H-m-l* 'carry'), but some roots have more or less than three. There are a number of biliteral (*y-d* 'hand'), quadriliteral (*t-r-j-m* 'translate'), and quinquiliteral (*b-n-f-s-j* 'violet') roots in Arabic, and there are even some monoliteral roots (for function words such as the preposition *ka-* 'as, like').

The verb citation form for dictionary use is **the third person masculine singular past tense**. There is no infinitive form of the verb in Arabic.

For example, all the following words having to do with "studying" are found in the dictionary under the root *d-r-s*, even though some begin with *ma-* or *mu-*, because all of them are located within the semantic field of *d-r-s*.

lesson	*dars*	درس
lessons	*duruus*	دروس

school	*madrasa*	مدرسة
teacher	*mudarris*	مُدَرِّس
studying	*diraasa*	دراسة
he studied	*daras-a*	دَرَسَ (the citation form)

Because of this major difference in dictionary organization, it is necessary for Western learners of Arabic to learn rules of Arabic word structure in order to be able to make sense of an Arabic or Arabic–English dictionary. Learners must be able to identify the root consonants in a word in order to find the main dictionary entry; then they need to know generally how the word pattern fits into the overall system of derivational morphology in order to locate that particular word within the abundant and sometimes extensive subcategories provided within the semantic field of the entry. The root-pattern system is fundamental for Arabic word creation and accounts for about 80–85 percent of Arabic vocabulary.

Using the Wehr Dictionary

In the most widely used Arabic–English dictionary, the *Dictionary of Modern Written Arabic* (DMWA) by Hans Wehr and edited by J. Milton Cowan, fourth edition (1979), the compilers assume that the users know and understand the system of Arabic derivational verb morphology based on the roman numerals I–X (or sometimes even up to XV). Wehr lists verbs first, in the I–X order, marked **only by the roman numeral**, not giving the actual verb spelling except for Form I.[1]

For example, under the root *q-b-l*, are listed roman numerals II, III, IV, V, VI, VIII, and X, and after each roman numeral are definitions for each of these forms of the verb. Thus, if the user is looking up an inflected verb form, such as *istaqbal-at*, the user needs to know that this is a Form X verb, that the root is *q-b-l*, and that it is inflected for third person feminine singular past tense. In this manner, the user can locate the verb root, find the roman numeral X and see that the listed definitions for this form include 'to face, to meet, to receive.' By putting together the lexical meaning from the dictionary information, contextual meaning from the text being read, and the grammatical meaning from the inflectional suffix, the user can deduce that the word *istaqbal-at* means 'she received.'

Note that the *DMWA* provides the present tense or imperfective stem vowel for Form I because it is not predictable. It does not do this for the derived forms, because they are predictable. It therefore includes, in romanization, after the Arabic script, under the entry for *k-t-b*, for example:

kataba   *u (katb, kitba, kitaaba)*

---

[1] Wehr provides a useful summary of the arrangement of entries in his introduction (1979, pp. vii–xvii).

That is, it gives the voweling for the past tense citation form, the present tense stem vowel, and, in parentheses, the most common verbal nouns for the Form I verb, all in romanization. The *DMWA* does not include short vowels in the Arabic script spelling of the entries; short vowels are indicated only by the romanization that directly follows the dictionary entry.

To look up the word *istiqbaal* استقبال, it is helpful to know that it is a verbal noun of Form X, since the *DMWA* lists nouns (including nouns of place and nouns of instrument, for example), adjectives, adverbs, and verbal nouns immediately after the verb definitions, in the I–X order. After that are listed active participles I–X and then passive participles, also in the I–X order. Note, however, that the *DMWA* does not identify the nouns or participles by number; it assumes that the user knows the derivational system.

It is also important for users to be able to recognize noun, adjective, and participle plurals because plurals are not listed as separate items in the dictionary, even though their word structure may differ substantially from the singular form, especially with broken plurals. Thus, coming across a word such as *mashaakil* مشاكل, the reader needs to know how to determine the root, *sh-k-l*, but also needs to recognize that this is a broken plural pattern, and will not be listed as a separate entry, but as a plural under the entry of *mushkila* مشكلة, 'problem' (a Form IV active participle).

Particular challenges emerge when lexical roots are weak or irregular in some way, that is, if they are geminate, hamzated, assimilated, hollow, defective, or doubly defective. In these cases, the nature of a root consonant may shift (from a long vowel to a *hamza*, for example as in the word *zaaʔir* زائر 'visitor' derived from the root *z-w-r*) or a root consonant may simply disappear (for example, the noun *thiqa* 'trust, confidence' from the root *w-th-q*). It is therefore crucial for learners to practice using the dictionary and to gain an understanding of the system of Arabic word structure in order to have quick and efficient access to vocabulary items. Having a knowledge of the basic derivational systems and the logic and rules within these systems is key to building vocabulary and to gaining access to the full range of the abundant Arabic lexicon.

Naturally, it is not possible for learners at the early stages to recognize all possible root variants, but understanding the logic of dictionary organization will help right from the beginning. While it is possible to simply scour all the entries under a particular root without knowing the I–X system or the part-of-speech information that tells one where to look, it takes a great deal more time, and can be very frustrating, if not defeating.

This reference grammar includes extensive analysis of the permutations of regular and irregular lexical roots, in the I–X system. Please consult these sections for analysis of word structure, paradigms, and examples of words in context.

Thus, to summarize, the *DMWA* lists entries for a lexical root in the following order:

1. the root (which resembles the third person masculine singular past tense Form I verb)
2. verbal nouns of Form I (listed directly after the root in romanization)
3. verbs I–X listed numerically by roman numeral only
4. nouns and other parts of speech derived from Form I
5. nouns derived from other forms of the verb (in II–X sequence)
6. active participles from Forms I–X
7. passive participles from Forms I–X

Using an Arabic–Arabic dictionary

Arabic-Arabic dictionaries are likewise organized by lexical roots and the roots are listed in alphabetical order. Note, however, that Arabic lexicons do not use the I–X roman numeral system and make no reference to it.

For example, a standard reference work in Arabic is *al-Munjid fii l-lugha wa-l-ʾaʿlaam*, a combination of dictionary and concise encyclopedia. In the dictionary part, it lists verb derivations in the I–X order by listing them as they are spelled.

It also introduces verbal nouns, especially of Form I, in context, used in a short sentence, for example:

كَتَبَ كَتْبا وكِتابا وكِتْبَةَ وكِتابةَ الكتابَ.

*katab-a **katb-an** wa-**kitaab-an** wa-**kitbat-an** wa-**kitaabat-an**-i l-kitaab-a.*

Literally: 'He wrote **writing and writing and writing and writing** the book.'

It is standard practice in Arabic reference works to use the verbal noun/s in a sentence with the verb in order to illustrate what they are (even though the example might not make logical sense). In the above example, there are four different verbal nouns displayed in boldface type.

This procedure is used with Form I verbs, but the verbal nouns of the derived forms II–X are not separately indicated because they are predictable. The *al-Munjid fii l-lugha wa-l-ʾaʿlaam* has an excellent introductory section summarizing Arabic derivational and inflectional morphology (pp. *haaʾ* to *faaʾ*).

Arabic dictionary structure has evolved over time, and some older dictionaries are organized in different ways.[2] Note also that some modern Arabic dictionaries are referred to as "*ʾabjadiyy*" or 'alphabetical,' meaning that their

---

[2] See Haywood 1965 for a history of Arabic lexicography. See also Shivtiel 1993 for a comparison of Arabic root dictionaries and alphabetical dictionaries.

entries are organized by word spelling (for example, *al-Munjid al-ʾabjadiyy*, 1968). Although this type of organization eases use somewhat for those who do not understand the derivational system of Arabic word structure, it is much less useful in helping the learner grasp semantic fields, word structure patterns, and meaning relationships among lexical items.

Appendix II: Glossary of technical terms

1. Glossary of Arabic grammatical terms

These entries are transliterated and organized in English alphabetical order with *ʿayn* and *hamza* discounted as orthographic elements.

ʿaamil	syntactic governor or 'operator'
ʾabjad; ʾabjadiyya	alphabet
ʾafʿaal	verbs (plural of *fiʿl*)
ʾafʿaal al-quluub/	verbs of perception or cognition, in particular,
ʾafʿaal qalbiyya	of emotions and intellect
ʾafʿaal taHwiil	verbs of transformation (of something from one state to another)
ʿamal	syntactic government; regime
ʾamr	imperative; command
ʾasmaaʾ	nouns (pl. of *ism*)
ʾasmaaʾ al-ʾishaara	demonstrative pronouns
ʾaxawaat	"sisters" – words similar in class and in governing effect
badal	apposition
Damiir/Damaaʾir	personal pronoun
Damaaʾir munfaSila	independent personal pronouns, subject pronouns
Damma	short vowel /u/
faDla	'extra' or 'surplus' parts of the sentence rather than the kernel or core of the predication
faaʿil	subject of a verbal sentence; agent; doer of the action
fatHa	short vowel /a/
fiʿl / ʾafʿaal	verb; action

fiᶜl ᵓajwaf	hollow verb
fiᶜl ghayr mutaᶜaddin	intransitive verb
fiᶜl laazim	intransitive verb
fiᶜl lafiif mafruuq	assimilated and defective verb
fiᶜl lafiif maqruun	hollow and defective verb
fiᶜl mahmuuz	hamzated verb
fiᶜl mithaal	assimilated verb
fiᶜl muDaᶜᶜaf	geminate verb, doubled verb
fiᶜl mutaᶜaddin	transitive verb
fiᶜl naaqiS	defective verb
fiᶜl SaHiiH saalim	sound verb; regular verb
fuSHaa	literary Arabic, classical Arabic
Haal	circumstantial accusative
hamzat al-qaTᶜ	strong *hamza*
hamzat al-waSl	elidable *hamza*
Haraka/-aat	short vowel
Harf / Huruuf	letter (of the alphabet); particle, function word
Huruuf qamariyya	"moon" letters; word-initial sounds that do not assimilate the *laam* of the definite article
Huruuf shamsiyya	"sun" letters; word-initial sounds that assimilate the *laam* of the definite article
ᵓiDaafa	annexation structure, noun construct, genitive construct
ᵓiDaafa ghayr Haqiiqiyya	"unreal" *ᵓiDaafa*, adjective *ᵓiDaafa*
ᵓiᶜraab	desinential (word-final) inflection
ishtiqaaq	derivational etymology
ism / ᵓasmaaᵓ	noun; name
ism al-faaᶜil	active participle
ism al-ᵓishaara	demonstrative pronoun
ism al-mafᶜuul	passive participle
ism maqSuur	indeclinable noun
ism mawSuul	relative pronoun
ism al-tafDiil	elative adjective; comparative or superlative
istithnaaᵓ	exception, exceptive

jamᶜ	plural
jamᶜ muʾannath saalim	sound feminine plural
jamᶜ mudhakkar saalim	sound masculine plural
jamᶜ al-taksiir	broken plural
jarr	genitive case
jazm	jussive mood
jawaab	answer; the apodosis, consequence clause
jumla	sentence
jumla fiᶜliyya	verbal sentence
jumla ismiyya	equational sentence; noun-initial sentence
kasra	short vowel /i/
laa nafy-i l-jins-i	the *laa* of absolute or categorical negation
laam al-ʾamr	permissive or hortative imperative
maa l-taᶜajjub	the *maa* of astonishment
maaDii	past, past tense; perfective aspect
madda/ ʾalif madda	*hamza* followed by a long /aa/; the symbol that indicates this sound (Ĩ)
mafᶜuul bi-hi	direct object of transitive verb; the accusative of direct object
mafᶜuul fii-hi	accusative adverb of time, manner, or place
mafᶜuul li-ʾajl-i-hi / *mafᶜuul la-hu*	accusative of purpose
mafᶜuul muTlaq	cognate accusative
majhuul	the passive voice
mamnuuᶜ min-a l-Sarf	diptote
majruur	genitive
manSuub	accusative/subjunctive
manquuS	defective
marfuuᶜ	nominative/indicative
maSdar	verbal noun
maSdar miimii	a verbal noun whose initial consonant is a prefixed *miim*
mustaqbal	future tense
maziid	"augmented"; extended verb form (II–X)

muʾannath	feminine
mubtadaʾ	subject of equational sentence
muDaaf	the first term of an *ʾiDaafa*, or annexation structure
muDaaf ʾilay-hi	the second term of an *ʾiDaafa*, or annexation structure
muDaariᶜ	present tense; imperfective aspect
mudhakkar	masculine
mufrad	singular
mujarrad	base form verb; Form I; literally 'stripped'
muᶜrab	triptote; fully inflectable
muTaabaqa	agreement or concord
muTaawaᶜa	'obedience; conformity'; verbal noun referring to verbs that are resultative, reflexive, passive, or semi-passive in meaning
muTaawiᶜ	'obedient, conforming' – that is, conforming with a particular, lexically related action; passive, resultative, reflexive, or semi-passive
muthannaa	dual
naaqiS	defective
nafy	negation
naHw	grammar; syntactic theory
naHt	compounding into one word
naaʾib al-faaᶜil	subject of a passive verb
naSb	accusative case (on substantives)/subjunctive mood (on verbs)
naᶜt	adjective
nawaasix	lexical items that convert substantives to the accusative case
nidaaʾ	vocative
nisba	relative adjective
rafᶜ	nominative case (on substantives)/indicative mood (on verbs)
rubaaᶜiyy	quadriliteral (root)

Sarf	derivational morphology and inflectional morphology that does not include case and mood marking
shadda	symbol that indicates doubling of a consonant (˝)
sharT	condition; protasis, conditional clause
Sifa	adjective
sukuun	absence of vowel; quiescence, symbolized by a small circle (˚)
tamyiiz	accusative of specification
tanwiin	nunation; pronunciation of an /n/ sound after the case-marking short vowel on a noun, adjective, or adverb
tarkiib	compounding
tashdiid	doubling of a consonant; the use of *shadda* (q.v.)
thulaathiyy	triliteral (root)
waaw al-ᶜaTf	conjoining *waaw*; conjunction *waaw*
waSf	descriptive adjective
waSla	symbol used to mark elision of *hamza*
wazn/ ʾawzaan	Form/s of the verb (I–X and XI–XV)
xabar	predicate of an equational sentence
xafD	genitive case (see also *jarr*)
Zarf	adverb generally derived from a triliteral lexical root
Zarf makaan	adverb of place
Zarf zamaan	adverb of time

2. Glossary of English grammatical terms

Many of these brief definitions are elaborated upon in various parts of this book. See the index for page and section references for more extended explanations and examples.

accusative	one of the three cases in Arabic noun and adjective declensions; it typically marks the object of a transitive verb but also serves to mark a wide range of adverbial functions

affix	an inflectional or derivational feature added to a word stem
agreement	a relationship between words where one word requires a corresponding form in another (e.g., agreement in gender or in case)
allophone	a contextually determined variant of a phoneme
annexation structure	a genitive noun construct; an *ʾiDaafa*
assimilated	referring to lexical roots, those whose initial phoneme is *waaw* or *yaaʾ*
assimilation	a phonological process wherein one sound acquires features of another (usually adjacent) sound
biliteral	having only two root phonemes
case	a form of word-final inflection on nouns and adjectives that shows their relationship to other words in a sentence
clause	a unit of sentence structure that includes a predication
construct phrase	a structure in which two nouns are juxtaposed in a genitive relationship; an annexation structure; an *ʾiDaafa*
cryptofeminine	a feminine noun not overtly marked for feminine gender
cryptomasculine	a masculine noun not overtly marked for masculine gender
circumfix	a combination of prefix and suffix used with a stem to create a lexical item, such as the English word "**en**lighte**n**," or an Arabic verb such as *ta-drus-uuna* 'you (m.pl.) study'.
defective	a term applied to lexical roots referring to those with a final *waaw* or *yaaʾ*
desinential inflection	word-final marking for syntactically determined case or mood
diptote	a term applied to certain indefinite nouns that do not take either *kasra* or nunation

elative	refers to the comparative and superlative forms of Arabic adjectives
geminate	a term applied to lexical roots wherein the second and third root consonants are identical
gemination	the process of doubling the length or strength of a consonant
genitive	one of the three cases in Arabic noun and adjective declensions; it typically marks the object of a preposition and also the second noun in the construct phrase
government	a syntactic principle wherein certain words ("governors") cause others to inflect in particular ways
hamzated	including the consonant *hamza* (glottal stop) as part of the root morpheme (e.g., ʾ-k-l , s-ʾ-l or q-r-ʾ)
hollow verb	a verb whose lexical root contains a semi-vowel in the medial position (e.g., q-w-l or S-y-r)
imperative	a mood of the verb expressing command
imperfect (also "imperfective")	as applied to a verb, denoting an incomplete action or referring in a general way to incomplete, ongoing actions or states
indicative	a mood of the verb that is ungoverned by a syntactic operator (ʿ*aamil*); it is characteristic of statements of fact and of questions
infix	an affix inserted into the body of a word stem
intransitive	describes verbs whose action or process involves only the doer
jussive	a mood of the Arabic verb required by certain governing particles (e.g., *lam*)
morphology	the study of word structure and word formation
morphophonemics	the study of how word structure interacts with phonological rules
nominative	one of the three cases in Arabic noun and adjective declensions; it typically marks the subject of a sentence

nunation	the pronunciation of an /n/ sound after the marker of case inflection; typically it denotes indefiniteness
object	a syntactic term that describes the recipient of an action (the object of a verb, also referred to as a "direct object"), or the noun or pronoun that follows a preposition
optative	expressing wish or desire
participle	a deverbal adjective that may function as a noun
active participle	describes the doer of the action
passive participle	describes the recipient or object of the action
pattern	the morphological framework into which an Arabic lexical root fits in order to form a word
perfect (also "perfective")	as applied to a verb, denoting a completed action in the past
phoneme	a distinctive language sound that carries a differential function
phonology	the study of the sound system of a language
phonotactics	the study of the rules of sound distribution in a language
phrase	a group of words that forms a syntactic unit but does not include a predication (noun-adjective phrase, prepositional phrase, demonstrative phrase, etc.)
prefix	an affix attached at the beginning of a word stem
quadriliteral	containing four root consonants
quinquiliteral	containing five root consonants
radical	a root consonant
resultative	referring to a verb form expressing the result of an action
root	the most elemental consonant structure of an Arabic word
semi-consonant	a *waaw* or *yaa'*; also referred to as "semi-vowels"; consonants that have some of the properties of vowels or which serve as vowels in certain contexts

sound (adj.)	regular in inflection or structure (*see also* "strong")
stem; word stem	the base form of a word without inflections
stem vowel	the vowel that follows the second root consonant in a verb stem
strong (*see also* "sound")	regular in inflection or structure
subjunctive	a mood of the Arabic verb typically used after expressions of wishing, desire, hoping, necessity, or other attitudes expressed toward the action of the verb
suffix	an affix attached at the end of a word stem
syntax	the relationship among words in a phrase, clause, or sentence
triliteral	containing three root consonants
triptote	a term applied to nouns meaning that they inflect for all three cases
transitive	describes verbs whose action affects an object (often referred to as "direct object")
verbal noun (also "deverbal noun")	a noun derived from a particular verb that describes the action of that verb (e.g., acceptance – *qubuul*; departure – *mughaadara*; swimming – *sibaaHa*); Arabic: *maSdar* or *ism fiʕl*

References

Abboud, Peter F. and Ernest N. McCarus, eds. 1968, 1975, 1983. *Elementary Modern Standard Arabic*. Parts One and Two. Cambridge: Cambridge University Press.

Abboud, Peter F., Aman Attieh, Ernest N. McCarus, and Raji M. Rammuny. 1997. *Intermediate Modern Standard Arabic (Revised Edition)*. Ann Arbor, MI: Center for Middle Eastern and North African Studies.

Abdo, Daud. 1969. *On Stress and Arabic Phonology: A Generative Approach*. Beirut: Khayat.

ʿAbd al-Latif, Muhammad Hamasa, Ahmad Mukhtar ʿUmar, and Mustafa al-Nahhas Zahran. 1997. *Al-naHw al-ʾasaasiyy* (Basic Grammar). Cairo: Daar al-fikr al-ʿarabiyy.

ʿAli, ʿAbdul Sahib Mehdi. 1987. *A Linguistic Study of the Development of Scientific Vocabulary in Standard Arabic*. London, New York: Kegan Paul International.

Alosh, Mahdi. 2000. *Ahlan wa-sahlan: Functional Modern Standard Arabic for Beginners*. New Haven/London: Yale University Press.

Anderson, Stephen R. 1992. *A-Morphous Morphology*. Cambridge: Cambridge University Press.

Anghelescu, Nadia. 1999. Modalities and grammaticalization in Arabic. In *Arabic Grammar and Linguistics*, ed. Yasir Suleiman. Surrey: Curzon.

Al-Ani, Salman. 1970. *Arabic Phonology: An Acoustical and Physiological Investigation*. The Hague: Mouton.

Arberry, A. J. 1957. *The Seven Odes*. London: George Allen and Unwin.

Aronoff, Mark. 1976. *Word Formation in Generative Grammar*. Cambridge: MIT Press.
　1994. *Morphology by Itself*. Cambridge: MIT Press.

Ayoub, Georgine and Georges Bohas. 1983. Les grammariens arabes, la phrase nominale et le bon sens. In *The History of Linguistics in the Near East*, ed. C. H. M. Versteegh. Amsterdam: John Benjamins.

Baalbaki, Ramzi. 1986. On the meaning of the *waaw al-maʿiyya* construction. *Al-ʿArabiyya* 19: 7–17.

Badawi, El-Said M. 1985. Educated spoken Arabic: A problem in teaching Arabic as a foreign language. In *Scientific and Humanistic Dimensions of Language*, ed. Kurt R. Jankowsky. Washington: Georgetown University Press.

Badawi, El-Said M., Ali El-Din Hillal, Mahmoud F . Hegazi, and Farouk Shousha, compilers. 1991. *Dictionary of Arab Names*. *Sultan Qaboos Encyclopedia of Arab Names (Muʿjam ʾasmaaʾ al-ʿarab)*. 2 vols. Muscat, Oman: Sultan Qaboos University and Beirut, Lebanon: Librairie du Liban.

Bahloul, Maher. 1994. *The Syntax and Semantics of Taxis, Aspect, Tense and Modality in Standard Arabic*. Ithaca: Cornell University Department of Modern Languages and Linguistics.
　1996. Extending the NegP hypothesis: Evidence from standard Arabic. In *Perspectives on Arabic Linguistics VIII*, ed. Mushira Eid. Amsterdam/Philadelphia: John Benjamins.

691

Al-Batal, Mahmoud. 1990. Connectives as cohesive elements in a modern expository Arabic text. In *Perspectives on Arabic Linguistics II,* ed. Mushira Eid and John McCarthy. Amsterdam/Philadelphia: John Benjamins.

1994. Connectives in Arabic diglossia: The case of Lebanese Arabic. In *Perspectives on Arabic Linguistics VI,* ed. Mushira Eid, Vicente Cantarino, and Keith Walters. Amsterdam/Philadelphia: John Benjamins.

ed. 1995. *The Teaching of Arabic as a Foreign Language.* Provo, UT: American Association of Teachers of Arabic.

Bateson, Mary Catherine. 1967; 2003. *Arabic Language Handbook.* Washington: Georgetown University Press.

Beeston, A. F. L. 1970. *The Arabic Language Today.* London: Hutchinson University Library.

1981. Languages of pre-Islamic Arabia. *Arabica* 28(2–3):178–86.

Bell, Allan. 1983. Broadcast news as a language standard. *International Journal of the Sociology of Language* 40:29–42.

Bell, Allan and Peter Garrett. 1998. *Approaches to Media Discourse.* Oxford: Blackwell.

Belnap, Kirk. 1986. Complementation in Modern Standard Arabic: A corpus-based approach. Unpublished Master's thesis, Brigham Young University.

Belnap, R. Kirk and Osama Shabaneh. 1992. Variable agreement and nonhuman plurals in classical Arabic and modern standard Arabic. In *Perspectives on Arabic Linguistics IV,* eds. Ellen Broselow, Mushira Eid, and John McCarthy. Amsterdam/Philadelphia: John Benjamins.

Benmamoun, Elabbas. 1996. Negative polarity and presupposition in Arabic. In *Perspectives on Arabic Linguistics VIII,* ed. Mushira Eid. Amsterdam/Philadelphia: John Benjamins.

Blachère, R. and M. Gaudefroy-Demombynes. 1975. *Grammaire de l'arabe classique: Morphologie et syntax.* Paris: Maisonneuve & Larose.

Blake, Barry J. 1994. *Case.* Cambridge: Cambridge University Press.

Blau, J. 1961. The importance of middle Arabic dialects for the history of Arabic. In *Scripta Hiersolymitana IX: Studies in Islamic History and Civilization,* ed. U. Heyd. Jerusalem: Magnes Press.

Bohas, Georges, J.-P. Guillaume, and D. E. Kouloughli. 1990. *The Arabic Linguistic Tradition.* London: Routledge.

Bolotin, Naomi. 1995. Arabic and parametric VSO agreement. In *Perspectives on Arabic Linguistics VII,* ed., Mushira Eid. Amsterdam/Philadelphia: John Benjamins.

Borer, Hagit. 1988. On the morphological parallelism between compounds and constructs. In *Yearbook of Morphology,* ed. Geert Booij and Jaap van Marle. Dordrecht: Foris.

Brame, Michael. 1970. Stress in Arabic and generative phonology. *Foundations of Language* 7: 556–91.

Bravmann, M.M. 1977. *Studies in Semitic Philology.* Leiden: Brill.

Brustad, Kristen, Mahmoud Al-Batal, and Abbas al-Tonsi. 1995. *Alif-Baa: Introduction to Arabic Letters and Sounds.* Washington. DC: Georgetown University Press.

1995. *Al-Kitaab fii taʿallum al-ʿarabiyya: A Textbook for Beginning Arabic.* Washington, DC: Georgetown University Press.

Bybee, Joan. 1988. Morphology as lexical organization. In *Theoretical Morphology,* ed. Michael Hammond and Michael Noonan. New York: Academic Press.

Cachia, Pierre. 1973. *The Monitor: A Dictionary of Arabic Grammatical Terms. Arabic–English, English–Arabic.* London: Longman and Beirut: Librairie du Liban.

Cantarino, Vicente. 1974, 1975, 1976. *The Syntax of Modern Arabic Prose.* 3 vols. Bloomington: Indiana University Press.

Cantineau, Jean. 1982. *Études de linguistique arabe.* Leiden: Brill.

Carstairs-McCarthy, Andrew. 1994. Inflection classes, gender and the principle of contrast. *Language* 70(4):737–88.

Carter, Michael G. 1972. Twenty dirhams in the *kitaab* of Sibawayhi. *Bulletin of the School of Oriental and African Studies (BSOAS)* 35:485–96.

1981. *Arab Linguistics.* Amsterdam: John Benjamins.

Chafe, Wallace L. 1970. *Meaning and the structure of Language.* Chicago: University of Chicago Press.

Comrie, Bernard. 1991. On the importance of Arabic for general linguistic theory. In *Perspectives on Arabic Linguistics II,* ed. Mushira Eid and John McCarthy. Amsterdam/Philadelphia: John Benjamins.

Corriente, F. 1976. From old Arabic to classical Arabic through the pre-Islamic koine. *Journal of Semitic Studies* 21:62–98.

Cotter, Colleen. 2001. Discourse and media. In *The Handbook of Discourse Analysis* eds. Deborah Schiffrin, Deborah Tannen, and Heidi E. Hamilton. Malden, MA/Oxford: Blackwell.

Cowan, David. 1964. *An Introduction to Modern Literary Arabic.* Cambridge: Cambridge University Press.

Cowan, George William. 1960. A reconstruction of proto-colloquial Arabic. Unpublished dissertation. Cornell University.

Cowell, Mark W. 1964. *A Reference Grammar of Syrian Arabic.* Washington DC: Georgetown University Press.

Crystal, David. 1997. *The Cambridge Encyclopedia of Language.* 2nd edn. Cambridge: Cambridge University Press.

al-Dahdah, Antwan. 1987. *Muʿjam qawaaʿid al-lugha l-ʿarabiyya fii jadaawil wa-lawHaat* (Encyclopedia of Arabic Grammatical Rules in Charts and Tables). Beirut: Maktabat Lubnaan.

Dahlgren, Sven-Olaf. 1998. *Word Order in Arabic.* Göteborg: Acta Universitatis Gothoburgensis.

Depuydt, Leo. 1997. Agent-less indirect adjectival verb forms in Egyptian and Arabic: The case for jrrw.n.f. and mafʿûl lahu, "for whom one acts." *Journal of the American Oriental Society* 117:487–505.

Dozy, Rheinhart Pieter Anne. 1967. *Supplement aux Dictionnaires Arabes.* 3rd edn. Leyde: E. J. Brill; Paris: G. P. Mainsonneuve et Larose.

Eid, Mushira. 1991. Verbless sentences in Arabic and Hebrew. In *Perspectives on Arabic Linguistics III,* ed. Bernard Comrie and Mushira Eid. Amsterdam/Philadelphia: John Benjamins.

Elgibali, Alaa. 1993. Stability and language variation in Arabic: Cairene and Kuwaiti dialects. In *Perspectives on Arabic Linguistics V,* ed. Mushira Eid and Clive Holes. Amsterdam/Philadelphia: John Benjamins.

El-Hassan, S. A. 1978. Educated spoken Arabic in Egypt and the Levant: A critical review of diglossia and related concepts. *Archivum Linguisticum* 8:112–32.

Emery, Peter. 1988. Compound words in modern standard Arabic. *Zeitschrift für Arabische Linguistik* 19:32–43.

Encyclopedia of Islam. New edn, 1960–. 10 vols. to date. Leiden: Brill.

Esseesy, Mohssen. 2000. Morphological and syntactic features of Arabic numerals as evidence of their diachronic evolution. Ph.D. Dissertation, Georgetown University.

Ferguson, Charles. 1956. The emphatic l in Arabic. *Language* 32:486–52.

1959a. Diglossia. *Word* 15:325–40.

1959b. The Arabic koine. *Language* 35:616–30.

1970. Myths about Arabic. In *Readings in the Sociology of Language,* ed. Joshua A. Fishman. The Hague: Mouton.

1990. Come forth with a surah like it. In *Perspectives on Arabic Linguistics I,* ed. Mushira Eid. Amsterdam/Philadelphia: John Benjamins.

1996. Epilogue: Diglossia revisited. In *Understanding Arabic,* ed. Alaa Elgibali. Cairo: American University in Cairo Press.

Fischer, Wolfdietrich. 1992. Arabic. In *International Encyclopedia of Linguistics,* vol. I. New York/Oxford: Oxford University Press.

2002. *A Grammar of Classical Arabic.* 3rd revised edn. Tr. by Jonathan Rogers. New Haven/London: Yale University Press.

Fleisch, Henri. 1957. Esquisse d'un historique de la grammaire arabe. *Arabica* 4:1–22.

1961, 1979. *Traité de philologie arabe I et II.* 2 vols. Beirut: Imprimerie Catholique 1961 (vol. I); Beirut: Dar al-Machreq 1979 (vol. II).

Frisch, Stefan A. and Bushra Adnan Zawaydeh. 2001. The psychological reality of OCP-Place in Arabic. *Language* 77(1): 91–106.

Fück, Johann. 1955. *Arabiyya.* Paris: Marcel Didier.

Gaballa, Hassan. 1999. Gender dispersal in the Qurʾan. *Al-ʿArabiyya* 32:87–116.

Gairdner, W. H. T. 1925. *The Phonetics of Arabic.* London: Oxford University Press.

Glinert, Lewis. 1989. *The Grammar of Modern Hebrew.* Cambridge: Cambridge University Press.

Golston, Chris. 1996. Direct optimality theory: Representation as pure markedness. *Language* 72(4):713–48.

Gordon, Cyrus H. 1970. The accidental invention of the phonemic alphabet. *Journal of Near Eastern Studies* 29(3):193–97.

Gray, Louis. 1934. *Introduction to Semitic Comparative Linguistics.* New York: Columbia University Press.

Greenberg, Joseph. 1950. The patterning of root morphemes in Semitic. *Word* 6:162–81.

Haegeman, Liliane. 1991, 1994. *Introduction to Government and Binding Theory.* 2nd edn. Oxford: Blackwell.

Haeri, Niloofar. 2003 *Sacred Language, Ordinary People.* New York: Palgrave Macmillan.

Hary, Benjamin. 1996. The importance of the language continuum in Arabic multiglossia. In *Understanding Arabic,* ed. Alaa Elgibali. Cairo: American University in Cairo Press.

Hasan, ʿAbbas 1987. *Al-naHw al-waafii* (The Complete Grammar). 4 vols. Cairo: Daar al-maʿaarif.

Haugen, Einar. 1976. *The Scandinavian Languages: An Introduction to Their History.* Cambridge: Harvard University Press.

Haywood, John A. 1965. *Arabic Lexicography: Its History and Its Place in the General History of Lexicography.* Leiden: Brill.

Haywood, John A. and H. M. Nahmad. 1962. *A New Arabic Grammar of the Written Language.* Cambridge: Harvard University Press.

Hetzron, Robert. 1987. Semitic languages. In *The World's Major Languages,* ed. Bernard Comrie. New York: Oxford University Press.

1992. Semitic languages. In *International Encyclopedia of Linguistics*, vol. III. New York: Oxford University Press.

Hijazi, Mahmoud. 1978. *Al-lugha al-ᶜarabiyya ᶜabr al-quruun* (The Arabic Language across the Centuries). Cairo: Daar al-thaqaafa li-l-Tabaaᶜa wa-l-nashr.

Holes, Clive. 1995. *Modern Arabic: Structures, Functions and Varieties*. London: Longman.

Howell, Mortimer Sloper. 1986 (reprint). *A Grammar of the Classical Arabic Language*. 4 vols. in 7. New Delhi: Gian Publishing.

Hurford, James R. 1994. *Grammar: A Student's Guide*. Cambridge: Cambridge University Press.

International Encyclopedia of Linguistics. 1992. 4 vols. New York: Oxford University Press.

Johnstone, Barbara. 1990. "Orality" and discourse structure in Modern Standard Arabic. In *Perspectives on Arabic Linguistics I*, ed. Mushira Eid. Amsterdam/Philadelphia: John Benjamins.

Kammensjö, Helène. 1993. Connectives in MSA and/or ESA: Suggestion for research. Gothenburg: University of Gothenburg Department of Oriental Languages.

Kaye, Alan S. 1987. Arabic. *The World's Major Languages*, ed. Bernard Comrie. New York: Oxford University Press.

Khaldieh, Salim. 2001. The relationship between knowledge of iᶜraab, lexical knowledge, and reading comprehension of nonnative readers of Arabic. *Modern Language Journal* 85(3):416–31.

Killean, Carolyn G. 1970. The false construct in modern literary Arabic. *An-Nashra* 4(2):2–17.
1978. Two mnemonic aids for the correct reading of weak verb forms. *Al-ᶜArabiyya* 11:5–9.

Kouloughli, D. E. 1994. *Grammaire de l'arabe d'aujourd'hui*. Paris: Pocket.

Lane, Edward William. 1863. *Arabic–English Lexicon*. 2 vols. Edinburgh: Williams and Norgate. [Reprint 1984, Islamic Texts Society, Cambridge]

Lecomte, Gerard. 1968. *Grammaire de l'arabe*. Paris: Presses Universitaires de France.

LeTourneau, Mark S. 1993. Case-marking and binding of subject clitics in Arabic complement clauses. In *Perspectives on Arabic Linguistics V*, ed. Mushira Eid and Clive Holes. Amsterdam/Philadelphia: John Benjamins.
1995. Internal and external agreement in quantified construct states. In *Perspectives on Arabic Linguistics VII*, ed. Mushira Eid. Amsterdam/Philadelphia: John Benjamins.
1996. The interaction of causativity and reflexivity in derived Arabic verbs. In *Perspectives on Arabic Linguistics VIII*, ed. Mushira Eid. Amsterdam/Philadelphia: John Benjamins.
1998. Implicit reciprocals in standard Arabic. In *Perspectives on Arabic Linguistics XI*, eds. Elabbas Benmamoun, Mushira Eid, and Niloofar Haeri. Amsterdam/Philadelphia: John Benjamins.

Lohmann, Johannes. 1972. M. Heidegger's "ontological difference" and language. In *On Heidegger and Language* ed. Joseph J. Kockelmans. Evanston: Northwestern University Press.

Mahmoud, Abdelgawad T. 1991. A contrastive study of middle and unaccusative constructions in Arabic and English. In *Perspectives on Arabic Linguistics III*, ed. Bernard Comrie and Mushira Eid. Amsterdam/Philadelphia: John Benjamins.

Matthews, P. H. 1974. *Morphology*. Cambridge: Cambridge University Press.

McCarthy, John J. 1981. A prosodic theory of nonconcatenative morphology. *Linguistic Inquiry* 12(3):373–417.

1986. OCP effects: Gemination and antigemination. *Linguistic Inquiry* 17:207–63.

1991. Semitic gutturals and distinctive feature theory. In *Perspectives on Arabic Linguistics III,* ed. Bernard Comrie and Mushira Eid. Amsterdam/Philadelphia: John Benjamins.

McCarthy, John J. and Alan Prince. 1990a. Prosodic morphology and templatic morphology. In *Perspectives on Arabic Linguistics II,* ed. Mushira Eid and John McCarthy. Amsterdam/Philadelphia: John Benjamins.

1990b. Foot and word in prosodic morphology: The Arabic broken plural. *Natural Language and Linguistic Theory* 8(2) :209–83.

McCarus, Ernest N. 1976. A semantic analysis of Arabic verbs. In *Michigan Oriental Studies in Honor of George G. Cameron,* ed. Louis L. Orlin. Ann Arbor: Department of Near Eastern Studies, University of Michigan.

McCarus, Ernest N. and Raji Rammuny. 1974. *A Programmed Course in Modern Literary Arabic Phonology and Script.* Ann Arbor: Department of Near Eastern Studies, University of Michigan.

McCarus, Ernest N. and Adil I. Yacoub. 1963. *Contemporary Arabic Readers: Newspaper Arabic.* Ann Arbor: University of Michigan Press.

McCarus, Ernest N. with Frederic J. Cadora. 1964. *Contemporary Arabic Readers: Formal Arabic.* Ann Arbor: University of Michigan Press.

McLoughlin, Leslie J. 1972. Towards a definition of modern standard Arabic. *Archivum Linguisticum: New Series* 3:57–73.

McOmber, Michael L. 1995. Morpheme edges and Arabic infixation. In *Perspectives on Arabic Linguistics VII,* ed. Mushira Eid. Amsterdam/Philadelphia: John Benjamins.

Mehall, David John. 1999. The verb morphology of unscripted media Arabic. PhD Dissertation, Georgetown University.

Middle East Centre for Arab Studies (MECAS), Shemlan, Lebanon. 1959. *A Selected Word List of Modern Literary Arabic.* Beirut: Daar al-Kutub.

1965. *The M.E.C.A.S. Grammar of Modern Literary Arabic.* Beirut: Khayats.

Miller, Ann M. 1986. The origin of the modern Arabic sedentary dialects: An evaluation of several theories. *Al-ʿArabiyya* 19:47–74.

Mitchell, Terence F. 1986. What is educated spoken Arabic? *International Journal of the Sociology of Language* 61:7–32.

Mitchell, Timothy. 1981. The phonology of weak verbs: A simple diagram of rules. *Al-ʿArabiyya* 14:1 and 2:11–18.

Mohammed, M. A. 1990. The problem of subject-verb agreement in Arabic: Towards a solution. In *Perspectives on Arabic Linguistics I,* ed. Mushira Eid. Amsterdam/Philadelphia: John Benjamins.

Monteil, Vincent. 1960. *L'arabe moderne.* Paris: Klincksieck.

Moore, John. 1990. Doubled verbs in Modern Standard Arabic. In *Perspectives on Arabic Linguistics II,* eds. Mushira Eid and John McCarthy. Amsterdam/Philadelphia: John Benjamins.

Moscati, Sabatino. 1958. On Semitic case-endings. *Journal of Near Eastern Studies.* 17:142–44.

1969. *An Introduction to Comparative Grammar of the Semitic Languages.* Weisbaden: Harrassowitz.

Nicholson, Reynold A. 1930. *A Literary History of the Arabs.* Cambridge: Cambridge University Press.

1987. *Translations of Eastern Poetry and Prose.* London: Curzon Press.

Nydell, Margaret K. (Omar). 2002. *Understanding Arabs: A Guide for Westerners.* Yarmouth, ME: Intercultural Press.

Owens, Jonathan. 1984a. Structure, class and dependency: Modern linguistic theory and the Arabic grammatical tradition. *Lingua* 64:25–62.

    1984a. The noun phrase in Arabic grammatical theory. *Al-ʿArabiyya* 17:47–86.

    1990. *Early Arabic Grammatical Theory: Heterogeneity and Standardization.* Amsterdam: John Benjamins.

Paoli, Bruno. 1999. Reflexions sur le traitment des pluriels internes de l'arabe. *Langues et litteratures du monde arabe* 1:43–56.

Parkinson, Dilworth. 1975. The agreement of *baʿD* and *kull* in modern literary Arabic. *Al-ʿArabiyya* 8:52–68.

    1981. VSO to SVO in MSA: A study in diglossia syntax. *Al-ʿArabiyya* 14:24–37.

    1991. Searching for modern *fusHa*: Real-life formal Arabic. *Al-ʿArabiyya* 24:31–64.

    1993. Knowing standard Arabic: Testing Egyptians' MSA abilities. In *Perspectives on Arabic Linguistics V,* ed. Mushira Eid and Clive Holes. Amsterdam/Philadelphia: John Benjamins.

Peled, Yishai. 1992. *Conditional Structures in Classical Arabic.* Wiesbaden: Harrassowitz.

Persson, Maria. 1999. Semantic considerations in the syntactic structures of complement clauses in modern literary Arabic. In *Arabic Grammar and Linguistics,* ed. Yasir Suleiman. Surrey: Curzon.

Procházka, Stephan. 1993. Some remarks on the semantic function of the reduplicated quadriliteral verb. *The Arabist: Budapest Studies in Arabic* 6–7:197–203.

Rabin, C. 1955. The beginnings of classical Arabic. *Studia Islamica* 4:19–37.

Rammuny, Raji M. 1994. *Advanced Standard Arabic through Authentic Texts and Audiovisual Materials.* Ann Arbor: University of Michigan Press.

Rammuny, Raji M. and Dilworth Parkinson. 1993. *Investigating Arabic: Linguistic, Pedagogical and Literary Studies in Honor of Ernest N. McCarus.* Columbus, OH: Greyden Press.

Ratcliffe, Robert R. 1990. Arabic broken plurals: Arguments for a two-fold classification of morphology. In *Perspectives on Arabic Linguistics II,* ed. Mushira Eid and John McCarthy. Amsterdam/Philadelphia: John Benjamins.

    1998. *The "Broken" Plural Problem in Arabic and Comparative Semitic.* Amsterdam/Philadelphia: John Benjamins.

Roochnik, Paul. n.d. A chart of quadriliteral Arabic verbs. Unpublished paper, Georgetown University.

Russell, Robert A. 1984. Historical aspects of subject-verb agreement in Arabic. ESCOL '84: Proceedings of the First Eastern States Conference on Linguistics (Columbus, OH: Ohio State Unviersity).

Ryding, Karin C. 1990. *Formal Spoken Arabic: Basic Course.* Washington: Georgetown University Press.

    1991. Proficiency despite diglossia: A new approach for Arabic. *Modern Language Journal* 75:2:212–18.

    1993. Case/mood syncretism in Arabic grammatical theory: Evidence for the split morphology hypothesis and the continuum hypothesis. In *Investigating Arabic.* ed., Raji Rammuny and Dilworth Parkinson. Columbus, OH: Greyden Press.

Ryding-Lentzner, Karin. 1977. Semantic and syntactic aspects of Arabic prepositions. Dissertation, Georgetown University.

Sara, Solomon. 1991. Al-Khalil, the first Arab phonologist. *International Journal of Islamic and Arabic Studies* 8(1):1–57.

Schiffrin, Deborah.1987. *Discourse Markers.* Cambridge: Cambridge University Press.

Schiffrin, Deborah, Deborah Tannen, and Heidi E. Hamilton. 2001. *The Handbook of Discourse Analysis.* Malden, MA and Oxford: Blackwell.

Schultz, Eckehard, Günther Krahl, and Wolfgang Reuschel. 2000. *Standard Arabic: An Elementary-Intermediate Course.* Cambridge: Cambridge University Press.

Semaan, Khalil. 1968. *Linguistics in the Middle Ages: Phonetic Studies in Early Islam.* Leiden: Brill.

Shahid, Irfan. 1981. *Rome and the Arabs: A Prolegomenon to the Study of Byzantium and the Arabs.* Washington, DC: Dumbarton Oaks.

1984. *Byzantium and the Arabs in the Fourth Century.* Washington, DC: Dumbarton Oaks.

1989. *Byzantium and the Arabs in the Fifth Century.* Washington, DC: Dumbarton Oaks.

1995. *Byzantium and the Arabs in the Sixth Century.* Washington, DC: Dumbarton Oaks.

Shivtiel, Avihai. 1993. Root-dictionary or alphabetical dictionary: A methodological dilemma. *The Arabist: Budapest Studies in Arabic* 6–7:13–25.

Sibawayhi, ʿAmr ibn ʿUthman. 1970. *al-Kitaab (Le Livre de Sibawayhi).* 2 vols. Paris: Derenbourg.

1991. *Kitaab Siibawayhi,* ed. Abd al-Salam Muhammad Harun. 5 vols. Beirut: Daar al-jiil.

Southwest Journal of Linguistics. 1991. Special volume: *Studies in Diglossia.* 10:1. University of North Texas Press.

Spencer, Andrew. 1991. *Morphological Theory.* London: Blackwell.

1994. Review of *Morphology by Itself,* by Mark Aronoff. *Language* 70(4):811–17.

Sterling, R. 1904. *A grammar of the Arabic language.* London: Kegan Paul, Trench, Trubner and Co.

Stetkevych, Jaroslav. 1970. *The Modern Arabic Literary Language.* Chicago: University of Chicago Press.

Stowasser, Barbara Freyer. 1981. Semantic analysis and the teaching of Arabic vocabulary. *Al-ʿArabiyya* 14(1 and 2):5–10.

Stubbs, Michael. 1983. *Discourse Analysis.* Chicago: University of Chicago Press.

Suleiman, Yasir, ed. 1999. *Arabic Grammar and Linguistics.* Surrey: Curzon.

2003. *The Arabic Language and National Identity.* Washington: Georgetown University Press.

Taha, Zeinab. 1995. The grammar controversy: What to teach and why. In *The Teaching of Arabic as a Foreign Language,* ed. Mahmoud Al-Batal. Provo, UT: American Association of Teachers of Arabic.

Testen, David. 1994. On the development of the Arabic subjunctive. In *Perspectives on Arabic Linguistics VI,* ed. Ellen Broselow, Mushira Eid, and John McCarthy. Amsterdam/ Philadelphia: John Benjamins.

1997. The suppletive imperative of Arabic "come." In *Perspectives on Arabic Linguistics X,* ed. Mushira Eid and Robert R. Ratcliffe. Amsterdam/Philadelphia: John Benjamins.

Thatcher, G. W. 1942. *Arabic Grammar of the Written Language.* 4th edn. London: Lund Humphries.

Versteegh, Cornelius H. M. 1977. *Greek Elements in Arabic Linguistic Thinking.* Leiden: Brill.

1978. The Arabic terminology of syntactic position. *Arabica* 25:261–80.

1983. *The History of Linguistics in the Near East.* Amsterdam: John Benjamins.

1984. *Pidginization and Creolization: The Case of Arabic.* Amsterdam/Philadelphia: John Benjamins.

1985. The development of argumentation in Arabic grammar: The declension of the dual and the plural. *Zeitschrift für Arabische Linguistik* 15:152–73.

1996. Linguistic attitudes and the origin of speech in the Arab world. In *Understanding Arabic,* ed. Alaa Elgibali. Cairo: American University in Cairo Press.

1997. *The Arabic Language.* New York: Columbia University Press.

Walters, Keith. 1996. Diglossia, linguistic variation and language change in Arabic. In *Perspectives on Arabic Linguistics VIII,* ed. Mushira Eid. Amsterdam/Philadelphia: John Benjamins.

al-Warraki, Nariman Naili and Ahmad Taher Hassanein. 1994. *The Connectors in Modern Standard Arabic/ ʾAdawaat al-rabT fii l-ʿarabiyya l-muʿaaSira.* Cairo: American University in Cairo Press.

Watson, Janet. 1999. The syntax of Arabic headlines and news summaries. In *Arabic Grammar and Linguistics,* ed. Yasir Suleiman. Surrey: Curzon.

Wehr, Hans. 1979. *A Dictionary of Modern Written Arabic. Arabic–English,* ed. J. Milton Cowan. Fourth edition. Wiesbaden: Harrasowitz.

Widdowson, H. G. 1988. Language, context and culture in the classroom *ERIC/CLL News Bulletin* 12:6–7

Wightwick, Jane and Mahmoud Gaafar. 1998. *Arabic Verbs and Essentials of Arabic Grammar.* Lincolnwood, IL: Passport Books.

Wright, Elizabeth K. 2000. Sound and Meaning in Medieval Arabic Linguistic Theory. PhD dissertation, Georgetown University.

Wright, William. 1966 (reprint). *Lectures in the Comparative Grammar of the Semitic Languages.* Amsterdam: Philo.

1967 (reprint). *A Grammar of the Arabic Language.* 3rd edn. 2 vols. in one. Cambridge: Cambridge University Press.

Yushmanov, N. V. 1961. *The Structure of the Arabic Language.* Washington, DC: Center for Applied Linguistics.

Zaborski, Andrzei 1992. Afro-Asiatic languages. In *International Encyclopedia of Linguistics.* New York: Oxford University Press.

Ziadeh, Farhat J. 1964. *A Reader in Modern Literary Arabic.* Princeton: Princeton University Press.

Ziadeh, Farhat J. and R. Bayly Winder. 1957. *An Introduction to Modern Arabic.* Princeton: Princeton University Press.

Zwettler, Michael 1978. *The Oral Tradition of Classical Arabic Poetry.* Columbus: Ohio State University Press.

Index

ʾaaxar, ʾuxraa 248–49
academies, Arabic 7–8, 95–96
accusative case 172–82
  absolute negation 179–80, 645–46
  adverbial use 165, 173–74, 276–97, 282–83, 289
  in apposition 225
  of astonishment 181
  circumstantial (Haal) 112–113, 174–75, 283–85, 454
  cognate accusative (mafʿuul muTlaq) 79, 83, 174, 285–86
  coverters to accusative (nawaasix) 176–79, 422–28, 645–46
  direct object (mafʿuul fii-hi) 172–73, 207
  of purpose or cause (mafʿuul li-ʾajl-i-hi) 175, 296
  of specification (tamyiiz) 175, 225, 249, 295–96, 340–44 (with counted nouns), 402 (with kam)
  of time 292–93
  verbs with double accusative 308
  with teens numbers 180, 339, 341–42
ʿadam 217–18, 650
adjectives 239–75
  adjective ʾiDaafa 221–23, 253–54, 274, 649–650
  agreement features 241
  attributive 239–40
  colors 270–73
  compound 274–75, 649–50
  comparative244–50
  derivation 254–58
  inflectional categories of 241–53
  nisba, or relative adjective 261–69
  non-gendered 244
  participles as adjectives 103, 105–07, 258–61
  predicative 240
  as substantives 240–41
  superlative 244, 250–53
  with nonhuman plurals 243
adverbs 276–97
  circumstantial (Haal) 283–85
  of degree 277–81
  locative (Zuruuf makaan and Zuruuf zamaan) 172–73, 289–95, 366–67, 386–400

  of manner 173, 281–87, 369–70 (bi-), 374–75 (ka-maa), 376 (fii)
  numerical adverbials 295
  as speech acts 297
Afro-Asiatic 1
agreement 57, 59, 64, 65–66
  adjectives 239–40, 241–44
  gender polarity (or reverse agreement) 334–39, 341–43, 345–46
  quantifier agreement 235–36
ʾalif 25–29
  spelling variants 26
    maqSuura 28–29
    otiose 28 (footnote), 443 (verbs)
    qaSiira 28
    Tawiila 26–28
  with accusative ending 163
alphabet 10–12
ʿamal (governance, regime) 57–58
ʾanna 425–26
annexation structure (see also ʾiDaafa) 81, 205–24
apposition 224–27, 286
aspect 51 (see also verbs)
assimilated roots/verbs 431 (see also verbs: root types)
assimilation 24–25
  of laam of definite article 40–41, 157
  of taaʾ in Form VIII verbs 570
  progressive 566
  regressive 567
auxiliary verbs 176–77, 446–49, 636–37
ʾayy(see also specifiers) 237–38, 402

baʿD(see also quantifiers) 231
bal 651
biDʿ(see also quantifiers) 232
biliteral roots 47
borrowed words 51, 95–96, 123, 204
  nisbas from 266–67
  plural 134, 138, 148–49
  as quadriliterals 599, 601

case 54, 56, 165–204
  accusative 172–82; 276, 278, 282, 286, 289
    (adverbials), 339, 341–42 (teens numerals)
  genitive 171–72, 212, 366–67
  nominative 169–71
case markers 167, 183–84
case and mood 56
circumfix 441
citation form
  of nouns 119, 171
  of verbs 435, 437 (*see also* verbs)
Classical Arabic 2–4
comparative adjective (see also adjective) 245–50
  periphrastic comparative 249–50, 296
compound or complex words 50, 99–101, 268,
    274–75, 293–94, 339, 341–43, 345–46, 348,
    446–48, 599–601, 647
concord (see agreement)
conditional sentence 449, 671–76
  apodosis (*jawaab*) 671
  contrary to fact 675–76
  with *maa* 674–75
  particles 671–72
  protasis (*sharT*) 671
conjunctions 411–17
  adverbial 413–17
  contrastive 411–12
  coordinating 410
  explanatory 412
  resultative 412–13
  subordinating 177 (see *'inna* and her sisters
    422–28)
connectives 407–21
  adverbial 413–17
    bayn-a-maa 'while,' 'whereas' 414
    baᶜd-a-maa 'after' 414
    baᶜd-a 'an 'after' 415
    baᶜd-a 'idhan 'after that,' 'then,' 'subsequently'
      415
    Hasab-a-maa 'according to,' 'in accordance
      with,' 'depending on' 417
    Hayth-u 'where' 413
    Hiin-a-maa, Hiin-a 'when,' 'at the time when'
      415
    ᶜind-a- 'idhan 'then,' 'at that point in time,'
      'at that time' 416
    ka-maa 'just as,' 'similarly,' 'likewise,' 'as' 416
    mithl-a-maa 'like,' 'just as,' 'as' 416
    qadr-a-maa 'as much as,' 'just as,' 'as . . . as'
      417
    rubb-a-maa 'perhaps,' 'maybe,' 'possibly' 417
    thumm-a 'then,' 'and then,' 'subsequently'
      416
  contrastive 411–12
    bal 'rather,' 'but actually' 411, 651

'inna-maa / *wa-'inna-maa* 'but,' 'but more-
      over,' 'but also,' 'rather' 412
  disjunctives 417–18
  explanatory 412
    'ay 'that is,' 'i.e.' 412
  fa- 'and so,' 'and then,' 'yet,' 'and thus'
      410–11
  resultive 412
    'idh 'since,' 'inasmuch as' 412
    'idhan 'therefore,' 'then,' 'so,' 'thus,' 'in that
      case' 412–13
    Hattaa 'until' 413
  sentence-starting 419–21
  wa- 'and' *waaw al-ᶜaTf* 409–10
consonants 12–16
construct phrase (see annexation structure and
    'iDaafa)
copula pronoun 61–62, 300–301, 319

Damma 31 (*see also* vowels, short)
  on adverbs 170, 277, 289 (*Hayth-u*), 291 (*baᶜd-u*)
  as indicative mood marker 441, 607
  as nominative case marker 183
  as stem vowel 457
days of the week 159, 362–63
declensions of nouns 54 (*see also* case), 167–68,
    182–204
  declension one (triptote) 183–87
  declension two (*see also* dual) 187–89
  declension three (sound masculine plural)
      189–91
  declension four (sound feminine plural)
      191–92
  declension five (diptote) 192–97
  declension six (defective) 197–99
  declension seven (indeclinable) 199–200
  declension eight (invariable) 200–204
defective roots/verbs 432 (*see also* verbs: Forms
    I–X: root types)
definite article 40–42, 156–60
  generic use 158
definiteness 54–55, 156–60
  and adjective inflection 241
  definite marker, spelling and pronunciation
      40–42
  indefinite marker, nunation 42–43, 161–65
  through annexation 160
  through pronoun suffix 160–61
demonstrative pronoun 214–15, 315–21
  of distance ("that"/"those") 316
  haa 'this' 320
  in *'iDaafa* 212, 214–15, 317–18
  locative demonstratives (*hunaa, hunaaka,*
      humaalika) 320–21
  of proximity ("this"/"these") 315

desinential inflection 165–66 (*see also* case and mood)
dhaat 313, 320
dhuu 312
dialects (*see* vernacular Arabic)
dictionary
  organization 49–50
  use 435, 677–81
diglossia 5–6
diphthongs 33
diptote 122, 167, 279 (*'ajma'-a*)
  broken plural patterns 150–55, 164
  comparative adjective 247
  declension 187, 192–97
  defective 197–99
  words not taking nunation 164
disjunctives 417–18
doubling (of consonant) 24–25, 40, 48, 105, 154, 157 (sun letters), 430 (in geminate verb/root)
dual 53–54, 129–31
  dual quantifiers "both" 230, 334
  in counting 332–33

Educated Spoken Arabic (Formal Spoken Arabic) 6, 8
elative 195 (*see also* comparative adjective), 244–53
equational sentence (*see also* nominal sentence) 59–63
ergative 669
exceptive expressions 181–82, 650–56
exclamations 171, 181, 518–19
existential 'there' 61, 288–89, 321

fatHa 31, 33 (*see also* short vowels)
  as accusative case marker 184
  as subjunctive mood marker 608–609
fa'al- as model root 436

geminate (doubled) root 430 (*see also* verbs: Forms I–X: root types)
gemination/consonant doubling 24–25, 40, 48, 105, 154, 157, 430
gender 53, 119–25
  adjectives 241–44
  of cities 122
  of countries 120, 122
  cryptofeminine 124
  cryptomasculine 120–21
  feminine 120–24
  masculine 120–21
  in nouns 119–25
  in pronouns 298 (personal), 315 (demonstrative) 322 (relative)
  in verbs 438
genitive case 54 (*see also* case), 171–72, 289–90 (in relation to adverbs)

markers of the genitive 183–84
  with prepositions and semi-prepositions 171, 289, 367
  on second term of *'iDaafa* 172, 212
ghayr 223–224, 274–75, 648–650
government (*'amal*) 57–58

Haal 112–13, 174–75, 283–85, 454
hamza 13, 16–21
  chair/seat rules (spelling) 16–21
  in definite article 40, 156
  hamzat al-waSl 19–21, 322 (relative pronouns), 322 (on *ithnaan*)
  imperative 623–25
  insertion in plurals 152, 154
  in *nisba* adjective 262, 266
hamzated root/verbs 431 (*see also* verbs: Forms I–X: root types)
Harakaat (see vowels: short)
Hayth-u 289
helping vowels (*see also* vowels: short), 32–33, 303 (plural pronoun suffix), 306 (second person plural helping vowel)
hollow root/verb 431 (see also verbs: Forms I–X: root types)
humanness 125–29
  as an agreement feature 125–27
hunaa/hunaaka 288, 320–21 (locative and existential)

'i'raab (case and mood marking) 53–54, 56
'iDaafa 205–24 (see also annexation structure)
  adjective *'iDaafa* ("false" or "unreal" *'iDaafa*) 221–23, 253–54
  complex (multi-term) 215–16
  compositional 209
  contents 209–10
  demonstrative pronoun in 214–15, 317 (in second term), 317–18 (in first term)
  ghayr as first term of *'iDaafa* 223–24
  joint annexation 217–18
  modification of 213–14, 221
  partitive 206–207
  possessive 206
  purpose 210
  rules for first term 211–12, 130–31, 141 (the five nouns), 186–87, 289, 317–18
  rules for second term 172, 212–13
  verbal noun in 207–208
'idda 226, 232–33
'illaa 651–653
imperative mood 444–45, 622–33
  negative imperative 632, 645
  permissive imperative 632
imperfect/imperfective aspect 53, 439–42

indefiniteness 54, 156, 161–65, 324–28 (with relative clauses/pronouns)
  indefinite marker (nunation) 42–43
indicative mood 606–608
inflection (overview) 51–55
  inflectional classes 55–56
ʾinna and her sisters 177–78, 422–28
  ʾanna 'that' 425–26
  buffer pronoun (*Damiir al-shaʾn*) 424
  ʾinna 'indeed,' 'truly,' 'verily' 425
  laʿalla 'perhaps,' 'maybe' 428
  laakinna 'but' 427
  li-ʾanna 'because' 427–28
  overt noun subject 423
  reduplicated pronoun subject 423–24
  separated subject 423
intransitive verbs 64
iyyaa- 308

jamiiʿ 229–30
jussive mood 53, 444–45, 616–22

kaan-a and her sisters 176–77, 446–49 (compound verbs), 634–40
kam 'how much/how many' 180, 296, 402–403
kasra 30–31
  as genitive case marker 183–84
  as helping vowel 32
kilaa 230, 334
kull 228–29

laa of absolute negation 179–80, 645–46
laakinna (see ʾinna and hers sisters) 427
laʿalla (see ʾinna and hers sisters) 428
lays-a 637, 641–644
law-laa 655–56
letters (of the alphabet) 10–12
  moon letters 40–41, 157
  names and shapes 11–12
  sun letters 40–41, 157
  transliteration 42
li-ʾanna (see ʾinna and hers sisters) 427–28
loanwords 51, 95–96, 123, 204 (see also borrowed words)

maa 227, 325–28 (relative pronoun), 374–75, 403–404, 647 (negative)
man 325–26 (relative pronoun)
maSdar (see also verbal noun) 75–83; for maSdars of specific verb forms (I–X, XI–XV, quadriliterals) see verbs: Forms
maziid min 234
mediopassive 530, 669
mimmaa 328, 380
Modern Standard Arabic 7

differences from Classical Arabic 4
definitions 8
pronunciation styles 34
mood 53, 444–45 (see also verbs: moods)
mundh-u 385–86, 447–48
muTaabaqa (see agreement)
muTaawiʿ 530, 555, 565, 657, 669

nafs 226, 236–37, 312
naHt 50, 99–100
names 97–99
  apposition 224
  days of the week 159
  demonstratives with proper names 318
  female proper 122, 138, 196
  masculine proper 120–21, 164, 197
  months 139
  non–Arabic proper 196, 204
  place names (with definite article) 158
  professions 143
nawaasix (converters to accusative) 176–79, 422–28 (see also ʾinna and her sisters)
negation 641–56
  ʿadam 217–18, 650
  exceptive expressions 181, 650–56
  ghayr 648–50
  laa 644–647, of absolute negation 179–80, 645–46 (see also accusative case)
  lam 622, 647
  lan 648
  lays-a 641–44
  maa 647
  neither . . . nor 646
nominal sentence 58–59
  equational sentence 58–63
nominative case 169–171
nouns
  abstract with /–iyya/ 90–92, 121, 126
  biliteral 92
  borrowed 95–96 (see also borrowed words)
  cases 165–204
  collective 94, 121
  common noun (ism) 121
  complex 90–101
  compound, complex 99–101, 218–19, 268, 274–75, 647
  diminutive 90
  "five nouns," the 92–93, 186–87, 305 (with -ii)
  generic (ism al-jins) 85, 89–90
  geographical names 96
  not derived from verb roots 92
  of instance 89–90, 121
  of instrument 87–88, 151, 154
  of intensity, repetition, profession 88, 143
  of place 86–87

participles as nouns 103–105
  active and passive 83–86
personal names 97–99
plurals 128, 132–56
primitive 92
proper 96–99
quadriliteral 93–94, 154–55, participles from
  111–12, 604–605
quinquiliteral 94, 152
unit nouns 94–95
verbal noun 75–83 (*see also* maSdar and verbs:
  verbal noun)
number (inflectional category) 53, 129–56
numbers and numerals 329–65
  cardinal 329–53
    1 330–31
    2 (*see also* dual) 332–34; *kilaa and kiltaa* 'both'
      230, 334
    3–10 334–39
    11–12 339–41
    13–19 180, 341–43
    20–99 343–46
    hundred(s) 346–49
    thousands 350–51
    millions and billions 353
  fractions 360–61
  number adjectives 363–64
  ordinals 354–60
    first 354–55
    2nd–10th 356–58
    11th–19th 358–59
    20th–99th 359–60
    100th 360
    'last'/final 364–65
  percent 347
  telling time 361–62
  years/dates 351–53
nunation 42–43 (*see also* indefiniteness), 161–65
  and *'iDaafa* 211–12
nuun-deletion 130–31, 141, 189, 191, 310, 333

object
  of a locative adverb 172
  of a preposition 171
  of a verb 172–73
"operative" particles 409
optative expressions 636, 676

participles 83–86, 102–18
  active 84–85, 103–13
  as first term of *i'Daafa* 209
  circumstantial accusative in 112–13, 174–75
    (*see also* accusative, circumstatial *Haal*)
  from verb Forms 1–X, XI–XV, and quadriliterals, *see* verbs: Forms: participles

"second" through "tenth" in pattern of
    active participle 356
    passive 85–86, 113–18
passive voice 657–70
  derivational 668–70
  internal/inflectional passive 658–68
  mention of agent 659, 668
  with potential meaning 668
  verb-preposition idioms 666–67
pattern
  definition 48–49
  root-pattern system 45–57
  verb derivation ('awzaan al-fi'l) 433–37
    ten-form template 434
perfect/ perfective aspect 439–40 (*see also* verbs)
person 52
  in pronouns, personal 298
  in verbs 438–39
pluperfect 448, 637
plurals 132–56
  broken plural 144–55, 193–95
  plural declensions 189–92
  plural of paucity 148
  sound feminine plural 132–40
    adjectives 243–44
    declension 191–92
    and two-way inflection 187–88
  sound masculine plural 128, 140–44
    adjectives 242
    declension 189–91
    pronoun suffixes 303–304, -*ii* 'my' 304
    and two-way inflection 187–88, 191–92
possession 61
  through *'iDaafa* 206
  'ind-a 399–400
  laam al-milk 371–72 (*li-*)
  ladaa 392–93
  ma'-a 394
  pronoun suffixes 301
predicate 59
  adjective *'iDaafa* as 223, 254
  complex 446–54
  of equational sentence 59–63
  of *kaan-a* 635–36
  of *lays-a* 637, 643–44
  predicate adjective 240
prepositions 287, 290, 297, 366–400
  objects of 171, 301, 305, 308
  true prepositions (*Huruuf al-jarr*) 366–86
    one-letter prepositions (*bi-, li-,* and *ka-*)
      367–75
    two-letter prepositions (*fii, min, 'an*)
      375–81
    three-letter prepositions (*'alaa, 'ilaa, Hattaa,*
      mundh-u) 381–87

prepositions (*Continued*)
  Zuruuf makaan wa-Zuruuf zamaan (derived
    prepositions - locative adverbs - semi-
    prepositions) 366, 386–400: *'amaam-a*
    386–87; *bayn-a* 387–88; *ba'd-a* 388–89;
    daaxil-a 390; *Didd-a* 390; *Dimn-a* 390;
    duun-a 390–91; *fawq-a* 391; *fawr-a* 391;
    Hasab-a 391; *Hawl-a* 391–92; *Hawaalii* 392;
    'ibaan-a 392; *'ithr-a* 392; *'izaa'-a* 392;
    ladaa 392–93; *ma'-a* 393–94; *mithl-a*
    394–95; *naHw-a* 395; *q-b-l* roots 395–96.
    qabl-a 395; *qubayl-a* 396; *qubaalat-a* 396;
    muqaabil-a 396; *min qibal-i* 396;
    q-r-b roots 396; *quraabat-a* 396; *qurb-a* 396;
    siwaa 397; *taHt-a* 397; *Tiwaal-a* 397; *tujaah-a*
    397; *waraa'-a* 397; *wasT-a* 398; *xalf-a* 398;
    xaarij-a 398; *xilaal-a* 398; *'abr-a* 398;
    'aqib-a 398; *'ind-a* 399–400
present tense 285, 439–42
  negation of 644
  passive 663, 665–66
pronouns
  buffer 424
  demonstrative 281–82, 315–21, 333 (see also
    demonstrative)
    dhaak-a 319
    dhaat-a 320
    of distance ("that"/"those") 316
    functions 316–19
    haa 'this' 320
    in *'iDaafa* 212, 214–15, 317–18
    with possessed nouns 318
    with proper names 318
    of proximity ("this"/"these") 315
  locative 288, 320–21
  personal pronouns 298–314
    object pronouns (suffixed) 305–12
    possessive (suffixed) 301–305: vowel
      shift 302; with noun and adjective
      303
    subject (independent) 298–301: *dhuu + noun*
      312–14
  relative 322–28
pro-drop 438
pronunciation (*see also* consonants and
    vowels)
  case endings 166–67
  full form 34
  pause form 34–35
  styles 34–35

qad 448–51
quadriliteral 364
  adjectives 258
  nouns 152, 154–55

participles active 111–12, 604–605; passive 117,
    142–43, 605
  roots 599–601
  verbs 429, 432, 599–605
    denominals 433, 602
    imperative 631–32
  verbal nouns 135–36, 604
quantifiers 228–38
  agreement features 235–36
  all, every, each (*kull*) 228–30
  ba'D 'some' 231
  biD' 232
  both (*kilaa* and *kiltaa*) 334
  'idda 226, 232
  mu'Zam, akthar 234–35
  shattaa, muxtalif, 'adad min, kathiir min 233
question words 401–406
  'ayn-a (where) 401–402
  'ayy-un (which, what) 402
  hal, 'a- (interrogative markers) 405–406
  kam (how many, how much) 402–403
  kayf-a (how) 403
  li-maadhaa (why, what for) 403
  maa, maadhaa (what) 403–404
  mataa (when) 405
quinquiliteral
  adjectives 266
  nouns 94, 152

raghm 654–655
reflexive expressions 312 (*nafs* + pronoun)
relative adjectives (*nisbas*) 261–69
  functioning as nouns 143–44
relative clause 322–28
  definite 323
  indefinite 324
  resumptive pronoun in 324–25
relative pronouns 322–28
  definite 322
  indefinite 325 (*maa* and *man*)
  maa (in apposition) 227
resultative 657
root, lexical 429, 434
  definition 47–48
  root-pattern system 45–47
  root types 430–433

semi-consonant 29–30
semi-prepositions (*Zuruuf makaan wa-Zuruuf
    zamaan*) or locative adverbs 289, 366–67,
    386–400 (see also prepositions: *Zuruuf*)
Semitic languages 1
semivowel/semi-consonant 29, 429
  waaw 30
  yaa' 30

sentence
  basic structures 57–73
  complex, components 72–73
  conditional sentence (*see* conditional)
  equational (*see also* nominal sentence) 58–63
  verbal (*see also* verbal sentence) 58, 63–65
shadda 24–25
"sisters" (see *ʾinna* and her sisters 422–28)
  of *ʾinna* 177–78, 422–28
  of *kaan-a* 176–77, 634–40
siwaa 653–54
solid stems 50–51
specifiers 228–38
  ʾayy 'any' 237–38
  nafs 'same; self' 236–37, 312
stress (word stress) 36–39, 307
subject
  of equational sentence 59–63
  overt noun subject 422 (*ʾinna* and her sisters)
  separated subject 423 (*ʾinna* and her sisters)
  of verbal sentence 63–64
subjunctive mood 444–45 (*see* verbs), 606, 608–15
  and auxiliary verb 636
  and negation 644–45, 648
subordinating conjunctions (*see ʾinna* and her sisters 422–28)
  buffer pronoun (*Damiir al-shaʾn*) 424–25
  ʾinna and her sisters (see *ʾinna*) 425–28
  reduplicated pronoun subject 423–24
  with *ʾan* 611–15
sukuun 31–32, 277
superlative adjectives 244–45, 250–53
syllables 35–36

taaʾ marbuuTa 21–24
  pronunciation in *ʾiDaafa* 24, 212
tashdiid 24–25
tense (*see also* verbs) 51–52, 439–44
thammat-a 289
transitive verbs 64–64
  doubly transitive 69–72
triliteral
  root 429–32
triptote 183–87

verbal noun (*maSdar*) 75–83, sound feminine
    plural 135, in cognate accusative 174,
    285–86 (*see also* under verbs: Forms)
verbal sentence 58, 63–70
verbs 429–640
  agreement markers 438–39
  of appropinquation 452
  citation form 435, 437
  compound verbs 446–49
  of continuation 453–54

derivation 433–34
Forms 434, 437
  I 455–90, participles 470–74, roots 456–65,
    verbal nouns in 465–70
  II basic characteristics 491–92, root types
    492–94, verbal nouns 494–96, participles
    496–98, conjugation tables 498–502
  III basic characteristics 503, root types
    503–506, verbal nouns 506–508, partici-
    ples 508–509, conjugation tables 510–14
  IV basic characteristics 515–16, root types
    516–18, exclamatory 518–19, verbal nouns
    519–21, participles 521–23, conjugation
    tables 524–29
  V basic characteristics 530–31, root types
    531–33, verbal nouns 533–34, participles
    534–39, conjugation tables 536–42
  VI basic characteristics 543, root types
    543–45, verbal nouns 546–47, participles
    547–49, conjugation tables 550–54
  VII basic characteristics 555–58, participles
    558–60, conjugation tables 561–64
  VIII basic characteristics 565–70, verbal
    noun 570–71, participles 571–73, conjuga-
    tion tables 574–78
  IX basic characteristics 584–86; verbal noun
    586–87; participles 587–89; conjugation
    tables 590–95
  X basic characteristics 579–80; verbal noun
    580–81; participles 581; conjugation tables
    582–83
  XI–XV 596–98
gender marking 438
inceptive verbs 453
inflection 438–46
  inflectional categories 51–52, 438–46
intransitive verbs 64
model root: *faaʾ - ʿayn - laam* 435–36
moods 53, 444–45
  imperative 445, 622–33
  indicative (*see* indicative mood) 445, 606–608
  jussive (*see* jussive mood) 445, 616–22
  subjunctive (*see* subjunctive mood) 445, 608–15
number marking 439
person marking 439
quadriliteral 432, 599–605
root types 430–33
  strong(sound) 430
  weak430; assimilated 431
  defective 432; doubly weak 432;
    geminate 430; hamzated 431; hollow 431
of 'seeming' 640
stem vowel 437, 455–57 (Form I)
tenses/aspects 52–53, 439–40
  future tense 442, 608: future perfect 449

verbs (*continued*)
  past perfect/pluperfect 448–49, 637:
    past progressive 446–47, 637
  past tense 285, 442–44: in conditional
    clauses 673
  present tense 441–42
  transitive verbs 64–64
    doubly transitive verbs 69–72
  verb strings 285, 451–54
  voice 52–53, 445–46, 658–59
  passive 445–46, 657–70
vernacular Arabic 5–6
vocative 170–71

voice 52–53, 445–46
vowels 25–34
  helping 32–33
  long 25–30
  phonemic chart 25
  short 30–34

*waaw al-ma*ᶜ*iyya* 308
waHd-a + pronoun 286–87
word order 66–69
writing system 10–34

Zuruuf 289–90, 366–67, 386–400

CPSIA information can be obtained
at www.ICGtesting.com
Printed in the USA
LVHW101533270721
693812LV00006B/330

9 780521 7777